Lecture Notes in Artificial Intelligence 2915

Edited by J. G. Carbonell and J. Siekmann

Subseries of Lecture Notes in Computer Science

Springer-Verlag Berlin Heidelberg GmbH

Antonio Camurri Gualtiero Volpe (Eds.)

Gesture-Based Communication in Human-Computer Interaction

5th International Gesture Workshop, GW 2003
Genova, Italy, April 15-17, 2003
Selected Revised Papers

Series Editors

Jaime G. Carbonell, Carnegie Mellon University, Pittsburgh, PA, USA
Jörg Siekmann, University of Saarland, Saarbrücken, Germany

Volume Editors

Antonio Camurri
Gualtiero Volpe
University of Genova
DIST, InfoMus Lab
Viale Causa 13, 16145 Genova, Italy
E-mail: music@dist.unige.it, volpe@infomus.dist.unige.it

Cataloging-in-Publication Data applied for

A catalog record for this book is available from the Library of Congress.

Bibliographic information published by Die Deutsche Bibliothek
Die Deutsche Bibliothek lists this publication in the Deutsche Nationalbibliografie; detailed bibliographic data is available in the Internet at <http://dnb.ddb.de>.

CR Subject Classification (1998): I.2, I.3.7, I.5, I.4, H.5.2

ISSN 0302-9743
DOI 10.1007/978-3-540-24598-8

Springer-Verlag is a part of Springer Science+Business Media

springeronline.com

MyCopy version of the original edition 2004

Typesetting: Camera-ready by author, data conversion by Olgun Computergrafik
Printed on acid-free paper 06/3142 5 4 3 2 1 0
www.springer.com/mycopy

Preface

Research on the multifaceted aspects of modeling, analysis, and synthesis of human gesture is receiving growing interest from both the academic and industrial communities. On one hand, recent scientific developments on cognition, on affect/emotion, on multimodal interfaces, and on multimedia have opened new perspectives on the integration of more sophisticated models of gesture in computer systems. On the other hand, the consolidation of new technologies enabling "disappearing" computers and (multimodal) interfaces to be integrated into the natural environments of users are making it realistic to consider tackling the complex meaning and subtleties of human gesture in multimedia systems, enabling a deeper, user-centered, enhanced physical participation and experience in the human-machine interaction process.

The research programs supported by the European Commission and several national institutions and governments individuated in recent years strategic fields strictly concerned with gesture research. For example, the DG Information Society of the European Commission (www.cordis.lu/ist) supports several initiatives, such as the "Disappearing Computer" and "Presence" EU-IST FET (Future and Emerging Technologies), the IST program "Interfaces & Enhanced Audio-Visual Services" (see for example the project MEGA, Multisensory Expressive Gesture Applications, www.megaproject.org), and the IST strategic objective "Multimodal Interfaces." Several EC projects and other funded research are represented in the chapters of this book.

A wide range of applications can benefit from advances in research on gesture, from consolidated areas such as surveillance to new or emerging fields such as therapy and rehabilitation, home consumer goods, entertainment, and audiovisual, cultural and artistic applications, just to mention only a few of them.

This book is a selection of revised papers presented at the Gesture Workshop 2003, the 5th International Workshop on Gesture and Sign Language-Based Human-Computer Interaction, held in Genoa, Italy, during April 15–17, 2003.

The International Gesture Workshop is a forum where researchers working on gesture-based interfaces and gestural interaction present and exchange ideas and research currently in progress, with a crossdisciplinary focus. GW2003 was the fifth workshop after the 1996 Gesture Workshop in York (UK), considered as the starting event. Thenceforth, International Gesture Workshops have been held roughly every second year, with fully reviewed postproceedings typically published by Springer-Verlag.

As an indicator of the continuously growing interest of the scientific community in gesture-mediated human-computer interaction and human-language technology, a large number of high-quality submissions was received. The program included invited talks, oral presentations of long and short papers, presentations of posters, and demonstrations: around 90 contributors from 20 different countries offered a broad overview of the state of the art in many research fields related to gesture-based communication. Over 170 delegates attended the workshop.

This workshop was organized by the InfoMus Lab at the DIST, University of Genoa, and was supported by the aforementioned EC IST MEGA project and by the Opera House Teatro Carlo Felice of Genova. We wish to thank Gennaro Di Benedetto, Sovrintendente of the Teatro dell'Opera Carlo Felice and his staff (with particular thanks to Rita Castello, Graziella Rapallo and Giampaolo Sperini), APT Genova and Agenzia Regionale per la Promozione Turistica della Liguria, the invited speakers Frank Pollick (Department of Psychology, University of Glasgow, UK) and Shuji Hashimoto (Department of Applied Physics, Waseda University, Tokyo, Japan), the Scientific Committee, the session chairs, Barbara Mazzarino and the other members of the Local Organizing Committee (Roberto Chiarvetto, Roberto Dillon and Paolo Coletta), the staff and the students of the DIST InfoMus Lab who helped in the organization, and all the presenters and attendees. We thank also Martino Musso (Lever) for the support to the organization of the event, Eidomedia and NumenSoft.

November 2003

Antonio Camurri
Gualtiero Volpe

International Programme Committee and Book Reviewers

Table of Contents

Foundational Issues

Gesture Tracking

Gesture Recognition

Gesture Notation and Synthesis

Multimodal Gestural Interfaces

Gesture Analysis: Invariant Laws in Movement

Sylvie Gibet, Jean-François Kamp, and Franck Poirier

Valoria, Université de Bretagne Sud, Campus de Tohannic, rue Yves Mainguy
F-56000 Vannes, France
{Sylvie.Gibet,Jean-Francois.Kamp,Franck.Poirier}@univ-ubs.fr

Abstract. This paper presents gesture analysis under the scope of motor control theory. Following the motor program view, some studies have revealed a number of invariant features that characterize movement trajectories in human hand-arm gestures. These features express general spatio-temporal laws underlying coordination and motor control processes. Some typical invariants are described and illustrated for planar pointing and tracing gestures. We finally discuss how these invariant laws can be used for motion edition and generation.

1 Introduction

With the massive development of Human-Computer Interaction (HCI), new systems try to take advantage of the expressive power of gestures. At first, gesture interaction has been reduced to simple command interfaces. More recently, techniques such as capturing body movements, recognizing and interpreting human actions, and animating virtual humans, have given rise to a number of virtual reality applications with more natural interfaces. In such applications, the produced gestures should be perceived as natural and should follow biomechanical or psychomotor laws characterizing human movement.

This paper presents gesture analysis results under the scope of motor control theory. The analysis leads to the identification of significant parameters that characterize some classes of gesture (simple pointing, point-to-point and rhythmic gestures), extracted from real data in the Cartesian space. The main issues are regarded as a way to understand the mechanisms underlying the control and coordination of movement, both in terms of general principles involving central processes of task planning and in terms of peripheral processes emerging from the bio-mechanical system. We examine the principles that can be expressed as invariant features in movement trajectories, the most well-known ones being the Fitt's law and the Two-Third Power law. The overview is restricted to planar pointing and tracing movements, with patterns which are not previously learnt. We don't intend to demonstrate that these laws prefigure organizational principles explicitly used by the Central Nervous System (CNS) to produce movement, but we give some elements that can be used for motion edition or generation in Human Machine interaction or computer animation.

A. Camurri and G. Volpe (Eds.): GW 2003, LNAI 2915, pp. 1–9, 2004.

2 Motor Control Theories

During the last decades, two main classes of control theories have been developed. The first one, related to the motor program concept, assumes that there exists a central instance of control which exploits an internal representation of motion to determine the appropriate motor control. The second class postulates that the processes responsible for motor control can be found in the organization of the biomechanical system itself rather than in imposed laws.

2.1 Motor Program

The motor program concept has been introduced by the cognitive science community [1]. It can be defined as the ability to build a set of organized commands in space and time before performing gesture. This notion support the hypothesis that there is no sensorial feedback during the execution of motion. For instance, goal-based gestures such as pointing gestures highlight some kind of pre-programmed activity, the corresponding motion being executed without visual or proprioceptive feedback. To take into account longer motion and also parametrical features, this notion of motor program has been replaced by Generalized Motor Programs (GMP) [2], [3], referring to a set of generic rules associated to specific motion classes. These rules could be issued from a learning process, mapping the efferent command, the sensory feedback, the environmental context and the result of the action. GMP partially explain invariant properties characterizing motion which could be coded in general schemes, the adaptation to the performing context being realized by the instantiation of specific parameters. The search for the invariant properties has given rise to the setting of motion laws which are presented in section 3.

2.2 Biomechanical Properties of the Effectors

Other approaches suggest that limb dynamics and biomechanical properties can contribute significantly to motion control. Within this point of view, the dynamical system paradigm considers that the control processes responsible for the formation of trajectories are not explicitly programmed, but are emerging properties of the dynamics of the system itself.

According to the equilibrium point hypothesis, movements arise from shifts in the equilibrium position of the muscles. The motor program specifies a succession of discrete equilibrium points [4]. Between two equilibrium points (targets), motion is generated according to the dynamics of the mechanical system. Several equilibrium point models have been proposed. The most weel-known is the Bizzi model [5], inspired from the Feldman model. These models are essentially exploited for discrete multi-point tasks, or for elliptical trajectories generated from the specification of via-points under isometric conditions. After observing that discontinuous displacement of equilibrium points did not lead to the production of realistic motion, Hogan suggested that these equilibrium points follow a virtual trajectory, thus forcing the muscular forces to satisfy this constraint [6].

Numerous research studies have been carried out for cyclic or rhythmic movements. The concept of Motor Pattern Generation MPG has been developed for respiratory movements or locomotion [7-8]. These MPG explain the activity of neuronal circuits easily identifiable.

Other theories lying on nonlinear dynamical systems try to show the importance of accounting for physical properties in generating motion. They have given rise to models of coordination structures including a set of nonlinear oscillating systems mutually coupled. But as opposed to MPG models, the oscillators are not directly associated to specific neural structures [9-10].

3 Invariant Laws

Despite the great variability of gestures, some invariant features of the motor performance have been highlighted in the past years. The enhanced hypothesis is that these spatio-temporal invariants express general laws underlying the organization of motricity. Several kinematic laws characterizing human volunteer movements have been proposed by cognitive scientists or neurophysiologists. These laws are satisfied for a large variety of gestures, including goal-directed gestures such as simple or multiple pointing gestures, but also repetitive cyclic gestures in two or three dimensions. Without trying to give an exhaustive view of these laws, we present in this paper the most typical invariants of movement trajectories. They include invariance of velocity profile, Fitts' law showing a relationship between kinematics and geometrical properties of the trajectory for pointing movements, two-third power law for rhythmic tasks and minimum jerk expressing smoothness of trajectories.

The presented laws have been highlighted from real signals captured with a pen on a graphical WACOM A3 tablet.

3.1 Invariance of the Velocity Profile

Multi-point movements produce velocity profiles whose global shape is approximately bell-shaped. Moreover, this shape presents an asymmetry which depends on the speed of the movement. As the speed increases the curve becomes more symmetrical until the direction of the asymmetry is reversed [11-13]. This law is shown in the figure 1 for pointing gestures with different speeds and distances to the target.

3.2 Isochrony Principle and Fitts' Law

The principle, originally established by Freeman [14], and known as the Isochrony principle, expresses the invariance of the execution duration of a movement in relation to its amplitude. It has been observed that there exists a spontaneous tendency to increase the velocity of the motion according to the distance to run, when no constraint on the mean velocity is imposed.

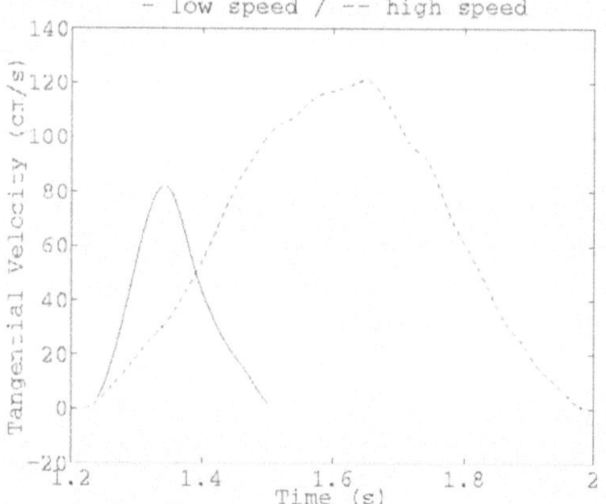

Fig. 1. Two velocity profiles: low speed (max ≈ 80 cm/s ; distance to target ≈ 10.3 cm) and high speed (max ≈ 120 cm/s ; distance to target ≈ 46.6 cm) for pointing gestures.

In this line of research, the Fitt's law has quantified this constancy in time duration for rapid movements between targets in a plane. First experiments, realized by Woodworth [15] and then by Fitts [16] consisted in executing back-and-forth movements with a pen, the distance between the targets and the width of the targets being varied over experiences. The Fitts' law (1) that can be referred to the task's index of difficulty I_d, expresses the relation between the duration of motion T, the amplitude required A and the target width W.

$$T = a + b.I_d = a + b.\log_2\left(\frac{2.A}{W}\right) \tag{1}$$

$$T = a + b.\log_2\left(\frac{A}{W} + c\right) \qquad c = ½ \text{ [17] or } \quad c = 1 \text{ [18]} \tag{2}$$

where a and b are constants determined in an empirical way.

This law is illustrated in the figure 2, for simple pointing gestures. In these experiments, the distance to the target varies from 10.3 cm to 38.4 cm and the target width W is constant.

The Fitt's law can be verified in diversified contexts for pointing gestures requiring a good accuracy of the hand endpoint. It is extensively used in its original form (1) or in variant forms (2), in particular to investigate the relative performance of devices used in Human-Machine interfaces. It can be extended to other classes of motion, as for example multi-scaled pointing gestures [19], [20].

3.3 Two-Third Power Law

For handwriting and drawing movements performed in a plane, studies by Viviani and Terzuolo shown that there is a relationship between the kinematics of elliptical

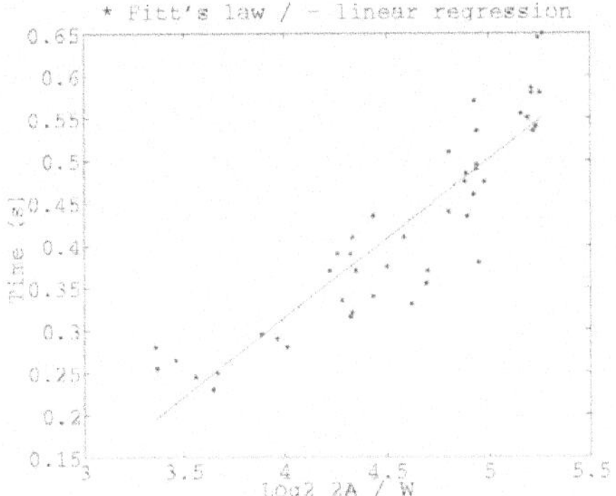

Fig. 2. Fitts' law: 45 pointing measurements (W = 2 cm and A = 10.3 cm … 38.4 cm). Linear regression of Time against $\log_2$ 2A/W gives a slope of 0.19. Correlation coefficient between measurements and linear regression = 0.9.

motion and the geometrical properties of the trajectory. This has given rise to the so-called Two-Third Power law [21-22] that establishes a relation between the angular velocity ω and the curvature C of the end-effector trajectory (3).

$$\omega(t) = kC(t)^{\frac{2}{3}} \tag{3}$$

Or equivalently :

$$v(t) = k\,R(t)^{\beta} \quad where\ \beta = \frac{1}{3} \tag{4}$$

$$v(t) = \sqrt{\dot{x}^2(t) + \dot{y}^2(t)} \tag{5}$$

$$R(t) = \frac{v(t)^3}{\left|\dot{x}(t).\ddot{y}(t) - \ddot{x}(t).\dot{y}(t)\right|} \tag{6}$$

where $v(t)$ is the tangential velocity and $R(t)$ the radius of curvature.

A more recent formulation of this law extends the validity of the original law, for a wider class of movements [23]:

$$v(t) = K\left(\frac{R(t)}{1+\alpha R(t)}\right)^{\beta} \quad \text{with } 0 < \alpha < 1 \text{ and } K > 0 \tag{7}$$

The exponent β takes values close to 1/3 (for adults). Figure 3 illustrates the power law for human elliptical movements.

The 2/3 power law has been suggested as a fundamental principle that the CNS may employ to constrain trajectory formation. Viviani supposes that complex movement can be decomposed into units of motor action. He suggests that the portions of movement over which the factor K is approximately constant correspond to chunks of motor planning. Thus, the velocity gain factor K can be used as a parameter to segment complex movements. In the case of tracing movements of ellipses with a given size and speed, K is constant during all the pattern ; its value depends among other factors on the frequency of the movement and on the eccentricity of the ellipse. For more complex graphical patterns with several loops, it is possible to identify several units corresponding to these loops.

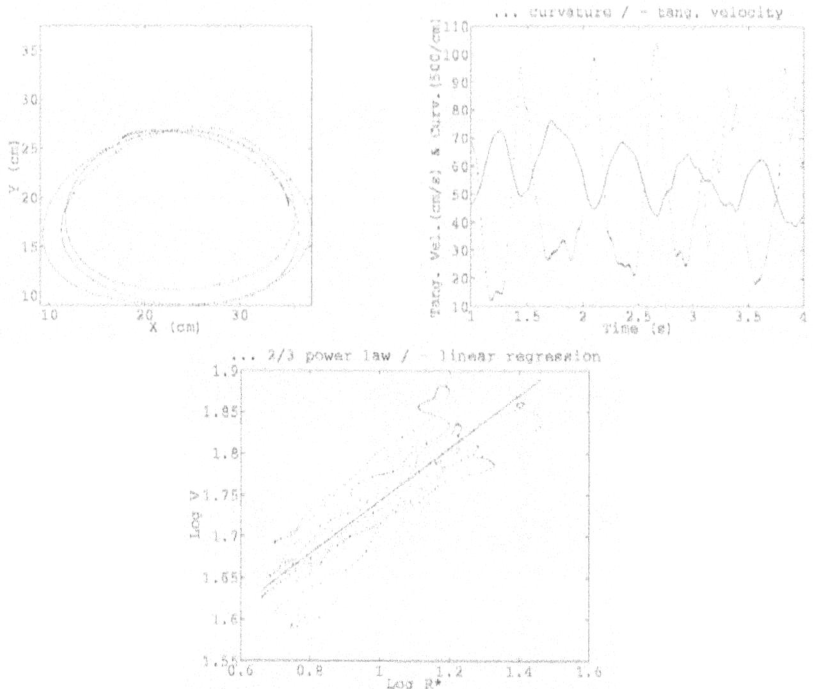

Fig. 3. Top left: human elliptical movement in the plane. Top right: tangential velocity and curvature displayed on the same scale. Bottom: log of tangential velocity versus log of R* where $R^* = R / (1+ \alpha R)$, $\alpha = 0.01$. Linear regression of log V against log R* gives a slope of $0.32 \approx 1/3$.

Supporting evidence for the power law has been provided in a large variety of studies. However, the law is most of the time obeyed for planar drawing patterns of relatively small size.

3.4 Smoothness Considerations

The Minimum Jerk model proposes another interpretation to motor production, providing a solution to the problem of trajectory formation. For point-to-point movements, it ensures that among all possible solutions for generating a trajectory, the motor control system chooses the one that maximizes the smoothness of the movement. This solution complies with the minimization of a global cost function C, expressed in terms of the mean square of the jerk (derivative of the acceleration) [24], [6]:

$$C = \frac{1}{2}\int_{t_1}^{t_2}\left[\left(\frac{d^3x}{dt^3}\right)^2 + \left(\frac{d^3y}{dt^3}\right)^2\right]dt \tag{8}$$

Some researchers think that the power law is a consequence of a constrained minimum jerk criterion along the end-effector trajectory.

Schaal argues that the 2/3 power law is a by-product of a movement system that favors smooth trajectories [25]. Therefore smoothness seems to be a major feature that generally characterizes natural movements. It can be attained by the minimization of the torque change criterion too [26]. Using the equilibrium point hypothesis, it has been shown that limb dynamics contributes significantly to producing power law.

4 Discussion and Perspectives

This paper presents a review of the most significant invariant laws in movement, i.e. the invariance of velocity profile, the Fitt's law and the Two-Third power law. These laws have been verified for real planar pointing or drawing gestures.

Rather than trying to discuss whether the motion invariants can explain or not some organizational principles employed by the brain for movement generation, we aim in our approach at using them for analysis, edition and synthesis of motion.

This issue is actually pertinent for the automatic animation of virtual characters with actions that reflect real human motions. Different sets of parameters are classically used to produce motion with a wide range of expressiveness. Among the different animation techniques, one of the most efficient is Inverse Kinematics [27], which is very used for its low computing cost and easiness of motion specification. In order to enhance the "naturalness" of the produced movements, this method can be linked to a trajectory specification in the end-effector space. In the EMOTE system for example [28], a series of key-postures are determined, and the Effort parameters, as defined by Laban Movement Analysis are used to generate the in-between postures.

In our work we exploit invariant laws as an alternative of interpolation techniques for motion specification, thus improving the realism of motion. We use a Sensory Motor Model for gesture generation, and a target-based control system that drives a geometrical hand-arm model [12], [29]. The targets are automatically extracted from real motion signals or calculated from the invariant laws. The position and timing occurrences of the targets are indeed directly calculated from Fitts' law for reaching tasks and from Two-Third Power law for cyclic tasks. Smoothness is achieved by introducing a coarticulation model associated to the target-based system. This approach has already proved to produce hand-arm realistic gestures [30-31].

In the near future we intend to study to what extent some of these invariant laws can be used to produce expressive parameterized gestures . We also want to evaluate the generation models, by comparing the motion captured trajectories with the synthesized trajectories.

References

1. Keele S.W. Movement control in skilled motor performance. Psychological Bulletin, 70, 387-403, 1968.
2. Schmidt, R.A. The motor program. In J.A.S. Kelso (Ed.) Human motor behavior: an introduction, pp. 187-218, Hillsdale NJ: Erlbaum, 1982.
3. Schmidt, R.A., Zelaznik H.N., Hawkins B., Franck J.S. et Quinn J.T. (197). Motor-ouput variability: a theory for the accuracy of rapid acts. Psychological Review, 86, pp. 415-451, 1975.
4. Feldman A.G. Once more on the equilibrium point hypothesis (lambda model) for motor control. Journal of Motor Behavior, 18, 17-54, 1966.
5. Bizzi E.N., Hogan N., Mussa-Ivaldi F.A et Giszer S. Does the nervous system use equilibrium point control to guide single and multiple joint movements. Behavioral and Brain Sciences, 15, pp. 603-613, 1992.
6. Hogan N. An organizing principle for a class of voluntary movements. Journal of Neuroscience, 4, 2745-2754, 1984.
7. Brown T.G. On the nature of the fundamental activity of the nervous centers ; together with an analysis of rhythmic activity in progression, and a theory of the evolution of function in the nervous system. Journal of Physiology, London, 48, pp. 18-46, 1914.
8. Stein P.S.G. A multiple level approach to motor pattern generation. In Ferrell W.R. and Proske U. edts., Neural control of movement. pp. 159-165. Plenum Press, New York, 1995.
9. Kelso J.A.S., Schöner, G. Self-organization on coordinative movement patterns. Human Movement Science, 7 : 27-46, 1988.
10. Kelso, J.A.S., Ding, M., Schöner, G. Dynamic pattern formation: a primer. In Baskin AB, Mitthenthal JE (eds.). Principles of Organization in Organisms, XII. Redwood City, CA, Addison-Wesley, 1992.
11. Zelaznick, H.N., Schmidt, R.A., Gielen, S.C.A.M. Kinematic properties of rapid aimed head movements, Journal of Motor Behavior, 18, pp. 353-372, 1987.
12. Gibet S. et Marteau P.F. A Self-Organized Model for the Control, Planning and Learning of Nonlinear Multi-Dimensional Systems Using a Sensory Feedback, *Journal of Applied Intelligence,* 4, pp. 337-349, 1994.
13. Morasso, P. Spatial control of arm movements. Exp. Brain Research, 42, pp. 223-227, 1981.
14. Freeman F.N. Experimental analysis of the writing movement. Psychological Review Monographs Supplement, 17, pp. 1-46, 1914.
15. Woodworth R.S. The accuracy of voluntary movement. Psychological Review 3, 1899.
16. Fitts, P.M. The information capacity of the human motor system in controlling the amplitude of movement, Journal of Experimental Psychology, 47(6), pp. 381-391, 1954.
17. Welford A.T. Fundamentals of Skill. New York : Methuen, 1968.
18. MacKenzie I.S. Fitts' Law as a Research and Design Tool in Human-Computer Interaction. Human Computer Interaction, vol. 7, Lawrence Erlbaum Associates Inc., pp. 91-139, 1992.
19. MacKenzie I.S. et Buxton W. Extending Fitts' law to two-dimensional tasks. Proceedings of the CHI'92 Conference on Human Factors in Computing Systems. New York :ACM, 1992.
20. Guiard Y., Beaudoin-Lafon M. et Mottet D. Navigation as Multiscale Pointing: Extending Fitts' Model to Very High Precision Tasks. Conference on Human factors in computing systems, CHI 1999, Pittsburgh, PA, pp. 450-457, 1999.
21. Viviani, P. et Terzuolo, C. A. Space-time invariance in learned motor skills. In G.E. Stelmach et J. Requin (eds). Tutorials in Motor Behavior. Amsterdam: North-Holland, 1980.

22. Viviani, P., Terzuolo, C. Trajectory determines movement dynamics, Neuroscience, 7, pp. 431-437, 1982.
23. Viviani, P., Cenzato, M. Segmentation and coupling in complex movements. Journal of Experimental Psychology, 11, pp. 828-845, 1985. Viviani P., Flash T. Minimum-Jerk, Two-Thirds Power Law, and Isochrony : Converging Approaches to movement planning. Journal of Experimental Psychology : Human Perception and Performance, vol. 21, n°1, pp. 32-53, 1995.
24. Flash T. & Hogan N., The coordination of arm movements : an experimentally confirmed mathematical model. Journal of Neuroscience 5, pp . 1688-1703, 1985.
25. Schaal S., Sternad D. Origins and Violations of the 2/3 Power Law in Thythmic 3D Arm Movements. Journal of Neurophysiology, 1999.
26. Uno Y., Kawato M. et Suzuki R. Formation and control of optimal trajectory in human multi-joint arm movement. Biological Cybernetics, 61, pp. 89-101, 1989.
27. Gribble P.L, Ostry D.J., Origins of the power law relation between movement velocity and curvature: modeling the effects of muscle mechanics and limb dynamics. The American Physiological Society, pp. 2853-2860, 1996.
28. Badler, N., Phillips, C., Webber, B.: Simulating Hulmans – Oxford University Press, Inc, 200 Madison Avenue, New York, 10016 (1993)
29. D. Chi, M. Costa, L. Zhao, and N. Badler: "The EMOTE model for Effort and Shape," ACM SIGGRAPH '00, New Orleans, LA, pp. 173-182, July 2000.
30. Lebourque, T., Gibet, S.: A complete system for the specification and the generation of sign language gestures, in Gesture-Based Communication in Human-Computer Interaction. Proc. GW'99, Gif sur Yvette (France), A. Braffort, R. Gherbi, S. Gibet, J. Richardson, D. Teil Eds., Springer-Verlag Pub. (1999) 227-251.
31. Julliard F. Spécification réactive pour l'animation de personnages articulés, PHD Thesis, University of South Paris, dec. 2001.

The Features People Use to Recognize Human Movement Style

Frank E. Pollick

Department of Psychology, University of Glasgow
58 Hillhead Street, Glasgow G12 8QB, UK
frank@psy.gla.ac.uk
http://www.psy.gla.ac.uk/~frank

Abstract. Observation of human movement informs a variety of person properties. However, it is unclear how this understanding of person properties is derived from the complex visual stimulus of human movement. I address this topic by first reviewing the literature on the visual perception of human movement and then discussing work that has explored the features used to discriminate between different styles of movement. This discussion includes work on quantifying human performance at style recognition, exaggeration of human movement and finally experimental derivation of a feature space to represent human emotion.

1 Introduction

As social beings we are keen to understand the intentions of those around us, and the observation of others' actions provides a window into their mental activities. Given this social context it is expected that humans would exhibit skill in parsing a variety of social signals from the observation of even mundane activities. However, if we start from the point of treating human movement as a visual signal it is difficult to understand how this decoding of human movement into intentions is achieved. Basic questions of what properties of human movement make it special and how these essential perceptual properties are organized to make cognitive representations remain active topics of research, and in this paper I review research that has addressed these questions

The paper is organized as follows: In Section 2 I review results on the visual perception of human movement that provide a basis for our understanding of human movement as a special class of motion. Then in Section 3 I address the issue of how the perceived features of movements can be used to support distinctions between different styles of movement. Finally, in Section 4 I summarize the findings.

2 Review of the Visual Perception of Human Movement

As a component of his research into the visual perception of motion Gunnar Johansson stimulated interest in the problem of human movement perception by demonstrat-

A. Camurri and G. Volpe (Eds.): GW 2003, LNAI 2915, pp. 10–19, 2004.

ing how it could be achieved by sparse displays. He showed that by placing lights on the joints and filming actors in a dark room it was possible to create point-light displays that produced a vivid impression of human movement [1]. There were two great technical advantages of this technique, the first is that the point-light displays still provide a vivid impression of human movement even though all other characteristics of the actor are subtracted away; the second is that by reducing human movement to the motions of a small set of points one has a motion stimuli that can readily be manipulated, controlled and compared to other simple motion stimuli. However, along with these technical advantages has come the yet unsolved puzzle as to how these points of light spontaneously organize themselves into human movement. While principles like rigidity can explain the perceptual organization of inanimate objects, there is no equivalent principle that can describe the organization of human point-light displays. From these simple point-light displays arose a variety of studies and in the following paragraphs I will present a rough chronology of this research.

Following on from the early results of Johansson that point light displays spontaneously organized themselves into the percept of human movement came the work of Cutting and colleagues who explored the conjecture that point light displays were sufficient to support the recognition of various person properties. Specifically it was shown that properties such as gender [2, 3] and identity [4, 5] could be identified from point-light walkers. These results solidified the belief that the perception of biological motion was special and motivated further theoretical work to explain the basis of this capability.

At least three different explanations were offered for the human capability to recognize point light walkers. Two of these exploited the unique structure of the human body using the constraints that although the body did not move rigidly, it did form a group of piecewise planar segments [6] or could be viewed as a hierarchy of body segments [7]. However, later experimental work did not find strong support that either of these constraints were by themselves critical for the perceptual organization of biological motion [8]. Another explanation of the perception of human movement was termed kinematic specification of dynamics and held that the perception of human movement should be formulated in terms of how the available motion kinematics could be used to infer the dynamics (forces, torques, etc) exhibited in the movements. Although convincing demonstrations were provided that showed how properties such as lifted weight were judged correctly, an elaboration of the specific mechanisms behind this capability was not provided [9, 10]. All three of these approaches shed light on the nature of the problem, but to date there still is no thorough and convincing theoretical construct to explain the perception of biological motion.

Additional evidence of the special nature of the perception of human movement came around the mid 1980s with a series of experiments in developmental psychology exploring infant perception of human movement [11, 12]. These studies revealed that infants as young as 4months old appeared to be sensitive to the human form displayed in motion by point light displays. Although this does not necessarily mean that the mechanisms for perception of human movement are innate it does illustrate that these capabilities develop early in life and might be considered as basic elements of our appreciation of the visual world.

If our ability to perceive human motion is a kind of primitive of motion perception then one could expect that some basic mechanism could be elucidated. However this has proved elusive. Two basic approaches have been examined that mirror the divisions among the perceptual and cognitive approaches they represent. The first approach is that specialized motion detectors are involved in the perception of human movement and that we can view the process in terms of bottom-up information that is specialized for representing human movement [13, 14] From these studies we can conclude that if such specialized detectors do exist then they have larger receptive fields that integrate over a longer temporal window. In distinction to these explanations based on specialized motion detectors are the results of experiments which suggest that it is the later impact of higher-level processing that organizes the motion signal into that of a human movement [15, 16, 17]. While it would seem likely that both approaches are to some extent correct there is hope that future studies of human brain imaging might be brought to bear on the topic.

In the past several years there has developed a vast literature investigating the brain areas and circuits involved in visual perception and the production of human movement. Although a thorough review of these areas is beyond the scope of this paper, (see [18] for a recent review) certain trends in this literature are significant enough to deserve mention. Starting with single-cell recording results from monkeys [19] and subsequent brain imaging experiments [20, 21, 22] studies have revealed a specific brain area in the human superior temporal sulcus (STS) that appears active when human movement is observed. This area in the STS has been implicated to be part of a larger system that is involved in social cognition [23, 24]. In addition to these visual and social regions, research into the production of human movement has found that certain brain areas traditionally thought of as motoric also serve a visual function. In particular the cells, termed mirror neurons [25], are activated by both producing a movement as well as seeing the same goal-directed movements performed. These results from neuropsychology are beginning to have impact on research into the perception of human movement since they suggest possible processing constraints. For example incorporation of the bidirectionality between movement production and recognition [26].

Finally, several studies have examined factors that influence the recognition of human movement. For example the effect of viewing position on recognizing human movement has been studied, revealing that recognition is viewpoint dependent [27]. Additional studies has explored the representation of human movement in egocentric and allocentric coordinate frames and revealed differences in how information is integrated across eye movements [28, 29]. It has also been shown that different types of human movements are recognized to different accuracy, for example, that locomotion is recognized better than instrumental actions [30].

3 Features for Style Recognition

This section examines the question of how different styles of movement are recognized. Movement style is defined broadly, akin to what is termed subordinate level categorization in object recognition. For example any given action could be done in a variety of ways, and this difference might signal differences in emotion, identity, vulnerability, gender, skill level, etc. For the most part, this section is a review of recent work in my laboratory and it is organized about three questions: How can we quantify human performance at style recognition? How can exaggeration of spatial and temporal properties of movements be used to obtain new movements with enhanced recognition? Is it possible to define a feature space for the recognition of emotional style? While each of these questions have their own particular methods they share the common method of examining the ability of observers to categorize different styles of movement and to relate this competency in categorization to the information available in the movements. They also share the common hope that finding the features that are salient for categorization will inform an understanding of what human movement properties are essential for the visual encoding and representation of human movement.

3.1 Quantifying the Efficiency of Style Recognition

One straightforward way to assess human performance at style recognition is to give observers a style recognition task and measure their accuracy at this task. However, there is an important issue with the use of accuracy as a measure of performance. This is that low accuracy might be due to exceptionally good performance at extracting information from an information-poor display or exceptionally bad performance at extracting information from an information-rich display. One way to deal with this issue is to obtain estimates of human efficiency, where human performance is compared to that of an algorithm that can be shown to use all the possible information. The efficiency measure generally used is the squared ratio of sensitivity (d') of the human observer to that of the ideal algorithm. This measure of efficiency can be used to compare performance across different tasks and it is generally accepted that efficiencies of over 10% indicate exceptionally good performance.

We performed two experiments examining the recognition of gender and affect from point light displays of arm movements performing knocking, lifting and waving actions in a neutral and angry style [31]. A database of approximately 1500 movements was collected from 26 actors (13 male, 13 female) and used in the study. At present it is impossible to come up with an algorithm that can be rigorously defined to be ideal. For this reason we used neural networks, trained on the subset of training movements from the database, to approach what ideal performance would be. Results showed that overall the network obtained d' values of approximately 3 regardless of whether recognizing gender or affect. However, human observers showed a large difference in performance - displaying d' values of around 1.5 for affect recognition and around 0 (chance level) for gender recognition. Computations of efficiency yielded upper-bound estimates of 32.5% for affect and 0.3% for gender recognition. From this we can reason that although the raw information was available to recognize both gender and affect, the perceptual system was not able to utilize the information that signaled gender.

Although in the study described above when arm movements were used as stimuli, observers were not able to use the available information to recognize gender there are numerous studies that have indicated that humans can recognize gender from point-light walkers. A meta-analysis of fifteen experiments examining the recognition of gender from the side view of a point light walker revealed an average percent correct of 67% with confidence intervals ($p<0.05$) spanning from 52% to 79%. [32]. While this supports the conclusion that we can recognize gender from point-light walkers it should also illustrate that we do not in general exhibit high accuracy on the task. However, this somewhat low accuracy might reflect exquisite performance on information-poor displays. To examine this we developed an optimal decision-maker based on body shape to use for the calculation of efficiency. The result of efficiency calculations revealed that efficiency was around 26% [32].

Taken together these two studies suggest that although we might not always have access to the information available in a movement, when we do we are very efficient at extracting the relevant information.

3.2 Spatial and Temporal Exaggerations of Movement

Movements unfold in both space and time and we wished to examine how the exaggeration of both spatial and temporal properties influenced the recognition of human movement style. The technique which we used to create these exaggerated movements was adapted from studies of face processing that have shown exaggerating facial features relative to a mean face to be useful in obtaining enhanced recognition [33, 34, 35, 36]. In essence the technique works by collecting a set of movements and then calculating averages of each style of movement as well as the grand average of all movements. By extrapolating in this movement space in the direction defined by the difference between a style average and the grand average it is possible to create movement exaggerations. We explored spatial exaggerations of the style of tennis serve [37], temporal exaggerations of identity from drinking movements [38] and spatial and temporal exaggerations of facial emotion [39].

Spatial exaggerations of tennis serve style was obtained by first obtaining 3D records of flat, slice and topspin tennis serves and animating these movements using tools of 3D human animation. Each tennis serve movement was specified by a vector with about 4000 dimensions corresponding to the 24 measurements with 3 spatial coordinates sampled at 60 Hz for around 1 second. Exaggerated displays were created by extrapolating to create exaggerated flat, slice and topspin serves. Results of this study showed an effect of the exaggeration technique, though the effect was clearest for the flat serves and individual difference indicated an effect of the exaggeration for slice serves only with the more "expert" tennis players. These measures of expertise were obtained independently on a dissimilarity rating task that showed that "experts" equally weighted all 3 serves equally, while "novices" had small weightings for at least one serve. While these results are encouraging, there is still the concern that since the exaggerated displays were created from individual frames, each that had been exaggerated, it was possible that enhanced recognition could have been due to a single frame rather than to the movement itself.

Temporal exaggerations of movement can be obtained which remove the previous concern about the effect of particular static frames. This temporal exaggeration technique requires that the movement being studied can be broken down into distinct phrases so that the relative timing of the different phrases can be manipulated. For the drinking movements we studied, the motion was decomposed into 5 segments based on minima of velocity of the wrist, these segments included: a) moving the hand from the side of the body to contact the glass, b) lifting the glass to the mouth, c) tilting the glass back, d) returning the glass to the table, and e) returning the hand to the side of the body. A database of 7 different drinkers was used to reveal that exaggerating the differences among the relative phrasing of the movements could be used to obtain enhanced recognition. For these displays the spatial pattern of every individual was identical for all exaggeration conditions, all that ever changed in the displays shown to observers was the timing of the segments. Thus, the exaggeration had to occur due to some property intrinsic to the motion. This study confirmed the use of temporal information in the recognition of human movement style.

The results of these two studies indicated that both spatial and temporal properties could be exaggerated to obtain enhanced recognition. One possible interpretation of this is that a spatiotemporal interaction such as velocity mediated the exaggeration effects obtained. Both of our exaggeration techniques change the velocity profile of the movement as they act to exaggerate the spatial or temporal information. We studied this effect further by performing both spatial and temporal exaggerations of facial emotion for point-light faces [39]. These results showed a clear effect of spatial exaggeration but no equivalent effect of temporal exaggeration. From this result with faces it is tempting to speculate that for different activities the essence of the movement style is present to different degrees in the spatial and temporal encoding of the movement.

3.3 Emotion and the Organization of Feature Space

The problem of recognizing emotion from human movement has been explored for the special case of the interpretation of stylized dance movements [40, 41]. Of the six emotions examined (surprise, fear, anger, disgust, grief/sadness, joy/happiness) it was found in both studies that anger was the most reliably identified emotion. Other differences among the recognition of the different emotions were noted though they fell into no particular pattern between the two studies. These studies provide good evidence that stylized movements can be seen as expressive, but do not address the more general case of movements that are not stylized. We performed experiments to see how well affect could be recognized from everyday movements such as knocking and drinking where only point-light displays of the arm were available [42].

To perform these experiments we first obtained recordings of the 3D motion of the arm from two actors as they performed movements in one of 10 affective styles (afraid, angry, excited, happy, neutral, relaxed, sad, strong, tired and weak). Participants viewed these displays and tried to correctly identify which of the 10 affects had been presented to them. Results were converted to a matrix of dissimilarities and input to a multidimensional scaling (MDS) algorithm. In a first experiment using the natural 3D recordings results showed that the structure of this MDS solution was similar to the two-dimensional circumplex structure of affect obtained by Russell [43] with one dimension varying along an activation axis and the other varying along a valence axis. In a second experiment we inserted a random phase delay into each point and inverted the display to show it to observers who made the same judgements as to the exhibited affect in the display. The results of this experiment showed that the ordering of affects along the activation axis was preserved but a reorganization along the valence axis was found. In both experiments we were able to show a strong correlation between the actual movement kinematics and the position of a movement along the activation axis - with more activation correlated positively to greater velocity. However, no strong correlation between kinematics and the valence dimension was obtained for either experiment.

The results generally indicated that activation was more robustly recovered than pleasantness. One possible reason for this is that by its nature movement is a more natural indicator of physiological arousal and its associated neural mechanisms. In addition, the continuous structure of the circumplex model parallels the smoothly varying range of speeds with which a movement can be performed. Thus, it would appear that the mapping between stimulus properties and representation of affect is a fairly direct one for the activation axis. However, such a direct connection between stimulus and representation has proven elusive for the second dimension of pleasantness. Other research has suggested that subtle phase relations between the joints might possibly carry information about affect [44]. Comparison of the results between our two experiments supports this view, however the present data does not indicate which aspect of the phase relations is the crucial one.

4 Summary

This paper has outlined what is known about the visual perception of human movement and how human movement can be decomposed into features for the recognition of movement style. Although these results fall short of the ultimate goal of a clear model of the transformation from visual input to understanding intent it does set down useful methodologies and results to guide research to this ultimate goal. In the following paragraph I give a brief summary of the paper.

The paper began with a review of the visual perception of biological motion, which revealed that there is no dominant theory to explain our capability to understand this special kind of motion. Although studies show that the appreciation of biological motion begins at an early age and appears to have dedicated neural circuits devoted to its functioning, it remains unknown whether these capabilities critically involve specialized detectors or input from higher cognitive centers. The paper next explored the study of categorization of movement style since it provides a means to understand what features of human movement are essential for its recognition. Studies into the goal of quantifying human performance of style recognition indicate that we aren't always able to decode the information available to recognize movements, but that when we can recognize movements then we exhibit high efficiency. Work on the manipulation of spatial and temporal properties show that enhanced recognition can be obtained by exaggerating relative to an average movement. While these studies did not isolate the specific spatial or temporal (or spatiotemporal) property key for recognition, the effectiveness of temporal exaggerations did indicate that properties intrinsic to the motion (i.e. not reliant on a single frame of the motion sequence) could be used for recognition. Finally, the exploration of emotion from everyday movements revealed a representation of emotion that was consistent with the two-dimensional circumplex model described in cognitive psychology. Moreover, it was shown that the activation axis of this circumplex model had a high correlation with movement kinematics.

References

1. Johansson, G.: Visual perception of biological motion and a model for its analysis. Perception and Psychophysics **14** (1973) 201-211.
2. Kozlowski, L.T., Cutting, J.E.: Recognizing the sex of a walker from a dynamic point-light display. Perception and Psychophysics **21** (1977) 575-580.
3. Barclay, C.D., Cutting, J. E., Kozlowski, L. T.: Temporal and spatial factors in gait perception that influence gender recognition. Perception and Psychophysics **23** (1978) 145-152.
4. Cutting, J.E., Kozlowski, L.T.: Recognizing friends by their walk: Gait perception without familiarity cues. Bulletin of the Psychonomic Society **9** (1977) 353-356.
5. Beardsworth, T., Buckner, T.: The ability to recognize oneself from a video recording of one's movements without seeing one's body. Bulletin of the Psychonomic Society **18** (1981) 19-22.
6. Hoffman, D.D., Flinchbaugh, B.E.: The interpretation of biological motion. Biological Cybernetics **42** (1982) 195-204.
7. Cutting, J.E., Proffitt, D.: Gait perception as an example of how we may perceive events. In: Walk, R., Pick, Jr. H. (eds.): Intersensory perception and sensory integration. Plenum, New York, New York (1981).
8. Bertenthal, B.I., Pinto, J.: Global processing of biological motions. Psychological Science **5** (1994) 221-225.
9. Runeson, S., Frykholm, G.: Visual perception of lifted weight. Journal of Experimental Psychology-Human Perception and Performance **7** (1981) 733-740.
10. Runeson, S., Frykholm, G.: Kinematic specification of dynamics as an informational basis for person and action perception: Expectation, gender recognition, and deceptive intention. Journal of Experimental Psychology-General **112** (1983) 585-615.
11. Fox, R., McDaniel, C.: The perception of biological motion by human infants. Science **218** (1982) 486-487.
12. Bertenthal, B.I., Proffitt, D.R., Kramer, S.J., Spetner, N.B.: Infants encoding of kinetic displays varying in relative coherence. Developmental Psychology **23** (1987) 171-178.
13. Mather, G., Radford, K., West, S.: Low-Level Visual Processing of Biological Motion. Proceedings of the Royal Society of London Series B-Biological Sciences **249** (1992) 149-155.

14. Neri, P., Morrone, M.C., Burr, D.C.: Seeing biological motion. Nature **395** (1998) 894-896.
15. Shiffrar, M., Freyd, J.J.: Apparent motion of the human body. Psychological Science **1** (1990) 257-264.
16. Shiffrar, M., Freyd, J.J.: Timing and apparent motion path choice with human body photographs. Psychological Science **4** (1993) 379-384.
17. Thornton, I.M., Pinto, J., Shiffrar, M.: The visual perception of human locomotion. Cognitive Neuropsychology **15** (1998) 535-552.
18. Giese, M.A., Poggio, T., Neural mechanisms for the recognition of biological movements and action. Nature Reviews Neuroscience **4** (2003) 179-192.
19. Oram, M.W., Perrett, D.I.: Responses of Anterior Superior Temporal Polysensory (Stpa) Neurons to Biological Motion Stimuli. Journal of CognitiveNeuroscience **6** (1994) 99-116
20. Decety, J., Grezes, J.: Neural mechanisms subserving the perception of human actions. Trends in Cognitive Sciences **3** (1999) 172-178.
21. Grezes, J., Fonlupt, P., Bertenthal, B., Delon-Martin, C., Segebarth, C., Decety, J.: Does perception of biological motion rely on specific brain regions? Neuroimage, **13** (2001) 775-785.
22. Grossman, E., Donnelly, M., Price, R., Pickens, D., Morgan, V., Neighbor, G., Blake, R.: Brain areas involved in perception of biological motion. Journal of Cognitive Neuroscience **12** (2000) 711-720.
23. Adolphs, R.: The neurobiology of social cognition. Current Opinion in Neurobiology **11** (2001) 231-239.
24. Allison, T., Puce, A., & McCarthy, G.: Social perception from visual cues: role of the STS region. Trends in Cognitive Sciences **4** (2000) 267-278.
25. Rizzolatti, G., Fogassi, L., Gallese, V.: Neurophysiological mechanisms underlying the understanding and imitation of action. Nature Reviews Neuroscience **2** (2001) 661-670.
26. Troje, N.F.: Decomposing biological motion: A framework for analysis and synthesis of human gait patterns. Journal of Vision **2** (2002) 371-387.
27. Verfaillie, K.: Orientation-Dependent Priming Effects in the Perception of Biological Motion. Journal of Experimental Psychology-Human Perception and Performance **19** (1993) 992-1013.
28. Verfaillie, K.: Transsaccadic memory for the egocentric and allocentric position of a biological-motion walker. Journal of Experimental Psychology-Learning Memory and Cognition **23** (1997) 739-760.
29. Verfaillie, K., Detroy, A., Vanrensbergen, J.: Transsaccadic Integration of Biological Motion. Journal of Experimental Psychology-Learning Memory and Cognition **20** (1994) 649-670.
30. Dittrich, W.H.: Action categories and the perception of biological motion. Perception **22** (1991) 15-22.
31. Pollick, F.E., Lestou, V., Ryu, J., Cho, S-B.: Estimating the efficiency of recognizing gender and affect from biological motion. Vision Research **42** (2002) 2345-2355.
32. Pollick, F.E., Kay, J., Heim, K., Stringer, R.: A review of gender recognition from gait. Perception **31** (2002) 118-118.
33. Perrett, D.I., May, K.A., Yoshikawa, S.: Facial shape and judgements of female attractiveness. Nature **368** (1994) 239-242.
34. Perrett, D.I., Lee, K.J., Penton-Voak, I., Rowland, D., Yoshikawa, S., Burt, D.M., Henzi, S.P., Castles, D.L., Akamatsu, S.: Effects of sexual dimorphism on facial attractiveness. Nature **394** (1998) 884-887.

35. Rhodes, G., Brennan, S., Carey, S.: Identification and ratings of caricatures: Implications for learning the mental representations of faces. Cognitive Psychology **19** (1987) 473-497.
36. Rhodes, G.: Superportraits: caricatures and recognition. Psychology Press, Hove, Sussex (1996).
37. Pollick, F.E., Fidopiastis, C.M., Braden, V.: Recognizing the style of spatially exaggerated tennis serves. Perception **30** (2001) 323-338.
38. Hill, H., Pollick, F.E.: Exaggerating temporal differences enhances recognition of individuals from point light displays. Psychological Science **11** (2000) 223-228.
39. Pollick, F.E., Hill, H., Calder, A., Paterson, H.: Recognizing facial expression from spatially and temporally modified movements. Perception **32** (2003) 813-826.
40. Walk, R.D. & Homan, C.P.: Emotion and dance in dynamic light displays. Bulletin of the Psychonomic Society **22** (1984) 437-440.
41. Dittrich, W.H., Troscianko, T., Lea, S.E.G., Morgan, D.: Perception of emotion from dynamic point-light displays represented in dance. Perception **25** (1996) 727-738.
42. Pollick, F.E., Paterson, H., Bruderlin, A., Sanford, A.J.: Perceiving affect from arm movement. Cognition **82** (2001) B51-B61.
43. Russell, J.A.: A circumplex model of affect. Journal of Personality and Social Psychology **39** (1980) 1161-1178.
44. Amaya, K., Bruderlin, A., Calvert, T.: Emotion from motion. In: Davis, W.A., Bartels, R. (eds.): Graphics Interface '96, (1996) 222-229.

Multimodal Analysis of Expressive Gesture in Music and Dance Performances

Antonio Camurri, Barbara Mazzarino, Matteo Ricchetti, Renee Timmers, and Gualtiero Volpe

InfoMus Lab, DIST - University of Genova
Viale Causa 13, I-16145, Genova, Italy
{toni,bunny,rtimmers,rmat,volpe}@infomus.dist.unige.it
http://infomus.dist.unige.it

Abstract. This paper presents ongoing research on the modelling of expressive gesture in multimodal interaction and on the development of multimodal interactive systems explicitly taking into account the role of non-verbal expressive gesture in the communication process. In this perspective, a particular focus is on dance and music as first-class conveyors of expressive and emotional content. Research outputs include (i) computational models of expressive gesture, (ii) validation by means of continuous ratings on spectators exposed to real artistic stimuli, and (iii) novel hardware and software components for the EyesWeb open platform (www.eyesweb.org), such as the recently developed Expressive Gesture Processing Library. The paper starts with a definition of expressive gesture. A unifying framework for the analysis of expressive gesture is then proposed. Finally, two experiments on expressive gesture in dance and music are discussed. This research work has been supported by the EU IST project MEGA (Multisensory Expressive Gesture Applications, www.megaproject.org) and the EU MOSART TMR Network.

1 Introduction

Expressive gesture is a key concept in our research (Camurri et al., 2001). This paper tries to face it and introduces two experiments aiming at understanding the non-verbal mechanisms of expressive/emotional communication.

Several definitions of gesture exist in the literature. The most common use of the term is with respect to natural gesture, which is defined as a support to verbal communication. For Cassel and colleagues (1990) "A natural gesture means the types of gestures spontaneously generated by a person telling a story, speaking in public, or holding a conversation". McNeill (1992) in his well-known taxonomy divides the natural gestures generated during a discourse in four different categories: iconic, metaphoric, deictic, and beats. In a wider perspective Kurtenbach and Hulteen (1990) define gesture as "a movement of the body that contains information". A survey and a discussion of existing definition of gesture can be found in (Cadoz and Wanderley, 2000).

In artistic contexts and in particular in the field of performing arts, gesture is often not intended to denote things or to support speech as in the traditional framework of natural gesture, but the information it contains and conveys is related to the affec-

A. Camurri and G. Volpe (Eds.): GW 2003, LNAI 2915, pp. 20–39, 2004.

tive/emotional domain. From this point of view, gesture can be considered "expressive" depending on the kind of information it conveys: expressive gesture carries what Cowie et al. (2001) call "implicit messages", and what Hashimoto (1997) calls KANSEI. That is, expressive gesture is the responsible of the communication of information that we call *expressive content*. Expressive content is different and in most cases independent from, even if often superimposed to, possible denotative meaning. Expressive content concerns aspects related to feelings, moods, affect, intensity of emotional experience.

For example, the same action can be performed in several ways, by stressing different qualities of movement: it is possible to recognize a person from the way he/she walks, but it is also possible to get information about the emotional state of a person by looking at his/her gait, e.g., if he/she is angry, sad, happy. In the case of gait analysis, we can therefore distinguish among several objectives and layers of analysis: a first one aiming at describing the physical features of the movement, for example in order to classify it (quite a lot of research work can be found in the computer vision literature about gait analysis, see for example Liu et al., 2002); a second one aiming at extracting the expressive content gait coveys, e.g., in terms of information about the emotional state that the walker communicates through his/her way of walking. From this point of view, walking can be considered as an expressive gesture: even if no denotative meaning is associated with it, it still communicates information about the emotional state of the walker, i.e., it conveys a specific expressive content. In fact, in this perspective the walking action fully satisfies the conditions stated in the definition of gesture by Kurtenbach and Hulteen (1990): walking is "a movement of the body that contains information". Some studies can be found aiming at analysing the expressive intentions conveyed through everyday actions: for example, Pollick (2001) investigated the expressive content of actions like knocking or drinking

If on the one hand expressive gestures partially include natural gestures, that is, natural gestures can also be expressive gestures, we face on the other hand a more general concept of expressive gesture that includes not only natural gestures but also musical, human movement, visual (e.g., computer animated) gestures. Our concept of expressive gesture is therefore somewhat broader than the concept of gesture as defined by Kurtenbach and Hulteen, since it considers also cases in which, with the aid of technology, communication of expressive content takes place even without an explicit movement of the body, or, at least, the movement of the body is only indirectly involved in the communication process (e.g. the allusion at movement in musical signals). This can happen, for example, also when using visual media. The expressive content is conveyed through a continuum of possible ways ranging from realistic to abstract images and effects: cinematography, cartoons, virtual environments with computer animated characters and avatars, expressive control of lighting and colour in a theatre context (e.g., related to actor's physical gestures). Consider, for example, a theatre performance: the director, the choreographer, or the composer can ask actors, dancers, musicians, to communicate content through specific expressive gestures (e.g., dance and/or music interpretation). At the same time, technology enables the director to extend artistic language: he can map motion or music features onto particular configurations of lights, on movement of virtual characters, on automatically generated computer music and live electronics. In this way, he can create an "extended" expressive gesture that - while still having the purpose of communicating an expressive content - it is only partially related to explicit body movement: in a way, such "extended expressive gesture" is the result of a juxtaposition of several dance, music, and visual gestures, but it is not just the sum of them, since it also includes the artistic point of view of the artist who created it, and it is perceived as a whole multimodal stimulus by human spectators.

Our research on expressive gesture is finalized to the development of interactive multimedia systems based on novel interaction paradigms enabling a deeper experience and participation of the user by explicitly observing and processing his/her (multimodal) expressive gesture. Since artistic performance uses non-verbal communication mechanisms to convey expressive content, we focused on performing arts, and in particular on dance and music, as the main test-beds where computational models of expressive gesture and algorithms for expressive gesture processing can be developed, studied, and tested.

In particular, our attention has been focused on two aspects:

- Expressive gesture as a way to convey a particular emotion to the audience;
- Expressive gesture as a way to induce intense emotional experience in the audience (see e.g. Scherer, 2003).

Each of them has been recently subject of experiments at our Lab aiming at understanding which features in an expressive gesture are responsible for the communication of the expressive content, and how the dynamics of these features correlates with a specific expressive content.

In this paper, we concretely illustrate our approach by presenting two experiments focused on these two aspects.

The first one aims at (i) individuating which motion cues are mostly involved in conveying the dancer's expressive intentions (in term of basic emotions) to the audience during a dance performance and (ii) testing the developed models and algorithms by comparing their performances with spectators' ratings of the same dance fragments.

The second one investigates the mechanisms responsible for the audience's engagement in a musical performance. The aim of this experiment is again twofold: (i) individuating which auditory and visual cues are mostly involved in conveying the performer's expressive intentions and (ii) testing the developed model by comparing its performance with spectators' ratings of the same musical performances.

For the analysis of expressive gesture in these experiments we developed a unifying conceptual framework, described it in the next section.

2 A Unifying Layered Conceptual Framework

The experiments presented in this paper address expressive gesture in music and dance performance.

While gesture in dance performance mainly concerns the visual/physical modality (even if the auditory components can be relevant as well), gesture in music performance uses both the auditory and the visual channels to convey expressive information, and, thus, it is multimodal in its essence. Gesture in music performance is not only the expressive and functional physical gesture of a performer, but it also includes expressive gesture present in the produced sound. When we define gesture in terms of structural units that have internal consistency and are distinguished in time and quality from neighbouring units, it is possible to analyse gesture in both (acoustic and visual) modalities. Multimodality is therefore a key issue. In order to deal with multimodal input a unifying conceptual framework has been adopted, derived from (Camurri, De Poli, Leman, 2001). It is based on a layered approach ranging from low-level physical measures (e.g., position, speed, acceleration of body parts for dance gestures; sampled audio signals or MIDI messages for music gesture) toward descriptors of overall gesture features (e.g., motion fluency, directness, impulsiveness for dance gestures; analysis of melodic, harmonic, agogic qualities of a music phrase for music gesture).

This layered approach is sketched in Figure 1. Each layer is depicted with its inputs, its outputs, and the kind of processing it is responsible for. In the following sections, each layer will be discussed with respect to its role in the two experiments.

Our conceptual framework, here presented for analysis, can also be applied for synthesis of expressive gesture: for example for the generation and control of the movement of avatars, virtual characters, or robots in Mixed Reality scenarios, as well as for the synthesis and interpretation of music. Examples of synthesis of expressive movement and expressive audio content are well documented in literature: see e.g. the EMOTE system (Chi et al., 2000) for generation of movement of avatars and virtual characters based on high level motion qualities, and the systems for synthesis of expressive music performances developed at KTH (Friberg et al, 2000) and by the DEI-CSC group at the University of Padova (Canazza et al., 2000).

Finally, it should be noticed that in the perspective of developing novel interactive multimedia systems for artistic applications, such a framework should be considered in the context of a broader scenario (Mixed reality, Distributed Collaborative Virtual Environments) in which virtual subjects (e.g., virtual characters) who behave both as observers and as agents perform the four layers of processing in the analysis of observed expressive gestures and in the synthesis of expressive gestures to communicate (directly or remotely) with other real and virtual subjects.

3 Analysis of Expressive Gesture in Dance Performance

As an example of analysis of expressive gesture in dance performance, we discuss an experiment carried out in collaboration with the Department of Psychology of the University of Uppsala (Sweden) in the EU-IST MEGA project.

The aim of the experiment was twofold: (i) individuating which motion cues are mostly involved in conveying the dancer's expressive intentions to the audience during a dance performance and (ii) testing the developed models and algorithms by comparing their performances with spectators' ratings of the same dance fragments.

In the case of this experiment, expressive gesture was analysed with respect to its ability to convey emotions to the audience. The study focused on the communication through dance gesture and recognition by spectators of the four basic emotions: anger, fear, grief, and joy.

The research hypotheses are grounded on the role of the Laban's dimensions in dance gesture, as described in Laban's Theory of Effort (Laban, 1947, 1963):

- The time dimension in terms of overall duration of time and tempo changes also elaborated as the underlying structure of rhythm and flow of the movement;
- The space dimension in its aspects related to Laban's "personal space" e.g., to what extent limbs are contracted or expanded in relation to the body centre;

High-level expressive information: (Experiment 1) Recognized emotions (e.g., anger, fear, grief, joy); (Experiment 2) Predict spectators' intensity of emotional experience.

Layer 4 – Concepts and structures
Modelling techniques (for example, classification in terms of basic emotions, or prediction of intense emotional experience in spectators): e.g., based on multiple regression, neural networks, support vector machines, decision trees, Bayesian

Segmented gestures and related parameters (e.g., absolute and relative durations), trajectories representing gestures in semantic spaces.

Layer 3 – Mid-level features and maps
Techniques for gesture segmentation: motion segmentation (e.g., in pause and motion phases), segmentation of musical excerpts in musical phrases. Representation of gestures as trajectories in semantic spaces (e.g., Laban's Effort space,

Motion and audio descriptors: e.g., amount of energy - loudness, amount of contraction/expansion - spectral width and melodic contour, low fluency - roughness etc.

Layer 2 – Low-level features
Computer vision techniques on the incoming images, statistical measures, signal processing techniques on audio signals.

- Images pre-processed to detect movement, trajectory of points (e.g., trajectories of body parts, trajectories of dancers in the space).
- MIDI and audio pre-processed to detect spectral and temporal low-level features.

Layer 1 – Physical signals
Analysis of video and audio signals: techniques for background subtraction, motion detection, motion tracking (e.g., techniques for colour tracking, optical flow based feature tracking), techniques for audio pre-processing and filtering, signal

Data from several kinds of sensors, e.g., images from videocameras, positions from localization systems, data from accelerometers, sampled audio, MIDI messages.

Fig. 1. The layered conceptual framework.

- The flow dimension in terms of analysis of shapes of speed and energy curves, and frequency/rhythm of motion and pause phases.
- The weight dimension in terms of amount of tension and dynamics in movement, e.g., vertical component of acceleration.

These cues were predicted to be associated in different combinations to each emotion category. Details can be found in (Camurri, Lagerlof, Volpe, 2003).

3.1 Description of the Experiment

An experienced choreographer was asked to design a choreography such that it excluded any propositional gesture or posture and it avoided stereotyped emotions.

In Uppsala, five dancers performed this same dance with four different emotional expressions: anger, fear, grief and joy. Each dancer performed all four emotions. The dance performances were video-recorded by two digital videocameras (DV recording format) standing fixed in the same frontal view of the dance (a spectator view). One camera obtained recordings to be used as stimuli for spectators' ratings. The second video camera was placed in the same position but with specific recording conditions and hardware settings to simplify and optimise automated recognition of movement cues (e.g., high speed shutter). Dancers' clothes were similar (dark), contrasting with the white background, in an empty performance space without any scenery. Digitised fading eliminated facial information and the dancers appeared as dark and distant figures against a white background.

The psychologists in Uppsala then proceeded in collecting spectators' ratings: the dances were judged with regard to perceived emotion by 32 observers, divided in two groups. In one group ratings were collected by 'forced choice' (chose one emotion category and rate its intensity) for each performance, while the other group was instructed to use a multiple choice schemata, i.e., to rate the intensity of each emotion on all four emotion scales for each performance.

At the same time, at the InfoMus Lab we proceeded in extracting motion cues from the video recordings and in developing models for automatic classification of dance gestures in term of the conveyed basic emotion.

3.2 Automated Extraction of Motion Cues

Extraction of motion cues followed the conceptual framework described in Section 2.

3.2.1 Layer 1

In the case of analysis of dance performance from video, layer 1 is responsible for the processing of the incoming video frames in order to detect and obtain information about the motion that is actually occurring. It receives as input images from one or more videocameras and, if available, information from other sensors (e.g., accelerometers). Two types of output are generated: processed images and trajectories of body parts. Layer 1 accomplishes its task by means of consolidated computer vision techniques usually employed for real-time analysis and recognition of human motion and activity: see for example the temporal templates technique for representation and recognition of human movement described in Bobick and J. Davis (2001). It should be noticed that in contrast to Bobick and J. Davis research, we do not aim at detecting or recognizing a specific kind of motion or activity. The techniques we use include feature tracking based on the Lucas-Kanade algorithm (Lucas and Kanade, 1981), skin color tracking to extract positions and trajectories of hands and head, an algorithm to divide a body silhouette in sub-regions, and Silhouette Motion Images (SMIs). A SMI is an image carrying information about variations of the silhouette shape and position in the last few frames. SMIs are inspired to motion-energy images (MEI) and motion-history images (MHI) (Bradsky and J. Davis, 2002, Bobick and J. Davis, 2001). They differ from MEIs in the fact that the silhouette in the last (more recent) frame is removed from the output image: in such a way only motion is considered while the current posture is skipped. Thus, SMIs can be considered as carrying information about the "amount of motion" occurred in the last frames. Information about time is implicit in SMI and is not explicitly recorded. We also use an extension of SMIs, which takes into account the internal motion in silhouettes. In such a way we are able to distinguish between global movements of the whole body in the General Space and internal movements of body limbs inside the Kinesphere.

3.2.2 Layer 2

Layer 2 is responsible of the extraction for a set of motion cues from the data coming from low-level motion tracking. Its inputs are the processed images and the trajectories of points (motion trajectories) coming from Layer 1. Its output is a collection of motion cues describing movement and its qualities. According to the research hypotheses described above, the cues extracted for this experiment include:

- Cues related to the amount of movement (energy) and in particular what we call Quantity of Motion (QoM). QoM is computed as the area (i.e., number of pixels) of a SMI (Camurri, Lagerlof, Volpe, 2003). It can be considered as an overall measure of the amount of detected motion, involving velocity and force.
- Cues related to body contraction/expansion and in particular the Contraction Index (CI). CI is a measure, ranging from 0 to 1, of how the dancer's body uses the space surrounding it. The algorithm to compute the CI (Camurri, Lagerlof, Volpe, 2003) combines two different techniques: the individuation of an ellipse approximating the body silhouette and computations based on the bounding region. The former is based on an analogy between the image moments and mechanical moments (Kilian, 2001): the eccentricity of the approximating ellipse is related to body contraction/expansion. The latter compares the area covered by the minimum rectangle surrounding the dancer with the area currently covered by the silhouette.
- Cues derived from psychological studies (e.g., Boone and Cunningham, 1998) such as amount of upward movement, dynamics of the Contraction Index (i.e., how much CI was over a given threshold along a time unit);
- Cues related to the use of space: length and overall direction of motion trajectories;
- Kinematical cues (e.g., velocity and acceleration) calculated on motion trajectories.

For those cues depending on motion trajectories a Lucas-Kanade feature tracker has been employed in Layer 1. A redundant set of 40 points randomly distributed on the whole body has been tracked. Points have been reassigned each time dancers stopped their motion (i.e., a pause was detected) so that a small and not significant amount of points is lost during tracking. Overall motion cues have been calculated by averaging the values obtained for each trajectory.

Figure 2 shows an example of extraction of motion cues using the EyesWeb open platform and specifically the EyesWeb Expressive Gesture Processing Library.

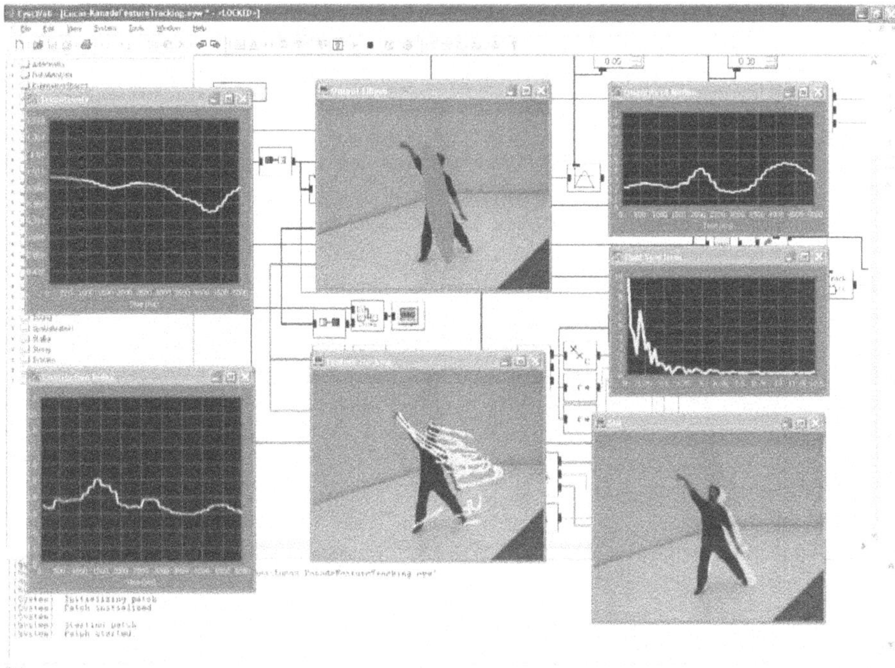

Fig. 2. An EyesWeb application extracting motion cues (QoM, CI, Kinematical cues).

3.2.3 Layer 3

Layer 3 is in charge of segmenting motion in order to individuate motion and non-motion (pause) phases. QoM has been used to perform such segmentation. QoM is related to the overall amount of motion and its evolution in time can be seen as a sequence of bell-shaped curves (*motion bells*). In order to segment motion, a list of these motion bells has been extracted and their features (e.g., peak value and duration) computed. An empirical threshold has been defined for these experiments: the dancer is considered to be moving if its current QoM is above the 2.5% of the average value of the QoM computed along each whole dance fragment.

Segmentation allows extracting further higher-level cues, e.g., cues related to the time duration of motion and pause phases. A concrete example is the Directness Index (DI), calculated as the ratio between the length of the straight trajectory connecting the first and the last point of a motion trajectory and the sum of the lengths of each segment constituting the trajectory. Moreover, segmentation can be considered as a first step toward the analysis of the rhythmic aspects of the dance. Analysis of the sequence of pause and motion phases and their relative time durations can lead to a first evaluation of dance tempo and its evolution in time, i.e., tempo changes, articulation (the analogous to music legato/staccato). Parameters from pause phases can also be extracted to individuate real still standing positions from active pauses involving low-motion (hesitation or subtle swaying or tremble e.g., due to instable equilibrium or fatigue).

Furthermore, motion fluency and impulsiveness can be evaluated. They are related to Laban's Flow and Time axes. Fluency can be estimated starting from an analysis of the temporal sequence of motion bells. A dance fragment performed with frequent stops and restarts (i.e., characterized by a high number of short pause and motion phases) will result less fluent than the same movement performed in a continuous, "harmonic" way (i.e., with a few long motion phases). The hesitating, bounded performance will be characterized by a higher percentage of acceleration and deceleration in the time unit (due to the frequent stops and restarts), a parameter that has been demonstrated of relevant importance in motion flow evaluation (see, for example, Zhao 2001, where a neural network is used to evaluate Laban's flow dimension).

A first measure of impulsiveness can be obtained from the shape of a motion bell. In fact, since QoM is directly related to the amount of detected movement, a short motion bell having a high pick value will be the result of an impulsive movement (i.e., a movement in which speed rapidly moves from a value near or equal to zero, to a peak and back to zero). On the other hand, a sustained, continuous movement will show a motion bell characterized by a relatively long time period in which the QoM values have little fluctuations around the average value (i.e., the speed is more or less constant during the movement).

Fluency and impulsiveness are also related to the spectral content of the QoM: a movement having significant energy at high frequencies is a candidate to be characterized by low fluency.

3.2.4 Layer 4

In this experiment, Layer 4 collects inputs from Layers 2 and 3 (18 variables have been calculated on each detected motion phase) and tries to classify a motion phase in term of the four basic emotions anger, fear, grief and joy.

As a first step, statistical techniques have been used for a preliminary analysis: descriptive statistics and a one-way ANOVA have been computed for each motion cue. Results of such preliminary analysis can be found in (Mazzarino, 2002; Camurri, Lagerlof, Volpe, 2003; Volpe, 2003).

Decision tree models have then been built for classification. Five training sets (85% of the available data) and five test sets (15% of the available data) have been extracted from the data set. The samples for the test sets were uniformly distributed along the four classes and the five dancers. Five decision trees have been built on the five training sets and evaluated on the five test sets. The Gini's index of heterogeneity has been used for building the decision trees. Decision trees have been selected for this study since they produce rules that can be used to interpret the results. Comparison with other classification techniques (e.g., Neural Networks, Support Vector Machines) remains for possible future work.

The above-described techniques in the four layers have been implemented in our EyesWeb open software platform (Camurri et al. 2000). Free download of technical documentation and full software environment are available at www.eyesweb.org. The Expressive Gesture Processing Library (Camurri et al., 2003) includes these and other processing modules.

3.3 Results

Results from spectators' ratings are described in (Camurri, Lagerlof, Volpe, 2003). The results obtained on the five decision trees can be summarized as follows (results for the best model are reported in Tables 1 and 2 showing the confusion matrices for the training set and for the test set respectively).

Table 1. Confusion matrix for the training set for the best decision tree.

Class	Total	%Correct	%Error	Anger	Fear	Grief	Joy
Anger	64	71.9	28.1	46	10	2	6
Fear	60	61.7	38.3	15	37	1	7
Grief	86	47.7	52.3	10	19	41	16
Joy	74	64.9	35.1	13	8	5	48

Table 2. Confusion matrix for the test set for the best decision trees.

Class	Total	%Correct	%Error	Anger	Fear	Grief	Joy
Anger	12	41.7	58.3	5	3	0	4
Fear	13	30.8	69.2	6	4	2	1
Grief	12	41.7	58.3	2	0	5	5
Joy	13	46.1	53.8	4	0	3	6

Two models (3 and 5) fit the data set quite well; the rates of correct classification on the training set for these two models averaged over the four classes are 78.5% and 61.6%, respectively). Three models (1, 2, and 4) have difficulties in classifying fear. The rates of correct classification on the training set for these three models averaged over the four classes are 41.9%, 38.7%, and 36.0%, respectively). Models 2 and 4 also have problems with joy, which means that they distinguish correctly only between anger and grief.

A similar situation can be observed in the evaluation carried out on the test set: only models 3 and 5 are able to classify all four emotions correctly. Model 1 cannot classify fear, while models 2 and 4 cannot classify fear and joy.

The rates of correct classification on the test set for the five models averaged on the four classes are respectively: 40%, 36%, 36%, 26%, and 40%. Thus the average rate of correct classification on the five models is 35.6%. Except for model 4, they are all above chance level (25%). Model 5 can be considered as the best model, since it has a rate of correct classification of 40% and is able to classify all four emotions.

These rates of correct classification that at a first glance seem to be quite low (40% the best model) should however be considered with respect to the rates of correct classification from spectators who have been asked to classify the same dances. In fact, spectators' ratings collected by psychologists in Uppsala show a rate of correct classification (averaged over the 20 dances) of 56%.

The rate of correct automatic classification (35.6%) is thus in between chance level (25%) and the rate of correct classification for human observers (56%).

Furthermore, if the rate of correct classification for human observers is considered as reference, and percentages are recalculated taking it as 100% (i.e., relative instead of absolute rates are computed), the average rate of correct automatic classification with respect to spectators is 63.6%, and the best model (i.e., model 5) obtain a rate of correct classification of 71.4%.

By observing the confusion matrix of the best model (both for the test set and for the training set) it can be noticed that fear is often classified as anger. This particularly holds for the test set, where fear is the basic emotion receiving the lowest rate of correct classification since 6 of the 13 motion phases extracted from fear performances are classified as anger. Something similar can be observed in spectators' ratings (Camurri, Lagerlöf, Volpe, 2003).

A deeper comparison with spectator's ratings shows that while anger is generally well classified both by spectators and by the automatic system (60% for automatic recognition vs. 60.6% for spectators), quite bad results are obtained for fear (below chance level for the automatic classification). The biggest overall difference between spectators and automatic classification was observed for joy (70.4% for spectators vs. 27.7%, just above chance level, for automatic classification). In the case of grief instead, automatic classification performs better than human observers (48.3% for automatic classification vs. 39.8% for spectators): this happens in five cases and mainly for grief. In seven cases, the rate of correct classification for the automatic system is below chance level (and this always happens for fear). In one case, automatic classification did not succeed in finding the correct emotion (Fear – Dancer 4), but spectators obtained 67% of correct classification. In another case, spectators' ratings are below chance level (Grief – Dancer 5), but automatic classification could obtain a rate of correct classification up to 50%.

Dancer 1 obtained the lowest rates of correct classification both from spectators and from the models. Dancer 5 obtains similar rates from both. Dancer 2 is the best classified by spectators and also obtains a quite high rate (with respect to the other dancers) in automatic classification.

4 Analysis of Expressive Gesture in Music Performance

The second experiment investigates the mechanisms responsible for the audience's engagement in a musical performance. The aim of this experiment is again twofold: (i) individuating which auditory and visual cues are mostly involved in conveying the performer's expressive intentions, and (ii) testing the developed model by comparing its performance to spectators' ratings of the same musical performances.

In this experiment, expressive gesture was analysed with respect to its ability to convey the intensity of emotion to the audience. The study focused on the communication through visual and auditory performance gesture of emotional intensity and the effect of it on spectators' emotional engagement.

The research hypotheses combine hypotheses from Laban's Theory of Effort (Laban, 1947, 1963) with hypotheses stemming from performance research (see Clarke and Davidson, 1998; Palmer, 1997; Timmers, 2002), from research on the intensity of emotion and tension in music and dance (see Krumhansl, 1996; 1997; Sloboda and Lehmann, 2001; Scherer, 2003):

1. Emotional intensity is reflected in the degree of openness (release) or contraction (tension) of the back of the performer;
2. Emotional intensity is communicated by the main expressive means for a pianist: tempo and dynamics;
3. Intensity increases and decreases with energy level (speed of movements, loudness, tempo);
4. Intensity is related to the performer's phrasing: it increases towards the end of the phrase and decreases at the phrase boundary with the introduction of new material.

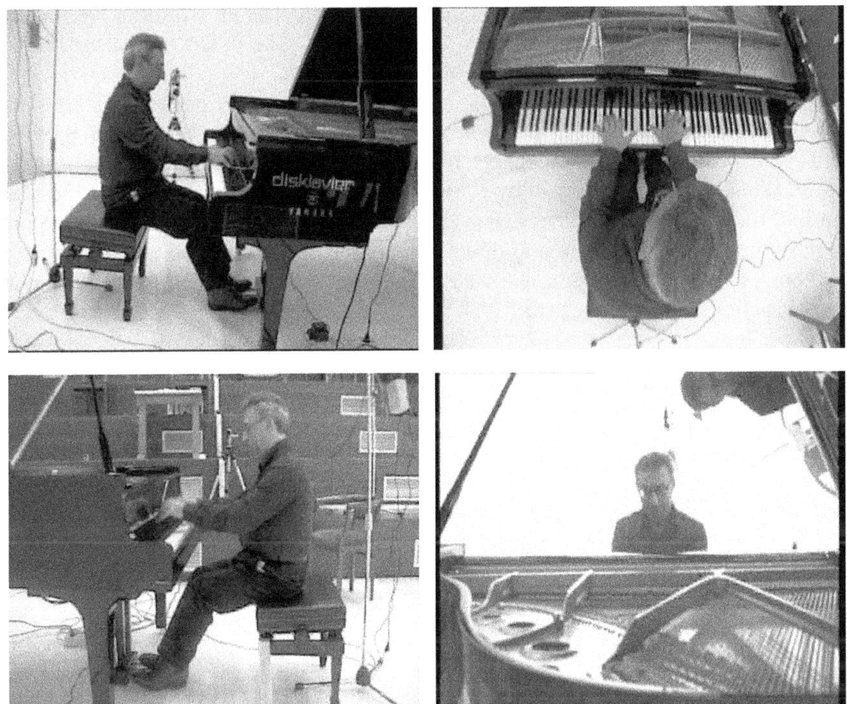

Fig. 3. Video recordings of the piano performances (left, top, right, and front views).

4.1 Description of the Experiment

A professional concert pianist (Massimiliano Damerini) performed Etude Op.8 No.11 by Alexandr Scriabin on a Yamaha Disklavier at a concert that was organized for the experiment's purpose. He performed the piece first without public in a normal manner and an exaggerated manner, and then with public in a normal, concert manner. Exaggerated means in this case with an increased emphasis in expressivity consistent with the style of performance of early 20th Century pianist style.

The Scriabin Etude is a slow and lyrical piece (Andante cantabile) in a late Romantic style that has a considerable amount of modulations. According to the pianist, the piece can be played with several degrees of freedom. Theoretically, the piece has a simple A B A with coda structure in which the A sections are repeated (A A' B A''

A''' C), but the pianist interpreted the line of the music differently: The first main target of the music is a release of tension halfway the B section. Everything preceding this target point is a preparation for this tension release. The A section is anyway preparatory; it leads towards the start of the B section, which is the real beginning of the piece. After this release of tension, the music builds up towards the dramatic return of the theme of the A section. This prepares for the second possible point of tension release halfway the coda at a general pause. The release is however not continued and the piece ends most sad.

The pianist performed on a grand coda piano (Yamaha Disklavier), which made it possible to register MIDI information of the performance. In addition, we did audio and video recordings from four sides (see Figure 3). The video recordings from the left were presented to the participants of the experiment.

Twelve students participated in the experiment; among them were four musicians. The participants saw the performances on a computer screen and heard them over high-quality (Genelec) loudspeakers twice. At the first hearing, they indicated the phrase boundaries in the music by pressing the button of the joystick. At the second hearing, they indicated to what extent they were emotionally engaged with the music by moving a MIDI-slider up and down. The order of the repeated performances was randomised over participants. The whole procedure was explained to them by a written instruction and a practice trial.

4.2 Analyses and Results

4.2.1 Layers 1 and 2

The key-velocity and onset-times of notes were extracted from the MIDI files (layer 1). From these data, the average key-velocity for each quarter note was calculated as well as inter-onset-intervals (IOI's) between successive quarter notes (layer 2). The quarter-note IOI is an accurate measure of local duration, while key-velocity corresponds well to local loudness.

The resulting profiles of quarter note key-velocity and quarter note IOI were highly similar for the three performances. The global pattern of increase and decrease in dynamics is indicated by arrows at the bottom of Figure 4. Local duration shows a similar pattern in the opposite direction. In addition, it shows the characteristic peaks of phrase-final lengthenings.

For the analysis of the movement of the pianist, we concentrated on the movement of the head, which shows both backward-forward movement (y-direction) and left-right movement (x-direction). The position of the head was measured, using the Lucas and Kanade feature-tracking algorithm (Lucas & Kanade, 1981) that assigns and tracks a specified number (in our case 40) of randomly assigned moving points within a region (layer 1). Velocity and acceleration has been calculated for each trajectory using the symmetric backward technique for the numeric derivative (layer 2). Average values of position and velocity among the forty trajectories were calculated for both the x and y component. In addition, the velocity values were integrated for the x and y movement to get a general measure of amount of movement over time. Redundancy in the number of points (i.e., forty points instead, for example, of just the barycentre of the blob) allowed us to get more robust and reliable values for velocity. A low-pass filter was applied to smooth the obtained data. Measures were summarized per quarter note in order to be comparable to the other measures.

The position of the head is plotted in Figure 5 for the two dimensions: left-right (upper panel) and backward-forward (bottom panel). The movement of the head was especially pronounced and especially consistent over performances in the left-right direction (correlation between p1 and p2 and between p2 and p3 was 0.79; it was 0.83 between p1 and p3). The periodic movement is relatively fast in the middle parts if the piece (B and A'') and slower in the outer parts. This suggests an intensification towards the middle followed by a relaxation towards the end.

As for the spectator ratings, firstly, the number of people who indicated a phrase-boundary was calculated for each quarter note in the performance by summing the number of boundary indications per quarter note over participants. This sum per quarter note was expressed as a multiple of chance-level, where chance-level corresponded to an even distribution of the total of segment-indications over quarter notes. This segmentation measure will be abbreviated as SM.

Secondly, the indication of emotional engagement was measured at a sampling rate of 10 Hz using a MIDI-slider that had a range from 0 to 127. The average level of the MIDI-slider (emotion measure, abbreviation EM) per quarter note was calculated for each participant separately. An EyesWeb patch application was developed to collect, process, and store participants data in real-time.

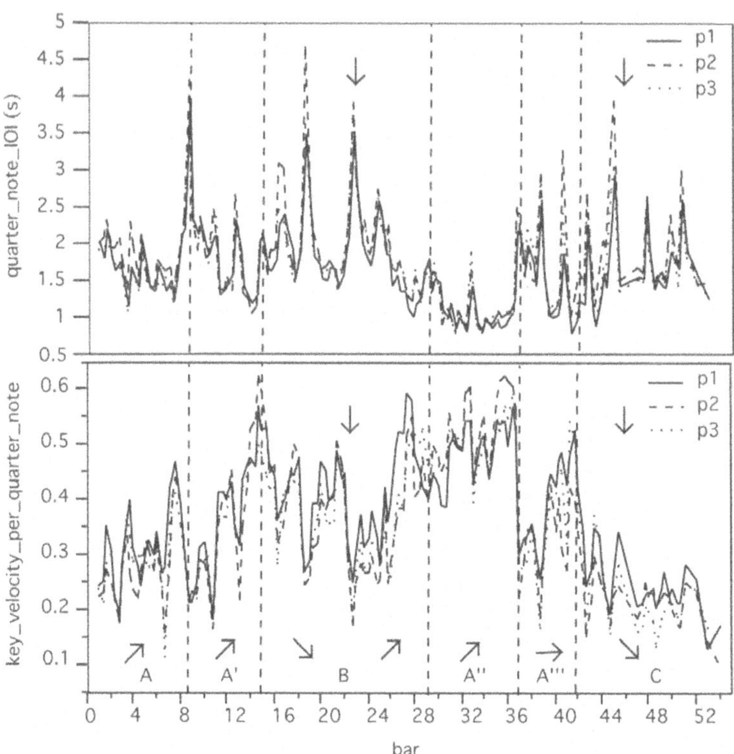

Fig. 4. The duration per quarter note and the key-velocity per quarter note as it varies throughout the Skriabin Etude. Separate plots for the three performances of the piece. Vertical lines indicate section boundaries. Arrows are explained in the text.

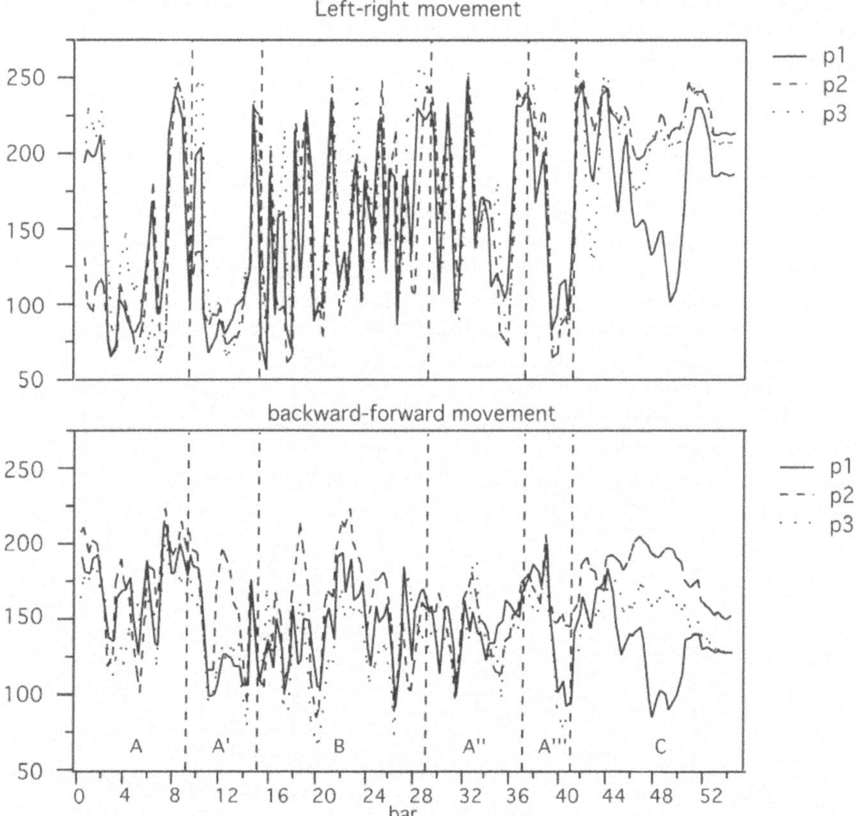

Fig. 5. The position of the head plotted per quarter note. Upper panel shows left-right position (x) and bottom panel the backward-forward position (y). Separate plots for the three performances of the piece. Vertical lines indicate section boundaries.

4.2.2 Layer 3

Correlations between performance measures were calculated to check the coherence between measures. Key-velocity and IOI were negatively correlated (r = -.51 on average). Velocity of head movement was positively correlated with key-velocity (r = .45 on average) and negatively with IOI (r = -.25 on average). The low correlation between values was partly due to the asynchrony between the periodicity of the measures. If peak-values (maximum for key and movement velocity and minimum for IOI) per two bars were correlated, agreement between movement and sound measures became higher. Especially the two velocity measures turned out to be highly correlated (r = .79 on average for key and movement velocity).

All performance measures showed a periodic increase and decrease. To check the relation between these periodicities and the musical structure, the location of mimima in key-velocity, and maxima in IOI, x-position and y-position were compared to the location of phrase-boundaries. Generally, the Skriabin Etude has a local structure of two-bar phrases. The forward and the left position of the performer were taken as start/end point for periodicity. IOI was most systematically related to the two-bar phrasing of the Skriabin-piece, followed by key-velocity. 55% of the phrase-boundaries were joined by a slowing down in tempo. The other phrase-boundaries were directly followed by a slowing down in tempo (a delay of 1 quarter note). For the key-velocity, 42% of the phrase-boundaries coincided with a minimum in key-velocity, 15% was anticipated by a minimum and 28% followed by a minimum. The period-boundaries of the movement of the pianist hardly synchronized with the score-phrasing. The location of these boundaries varied greatly with respect to the two-bar score-phrasing.

4.2.3 Layer 4

In this study, we had four hypotheses concerning the communication of intensity of emotion in musical performances.

Hypothesis 1 predicts that intensity of emotion is positively correlated with backward-forward movement (y). This hypothesis is easily tested and contradicted: the correlation between listeners' indication of intensity of emotion and backward-forward position is negative (r is -.23, -.50, -.29 for p1, p2 and p3, respectively). It is also contradictory with respect to the other performance data: y-position is negatively correlated with velocity and positively with IOI, this means that the performer moves forward in soft and slow and therefore less intense passages and backwards in louder and faster and therefore more intense passages (see hypothesis 3).

Hypothesis 2 predicts that tempo and dynamics cooperate to communicate intensity of emotion. This is made problematic by the fairly low correlation between IOI and key-velocity and by its different relation towards the score-phrasing. Instead the performance data suggests a differentiation in function between the two expressive means, whereby tempo strongly communicates phrasing.

Hypothesis 3 predicts high movement to correspond with intense dynamics and fast tempi. As we have seen in the previous section, dynamics and movement-velocity agree more strongly than movement-velocity and tempo. Especially the variation in velocity-peaks corresponds.

Hypothesis 4 relates phrasing to intensity of emotion. A clear phrase ending is predicted to coincide with a release in emotional intensity.

A series of multiple regression analyses were done. In the first analysis, quarter note IOI, key velocity, and movement velocity were used to predict EM. In the second analysis, the same variables were used to predict SM. In the third analysis, peak values per hyper-bar were used to predict average emotion measure per hyper-bar. All analyses were done directly and with a time-delay of one, two and three quarter notes of the performance data with respect to the listeners' data. The best R^2 obtained will be reported..

The subjective segmentation measure was rather well predicted by the model given the Rs^2 of .34, .33, .30 for p1, p2 and p3, respectively. From this model, IOI was the only significant variable. In other words, duration was a fairly good predictor of the variation in number of participants indicating a section-boundary. More participants indicated a phrase-boundary for longer durations.

EM was well predicted by the quarter note model, but even better by the second model that took the peak-values per hyper-bar to predict the average EM per hyper-bar. The quarter-note regression analysis had an R^2 of .45, .68, .50 for p1, p2, and p3 respectively, while the hyper-bar peak-value regression had an R^2 of .53, .82, and .56. Velocity was always the most significant variable and was the only significant variable for the hyper-bar peak-value regression. For the quarter-note regression movement velocity also reached significance for p2 and p3, and IOI for p2. All R^2 were relatively high for p2, which suggests that the exaggerated expression of this performance increased communication.

As a comparison, the analyses were repeated with x-position and y-position as independent movement variables instead of the more general movement velocity variable. The results did not improve or change from this alteration, instead x and y-position did not contribute significantly to any of the regressions.

These results confirm a differentiation between expressive means: tempo primarily communicated segmentation, while dynamics communicated emotion. Velocity of the movement was correlated with dynamics and may therefore also have reflected emotional intensity, but the sounding parameters were the main communicative factors.

The results are suggestive counter-evidence for hypothesis 4. The lack of tempo to explain variations in emotional intensity contradict that phrase-final lengthenings caused a release in emotional intensity. There was however another way in which phrasing and the dynamics of tension and release did relate, which was at a higher and more global level. Phrase final lengthenings occurred at a high rate and a local scale. At this scale the relation was weak. Major phrase boundaries that were indicated by a drop in tempo and dynamics were however followed by a clear release in intensity. Moreover the global variation of dynamics to which the variation in emotional intensity was so strongly related was the performer's way of communication of the overall-form: the first part is an introduction and builds up to the B section, which he considered as the real beginning of the piece. This beginning is again a preparation for the first target of the piece: the release of tension at the middle of the B section (see downward pointing arrows in Figures). Hereafter tension builds up towards the dramatic return of the theme, which leads via a repeat of the theme in contrasting dynamics to the second important target of the theme: the second possible release of tension at the general pause. After the general pause, the release is not given and all hope is lost. The piece ends most sad. The pianist most skilfully expressed this interpretation in the patterning of dynamics (see arrows in the key-velocity panel of Figure 4). The resulting phrasing is over the entire piece with subdivisions at measures 22 and 36. The return of the theme is the culminating point of the piece where after tension can release. According to the pianist, this tension cannot however be fully resolved.

4.4 Summary and Conclusions from the Experiment

This study had two aims (i) individuating which auditory and visual cues are mostly involved in conveying the performer's expressive intentions and (ii) testing the developed model by comparing their performances with spectators' rating of the same musical performances. The auditory and visual cues most involved in conveying the performer's expressive intentions were hypothesised to be key-velocity, IOI, movement velocity, and the openness or contraction of the performer's posture. In addition, a relation between phrasing and emotional tension-release was expected.

The analyses of performance data suggested an opposite relation between emotional intensity and the performer's posture. The pianist leaned forward for softer passages and backward for intensive passages. In addition it suggested a differentiation in expressive means with tempo on one side and key-velocity and movement velocity on the other side.

When relating the performers data to the listeners' data, this differentiation in expressive means was confirmed. Tempo communicates phrase boundaries, while dynamics is highly predictive for the intensity of felt emotion. Hardly any evidence was found for movement cues to influence listeners' ratings. The sound seemed the primary focus of the participants and vision only subsidiary. The local phrase-boundaries indicated by tempo did not lead to release of emotional intensity. The modulation of dynamics over a larger time-span communicates the overall-form of the piece and, at that level, intensity did increase and decrease within phrases.

5 Discussion

The modelling of expressive gesture is receiving growing importance from both research and industry communities, even if we can consider it at its infancy. The main contributes of our research are to the definition of a unified multimodal conceptual framework for expressive gesture processing, to the results obtained from the two types of experiment described in the paper. Further, a collection of software modules for cue extraction and processing has been developed to support such research. The conceptual framework proved to be useful and effective in two different scenarios, well represented by the two experiments described in the paper.

In the first experiment, we focused on the communication of basic emotions from a dancer to the audience, while in the second experiment we focused on the mechanisms that possibly cause emotional engagement in the audience.

The dance experiment can be considered as a first step and a starting point toward understanding the mechanisms of expressive gesture communication in dance. A collection of cues that have some influence in such a communication process has been individuated, measured, and studied. A first attempt of automatic classification of motion phases has been carried out and some results have been obtained (e.g., an average rate of correct classification not particularly high, but well above chance level). Some directions for future research also emerged. For example, other classification techniques could be employed and their performances compared with what we obtained with decision trees. Some aspects in dance performance that were only marginally considered should be taken into account. In particular, aspects related to rhythm should be further investigated. Expressive cues like impulsiveness and fluency should be further worked out. Moreover, perceptual experiments would be needed to empirically validate the extracted expressive cues.

The music experiment can be considered as a first step towards the understanding of the relation between movement and sound parameters of a performance, their expressive forms and functions, and their communicative function for spectators. A next step, should involve a larger variety of performances and a larger collection of calculated cues. Cues should be fitted to the responses of individual spectators in order to get a deeper as well as broader understanding of these complex phenomena.

Acknowledgements

We thank Ingrid Lagerlöf and Marie Djerf for the joint work carried out in the experiment on expressive gesture conveying emotions in dance performances, Roberto Dillon and other colleagues at the DIST - InfoMus Lab, the EyesWeb development team (Paolo Coletta, Massimiliano Peri, and Andrea Ricci), the students Andrea Pertino and Riccardo Casazza for their contribute in the set up of the music performance experiment and in the extraction and analysis of data, and last but not least Massimiliano Damerini for discussion and his artistic contributes in providing the material of the studies.

References

1. Bobick, A.F., Davis J. (2001), "The Recognition of Human Movement Using Temporal Templates", in IEEE Transactions on Pattern Analysis and Machine Intelligence, 23(3): 257-267
2. Bradsky G., Davis J. (2002), "Motion segmentation and pose recognition with motion history gradients", Machine Vision and Applications 13:174-184.
3. Cadoz C., and Wanderley, M. (2000), "Gesture – Music", in Wanderley, M. and Battier M. eds. (2000), "Trends in Gestural Control of Music." (Edition électronique) Paris: IRCAM.
4. Camurri A., Lagerlof I., and Volpe G. (2003), "Emotions and cue extraction from dance movements", International Journal of Human Computer Studies, Vol.59, No.1-2. pp.213-225, Elsevier.
5. Camurri, A., De Poli G., Leman M. (2001), "MEGASE - A Multisensory Expressive Gesture Applications System Environment for Artistic Performances", Proc. Intl Conf CAST01, GMD, St Augustin-Bonn, pp.59 – 62.
6. Camurri A., Hashimoto S., Ricchetti M., Trocca R., Suzuki K., Volpe G. (2000) "EyesWeb – Toward Gesture and Affect Recognition in Interactive Dance and Music Systems." Computer Music Journal, 24:1, pp. 57-69, MIT Press, Spring 2000.
7. Canazza S. De Poli G., Drioli C., Rodà A., Vidolin A. (2000), "Audio morphing different expressive intentions for Multimedia Systems", IEEE Multimedia, July-September, Vol. 7, N° 3, pp. 79-83.
8. Chi D., Costa M., Zhao L., and Badler N. (2000), "The EMOTE model for Effort and Shape", ACM SIGGRAPH '00, New Orleans, LA, pp. 173-182.
9. Clarke, E. F. Davidson, J. W. (1998), "The body in music as mediator between knowledge and action", in W. Thomas (Ed.).Composition, Performance, Reception: Studies in the Creative Process in Music, Oxford University Press, 74-92
10. Cowie R., Douglas-Cowie E., Tsapatsoulis N., Votsis G., Kollias S., Fellenz W. and Taylor J. (2001), "Emotion Recognition in Human-Computer Interaction", IEEE Signal Processing Magazine, no. 1.
11. Friberg A., Colombo V., Frydén L., and Sundberg J. (2000), "Generating Musical Performances with Director Musices", Computer Music Journal, 24(3), 23-29.
12. Hashimoto S., (1997), "KANSEI as the Third Target of Information Processing and Related Topics in Japan", in Camurri A. (Ed.) "Proceedings of the International Workshop on KANSEI: The technology of emotion", AIMI (Italian Computer Music Association) and DIST-University of Genova, pp101-104.
13. Kilian J. (2001), "Simple Image Analysis By Moments", OpenCV library documentation.
14. Krumhansl, C. L. (1996), "A perceptual analysis of Mozart's piano sonata K.282: Segmentation, tension and musical ideas", Music Perception, 13 (3), 401-432.
15. Krumhansl, C. L. (1997), "Can dance reflect the structural and expressive qualities of music? A perceptual experiment on Balanchine's choreography of Mozart's *Divertimento* No. 15", Musicae Scientiae, 1, 63-85.
16. Kurtenbach and Hulteen (1990), "Gesture in Human-Computer Interaction", in Benda Laurel (Ed.) The Art of Human-Computer Interface Design.
17. Laban R., Lawrence F.C. (1947), "Effort", Macdonald&Evans Ltd. London.
18. Laban R. (1963), "Modern Educational Dance" Macdonald & Evans Ltd. London.

19. Lagerlof, I. and Djerf, M. (2001), "On cue utilization for emotion expression in dance movements", Manuscript in preparation, Department of Psychology, University of Uppsala.
20. Liu Y., Collins R.T., and Tsin Y. (2002), "Gait Sequence Analysis using Frieze Patterns", European Conference on Computer Vision.
21. Lucas B., Kanade T. (1981), "An iterative image registration technique with an application to stereo vision", in Proceedings of the International Joint Conference on Artificial Intelligence.
22. McNeill D. (1992), "Hand and Mind: What Gestures Reveal About Thought", University Of Chicago Press,
23. Palmer, C. (1997). "Music Performance", Annual Review of Psychology, 48, 115-138.
24. Pollick F.E., Paterson H., Bruderlin A., Sanford A.J., (2001), "Perceiving affect from arm movement", Cognition, 82, B51-B61.
25. Scherer, K.R. (2003) "Why music does not produce basic emotions: pleading for a new approach to measuring the emotional effects of music", in Proc. Stockholm Music Acoustics Conference SMAC-03, pp.25-28, KTH, Stockholm, Sweden.
26. Sloboda J.A., Lehmann A.C. (2001) "Tracking performance correlates of changes in perceived intensity of emotion during different interpretations of a Chopin piano prelude", Music Perception, Vol.19, No.1, pp.87-120, University of California Press.
27. Timmers, R. (2002). "Freedom and constraints in timing and ornamentation: investigations of music performance". Maastricht: Shaker Publishing.
28. Wanderley, M. and Battier M. eds. (2000), "Trends in Gestural Control of Music." (Edition électronique) Paris: IRCAM.
29. Zhao, L. (2001), "Synthesis and Acquisition of Laban Movement Analysis Qualitative Parameters for Communicative Gestures", Ph.D Dissertation, University of Pennsylvania.

Correlation of Gestural Musical Audio Cues and Perceived Expressive Qualities

Marc Leman, Valery Vermeulen, Liesbeth De Voogdt,
Johannes Taelman, Dirk Moelants, and Micheline Lesaffre

IPEM - Dept. of Musicology, Ghent University
Blandijnberg 2, B-9000 Ghent, Belgium
Marc.Leman@UGent.be
Tel:+32 9 2644125

Abstract. An empirical study on the perceived semantic quality of musical content and its relationship with perceived structural audio features is presented. In a first study, subjects had to judge a variety of musical excerpts using adjectives describing different emotive/affective/expressive qualities of music. Factor analysis revealed three dimensions, related to valence, activity and interest. In a second study, semantic judgements were then compared with automated and manual structural descriptions of the musical audio signal. Applications of the results in domains of audio-mining, interactive multimedia and brain research are straightforward.

1 Introduction

Theorists conjecture that music appears as an organism to which particular gestural properties and associated qualifications can be attributed (Broeckx, 1981). The aesthetic nature of this musical gestural semantics has received attention in the past (e.g. Coker, 1972), and studies have been based on empirical investigations, relating aspects of this semantics with particular musical structures (e.g. Hevner, 1936; Wedin, 1972; Gabrielsson, 1973; Nielzén & Cesarec, 1981). There is a general agreement among music researchers that the emotional and qualitative nature of musical gestures is an important, if not, the most important, aspect of human involvement with music.

A semantics of perceived gestural qualities is a meaningful space of relationships among emotive, affective, and expressive attributes of gestures which composers, musicians and listeners are assumed to share and exchange during life long experiences with music. This semantics is furthermore assumed to provide the basis of communication about expressive gestures. Attributes of perceived expressiveness in gestures may furthermore relate to a fairly general and high-level gestural meaning such as *majestic* gestures, *lively*, *desperate* or *vulnerable* gestures.

The present paper gives an account of relationships found between perceived gestural qualities and audio-structural cues. Section 2 and 3 overview different approaches to gestural expressive semantics and present a taxonomy for music

A. Camurri and G. Volpe (Eds.): GW 2003, LNAI 2915, pp. 40–54, 2004.

description. Starting from an experimental study, Sect. 4 addresses the structure of the perceived gestural semantics. This is followed by an overview of the automated and manually extracted cues in Sect. 5, and finally by an analysis of the relationships between perceived gestural semantics and the audio structural cues (Sect. 6). The conclusion summarizes results and provides pointers to future research and applications.

2 Approaches to Gestural Expressive Semantics

The study of qualitative descriptions of music, in particular emotions and music, has been approached from different viewpoints, including philosophy, musicology, psychology, biology, anthropology, sociology, and music therapy (see Juslin & Sloboda, 2001 for an overview). Experimental work on music and emotions aims at clarifying the underlying semantics in terms of cognitive maps or qualitative spaces induced from listener responses. If the semantic spaces are known, they can be correlated with perceived musical acoustical features which reflect the physical characteristics of performed structural gestures.

Three approaches can be distinguished, called *categorical*, *dimensional*, and *componential* (Scherer, 2003). In the *categorical* approach, the perceived emotive/affective properties are cast using a set of basic emotions such as fear, sadness, joy, anger. In the *dimensional* approach, the perceived emotive and affective qualities of music are mapped out using a differentiated set of adjectives from which main factors of the underlaying emotive/affective space are deduced. Finally, the *componential* approach advocated by Scherer (2003) holds that qualitative descriptions may rely on a variety of components or appraisal patterns, rather than the classical subjective feeling states of the dimensional approach or a limited number of supposedly basic emotions of the categorical approach. Examples of component patterns are the degree of novelty, pleasantness, consistency, and control, which, serve as predictors for the particular qualification or emotion.

Straightforward modelling of the relationship between perceived emotive and affective qualities in natural music, however, is often obscured by difficulties in finding the relevant audio-structural cues. This paper first explores different aspects of audio-structural cues. We then report the results of a large scale study on perceived musical qualities[1].

3 Low, Mid, and High-Level Descriptors of Musical Audio

Most music researchers agree that music allows a description at different representational levels (Marsden & Pople, 1989; Todd & Loy, 1991; De Poli, Piccialli, & Roads, 1991; Balaban, Ebcioglu, & Laske, 1992; Haus, 1993; Roads, De Poli,

[1] A more detailed account of this experiment will be given in Leman et al. (submitted).

<table>
<tr><th colspan="2">STRUCT</th><th colspan="2">CONCEPT LEVEL</th><th colspan="5">MUSICAL CONTENT FEATURES</th></tr>
<tr><td rowspan="3">CONTEXTUAL</td><td rowspan="2">global beyond 3 sec</td><td>HIGH II</td><td>EXPRESSIVE</td><td colspan="5">cognition | emotion | affect = syntactic+semantic concepts</td></tr>
<tr><td>HIGH I</td><td>FORMAL</td><td>melody
key
profile</td><td>harmony
tonality
cadence</td><td>rhythm
rhythmic patterns
tempo</td><td>source
instrument
voice</td><td>dynamics
trajectory
articulation</td></tr>
<tr><td>global < 3 sec</td><td>MID</td><td>PERCEPTUAL</td><td>successive intervallic pattern</td><td>simultane intervallic pattern</td><td>beat
IOI</td><td>spectral envelope</td><td>dynamic range
sound level</td></tr>
<tr><td rowspan="2">NON-CONTEXTUAL</td><td>local + spatial</td><td>LOW II</td><td>SENSORIAL</td><td colspan="2" rowspan="2">pitch
periodicity pitch
pitch deviations
fundamental frequency
frequency</td><td rowspan="2">time
note duration
onset
offset
duration</td><td rowspan="2">timbre
roughness
spectral flux
spectral centroid
spectrum</td><td rowspan="2">loudness
neural energy
peak
intensity</td></tr>
<tr><td>local + temporal</td><td>LOW I</td><td>PHYSICAL</td></tr>
</table>

Fig. 1. Conceptual framework used within the context of audio mining. A distinction is made between low-level, mid-level and high-level audio descriptors

& Pope, 1997; Leman, 1997; Zannos, 1999; Godøy & Jørgensen, 2001): A taxonomy of audio descriptors may typically involve the distinction between low level, mid level, and high level aspects (Leman, Lesaffre, & Tanghe, 2001). Figure 1 shows the conceptual framework of a taxonomy worked out within the context of audio mining (Lesaffre et al., 2003).

Low level descriptors are obtained from a frame-based analysis of the acoustical wave, using time-frequency techniques such as Fourier analysis, wavelets, or auditory models (e.g. Van Immerseel & Martens, 1992). Conceptually speaking, these features imply the specification of so-called *distal* cues (Scherer, 2003), that is, cues as analyzed from the viewpoint of the information receiver. Low level audio cues encode basic spatial, temporal and local (non-contextual) features of the signal and they can be given a meaningful interpretation whenever they are related to sensorial or perceptual properties of the signal such as pitch, loudness, onset, offset, roughness.

Mid level descriptors are derived from musical context dependencies within time-scales of about 3 seconds, which accounts for the musical present, the *now*. Examples of descriptors at this level are beat, short rhythmic patterns, and melodic features such as short interval sequences, contour, tonal tension. The latter can be calculated by comparing pitch images that reflect the development of musical pitch at a local level with pitch patterns at a global level (Leman, 2000).

Mid level descriptors may also be based on segmented patterns. Segmented mid level descriptors allow for the event-based representation of musical objects. Object-descriptors have attributes such as beginning, end, duration, pitch, loudness, timbre, vibration frequency, vibration index etc..., and can be related to super-object descriptors such as intervallic pattern, contour, pitch distribution etc...

Gesture-based representations can be conceived of as movement induced patterns such as, for example, the galloping of a horse. The galloping pattern, however, may be calm or restless and the gesture may appeal to affective, emotive and expressive appreciations of the listener. Though gestures may be found using advanced segmentation procedures (Cambouropoulos, 2000) or episodic statistics (Eerola, Jarvinen, Louhivuori, & Toiviainen, 2001), in general however, a precise verbal definition and specification of gestural appreciation in music is difficult and musicologists may disagree on particular examples. Yet on the other hand, a study of the inter-subjective appreciation of expressiveness in gestures seems to be a feasible objective (see below).

High level descriptors typically involve learning and categorization beyond the representation of the *now* (> 3 seconds). High level descriptors are related to the cognitive as well as emotional and affective domains. They are determined by cultural context and relate to long term memory processing. Up to now, however, there is insufficient knowledge of how high level descriptors may be associated with perceived structural properties of audio.

High level concepts related to expressiveness are typically characterized by terms that describe qualities such as *dark*, *bright*, *sharp*, *rough*, *dissonant*, *graceful*, etc... Some authors (Broeckx, 1981) are inclined to make a distinction between primary concepts, such as *high*, *low*, *far*, *near*, *accelerando* or *ritardando* that describe perceived physical features of a musical pattern or event on the basis of its formal audio structural aspects, and secondary concepts, which have an associative or metaphorical origin rooted space, movement, and affect. The latter, following Broeckx, are the so-called kinaesthetic (Laban, 1963), synaesthetic (Cytowic, 1989), and cenaesthetic concepts which actually belong to a particular domain of experience such as movement or color perception, or particular sensations, but which are easily transferred to the musical domain. Examples are *pressing*, *gliding*, *flicking* , or concepts such as *labile*, *bright*, *conflicting* , *extinction*, ...

High level concepts form part of the expressive gestural semantics which people use when they speak about music. The structure is still badly understood, and the inter-subjective consistency of this semantics has rarely been investigated on a large scale. The question addressed in this paper is whether the verbal expressive concepts from this highest level (Fig. 1: HIGH II) can be related to lower level cues.

4 The Structure of Perceived Emotive/Affective Qualities

The structure of perceived emotive/affective qualities in a large set of musical stimuli was addressed using the method of semantic differentials. The semantic differential is a contrasting pair of adjectives which can be used as a scaling instrument to quantitatively measure the perceived quality of an object. A set

Table 1. Bipolar adjectives in Dutch and English

Dutch (English)	Dutch (English)
Groots (Majestic)	Luchtig (Light)
Chaotisch (Chaotic)	Geordend (Orderly)
Vrolijk (Gay)	Droevig (Sad)
Kwetsbaar (Fragile)	Krachtig (Powerful)
Zorgeloos (Carefree)	Angstig (Anxious)
Brutaal (Bold)	Teder (Tender)
Kalm (Calm)	Rusteloos (Restless)
Sober (Simple)	Weelderig (Sumptuous)
Aangenaam (Pleasing)	Storend (Annoying)
Ontroerend (Moving)	Onverschillig (Indifferent)
Koel (Restrained)	Passioneel (Passionate)
Wanhopig (Desperate)	Hoopvol (Hopeful)
Opwindend (Exciting)	Saai (Boring)
Levendig (Lively)	Doods (Dead)
Positief (Positive)	Negatief (Negative)

of semantic differentials spans a multidimensional space, which can be reduced to a space defined by a few dimensions using factor analysis.

100 students from the Faculty of Letters and Arts (section Art Sciences, second year) from Ghent University participated in the experiment. The mean age was 21 years, 73% were females and about 60% of the subjects did not have any active musical experience. The test took place within the context of an introductory course in computer applications in the art sciences.

Subjects were asked to fill in a form on which to rate the musical excerpts using a set of semantic differentials. The test used adjectives in Dutch language, here translated into English (Table 1).

Out of 60 different musical excerpts, chosen from many musical genres (pop, rock, ethnic, jazz, classical, ...) and on the basis of an assumed wide variety of emotional expressiveness, each student evaluated 24 randomly selected pieces (24*100 = 2400 responses). In total, each excerpt was evaluated 40 times. The evaluation was done with 15 bipolar adjectives using a 7-point scale. The scales where constructed according to the semantic differential method in which -3 represents for example very happy, 3 very sad and 0 stands for neutral or undecided.

4.1 Factor Analysis

Factor analysis, using maximum likelihood estimation and varimax rotation, was performed to reveal underlying structure in listener responses. The question investigated here is whether the 15-dimensional space used for the description of the perceived qualities in music can be reduced to a lower dimensional space. The inter-correlations between the 15 semantic differentials indeed reveal three main factors shown in Fig. 2.

The first dimension (first factor) refers to the contrasting poles of Carefree and Anxious, Gay and Sad, Desperate and Hopeful, and Positive and Negative. Given the bipolar nature of the adjectives, it means that the adjectives Carefree,

Fig. 2. Factor Loadings. The first factor explains 19.5 % of the variance in the data, the second and third factor explain 19% and 18% of the data

Gay, Hopeful, Positive are on one side of the axis, and Anxious, Sad, Desperate, Negative on the other side. The adjectives come down to the distinction between favorable and unfavorable qualifications. The dimension is therefore related to the *valence* of perceived qualifications. This dimension explains 19.5% of the total variance in the data.

The second dimension (second factor) refers to the contrasting poles of Tender, Calm and Fragile versus Bold, Restless, Powerful. The adjectives come down to the distinctions based on power and energy. The dimension is called *activity* and it explains 19% of the total variance.

The third dimension (third factor) refers to the contrasting poles of Moving, Exciting, Pleasing, Passionate, versus Indifferent, Boring, Annoying, and Restrained. The adjectives relate to *interest* and this dimension explains 18% of the total variance.

4.2 Discussion

The space formed by the dimensions of *valence*, *activity*, and *interest* explains 56.5% of the variance in the data. The three dimensions explain an almost similar amount of the variance. The results are in agreement with Osgood, Suci, and Tannenbaum's theory (1957) and subsequent research in which the communication of affect can be seen as having three major dimensions of connotative meaning.

All 15-dimensional subject responses were then projected onto the 3-dimensional emotive/affective quality space, for further use in a regression analysis (see Sect. 6).

5 Musical Acoustical Cues

The question whether the expressive gestural semantic space can be related to features extracted from audio has been addressed in terms of automated and manual methods. One set of features has been extracted using an auditory model and provides low level (surface) distal cues. Another set of features has been extracted by human experts in a manual annotation task and provides perceived mid level (in depth) distal cues.

5.1 Auditory-Based Feature Extraction

Low level features have been obtained from an auditory model[2]. The auditory model consists of a cochlear filter bank front-end followed by low-level feature extractors in each band. The cochlear filter bank is implemented in multirate DSP for a good trade-off between precision and efficiency. It computes 40 bands spread over the range of 50Hz to 18kHz according to ERB rate.

In the present context, loudness, roughness, pitch, and centroid extraction have been considered. The low-level features are summarized over all bands at frame-rate. The loudness extractor is based on a low-pass filter on the amplitude in each band. The roughness is the amplitude after a high-pass filter on the amplitude. Pitch and pitch prominence are computed from an FFT in each band. Over a window of frames, onsets are detected by comparing the average loudness with the peak loudness. The centroid is the center-of-gravity of the amplitudes in the bands. Though feature extraction is based on available data from psychoacoustics, their particular effectiveness on a wide range of musical examples has not yet been fully tested, although comparison with manually annotated cues reveals interesting correlations (see Sect. 5.2). Errors, however, are also compensated for by the statistical methods used.

Though each feature is extracted in a continuous way over the total duration of an excerpt, only basic statistics has been taken into account. The loudness values, for example, are averaged over the whole excerpt, and standard deviation is computed. As such, a low-level descriptor is just one single numeric value for the entire musical excerpt. Table 2 gives a list of 11 low-level feature extracted. Single value descriptors are here justified on the basis of homogeneous expressiveness in each of the 60 excerpts.

5.2 Manually-Based Feature Extraction

The manually extracted features have been obtained from a team of ten musicologists at Ghent University. Attention has been focused on structural features, in particular: tempo, the perceived harmonicity, and the softness/loudness characteristics. Loudness is characterized as a mid level feature in Figure 1, whereas

[2] Developed at IPEM in the context of the MEGA-IST project (see www.megaproject.org). The project has a focus on the modelling and communication of expressive and emotional content in non-verbal interaction by multi-sensory interfaces in shared interactive mixed reality environments.

Table 2. Auditory-based features

aL.m	average loudness (from less loud to very loud)
aR.m	average relative roughness (from very rough to less rough)
aP.m	average pitch prominence
aC.m	average centroid
aI.m	average inter onset interval
aO.m	number of onsets in 30 seconds
aL.s	standard deviation of loudness
aR.s	standard deviation of roughness
aP.s	standard deviation of pitch prominence
aP.m.s	standard deviation of the mean pitch prominence per frame
aC.s	standard deviation of centroid

Table 3. Manually-based features

mH.m	average harmonicity (consonance/dissonance)
mH.s	standard deviation of harmonicity (consonance/dissonance)
mL.m	average soft/loud
mL.s	standard deviation of soft/loud
mT.m	average tempo
mT.s	standard deviation of tempo

tempo and harmonicity can be considered high level formal features. Tempo annotations were processed in the sense that doubling or halving was taken into account (van Noorden & Moelants, 1999). Harmonicity, however, may be expected to have a less stable inter-subjective interpretation than loudness and tempo because of its association with either cognitive or musical consonance or dissonance, or with sensory consonance and dissonance (Terhardt, 1976). In the latter case, it refers to roughness, whereas in the former case, it refers to harmonic chords and harmonic sequences. From these annotations, we took the mean and the standard deviation (see Table 3) over the 10 subjects, so we get 6 manually annotated cues for each excerpt.

5.3 Correlation between Automated (Surface) and Manual (In-Depth) Features

Table 4 gives an overview of the correlations between automatically (auditory-based) extracted and manually extracted features. Each label is associated with an extracted feature and represents a vector of 60 components. Each component accounts for the measured value of the extracted feature in one single excerpt. The correlation matrix can be read as a test of the cues obtained with the auditory model.

Manually annotated harmonicity (mH.m) correlates with roughness (aR.m) and inter-onset intervals (aI.m) ($r = -0.31$, $p = 0.015$ and $r = 0.29$, $p = 0.026$), whereas variance in estimated harmonicity has no significant correlation with any of the auditory-based features.

Manually annotated loudness (mL.m) has a very high correlation with auditory-based loudness (aL.m) and roughness (aR.m) ($r = 0.59$ and $r = -0.73$, $p < 0.001$). Apparently, the estimated loudness is more complex and involves also the variation in auditory-based loudness (aL.s) and the variation in roughness (aR.s) ($r = -0.42$ and $r = -0.38$, $p < 0.01$), and to a certain degree also the

Table 4. Correlation between auditory-based and manually-based features. Signficance levels: ** < 0.001, * < 0.01, . < 0.05

Features	mH.m	mH.s	mL.m	mL.s	mT.m	mT.s
aL.m	0.14	0.26	0.59**	-0.22	0.19	-0.21
aR.m	-0.31.	0.03	-0.73**	0.24	-0.38.	-0.09
aP.m	0.03	0.06	0.16	-0.17	-0.14	-0.15
aC.m	0.08	-0.11	0.13	0.06	0.04	0.19
aI.m	0.29.	-0.04	-0.09	0.20	-0.46**	0.13
aO.m	-0.13	-0.03	0.22	-0.11	0.60**	-0.17
aL.s	-0.22	-0.05	-0.42*	0.28.	-0.06	-0.01
aR.s	-0.22	-0.07	-0.38*	0.33.	-0.06	-0.01
aP.s	-0.13	-0.04	-0.23	0.09	-0.10	-0.01
aP.m.s	-0.04	-0.04	-0.11	-0.06	-0.14	-0.14
aC.s	-0.13	-0.06	-0.30.	0.24	0.01	0.04

variance of auditory-based centroid, which is a feature related to timbre ($r = -0.30$, $p = 0.019$).

The variation of manually annotated loudness (mL.s) is related to variation in auditory-based loudness (aL.s) and the variation in roughness (aR.s) as well ($r = 0.28$, $p = 0.029$ and $r = 0.33$, $p = 0.011$).

Manually annotated tempo (mT.m) correlates in a very significant way with inter-onset intervals (aI.m) and number of onsets (aO.m) ($r = -0.46$ and $r = 0.60$, $p < 0.001$), less significantly with auditory-based roughness (aR.m) ($r = -0.38$, $p = 0.0024$). Changes in tempo have no significant relationships to any of the auditory-based features.

As a conclusion, it appears that significant relationships exist between manually annotated features of average loudness and average tempo and their low-level automatically extracted counterparts of loudness and roughness, and inter-onset intervals and number of onsets. The relationships imply that the high level concepts relate multiple though related low level features, and that low level features contribute to multiple though related high level features.

6 Individual Ratings of Perceived Emotive/Affective Qualities

In order to carry out the regression analysis on an individual basis, a second experiment was set up with 8 new subjects that rated all 60 musical excerpts using the above 15 semantic differentials. The conditions were similar as in the first experiment. The responses of each individual were then mapped onto the 3-dimensional space (valence, activity, interest) obtained from the large group of students. Each factor was then taken as an dependent variable for the analysis, first, of the relationships with the automatically extracted auditory-based features, secondly, of the relationships with the manually annotated features.

The rationale behind this approach relies on the distinction between the inter-subjective and subjective aspects involved. The expressive gestural semantics is clearly an inter-subjective space which shows structural relationships among adjectives based on collective responses. The study of the relationships between evaluations and physical attributes, however, must be based on individual eval-

Table 5. Regression analysis using auditory-based features. Labels refer to the low-level auditory cues summarized in Table 2 The Id refers to the subject identification (8 subjects). The values shown are β-values of the regression analysis. Stars specify the statistical significance of the values

Factor 1												
Id	R^2	aL.m	aR.m	aP.m	aC.m	aI.m	aO.m	aL.s	aR.s	aP.s	aP.m.s	aC.s
1	0.41	-0.057				0.009	-0.0038*		-0.12			
2	0.07					0.012						
3	0.23						-0.0031**					
4	0.18					0.13**						
5	0.19	-0.092					-0.0025		-0.13			
6	0.25	-0.028					-0.0028**					
7	0.19		0.19		0.0009		-0.0015					-0.006
8	0.36					0.0085	-0.0031*					
Factor 2												
Id	R^2	aL.m	aR.m	aP.m	aC.m	aI.m	aO.m	aL.s	aR.s	aP.s	aP.m.s	aC.s
1	0.44		-0.48**						-0.083			
2	0.52	0.089	-0.27	-0.604**		-0.11*			-0.3			0.0016*
3	0.57	0.07	-0.42**	-0.26			-0.0013		0.12	-0.28		
4	0.43		-0.55**					0.33	-0.35			
5	0.49	0.09	-0.32*	-0.49*		-0.0069	-0.0023	-0.24		0.403		0.001
6	0.39		-0.47**				-0.0013				-0.42	
7	0.36		-0.46**									
8	0.46		-0.66**					0.45	-0.42			
Factor 3												
Id	R^2	aL.m	aR.m	aP.m	aC.m	aI.m	aO.m	aL.s	aR.s	aP.s	aP.m.s	aC.s
1	0.14	0.04					0.0017					
2	0.16		-0.31	0.29								
3	0.08		-0.11									
4	0.13			-0.39	0.0005			-0.19			1.14	
5	0.12	0.067						-0.39	0.47			
6	0.16				-0.0007					-0.35		0.0007*
7	0.18	0.061						-0.4	0.53*	-0.61		
8	0.26				-0.0005		0.0034**			-0.5		

Table 6. Summary of all subjects

	aL.m	aR.m	aP.m	aC.m	aI.m	aO.m	aL.s	aR.s	aP.s	aP.m.s	aC.s
Factor 1	0.031	0.056	0.000	0.027	0.253	0.260	0.041	0.038	0.066	0.018	0.0344
Factor 2	0.200	0.562	0.015	0.053	0.054	0.057	0.152	0.144	0.043	0.013	0.088
Factor 3	0.104	0.125	0.035	0.006	0.033	0.056	0.091	0.093	0.044	0.028	0.039

uations. Taking the mean of all individual evaluations would blur the effects. Mapping the individual responses into the expressive gestural space reduces the 15 adjectives to 3 underlying factors according to the collectively established semantic rules, and relates the individual measurements to other individuals in terms of this semantics.

6.1 Regression Analysis Using Automatically Extracted Auditory-Based Features

The result of a stepwise (both directions) multiple regression analysis is shown in Table 5. The table gives the regression models for each subject and each factor. The left column gives the subject identification, the second column provides the R^2, which is a measure of the explained variance versus the total variance.

β values are then given for each feature. The significance of these values was tested and indicated using * for $p < 0.01$, ** for $p < 0.001$.

Factor 1 (valence) has a significant correlation with aO.m (number of onsets) in half of the cases and once with aI.m (inter onset interval). Factor 2 (activity), however, shows a very significant correlation with aR.m (roughness) in 7 out of the 8 cases. Factor 3 (interest) shows only one significant correlation with aO.m, aR.s, aC.s for different subjects, and therefore these results are not conclusive. As to Factor 1 and Factor 2, however, the results are straightforward.

In order to estimate this tendency in the large group of 100 subjects, we performed a linear regression with Factor 1, 2, 3 as respective dependent variable, and the features as independent variables. This analysis used the 24 estimated excerpts for each subject. From each result, we took the correlation coefficient and tested its significance so that for each factor and each subject, we got correlation coefficient and significance for each feature. Table 6 shows the weighted mean over all subjects for each factor and feature. Only significant correlations at $p < 0.01$ are taken into account.

The results confirm the observations of the 8 individual cases, except that Factor 1 is correlated with aO.m and also with aI.m. Factor 2 is highly correlated with aR.m, while Factor 3 doesn't show a high correlation with any of the features.

6.2 Regression Analysis Using Manually Annotated Features

Regression models based on manually annotated features are shown in Table 7. As in the previous section, the analysis uses the results of 8 individual subjects whose evaluations, using 15 semantic differentials to qualify all 60 excerpts, have been projected onto the 3-dimensional space of expressive gestural semantics that was obtained in Section 4.1. The factors 1 to 3 refer to the factors that have previously been identified as valence, activity and interest. The regression models for factor 1 (valence) show that both harmonicity and tempo are relevant, though these factors are somehow distributed among an equal amount of subjects. One group seems to interpret valence more in terms of tonal aspects (harmonicity), while the other focuses more on rhythmic aspects (tempo). Only two students take both features into account. Notice that the corresponding low-level feature of valence is the number of onsets. As a general trend, the higher the note onsets, the harmonic consonance, and/or the tempo, the higher the positive perceived quality of the music.

As to the second factor (activity) it is clear that all subjects relate qualifications of bold, restless, and powerful with the manually annotated loudness. The higher the perceived loudness, the higher the aggressive impact of the music. The corresponding low-level feature was more related to roughness (see Table 5, factor 2). However, the manually annotated loudness seems to incorporate more than just intensity (see Table 4).

The third factor (interest), again, shows no significant relationships.

Table 7. Regression analysis using manually annotated features. Labels refer to the cues summarized in Table 3 The Id refers to the subject identification (same 8 subjects as in Table 5). The values shown are β-values of the regression analysis. Stars specify the statistical significance of the values

Factor 1							
Id	R^2	mH.m	mH.s	mL.m	mL.s	mT.m	mT.s
1	0.34	0.40**	0.84			-0.012**	
2	0.25	0.47**				-0.0058	
3	0.31	0.19				-0.0086**	
4	0.38	0.46**	0.79	-0.21			
5	0.15	0.45*		-0.23			
6	0.22	0.13				-0.0075**	
7	0.26	0.25*	0.62			-0.0064*	
8	0.46	0.40**	0.89*	-0.18		-0.0089**	
Factor 2							
Id	R^2	mH.m	mH.s	mL.m	mL.s	mT.m	mT.s
1	0.71			0.69**			0.031*
2	0.67			0.44**		0.01**	
3	0.69			0.50**			
4	0.71	0.21*		0.55**			
5	0.68			0.60**			
6	0.63			0.53**			0.04**
7	0.61			0.59**			
8	0.76			0.74**			
Factor 3							
Id	R^2	mH.m	mH.s	mL.m	mL.s	mT.m	mT.s
1	0.12		0.62	0.15			
2	0.29		1.20	0.43**	0.80		
3	0.10	0.14					
4	0.22	0.41**				0.0058	
5	0.21		0.96	0.19			
6	0.04		0.87		0.46		
7	0.26	0.25			0.76		
8	0.062						

7 Conclusions

The results of this study are (1) that the listener's perception of qualitative (emotional, affective, expressive) musical content tends to be inter-subjectively consistent, (2) that the underlying semantics tends to be structured in a low-dimensional space, (3) that part of this semantics can be brought into connection with automatically extracted low level and mid level acoustical cues, and (4) that this semantics reflects perceived qualities of musical gestures.

The high level expressive gestural semantics is structured along three dimensions called valence, activity and interest. Valence adjectives, such as carefree, gay, hopeful, are related to the low level (auditory-based) cue of number of onsets, and to perceived (manually annotated) cues of tempo, and musical harmonicity. It seems that faster tempo and a higher degree of musical consonance enhances the perception of positive qualities. Activity adjectives, such as bold, restless, powerful, are related to the surface feature of roughness and the in-depth feature of soft/loud. The higher the degree of roughness and loudness, the more bold, restless, and powerful the music is perceived. Less good results have been obtained with the interest dimension in that no significant relationships could be established. This is probably due to the fact that the method is calling for cognitive evaluation, or qualitative attributions, whereas interest adjectives may probe personal experiences (arousal) as well. Further research is needed to clarify this problem.

The origin and nature of the expressive gestural semantics of real music requires further study in the future. The semantic space used in this paper was restricted to 15 dimensions and might be extended or focused on different aspects. It will be of interest to know whether this semantics is the same for different groups of users (age, gender, social background, musical background, etc...), and whether this semantics is different when applied to specific musical genres.

As it stands now, the semantic features are quite general and further specification of their meaning should be given with respect to the particular dynamics of gestures. Due to the fact that the semantic space is reduced to a low-dimensional space, this approach does not allow a very fine specification of gestural traits. In future research, it will be of interest to consider different components of gestural traits in relation to found acoustical cues. Hence, the dimensional approach adopted here may be extended towards a componential approach. As to the automatically extracted acoustical cues used in this study: they are all rather low-level cues and more research is needed to develop reliable mid-level cues. The difficulty with manually annotated cues is that they involve qualitative assessments.

The results of this study are promising. Though further refinement of semantic space and feature extraction has to be developed, some of the found relationships may be quite useful in audio-mining applications, interactive multimedia, and brain research. Applications in data-mining aim at allowing consumers to use emotive and affective descriptors to retrieve music (Leman et al., 2002; Leman, 2002). Interactive software/hardware environments are becoming available for direct motoric annotation of qualitative responses (Camurri & Ferrentino, 1999). Interactions between the high level gestural semantics and low level features in audio are furthermore useful in artistic applications where dancers, actors and musicians interact with machines on the basis of expressive emotional and affective cues (Camurri, De Poli, & Leman, 2001). In that context, it is straightforward to use the reduced dimensional representation of the expressive gestural semantics as a space for controlling qualitative processing in audio, and from there in other domains such as computer animation. Finally, the results can be relevant to brain research, where correlations between audio cues and brain responses give insight into the cortical representation of musical content. Recent findings by Janata et al. (2002) show that the sense for tonality, for example, is processed in an area in the brain (the pre-frontal rostromedial cortex) where motoric and affective processing are located. It is likely that the processing underlying expressive gestural semantics is in a similar way connected to motoric and affective centers in the brain.

References

Balaban, M., Ebcioglu, K., & Laske, O. (Eds.). (1992). *Understanding music with AI: Perspectives on music cognition.* Cambridge, MA: The MIT Press.

Broeckx, J. (1981). *Muziek, ratio en affect: Over de wisselwerking van rationeel denken en affectief beleven bij voortbrengst en ontvangst van muziek.* Antwerpen: Metropolis.

Cambouropoulos, E. (2000). Melodic cue abstraction, similarity and category formation: A computational approach. *Music Perception, 18*(3), 347-370.

Camurri, A., De Poli, G., & Leman, M. (2001). MEGASE: a multisensory expressive gesture applications system environment for artistic performances. In *Proceedings of CAST01 - Living in mixed reality - Conference on communication of art, science and technology, september 21-22.* Schloss Birlinghoven, Sankt Augustin, Bonn: Fraunhofer-Institute for Media Communication IMK.

Camurri, A., & Ferrentino, P. (1999). Interactive environments for music and multimedia. *Multimedia Systems, 7*, 32-47.

Coker, W. (1972). *Music and meaning - a theoretical introduction to musical aesthetics.* New York: The Free Press.

Cytowic, R. (1989). *Synesthesia.* Berlin, Heidelberg: Springer-Verlag.

De Poli, G., Piccialli, A., & Roads, C. (Eds.). (1991). *Representations of musical signals.* Cambridge, MA: The MIT Press.

Eerola, T., Jarvinen, T., Louhivuori, J., & Toiviainen, P. (2001). Statistical features and perceived similarity of folk melodies. *Music Perception, 18*(3), 275-296.

Gabrielsson, A. (1973). Adjective ratings and dimension analysis of auditory rhythm patterns. *Scandinavian Journal of Psychology, 14*, 244-260.

Godøy, R., & Jørgensen, H. (Eds.). (2001). *Musical imagery.* Lisse: Swets & Zeitlinger.

Haus, G. (Ed.). (1993). *Music processing.* Madison, Wisconsin: Oxford University Press & A-R Editions.

Hevner, K. (1936). Experimental studies of the elements of expression in music. *American Journal of Psychology, 48*, 246-248.

Janata, P., Birk, J., Van Horn, J., Leman, M., Tillmann, B., & Bharucha, J. (2002). The cortical topography of cognitive structures underlyingwestern tonal music. *Science, 298*, 2167-2170.

Juslin, P., & Sloboda, J. (Eds.). (2001). *Music and emotion - theory and research.* New York: Oxford University Press.

Laban, R. (1963). *Modern educational dance.* London: MacDonald & Evans.

Leman, M. (Ed.). (1997). *Music, Gestalt, and computing - studies in cognitive and systematic musicology.* Berlin, Heidelberg: Springer-Verlag.

Leman, M. (2000). An auditory model of the role of short-term memory in probe-tone ratings. *Music Perception, 17*(4), 481-509.

Leman, M. (2002). Musical audio-mining. In J. Meij (Ed.), *Dealing with the data flood: Mining data, text and multimedia.* The Hague, Netherlands: STT Netherlands Study Centre for Technology Trends.

Leman, M., Clarisse, L., De Baets, B., De Meyer, H., Lesaffre, M., Martens, G., Martens, J., & Steelant, D. V. (2002). Tendencies, perspectives, and opportunities of musical audio-mining. In A. Calvo-Manzano, A. Pérez-López, & J. S. Santiago (Eds.), *Forum Acusticum Sevilla 2002, 16-20 september, 2002.* Madrid: Sociedad Española de Acústica -SEA. (Special issue of Journal Revista de Acústica Vol XXXIII, no. 3-4)

Leman, M., Lesaffre, M., & Tanghe, K. (2001). *A toolbox for perception-based music analysis (http://www.ipem.ugent.be/toolbox).* Ghent: IPEM - Dept. of Musicology, Ghent University.

Leman, M., Vermeulen, V., De Voogdt, L., Taelman, J., & Moelants, D. (submitted). *Acoustical and computational modelling of musical affect perception.*

Lesaffre, M., Leman, M., Tanghe, K., De Baets, B., De Meyer, H., & Martens, J. (2003). User dependent taxonomy of musical features as a conceptual framework for musical audio-mining technology. In R. Bresin (Ed.), *Proceedings of the Stockholm Music Acoustics Conference (SMAC 03), august 6-9, 2003* (p. 635-638). Royal Institute of Technology (KTH).

Marsden, A., & Pople, A. (1989). Towards a connected distributed model of musical listening. *Interface - Journal of New Music Research, 18*(1-2), 61-72.

Nielzén, S., & Cesarec, Z. (1981). On the perception of emotional meaning in music. *Psychology of music, 9*, 17-31.

Osgood, C., Suci, G., & Tannenbaum, P. (1957). *The measurement of meaning.* Urbana, IL: University of Illinois Press.

Roads, C., De Poli, G., & Pope, S. (1997). *Musical signal processing.* Lisse, The Netherlands: Swets & Zeitlinger.

Scherer, K. (2003). Vocal communication of emotion: A review of research paradigms. *Speech Communication, 40*, 227-256.

Terhardt, E. (1976). Ein psychoakustisch begründetes konzept der musikalischen konsonanz. *Acustica, 36*, 122-137.

Todd, P., & Loy, D. (1991). *Music and connectionism.* Cambridge, MA: The MIT Press.

Van Immerseel, L., & Martens, J. (1992). Pitch and voiced/unvoiced determination with an auditory model. *The Journal of the Acoustical Society of America, 91*, 3511–3526.

van Noorden, L., & Moelants, D. (1999). Resonance in the perception of musical pulse. *Journal of New Music Research, 28*(1), 43-66.

Wedin, L. (1972). Multidimensional scaling of emotional expression in music. *Swedish Journal of Musicology, 54*, 1-17.

Zannos, I. (Ed.). (1999). *Music and signs – semiotic and cognitive studies in music.* Bratislava: ASKO Art & Science.

Gestural Imagery in the Service of Musical Imagery

Rolf Inge Godøy

Section for musicology, University of Oslo
P.O.Box 1017 Blindern, N-0315 Norway
r.i.godoy@imt.uio.no
tel. (+47)22854064, fax. (+47)22854763

Abstract. There seem to be strong links between gestural imagery and musical imagery, and it is suggested that gestural imagery can be instrumental in triggering and sustaining mental images of musical sound. Gestural images are seen as integral to most experiences of music, and several practical and theoretical musical disciplines could profit from focusing on these gestural images. Research in support of this is reviewed, and some topics for future research are presented.

1 Introduction

The topic of this paper is how gestural imagery, meaning imagining or mentally simulating various gestures, can trigger, sustain, and enhance images of musical sound in our minds. This is part of a long-term research project, *Motor-mimesis*, which aims at enhancing our means for thinking musical sound in various tasks (composing, arranging, improvisation, performance, analysis, music education, etc.) through mental images of sound-associated actions, including both sound-producing actions such as hitting, stroking, plucking, bowing, blowing, etc., and other sound-related body movements such as dancing and various kinds of sound tracing gestures.

In the call for papers prior to a conference on musical imagery some years back, we tentatively defined musical imagery as 'our mental capacity for imagining musical sound in the absence of a directly audible sound source, meaning that we can recall and re-experience or even invent new musical sound through our 'inner ear'.' [1]. It could now be useful to propose a similar definition here of gestural imagery as 'our mental capacity for imagining gestures without seeing them or actually carrying them out, meaning that we can recall and re-experience or even invent new gestures through our 'inner eye' and inner sense of movement and effort.' It must be emphasized that imagery is not just a matter of daydreaming or arm-chair contemplation, but is in fact the very basis for thinking and feeling: Memory, and hence, imagery, is at work in all perception and cognition, and, as pointed out already by the phenomenologists at the end of the 19th century [2], there simply would be no perception and cognition at all without mental images of past and expected (future) events.

Although there has been a number of studies of musical imagery during the last decades [3], the most intriguing, and also most practically oriented question is in my opinion that of what actually triggers and sustains images of musical sound in our minds. This question of what is the 'engine' of musical imagery has oddly enough

A. Camurri and G. Volpe (Eds.): GW 2003, LNAI 2915, pp. 55–62, 2004.

been given little attention by researchers, however, the prime suspect for this triggering agent which emerges from various studies of musical imagery, is actually gestural imagery. In other words: *Images of gestures seem to be efficient in evoking images of sounds.* The challenge now is to substantiate this claim, both by providing evidence from available research reports on the neurophysiological and cognitive bases for the gesture-sound interaction in imagery, and to design schemes for practical applications which can demonstrate that imagining gestures is actually an efficient strategy for evoking lucid and vivid images of musical sound in various music related tasks.

2 Gesture-Sound Links in Perception and Cognition

Many musicians are familiar with the experience that recall of music is facilitated by mimicking the sound-producing movements or other kinds of movements associated with a musical work, e.g. moving hands and fingers as if actually playing when recalling a piano piece, playing 'air guitar' or 'air drum' when recalling a song, making dance movements when recalling a dance tune, etc. In other words, there can hardly be any doubt that gestures are effective in triggering images of musical sound, something which has in fact been documented through a series of experiments by Mariko Mikumo [4], and something which has been remarkably depicted by David Sudnow in his introspective account of jazz improvisation [5].

Generally, imagery research in any domain, be that visual, auditive, motor, etc., has inherently significant methodological problems because it is difficult to study what goes on within the mind, i.e. we can not place an 'observer' in people's minds to register what is going on when people imagine various scenes, gestures and sounds. However, the last couple of decades has seen the emergence of some clever methods for capturing what is assumed to go on in processes of imagery, such as measuring reaction times, and effects of mental preparation and rehearsal, for various tasks [6]. In addition to such indirect methods, advances in methods for non-invasive neurophysiological observation, such as fMRI, PET and ERP [7], have given us more information on the workings of mental imagery. One significant finding here is that of 'functional equivalence', meaning the close resemblance between the neuronal apparatus involved in actual actions and/or perceptions and in the imagined actions and/or perceptions. One possible interpretation of this could be that imagery does share many features with actual experience, hence, that studying the links between gestures and sound in actual experience could also give us clues as to the links between gestures and sound in imagery. Also, another interesting finding here is that certain motor areas of the brain seem to be activated when imagining sound, hence that action imagery is activated concurrently with tasks of musical imagery.

Neurophysiological research will in the near future no doubt come up with interesting findings on gesture-sound links in imagery. However there is also a considerable amount of existing audition research which suggests close links between gesture and sound in perception and cognition. This research could be summarized as 'ecological' in the sense that its basic paradigm is to understand human audition as embedded in evolutionary constraints, hence, as trying to understand human audition as a holistic and cross-modal phenomenon where the different sense-modalities cooperate in order to extract meaning from what we hear in our environment. There are many instances of this in the domain of Auditory Scene Analysis [8], and just to mention one classic example, the so-called 'McGurk effect' demonstrates that we may be tricked when seeing a certain sound-producing gesture to believe that we have heard something else than we actually have been presented with in the acoustic signal [9].

However, the most persistent project to explore and exploit gesture-sound links is that of the so-called 'motor theory' of perception [10]. Going back more than three decades, the advocates of this theory have claimed that the various features in the signal alone are not sufficient to account for perception and discrimination of language sounds, and that the listener actually mentally mimics the sound-producing gestures when trying to make sense of what is spoken, projecting gestural images on to the sound input in a top-down manner. The motor theory thus claims that perception involves a gestural simulation in the mind of the listener, and that learning to understand a language is actually a process of learning to imagine the sound-producing gestures of that particular language. The motor theory has been controversial. However, the above-mentioned advances in neurophysiological research is now increasingly giving support for this theory [11].

Ideas from motor theory are fundamental here, not only for exploring gesture-music links, but also for structuring our images of musical sound as *gesture units* (see section 5 below). In this connection, research into the role of gestures in language is also relevant [12], as this indicates how gestures not only amplify certain rhetorical elements of speech, but suggests that gestures may have been the evolutionary basis for spoken language [13], and may be instrumental in actually generating utterances [14], i.e. that gestures in speech may play a cognitive role similar to the role of gestures in music. As to this last point, there is of course also a fast growing body of research into practical applications of gesture control in music [15], and experiences here can no doubt tell us more about the links between gestural imagery and musical imagery as well.

3 Separating Gestures and Sound

Although the classical separation of sense-modalities such as vision, hearing, balance, etc. may now seem questionable from what is known about the cooperation of many channels of sensory input in the brain [16], it will for strategic reasons be useful to conceptually separate gestures and sound here [17]. This means *separating images of what we do* from *images of the effects of what we do*, or separating the *silent choreography of sound-producing and sound-accompanying actions* from *sonorous images*. This means furthermore that we separate ecological knowledge of actions that we all have accumulated since our births (or even from a pre-natal stage), i.e. knowledge of action-trajectories and effort in stroking, blowing, hitting, kicking, etc., from ecological knowledge of resonant features of whatever sounding body (strings, tubes, vocal tract, etc.) and environment (rooms, ambient sounds, transducing medium, etc.) that we similarly have experienced by being in the world [18, 19].

First of all, this separation of gestures and resultant sound reveals quite clearly that what we often (or in most cases) think of as the meaning or content of music is actually a matter of gestural images: Images of effort, velocity, contours, trajectories, gait, etc., could all be understood as gestural phenomena, as gestural images transmitted by sound and 'decoded' in listening back to a gestural language as in ballet or pantomime

[20]. For example, when listening to the ferocious beating of drums, it is probably almost impossible to avoid having images of an equally ferocious activity of hands and mallets hitting the drum membranes, and conversely, listening to a slow, quiet, and contemplative piece of music would probably evoke images of slow and smooth sound-generating gestures. For disciplines such as musical aesthetics and musical semiotics, a focus on gesture could be very useful to characterize musical meaning. In our context here, such a shift of focus reveals that gestural scripts are deeply embedded in what we think of as musical imagery, making the 'pure' sound a kind of 'residue' which is left over once we remove gestural images. The consequences of this is that a cultivation of gestural images is not only legitimate, but can have some very attractive features in practical applications as well (see section 5 below).

Secondly, this separation of gesture and sound may encourage us to understand music as organized not only by traditional principles for pitch, harmony, consonance-dissonance, motives, melodies, thematic development, etc. but equally well by principles for motor cognition, i.e. action-units or action-gestalts, motor programmes, motor-hierarchies, coarticulation, etc., as I shall briefly present in the next section. There can be no doubt that human motor cognition has a number of constraints on music making, e.g. need for alternating between effort and rest, need to conserve energy, thresholds for velocity, phase transitions with changes in tempi [21], etc., and that human motor cognition exerts schematic constraints on melodic, rhythmic and textural grouping [22, 23].

Thirdly, separating gesture and sound opens up the fascinating domain of motor imagery [24], hence, opens up for thinking musical imagery as *simulation of gestures*. This in turn opens up for all the advantages inherent in the dynamics of motor imagery, such as imagining actions at *variable resolution* (mentally fast running through a sequence of actions or slowly replaying all the details) and *variable acuity* (vague, approximate, sketch-like recollections of actions and effort or very precise, salient images of trajectories). Musical sound can not (in principle) unfold faster than what it does without distorting its features, but motor programmes may create compressed overview images of gestures in the form of scripts or lists of highlights, similar to trailers in the promotion of films where the point is to pack as many salient scenes as possible (often the most spectacular and/or violent) into a 30 second advertisement. In fact, scores in common practice western notation are partially such gesture scripts, allowing for rapid running through or 'at a glance' rough impression of what the music is like (making some suspicious conductors prefer a quick glance at a score rather than spending time on actually listening through a work).

This separation of gesture and musical sound prepares the ground for talking about *mental simulation* as the substance of musical imagery, meaning that musical imagery is not a kind of abstract representational or propositional system, but is a matter of reenacting from a first-person, egocentric perspective what we have perceived in the world. This simulation view of cognition [16, 25] seems fortunately now to be gaining plausibility, and means that whatever kind of music we imagine, and regardless our level of expertise and/or the complexity of the music, there is always the possibility of mentally mimicking gestures we think belong to the music (although perhaps only in a low-acuity, sketchy manner).

4 Motor Cognition

Accepting that gestural images are integral to musical imagery, it could be useful to have a brief look at some principles of motor cognition [26]. There are physiological constraints on human action which are obvious in musical situations (e.g. singers, brass and woodwind players need to breathe, velocity of bow, hand and finger movements are limited within a certain range, etc.), but most of all, there are some cognitive constraints and principles of organization which are highly relevant for gestures in music, hence also for gestural imagery in music.

The most important concept here is that of *motor programmes*. A motor programme is a mental image of an action or a sequence of actions, such as opening a door, sitting down, walking to work, or hitting a drum, playing a tune on the flute, or playing a long piece on the piano. A motor programme is thus a kind of script for how something is to be done, and this script may, as mentioned above, have a *variable resolution*, e.g. I can very quickly envisage the walk to my place of work, or I can go through the entire trajectory quite slowly, envisaging every little part of the trajectory and how my feet will be moving at any point of time. This variable resolution is interesting for musical purposes, as it shows how it is possible to quickly run through the gestural script of some music, or to go through it very slowly, focusing on every single detail.

Also, motor programmes are flexible and allow for alternatives when needed. For instance, I can push open the door with my shoulder or my foot when I am carrying something in my hands, or to take a more musical example, I can play a melody on the piano with my left hand if I have injured my right hand. This possibility of alternative executions is called *motor equivalence*, and is important for music cognition as it may be a model for understanding how alternative renderings of similar musical ideas are possible. The idea of motor equivalence could allow for generalizations of musical gestures, e.g. a rapid glissando on a harp would be quite similar to a rapidly played series of tones on a piano, although in detail the actions would be rather different in these two cases.

Furthermore, motor programmes are *hierarchical* in the sense that they provide overviews of entire actions, i.e. provide executive control, yet at the same time allow for control of detail through 'sub-routines'. With practice and increased level of skill in various tasks, there is a tendency to group actions into larger units, i.e. into *chunks*, making detail actions automatic and attention to these details unnecessary. These action-based groupings are significant in musical contexts, and it can be shown that rhythmical groupings often follow these principles of action-chunking [22, 23]. Furthermore, chunkings of action seem also to have a basis in physiological optimalization, meaning that with practice, there is usually a tendency towards maximum efficiency or energy conservation, resembling a mass-spring model with alternations between peaks effort and phases of relaxation.

Related to chunking of musical sound on the basis of physiological and cognitive optimalization, is the phenomenon of *coarticulation*, meaning that several otherwise separate actions are fused or embedded into larger scale action-units. The concept of coarticulation was probably first used in linguistics to denote the preparation of the next phoneme by shaping the vocal apparatus in advance, but it has now also been applied to other areas of human movement, such as when my arm is moving towards an object to pick it up, my fingers simultaneously move to anticipate the optimal way of grasping the object [27]. The occurrences of coarticulation in music are numerous, as in phrasing, articulation, and even in intonation, and naturally occurring coarticulation in vocal and instrumental music is in fact that which makes naturally sounding melodic phrases on sampled wind, brass and string instruments practically impossible.

5 Advantages and Applications of Gestural Imagery

A focus on gestural imagery in music will have many advantages. As I have tried to suggest, the gestural component is a significant component of musical listening in general, and deserves much more attention as a carrier of meaning in studies of musical aesthetics, semiotics, analysis, performance, music education, etc., and it could be tempting to speak of a 'gestural hermeneutics' in musical thinking, meaning gesture as the mediating element between music and other modes of thought. Furthermore, gestural imagery could also shed light on enigmatic issues in music cognition and aesthetics such as temporality and experience of musical form through the possibility of thinking gestures at various levels of resolution as gesture scripts. Actually, a cultivation of gestural imagery could be seen as a contribution to phenomenological approaches to music theory, related to the project of Pierre Schaeffer [28], with mental gestural tracing or sketching of the shapes of sound objects as an extension of Schaeffers typo-morphological characterizations. Furthermore, gestural images may also help us understand categorization in music because gestures can be easily recognized yet at the same time be variation-tolerant in detail, meaning there can be variant versions of a gesture such as in hitting a drum, yet the gesture retains the general feature of a sudden, ballistic movement. This possibility of categorizations by actions was suggested by Elanor Rosch and co-workers [29], and is similarly reflected in the motor theory of perception [10].

Finally, gestural imagery can also have some more specific, practical applications, and now just to mention some:

- Thinking melodic contours as gestures, hence, as holistic entities and not as collections of pitches, and thus enhance our understanding of melodic phenomena.
- Thinking musical textures as complex, multi-dimensional patterns of gestures, all seen from the egocentric, first-person perspective, and thus help us grasp the workings of different texture types.
- Thinking orchestration (and score reading) as similarly complex, multi-dimensional patterns of gestures, however with the addition of the resultant sound from these gestures, generating more lucid predictions of how scores are going to sound.
- Providing a better basis for music education in general, and ear-training in particular, by specifically cultivating the musical imagery triggering capabilities of gestural imagery.
- Helping to understand and master rhythmical grouping, expressivity, and phrasing in musical performance by mental practice of gesture chunks.
- Helping to understand the mental and motor processes of improvisation, i.e. how it is possible to simultaneously have images of the immediate past and images of what is to come in the immediate future, by simultaneously thinking different gestural scripts.

6 Conclusion and Ideas for Further Research

Altogether, there is reasonable grounds for assuming that there are quite close links between gestural images and images of musical sound, and it is easy to see how these links could be exploited in a number of theoretical and more practical challenges in music. Needless to say, there are a large number of unanswered questions here, and in the overseeable future, research within the following domains could be useful to substantiate our knowledge of the links between gestural and musical imagery:

- Compiling relevant data from existing observational (non-invasive) neurophysiological studies. There is a fast growing body of research here, and increasingly so, there seems to be much interest in the subjects of motor imagery and mental simulation.
- Gathering data on performance gestures, meaning that we need to know more about both the physiological and cognitive constraints and schemata which are at work in performance gestures, as well as developing suitable representations for this data.
- Physical model synthesis with incremental changes of the excitatory gestures followed by listening judgements, i.e. an 'analysis by synthesis' approach to studying the relationship between gestures and timbral qualities.
- Various kinds of experiments on the links between gestural and musical memory, e.g. along the lines of [4], and on the priming and mental practice effects of gestural imagery in practical tasks such as orchestration, improvisation and performance.

All through this gathering of data from various sources, the unifying principle here should be that of *mental simulation*, i.e. that of understanding perception, cognition and imagery in music as an active, embodied re-enactment of the gestures we believe belong to musical sound.

References

1. Godøy, R. I., Jørgensen, H. (eds.): Musical Imagery. Swets and Zeitlinger, Lisse (Holland) (2001) p. ix
2. Husserl, E.: Vorlesungen zur Phänomenologie des inneren Zeitbewusstseins. Max Nimeyer Verlag, Tübingen (1980)
3. For an overview, see Godøy, R. I., Jørgensen, H. (eds.): Musical Imagery. Swets and Zeitlinger, Lisse (Holland) (2001)
4. Mikumo, M.: Encoding Strategies for Pitch Information. Japanese Psychological Monographs No. 27 (The Japanese Psychological Association) (1998)
5. Sudnow, D.: Ways of the Hand. Harvard University Press, Cambridge, Mass. (1978)
6. Kosslyn, S. M.: Image and Brain. The MIT Press, Cambridge, Mass. (1994)
7. Janata, P.: Neurophysiological Mechanisms Underlying Auditory Image Formation in Music. In: Godøy, R. I., Jørgensen. H. (eds.): Musical Imagery. Swets and Zeitlinger, Lisse (Holland) (2001) pp. 27-42
8. Bregman, A. S.: Auditory Scene Analysis. The MIT Press, Cambridge, Mass. & London (1990)
9. McGurk, H., MacDonald, J.: Hearing Lips and Seeing Voices. Nature, 264 (1976) 746-748

10. Liberman, A. M., Mattingly, I. G.: The Motor Theory of Speech Perception Revised. Cognition, 21 (1985) 1-36
11. Fadiga, L., Craighero, L., Buccino, G., Rizzolatti, G.: Speech Listening Specifically Modulates the Excitability of Tongue Muscles: a TMS Study. European Journal of Neuroscience, Vol. 15 (2002) pp. 399-402
12. McNeill, D.: Hand and Mind: What Gestures Reveal About Thought. University of Chicago Press, Chicago, IL (1992)
13. Rizzolatti, G., Arbib, M. A.: Language Within Our Grasp. Trends in Neuroscience Vol. 21 (1998) 188–194
14. Kita, S.: How representational gestures help speaking. In: McNeill, D. (ed.): Language and Gesture. Cambridge University Press, Cambridge (2000) pp. 162-185
15. Cadoz, C., Wanderley, M.: Gesture-Music. In: Wanderley, M. M., Battier, M. (eds.): Trends in Gestural Control of Music (CD-ROM). IRCAM, Paris (2001) pp. 28-65
16. Berthoz, A.: Le sens du mouvement. Odile Jacob, Paris (1997)
17. Godøy, R. I.: Imagined Action, Excitation, and Resonance. In: Godøy, R. I., Jørgensen. H. (eds.): Musical Imagery. Swets and Zeitlinger, Lisse (Holland) (2001) pp. 239-252
18. Freed, D. J.: Auditory Correlates of Perceived Mallet Hardness for a Set of Recorded Percussive Sound Events. Journal of the Acoustical Society of America, 87 (1990) 311-322
19. Handel, S.: Timbre Perception and Auditory Object Identification. In: Moore, B. C. (ed.): Hearing. Academic Press, San Diego (1995) pp. 425-461
20. Laban, R.: The Mastery of Movement (fourth edition by Lisa Ullmann). Northcote House Publishers Ltd., Plymouth (1980)
21. McAngus Todd, N. P., O'Boyle, D. J., and Lee, C. S.: A Sensory-Motor Theory of Rhythm, Time Perception and Beat Induction. Journal of New Music Research,Vol. 28, No. 1 (1999) pp. 5-28
22. Godøy, R. I.: Knowledge in Music Theory by Shapes of Musical Objects and Sound-Producing Actions. In M. Leman (ed.): Music, Gestalt, and Computing. Springer Verlag, Berlin (1997) pp. 106-110
23. Godøy, R. I.: Cross-modality and Conceptual Shapes and Spaces in Music Theory. In I. Zannos (ed.): Music and Signs. ASCO Art & Science, Bratislava (1999) pp. 85-98
24. Jeannerod., M.: Mental Imagery in the Motor Context. Neuropsychologia, Vol. 33, No. 11 (1995) 1419-1432
25. Dokic, J. & Proust, J. (eds.): Simulation and Knowledge of Action. John Benjamins Publishing Company, Amsterdam/Philadelphia (2002)
26. Rosenbaum, D. A.: Human Motor Control. Academic Press, Inc, San Diego (1991)
27. Rosenbaum, D. A., Loukopoulos, L. D., Meulenbroek, R. G. J., Vaughan, J., Engelbrecht, S. E.: Planning Reaches by Evaluating Stored Postures. Psychological Review, Vol 102, No. 1 (1995) 28-47
28. Schaeffer, P.: Traité des objets musicaux. Éditions du Seuil, Paris (1966)
29. Rosch, E., Mervis, C. B., Gray, W. D., Johnson, D. M., Boyes-Braem, P.: Basic Objects in Natural Categories. Cognitive Psychology, 8 (1976) 382-436

The Interaction of Iconic Gesture and Speech in Talk

Judith Holler and Geoffrey Beattie

University of Manchester
United Kingdom

Abstract. One traditional view of how speech and gesture interact in talk is that gestures represent information, which is largely redundant with respect to the information contained in the speech that they accompany. Other researchers, however, have primarily stressed a complementary interaction of gesture and speech, and yet others have emphasised that gesture and speech interact in a very flexible manner. These discrepant views have crucially different implications with regard to the communicative role of gestures. The study reported here offers a systematic and detailed investigation of this issue to gain further insights into how the two modalities interact in the representation of meaning. The findings support the notion of gesture and speech interacting in a highly flexible manner.

1 Introduction

Iconic gestures are spontaneous movements of the hands and arms that accompany talk, and they represent concrete meaning that is closely associated with the semantic information in the speech. The way in which these hand gestures interact with speech in the representation of meaning has been described in the literature in quite different ways. Whereas one view of the gesture-speech relationship is that gestures convey mainly information that is redundant with respect to the speech (e.g., [1], [2]), others have stressed their complementary relationship with speech (e.g., [3]). Yet other investigators have been rather vague about the exact relationship of iconic gesture and speech by saying that these gestures 'illustrate' what is being said (e.g., [4], [5]) – which can be understood in a variety of ways, for example in terms of the gestural information emphasising what is said (i.e., representing the same information) or it could be understood as meaning that the gestural information complements the verbal information (i.e., by representing additional semantic information).

An example of a gesture representing information which can be considered as largely redundant with regard to the speech, is the following (example 1):

(1)

'a group of..of men, kind of around a [big table]'[1]

[both hands rise to about stomach height, they are held in parallel at the right and the left side of the body, the palms are facing towards the middle]

(Extracted from authors' corpus)

[1] For transcription conventions, please see Appendix.

A. Camurri and G. Volpe (Eds.): GW 2003, LNAI 2915, pp. 63–69, 2004.

In this example, the gesture refers to the table that the speaker is talking about and it emphasises its size. Thus, the gesture can be considered as not providing any information over and above the speech, which also contains the information that the table is big. This gesture would therefore correspond to Birdwhistell's [1] and Krauss, Morrel-Samuels and Colasante's [2] view that the information represented by gesture and speech is largely redundant. Although Birdwhistell [1] did not explicitly refer to iconic gestures, he did include in his analyses hand gestures that are essentially iconic in that they represent concrete semantic information. For example, Birdwhistell referred to gestures that show how an action is being carried out (e.g., 'swiftly' or 'slowly'), which he referred to as kinesic markers of the 'manner of action'. Krauss *et al.* ([2], p.743) also stated that 'although gestures can convey some information, they are not richly informative, and the information they convey is largely redundant with speech'. (Although Birdwhistell and Krauss *et al.* arrived at a similar conclusion concerning the semantic interaction of gesture and speech, it has to be noted that their views of the communicative role of gestures differ crucially.)

McNeill [3] seemed to stress a rather strict complementary pattern of gesture-speech interaction. In arguing for a broader view of language that takes into account gesture McNeill explained that gesture and speech often provide information about *different* semantic aspects of the same scene to make clear that a crucial part of a speaker's message might be ignored if only the speech is considered as conveying semantic information. The following example represents a case of speech and iconic gesture being complementary in their representations (example 2):

(2)

'she [chases him out again]'

[hand appears to swing an object
through the air]

(Extracted from [3], p.13)

Whereas the speech provides here the information that one character is chasing another, the accompanying iconic gesture shows that an instrument (an umbrella) is being used to do so. Although speech and gesture have here the same semantic reference point as they both represent information relating to the same event, they provide information about different aspects of this event so that they interact in a very complementary fashion. Hence, McNeill [3] argued that speech and gesture together reveal a fuller insight into a speaker's thoughts.

Rather than emphasising either a redundant or a complementary pattern of gesture-speech interaction, Kendon (e.g., [6], [7]) argued for a very flexible interaction of gesture and speech, with gesture representing an 'available resource' that speakers can use to respond to very different communicational demands.

Overall, it appears that the views of how speech and gesture predominantly interact are somewhat discrepant, and it thus seems necessary to investigate this issue further to gain more of an idea how these two channels of communication interact in the representation of meaning. However, instead of providing a number of individual examples, which show that speech and gesture can interact in one way or the other, as many previous investigations into this issue have done, this study systematically analyses a larger corpus of gestures.

2 Experimental Investigations into the Semantic Interaction of Gesture and Speech

2.1 An Attempt to Quantify the Interaction of Iconic Gesture and Speech

An experimental investigation was carried out investigating the interaction of gesture and speech by using a detailed analysis of a corpus of gesture-speech compounds produced in the context of narratives. These narratives stemmed from speakers telling cartoon stories, which were projected onto a wall in front of them, to the experimenter (JH). The gestural and verbal utterances referred to six 'semantic events' that formed part of two different Tom and Jerry cartoon stories (for example, 'Jerry stabbing Tom in the tail with a sharp instrument', 'Spike, the dog, dangling Jerry by his tail', etc.). For the analysis, 58 verbal utterances accompanied by 58 iconic gestures (stemming from 27 different speakers) were selected and the semantic information represented by gesture and speech was scored according to 20 detailed semantic categories (the general idea of applying a semantic feature approach was derived from Beattie and Shovelton [e.g., 8, 9, 10, 11]. The semantic categories used referred to, for example, information about the kinds of entities involved in the event that the speakers talked about (such as 'agent', 'object [in terms of an entity that is being acted upon] and 'instrument'), the direction of, or the force associated with, a movement, the position of individual entities relative to each other and the surrounding space, as well as the shape and the size of the individual entities that formed part of the event (see Table 1; for more detail on the individual semantic categories, please see [12]). An important aspect of the study is also that it took into account information that was only implicitly represented in speech, as well as explicitly represented information. The scoring scheme applied in the study was designed to capture such subtle differences.

The mathematical scoring scheme was developed to quantify the information represented by gesture and speech. It consisted of certain 'informational values', namely 0 (meaning that information was not represented), 0.5 (meaning that information was *implicitly* represented) and 1 (meaning that information was *explicitly* represented). Scores were given for all 58 gestures and 58 speech extracts in separate, and each gesture and speech extract was scored according to the 20 semantic categories displayed in Table 1 (for more detail concerning the criteria used for scoring the information, please see [12]). The inter-observer reliability for scoring the information represented by the gestures and the speech extracts was calculated using Cohen's Kappa, which resulted in K=.96 for speech and K=.97 for gesture.

The informational value 0.5 did not find appliance in the scoring of the gestural information. Hence, the possible interaction patterns of gesture and speech could be categorised into six different types, as displayed in Table 2.

The next step in the analysis involved calculating how often gesture and speech had interacted in the six different ways identified here concerning each of the semantic categories. In order to simplify the rather complex database resulting from this procedure (i.e., a 6x20 matrix), the predominant interaction pattern was identified for each semantic category. Those semantic features with clear peaks concerning one of the interaction patterns are shown in Table 3.

Table 1. Overview of the basic and their related, more detailed semantic categories applied

Entity	1. Agent 2. Object 3. Instrument
Action	4. Body-parts involved in the movement 5. Direction of the movement 6. Point of contact defined 7. Force
Relative position	8. Relative position: Agent – Object 9. Relative position: Agent – Instrument 10. Relative position: Object – Instrument 11. Relative position: Object – Space
Size	12. Size: agent 13. Size: object 14. Size: instrument
Shape	15. Agent 16. Object 17. Instrument
Shape of a part	18. Agent 19. Object 20. Instrument

(From [12])

Table 2. Overview of the six types of speech-gesture interaction patterns resulting from the scoring scheme applied

Speech - Gesture	
0-0	The information is represented *neither by speech nor by gesture.*
0-1	The information is represented *only gesturally.*
1-0	The information is represented *only verbally.*
0.5-0	The information is *implicitly* represented *in speech, but not in gesture.*
0.5-1	The information is *implicitly* represented *in speech and explicitly in gesture.*
1-1	The information is *explicitly* represented *in both gesture and speech.*

(From [12])

Complexity and Flexibility – Two Important Aspects Characterising the Interaction of Iconic Gesture and Speech. What can be seen from Table 3 is, first of all, that the interaction of gesture and speech seems rather complex, as gesture and speech were shown to interact in at least five different ways, and these include that gesture and speech represent both complementary as well as redundant information. The analysis also reveals that it is necessary to be more precise when we talk about 'complementarity' in association with the semantic interaction of gesture and speech. This is because the gestural and the verbal information can be strictly complementary in

Table 3. Overview of the semantic features that were predominantly represented by one of the six gesture-speech interaction patterns identified

Speech - Gesture	Semantic feature
0-0	Action: force Rel. position: O-S Size: instrument
0-1	Rel. position: A-O Rel. Position: A-I Shape of a part: object
1-0	----
0.5-0	Size: object Shape: object
0.5-1	Action: body-parts Shape of a part: agent
1-1	Entity: agent Entity: object Entity: instrument

(From [12])

that each of the two communicational channels represents information that is not at all represented in the respective other (for example, as in the case of the gesture-speech example from McNeill described above). However, they can also complement in that speech represents some (i.e., implicit) information, while the gesture represents the same information more explicitly. Furthermore, although some of the semantic features were shown to be predominantly represented by gesture and speech interacting in one certain way, each individual semantic feature was represented by iconic gesture and speech interacting in a variety of different ways.

Overall, it seems that stressing either a redundant or a complementary interaction of iconic gesture and speech does not provide an accurate picture of how the two modalities actually interact in the representation of meaning. Rather, it seems necessary to stress the complexity that characterises the interaction of iconic gesture and speech. Furthermore, it is important to note that iconic gesture and speech can interact in a very flexible manner, even concerning the representation of the same semantic aspects. Hence, the findings of this quantitative analysis support Kendon's (e.g., [6], [7]) notion of how speech and gesture interact.

Having come to this conclusion, the question remains as to what factors do then have an impact on how gesture and speech interact. One such factor could of course be the social context in which spoken discourse is embedded, and in line with Kendon, it could be assumed that this context is directly involved in shaping the communicational demands that a speaker responds to using gesture.

Based on the observation that in some cases in which speech provided only implicit information, this information was explicitly represented by gesture, one could assume that one communicative function of gesture may be the facilitation of inferences that listeners have to make when information is only implicitly provided. In other words, the gestures in these cases might provide the recipient with semantic cues as to what the correct inferences are. If future investigations could provide evidence that hand gestures really do function as an aid for the recipient to draw inferences during talk, this would be evidence for a very important communicative function of gesture, because inferences play such a crucial role in the understanding of everyday talk. Moreover, it would show that gestures are indeed used by speakers to facilitate the listener's understanding and thus that the use of gesture is influenced by the social context. Hence, the findings of the present study suggest a potential pragmatic use of gesture, which calls for further investigation, particularly considering that there is still much debate about whether gestures are communicatively intended or not (cf. [13], [14]).

3 Conclusions

Overall, the investigation reported here shows that the interaction of iconic gesture and speech is complex as well as flexible. It thus clarifies the issue of how iconic gesture and speech interact in the representation of meaning somewhat by showing that views emphasising either a predominantly complementary or a predominantly redundant pattern of interaction do not reflect the most crucial aspect that seems to characterise the interaction of iconic gesture and speech, namely flexibility. Furthermore, the findings support the notion that speakers draw on gesture in order to fulfil certain communicational functions. Because the scoring scheme applied in this study took into account inferences that listeners might have to make in order to comprehend spoken discourse, it was possible to identify an important potential use of gesture, namely the facilitation of inferences. Future research is needed to further test whether gestures are indeed used by speakers for this purpose.

References

1. Birdwhistell, R. L.: Kinesics and Context. Essays on Body-Motion Communication. Allen Lane The Penguin Press, London (1970).
2. Krauss, R. M., Morrel-Samuels, P., Colasante, C.: Do conversational hand gestures communicate? Journal of Personality and Social Psychology (1991), 61, 743-754.
3. McNeill, D.: Hand and Mind: What Gestures Reveal about Thought. University of Chicago Press, Chicago (1992).
4. Ekman, P., Friesen, W. V.: The Repertoire of Nonverbal Behaviour: Categories, Origins, Usage and Coding. Semiotica (1969), 1, 49-98.
5. Argyle, M.: Bodily Communication. Methuen and Co Ltd., London (1975).
6. Kendon, A.: Gesticulation and speech: Two aspects of the process of utterance. In: Key, M. R. (ed.). The Relationship of Verbal and Nonverbal Communication. Mouton, The Hague (1980), 207-227.
7. Kendon, A.: Some Uses of Gesture. In: Tannen, D. and Saville-Troike, M. (eds.), Perspectives on Silence. Ablex Publishing Corporation, Norwood New Jersey (1985) 215-234.
8. Beattie, G., Shovelton, H.: Do Iconic Hand Gestures Really Contribute Anything to the Semantic Information Conveyed by Speech? An Experimental Investigation. Semiotica (1999), 123, 1-30.
9. Beattie, G., Shovelton, H.: Mapping the Range of Information Contained in the Iconic Hand Gestures that Accompany Spontaneous Speech. Journal of Language and Social Psychology (1999), 18, 438-462.

10. Beattie, G., Shovelton, H.: An experimental investigation of the role of different types of iconic gesture in communication: A semantic feature approach. Gesture (2001), 1, 129-149.
11. Beattie, G., Shovelton, H.: An Experimental Investigation of Some Properties of Individual Iconic Gestures that Mediate their Communicative Power. British Journal of Psychology (2002), 93, 179-192.
12. Holler, J., Beattie, G.: How Iconic Gestures and Speech Interact in the Representation of Meaning: Are Both Aspects Really Integral to the Process? Semiotica (2003), 146, 81-116.
13. Butterworth, B., Hadar, U.: Gesture, speech, and computational stages: A reply to McNeill. Psychological Review (1989), 96, 168-174.
14. Krauss, R. M., Chen, Y., Gottesman, R. F.: Lexical gestures and lexical retrieval: A process model. In: McNeill, D. (ed.), Language and Gesture. Cambridge University Press: Cambridge (2000), 261-283.

Appendix

Transcription conventions:

Segments of speech analysed are marked using 'single quotes'. That part of the verbal utterance that was accompanied by the iconic gesture is marked using [square brackets]. The iconic gesture that accompanied the verbal utterance is described underneath the extract of speech and this description is also contained within square brackets.

Conceptual and Lexical Factors in the Production of Speech and Conversational Gestures: Neuropsychological Evidence*

Carla Cristilli[1] and Sergio Carlomagno[2]

[1] Dpt. di Studi Americani, Culturali e Linguistici
Università degli Studi di Napoli "L'Orientale"
P.zza S.Giovanni Maggiore, 30, 80134 Napoli
cristill@unina.it

[2] Dpt. di Scienze Neurologiche, Seconda Università di Napoli
Via Pansini, 5, 80131 Napoli
sergio.carlomagno@unina2.it

Abstract. Parallel breakdown of gestures and speech following neurological damage supports the notion that "....gestures and speech ... share a computational stage..." (McNeill, 1992) and emphasizes the role of neuropsychological approach for studying gestures. In this study patterns of conversational gestures were analysed in subjects with Alzheimer's dementia, whose communicative performance indicated either primary lexical deficit or deficit in pragmatic/conceptual elaboration of discourse. Two gesture patterns were identified. The demented subjects with lexical deficit mostly produced iconic gestures which accompanied paraphasic expressions related to discriminating information. Conversely, the pragmatic/conceptual deficit corresponded to reduced production of iconic and increased production of deictic gestures. These findings indicate that the cognitive impairment underlying communicative deficit constrains the production of conversational gestures in brain-damaged patients. They also support the hypothesis that the early conceptual processes of speech production system play a central role in producing gestures.

1 Introduction

When speaking, people ordinarily perform a variety of movements: they change postures, they nod their heads or they gesture with arms and hands. Within the latter class of movements some are clearly tied to the speech rhythm or used to emphasise some speech content (beats); some have definite accepted meaning, as the gestures signalling "Yes", "No", "OK" (emblems); others have some ideational content (iconic gestures). The last are particularly interesting for psychologists as, being more motivated

* This study has been supported by a PRIN Cofin-2000 Grant from MURST (Italy) to Sergio Carlomagno.
This paper is the result of the joint research of the two authors. The first two paragraphs of Part I (Introduction) and Part 3 (Results and Discussion), however, have been written by Carla Cristilli, while the Abstract, the last two paragraphs of Part I (Introduction) and Part 2 (Methods and Subjects) have been written by Sergio Carlomagno.

A. Camurri and G. Volpe (Eds.): GW 2003, LNAI 2915, pp. 70–76, 2004.

than linguistic signs, they offer the possibility of inferring the processes of symbolic representation of reality (McNeill, 1992).

The potential of a neuropsychological approach for enhancing our understanding of these gestures has long been recognised in studies which examined expressive movements of this type in fluent and non-fluent aphasia syndromes (Cicone, Wapner, Foldi, Zurif & Gardner, 1979; McNeill, 1992), right hemisphere damaged subjects (McNeill, 1992) or in patients with Alzheimer's Type Dementia (DAT) (Glosser, Wiley & Barnoskj, 1998). These studies have pointed out a parallel dissolution of language and iconic gestures in these syndromes, which supports the notion that gestures and speech share a computational stage in the process of discourse construction, being, perhaps, different aspects of a single process (McNeill, 1992). For instance, DAT patients have been shown to produce proportionately more referentially ambiguous gestures (gestures which do not show in their form a semantic content clearly related to a word or a phrase), just as they produce “empty speech”, i.e. speech with poor semantic content and/or lack of reference (Glosser et al., 1998).

It is currently assumed, however, that speech production involves different steps of processing relating to 1) pre-verbal (conceptual) message construction (say selecting information and ordering it to accomplish the communicative intention); 2) linguistic processing (say lexical and morpho-syntactic encoding of information) and 3) phonetic execution (see for instance Levelt, 1989). Language disturbances in brain damaged patients may arise from damage to different cognitive components of speech processing system. Then, if a particular linkage exists between one (or more) of these cognitive components and the gesture production system, correlation would emerge between the particular cognitive deficit of the patient and his production of iconic gestures. DAT "empty speech", for instance, may be due to faulty lexical encoding of information and/or poor conceptual elaboration of discourse information content (Blanken, Dittanem, Haas & Wallesch, 1988). Thus, in a previous study (Carlomagno et al., 2002b) we attempted to find out whether different cognitive impairments which may underlie the DAT language deficit were correlated to differences in gestural behaviour.

The communicative behaviour of DAT patients in a referential communication task made it possible to analyse conceptual and lexical factors affecting the discourse information content of DAT subjects. Following this method, it was possible to show that defective lexical encoding of information resulted in reduced production of target words and increased paraphasic errors, while defective conceptual elaboration of discourse information content gave rise to production of confounding information and irrelevant details (Carlomagno et al., 2002a). Furthermore, it was found that some DAT patients could show dissociated performance probably due to the multiform distribution of DAT pathology in the different areas of the brain. For instance, in some DAT patients performance indicated a significant lexical deficit with preserved conceptual elaboration of discourse information content. For other patients, the reverse pattern was found. Such a double dissociation provided unique opportunities for testing whether damage to different components (lexical or conceptual) of language production system differed in the way they constrained production of gestures in DAT subjects. Gestures performed in the referential communication task were thus analysed in two DAT subjects with primary deficit in lexical encoding of information and in two DAT subjects with primary deficit in pragmatic conceptual elaboration of discourse, two fluent aphasic (FA) patients and two normal controls. It was shown that the two FA and the two DAT patients with lexical deficit produced twice as many gestures as the normal participants with a normal percentage of iconic gestures. Conversely, the defective conceptual elaboration of message in the other two DAT patients corresponded to a normal gesturing rate but a reduced percentage of iconic gestures and a corresponding increase in deictic (pointing) ones. These findings indicated that the nature of cognitive impairment underlying the DAT "empty speech" constrained production of conversational gestures in these patients. These findings also indicated the role of early conceptual processes in producing iconic gestures. Indeed, defective conceptual representations of message information in the DAT patients with conceptual deficit were accompanied by poor semantic gestures content (less iconic gestures) while, in the DAT patients with poor lexical encoding of information, a possible compensatory hyperactivation of conceptual representations of information to be conveyed led to increased production of iconic gestures.

The present study attempted to check this hypothesis further by detailing relationships between speech propositional content and gestures in DAT patients with "pure" lexical deficit or "pure" defective conceptual elaboration of discourse information content.

2 Method and Subjects

In the referential communication task participants were requested to act as speakers on 25 stimuli, each consisting of a target picture marked with a red circle (the referent) and three distracters. They had to send discriminating information (from one to three information units) to a naive listener by verbal and non-verbal means so that the listener could identify the referent. The speakers were allowed up to two repairs for each stimulus. The testing session was videotaped focusing on the patient's upper body so that all arm/hand movements could be recorded. These tapes were analysed with a standardised scoring procedure which took into account lexical encoding of information and accuracy in selecting information (Carlomagno et al. 2002b).

Since the aim of the present study was to check for visible trends of gesture patterns in DAT with respect to lexical or conceptual deficit, two DAT patients were chosen as having a communicative performance that indicated primary lexical or conceptual deficit. For instance, in the patient R.O. reduced production of target words (18/40) and significant production of paraphasic errors (16) indicated impaired lexical processing. This patient, however, did not produce confounding information (information pertaining to distracters. Normal value $\overline{x}$ = 0.2) and she sent non-discriminating information only on 5 occasions (normal value $\overline{x}$ = 4.2). This indicated preserved conceptual elaboration of discourse information content. For another patient, B.R., the reverse pattern was found, as she produced 31 out of the 40 words which were predicted to identify the item (normal value $\overline{x}$ = 37.1), while on 5 occasions confounding information and 13 irrelevant details were scored (see above).

A detailed gesture analysis was performed on the same eight stimuli for all the participants. These tape segments were analysed by two trained independent examiners, unaware of the project. They were requested to mark the occurrence and duration of each movement with respect to the alphabetic transcription of concurrent verbal output. This had been previously arranged so that it contained the temporal structure of pause/phonation components of the speech sample. The description of physical aspects of each hand/arm movement that could be related to speech was made according to Kendon (1995). These movements were further analysed as to their semantic content and classified into representative (iconic), deictic (pointing) and metalinguistic. The last category included gestures related to the personal feeling of the speaker, e.g. gestures which expressed uncertainty about the linguistic referential expression produced or to be produced; gestures expressing the intended speech act and gestures marking the speech rhythm. All these gestures were considered with respect to the accuracy of the concurrent verbal output (correct information, paraphasic expression, anomic incident, non-informative comment and incorrect or irrelevant information; see later for related examples). Self-touching movements and "emblematic gestures", i.e. gestures having a conventional meaning (Yes, No, OK.), were rare and were not be further considered. The percentage of agreement between the two examiners ranged from 88 to 93%.

3 Results

Gesture and verbal production of the two patients is shown in the following Tables 1 and 2, where the two gesture and verbal patterns are respectively illustrated by the results from the present analysis.

Table 1. Speech and Gesture Analysis of Patient RO: number of occurrences

Speech	Gesture		
	ICONIC	DEICTIC	META-LINGUISTIC
Correct Information	2	–	1
Paraphasic Expressions	16	–	2
Anomia	5	2	–
Incorrect Information	1	–	2
Non-informative Speech	1	–	2
Total	25	2	7

Patient R.0. produced 35 gestures. Twenty-five of these (71%) were representative, seven (20,5%) metalinguistic and the remaining ones were gestures pointing to the stimulus pictures. The majority of representative gestures (21) accompanied paraphasic verbal attempts to identify the referent or anomic incidents. For instance, for the item "a squirrel under a swing" she said (underlined speech segments correspond to a gesture): "this is a little animal which I don't know, a little animal is here with (...) and with the little tail. Then there are two thing which come down ... they are tied up like....a thing which one makes boom boom boom...(listener's prompt)...it lies down...under...". Only the first movement was an indefinite gesture which stressed uncertainty about her verbal referential expression. The other four gestures in the first message represented the shape of the ears and the tail of the squirrel, the swing vertical axes of the swing and the swing movement. Then, after the listener's prompt, again information was given by paraphasic expressions. Once more these were accompanied by gestures (those depicting the down position of the squirrel and the swing chair). It should be noted that, on the eight items of the analysis, this patient was able to name only 3 out of the 12 information units which were predicted to identify the referents. Such a difficulty in lexical encoding of information was in marked contrast with the adequate conceptual elaboration of the information she had to transmit. Note that distracters illustrated a dog under the swing, a squirrel near a tree and a squirrel on the swing chair. Furthermore, six out of the seven metalinguistic gestures expressed uncertainty about the verbal expression she was producing, e.g., "little animal" instead of squirrel.

A quite different pattern was observed in the case of patient B.R (Table 2).

First, her gesturing rate was about half of that observed in the case of R.O., in spite of her producing the same amount of words. Second, representative gestures were replaced by deictic gestures (78.9%), which accompanied production of correct information (on 6 occasions) as well as confounding (5 times) and paraphasic expressions (3 times).

Table 2. Speech and Gesture Analysis of Patient BR: number of occurrences

Speech	**Gesture**		
	ICONIC	DEICTIC	META-LINGUISTIC
Correct Information	–	6	–
Paraphasic Expressions	2	3	–
Anomia	1	–	–
Incorrect Information	–	5	1
Non-informative Speech	–	1	–
Total	3	15	1

For instance, still about the "squirrel" item, he said: "there is …a … a squirrel and then a swing … a squirrel…(listener's prompt: "but where is it?) …near the swing? Yes the dog… (listener's prompt: "please, could You talk about the figure with the red circle?") …Ah Ah! a squirrel ". All gestures pointed to the picture array. Moreover, it should be noted that in our referential communication task deictic gestures had no referential value as the listener could not see which item the speaker was pointing to. Only in relation to one of the eight items of the gesture analysis did the patient produce a representative gesture (handling a camera), which accompanied an anomic incident and a subsequent paraphasic expression.

4 Discussion

The analysis of the communicative performance of DAT patients in the referential communication task suggested that the "empty speech" of these patients could originate from damage to separate (lexical or conceptual) components of speech production system (Carlomagno et al., 2002b). The analysis of the gesture pattern in the DAT patients with selective impairment of one of the two components indicated that the nature of cognitive impairment underlying their speech production deficit constrained the gesture pattern in these patients.

The explanation proposed by Carlomagno et al. (2002a) for the two gesture patterns focused both on the nature of the DAT conceptual deficit and on the role of early conceptual processes of discourse construction as a common computational stage in gesture and speech production system (see for instance Krauss, Chen and Chawla, 1996, De Ruyters, 2000). The DAT patient with conceptual deficit, indeed, appeared to be unable to maintain activated relevant information from the referent (squirrel, under and swing) and to disregard competing information from distracters (dog) until the discriminating information was adequately organised for linguistic encoding. Such a defective activation of information processing corresponded to reduced activation of gestures with semantic content (iconic). We would stress indeed that the large amount of deictic gestures we observed suggests that the subject was simply naming arguments from the picture array without focusing those which discriminated the referent picture. Conversely, in the DAT patient with lexical deficit, the greater production of gestures was related to paraphasic expressions regarding discriminating information units. In order to compensate for the defective lexical encoding of this information, the DAT patient with lexical deficit attempted to describe physical aspects of the argument (the swing axes and chair or the ear and the tail of the squirrel) she had focused. This probably entailed compensatory hyperactivation of conceptual representations of information included in the referring expression. Such hyperactivation resulted, on one hand, in paraphasic expressions and, on the other, in a significant production of representative (iconic) gestures.

Our finding of a normal percentage of iconic gestures in the DAT patient with primarily lexical deficit is at variance with the results obtained by Glosser et al. (1998). They found that DAT subjects, as a group, exhibited a parallel dissolution of language (empty speech) and gesture (production of referentially ambiguous gestures). Glosser et al. (1998), however, did not take into selective account factors which could underlie the communicative deficit in individual DAT subjects and only searched for group differences between the DAT and normal subjects at syndromic level. However, such a description probably obscured individual differences in gestures produced by DAT subjects. Furthermore it only suggested general relationships between speech and gesture production. In the present study, predictions have been made about the role of the particular cognitive deficit in producing the gesture pattern in individual DAT patients according to current models of speech/gesture production (Krauss, Chen and Chawla, 1996, De Ruyters, 2000) which assume separate components of speech production system. The heterogeneous patterns of gestures we found indicate that conceptual and lexical factors differ in the way they constrain gesture production. These differences fit well with these models of speech/gesture production. We argue that such a model-based neuropsychological approach to the study of co-verbal gestures may offer a new possibility for analysing the relationships between the different processes involved in communication.

References

1. Blancken G., Dittanem J., Haas J. C., & Wallesch C. W.: Spontaneous speech in senile dementia and aphasia: implication for neurolinguistic model of language production. Cognition, 27.3. Elsevier Science (1998) 247-274
2. Carlomagno, S., Santoro, A., Menditti, A., Pandolfi, M. & Marini, A.: Referential Communication in Alzheimer's Type Dementia (2002a). Cortex, Masson, Milano. Submitted
3. Carlomagno, S., Pandolfi, M., Marini, A., Di Iasi, G. & Cristilli, C.: Coverbal Gestures in Alzheimer's Type Dementia (2002b). Cortex, Masson, Milano. Submitted
4. Cicone, M., Wapner, W., Foldi, N., Zurif, E. & Gardner, H.: The relation between gesture and language in aphasic communication. Brain and Language, Vol. 8. Academic Press, New York (1979) 324-349.

5. Glosser, G., Wiley, M.J. & Barnoskj, E.J.: Gestural communication in Alzheimer's disease. Journal of Clinical and Experimental Neuropsychology, Vol. 20.1. Swets Zeitlinger, Lisse (1998) 1-13.
6. Kendon, A.: Gestures as illocutionary and discourse structure markers in southern Italian conversation. Journal of Pragmatics, Vol. 23.3. Elsevier Science (1998) 247-279
7. Krauss, R.M., Chen, Y. & Chawla, P.: Nonverbal behaviour and nonverbal communication: what do conversational gestures tell us? In: Zanna, M. (ed.): Advances in experimental social psychology, Vol. 28. Academic Press, New York (1996) .
8. Levelt, W.J.M.: Speaking. The M.I.T. Press, Cambridge (MA) (1989)
9. McNeill, D.: Hand and Mind. University of Chicago Press, Chicago (IL) (1992).
10. De Ruyter, J.P.: The production of gesture and speech. In: McNeill, D. (ed.): Language and Gesture. Cambridge University Press, Cambridge (2000) 284-311

The Communicative System of Touch. Alphabet, Lexicon, and Norms of Use

Isabella Poggi, Filomena Cirella, Antonietta Zollo, and Alessia Agostini

Dipartimento di Scienze dell'Educazione - University Roma Tre
poggi@uniroma3.it

Abstract. The paper argues that the communicative system of touch includes a lexicon, an alphabet and some norms of use, and presents a research aimed at making them explicit. 104 items of touch were analysed in terms of their formational parameters, various semantic criteria, and norms of use, and some hypotheses on the structure of the communicative system of touch in Italy were tested in a pilot study. Then the communicative use of touch in 3 mother-child couples was analysed, showing how the criteria of analysis proposed allow to distinguish different styles of mother-child interaction.

1 Introduction

Touch is one of the most primitive but still most important ways of communicating; a kiss or a caress may communicate love, a push or a kick rejection, a pat on the back encouragement. In this paper we propose to study touch, as other communication systems, by singling out its alphabet, its lexicon, and its norms of use. After presenting our view of communication and communication systems (Section 2), and a distinction between communicative and non-communicative uses of touch (3), we illustrate some research aimed at studying the alphabet, the lexicon and the norms of use of touch in Italy (4 – 7), and show how the categories proposed can be used to analyse touch in mother-child interaction (8).

2 Communication and Communication Systems

In terms of the Model we adopt here [1], communication is defined as a process in which a Sender has the goal to have an Addressee believe some meaning, and in order to achieve this produces a signal with that meaning. A signal is any perceivable stimulus produced by the Sender's muscular actions or morphological features: a word, a beat gesture, a blush, a gaze, a slap, a posture are signals. The meanings may concern Information on the World – beliefs about concrete or abstract events, their actors and objects, time and space relations, Information on the Sender's Identity – sex, age, social and cultural roots, personality, and Information on the Sender's Mind – his/her beliefs, goals, and emotions (Poggi et al., this vol.). The goal of communicating some meaning may be a conscious goal, as when I utter a sentence; an unconscious one, in a neurotic symptom; a "tacit" goal, outside the focus of attention, in a baton, or in

A. Camurri and G. Volpe (Eds.): GW 2003, LNAI 2915, pp. 77–89, 2004.

walking hand in hand with a friend; a biological goal (the seagull's flight that warns the flock of a predator, or the blushing that apologises for a shameful act [2]); or a social goal (uniforms or status symbols, that provide information about role or group identity).

A communication system is a system of rules to link a set of signals to a set of meanings. Communication systems are either "codified" or "creative" [3]. In a "codified" system, such as words or symbolic gestures, the rules of correspondence between signals and meanings are shared by a Sender and an Addressee, and codified in their long-term memory, so as to make lexicon of different modalities. In a "creative" system, what is coded in memory is a small set of inference rules about how to create a new signal starting from a given meaning, or how to retrieve a meaning from a given signal: like in pantomime [4] and in "iconics" [5], or in the creation of new words in natural languages.

To investigate the structure of communicative systems implies finding out the rules that link signals to meanings. For "creative" communication systems it means finding out the inference rules that state how new signals can be created by a Sender and understood by an Addressee: for example, how we invent an iconic gesture to represent the idea of climbing, of a spiral staircase, a cello, the wind [5], [3], [6]. [7], [8]. For "codified" systems, or "lexicons", the task is to compile lexicons of systems in all modalities. Some examples in this field are the dictionaries of Sign Languages and the dictionaries of symbolic gestures of different cultures [9], [10].

Yet, in our view not only words or symbolic gestures, as it is generally accepted, but also other kinds of gestures, like batons, affect displays or some adaptors (with the exception, perhaps, only of iconics and metaphorics), and even gaze, facial expression, posture shifts, intonation are "lexical" systems. We claim that the job of Communication scholars is to disclose and to inventory all of these subtle but precise lexicons. In this sense, Ekman and Friesen's FACS [11] is a sort of lexicon, since it states the correspondences between patterns of facial muscular actions (Action Units), and the meanings of different emotion expressions. But also other lexicons or fragments of lexicons have been proposed: for deictic gestures [12], performative facial expressions [13], gaze [14]. And a lexicon can be found also for the communicative system of touch.

Now, a lexicon is a list of rules of correspondence between signals and meanings, where the meanings can be analysed in terms of mental images or semantic components to be expressed in a propositional format. But how can the signal be analysed? To analyse the signal side of a lexicon one has to find out the "alphabet" that composes its signals, that is, the set of sub-lexical components, parts or aspects of signals, that, variously combined simultaneously or in sequence, form all the possible signals in that lexicon.

For signals produced by the whole body, relevant works in this field are Birdwhistell's system [15], Laban notation [16], FACS [11]. For gestures, an important impulse has been provided by the seminal work of Stokoe [17] and his notion of formational parameters to analyse signs in Sign Languages of the Deaf. Formational parameters are dimensions in terms of which one can analyse and classify all signals in a communication system. A parameter can assume some values, and each signal may be described as a combination of the values in all parameters. Each value has a "phonological" status, in that changing a value may result in a different signal or a non-signal. For example, gestures are produced by a particular handshape, movement, location, and orientation, and each gesture takes a particular value with respect to each of these parameters. The notion of formational parameters, already applied to the symbolic gestures of Italian Hearing People [18] and to gaze [14], can also be used to analyse the signals of touch [19].

Coming to the meaning side of a lexicon, it includes two kinds of rules: semantic rules and norms of use. The former are rules of this type:

> if you want to communicate the meaning "I greet you", say "Hello",
> if you want to communicate the meaning "I greet you", raise your eyebrows,
> if you want to communicate the meaning "I greet you", wave your hand.

Norms of use, instead, do not state how some meaning has to be conveyed, but if some meaning can, should or should not be conveyed in a given situation, by whom and how. A such rule might sound:

> if you meet a person you know, apply the rule for the meaning "I greet you";
> if you meet an unknown person, do not apply the rule for the meaning "I greet you".

3 Touch as Action, Touch as Communication

As other communication systems different from verbal and sign languages, like gaze [14], touch calls for distinguishing between communicative signals and non-communicative behaviour.

We define an act as *touch* when a physical contact occurs between a part of the body of an Agent and a part of an object or a person (other than that Agent). The act of touching may be performed out of four different goals: to sense, to grasp, to feel, or to communicate:

To Sense. Touching is sometimes performed simply for the goal of getting information about an object or person. I touch a tissue to sense if it is soft or raw; in the Bible Isaac touches his son to tell if he is Jacob or Esau;

To Grasp. I may touch an object or person not just to get information about it, but because touching is necessary to grasp it: I do not touch an apple to know how smooth it is (I already know) but to grasp it and chew it; if I touch a man who has just stolen my camera on the bus it is not to get information about his skin but to grasp him and stop him;

To Feel. Touching things, other people or ourselves, may give us pleasure or pain. We may caress soft fur or smooth skin, just to feel the pleasure of this contact. I could even touch something burning or sharp out of a goal of self-punishment.

To Communicate. We define an act of touch as "communicative touch" when a physical contact occurs between a part of the body of a Sender and a part of the body of an Addressee, and when this physical contact is caused by the Sender with the goal of communicating something to the Addressee (that is, of having the Addressee believe some meaning). For instance, a *caress* communicates something like "I want to give you pleasure – then – I love you tenderly"; a *slap* means "I want to hurt your (physical, but also symbolic) face". In other words, touch is a way of performing a communicative act, that is, of communicating something which could be paraphrased with a sentence. Of course, the communicative goal of a Sender in "telling something" through touch is usually a tacit – not totally aware – communicative goal; in the same vein, when the Addressee "understands" the meaning of an act of touch s/he may not "understand" it at a cognitively sophisticated level. This is also why in some cases it is not straightforward to tell whether an act of touch is a communicative act or not. When a mother takes her 2 year child under his armpits, how can you tell if she is only trying to hold him or she is also communicating "I am holding you" to reassure him?

A research on the communicative system of touch in Italy was carried out by the Authors to discover its lexicon, its alphabet and its norms of use [19], [20]. To single out the lexical items of the Italian lexicon of touch, 104 names of acts of touch in Italian were collected, like *bacio* (kiss), *schiaffo* (slap), *calcio* (kick), *carezza* (caress), and analysed as for their meaning, their signal and their use.

4 The Alphabet of Touch

On the signal side, the formational parameters that seem relevant to distinguish the 104 different items of touch are the following:

1. *touching part*. Different from gesture or gaze, touch is a communication system that cannot be located in a single body organ: the touching part is a hand in a caress, a foot in a kick, the mouth in a kiss. The parts of our body by which we touch represent one parameter of the touch system.
   The values found for this parameter in Italian touch signals are 23: hair, forehead, head, eyelash, nose, cheek, beard, lips, teeth, tongue, shoulder, arm, back, elbow, hand, fingers, nails, hip, genitals, glutei, thigh, knee, foot.
2. *touched part*. The values in this parameter, that is, the parts of the other's body we can touch, are 32: hair, forehead, head, eyebrows, eyelashes, eye, temple, nose, cheek, ear, beard, lips, tongue, neck, shoulder, arm, forearm, breast, trunk, stomach, back, elbow, hand, fingers, hip, genitals, glutei, thigh, knee, calf, ankle, foot;
3. *location or space* touched. We can touch on a point, a line, an area. A kick, a slap fall on a point; a caress, a lick move along a line; scratching over an area;
4. *movement*. An act of touch in a sense is a gesture, so, as for gestures, the parameter of movement is very important and articulated. For touch, we can distinguish a *movement 1* (before skin contact takes place) and a *movement 2* (during contact). In some acts of touch, like in a slap, there is no *movement 2*. Both movements, 1 and 2, include the same sub-parameters, path, duration, speed and frequency, but with slightly different values.

4.1 *movement 1*.
   a. *path*: the direction of the touching part with respect to the touched part, with 4 values: perpendicular, oblique, oblique circular, oblique arched.
   b. *tempo*: how long, frequent or repeated is the physical contact between touching and touched part. It includes:
      duration (short, medium, long)
      speed (slow, medium, fast)
      rhythm, which has 5 values:

- unique, when skin contact is very short and not repeated (as for a slap, a punch, a kiss on the forehead);
- single, when skin contact is somewhat persistent but not repeated (caress, rub, drying the other's tear);
- repeated in jerks, when contact is repeated twice or more (burping a baby, giving a pat on the back);
- standing, when contact persists quite long without the touching part moving away from the touched part (keeping the other's hand, walking arm-in-arm);
- continuous, if the movement is repeated with no pause (massaging, rubbing).

4.2 *movement 2*: within *path* it only allows the values *parallel along a line* (caress) and *parallel circular* (rubbing).

5. *pressure*: an aspect of movement, it applies to either movement 1 or movement 2, and includes two sub-parameters, *tension* and *impact*.
   a. *tension*: muscular tension of the touching part: tense, delicate, relaxed, normal.
   b. *impact*: the way in which the act of touch ends: normal, block, skim.

Pressure is quite an important parameter since it typically distinguishes friendly from aggressive touch.

Each of the 104 items was analysed in terms of all parameters, as in Figure 1.

5 The Lexicon of Touch

Besides finding out the formational parameters of touch, the 104 items of communicative touch were analysed in terms of 6 semantic criteria, starting from the assumption that any communicative (thus meaningful) act – even an act of touch – can be paraphrased in a verbal language. It was also assumed that for some meanings it is possible to find out both their origin in action [21] and the possible communicative inferences they elicits, that is, their indirect meaning. Often, in verbal lexicons but also in other modalities, a lexical item may have, besides its literal meaning, a meaning that can be inferred from the literal one, and that sometimes is idiomatised, stored in memory as one more (sometimes the only) meaning of the item. For instance, clapping hands has a literal meaning of praise, but it has also acquired a further ironical meaning of blame.

For each item of touch, the following information was provided (Figure 2):

1. **name** or **verbal description**: e.g. *bacio* (kiss), *schiaffo* (slap), *calcio* (kick), *carezza* (caress), *asciugare le lacrime* (drying the other's tears);
2. **verbal paraphrase** or other verbal expression that may accompany the act of touch. *Drying the other's tears* may be accompanied by the expression "*C'mon, don't cry*"; while caressing someone we may tell him *"I love you"*;
3. **literal meaning**: *drying the other's tears* means "I want to console you"; a *caress*, "I want to give you serenity and pleasure";
4. **indirect idiomatic meaning**: sometimes a caress has a further goal of letting one be calmer, so its indirect meaning is "I want to calm you";

5. **original meaning**: the primitive goal of the act from which the literal meaning might have evolved (e.g., through ritualization). *Embracing* might derive from a desire to enfold the other, to incorporate her in oneself.
6. **social goal**: the toucher's social disposition towards the touched person. Four types of social goal were distinguished: one aggressive goal, as it aims at hurting or causing harm to the other (say, a *slap*), and three positive goals, differing for the power relationship they claim with the touched person. Protective touch offers help or affect (a *kiss* or *to hand one's hand to another*); when affiliative it asks for help or affect (a wife leaning on her husband's arm); a friendly touch offers help or affect without implying difference in power.

Since some acts of touch, if performed by different actors, may imply a difference in meaning, for some items different semantic analyses were provided according to their possible actors.

6 The Norms of Use of Touch

For each act of touch a hypothesis was formulated as to its norms of use (Table 1), concerning:

1. **time**: at which point in an encounter a touch is usually performed: the welcome, the opening, during the encounter, the closing;
2. **social frame**: the type of social situation in which that touch is most typically performed: *affective*, if used to communicate a sincere, really emotionally loaded, positive or negative affect (*embracing*, *punch*); *erotic*, if it is part of or anticipates sexual intercourse (*kiss on neck*); *ritual* if it aims at goals of politeness and at making social relationships smooth (*kiss on both cheeks* between presidents of two States); *kidding*, if it is not serious but performed in a playful way (*slap on glutei* between females).
3. degree of **intimacy**: whether each gesture of touch can be used only between lovers, or with friends, acquaintances, unknown people.
4. **power** relationship between toucher and touched person: whether an act of touch is performed only with lower status (toucher > touched), peers (toucher = touched), or also with upper status persons (toucher < touched).

Table 1. Norms of use of touch

Touch	Time	Social Frame	Intimacy	Power Relationship		
				>	=	<
kiss on neck	during the encounter	erotic	Lovers	x	x	
kiss on both cheeks	welcome, closing	affective, ritual	Friends, acquaintances	x	x	x
Poke	during the encounter	affective	Friends, strangers	x	X	

7 Meanings and Norms of Use of Touch. An Empirical Research

Among the methods for analysing the items of a lexicon, the one adopted so far is the Chomskian method of the Speaker's Judgements: you inquire how an item can be paraphrased in words, if it is acceptable in a given context, or so. But after the lexical items of a touch lexicon were hypothesised, some were tested through questionnaires: 46 subjects, 23 male and 23 female Italian University students, answered multiple choice questions on the meanings and norms of use of 21 items out of the 104 analysed [20].

For all 21 acts of touch the meanings chosen by subjects confirmed the hypotheses between 45% and 89% of cases. The act of touch for which the meaning hypothesised was most frequently chosen is "gimme five" (S, with open hand palm to A, beats palm to A's palm), that was attributed a meaning of complicity. Nine acts out of 21 were attributed the meaning hypothesised by more than 65% subjects. Anyway, in spite of this first partial confirmation, further investigation is required.

To test the norms of use of touch, subjects were asked: if they like to touch other people, whom they touch the most, on what parts of the body, why; why they do not touch, and whether and why they like it or not. As for the persons subjects touch and are touched by, frequency reported for touching and being touched is usually the same, for both males and females. More than 50% of females report they never touch and are never touched by strangers, rarely by acquaintances, between rarely and often or very often by friends and relatives; 78% touch or are touched very often or always by their partners. One third of subjects both touch and are touched rarely by relatives; yet touch does have a meaning of intimacy, since both males and females touch known but non-intimate people rarely.

What parts of the body are touched most, and by whom? Both males and females do not touch nor are touched on any part of their body by unknown people. For males, the parts of the body most frequently touched are shoulders (19% by acquaintances, 30% by friends, 30% by relatives). With increasing degrees of intimacy there is a corresponding increase in the body parts touched: for example, a woman touches friends' and relatives' hair, cheeks, shoulders, arms, hands.

But why do we tend to touch or not to touch? A reason not to touch is for 34% of our subjects lack of intimacy, and 26% because the contact could be disliked. The most frequent reasons why males like to be touched are that they feel considered (28%) or loved (28%), for females, mainly that they feel loved (39%). Thirty percent of females against 19% of males feel annoyed at being touched quite often, often, very often or always. 28% of both males and females do not like or feel annoyed at being touched for lack of intimacy, and 28% of females do when the toucher causes morbid or intrusive sensations. An interesting result is that, comparing answers about being touched by unknown people vs. by acquaintances on body parts that are usually more involved in sexual behaviour, like lips, thighs or hips, quite paradoxically subjects are less annoyed if touched there by unknown people than by acquaintances or even friends. This might mean that as a stranger touches us on an intimate body part we may think it is accidental, but when someone we know does so, we feel he or she is going beyond the barrier of intimacy between personal and intimate relationship [22], and this alarms us more.

8 Touch between Mother and Child

It is well-known the importance of physical contact with mother for the child's affective and relational development [23], [24]. Since the interaction and the relationship between mother and child acquire a different quality and intensity depending on the amount and type of their reciprocal physical contact, the analysis of touch could provide a tool for the analysis of mother-child interaction. To create such a tool, in an observational study we analysed touch in mother-child interaction [25].

8.1 Procedure

Three mother-child couples were videotaped during spontaneous interactions at home. The children were two females (M, 36 months, and S, 37), and one male (T, 32 months). Each couple was videotaped for 3 hours, and all items of touch of both mother and child, in a 20' fragment per couple, were analysed as in Figure 3.

Col.1 states the time of the fragment under analysis, 2 a global description of the act of touch, cols. 3-11 describe it in terms of the formational parameters above (with the addition of handshape, col.5), and cols. 12-16 provide an analysis of the meaning. Let us focus on these 5 columns. Col.12 contains a verbal formulation of the information provided by the act and col.13 classifies this information as communicative or not. This is a nontrivial theoretical issue. Since touch is a quite primitive act of communication, one, so to speak, on the border between action and communication, sometimes it is not straightforward to tell whether it has a communicative goal or not. The mother tickling her daughter (line 3, time 6'39"), or the daughter touching her mother's nose to let her smell an object (line 4, time 10'10") are surely communicative, so we write + in col.13. But take line 2, where R sustains M holding her hand: she might be simply performing the non-communicative act of sustaining her, or be (also) communicating "I am here to sustain you". So we write ? in col.13.

In all cases where col. 13 contains a + or ? (that is, when we are sure or suspect that the act of touch does have a communicative goal), in col.14 we write the type of communicative act performed. The acts uncovered are of 8 kinds: *offer of help*, *offer of affect*, *request*, *proposal*, *request of help*, *request of affect*, *negative request*, and *sharing*. In an *offer of help* or *offer of affect*, the act of touch is aimed at fulfilling the Addressee's goals – letting him/her feel helped of loved; in a *request*, *request of help*, *of affect* or a *proposal*, the Sender asks the Addressee to fulfil the Sender's goal, and a proposal differs from a request in that for the Addressee to do what Sender asks is also in the interest of the Addressee; a *negative request* occurs when the Sender prevents or forbids the Addressee to do something. In *sharing* the Sender does something to induce in the Addressee the same experience (sensation, emotion, information) as s/he is feeling, to enhance commonality.

Col. 15 mentions the power relationship to the touched person maintained by the toucher, and col. 16 the social goal of the toucher in performing the communicative act of touch. Information in columns 14, 15 and 16 is generally congruent: at line 1, where the power relationship maintained is that the touched has less power than the touched one, the communicative act performed is a request, and the social goal is one of affiliation; at line 2, the communicative act is an offer of help (col.14), mother maintains more power than daughter (15), and her social goal is protective (16). In both cases of sharing (lines 3 and 4) the maintained power relationship is one of equal power (col. 15) and the social goal is friendly. At line 5, the (eventual) communicative act is a prohibition, M maintains herself in a dominant position (col.15), and her social goal is aggressive.

8.2 Results

The analysis of the acts of touch by the three mother-child couples allowed us to distinguish their different styles of interaction. Tables 2 and 3 show the three couples' patterns of, respectively, communicative goals and social attitudes: couple T+L (with the male child) has a more intense and affective interaction than the other couples, both for the overall number of touch cases, higher than in the other couples, and for the amount of mother's friendly and protective touch. Couple S+N, particularly the child, is the poorest in touch. Couple M+R shows the most articulated profile: 1. the initiative comes more from child than from mother (13 for M and 7 for R), as opposed to the other couples, where the opposite is the case; 2. M is the only child who performs aggressive acts of touch towards the mother; and more generally, M performs a higher quantity and variety of acts of touch than the other two children do.

Table 2. The communicative acts of touch

	M	MR	Tot M+R	S	mN	Tot S+N	T	mL	Tot T+L	Tot Child	Tot Mother	Tot Ch+M
offer of help		4	4		7	7		4	4		15	15
offer of affect	1		1		1	1		7	7	1	8	9
Sharing	3	1	4					7	7	3	8	11
Request	5	2	7	2	2	4		2	2	7	6	13
Proposal							1	4	5	1	4	5
request of help	3		3							3		3
request of affect							4	5	9	4	5	9
negative request	1		1							1		1
Tot.	13	7	20	2	10	12	5	29	34	20	46	66

Table 3. The social goals of touch

	M	mR	Tot M+R	S	mN	Tot S+N	T	mL	Tot T+L	Tot Child	Tot Mother	Tot Ch+M
Affiliative	3		3				4		4	7		7
Friendly	3	2	5	2	4	6	1	16	17	6	22	28
Protective	2	5	7		6	6		13	13	2	24	26
Aggressive	5		5							5		5
Tot.	13	7	20	2	10	12	5	29	34	20	46	66

9 Conclusion

We have argued that the behaviour of touch can be in some cases communicative behaviour, and that a set of acts of touch form a lexicon of touch, that is, a list of touch-meaning pairs codified in people's long-term memory. In order to discover this lexicon, for 104 acts of touch used by Italian people the signal was analysed in terms of formational parameters, the meaning in terms of a number of semantic criteria, and for the norms of use some hypotheses were put forward and then tested in an empirical study. Then this semantic and pragmatic analysis of touch was applied in an observational study of mother-child interaction, showing how it allows to single out the different styles of interaction of three mother-child couples.

We think that the idea of touch as a "lexical" communicative behaviour, and its analysis in terms of semantic, pragmatic and semiotic criteria presented in this paper can be usefully adopted in empirical research on communicative interaction, but also provides new challenges to communication theory.

References

1. I. Poggi. Mind, Hands, Face, and Body. A goal and belief view of Multimodal Communication. John Benjamins, Amsterdam (in press)
2. C. Castelfranchi and I. Poggi. Blushing as a Discourse: Was Darwin Wrong?. In R.Crozier, ed.: Shyness and Embarrassment. Perspectives from social Psychology. Cambridge University Press, New York (1990) 230-251
3. E. Magno Caldognetto and I. Poggi. Creative iconic gestures: some evidence from Aphasics. In R.Simone, ed.: Iconicity in Language. John Benjamins, Amsterdam (1995)
4. E. Klima and U. Bellugi. The Signs of Language. Harvard University Press, Cambridge (Mass.) (1979)
5. D. McNeill. Hand and Mind. University of Chicago Press, Chicago (1992)
6. I. Poggi and E. Magno Caldognetto. Mani che parlano. Unipress, Padova (1997)
7. H. Yan. Paired speech and gesture generation in Embodied Conversational Agents. PhD. Thesis, MIT, Cambridge (Mass.) (2000)
8. T. Sowa and I. Wachsmuth. Coverbal iconic gestures for object descriptions in virtual environments: an empyrical study. In M.Rector, I.Poggi and N.Trigo, eds.: Gestures. Meaning and Use. Universidad Fernando Pessoa Press, Porto (2003)
9. D. Morris, P. Collett, P. Marsh and M. O'Shaughnessy. Gestures. Their origins and distribution. University of Chicago Press, Chicago (1979)
10. M. Rector, I. Poggi and N. Trigo (eds.): Gestures. Meaning and use. Universidad Fernando Pessoa Press, Oporto (2003)
11. P. Ekman, W. Friesen. Facial Action Coding System. Consulting Psychologist Press, Inc., Palo Alto, CA (1978)
12. W. Johnson, J. Rickel and J.C. Lester. Animated pedagogical Agents: Face-to-face interaction in interactive learning environments. International Journal of Artificial Intelligence in Education, 11, (2000) 47-78
13. I. Poggi and C. Pelachaud. Performative facial expressions in Animated Faces. In J.Cassell, J.Sullivan, S.Prevost and E.Churchill, eds.: Embodied Conversational Agents. MIT Press, Cambridge (Mass.) (2000)
14. I. Poggi and C.Pelachaud. The Meanings of Gaze in Animated Faces. In P.McKevitt, S.Nuallàin and C.Mulvihill, eds.: Language, Vision and Music. John Benjamins, Amsterdam (2002) 133 – 144

15. R. Birdwhistell.: Kinesics and Context. University of Pennsylvania Press, Philadelphia (1970)
16. R. Laban and F.Lawrence. Effort: Economy in Body Movement. Plays, Inc., Boston (1974)
17. W.C. Stokoe. Sign Language Structure: An Outline of the Communicative Systems of the American Deaf. Linstock Press, Silver Spring (1978)
18. M. Romagna. L'alfabeto dei gesti. I parametri formazionali nei gesti degli udenti italiani. Unpublished Degree Thesis. University Roma Tre (1998)
19. A. Zollo. Contatto fisico come comunicazione. L'alfabeto del toccare. Unpublished Degree Thesis. University Roma Tre, Roma (2001)
20. F. Cirella. Contatto fisico come comunicazione. Il significato del toccare. Unpublished Degree Thesis. University Roma Tre, Roma (2001)
21. I. Poggi. The lexicon of the Conductor's Face. In P.McKevitt, S.Nuallàin and C.Mulvihill (eds.): Language, Vision and Music. John Benjamins, Amsterdam (2002) 271 – 284
22. E.T. Hall. The hidden Dimension. Doubleday, New York (1966)
23. J. Bowlby. Attachment and Loss. Hogarth Press, London (1969)
24. A. Montagu. Il Linguaggio della pelle. Garzanti, Milano (1971)
25. A. Agostini. Il contatto fisico tra madre e figlio. Unpublished Degree Thesis. University Roma Tre, Roma (2003)

Fig. 1. The formational parameters of touch

Touch	toucher	touched	space	Movement 1				Movement 2				pressure	
				Path	duration	speed	rhythm	Path	duration	speed	rhythm	tension	impact
Drying the other's tears	index	tears, eye region	line	perp.	medium	slow	single	parallel circular	medium	slow	continuo us	delicate	skim
Caress	Palm or back of open hand	all body	line	perp.	long	slow	single	parallel	long	slow	continuo us	delicate	normal or skim
Slap	open hand	cheek	point	perp.	short	speedy	unique	/	/	/	/	tense	block
Embracing	Hands, arms, trunk and breast	trunk, should-ers	area	perp. or oblique	long	slow	standing	/	/	/	/	tense	normal

Fig. 2. The meaning of touch

1 Touch	**2** paraphrase or verbal coocurrent phrase	**3** literal meaning	**4** indirect idiomatic meaning	**5** originary meaning	**6** Social Goal
Drying the other's tears	*c'mon, don't cry*	I want to console you		I want to wipe your pain away as I wipe your tears	protective
Caress	*oh nice, I love you*	I want to give you serenity	I want you to be calm	I want to give you a pleasant sensation	friendly
Slap		I want to punish you	I want to take you your "face" (your dignity) away	I want to send your face away from me violently	aggressive
Embracing	*I love you*	I love you		I want to wrap you all, I want to incorporate you in me	friendly / protective

Fig. 3. Touch in Mother – Child interaction

1 Time	2 Description	3 Toucher	4 Touched	5 Handshape	6 Pressure	7 Space	8 Path	9 Duration	10 Speed	11 Rhythm	12 Verbal Formulation	13 +/- Com	14 Com. Act	15 Power	16 Social Goal
20''	M leans with her hand on R's hand	Hand	Hand	M's hand palm down. R's hand palm down	Soft	Area	Perp.	long	slow	stand-ing	I hold myself upon you	+	Request	<	Affiliative
31''	R sustains M Holding M's hand in her hand	Hand	Hand	R hand open curve. palm up; M palm down	Medium	Area	Perp.	long	slow	stand-ing	I am here ready to sustain you	?	Offer of help	>	Protective
6'39''	R tickles M	Fing-ers	all the body	Curve fingers	Soft	Area	Perp.	long	speed	continuous	I want you to laugh; I want to play with you;	+	Sharing	=	Friendly
10'10''	M approaches an object to R's nose	Hand / Ob-ject	Nose	Hand palm up	Soft	Point	Perp.	medium	slow	unique	see how it smells (I just washed it)	+	Sharing	=	Friendly
10'13''	M takes away a doll from R's hands	Hands /Doll	Hands /doll	closed hand	Hard	Area	Perp.	short	speed	unique	do not touch it! leave it!	?	Forbid (?)	>	Aggressive
1'44''	T takes an object before his mother L does	Hand	Hand Object	curve fingers	Soft	Point	Parallel	short	speed	single	I take it	?	Request	=	Friendly
2'26''	T inserts his arm between L arms	Arm	Arms	extended arm	Soft	Area	Perp.	medium	slow	single	I need love	+	request of affect	<	Affiliative

Legenda: M = daughter; R = M's mother; T = son; L = T's mother

Some Issues in Sign Language Processing

Bruno Bossard, Annelies Braffort, and Michèle Jardino

LIMSI-CNRS, Bat 508, BP 133, F-91403 Orsay cedex, France
{Bossard.Bruno,Annelies.Braffort,Michele.Jardino}@limsi.fr

Abstract. The aim of this paper is to specify some of the problems raised by the design of a gesture recognition system dedicated to Sign Language, and to propose suited solutions. The three topics considered here concern the simultaneity of information conveyed by manual signs, the possible temporal or spatial synchronicity between the two hands, and the different classes of signs that may be encountered in a Sign Language sentence.

1 Introduction

Gestures are a communication channel which can be used alone to form a full communication channel, or can be combined with other communication channels like speech. Different kinds of gestures exist, with different levels of expressivity which meet various situations and needs. Simplest are isolated gestures which replace speech in order to give commands or simple instructions (for example diver's gestures). At a higher level of expressivity, there are co-verbal gestures and mimics. Iconic structures are used for descriptions, and gestures can be combined with speech or with other gestures. At the top level, there is Sign Language. This language owns lexicons and grammar rules, and signs are combined to form sentences. This continuous spread of the expressivity is knows as the Kendon's continua [1, 2].

Obviously, any increase of expressivity makes gesture recognition more difficult. In this paper, we focus only on problems encountered in recognition of manual signs, and more particularly on synchronisation problems. The two hands are two communication channels which can be combined in synchronous or asynchronous ways, and these channels can be also completely independent. The synchronisations arise as spatial and/or temporal relationships between the hands. To tackle the different kinds of manual signs, we need to be able to decide if the hands are synchronised or not.

Section 2 describes different kinds of signs and their features in order to be able to show in section 3 the different problems we can meet in recognition. In section 3 we also detail synchronisation problems. And finally, section 4 proposes an architecture (still in development) to solve the synchronisation problems.

A. Camurri and G. Volpe (Eds.): GW 2003, LNAI 2915, pp. 90–100, 2004.

2 Sign Language Features

Sign Language is used by Deaf people to communicate with each other. Sign Language is a full featured language (with lexicons, a grammar, etc) and it is the most advanced form of gestural communication [3, 1].

Sentences in Sign Language are not only made up of hand gestures. There are also face mimics, as well as gaze and torso movements. In this paper, we only focus on hands, and other body's parts will not be considered.
Our interest is mainly in signs translation and in interpretation of relationships between those signs. Thus let us first describe signs features and interactions which can arise between signs.

2.1 Sign Composition

Any manual sign can be broken up into four parameters. Each of these parameters is independent of each other, and is dynamic or static during a sign.

- The ***handshape*** is defined by fingers and palm (see examples in Fig. 1). Signs are often iconic [3] and handshape is related to what the sign describes.

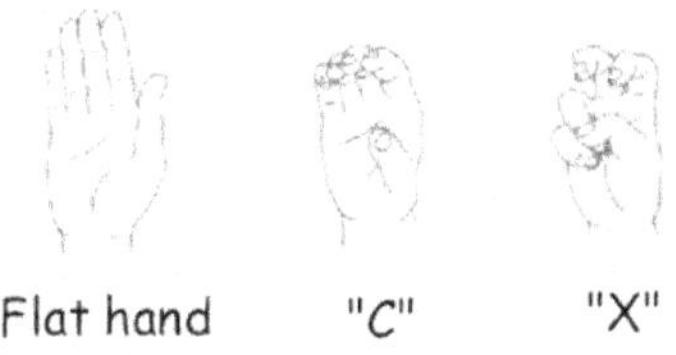

Fig. 1. Examples of handshapes.

- The ***orientation*** is defined by two axes of the hand, as shown in Fig. 2.
- The ***movement*** is the hand trajectory (line, circle, curve, etc.)(see Fig. 2).
- The ***location*** is the hand position in relation to the body. The location is mainly used to express spatial and temporal information or relationship and the location granularity is more or less according to needs. In Fig. 3 the first sign means [BOY], and the second sign gives the information that the boy is located in the ***narration scene*** at the right side of signer.

Each of the four parameters carries information and is part of the sign meaning.

2.2 Interaction and Relationships between the Hands

A sign can be performed by one hand or by the two hands, and hands can interact in different ways. When the two hands are implied in a sign, two cases arise.

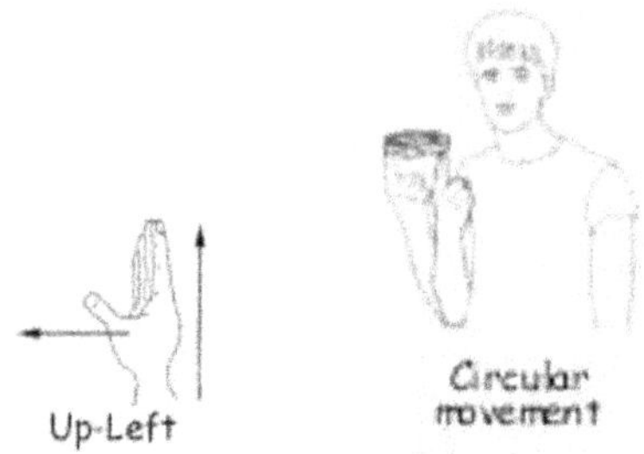

Fig. 2. Orientation and movement example.

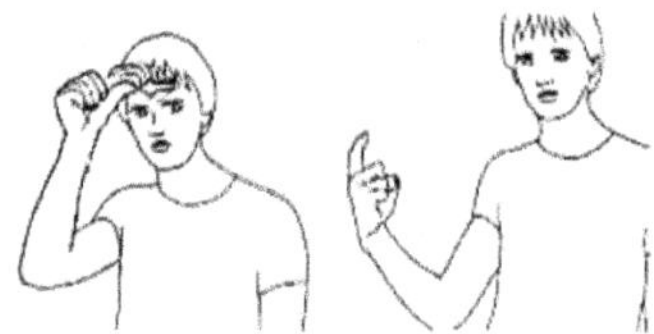

Fig. 3. Sentence "The boy at the right-hand side." composed by signs [BOY] and [HERE].

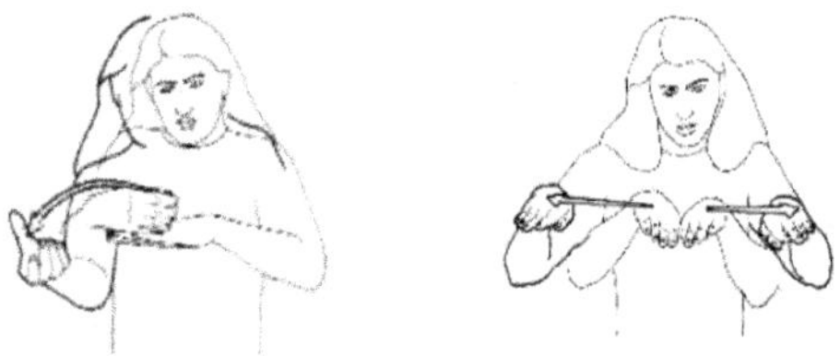

Fig. 4. Signs [FALLING FROM] and [TABLE] (French Sign Language).

- In the first case, each hand appears to have a role. One hand is called ***dominant*** hand and the other ***dominated*** hand. The dominant hand is used to describe "the action", when the dominated hand gives a reference to this action. For example, in sign [FALLING FROM] (figure 4, at left), we see the dominant hand (right hand) playing the action of falling from something. The dominated hand (left hand) gives the reference from which the dominant hand is falling. The dominant hand often has a dynamic role, while the dominated hand convey a static information.
- In the second case, hands are completely synchronised: their parameters are identical or symmetric. For example, with sign [TABLE] (figure 4, at right), the two hands have the same handshape and orientation but symmetric movements.

When only one hand is used to performed a sign, there are also two cases:

- Either the second hand does nothing (like in Fig. 3).
- Or the hand performs another sign (see three last pictures in Fig. 6). When the second hand does another sign, it is possible to have a dominant-

Fig. 5. Sentence *A crate full of apples.*

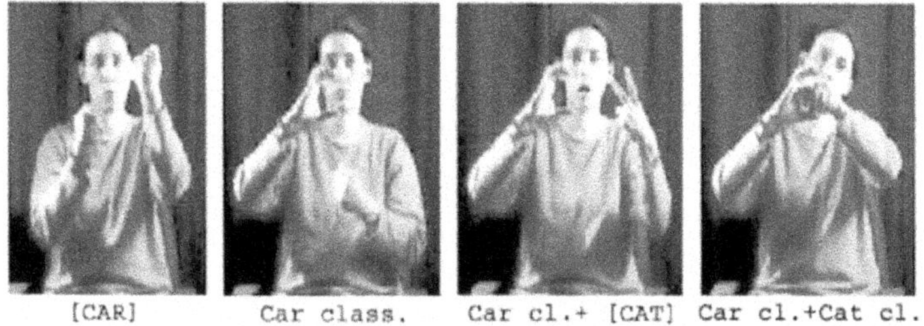

Fig. 6. *The cat is inside the car.* (French Sign Language).

dominated interaction (last picture in Fig. 6). Temporal and/or spatial relationships between the manual signs are used to provide information(s) on the entities represented by the signs.

We see that hands can be synchronous as well as asynchronous, and even if the two hands perform signs, that does not mean that they are doing a single sign. Perhaps they are making two signs and those signs can be independent or have relationships.

2.3 Different Classes of Signs

In Sign Language, we can distinguish different classes of signs. Each one suits to a particular use. Signs named "standard signs" fit to words (noun, verb, adjective) which have a well-defined meaning. We can give a pretty good association between those signs and words from the oral-language. Therefore many studies have been made on automatic translation of ***standard signs***. At present, there are reliable standard signs recognition systems, and they are able to translate hundreds of signs. For example in [4] the recognition rate is a little more than 90% with a lexicon of a hundred or so signs.

Two other classes exist. Signs of those classes cannot be translated "directly" in oral-language words. Those signs are called ***shape and size specifiers*** and ***classifiers***. They are iconic signs and are part of ***great iconic structures*** [3]. With specifiers we can describe entities like objects, animals, scenes, etc. The signer uses handshape, orientation and movement of his hands to describe an entity shape or size. Classifiers are similar to specifiers because they are also used to represent entities (objects, persons, animals, etc). Therefore the handshape is in relation to the entity shape or function. But classifiers represent entities in a more symbolic way than specifiers: they are kinds of pronouns. When something has been expressed in a sentence (standard sign or description with specifiers), it can be substituted by a classifier. The classifier is used in the rest of the sentence to represent the original(s) sign(s). For example, a classifier substituted to a sign representing an object, can be used to specify the object position, or to describe the object trajectory.

In Fig. 5, we can see a sentence which contains the three kinds of signs. The first sign is a shape and size specifier, describing a crate by depicting the sides of the crate. The second sign is a standard sign [APPLE]. The third sign is a classifier representing the apple. The signer places the classifier at different positions to represent the heap of apples contained by the crate.

All those Sign Language features (diversity of signs, hands interactions, etc.) will raise problems for sign recognition. The following section will discuss those recognition problems.

3 Manual Sign Recognition Issues

In a traditional pattern recognition system, data are often processed together in a single block. In this case the two hands would be considered as a single entity. Here we will show that this kind of recognition system seems not well suited to Sign Language features.

3.1 Lexicon Complexity

Complexity is a recurrent problem in pattern recognition systems when the lexicon has a significant size. Because a sign is made up of many elements occurring at the same time, Sign Language lexicon can contain a great number of signs [5]. With a hand, we can have N possible handshapes, M kind of movements, P locations, and Q possible orientations. Thus $N * M * P * Q$ signs are possible[1]. Moreover hands can be combined together, so we can obtain a very large lexicon. Creating a recognition system for such a lexicon is difficult, and the learning curve is tiresome.

In fact, not all possible combinations are used by signers. Parameters of signs are combined following grammatical and semantical rules. However, the size of the resulting lexicon remains large. To solve this problem, rather than processing parameters of signs together we choose to process them separately as in [7, 8]. We can establish a parallel with speech recognition where phonemes rather than words are recognised. But in speech processing, phonemes are successive while in Sign Language parameters are simultaneous, so creating a recognition system remains difficult.

---

[1] Theoretically there is no limit (apart from articulatory constraints) to the number of possible values for hand parameters. This is particularly obvious for shape and size specifiers, because parameters are linked to what the sign describes. For French Sign Language's standard signs, we approximately count 140 handshapes, 300 orientations, and 50 locations [6].

3.2 Relationships between the Two Hands

Previously we saw (section 2.2) that four kinds of interactions exist between the two hands. Either the hands produce a sign together, or a hand does a sign and the other is "asleep", or each hand produces a sign and those signs can have relationships or be completely independent.
The problem is to be able to set apart each case. Thus we will not recognise a two-handed sign when there are two different signs performed at the same time (and vice versa). To discriminate between these two cases, the measure of parameters similarity between the two hands is useless, because we saw in the first section that hands, with two-handed signs, can be completely synchronous (sign [TABLE] in Fig. 4), as well as correlated and not having parameter similarity (sign [FALLING FROM] in Fig. 4).

Two other relationships between hands exist, and we need to detect them. When the two hands perform two different signs with a dominant hand-dominated hand relationship, there are ***synchronisation points*** between the signs. During a moment, the two hands will be organised in a way that provides information. For example in the sentence *The cat is inside the car* (figure 6), the sign [CAR] is first expressed (first picture), then the *C* classifier is used to substitute the car as a "container" and to give the car position in the scene (second picture). In the third picture we see the left hand doing the sign [CAT]. The sign is substituted by the *X* classifier which symbolises legs and this classifier is positioned inside the *C* classifier representing the car (last picture) [9].

We can see in the last three pictures that the dominated hand keeps the *C* classifier when the dominant hand performs three signs in a row. Thus we could think that the two hands are completely independent. However during a short time, hands are organised in order to provide the spatial information that the cat is inside the car (picture four in Fig. 6). Therefore we need to be able to detect this particular moment in order to interpret this spatial relationship. Even if the information conveyed by the hands is only spatial, the relationship between the hands is spatiotemporal.

3.3 Non-standard Sign Translation

A third problem concerns the translation of non standard signs, and this is a particularly difficult problem. At present, only a tiny part of those signs (directional verbs) has been considered by sign recognition systems [10, 11]. Classifiers and shape and size specifiers are part of non standard signs, and have not been considered yet (only a few classifiers in [10]). We saw in part 2.3 that classifiers and specifiers do not have their own meaning. The sentence and its context give this meaning, and that makes the recognition problem particularly difficult.

Classifiers are often linked to a standard sign which has been previously performed, so in this case giving a meaning to the sign is easy. Unfortunately, sometimes classifiers are related to signs which are performed after them or they are related to descriptions made with specifiers. However, we can establish a list of possible classifiers for signs. For example, in the sentence *The cat is in the car* (figure 6), there are two classifiers : C and X. The C classifier symbolizes a container, and the X symbolizes legs. Thus, if we have additional informations for signs (such as: the sign [CAT] is related to an animal with legs, [CAR] is a vehicle, it can contain something, etc), we can create the associations [CAT]-X and [CAR]-C.

Finding a specifier meaning is more difficult, because they are peculiar to what they describe. Then from one description to another these signs can vary to a large extent. Unlike oral languages which have limited lexicons, in Sign Language, signs can be "invented" according to needs. By definition, the parameters of the specifiers signs are related to what they describe. Thus for each description, "new signs" can appear. Moreover, the way the description is done depends on the signer's social and cultural context [12].

To translate these non standard signs, we need to analyse the sentence and its context. We also need to analyse parameters of those signs in order to be able to link them with what is being described. This is not obvious, and can only be dealt at the syntactic and semantic level. Because recognition systems mainly work at the lexical level, they are not able to deal with such signs which are rejected or badly translated. We need to store these signs and to transmit them to a higher level analyser.

At present the problems presented in sections 3.2 and 3.3 are still unsolved. Next section presents an architecture which tries to take into account these problems.

4 Recognition System Design

4.1 Suggested Architecture

Here, we propose an architecture which process the signs in three steps. Each of these steps match to a level of the architecture, and they intervene from lexicon to syntax.

First Level: Sign Recognition. Sign recognition will be broken up into four parts, each one corresponding to one parameter. This will allow to bring down complexity (cf section 3.1), but also to model any kind of sign. Indeed if we can not recognise non standard signs (like classifiers or specifiers) we can extract their parameters, so that the information will still be available for a later sign analysis.

Figure 7 shows the four modules which process data in parallel (for two handed signs, there will be eight modules). A fifth part (in dotted line) will receive the four outputs and perform the following tasks : building quadruplets from the outputs, trying to find the signs which suit to quadruplets (by searching connections in a quadruplet database or using stochastic methods), and computing a score. If no connection is found between the quadruplet and learned signs (it is probably a non standard sign), the quadruplet is transmitted just as it is, else it is labelled with the recognised sign. With the score, the sign duration is also joined to the quadruplet (the time at which the sign starts and the time it stops).

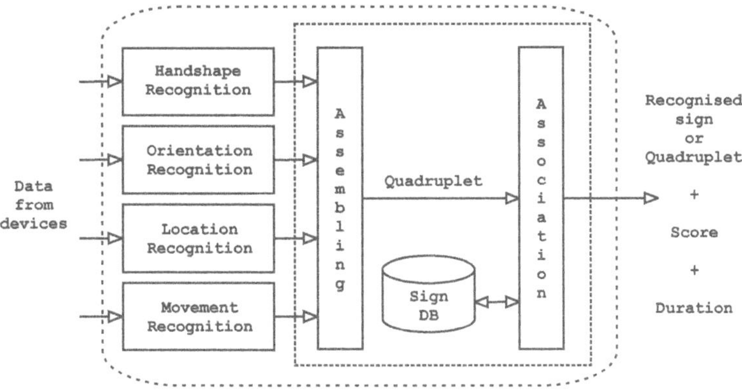

Fig. 7.

The kind of the recognition modules can change according to the sentences and the vocabulary size we want to recognise. Statistic recognition systems [13] as well as stochastic models like hidden Markov chains [8] are candidates for the modules.

Second Level: Sign Selection. We distinguish three classes of signs: two-handed signs, left-handed signs and right-handed signs. In order to perform a correct sign translation, we have to classify the sign in one of those three classes. The suggested solution is as follow: for each sign received, three recognitions systems (as described in section 4.1.1) try to translate the sign(figure 8). Each system has his own learning lexicon and works in parallel of the two others systems. We get three outputs from these three recognition systems, and we keep the two-handed output or left and/or right output. A dedicated system uses an evaluation function in order to compare the signs and choose the best sign(s). This function can be more or less advanced. A simple evaluation will be based on sign's scores, a more advanced evaluation will take into account previous signs (with grammatical and semantical rules we can give hypothesis on the following signs).

Third Level: Detection of Relationships between Signs. According to the results obtained at the comparison step (see section 4.1.2), we have to search relationships between signs: if a left-handed sign and a right-handed sign have been recognised, they could have respectively a dominant hand role and a dominated hand role. Then we need to check if there is any synchronisation point (i.e. a spatiotemporal relationship) between the two hands.

In order to detect this particular moment, proposed the following solution. A first step will "synchronise" right-handed signs with left-handed signs, because signs do not have the same duration and thus do not come out from recognition system (see section 4.1.2) at the same time. The "synchronisation" consists with doing pairs of signs according to their start and end time. For example, if the

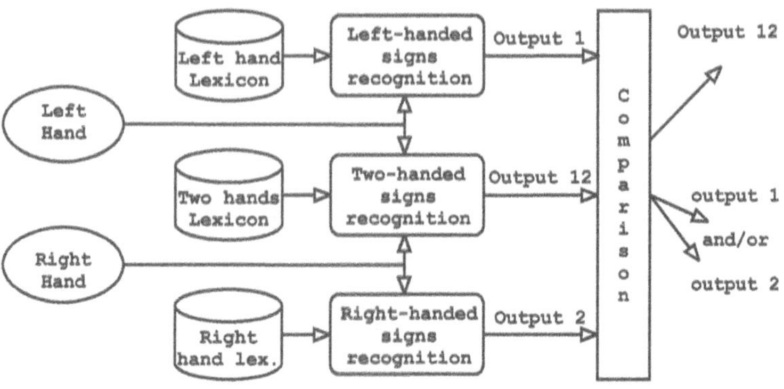

Fig. 8. The three recognition systems which can recognise the three sign classes.

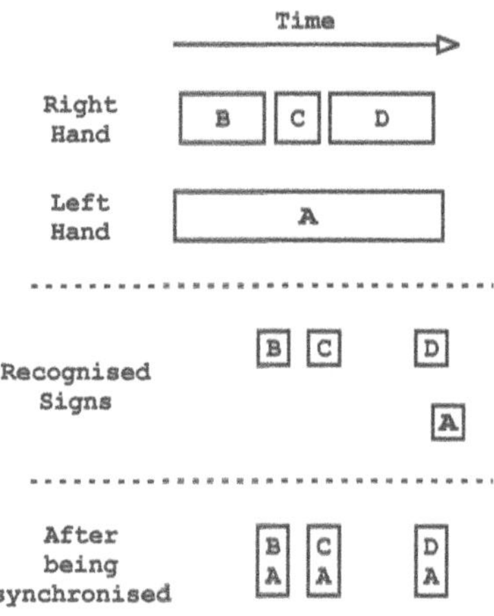

Fig. 9.

left hand does a sign A when the right hand does the signs B,C and D, we obtain the following pairs : (A,B),(A,C),(A,D).

The next step is to detect position, orientation or movements similarities among all those pairs. Then we give this information to syntactic and semantic levels, in order to find the meaning of the relationships.

4.2 Experimentation and Future Work

To test this architecture, we choose sentences which contain standard signs and classifiers. Those sentences give position of objects or animals in relation to other objects. For example the sentence *The cat is inside the car* (figure 6) contains two classifiers (C and X) and two standard signs ([CAR] and [CAT]) and gives position of the cat. Those sentences have advantage of bringing up problems explained in part 3: one-handed and two-handed signs are mixed up, there are synchronisation points in order to give spatial informations, and classifiers are part of non standard signs.

Sentences are recorded with datagloves and 6 degrees of freedom sensors. With such devices, we can have more numerous and accurate data than with video devices. But they operate at different rates, and are not plugged in the same computer. Therefore a part of the work has been to synchronise data from devices, before to send the data to the recognition systems. Otherwise recognised signs for the left and the right hands can be slightly shifted.

At present, only first parts of the architecture (section 4.1.1) are achieved. To recognise signs, we use recognition systems based on a statistical classification system [13]. Comparison part is under development. We test different kind of classification distances, in order to compare outputs from recognition systems. First results lead us to rather choose distances like Manhattan or Euclidian distances than Mahalanobis distance which is too dependent on the quality of the learning step.

The system is based on statistical classification, and this do not suit well to gestural sentences. In the long-term range, we want to use a stochastic model based on hidden Markov model, because it can model sign's coarticulation.

5 Conclusion

The fact that the hands are two independent communication channels produces the possibility of having different relationships between right-handed signs and left-handed signs. We can not ignore those relationships because they bring informations which are necessary to the translation process. In addition we need to be able to set apart one-handed signs from two-handed signs, else we will do a wrong translation of the signs.

The architecture introduced in this paper, aims at solving these problems. Moreover it takes into account other existing problems (complexity and difficulty to translate non standard signs) by use of existing solutions and the transmission of non recognised signs. At present, the first level is achieved and the second one is in progress.

Sign Language and the other gestural communications ways have common points, so this work could be extended over other application fields. Especially, this work will be extended to the gestural interaction in an immersive environment (VENISE, project of LIMSI). Moreover, work that will be done for synchronisation points can be adapted to the other fields where are limited synchronisations between channels carrying information.

References

1. McNeil, D. : Hand and Mind : What gestures reveal about thought, University of Chicago Press, (1992).
2. Kendon, A. : How gestures can become like words. In : Poyatos, F. (Ed.), Crosscultural perspectives in nonverbal communication, Toronto : Hogrefe, (1988), 131-141.

3. Cuxac, C. : La langue des Signes Française (LSF), les voies de l'iconicité. chap. 3, Faits de Langues, OPHRYS, (2000).
4. Hienz, H., Bauer, B. : Video-Based Continuous Sign Language Recognition Using Statistical Methods. In : Proc. of International Conference on Automatic Face and Gesture Recognition FG 2000, (2000), 440-445.
5. Vogler, C., Metaxas, D.N. : Toward Scalability in ASL Recognition: Breaking Down Signs into Phonemes. In : Proc. of Gesture Workshop'99, Lecture Notes in Artificial Intelligence, Vol. 1739. Springer-Verlag, Gif sur Yvette France, (march 1999), 211-224.
6. Braffort, A. : Reconnaissance et compréhension de gestes, application à la Langue des Signes. PhD thesis, Université Paris XI - Orsay, (1996).
7. Liang, R.H., Ming, O. : A Sign Language Recognition System Using Hidden Markov Model and Context Sensitive Search. In : Proc. of ACM Symposium on Virtual Reality Software and Technology'96, (1996), 59-66.
8. Vogler, C., Metaxas, D.N. : Parallel Hiden Markov Models for American Sign Language Recognition. In : Proc. of International Conference on Computer Vision, (1999), 116-122.
9. Lejeune, F., Braffort, A., Descles. J.P. : Study on Semantic Representations of French Sign Language Sentences. In : Proc. of Gesture Workshop'01, Lecture Notes in Artificial Intelligence, Vol. 2298. Springer-Verlag, London UK, (April 2002), 197-201.
10. Braffort, A. : ARGo: An Architecture for Sign Language Recognition and Interpretation. In : Proc. of Gesture Workshop'96, Harling, P.A., Edwards, A.D.N. (eds.), Springer-Verlag, (March 1996), 17-30.
11. Sagawa, H., Takeuchi, M. : A Method for Analyzing Spatial Relationships Between Words in Sign Language Recognition. In : Proc. of Gesture Workshop'99, Lecture Notes in Artificial Intelligence, Vol. 1739. Springer-Verlag, Gif sur Yvette France, (march 1999), 197-210.
12. Cuxac, C., Fusellier-Souza, I., Sallandre, M.A. : Iconicité des Langues des Signes et Catégorisations. In: SEMIOTIQUES, Num. 16, (1998).
13. Rubine, D. : The Automatic Recognition of Gestures, PhD thesis, Carnegie Mellon University, (1991).

Multimodality and Gestures in the Teacher's Communication

Giorgio Merola[1] and Isabella Poggi[2]

[1] Dipartimento di Psicologia , Università di Roma "La Sapienza"
merogio@hotmail.com
[2] Dipartimento di Scienze dell'Educazione, Università Roma Tre
poggi@uniroma3.it

Abstract. The paper presents a research on the multimodal communication of teachers in the classroom. The "musical score", a procedure for the analysis of multimodal communication, is used to analyse aspects of the signals produced and of the meanings conveyed by teachers while interacting with their pupils, by focusing not only on affective and interactional aspects, but also on the cognitive effects of nonverbal communication. Finally, the paper shows how, based on this procedure, it is possible to analyse chunks of teachers' communication, and to distinguish different multimodal communicative styles among different teachers.

1 Multimodality in the Classroom

Among studies on everyday interaction, an interesting area for the study of multimodal communication is teacher-pupil interaction, a topic generally studied in the domains of education, linguistics, sociolinguistics, pragmatics, and social psychology [1], [2], [3], [4]. [5] applied Ekman and Friesen's analysis [6], mainly stressing the affective and interactional aspects of the teacher's nonverbal communication. But the action of multimodality is not limited to affective issues: it has important effects in at least three domains of educational interaction:

a. Conversational interaction
The teacher's facial, gestural and bodily communication has an important role in turn-taking management and in providing feed-back to pupils.

b. Cognitive import
Gestures sometimes convey conceptual, concrete and abstract information [7], [8]; and even gaze signals may convey propositional concrete and abstract contents [9]. Moreover, gesture, gaze and posture may help students to understand the teacher's discourse [10].

c. Teacher's prejudice
As shown by [4], the "Pygmalion effect", a typical case of a teacher's prejudice that affects a pupil's performance, is caused at a large extent by the feed-back the teacher provides to the pupil, which is mainly conveyed by his/her multimodal communication.

All of these aspects of teacher-pupil interaction point at the necessity of studying the teacher's multimodal communication 1. to enhance teachers' self-consciousness,

A. Camurri and G. Volpe (Eds.): GW 2003, LNAI 2915, pp. 101–111, 2004.

self-modeling and regulation, 2. to develop Pedagogical Agents, for simulation purposes [11]. Scholars at the crossroads of Psychology, Artificial Intelligence, Autonomous Agents and Computer Graphics engage in building Embodied Believable Conversational Agents [12], [13], Artificial Agents able to interact with the User through voice, facial expression and gaze, gesture and body posture.

In this view, studying the human teacher's communicative behaviour is a necessary step to discover the rules that govern her or his multimodal communication, not only because it is useful in building Artificial Teachers (would we all like to learn things only from a virtual Mentor?), but also because the approach of simulation, the effort to reconstruct human intelligence and behaviour in machines, is one of the best means to obtain a deeper knowledge of human behaviour. For both these purposes, one has to single out the most typical features of teachers' multimodal communication: what verbal and nonverbal signals they use most frequently, what meanings they convey, and how they combine signals in the different modalities, to communicate the meanings required in their educational interaction.

2 A Human's Meanings

To find out the specific features of the teacher's communication, we start from a theoretical model of communication that makes some hypotheses about all the meanings that human need in general to communicate, and the verbal and nonverbal signals devoted to conveying them, and we predict what meanings a teacher might specifically need to communicate most frequently. Finally, we test these predictions by analysing real data collected in empirical research on teachers' multimodal communication.

We distinguish three classes of meanings Humans generally convey during communication: Information on the **World**, on the **Speaker's Identity**, and on the **Speaker's Mind** [14].

Information on the World. As we talk we provide information about the concrete and abstract events we mention, their actors and objects, and the time and space relations among them. This is provided mainly through the words of sentences and their syntactic structure; but often also by deictic, iconic and symbolic gestures. A deictic gesture indicates something in the surrounding environment: a way to set the reference of our discourse, then a way to explain what, in the external world, we are going to talk about. An iconic gesture instead describes the shape, size or movements of some referent we are mentioning; and this description can be sometimes metaphorically extended to refer to some abstract referent. Finally, some symbolic gestures directly mention some object, feature or action. But not only gesture can indicate or describe; sometimes we point at things or persons by eye, lip or chin direction, and we may refer to features of objects or persons also by gaze, prosody and body movement: we squeeze our eyes to refer to something small or difficult, we open eyes wide to refer to something huge, we utter a longer vowel to say something is long, we speak in a "staccato" way to indicate precision, we refer to a person we know by moving as she does. And also a teacher can add these kinds of information to her verbal discourse by using hands, voice and gaze.

Information on the Speaker's Identity. As we talk, physiognomic traits of our face, eyes, lips, the acoustic features of our voice, and often our posture, provide information on our sex, age, socio-cultural roots, and personality. But besides providing information on our objective identity, we also inform about the Identity we claim is ours: our image, that is, how we want others to see us. In other words, in any moment of our life and communication we have a goal of Self-presentation: we inform not only about how we are, but about how we want to be seen. This is often done without awareness; but a teacher, at her first class with new pupils, might monitor her appearance and behaviour to project a particular image of herself, to set the basis for future interaction.

Information on the Speaker's Mind. While talking about events of the external world, we also communicate why we want to talk about those events, what we think and feel about them, how we plan to talk about them: we provide information on the **beliefs** we're mentioning, our **goals** concerning how to talk about them, and the **emotions** we feel while talking [15].

a. Among information concerning our own **beliefs**, we inform:
   1. on the degree of certainty of the beliefs we are mentioning, by words like *perhaps*, *certainly*, or the conditional or subjunctive verb mode, but also by *frowning*, which means: "I am serious in stating this" [10], or by *open hands palms up*, which means "this is self-evident"[16];
   2. on the source of the beliefs we mention, whether they come from memory, inference, or communication [17]: we *look up* when trying to make inferences, *snap fingers* while trying to remember, we make the gesture "*quote*" with index and middle fingers curved twice to mean that we are quoting other people's words for which we are not responsible.
b. While talking we inform about our **goals** concerning our sentence (b.1., b.2.), our discourse (b.3.), and the ongoing conversation (b.4.), then about:
   1. the performative of our sentence, that may be conveyed by performative verbs [18], [19] but also through intonation or performative facial expression [20];
   2. the topic-comment distinction within a sentence or discourse, which may be conveyed by *batons, eyebrow raising*, *high intensity* or *pitch* of a tonic vowel;
   3. the discourse rhetorical relationships: a list may be scanned by words (*first*, *second*, *third...*), but also by *counting on fingers*, or marking all the items in the list with the *same intonational contour*; topic shift may be expressed through *posture shift*;
   4. the turn-taking and back-channel structure of conversation: we *raise our hand* to ask for turn; we *nod* to reassure the Interlocutor we are following, understanding, approving of what he's saying.
c. Finally, we inform on the **emotions** we are feeling while talking, not only by affective words, but with gestures, emotional intonation, facial expression, gaze and posture.

3 A Teacher's Meanings

A teacher in classroom interaction may convey all of these meanings; but some are conveyed more frequently, because of the teacher's particular role. Starting from the taxonomy above, then, we can predict the specific communicative profile of a teacher's communication. Of course these predictions stem from our stereotype of the teacher's role, but they can be tested on real data.

3.1 Information on the World

A great part of the teacher's classroom communication informs about the contents of different disciplines, that include both concrete and abstract information. In some cases, concrete information like the shape of an object or a space, or a sequence of actions is better conveyed by iconic signals, like pictures, paintings, pantomime or iconic gestures. But gestures have proved to be useful also in the explanation of abstract (for example, mathematical) concepts [8].

3.2 Information on the Speaker's Mind

This is the realm in which teacher's multimodal communication is most informative.

Beliefs. Starting from information on the Speaker's beliefs, namely the degree of certainty of the beliefs she mentions (a.1.), we predict a teacher will not convey uncertainty or doubt so often, given the image of a self-confident person she must generally project in front of her pupils. So, her most frequent expression will be the *small frown* showing that she is serious in what she says, and that she believes it strongly. As to the metacognitive information about the source of her current knowledge (a.2.), during a lecture the teacher will rarely *gaze side-downward*, or *raise eyes up*, because she is usually supposed to remember the things she reports very well, without needing to retrieve them from long-term memory, or to reason long about them.

Goals. The teacher's communication (as opposed to the layperson's) is supposedly particularly rich in providing information about her sentence, discourse and conversational goals. As shown by studies on teachers' behaviour [1], the teacher's performatives, i.e. the specific communicative intentions of her sentences, are a great number: question, peremptory order, advice, approval, praise, blame, reproach, question with an indirect meaning of command, praise with an ironic meaning of blame; but they are rarely conveyed by the classical performative verbs (*I order, I advice, I propose...* [18], [19]); they are generally expressed by intonation, gaze or facial expression. Instead of saying *"I order you to turn off you cellular"*, the teacher will express the propositional content of the speech act (*"Turn off your cellular"*) while conveying its performative by a severe directive intonation, and/or by a serious face, no smile, head up, gaze staring at he pupil. Performative intonation and performative facial expression [20] are sophisticated devices of human communication, devoted to convey even the most subtle nuances that distinguish performatives from one another. This is why the teacher's voice and face behaviour are important in educational interaction.

One more frequent and important information the teacher conveys, but mostly not by verbal language, is about the relative importance of the different parts of a sentence of discourse: the topic-comment distinction. More than in everyday communication, the teacher needs to distinguish, within her sentence or discourse, the beliefs that pupils have to retrieve from their long-term memory (topic) from the new beliefs to connect with them that are the object of the teacher's present communication (comment). Often, to explain new concepts that to be understood require reference to previous contents, the teacher has to recall a lecture or an activity performed even months before. This distinction between what is to be retrieved from memory and what is coming as new is generally expressed by facial and intonational devices [10].

Again, gesture and intonation are of help when the teacher makes explicit the rhetorical relationships among different parts of the discourse she is delivering. An aid to understand and memorise a discourse is to know the Author's outline. This is why a teacher often says: "I'll now speak of X... now I come to topic Y...". But this can also be done in nonverbal ways: a posture shift, for instance, signals we are moving to another topic or starting a digression [21]. Another way to stress transition to another sub-topic is counting paragraphs, not only verbally (*"first... second.... third..."*) but also gesturally, by *counting on fingers*. Intonation has an important role too: a recurrent intonational contour signals we are listing different items of the same class, while we can mark a parenthetic clause through lower pitch and intensity [22].

The signals to regulate turn-taking and to provide back-channel are particularly important in classroom interaction, both for teacher and pupils; and the teacher must be particularly aware of these signals, whether delivered from herself or the pupils. A trivial example is when a pupil *raises a hand* to ask for a speaking turn. But while this holds in a classroom with a quite asymmetrical structure and rigid interactional norms, it could not hold in a democratic group or while working in a small team. In this case, a teacher that wants all members to talk must be aware of more subtle ways of asking for a speaking turn: *leaning forward*, *opening mouth* as in starting to speak, *opening eyes wider.*

Finally, a back-channel signal is any communicative verbal or nonverbal act performed by an Interlocutor to provide a feed-back to the present Speaker about whether the Interlocutor is *a.* understanding, *b.* believing, *c.* approving, and *d.* finding interesting what the Speaker is saying. I can say *"I see"* or simply *nod* to tell you I understand what you are saying; if I don't understand I'll say *"I can't follow you"* or *frown*; if I understand but I don't believe it, I can say *"I don't believe it"*, *shake my head* or show a *facial expression of doubt or perplexity*; I can *nod* also for approving, and *shake head, shake index finger*, or *frown* for disapproving; if what you say is very interesting I'll say *"You don't say!"*, or *"Oh!"* emphatically, or *raise eyebrows* to show surprise; but if I am not very much concerned or definitely bored, I can cyclically repeat *"oh"*, with a very flat intonation, or even *yawn.*

Now, some back-channel signals may be emotionally loaded, since they imply an evaluation and then may touch or hurt the Speaker's image or self-image: letting the speaker know that I don't believe what she says, or that her talk is boring, may be offensive. So we can predict 1. what back-channel signals are more frequently provided by teachers and pupils, respectively, and 2. what back-channel signals are more relevant for, respectively, teachers' and pupils' behaviour. A very young pupil will not perform many back-channel signals of incredulity, not only because it is implausible for him to have a knowledge base sufficiently larger than the teacher's enabling him to know things contrasting with what she says; but also because, even if the pupil really does not believe the teacher, he might be afraid to offend her by showing it. Again, a pupil will be particularly sensitive to back-channel signals of approval and disapproval. Conversely, if a teacher thinks motivation is an important basis for learning, she will pay attention to signals of interest or boredom.

Emotions. As to information about emotions, a teacher may feel various kinds of emotions during class work: joy, stress, anxiety, enthusiasm; tenderness, compassion, love, hatred, worry, anger, interest, curiosity, boredom. Of course, the very fact that a teacher expresses her emotions may be subject to sanction; so some teachers may claim they do not express their emotions to pupils, but yet their emotions can leak out from nonverbal behavior: anxiety or anger may be not expressed by a specific signal, but by some aspects of how one performs verbal or nonverbal signals: some sub-parameters of gestural or bodily behaviour like rhythm or muscular tension may vary producing a particular muscular tension in making gestures, a higher pitch of voice in speaking, a higher speed in moving around in the classroom.

3.3 Information on the Speaker's Identity

The teacher's multimodal communication provides information about her identity: the image she wants to project of herself as an easy, serious, rigorous teacher may be conveyed by her exterior look (clothing, hairdo) but also, once more, by the way she produces verbal and nonverbal signals: smooth movements may provide an image of a relaxed and easy-going person, jerky movements tell of a hectic behaviour.

4 The Musical Score of the Teacher's Communication

Testing our predictions about the teacher's multimodal communication requires us to assess the quantity and quality of multimodal communication in different teachers and to single out the communicative and teaching style of different teachers. To this goal, a tool is needed that is capable of showing how many and what meanings the teacher conveys, but also how these different meanings are related to each other.

In a previous work, [14] proposed the "musical score", a procedure for the transcription, analysis and classification of signals and their interaction in multimodal communication. This procedure (Poggi, Pelachaud & Magno, this volume), has been applied to the study of the teacher's multimodal communication.

5 A Research Study on the Teacher's Multimodal Communication

We conducted a research study on the teacher's gestural communication in four classes of a Primary School in a village of the province of Rome, Italy.

5.1 Method

The behaviour of 4 female teachers in 3 different classes was videorecorded. For each teacher, 40 minutes per class were collected and 10 minutes out of these were thoroughly analysed with the "musical score". The classes are three 2nd grades (7 year old pupils) of around 25 pupils each.

The aims of our research were: 1. to state how many and what types of meanings are conveyed by the teachers' gestures, and 2. to single out different communicative styles of the teachers. Using the "musical score", all gestures of each teacher were analysed and classified as to three features:

1. type of gesture: following [23] we distinguished deictics, symbolic, iconics (pantomimics, pictographics, spatiographics), batons and self-manipulations;
2. type of meaning conveyed: according to the typology above, the teacher's gestures were classified as providing Information on the World (IW), Information on the Speaker's Mind (ISM), and Information on the Speaker's Identity (ISI);
3. gesture function, that is, the relationship between the meaning of the gesture and that of the concomitant word or sentence: repetitive, if it provides the same information as the other item; additive if it provides additional but congruent information; substitutive if it tells something that is not told in the other modality; contradictory, if the information it expresses is incompatible with that of the other item; or indifferent, as it makes part of a different communicative plan [14].

5.2 Data Analysis: The Teacher's "Musical Score"

Let us see a fragment of the teacher's communication analysed through the "score" (Fig.1).

In the prosodic modality, the teacher stresses the words *I*, *tree*, *my*, *paper*, as if pointing at the key words she wants the pupils to pay attention to (an Information on her goal of emphasising these words, then an Information on the Speaker's Mind, ISM). But at the indirect level, she invites the class to compare these objects, and this aims at showing how different in size they are (an Information on the World, IW). Both direct and indirect meaning have an additive function, because this concept of the difference in size (quite important for the teacher's goal of explaining the concept of symbolic representation) is not conveyed verbally. This is a typical example of how prosodic communication may tell much more than the verbal signal.

In the gestural modality, the first gesture is a deictic, more specifically a case of abstract deixis [8]: it points out the window, where a tree might be, but in fact is not. Its indirect meaning is that, even if a tree is not there, trees do exist: an Information on the World. The following gesture, lowering arms with palms inward, as if limiting the borders of the paper, is a pictographic gesture, representing the shape of the paper; at an indirect level it means that the big tree outside can be reproduced in a place within reach and with a small size. Both meanings provide an additive Information on the World.

5.3 Results

The "score" analysis of all fragments allowed us to distinguish the different communicative styles of the four teachers. First we computed the amount of occurrences for each different type of gesture (see Table 1).

Teacher M uses gestures much less than the other teachers do. She produces more batons (17,2%) and self-manipulations (24,1%) than all other teachers, while among her own gestures, the most frequent are deictics (27,6%). A and R produce more gestures than the other two, both with the highest percent for symbolics (R=39,1%, A 30,4%), followed by deictics (R=34,8%, A=28,3%). Teacher C differs from the others since her iconic gestures exceed even symbolics in percent (29,2 vs. 26,8%). As to the distribution of gesture types, symbolics and deictics are far the most frequent (29,6 and 26,5%).

Teacher C explains that even very large objects can be represented in small graphic representations; to do this one can use iconic signals equivalent but not equal to their referents, by maintaining some similarities, while abandoning others.

v. SD *Se io volessi riportare un albero sul mio foglio*
Suppose **I** want to reproduce a **tree** on **my paper**

p. SD *Increasing intensity*
word stress on ***io,*** ***albero*** ***mio foglio***

MD I You should pay attention to these words
II I want you to realise how different in size these things are

MT I ISM
II IW

F I Additive
II Additive

g. SD g.1: raises r.arm up (toward the window), holding a pen with cupped palm and ind..and mid..finger — g. 2: lowers arms in neutral space, palms inward

ST I g. 1: deictic, — g. 2 pictographic
II

MD I g.1: I refer to a hypothetical tree out there; g.2: I represent it on my paper
II g.1: the tree I refer to really exists; g.2: I represent it in something small and within reach

MT I g.1: IW — g.2: IW
II g.1: IW — g.2: IW

F I Additive
II Additive

Legenda:
v.= verbal modality; p-i.= prosodic-intonational modality; g= gestural m.; f.= facial m.; b.= bodily m.
SD= Signal Description; ST= Signal Type (not considered for prosodic modality); MD= Meaning Description; MT= Meaning Type; F= Function
IW= Information on the World; ISM= Information on the Speaker's Mind; ISI=Information on the Speaker's Identity

Fig. 1.

Let us see the distribution of gestures with respect to their Meaning Type (Table 2).

All in all, the four teachers convey more Information on the Speaker's Mind (50%) than Information on the World (45%), and the amount of Information on the Speaker's Identity is quite low; but with individual differences. C conveys more IW than ISM, while A differs from the other teachers for her relatively high percentage of Information on the Speaker's Identity (10%): a striking difference if compared to 5%

ISI for R and 1,4% for C, but, especially, to the total absence of these kinds of signals in M. Teachers A and M represent two completely opposite patterns. A is very expressive and extroverted: as we have seen in Table 2, she makes a lot of symbolic and iconic gestures, and she has a highly dramatic behaviour. She also performs many gestures of self-manipulation, but a great part of them belongs to the class of Information on the Speaker's Identity, because they indirectly aim at self-presentation, namely at a good presentation of her physical appearance: she often smoothes her hair, she arranges her suit by touching her buttons. She seems in fact like a highly narcissistic teacher. M's self-manipulations, on the contrary, even if they are her relatively most frequent gestures (24,1%), never aim at self-presentation, as shown in Table 3, where she never provides Information on the Speaker's Identity.

Let us now see what functions are fulfilled by gestures with respect to verbal communication in the four teachers (Table 3).

Table 1.

	A		C		M		R		Tot.	
	n.	%	n.	%	n.	%	n.	%	n.	%
deictics	13	28,3	6	14,6	8	27,6	16	34,8	43	26,5
symbolics	14	30,4	11	26,8	5	17,2	18	39,1	48	29,6
pantomimics	7	15,2	6	14,6	3	10,3	4	8,7	20	12,3
pictographics			4	9,7	1	3,4			5	3,1
spatiographics	1	2,2	2	4,9			1	2,2	4	2,5
iconics	8	17,4	12	29,2	4	13,8	5	10,9	29	17,9
batons	6	13	5	12,2	5	17,2	6	13	22	13,6
self-manipulations	5	10,9	7	17	7	24,1	1	2,2	20	12,3
Tot.	46		41		29		46		162	100

Table 2.

	A		C		M		R		Tot.	
	n.	%	n.	%	n.	%	n.	%	n.	%
IW	34	42,5	36	50	24	50	33	41,2	127	45,3
ISM	38	47,5	35	48,6	24	50	43	53,7	140	50
ISI	8	10	1	1,4	0		4	5	13	4,6
Tot.	80		72		48		80		280	100

Table 3.

	A		C		M		R		Tot.	
	n.	%	n.	%	n.	%	n.	%	n.	%
repetitive	27	58,7	20	48,8	15	51,7	24	52,2	86	53,1
additive	12	26,1	10	24,4	14	48,3	18	39,1	54	33,3
substitutive	1	2,2	8	19,5			4	8,7	13	8
contradictory	6	13	3	7,3					9	5,6
Tot.	46		41		29		46		162	100

From Table 3 it results a clear-cut prevalence of gestures with a repetitive function (53,1%), but also gestures providing additional information are quite frequent: a third of all gestures. The most striking difference among teachers is the high amount of substitutive gestures in C: 19,5% of her total gestures, as opposed to 8,7% for R, 2,2% for A, and none for M. This substitutive use of gestures by C is very peculiar: quite often she uses gestures instead of words not because she cannot or does not want to use the corresponding words (as it has been shown to happen with Aphasic patients, [24]): she makes the gesture before saying the word as a pedagogical ploy, to give the pupils the time to utter the word themselves, before she does. She invites the children to actively participate in her lecture by completing her explanations and reaching solutions thanks entirely to these nonverbal helps she offers them.

One more interesting result is the presence of a fair amount of contradictory gestures (13%) in A's behaviour: a quite high percent if compared to C who contradicts herself quite less (7,3%) and to M and R whose gestures never contradict speech.

From the quantitative but also qualitative analysis of the fragments collected, semantically enriched by the use of the "score", the profiles of the four teachers stand out clearly. Teacher A is quite focused on her own image, but she has a considerable charisma over pupils; yet at times, as we have seen, she happens to convey contradictory commands that may puzzle children. Teacher C tends to focus specifically on her work of teaching, not so much on her pupils; nonetheless, she looks quite passionate and expressive during classes. Teacher M looks quite shy, almost depressed, in her classroom behaviour, and she is not expansive even with pupils. Teacher R, finally, tends to establish exclusive relations with single children, for example as she sits down close to a handicapped girl, and talks to her in a low voice, thus establishing intimacy and complicity; or as she reprimands a disobedient child.

Do these different styles affect the classroom social climate? In fact, A's classroom is very lively and noisy, while B's class is very quiet and silent. Might this depend from the teacher's style? Further investigation is needed to answer this question.

6 Conclusion

Teaching is a typical human behaviour; a complex behaviour, because in teaching you must take into account not only what you want to teach, but also those whom you teach, as well as the context of learning. And while teaching you have to communicate knowledge, but you also have to elicit and sustain passion, motivation, and positive emotions in those whom you teach; finally, to manage their relationship with you. Communication in all modalities is the medium of this complex transaction of beliefs, feelings, and relations. Clearly, then, there is good reason to study teachers' multimodal communication, in order to train better teachers in both the Artificial and the Human domain. But to study all the subtleties of the teacher's communication requires sophisticated tools that allow the researcher to capture all the signals produced by a teacher, all their meanings, and all the complexities of their combination. We have reported a research on teachers' communication where thanks to the "score", a tool for the analysis of multimodality, we analysed some of the complexities of this behaviour, and outlined the different styles of different teachers. An interesting issue to investigate in future research is how these different styles affect important aspects of classroom interaction, such as the pupils' emotions, motivation, and cognitive development.

References

1. N. A. Flanders. Interaction Analysis in the Classroom: A Manual for Observers. University of Michigan Press, Ann Arbor (1966)
2. E. Amidon and E. Hunter. Improving Teaching. Holt, Rinehart & Winston, New York (1966)
3. F. Orletti. La conversazione diseguale. Carocci, Roma (2000)
4. R. Rosenthal and L. Jacobson: Pygmalion in the Classroom. Holt, Rinehart & Winston, New York (1968)
5. G. De Landsheere and A. Delchambre. Les comportements non verbaux de l'einsegnant. Labor, Bruxelles (1979)
6. P. Ekman and W. Friesen. Facial Action Coding System. Consulting Psychologist Press, Inc., Palo Alto, CA (1978)
7. A. Kendon. Gesticulation and Speech: two aspects of the Process of Utterance. In M.R.Key, ed.: The relationship of Verbal and Nonverbal Communication. Mouton, The Hague (1980)
8. D. McNeill. Hand and Mind. University of Chicago Press, Chicago (1992)
9. I. Poggi and C. Pelachaud. Signals and meanings of gaze in Animated Faces. In P. McKevitt, S. O' Nuallàin, Conn Mulvihill, eds.: Language,Vision, and Music. Selected papers from the 8th International Workshop on the Cognitive Science of Natural Language Processing, Galway, 1999. John Benjamins, Amsterdam (2002) 133-144
10. I. Poggi. Le sopracciglia dell'insegnante: un contributo al lessico della faccia. Atti delle XI Giornate di Studio del Gruppo di Fonetica Sperimentale. Multimodalità e Multimedialità nella Comunicazione. Padova, 29 novembre-1 dicembre 2000. Padova, Unipress (2001) 57-65
11. W. Johnson, J. Rickel and J.C.Lester. Animated pedagogical Agents: Face-to-face interaction in interactive learning environments. International Journal of Artificial Intelligence in Education 11 (2000) 47-78
12. J. Cassell, J. Sullivan, S. Prevost and E. Churchill, eds.: Embodied Conversational Agents. MIT Press, Cambridge (Mass.) (2000)
13. C. Pelachaud and I. Poggi (eds.): Multimodal Communication and Context in Embodied Agents. Proceedings of the Workshop W7 at the 5th International Conference on Autonomous Agents, Montreal, Canada, May 29, 2001.
14. I. Poggi and E.Magno Caldognetto. Mani che parlano. Gesti e Psicologia della comunicazione. Unipress, Padova (1997)
15. I. Poggi. Mind Markers. In M.Rector, I.Poggi and N.Trigo, eds.: Gestures. Meaning and use. Universidad Fernando Pessoa, Porto (2003)
16. C. Mueller. Conventional gestures in speech pauses. In C.Mueller and R.Posner, eds.: The semantics and pragmatics of everyday gestures. Berlin Verlag Arno Spitz, Berlin (2003)
17. C. Castelfranchi and I. Poggi. Bugie, finzioni, sotterfugi. Per una scienza dell'inganno. Carocci, Roma (1998)
18. J.L. Austin. How to do things with words. Oxford University Press, Oxford (1962)
19. J. Searle. Speech Acts. Cambridge University Press, Cambridge (1969)
20. I. Poggi and C. Pelachaud. Performative facial expressions in Animated Faces. In J.Cassell, J.Sullivan, S.Prevost and E. Churchill, eds.: Embodied Conversational Agents. MIT Press, Cambridge (Mass.) (2000)
21. J. Cassell, Y. Nakano, T. Bickmore, C. Sidner and C. Rich. Annotating and Generating posture from Discourse Structure in Embodied Conversational Agents. In Multimodal Communication and Context in Embodied Agents. Proceedings of the Workshop W7 at the 5th International Conference on Autonomous Agents, Montreal, Canada, 29 May 2001.
22. M. Payà Canals. Incidental clauses in Spoken Catalan: Prosodic Characteristics and Pragmatic Function. In B. Bel and I.Marlien, eds.: Proceedings of the Speech Prosody 2002 Conference, 11-13 Aprile 2002. Aix-en-Provence: Laboratoire Parole et Langage (2002) 559-562.
23. P. Ekman and W. Friesen. The repertoire of nonverbal behavior. Semiotica, 1 (1969) 49-98
24. E. Magno Caldognetto and I. Poggi. Creative iconic gestures: some evidence from Aphasics. In R.Simone, ed.: Iconicity in Language. John Benjamins, Amsterdam (1995)

Deixis in Multimodal Human Computer Interaction: An Interdisciplinary Approach

Alfred Kranstedt[1], Peter Kühnlein[2], and Ipke Wachsmuth[1]

[1] Artificial Intelligence Group, Faculty of Technology, University of Bielefeld, D-33594 Bielefeld, Germany
{akranste,ipke}@techfak.uni-bielefeld.de
[2] Linguistics Dept., Faculty of Linguistics & Literary Science, University of Bielefeld, D-33594 Bielefeld, Germany
p@uni-bielefeld.de

Abstract. Focusing on deixis in human computer interaction this paper presents interdisciplinary work on the use of co-verbal gesture . Empirical investigations, theoretical modeling, and computational simulations with an anthropomorphic agent are based upon comparable settings and common representations. Findings pertain to the coordination of verbal and gestural constituents in deictic utterances. We discovered high variability in the temporal synchronization of such constituents in task-oriented dialogue, and a theoretical treatment thereof is presented. With respect to simulation we exemplarily show how the influence of situational characteristics on the choice of verbal and nonverbal constituents can be accounted for. In particular, this depends on spatio-temporal relations between speaker and the objects they refer to in dialogue.

1 Introduction: Interdisciplinary Gesture Research

The formation of new fields of applications, e.g. in virtual reality, raises new demands on how to interact with computational systems. In response, there are numerous attempts at utilizing natural multi-modal communication skills humans employ in face-to-face conversation. This includes the reception and generation of synchronized verbal and nonverbal utterances. The development of computational models requires detailed knowledge about the involved mechanisms, in particular the deep coordination of speech and gestures and their formation throughout the production of utterances. Specific investigations induced by the needs of simulation work can help close knowledge gaps.

In this paper, we present our research into the use of multi-modal deixis in a restricted domain of assembly tasks. From the viewpoint of linguistics there is quite a remarkable extent of theoretical discussion concerning the way deixis works. The status of gestures is not unequivocally accounted for by the different theories in the philosophy of language community, cf. Section 2. The works of Kaplan [5] and his successors serve as a model for linguistic reference by

A. Camurri and G. Volpe (Eds.): GW 2003, LNAI 2915, pp. 112–123, 2004.

demonstratives that in our view can plausibly be accommodated to cover pointing. There is no comparably easy way to translate other manners of gesturing into linguistic theories without begging certain relevant questions. On the other hand, simulative work dedicated to deixis offers an opportunity to develop exemplary computational production models of utterances most often expressed in more than one modality and structured in direct relation to the spatio-temporal environment.

The interdependence between the empirical, theoretical and simulative parts and their methodical connection described in Section 3 is based on a common setting called pointing games. We describe empirical studies realized in these setting concerning (1) the temporal synchronization between speech and pointing gestures; (2) the influence of the spatio-temporal restrictions of the environment, in particular the density of the objects referred to, on deictic behavior. The transfer between empirical, theoretical, and simulative work is fostered by the creation of translations between the annotations we use in our empirical studies and a common representation language for utterance descriptions, MURML[9].

In Section 4 we outline some findings and their implications on theoretical modeling of the phenomenon deixis. An extension of our theoretical framework is proposed to deal with the high temporal variability in synchronization we found in the task-oriented dialogues we investigated. Moreover, it is shown how the empirical results guide the enhancement of the virtual anthropomorphic agent MAX. MAX was developed as a mediator in an immersive 3D virtual environment for the simulation of assembly tasks [25,11]. He is able to grasp simple multimodal instructions which may include deictic and iconic gestures, and to produce smooth co-verbal gestures in synchrony with synthetic speech from descriptions of their surface form in real time [7,8]. For deixis these descriptions can be generated from abstract prototypical templates in a situated planning process.

2 Related Work

There is hardly any research dedicated to the phenomenon of deixis with the goal of computational simulation that implicates more than simple pointing. As a subcase of co-verbal gesture, pointing is usually treated as a putatively simple case. The concurrence of deictic gestures and corresponding verbal expressions, however, is not explicitly acknowledged.

The empirical data available in this area of research is also quite sparse. There is noteworthy work by Paul Piwek from ITRI in Brighton and co-workers, cf. [21,22], that aims in the same direction as our work does. A problem is that their findings seem to be specific for Dutch.

There is not much work comparable to our approach in the field of the theoretical investigations reported, either. Philosophically, the status of gestures is a matter of controversy. Researchers in the line of Kaplan [5], take the stance that (1) gestures are logically irrelevant for determining the meaning of demonstrative expressions and (2) the speaker's intentions already suffice to fix meanings. In contrast, we adopt in our theoretical work what we call a *neo-Peirce-Quine-*

Wittgenstein view. According to this position, gestures are part of more complex signs and have to be treated on a par with speech. Few other researchers in the linguistics community adopt this view when it comes to formal modeling. E.g., in the STAGING project a related integrative account is pursued, utilizing attribute-value grammar and unification [20]. However, an elaborate theory of integration is still missing.

In simulative work on utterance generation, the production of speech has gained most attention, in recent work replenished, modified or partly substituted by gesture. Current approaches, e.g. [19,2], enrich speech with nonverbal behaviors fetched from a database. But investigations on human-human communication reveal an intricate temporal synchronization between speech and gesture related to semantic and pragmatic synchronization.

In recent psycholinguistic work several models of speech-gesture production have been proposed to approach this problem. While *RP-models*[1] [4,3,10] extend the speech-production model of Levelt [12] and suggest a parallel production process in specialized modules, McNeill [16,17] emphasizes the inseparable connection of the modalities. If we want to follow the computationally more manageable RP-approach the examplary treatment of deixis can help to realize the cross-modal interactions on the different levels of the production process which are inexplicit in the suggested models. In section 4 we describe how the environmental restrictions on successful pointing influence the conceptualization of the co-articulated speech.

3 Methodological Issues

3.1 The Pointing Game Scenario

We investigate deixis in a reduced setting of interaction between two agents we call pointing games. Pointing games inherit their names from the dialogue games as proposed by [13,14]. We start with the minimal form of these games consisting only of two turns. The underlying idea of pointing games is to integrate signal interpretation and the generation of an answer in one unique setting. This gives the chance to investigate deixis in dialogue imagined as part of an interactive process of fixing reference.

Pointing games are embedded in instructor-constructor settings involving the assembly of *Baufix*[2]-aggregates, e.g. toy airplanes, investigated in the Collaborative Research Center "Situated Artificial Communicators" (SFB 360).

In parallel to the empirically investigated human-human setting we build a human-computer interaction scenario embedded in immersive virtual reality (VR), realized in a three side cave-like installation (see Fig. 1). MAX and the user are located at a table with Baufix parts and communicate about how to assemble them.

[1] **R**epresentations and **P**rocesses, models related to the information processing approach.

[2] Baufix is the trade name of a children's construction toy used in our scenario.

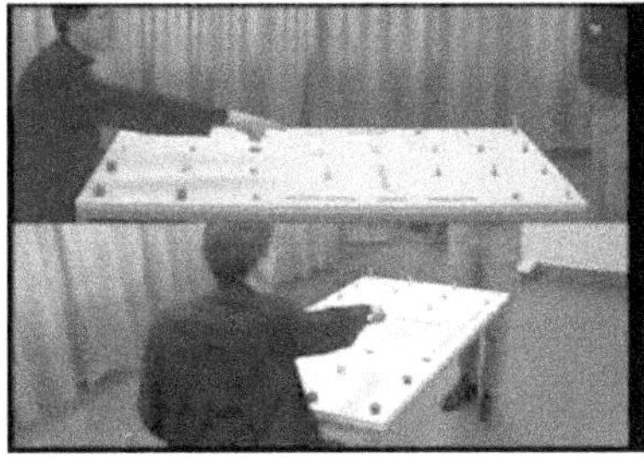

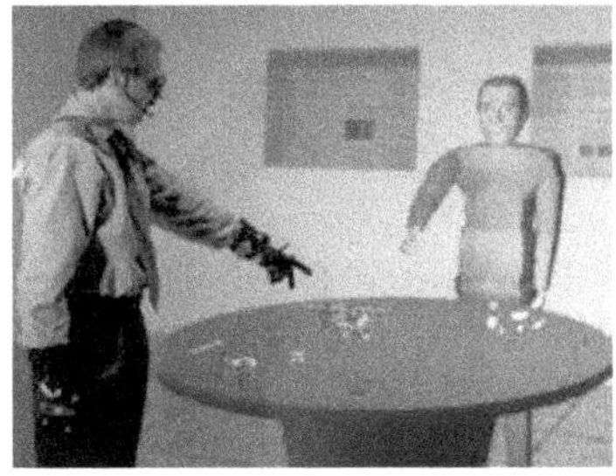

Fig. 1. The pointing game scenario: Comparable settings for empirical studies and VR

Intended empirical studies realized in this VR-setting are aimed at evaluating MAX capacity to interpret and generate situated co-verbal gesture and testing for the naturalness and acceptability of the simulation.

3.2 From Data to Qualitative Descriptions: Empirical Settings and Preparation of the Collected Data

We conducted a number of studies to obtain data concerning the timing relations and spatial conditions for successfully received pointing. A central question was whether in construction dialogues the temporal relations are the same as reported in the literature for narratives and related gestures. It was not clear if the timing would be the same, given the fact that the task was completely different and gestures serve a different purpose during pointing. The spatial conditions we investigated concern how the perceived density of objects influenced the pointing behavior of subjects.

For our studies we used a carefully selected setting. Two subjects, one called instructor, the other constructor, were to cooperate in identifying the atomic parts of a toy airplane distributed on a table. Instructor had to tell constructor via some multi-modal utterance which of the parts s/he had in mind, and constructor in turn had to briefly lift the object to indicate that s/he had identified it and then put it back in place.

The physical density of the objects on the table (though not the *perceived* density) was constant all over the area and did not change over time. The gestures performed to identify objects were very likely to be simple pointing gestures with the fingers. The dialogue patterns were expected to be simple, as were the sentential constructions.

The studies were video-graphed and annotation was done using the TASX annotator, cf. [18], a tool that allows to annotate of sound and video data without prescribed categories. We can thus use the inventory of MURML [9], a symbolic description of the surface shape of utterances developed for the simulation of speech and gesture with MAX. We devised an XSLT script as an output filter for TASX that produces complete MURML descriptions. The XSLT script serves the purpose of transforming the TASX output by reduction of information, extracting qualitative description from quantitative data, and ordering them in a hierarchical structure. This step opens the path to the inverse of the generation of quantitative data by the empirical part of the project in that the behavior of MAX can be studied using qualitative judgments in turn.

3.3 Utterance Form Descriptions as a Link between Analysis of Coverbal Gestures and Their Simulative Synthesis

Organizing utterance generation as a process on several levels, a qualitative description of their overt shape can be an important link between the mental planning process and the physical realization of utterances. A notation system of such descriptions, MURML, was developed as starting point for MAX's generator modules which form a hierarchical system of controllers computing the upper-limb movements and feed the text-to-speech system [7,8].

We adopt the empirical assumption [16] that continuous speech and gesture are co-produced in successive units each expressing a single idea unit. The correspondence between gesture and speech at the surface realization is commonly assumed to depend on a correspondence between certain units on different levels of the hierarchical structure of both modalities [6,16]. As introduced in [9], we define *chunks* of speech-gesture production to consist of an intonational phrase in overt speech and a co-expressive gesture phrase (see Fig. 2). Within each chunk, the gesture stroke corresponds to the focused constituent in the intonational phrase (the *affiliate*) that carries the nuclear accent. Complex utterances with multiple gestures are conceived as being divided in several chunks.

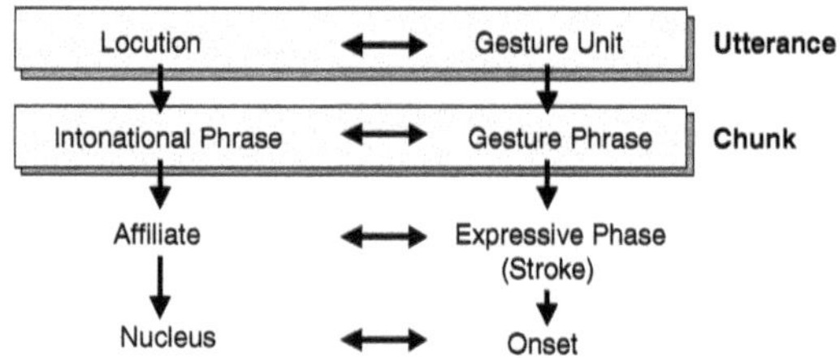

Fig. 2. Units of speech-gesture correspondence (taken from [9])

MURML utterance specifications are hierarchically organized in an XML-notation [9]. They start from the textual output augmented with certain points in time expressing the correspondence between speech and the subsequently defined gesture by specifying the affiliate's onset and end. Gestures can either be stated by specifying a communicative function or be explicitly described symbolically in terms of their spatiotemporal features. We use an inventory derived from the sign language notation system HamNoSys [23]. The optional parametrization of all features give us the possibility to define prototypical templates for frequently used utterances and instantiate them during the generation process, adapting the situational requirements. This will be exemplified in Section 4.3.

4 Results and Discussion

4.1 Empirical Findings

The results of the described studies were in part unexpected. E.g., pointings occurred that had their onset *after* the associated expression. In other cases the pointing took place after all the linguistic material was uttered. This is evidence that the timing relations in construction dialogues are more varied than timing relations during narratives, with no such events reported there [16].

"Good"[3] cases are those where the stroke of the gesture lies before or on the noun phrase that is its affiliate. These cases are good, because the gesture can be understood as being a normal modifier for the noun phrase. Compare the following linguistic constructions:

(1) Take the yellow bolt.
V Det Adj N

(2) Take the ↘ bolt.
V Det – *N*

Yellow is an adjective that modifies the noun *bolt*. This modifier can be seen as an operator that takes the following phrase as an argument, hence binds to the right (cf. section 4.2). The symbol "↘" is used to represent the stroke of a pointing gesture, and is intended to indicate that the stroke occurs at the time between uttering "the" and "bolt" in the present example. So, when the gesture is a semiotic object on a par with linguistic signs, the gestures stroke and the modifying adjective are of the same category here.

Pointings with strokes *after* the linguistic material are called "bad", because the model of the modifying adjective that is supposed to be of the same category breaks down. An utterance like (3) simply is not well-formed in English[4], but pointings like (4) are perfectly possible. Cf. section 4.2 for discussion.

(3) * Take the bolt yellow.
V Det N Adj

(4) Take the bolt ↘.
V Det N –

Concerning the spatial conditions, we observed a two-way interaction between perceived density and complexity of linguistic material that can be measured counting the frequency of pointing behavior, cf. Fig. 3. Whenever the perceived density is very low, instead of pointing with fingers, subjects seem to use gaze direction as a pointing device. When there is a mid-density of objects, they use noun phrases with low complexity and frequently point with their fingers. High density surprisingly leads to a slight decrease in pointing and an increase of the complexity of noun phrases.

The borderline between the far and the mid area is an indicator of the resolvability of human pointing. On the evidence of these data, we could determine the size of a *pointing cone* as being of $\approx 8^\circ$ around the axis of the pointing finger. The

[3] "Good" in the sense that they are simple to treat with our theoretical apparatus.

[4] As one of the reviewers pointed out, adjectives in post-position are perfectly acceptable in, e.g., French. Our claim that the meaning of pointing gestures can be assimilated to linguistic meanings is, however, not touched by that fact. Our model is in this regard parametried for English (and German) grammar.

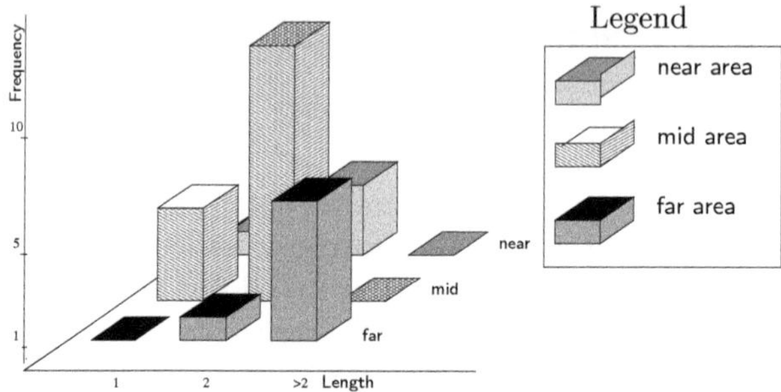

Fig. 3. The two-way interaction between perceived density and complexity of the linguistic material. "Frequency" denotes the frequency of successful gestures, "Length" the length of their affiliate in speech

behavioral clues we used were the conditions under which instructors were able to point out objects to constructors successfully. The results were correlated with the perceived object density, the distance between the intended object and the closest one relative to the distance of the finger root to the object and the angle between object plane and pointing ray. We hypothesize that a similar pointing cone can be found for the case where eye gaze is used for pointing[5].

4.2 Theoretical Modeling: What about the Bad Cases?

Theoretical modeling at the moment is restricted to deal with the temporal phenomena observed, and does not comprise the spatial structure of the domain. Doing that step will involve using structured models for the semantics, planned at a later time.

Our current interest is to find a sound and up-to-date explanation of the interface between syntax and semantics of speech-gesture complexes. Facing the problem that we want to obtain computer-implementable results we strive for mathematically tractable methods. We adopted a constraint-based version of HPSG, which had to be enriched in a multitude of ways. The typed feature structure descriptions that form the representations of the HPSG analyses spell out under which conditions a given (multi-dimensional) sign is well-formed. We set up a type-logical interpretation for the syntax, instead of the flat semantics currently favored.

From a logical point of view the results reported in section 4.1 mean that the gesture corresponds to a polymorphic operator. The standard case for operators in linguistics is that they are taken to bind to the right, which means that subsequent material can be in the scope of the operator. It is hence straightforward to give a semantics for a pointing gesture in the "good" cases. It is not even difficult in principle to define an operator as binding to the left and then use it as an interpretation for a gesture in the "bad" cases. But it is unsatisfactory to have a multiplicity of interpretations in contrast to uniform interpretations.

[5] This will be verified in future studies using eye tracker technology.

For a type-logical treatment this multiplicity means that there have to be multiple solutions at first, and some subsequent filter. Things here are not even easy for the "good" cases, as different realizations of gesture positions are possible. Accordingly, for the "good" cases like (1), there could be six possible interpretations for the pointing gesture, four of which would be different in logical type. The various interpretations that are possible at each of the positions of the gesture imply that the corresponding logical operator is not only polymorphic, but also polysemous.

For the "bad" cases (where ↘ follows the relevant linguistic material in temporal order) we have all the interpretations that are possible for the "good" cases, except that the binding is in the other direction. An example that is close enough to the "bad" case (4) could be (5):

(5) Take the bolt that lies rightmost
V *Det N* *RC*

It is obvious that post-modification as exemplified in (5) is possible. (For a discussion of the use of post-modification in Dutch and English in the context of task oriented dialogues and pointing see [21,22].) And it is obvious that this parallels the "bad" cases again, cf. (4). Note that mixed cases again add one dimension of complexity. Let this suffice as an indication of how the semantics of the gesture is treated and how the results of the studies influence and inform the semantic representation. Analogously, if a syntactic representation of speech plus gesture is desired, it has to respect the complex data that were found in the studies.

In our project – and in contrast to [20] – we developed a syntactic apparatus, based on the suggestions by [24], which uses constraints in order to define well-formed multi-modal expressions. The interface we got thus far contains a lexical component with definitions of the logical types of the linguistic and gestural material as discussed above. To be clear, "lexical component" here means that the entries for the lemmas contain rules for the uses of expressions (for the gestures, e.g.) and only in cases of rigid designators it contains also the values for reference. Following logical tradition, we view pronouns as carrying values only if they were uttered on a certain occasion. Analogously, pointing gestures are in a sense lexicalized, but this does by far not mean that their reference is fixed in the lexicon. Rather, we have a multiplicity of rules for uses of pointing gestures in order to capture the polysemy and polymorphy discussed above.

The calculation of utterance meanings then is rather straightforward. The semantic composition follows the syntactic analysis just as usual. Here it proves useful to have a type-logical apparatus, as the calculations done within this framework have been especially well-studied.

4.3 Simulative Synthesis

The empirical results with respect to the "bad cases" of synchronization and the high failure rate in human-human communication give us an idea of the difficulties and the limits of getting machines to understand multimodal utterances.

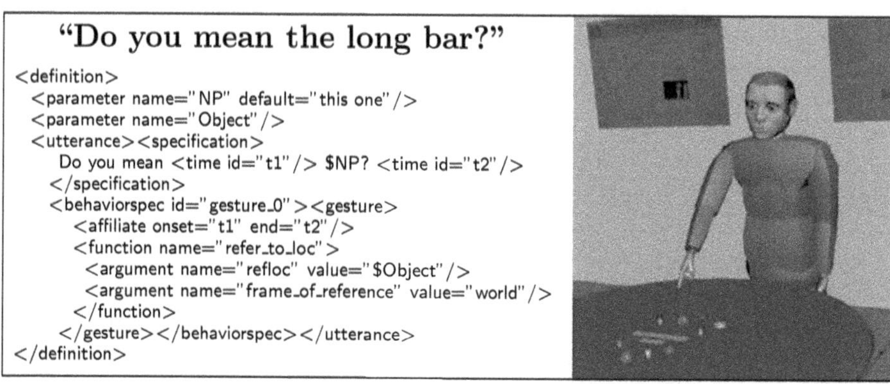

Fig. 4. Sample abstract MURML specification of a deictic utterance fetched from a database and the simulative realization. The variable "Object" is instantiated with the identifier of the intended object and in a further step by its coordinates. The variable "NP" in the speech specification is substituted in the planning process by an object description that allows the user to identify the intended object in the scene. This depends on the discriminating power of the pointing gesture. For a more detailed description see the text

But we can learn from the way humans handle misunderstandings, namely, they clarify them in dialogue. Analogously, we reduce the analytic process w.r.t. synchronization on the frequent "good cases" and relocate gaps of understanding in the interaction. In most cases, these apply to a further enquiry. Furthermore, there are no cues which suggest that the "bad cases" are an indispensable part of human communication. This allows reducing the range of our agents' communicational behavior to the "good cases" and automatizing them in the generation process. Thus, we have defined an implicit parameter representing the offset between the beginning of the gesture stroke and the affiliate in the co-expressive speech that has the default value 0.2 seconds, but can optionally be redefined in MURML.

The described empirical investigations suggest a "zoning" of the pointing area depending on the perceived object density. We can make these results fruitful for utterance planning using the pointing cone as a central concept. This approach has the advantage of offering a distance-invariant description of the observed phenomena. The *near* area then is that area where all pointing is unambiguous, meaning only one object is in the pointing cone, the perceived object density is low. The *far* area is the area where an unambiguous pointing gesture is impossible, the perceived object density being high.

This view can be used for the assignment of information to the modalities and the adaption of the overt shape of the planned utterance to conditions resulting from the environment. A reasonable heuristics in utterance planning should be the minimization of the extent and complexity of the target utterance. Deixis is a very good example of utterance types we could build up from prototypical templates representing the simplest form to utter, here a simple pointing gesture connected to a short unspecific noun phrase in speech like "this one".

Beginning with a prototypical template fetched from an utterance database we can describe the realization in two planning steps. In the example illustrated in Fig. 4 the MURML description of the template scripted on the left contains an abstract function for a pointing gesture and a parametrized speech specification. The first step is the assignment to the modalities beginning with a check if a pointing gesture with only the desired object in the pointing cone is possible. To check this, an approximate hand position on the line from a point between the shoulders to the intended object is anticipated. If more than one object is detected in the estimated pointing cone, an adequate verbal restrictor is chosen discriminating the objects in the pointing cone by a comparative analysis of the object knowledge in the following order: *color, general type* (typically descriptions in natural speech), *shape, size*, and *location*. For a discussion of order of adjectives and an overview of the literature for German see [26]). The first discriminating attribute, preferably the color, is used to specify the reference-object. In our example there are two bars with the same color, so the first discriminating attribute is size relative to the shape, that is, length.

The second step contains the parallel realization in the involved modalities. A text production module replaces the variables in the speech specification with a syntactical correct combination of the chosen verbal restrictors. The function "refer_to_loc" in the behavior specification is substituted by a shape description containing parametrized hand/arm configurations and movement constraints in terms of the three features hand shape, hand orientation, and hand position. In a further step this feature descriptions must be adapted to the spatial requirements, in the case of a pointing gesture the direction and distance of the referred object. Finally, cross-modal correspondence is established by appending the coverbal behavior to its respective chunk. Its affiliate in speech receives a pitch accent. The resulting utterance plan feeds the text-to-speech system and the motor planner that generates a hierarchical system of movement control primitives (for details see [8]).

5 Conclusions and Perspective

It was explained how the interdisciplinary approach taken in our project furthers the understanding of the functioning of deictic gestures and leads way to their natural simulation. The empirical data have guided theoretical modeling in that they made salient the relevant cases concerning timing. They also revealed findings to support simulations for natural human-machine interactions.

In future work we will intensify the role of the virtual agent MAX in the empirical investigations. As an example, MAX can be programmed to perform the gesture-to-speech synchronization at different points in time for uttering one and the same sentence in multiple ways. When Max interacts with subjects under varied conditions, their reactions are expected to show whether the changes in MAX's behaviour are comparable to effects in human-human interactions.

We are currently exploring dialogue models that go beyond two-turn sequences of speech acts based on the *dialogue games theory* as proposed by [13] and extended by [15]. The syntax-semantics interface developed in the theoretical part of the project is well suited for an extension in that line.

Acknowledgement

This research is partly supported by the Deutsche Forschungsgesellschaft (DFG) in the Collaborative Research Center "Situated Artificial Communicators" (SFB 360).

References

1. Niels Ole Bernsen and Oliviero Stock, editors. *Proceedings of the International Workshop on Information Presentation and Natural Multimodal Dialogue* – IPNMD *2001, Verona, Italy*. ITC-irst, December 14–15, 2001.
2. J. Cassell, H. Vilhjalmsson, and T. Bickmore. BEAT: the Behavior Expression Animation Toolkit. In Eugene Fiume, editor, *Proceedings of SIGGRAPH 2001*, pages 477–486. ACM Press/ACM SIGGRAPH, 2001.
3. Justine Cassell and Scott Prevost. Distribution of Semantic Features Across Speech and Gesture by Humans and Machines. In *Proceedings of the Workshop on the Integration of Gesture in Language and Speech*, 1996.
4. Jan Peter deRuiter. The production of gesture and speech. In David McNeill, editor, *Language and gesture*, chapter 14, pages 284–311. Cambridge University Press, 2000.
5. David Kaplan. On the Logic of Demonstratives. *Journ. Phil. Logic*, 8:81–98, 1979.
6. Adam Kendon. Gesticulation and speech: Two aspects of the process of utterance. In M. R. Key, editor, *The Relationship of Verbal and Nonverbal Communication*, pages 207–227. The Hague, Mouton, 1980.
7. S. Kopp and I. Wachsmuth. A Knowledge-based Approach for Lifelike Gesture Animation. In W. Horn, editor, *ECAI 2000 - Proceedings of the 14th European Conference on Artificial Intelligence*, pages 663–667, Amsterdam, 2000. IOS Press.
8. S. Kopp and I. Wachsmuth. Model-based Animation of Coverbal Gesture. In *Proceedings of Computer Animations 2002*, pages 252–257. IEEE Press, 2002.
9. A. Kranstedt, S. Kopp, and I. Wachsmuth. MURML: A Multimodal Utterance Representation Markup Language for Conversational Agents. In *Proceedings of the AAMAS02 Workshop on Embodied Conversational Agents – let's specify and evaluate them*, Bologna, Italy, July 2002.
10. R. Krauss, Y. Chen, and R. Gottesman. Lexical gestures and lexical access: a process model. In D. McNeill, editor, *Language and gesture*, chapter 13, pages 261–283. Cambridge University Press, 2000.
11. Marc Erich Latoschik. A Gesture Processing Framework for Multimodal Interaction in Virtual Reality. In A. Chalmers and V. Lalioti, editors, *Afrigraph 2001, 1st International Conference on Computer Graphics, Virtual Reality and Visualization in Africa, 5 - 7 November 2001*, pages 95–100, New York, NY 10036, 2001. ACM SIGGRAPH.
12. W. J. Levelt. *Speaking*. MIT Press, Cambridge, Massachusetts, 1989.
13. James A. Levin and James A. Moore. Dialogue Games: Metacommunication Structures for Natural Language Interaction. *Cognitive Science*, 1(4):395–420, 1978.

14. William C. Mann. Dialogue Games: Conventions of Human Interaction. *Argumentation*, 2:512–32, 1988.
15. William C. Mann. Dialogue macrogame theory. http://www-rcf.usc.edu/~billmann/dialogue/dmt-paper1.htm, 2002. Revised version of a paper presented at SIGdial, Philadelphia, Pennsylvania USA, July 2002.
16. David McNeill. *Hand and Mind: What Gestures Reveal about Thought.* University of Chicago Press, Chicago, 1992.
17. David McNeill. Models of speaking (to their amazement) meet speech-synchronized gestures. Obtained from the cogprints archives: http://cogprints.soton.ac.uk/, 1998.
18. Jan-Torsten Milde and Ulrike Gut. The TASX-environment: an XML-based corpus database for time aligned language data. In *Proceedings of the IRCS Workshop on linguistic databases, Philadelphia*, 2001.
19. T. Noma and N. Badler. A Virtual Human Presenter. In *Proceedings of the IJCAI Workshop on Animated Interface Agents: Making Them Intelligent*, pages 45–51, 1997.
20. Patrizia Paggio and Bart Jongejan. Multimodal communication in the virtual farm of the STAGING project. In: [1], pages 41–45, 2001.
21. P. Piwek, R.J. Beun, and A. Cremers. Demonstratives in Dutch Cooperative Task Dialogues. IPO Manuscript 1134, Eindhoven University of Technology, 1995.
22. P. Piwek and R. J. Beun. Multimodal Referential Acts in a Dialogue Game: From Empirical Investigation to Algorithm. In: [1], pages 127–131, 2001.
23. Siegmund Prillwitz. *HamNoSys. Version 2. Hamburger Notationssystem für Gebärdensprachen. Eine Einführung.* SIGNUM-Verlag, 1989.
24. Ivan Sag and Thomas Wasow. *Syntactic Theory – A Formal Introduction.* CSLI, 1999.
25. T. Sowa, S. Kopp, and M.E. Latoschik. A Communicative Mediator in a Virtual Environment: Processing of Multimodal Input and Output. In: [1], pages 71–74, 2001.
26. Petra Weiß and Stefan Barattelli. Das Benennen von Objekten. In Th. Herrman and J. Grabowski, editors, *Enzyklopädie der Psychologie: Themenbereich C, Theorie und Forschung*, volume III of *Sprache.* Hogrefe, 2003.

The Analysis of Gesture: Establishing a Set of Parameters

Nicla Rossini

Department of Linguistics, University of Pavia
tattvamasi@libero.it

Abstract. Studying gesture has always implied the application of different methods concerning the selection of suitable parameters for gesture. Several solutions to this problem have been proposed by scholars over the years. These contributions will be briefly reviewed and discussed with the aim of retrieving a common method for the analysis and definition of gesture.

Introduction

Studying gesture has always implied the application of different methods concerning the selection of suitable parameters for gesture analysis. Several solutions to the problems concerning gesture analysis and coding have been proposed by scholars over the years, but, since these solutions were usually aimed at studying different aspects and properties of gesture, no standard set of parameters is nowadays available for the interdisciplinary analysis of gesture. The proposal for gesture analysis here described constitutes an attempt to solve the problems posed by the interdisciplinary character of gesture studies by establishing a set of parameter both accurate and suitable for different areas of research.

This paper is structured as follows: in the first section (***Gesture analysis: a review of the main contributions***), the main approaches to gesture analysis and coding are reviewed and discussed, while in the second section (***The analysis of gesture: establishing a set of parameters)***, an interdisciplinary set of parameters for gesture analysis including ***timing, size, point of articulation*** , and ***locus***, is presented. Lastly, a sample of gesture analysis and transcription following these parameters is provided and explained.

Gesture Analysis: A Review of the Main Contributions

As mentioned in the introduction, several studies have focused, so far, on the analysis and coding of gesture. Still, since the methodologies so far developed for the analysis of gestural phenomena were mainly aimed at studying particular aspects of gesture, no inter-disciplinary standardized set of parameters is available. In this section, a brief review is provided of the main methodologies for gesture analysis and coding. Taking these contributions as a valuable starting point, an interdisciplinary set of parameters is proposed in the next section.

A. Camurri and G. Volpe (Eds.): GW 2003, LNAI 2915, pp. 124–131, 2004.

Birdwhistell (1952)[1] was the first in developing a method for the transcription of gesture: he worked it out following the method for phonetic transcription. Condon & Ogston (1966)[2] introduced their well-known, and still used, method of transcribing both gestures and speech flow, noting and analyzing the relationships existing between them. Also Kendon (1972)[3] successfully followed this path: he adopted Condon & Ogston's approach to the analysis of gestures, although his interest was mainly focused on a more technical issue, that is, the way speech and movements are organized and synchronized in speech acts[1].

Kendon's method of analysis is structured as follows: during film analysis, two "maps" are made. In the first one, speech is transcribed and changes of sound are recorded, while in the second a description of movement changes (each of them labeled by means of a set of terms relating joint function) are thoroughly matched with the speech segment they occur with. He also introduced fundamental concepts for the interpretation of gesture morphology and a pattern for the analysis of gesture-speech synchronization. In fact, he analyzed gesture as composed of "a ***nucleus*** of movement having some definite form and enhanced dynamic qualities, which is preceded by a preparatory movement and succeeded by a movement which either moves the limb back to its rest position or repositions it for the beginning of a Gesture Phrase"[2]; a ***Gesture Phrase*** being composed of ***preparation***, ***nucleus***, and ***retraction/reposition***. He also defined a correspondence pattern between ***Gesture Phrases*** and ***Tone Units***, or "phonologically defined syllabic groupings united by a single intonation tune"[3].

McNeill (1992)[4] also focused on gesture transcription and analysis: he and his lab developed a method for transcription mainly based on the same assumptions as Condon & Ogston. In this case, speech and gestures transcriptions are perfectly matched: the first line shows speech flow, with symbols representing hesitations, breath pauses and laughter. Square brackets clearly determine the part of speech flow a gesture is related with. Boldface in transcription precisely shows the syllables synchronizing with each gesture stroke. Right below speech flow report, an accurate description of the gesture is made following the same method as for A.S.L. transcription. As for Kendon's method, the major parameter for McNeill's gesture analysis is timing. He divided gesture into different phases, which he named ***preparation,*** (eventual) ***pre-stroke hold, stroke,*** (eventual) ***post-stroke hold*** and ***retraction.***

Establishing a Set of Parameters

An attempt to define interdisciplinary parameters for gesture analysis may thus start from the methods achieved by these scholars. Of course, a set of interdisciplinary parameters for the analysis of gesture must consider a wider set of features in order to guarantee accuracy and exhaustiveness of analysis. A possible method to guarantee these standards in gesture analysis is the introduction of further parameters, which are listed as follows:

---

[1] "[...]The primary aim here is to describe how the movements observed to occur as X speaks are organized, not from the point of view of their possible significance as gestures..." (Kendon 1972[3]).

[2] Kendon, 1986:34[5]. Emphasis theirs.

[3] Kendon, 1986:34[5].

- ***Size:*** the angle determined by the moving part of the joint with respect to the horizontal plane during the stroke phase. Since gestures are non-markedly performed at a major point of articulation which is the elbow, gesture size will be measured at the elbow, when possible. The horizontal plane is thus located at the level of the elbow, when the elbow is in rest position. The stroke phase is here defined as the phase occurring between the full acquisition of the handshape, and the phase immediately preceding handshape loosing. This method will only apply when the hand starts from a rest position whish is situated below the horizontal plane. Whenever the hand movement starts from a rest position which is already located above this plane (see ***table 1, figures 1-2***), the angle already formed by the forearm will be deducted from the angle determined is stroke phase. Moreover, the size of each phase following a reposition will be measured form the position immediately preceding handshape change (***see table 1, figures 3-6***). In this case, the angle determined by the forearm in the phase immediately preceding handshape change will be deducted form the angle determined in stroke phase. In case of gestures whose major point of articulation is the shoulder, gesture size will be expressed is means of angles determined by the upper arm with respect of the bust. When, on the other hand, the gesture is articulated at the wrist, gesture size will be expressed in means of rotation.

Table 1. The determination of gesture ***Size***

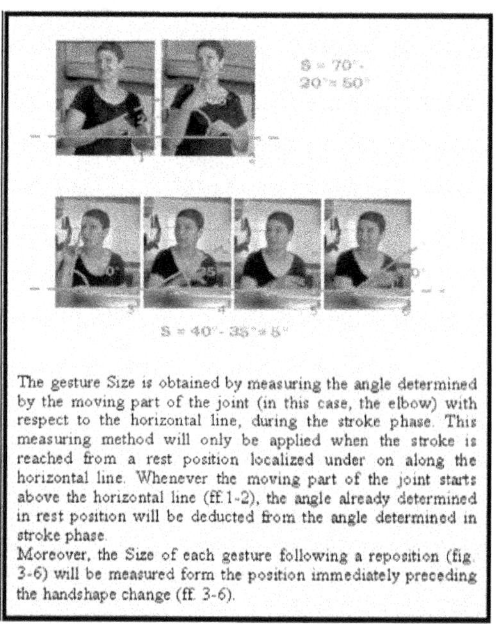

The gesture Size is obtained by measuring the angle determined by the moving part of the joint (in this case, the elbow) with respect to the horizontal line, during the stroke phase. This measuring method will only be applied when the stroke is reached from a rest position localized under on along the horizontal line. Whenever the moving part of the joint starts above the horizontal line (ff. 1-2), the angle already determined in rest position will be deducted from the angle determined in stroke phase.
Moreover, the Size of each gesture following a reposition (fig. 3-6) will be measured form the position immediately preceding the handshape change (ff. 3-6).

- ***Gesture Timing:*** the ***gesture phrase*** (which begins with the hand onset and ends when the hand goes back to rest position/reposition) should be further divided into different phases, which will be noted in transcriptions with their timing. These phases are as follows: ***pre-stroke phase,*** which is the ***preparation*** phase. It is defined as the phase in which the hand leaves the rest position and achieves the area

in which the meaningful part of the gesture will be performed (usually the bust area. See McNeill, 1992[4]). During this phase, the hand may begin to acquire the shape needed for the gesture performance; ***stroke phase***, or the meaningful part of gesture. During this phase the hand acquires the full shape needed for the gesture performance, and the ***gesture size*** is maximum. The intrinsic morphology of some gestures requires repeated strokes, or ***oscillations***. In these cases, although the stroke phase covers the whole period, ***oscillations*** will be noted separately. This device will help the determination of synchronization patterns between ***Gesture Phrase*** and ***Tone Unit***; ***post-stroke phase,*** or ***retraction***, when the hand loses the configuration needed for the gesture performance and goes back to rest position.
- ***Point of Articulation:*** main joint involved in the gesture movement;
- ***Locus:*** the body space involved by the gesture (See McNeill, 1992[4], based on Pedelty, 1987[6]). ***Locus*** will be identified by giving the name of the body part the space of which is interested by hand movement, i.e.: L: lower bust. For further indications, see figure 1.

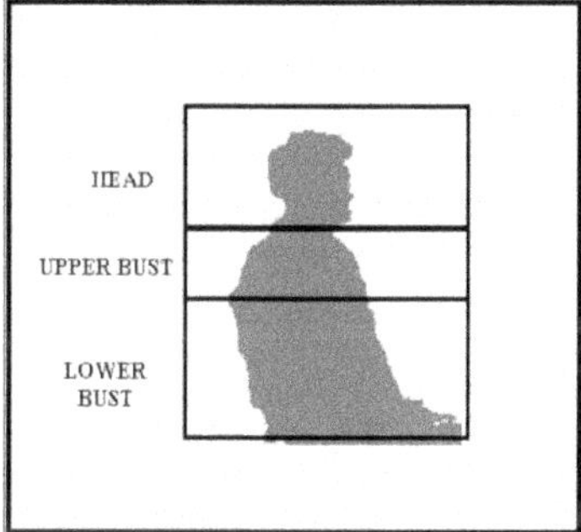

Fig. 1. ***Loci*** in gesture

Note that this proposal for the analysis of locus in gesture is only applicable to a bi-dimensional study. For tri-dimensional analyses, a different model, which is shown in figures 2 and 3. In order to have a suitable model for tri-dimensional analysis, not only the subject's body space, but also his/her personal space has to be considered, , personal space being here defined as the space which one would occupy by extending hid arms both frontally and laterally (see figure 3).

According to this model, the personal space is sub-divided into smaller volumes, which correspond to the bust areas shown in figure 1. The ***body space*** is analysed by means of the classical Cartesian axes:
- the ***x axis*** (see figure 2) is subdivided into a central space (roughly corresponding to the area occupied by the trunk of the speaker), and left and right peripheries. Each periphery is, in its turn, subdivided into ***periphery 1*** (roughly corresponding to area taken up by the elbow in a full lateral extension of the speaker's arm), and ***periphery 2***, which is the area taken up by the hand in a full lateral extension;
- the ***y axis*** (see figure 2) is divided into different body areas. These areas are named by means of the same labels shown in figure1, with the addition of a new area, namely the ***over-head area***, which covers the whole space over the speakers' head involved in the full up extension of his/her arms;

the *z* ***axis*** (see figure 3) is further divided into three different areas, namely, the ***trunk area***, the ***middle distance from the trunk*** (roughly corresponding to the area involved in a full frontal extension of the upper arm), and ***full distance form the trunk***, which is the area taken up by the hand in a full frontal extension of the speaker's arms.

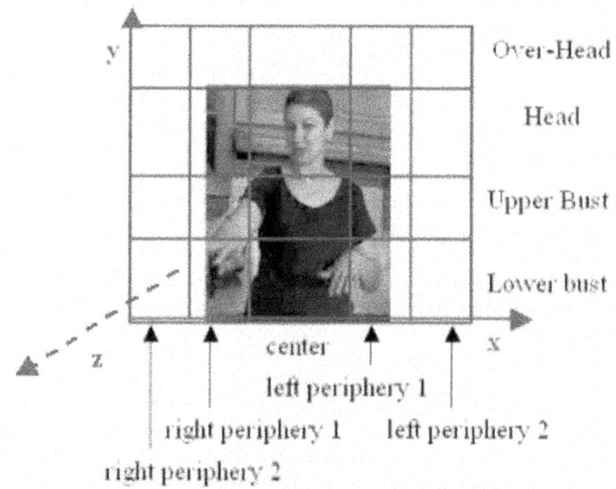

Fig. 2. Model for a contrastive study of the personal space used in gesture (frontal perspective)

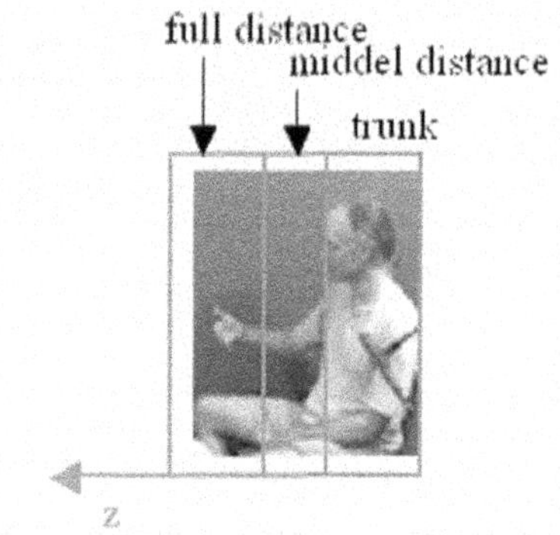

Fig. 3. Model for a contrastive study of the personal space used in gesture (lateral perspective)

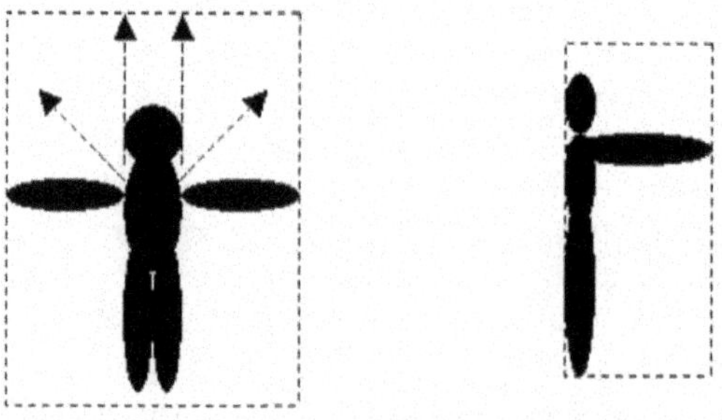

Fig. 4. Defining the ***personal space***

Transcription Sample

In this section, a sample of transcription is provided. The key to abbreviations is shown below, while transcripts are provided in table 2.

Key to Abbreviations

I_1 : Interviewer n.1
I_2 : Interviewer n. 2
S_1 : subject n. 1
E: emblem
D: deictic
M: metaphor
C: conduit
I: iconic
B: beat
a̲: stressed syllable
a̲: more relevant stressed syllable within the Tone Unit
a: : prolonged vowel
/: speech silent pause (<0.20")
//: speech silent pause (0.20"- 0.30")
///: speech silent pause (> 0.30")
{ }: part of speech co-occurring with a gesture phrase
[ ]: part of speech synchronizing with gesture stroke
* : *locus desperatus*
ff.: frames
osc: oscillation
Yhs: YES head sign
Nhs: NO head sign
ps: pre-stroke phase
sh: stroke hold
bp: retraction phase
S: size
PA: point of articulation
e: elbow
s: shoulder
w: wrist
L: locus
ub : upper bust
lb: lower bust
h: head
bh: both hands
rh: right hand
lh: left hand

As one may see, Magno Caldognetto & Poggi's (1997)[7] full score pattern is adopted. The first line provides numbered frames captured from the video, whose function is to supply a visual description of the gesture performed. In the second line, speech flow is transcribed, including hesitation pauses, silent pauses, and vocalic prolongations. Conventional marks show the stressed syllables of the tone units[4] in the speech flow. The segments of speech flow synchronizing with a kinetic unit, a

[4] See for this Kendon (1986)[5].

gesture phrase[5] and a stroke phase are also marked out. In the third line, each gesture phrase is labeled and analysed.

Labels refer to the gesture typology discussed in Rossini (***in progress***)[8]: although this typology shows a certain degree of arbitrariness, I consider it the most suitable for the purposes of this research, which has no taxonomic aims.

Table 2. Transcription sample

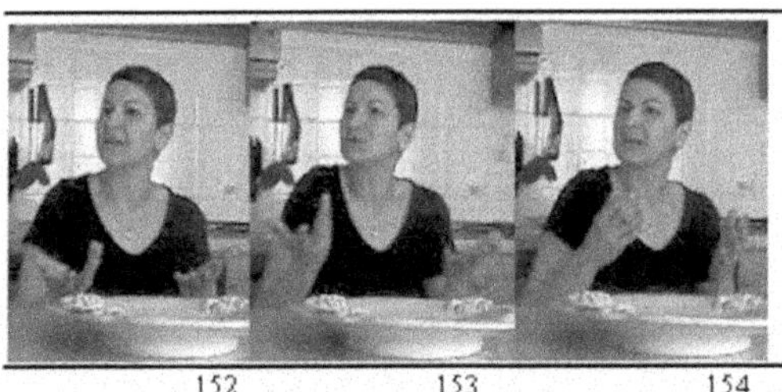

152 153 154

$\mathbf{I_1}$: ma: i **com**piti non glielo danno a **ca**sa? $\mathbf{S_1}$: eh! $\mathbf{I_1}$: i compiti a casa $\mathbf{S_1}$:{‡ma‡ a [ca]sa/[sì ma/]/

$\mathbf{I_1}$: don't they give him homework? $\mathbf{S_1}$: yes $\mathbf{I_1}$: homework $\mathbf{S_1}$: homework. Yes, but he

D+E+M+M+E (ff.143-54):
0.40" ps+0.12"sh (PA: e/w L: lb)
0.16"ps+ 2 osc/0.20"+0.48"r
(S: 10° e PA:e/w/f L: h)
0.48"ps+0.08"sh (S: nd PA: e/w
L:lb) 0.16"ps+ 0.24"sh+

Conclusion

In conclusion, these parameters have been successfully applied to different gesture studies, such as experiments on deaf orally educated subjects (see Rossini, ***in progress***[8]), and the socio-cultural variation of gesture performance in the Italian area (see Rossini, 2003[9]) . In particular, ***Point of Articulation*** and ***Size*** have been helpful in the determination of E***mphasis*** in gesture (see Rossini, 2003[9]). The measurement of gesture ***Size*** also helped to highlight mobility patterns in deaf signing subjects who acquired Italian as their second language[6].

References

1. Birdwhistell, R. L.: Introduction to Kinesics. U. S. Department of State Foreign Service Institute Washington, D. C. (1952).
2. Condon, W. S., Ogston, W. D.: Sound Film Analysis of Normal and Pathological Behaviour Patterns. Journal of Nervous and Mental Diseases, CXLII (1966) 338-47.
3. Kendon, A.: Some Relationships between Body Motion and Speech. An Analysis of an Example' in Wolfe, A., Pope, B. (Eds.): Studies in Dyadic Communication. Pergamon Press New York (1972).

[5] For the notion of ***gesture phrase***, see Kendon (1986)[5].

[6] See Rossini, ***in progress*** [8].

4. McNeill, D.: Hand and Mind: What Gestures Reveal about Thought. University of Chicago Press, Chicago and London (1992).
5. Kendon, A.: Current Issues in the Study of Gesture. In Nespoulous, J. L., Perron, P., Lecours, A. R. (Eds.): The Biological Foundations of Gestures : Motor and Semiotic Aspects. Erlbaum Hillsdale, New Jersey (1986).
6. Pedelty, L.L.: Gesture in aphasia. Ph.D. diss., Department of Behavioral Sciences, University of Chicago.
7. Magno caldognetto, e. & Poggi, I.: Il sistema prosodico intonativo e l'analisi multimodale del parlato in Poggi, I., Magno Caldognetto,E.: Mani che parlano. Gesti e psicologia della comunicazione. Unipress, Padova (1997).
8. Rossini, N.: Gesture and its Cognitive Origin: Why do We Gesture? Experiment on Hearing and Deaf People (in progress. Ph.D. Thesis).
9. Rossini, N.: Gesture and Sociolinguistics: How about the ***Mano a Borsa***? Paper presented at the 9th International Conference on Cross- Cultural Communication (CSF 2003).

Holistic Body Tracking for Gestural Interfaces

Christian Lange, Thomas Hermann, and Helge Ritter

Neuroinformatics Group, Faculty of Technology, Bielefeld University,
Postfach 100131, D-33501 Bielefeld, Germany
{clange,thermann,helge}@techfak.uni-bielefeld.de
http://www.TechFak.Uni-Bielefeld.DE/ags/ni/index.html

Abstract. In this paper we present an approach to track a moving body in a sequence of camera images by model adaptation. The parameters of a stick figure model are varied by using a stochastic search algorithm. The similarity of rendered model images and camera images of the user are used as quality measure. A refinement of the algorithm is introduced by using combined stereo views and relevance maps to infer responsible joint angles from the difference of successive input images. Finally, the successful application of various versions of the algorithm on sequences of synthetic images is demonstrated.

1 Introduction

In human-human communication gestures are frequently used to simplify communication or to emphasize and disambiguate verbal utterances [1]. While humans are able to interprete gestures from just seeing their communication partner, currently existing gesture recognition systems have to solve the complex problem of (i) understanding a visual scenery, (ii) analyzing the body motion for gestures and (iii) interpreting the gesture correctly in the context of other modalities like speech. Many approaches circumvent (i) by using tracking systems or markers. But sensors that need to be placed at the user are inconvenient. To enable a more natural human-computer interaction, we prefer gesture recognition by only using visual sensors. This leads to the task of extracting gestures from image sequences. An overview of vision-based gesture recognition systems can be found in [2,3]. Most of the existing approaches use a fixed set of predefined gestures that are used like a command language. For natural human computer interaction, such restriction, however, should be avoided.

In general, gestures can be described by a sequence of body postures and each posture can be represented by a vector of joint angles of a stick figure model. From this perspective the first task of gesture recognition is to determine the vector of joint angles for the stick figure model from an image or a sequence of images.

Our system will have two or more cameras to observe the user. An internal model is used to represent and visualize the body posture which is represented by 34 angles. The model is updated about 100 times per frame by moving some

A. Camurri and G. Volpe (Eds.): GW 2003, LNAI 2915, pp. 132–139, 2004.

selected angles until the similarity between the rendered image and the input image reaches a (local) maximum, using a given similarity measure.

Section 2 describes details about the body model as well as our holistic tracking algorithm. Section 3 describes the environment for testing and tuning parameters of the holistic tracking algorithm. Results for different tracking approaches are presented in Section 4. The paper closes with conclusions and prospects for ongoing research.

2 Tracking by Image Adaptation

The problem of body posture recognition can be divided into two different cases, concerning the available context: (a) *single image posture estimation:* given a new image without any context and knowledge about the body posture, and (b) *tracking:* given a series of images and a valid model posture at time t, adapt the model so that it most likely describes the observations in the image at time $t+1$. The problem (a) has to be solved for instance at system start and is computationally much harder than (b), since much less prior knowledge is available. We plan to employ a hierarchical artificial neural network architecture based on work reported in [4] for learning the mapping from images to configurations. However, for a running system, tracking may offer better results in terms of an error measure in configuration space.

The system renders an image of its human model and compares it with the segmented input image. This is illustrated in the box "Adaptation loop" in the signal flow diagram (Fig. 3). To keep the angle vector of the model up to date, the system generates trials for new postures by varying individual angles by adding a Gaussian random number with zero mean and suitably scaled standard deviation. A trial is accepted, if it increases the similarity between the input and the current model image. This similarity is measured by the quality function (see Section 2.4). If performed at a sufficiently high rate, the stochastic optimization steps cause the configuration to follow/imitate the external person' s motions. A major question to be addressed to make this technique efficient for practical situations is deciding which angles should be varied and how far. This issue is taken up in the next section.

2.1 Algorithms for Model Adaptation

The adaptation algorithm changes the angles of the model and computes the difference between the input image and the rendered image of the model. Without any assumption which of the angles should be moved, the algorithm has to select one randomly. However, with such a simple strategy many trials modify "wrong" angles. The stochastic search can be accelerated by using a suitable measure that tells which angle (or angles) should be preferably changed.

One possible measure could be obtained as follows: Find out where in the image changes are located, and then infer from these local image differences to the angles whose modification is likely to cause changes in that region.

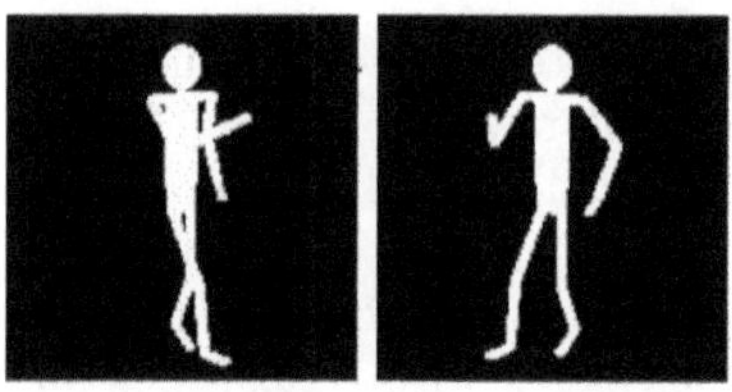
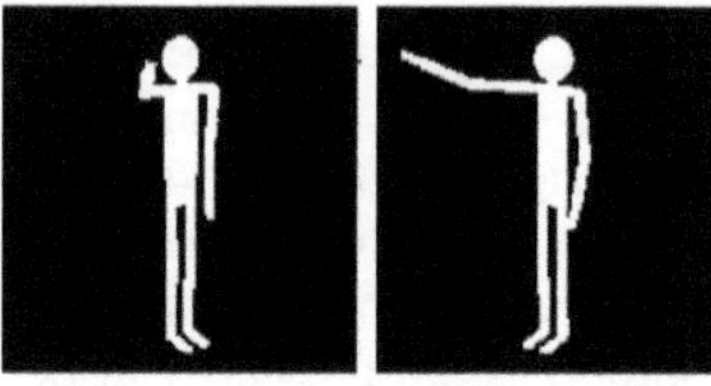

Fig. 1. Two postures of the stick figure (each rendered from two different points of view). Such images are compared to segmented input images to identify the posture of the input figure. Obviously it is helpful to have at least two views of a scene to disambiguate (self-)occlusions.

The ideal algorithm, however, should minimize the distance in configuration space from measuring distances in image space, because the distance in angle space indicates whether the posture of the internal model matches the observed person and the image space is the available input for the system.

2.2 Human Model

For an internal representation of body postures, it is necessary to agree upon a common body model. The more a model respects physical constraints of the human example, the more likely it will behave similar. The simplest model might characterize a human by its hand, shoulder and head coordinates in 3d space. Such a model is computationally not far from what a skin-color-based pattern detection algorithm can provide as its output, but it still is vulnerable to the possibility of representing impossible configurations, for instance a hand-head distance longer than the length of an arm. A much better description can be given by a skeleton model or stick figure model. A posture then is characterized by a vector of joint angles, and physical limitations can be incorporated into angle ranges. Our approach adopts this stick figure model, using length and angle range parameters as described by Badler (see [5] for details). The structure is shown in Figure 2. In practical situations, two different time scales for model adaptation have to be considered: (i) the model dynamics covers the joint angles and time-variant changes of the posture, while (ii) the model parameters cover person specific details like relative arm length or the person's total size. For reason of simplicity, model parameters are considered fixed for the following discussion.

Given a vector $\vec{\Theta}$ of 34 values for the bodies angles (see Fig. 2 for a list), a 3d rendering module based on the GL-library renders a corresponding image of the stick figure. For the further algorithms we binarized those images (see Fig. 1 for some examples). The size of the images was varied between 50×50 and 100×100 during the experiments. First results indicate that the adaptation is less accurate for smaller images, so a trade-off between efficiency and quality must be found. For most of the experiments two different views of the stick figure are used, since this can overcome problems with degeneracy from special single views and therefore leads to better adaptation than a single image. The displacement of the viewpoints is chosen as if the cameras are placed beside a

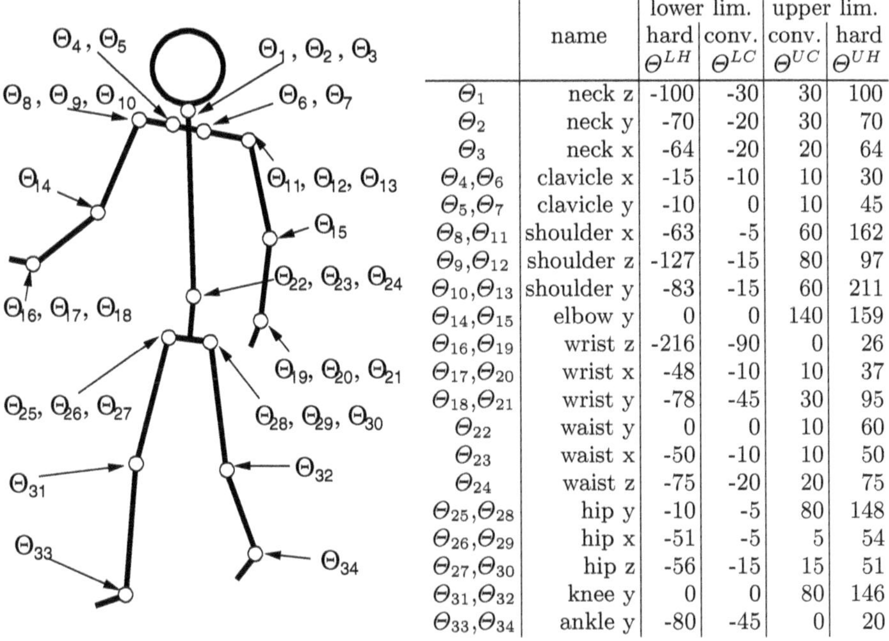

	name	lower lim. hard Θ^{LH}	lower lim. conv. Θ^{LC}	upper lim. conv. Θ^{UC}	upper lim. hard Θ^{UH}
Θ_1	neck z	-100	-30	30	100
Θ_2	neck y	-70	-20	30	70
Θ_3	neck x	-64	-20	20	64
Θ_4,Θ_6	clavicle x	-15	-10	10	30
Θ_5,Θ_7	clavicle y	-10	0	10	45
Θ_8,Θ_{11}	shoulder x	-63	-5	60	162
Θ_9,Θ_{12}	shoulder z	-127	-15	80	97
Θ_{10},Θ_{13}	shoulder y	-83	-15	60	211
Θ_{14},Θ_{15}	elbow y	0	0	140	159
Θ_{16},Θ_{19}	wrist z	-216	-90	0	26
Θ_{17},Θ_{20}	wrist x	-48	-10	10	37
Θ_{18},Θ_{21}	wrist y	-78	-45	30	95
Θ_{22}	waist y	0	0	10	60
Θ_{23}	waist x	-50	-10	10	50
Θ_{24}	waist z	-75	-20	20	75
Θ_{25},Θ_{28}	hip y	-10	-5	80	148
Θ_{26},Θ_{29}	hip x	-51	-5	5	54
Θ_{27},Θ_{30}	hip z	-56	-15	15	51
Θ_{31},Θ_{32}	knee y	0	0	80	146
Θ_{33},Θ_{34}	ankle y	-80	-45	0	20

Fig. 2. Angles and limits of the human model (angles of the left hand side have the same ranges as their counterpart on the right side). The larger ranges of hard limits will never be exceeded by a human, whereas the tighter range of convenience limits can.

projection wall or a big screen, because the real world scenario will be a user in front of such a display as described in Nölker [6].

2.3 Convenience of a Posture

The space of possible configurations is only very sparsely filled with realized gestures for two reasons: firstly angle ranges restrict the postures to a 34-dimensional hypercube. Secondly, even when assuming only 3 different, discrete settings per angle, the resulting 34-dimensional state grid would offer 3^{34} or more than 10^{16} configuration points, of which only a tiny fraction can be generated within human lifetime. Thus the actually occurring configurations are likely to live only on a limited submanifold of much lower dimension.

Our system has some mechanisms to avoid unnatural postures. Firstly, for all angles there are hard limits (Θ^{LH} and Θ^{UH}) that average people can't exceed. Secondly, tighter "convenience limits" (Θ^{LC} and Θ^{UC}) are introduced that most people won't exceed for a long time. The values are listed in Figure 2.

The convenience $\text{conv}(\vec{\Theta})$ of a posture $\vec{\Theta}$ is defined to be 1 if all angles are within their convenience limits, between 0 and 1 if at least one angle is out of its convenience limits and 0 if at least one angle is beyond its hard limits:

$$\mathrm{conv}(\vec{\Theta}) = \prod_{i=1}^{34} \mathrm{conv}_i(\Theta_i) \tag{1}$$

$$\mathrm{conv}_i(\Theta) = \begin{cases} 0 & \forall \ \Theta \notin [\Theta_i^{LH}, \Theta_i^{UH}] \\ \dfrac{\Theta - \Theta_i^{LH}}{\Theta_i^{LC} - \Theta_i^{LH}} & \forall \ \Theta \in [\Theta_i^{LH}, \Theta_i^{LC}[\\ 1 & \forall \ \Theta \in [\Theta_i^{LC}, \Theta_i^{UC}] \\ \dfrac{\Theta_i^{UH} - \Theta}{\Theta_i^{UH} - \Theta_i^{UC}} & \forall \ \Theta \in]\Theta_i^{UC}, \Theta_i^{UH}] \end{cases} . \tag{2}$$

Thus the convenience measure gives higher values for postures that are closer to the normal center position.

2.4 Quality Measure

To decide whether an adaptation step has improved the model posture, the similarity of the two images must be computed. There are different possibilities of quality measures. Since images can be seen as large vectors of pixel values the euclidian distance is one way to compute their difference. Afterwards the reciprocal is computed, because the term "quality" implies to have higher values for more similar images. In case of two views the distances are added before computing the reciprocal:

$$Q = \frac{1}{||\vec{I}_{in}^{l} - \vec{I}_{model}^{l}|| + ||\vec{I}_{in}^{r} - \vec{I}_{model}^{r}||} . \tag{3}$$

The nonlinear transformation/mapping of the functions doesn't bother the adaptation algorithm because it just checks whether a trial increases the quality.

2.5 Adaptation Step Generator

To adapt the internal model to the input, the adaptation step generator randomly selects an angle j, and adds a Gaussian increment to it:

$$\Theta_j := \Theta_j + \mathcal{N}(0, \sigma) \cdot (\Theta_j^{UC} - \Theta_j^{LC}). \tag{4}$$

Then a model image is rendered and the quality of the new posture is measured. If the quality has increased, the step is accepted, otherwise it is rejected and taken back. Steps that lead to a posture with convenience less than 0.8 are also taken back. After trying a fixed number of N_{adapt} steps, the generator stops and should have reached a good approximation to the input image.

The parameters in this algorithm are the number of adaptation steps N_{adapt}, the variance for the Gaussian increment of those steps and the size of the images.

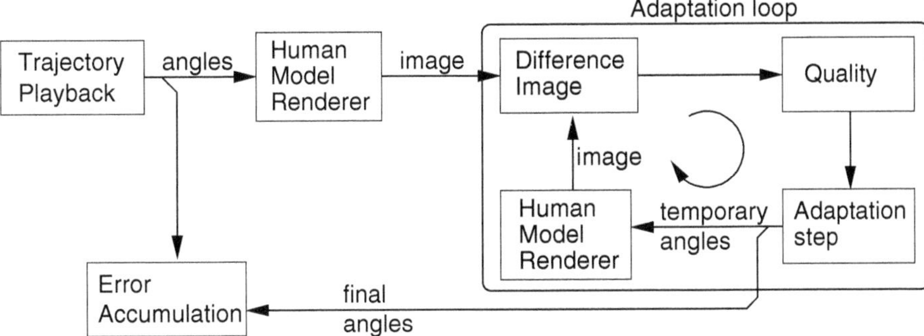

Fig. 3. Signal flow diagram to illustrate the testing environment. For each step of the presented trajectory, the "Adaptation loop"-algorithm tries to adapt the internal model to the input by analyzing the difference image.

3 Testing Environment

To test and optimize the algorithm we use rendered images as input instead of camera images. So we can easily compute the difference between the given angle vector and the adapted one in the model (see Fig. 3). Within this framework, we tried several adaptation algorithms. The distinctive features between the algorithms were the following: the computation of the difference between the images, the decision which angles are changed, the kind of image preprocessing and the size (variance) and number of the random steps.

3.1 Trajectory Generator

The trajectory generator creates a random sequence of postures. For each step it selects some angles at random. Then all of those angles are moved by small Gaussian steps with random size and direction. Steps that would lead to a posture with convenience less than 0.85 are rejected and not recorded.

To compare the different adaptation algorithms, we once generated a trajectory of $N_{traj} = 1000$ steps as a test dataset. The examined algorithm successively gets the images as input and tries to adapt the model to them.

3.2 Comparative Runs

Input trajectory and internal model both are initialized to a central rest position. After every 100 trajectory steps, the model is readjusted to the actual angle values of the input stick figure. Thus each algorithm has up to 10 trials to follow the trajectory. This adjustment is done because we want to compare the capability of following a given trajectory when starting close to it. After a sequence of 100 steps some algorithms are not close to the input anymore. After each step the difference in angle space between the given figure and the model

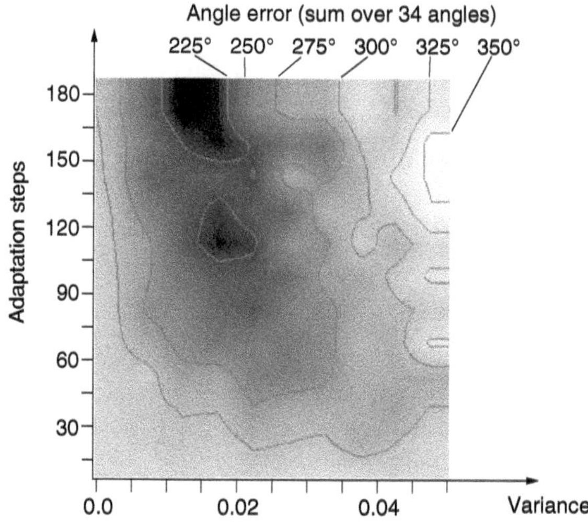

Fig. 4. Error surface with variance and number of adaptation steps as parameters shows that the default algorithm (two views, each 100×100 and unconstrained random selection of varied angle) causes smallest errors when having more than 100 adaptation steps and variance between 0.01 and 0.02.

is recorded as the sum of the deviations of all angles. We denote this error after step i by $E_i = ||\vec{\Theta}_{desired} - \vec{\Theta}_{model}||_1$. The mean error for the dataset

$$\overline{E} = \frac{1}{N_{traj}} \sum_{i=1}^{N_{traj}} E_i \quad (5)$$

is used to compare the different algorithms and parameters.

4 Results

The qualitative observation of the images shows that the adaptation of the model works fine most of the time.

The adaptation algorithm using equidistributed random choices to select an angle is the most simple method, because it needs no heuristic. It will be used as reference to rate the other algorithms. Applying it on several values for jumping variances and different numbers of adaptation-steps gives an error surface (Fig. 4).

The figure shows that the ideal variance is between 0.01 and 0.02 and the algorithm should use more than 100 adaptation steps. These results are obtained by using a stick figure renderer creating images from two views of the person of 100×100 pixels each. Using smaller images reduces the processing time but results in similar shaped error surfaces with a higher total error value. The two-views algorithm is superior to a one-image variant, even when using a higher image resolution such that the processing times become equivalent.

One starting-point for further enhancement should be the quality function. The current version tends to vary very strongly even if the input images differ only slightly. The attempt to smooth the images before computing the difference doesn't solve the problem, but leads to higher errors.

The testing environment not only accumulates the error but also counts how many of the final model steps reduce the error measured as the difference in configuration space. The algorithm using two views of 100×100 pixel each, did 70% steps towards a lower error. All other versions achieved more than 50%.

5 Conclusion

This paper presents an approach for tracking a human model by using an adaptive stochastic search in model space. For investigating and optimizing the performance of the algorithm, we generated test images by using the model itself. The results shed light on important aspects to be addressed in stochastic tracking, namely the trade-off between acceptance rate and search radius (represented by covariance structure of the transition distribution). Optimal values for jumping covariance and number of steps were experimentally derived for different similarity measures and search algorithms.

The next step will be to replace the currently used synthetically rendered input images by camera images. Necessary prerequisite is a segmentation of camera pictures into foreground and background. For the process of image segmentation, we intend to incorporate both knowledge of the model, skin color and the distribution patterns for image regions.

References

1. McNeill, D.: Hand and Mind: What Gestures Reveal about Thought. University of Chicago Press, Chicago (1992)
2. Moeslund, T.B., Granum, E.: A survey of computer vision-based human motion capture. Computer Vision and Image Understanding: CVIU **81** (2001) 231–268
3. Lenman, S., Bretzner, L., Thuresson, B.: Computer vision based recognition of hand gestures for human-computer interaction. Technical Report TRITA-NA-D0209, University of Stockholm, Department of Numerical Analysis and Computer Science, CID, Centre for User Oriented IT Design (2002)
4. Nölker, C., Ritter, H.: Visual recognition of continuous hand postures. IEEE Transactions on Neural Networks, Special Issue Multimedia **13** (2002) 983–994
5. Grosso, M., Quach, R., Otani, E., Zhao, J., Wei, S., Ho, P., Lu, J., Badler, N.: Anthropometry for computer graphics human figures. Technical Report MS-CIS-87-71, University of Pennsylvania, Dept. of Computer and Information Science, Philadelphia, PA (1987)
6. Nölker, C., Ritter, H.: Illumination independent recognition of deictic arm postures. In: Proceedings of the 24th Annual Conference of the IEEE Industrial Electronics Society, Aachen. (1998) 2006–2011

Recovering Articulated Motion with a Hierarchical Factorization Method

Hanning Zhou and Thomas S. Huang

University of Illinois at Urbana-Champaign
405 North Mathews Avenue, Urbana, IL 61801, USA
{hzhou,huang}@ifp.uiuc.edu

Abstract. Recovering articulated human motion is an important task in many applications including surveillance and human-computer interaction. In this paper, a hierarchical factorization method is proposed for recovering articulated human motion (such as hand gesture) from a sequence of images captured under weak perspective projection. It is robust against missing feature points due to self-occlusion, and various observation noises. The accuracy of our algorithm is verified by experiments on synthetic data.

1 Introduction

Hand gesture can be a more natural way for human to interact with computers. For instance, one can use his or her hands to manipulate virtual objects directly in virtual environments. However, capturing human hand motion is inherently difficult due to its articulation and variability. One way to solve the problem is to decompose the hand into linked objects, track them hierarchically and derive the configuration afterwards. This kind of decomposition method was first used in human motion analysis by Webb et al.[15]. Holt and Huang [7] proposed a more general approach which used perspective (instead of orthogonal) projection. They found a closed form solution using an algebraic geometry method [6].

In this paper, a hierarchical factorization method is proposed for recovering articulated hand motion from a image sequence. Both global motion and local articulation are recovered simultaneously.

Section 2 summaries previous work on the factorization methods, especially for multiple object and non-rigid object. Section 3 describes the extension of the factorization method to articulated object. Section 4 introduces the hierarchical factorization method to handle occlusion and feature point correspondences. Section 5 provides experimental results in both quantitative and visual forms. Section 6 concludes with applicable situations, the limitation of this approach and future directions for extension and improvement. The appendix gives some computational details.

A. Camurri and G. Volpe (Eds.): GW 2003, LNAI 2915, pp. 140–151, 2004.

2 Previous Work in Factorization Methods

Factorization-based structure from motion of a single object under orthographic projection was introduced by Tomasi et al. [14], and later extended to para-perspective projection model [12]. A sequential version was proposed in [11]. Attempts were made to generalize the technique for full perspective [13], but due to the inherent nonlinearity of camera projection, some preprocessing (especially depth estimation) is necessary, which leads to a sub-optimal solution.

Costeira et al. proposed an algorithm for multi-body segmentation based on factorization technique [2]. Similar approaches were later developed for linearly moving objects [5] and for deformable objects [1]. Costeira [2] based their segmentation algorithm on a so-called shape interaction matrix $\mathbf{Q}$ (see below). If two features belong to two different objects, their corresponding element in $\mathbf{Q}$ should be zero; otherwise, the value should be non-zero. They then grouped feature points into objects by thresholding and sorting $\mathbf{Q}$. Gear [4] formulated the task as a graph matching problem by placing appropriate weights on the graph edges. Unfortunately, the performance of both techniques degrades quickly when data points are corrupted with noise, because the relationship between data noise and the coefficients of $\mathbf{Q}$ (or weights of the graph edges) is so complicated that it is hard to determine an appropriate threshold. Ichimura [8] proposed an improved algorithm by applying a discriminant criterion for thresholding, but the discriminant analysis is still performed on the elements of $\mathbf{Q}$, resulting a similar degradation with noise. To avoid this problem, Kanatani [9] proposed to work in the original data space by incorporating such techniques as dimension correction (fitting a subspace to a group of points and replacing them with their projections onto the fitted subspace) and model selection (using a geometric information criterion to determine whether two subspaces can be merged). Wu and Huang in [16] proposed a new grouping technique based on orthogonal subspace decomposition, which introduces the shape signal subspace distance matrix $\mathbf{D}$, for shape space grouping, based on a distance measure defined over the subspaces. Robust segmentation results are achieved.

Following the exploration of multi-body factorization, it is natural to extend the multi-body factorization method to articulated objects, which can be treated as a group of linked rigid bodies. This paper mainly discusses the integration of kinematic constraints into the multi-body factorization method.

3 Factorization Method for Articulated Objects

Although the factorization method here can be applied to arbitrary articulated objects, we describe the algorithm using human hand as an example. The kinematic hand model has 21 degrees of freedom (DOF) for joint angles and 6 DOF for global pose. Figure 1 shows a kinematic hand model. The distal interphalangeal (DIP) joint and proximal interphalangeal (PIP) joint each of the four fingers has one DOF and the metacarpophalangeal(MCP) joint has two DOF due to flexion and abduction. The thumb has a different structure from the other four fingers and has five DOF, one for the interphalangeal (IP) joint and two for each of the thumb MCP joint and trapeziometacarpal (TM) joint both due to flexion and abduction. The palm is approximated by a rigid polygon.

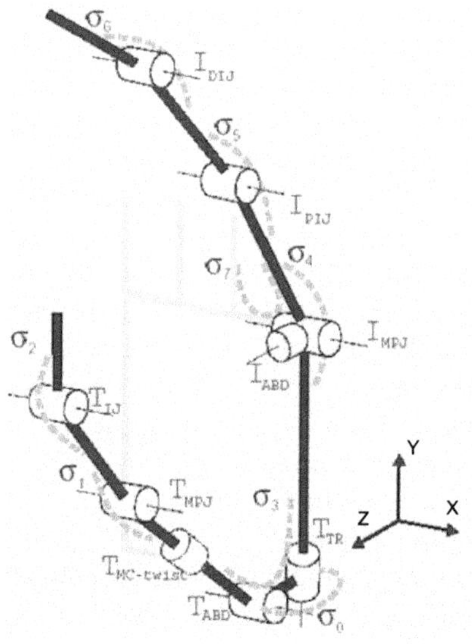

Fig. 1. Kinematic hand model and joint notations

3.1 Rank Constraints for Articulated Motion

According to the kinematic model, we treat the hand as 16 linked objects (15 phalanxes and 1 palm). Upon the F images of hand articulation, we track P^c (at least four non-coplanar) feature points on the c-th object. Given the $P = \sum_{c=1}^{N} P_c$ feature points and their pixel coordinates $(u_{f,p}, v_{f,p})$ in each frame f, we collect all the image measurements into matrix

$$W_{2F\times P} = [\, W^1 \ldots W^N \,] \tag{1}$$

where $W^c_{2F\times P_c} = \frac{1}{\zeta}\begin{bmatrix} u^c_{1,1} & \cdots & u^c_{1,P^c} \\ \vdots & \cdots & \vdots \\ u^c_{F,1} & \cdots & u^c_{F,P^c} \\ v^c_{1,1} & \cdots & v^c_{1,P^c} \\ \vdots & \cdots & \vdots \\ v^c_{F,1} & \cdots & v^c_{F,P^c} \end{bmatrix}$ and ζ is the focal length. Applying the multi-body factorization method [3] without considering the kinematic constraints, W can be factorized as:

$$W_{2F\times P} = \left[M^1 \dots M^N\right] \begin{bmatrix} S^1 & 0 & \dots & \dots & 0 \\ 0 & S^2 & \dots & \dots & 0 \\ 0 & \dots & \ddots & \dots & 0 \\ 0 & \dots & \dots & S^{N-1} & 0 \\ 0 & \dots & \dots & 0 & S^N \end{bmatrix} \tag{2}$$

Where

$$M^c_{2F\times 4} = \left[\begin{array}{c|c} \frac{1}{t^c_{z,1}}\mathbf{i}^c_1 & \frac{t^c_{x,1}}{t^c_{z,1}} \\ \vdots & \vdots \\ \frac{1}{t^c_{z,F}}\mathbf{i}^c_F & \frac{t^c_{x,F}}{t^c_{z,F}} \\ \frac{1}{t^c_{z,1}}\mathbf{j}^c_1 & \frac{t^c_{y,1}}{t^c_{z,1}} \\ \vdots & \vdots \\ \frac{1}{t^c_{z,F}}\mathbf{j}^c_F & \frac{t^c_{y,F}}{t^c_{z,F}} \end{array}\right] \tag{3}$$

consists of

$$\mathbf{i}^c_f = \begin{bmatrix} i^c_{x,f} \\ i^c_{y,f} \\ i^c_{z,f} \end{bmatrix} \tag{4}$$

and

$$\mathbf{j}^c_f = \begin{bmatrix} j^c_{x,f} \\ j^c_{y,f} \\ j^c_{z,f} \end{bmatrix} \tag{5}$$

which are the axes of the camera coordinate frame expressed in the object c's frame. $t^c_{x,f}, t^c_{y,f}, t^c_{z,f}$ represent the translation from the origin of the object c's frame to that of the camera frame.

$$S^c_{4\times P_c} = \begin{bmatrix} x^c_1 & \dots & x^c_{P_c} \\ y^c_1 & \dots & y^c_{P_c} \\ z^c_1 & \dots & z^c_{P_c} \\ 1 & \dots & 1 \end{bmatrix} \tag{6}$$

is the homogeneous 3D coordinates of the feature points in phalanx c's frame.

It is obvious that $W_{2F\times P}$ has at most rank $4N$. The motion estimation problem is formulated as finding the corresponding sequence of rotation-translation matrices $M_f = [R_f \; T_f]$ with respect to the initial pose.

3.2 Solving Motion $[R_f T_f]$ by Factorization

Singular value decomposition is proved to be a robust method for recovering M matrix.

$$W = U\Sigma V^T \tag{7}$$

Take the largest $4N$ singular values in Σ to form diagonal matrix $\hat{\Sigma}$. We define

$$\hat{M} = U\hat{\Sigma}^{\frac{1}{2}} \tag{8}$$

$$\hat{S} = \hat{\Sigma}^{\frac{1}{2}}V^T \tag{9}$$

This factorization is unique up to a nonsingular matrix $A_{4\times4}$, since $MS = (\hat{M}A)(A^{-1}\hat{S})$. For a single rigid body, if we choose the centroid of the object as the origin of the world coordinate, we can solve A using the constrains on M (as given in the appendix). However, in the case of articulated object, different constraints must be applied, which will be discussed in Section 4.

Given $M = \hat{M}A$, the two axes of the camera frame at instant f in object c's frame are given by $\mathbf{i}_f^c$ and $\mathbf{j}_f^c$. And the third axis

$$\mathbf{k}_f^c = \mathbf{i}_f^c \times \mathbf{j}_f^c \tag{10}$$

The Full rotation matrix from object c's frame to the camera frame is

$$R^c_{f\,3\times3} = [\mathbf{i}_f^c\ \mathbf{j}_f^c\ \mathbf{k}_f^c] \tag{11}$$

3.3 Recovering Local and Global Motion

Recovering of 20 joint angles of the hand model equivalent to solve the rotation matrix between adjacent phalanxes. Assuming phalanxes c_1, c_2 are adjacent, we can solve the relative rotation at instant f as $R_f(c_1, c_2) = {R_f^{c_1}}^{-1} R_f^{c_2}$, and recover the joint angles from $R_f(c_1, c_2)$.

If we define the world coordinates as that of the palm (object c_0), the global hand pose is $R_f = R_f^{c_0}$.

4 Hierarchical Factorization

The ideal solution in Section 3 has two difficulties in practice. First it is very hard to track all the feature points reliably and measure their local coordinates, due to self-occlusion and observation noise. The feature points of different objects will be randomly mixed in matrix W. There have been many methods to address this problem as listed in Section 2.

The second difficulty is more specific for articulated object: since we treated each object as independent objects, there is no guarantee that the ends of consecutive objects are linked in the recovered motion. We propose a hierarchical factorization method to solve this problem.

Given F images with $P = \sum_{c=1}^{N} P_c$ feature points and their pixel coordinates $(u_{f,p}, v_{f,p})$ in each frame f, we collect all the image measurements into matrix

$$W_{2F\times P} = \frac{1}{\zeta}\begin{bmatrix} u^c_{1,1} & \cdots & u^c_{1,P^c} \\ \vdots & \cdots & \vdots \\ u^c_{F,1} & \cdots & u^c_{F,P^c} \\ v^c_{1,1} & \cdots & v^c_{1,P^c} \\ \vdots & \cdots & \vdots \\ v^c_{F,1} & \cdots & v^c_{F,P^c} \end{bmatrix} \tag{12}$$

Using the multi-body factorization method in [2], $W_{2F\times P}$ can be factorized as following

$$W_{2F\times P} = \begin{bmatrix} \hat{M}^1 \dots \hat{M}^N \end{bmatrix} \begin{bmatrix} \hat{S}^1 & 0 & \dots & \dots & 0 \\ 0 & \hat{S}^2 & \dots & \dots & 0 \\ 0 & \dots & \ddots & \dots & 0 \\ 0 & \dots & \dots & \hat{S}^{N-1} & 0 \\ 0 & \dots & \dots & 0 & \hat{S}^N \end{bmatrix} \tag{13}$$

Where

$$\hat{M}^c_{2F\times 4} = M^c A^c \tag{14}$$

and

$$\hat{S}^c_{4\times P_c} = (A^c)^{-1} S^c \tag{15}$$

where A_c is a full rank 4×4 matrix.

In the matrix $M_f^{c2} = \begin{bmatrix} \frac{1}{t^{c2}_{z,f}} \mathbf{i}_f^{c2} & \frac{t^{c2}_{x,f}}{t^{c2}_{z,f}} \\ \frac{1}{t^{c2}_{z,f}} \mathbf{j}_f^{c2} & \frac{t^{c2}_{y,f}}{t^{c2}_{z,f}} \end{bmatrix}$, we have

$$\mathbf{i}_f^{c_2} \perp \mathbf{j}_f^{c_2} \tag{16}$$

$$|\mathbf{i}_f^{c_2}| = 1 \tag{17}$$

$$|\mathbf{j}_f^{c_2}| = 1 \tag{18}$$

Denote the 4×4 matrix A^c as the concatenation of two blocks.

$$A^c = [A^c_R | \mathbf{a}^c_t] \tag{19}$$

A^c_R is the first 4×3 submatrix related to rotational component. And $\mathbf{a}^c_t$ is a 4×1 vector related to translations. From Equation (16)(17)(18), A^c_R can be solved (the details are given in the appendix). To recover $\mathbf{a}^c_t$, [2] used the centroid of the feature points on object c, that is, the average of each row of W^c:

$$\bar{\mathbf{w}^c} \equiv \frac{1}{P^c} \sum_{p=1}^{P^c} \begin{bmatrix} u^c_{1,p} \\ \vdots \\ v^c_{F,p} \end{bmatrix} = [\hat{M} A^c_R | \hat{M} \mathbf{a}^c_t] \begin{bmatrix} \bar{\mathbf{s}^c} \\ 1 \end{bmatrix} \tag{20}$$

where $\bar{\mathbf{s}^c} = \frac{1}{P^c} \sum_{p=1}^{P^c} \begin{bmatrix} x^c_p \\ y^c_p \\ z^c_p \\ 1 \end{bmatrix}$ is the 3D centroid of the object c. The traditional method [2] assumes the centroid of the object to be the origin of the object, that is $\bar{\mathbf{s}^c} = 0$. Then $\bar{\mathbf{w}^c} = \hat{M}^c \mathbf{a}^c_t$ and $\mathbf{a}^c_t$ is solved to be $\mathbf{a}^c_t = (\hat{M^c}^T \hat{M})^{-1} \hat{M^c}^T \bar{\mathbf{w}^c} = \Sigma^{c-\frac{1}{2}} U^{cT} \bar{\mathbf{w}^c}$. However, if we solve $\mathbf{a}^c_t$ this way, the results will usually violate the linked-ends constraints.

Step(1): Solving motion of the palm as the root object
Track at least 4 feature points in general position on the palm; solving transformation matrix for palm M^1 as described in Section 3
Step(2): Solving motion of the five proximal phalanxes
Based on M^1, we can solve the M matrices for the five proximal phalanxes (the phalanxes attached to the palm).
Step(3): Solving the motion of the five medial phalanxes (the second row)
Step(4): Solving the motion of the five distal phalanxes (on the third row)

Fig. 2. The hierarchical factorization algorithm

To solve this problem, we propose the hierarchical factorization algorithm for solving A^c ($c = 1 \dots N$) as shown in Figure 2. In each step, the solution for A^c_R is still the same as the multi-body factorization method described in the appendix, but for $\mathbf{a}^c_t$, we introduce the translational constraint as shown in Figure 3.

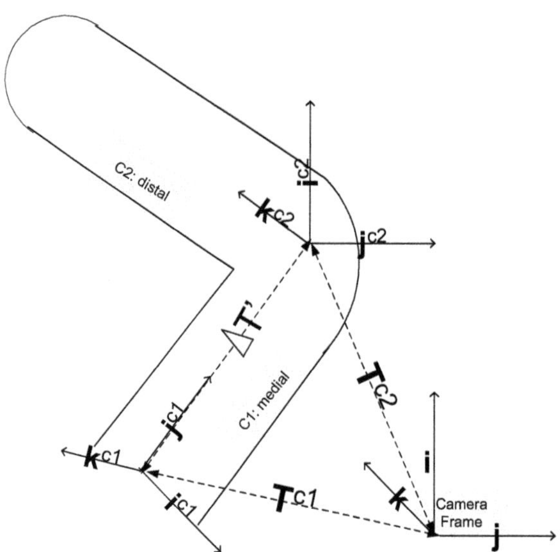

Fig. 3. An example of two linked phalanxes c_1 and c_2 (the medial phalanx and the distal phalanx) and the translational relation between their local coordinates

Table 1 lists the notations used in Figure 3. As M^{c_1} is solved from the previous step, we can express the translational constraint due to the linked-ends of c_1 and c_2 as:

$$\Delta T_f = \begin{bmatrix} t^{c_1}_{x,f} - t^{c_2}_{x,f} \\ t^{c_1}_{y,f} - t^{c_2}_{y,f} \\ t^{c_1}_{z,f} - t^{c_2}_{z,f} \end{bmatrix} \tag{21}$$

where $f = 1 \dots F$.

Table 1. Notations used in Figure 3

notation	physical meaning
c_1	medial phalanx
c_2	distal phalanx
ΔT	translation between the local coordinates of c_1 and c_2 in the camera frame
$\Delta T'$	translation between the local coordinates of c_1 and c_2 in sub_object c_1's frame

According to the kinematic hand model

$$\Delta T' = \begin{bmatrix} 0 \\ l^{c_1} \\ 0 \end{bmatrix} \tag{22}$$

where l^{c_1} is the length of c_1.

$$\Delta T_f = \left[\mathbf{i}_f^{c_1}\ \mathbf{j}_f^{c_1}\ \mathbf{k}_f^{c_1}\right] \Delta T' \tag{23}$$

where $\mathbf{i}, \mathbf{j}$ and $\mathbf{k}$ are defined in Equation (4), (5) and (10). Therefore, $[t_{x,f}^{c_2}\ t_{y,f}^{c_2}\ t_{z,f}^{c_2}]^T$ satisfies

$$\begin{bmatrix} t_{x,f}^{c_1} \\ t_{y,f}^{c_1} \\ t_{z,f}^{c_1} \end{bmatrix} = \left[\mathbf{i}_f^{c_1}\ \mathbf{j}_f^{c_1}\ \mathbf{k}_f^{c_1}\right] \begin{bmatrix} 0 \\ l^{c_1} \\ 0 \end{bmatrix} \tag{24}$$

From Equation (24), we obtain the origin of object c's local coordinates, which is not the centroid of the feature points, but the joint where current object is linked with the previous one. We take the ratio between their x-y coordinates and the coordinates and stack them into vector $\mathbf{t}^c = \begin{bmatrix} \frac{t_{x,1}}{t_{z,1}} \\ \vdots \\ \frac{t_{x,F}}{t_{z,F}} \\ \frac{t_{y,1}}{t_{z,1}} \\ \vdots \\ \frac{t_{y,F}}{t_{z,F}} \end{bmatrix}$, which *is* the fourth column of M^c. Therefore $\hat{M}\mathbf{a}_t^c = \mathbf{t}$ and $\mathbf{a}_t^c$ can be solved as:

$$\mathbf{a}_t^c = (\hat{M^c}^T \hat{M^c})^{-1} \hat{M^c}^T \mathbf{t}^c = \Sigma^{c-\frac{1}{2}} U^{cT} \mathbf{t}^c \tag{25}$$

5 Experimental Results

Figure 4 shows a synthetic sequence of hand motion rendered with OpenGL. The joint angle data is collected with $CyberGlove^{TM}$.

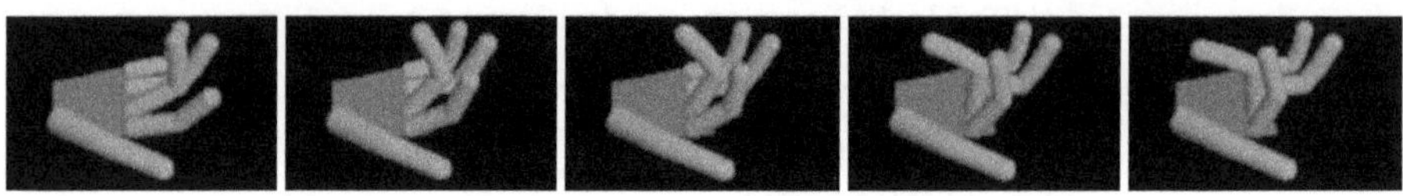

Fig. 4. Synthetic image sequence of hand motion

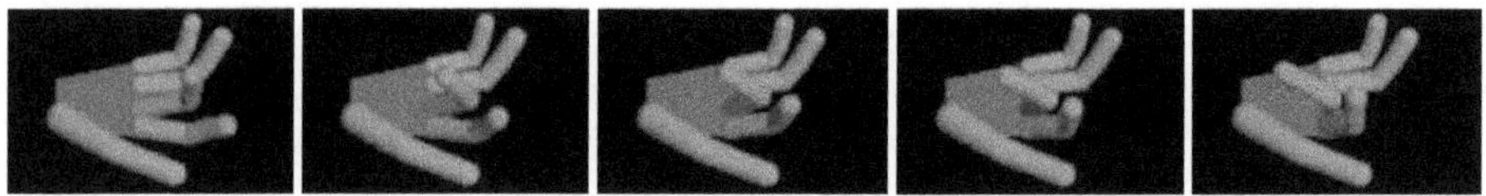

Fig. 5. Hand motion recovered with the hierarchical factorization method

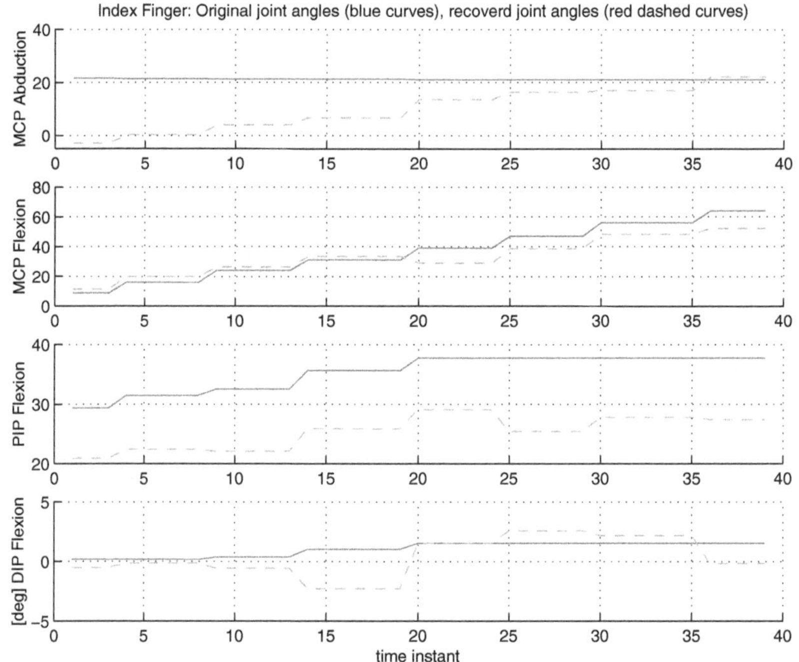

Fig. 6. Original joint angles and joint angles recovered with hierarchical factorization method

Figure 5 shows Hand motion recovered with hierarchical factorization method, rendered from the same view point. It can be seen that the metacarpophalangeal (MCP) abduction angle is a bit off, which also shows in the first subplot in Figure 6.

Finger 6 shows the comparison between the original joint angles and the recovered joint angles of the index finger.

The blue curves show the original joints angles over 38 frames. The red curves show the recovered joint angles. The 4 subplots corresponds to 4 angles, i.e. MCP Abduction (MCPA), MCP Flexion (MCPF), PIP Flexion (PIPF) and DIP Flexion (DIPF) respectively, at 3 joints of the index finger. All the values shown in the plots are in degree angle.

Table 2. RMSE, std, range of motion(ROM) and rRMSE between the ground truth and recovered joint angles

joint angle	RMSE	std	ROM	rRMSE
MCPA	2.186	7.727	0.635	344.156%
MCPF	1.125	3.480	55.144	2.040%
PIPF	1.601	1.121	8.358	19.159%
DIPF	0.247	1.054	1.376	17.956%

In Table 2, RMSE denotes the rooted mean square error between the ground truth joint angles and the recovered ones, the mean is taken across all the frames within the test sequence. And std denotes the standard deviation of the absolute difference between the ground truth joint angles and the recovered ones, taken across all the frames within the test sequence. ROM denotes the range of motion, that is, the difference between the joint angle in the first frame and that in the last frame. rRMSE is the ratio between RMSE and ROM. As the table shows, the results for MCPF are the best, while the relative MSE for MCPA is the largest among all joint angles, which shows that most of the noise is in MCPA and the noise is changing dramatically with the motion. This is due to the fact that most sample points are chosen at similar relative depth. Nearly coplanar structure matrix will cause rank deficiency in singular value decomposition and thus cause majority of the noise in z direction: the main direction of MCPA.

As for PIPF, the MSE is 1.601, the standard deviation of the difference is very small (only 1.121), which shows there is an almost constant offset between the original angle and recovered angle. This suggests that the noise is global and irrelevant to the particular motion. By increasing the feature points on the medial and proximal phalanxes, this error can be reduced. For DIPF, both ROM and MSE are very small.

6 Conclusions

In this paper, we propose a hierarchical factorization method for recovering the articulated human motion. The kinematical constraints are utilized to grantee the ends of consecutive objects are linked. The limitation for this algorithm is that at least 4 non-coplanar feature points on the palm must be tracked reliably in order to recover the global pose and initiate the hierarchical algorithm. After factorization-based segmentation, labelling of each object is also nontrivial.

In the future we will concentrate on integrate more constraints into the factorization method. For example, in each proximal interphalangeal (PIP) joint and each distal interphalangeal (DIP) joint, there are only 1 DOF in the rotation matrix R, while for MCP joints, there are only 2 DOF in R. By projecting the corresponding rotation matrix the subspace of SO(1) and SO(2) [10], we can get more accurate recovering results.

References

1. C. Bregler, A. Hertzmann, and H. Biermann. Recovering non-rigid 3D shape from image streams. In *Proc. IEEE Conf. on Computer Vision and Pattern Recognition*, pages 690–696, Hilton Head Island, SC, June 2000.
2. J. Costeira and T. Kanade. A multibody factorization method for independently moving objects. *International Journal of Computer Vision*, 29:159–179, 1998.
3. Joao Costeira and Takeo Kanade. A multibody factorization method for motion analysis. Technical Report CMU-CS-TR-94-220, Computer Science Department, Carnegie Mellon University, Pittsburgh, PA, September 1994.
4. C. Gear. Multibody grouping from motion images. *International Journal of Computer Vision*, 29:133–150, 1998.
5. M. Han and T. Kanade. Reconstruction of a scene with multiple linearly moving objects. In *Proc. IEEE Conf. on Computer Vision and Pattern Recognition*, volume II, pages 542–549, Hilton Head Island, SC, June 2000.
6. R. J. Holt and T. S. Huang. Algebraic methods for image processing and computer vision. *IEEE Transactions on Image Processing*, 5:976–986, 1996.
7. R. J. Holt, T. S. Huang, A. N. Netravali, and R. J. Qian. Determining articulated motion from perspective views: A decomposition approach. *Pattern Recognition*, 30:1435–1449, 1997.
8. N. Ichimura. Motion segmentation based on factorization method and discriminant criterion. In *Proc. IEEE International Conference on Computer Vision*, pages 600–605, Greece, Sept. 1999.
9. K. Kanatani. Motion segmentation by subspace separation and model selection. In *Proc. IEEE International Conference on Computer Vision*, Vancouver, Canada, July 2001.
10. Yi Ma, Jana Kosecka, Stefano Soatto, and Shankar Sastry. *An Invitation to 3-D Vision.* Springer-Verlag, New York, 2002.
11. T. Morita and T. Kanade. A sequential factorization method for recovering shape and motion from image streams. *IEEE Transactions on Pattern Analysis and Machine Intelligence*, 19:858–867, 1997.
12. C. Poelman and T. Kanade. A paraperspective factorization method for shape and motion recovery. *IEEE Transactions on Pattern Analysis and Machine Intelligence*, 19:206–218, 1997.
13. P. Sturm and B. Triggs. A factorization based algorithm for multi-image projective structure and motion. In *Proc. European Conference on Computer Vision*, volume II, pages 709–720, 1996.
14. C. Tomasi and T. Kanade. Shape and motion from image streams under orthography – a factorized method. *International Journal of Computer Vision*, 9:137–154, 1992.
15. J. A. Webb and J. K. Aggarwal. Structure from motion of rigid and jointed objects. *Artificial Intelligence*, 19:107–130, 1982.
16. Y. Wu, Z. Zhang, T. S. Huang, and J. Y. Lin. Multibody grouping via orthogonal subspace decomposition. In *IEEE Conf. on Computer Vision and Pattern Recognition*, volume II, pages 252–257, Kauai, Hawaii, Dec 2001.

Appendix: Solving A_R^c

The following equations hold for all c, so the superscript c are omitted.

Define

$$\begin{bmatrix} l_1 & l_2 & l_3 \\ l_2 & l_4 & l_5 \\ l_3 & l_5 & l_6 \end{bmatrix} = L = {A_R}^T A_R \tag{26}$$

$$m_{1,f} = [\hat{M}(1,1)_f \hat{M}(1,2)_f \hat{M}(1,3)_f] \tag{27}$$

$$m_{2,f} = [\hat{M}(2,1)_f \hat{M}(2,2)_f \hat{M}(2,3)_f] \tag{28}$$

According to Equation (16) (17)(18), we have

$$\hat{m}_{1,f}^T \ L\hat{m}_{2,f} = 0 \tag{29}$$

$$\hat{m}_{1,f}^T \ L\hat{m}_{1,f} = \frac{1}{t_z} \tag{30}$$

$$\hat{m}_{2,f}^T \ L\hat{m}_{2,f} = \frac{1}{t_z} \tag{31}$$

According to [11], for each c, there are $3 \times F$ equations and they can be rewritten as

$$G\mathbf{l} = \mathbf{c} \tag{32}$$

where

$$G = \begin{bmatrix} g(m_{1,1}, m_{1,1}) \\ \vdots \\ g(m_{1,F}, m_{1,F}) \\ g(m_{2,1}, m_{2,1}) \\ \vdots \\ g(m_{2,F}, m_{2,F}) \\ g(m_{1,1}, m_{2,1}) \\ \vdots \\ g(m_{1,F}, m_{2,F}) \end{bmatrix}, \ \mathbf{l} = \begin{bmatrix} l_1 \\ \vdots \\ l_6 \end{bmatrix} \tag{33}$$

$$\mathbf{c}^T = [\underbrace{1 \ \dots \ \dots \ \dots \ 1}_{2F} \ \underbrace{0 \dots \ 0}_{F}]^T \tag{34}$$

and

$$g(a,b) = [a_1 b_1 \ 2a_1 b_2 \ 2a_1 b_3 \ a_2 b_2 \ 2a_2 b_3 \ a_3 b_3] \tag{35}$$

Using Least Square Method, $\mathbf{l}$ can be solved

$$\mathbf{l} = (G^T \ G)^{-1} G^T \mathbf{c} \tag{36}$$

The eigen-decomposition of matrix L gives matrix A_R.

An Experimental Comparison of Trajectory-Based and History-Based Representation for Gesture Recognition

Kenny Morrison and Stephen J. McKenna

Division of Applied Computing
University of Dundee
Dundee DD1 4HN, Scotland
{kmorrison,stephen}@computing.dundee.ac.uk
http://www.computing.dundee.ac.uk

Abstract. Automatic visual recognition of gestures can be performed using either a trajectory-based or a history-based representation. The former characterises the gesture using 2D trajectories of the hands. The latter summarises image sequences using values computed from individual pixel histories. A direct experimental comparison of these two approaches is presented using skin colour as a common visual cue and recognition methods based on hidden Markov models, moment features and normalised template matching. Skin history images are proposed as a useful history-based representation. Results are reported on a database of sixty gestures and the relative advantages and disadvantages of the different methods are highlighted.

1 Introduction

This paper compares two very different types of visual representation useful for real-time recognition of human gestures and actions. These will be refered to here as *trajectory-based* and *history-based* representations. These two types of representation result in quite different approaches to recognition. Each has its strengths and weaknesses. The approaches are somewhat complementary and can be combined to form a more effective overall system.

A *trajectory-based representation* relies on a tracking system to provide temporal feature trajectories that summarise the movement of the body parts of interest. A simple example of such a trajectory might consist of the image coordinates of the centroids of the hands in each image of a sequence. Recognition based on such trajectories is typically performed using hidden Markov models (HMMs). A *history-based representation* takes a quite different approach. It summarises an image sequence using values computed from pixel histories. Recognition based on history images has typically been performed by statistical matching of Hu moment features computed from the history images, although other matching algorithms are also applicable.

Results of experiments are reported here that characterise the recognition performance resulting from these two different approaches to representation.

A. Camurri and G. Volpe (Eds.): GW 2003, LNAI 2915, pp. 152–163, 2004.

This is an attempt to directly compare them under identical conditions using the same data sets and visual cues. Comparisons of this kind are badly needed in the literature in order to enhance understanding of the different approaches and to highlight their strengths and weaknesses.

The task here is recognition of temporal gestures as opposed to the recognition of static postures of the hands. The gestures are performed with the user oriented towards the camera so the task is view-specific. Furthermore, recognition is based upon a single monocular, colour view. All the methods reported here use representations based on skin colour detection. A preprocessing step common to all the methods provides a classification of each pixel in each image as skin or non-skin. While other visual cues such as temporal differencing [1,2], optical flow [3], shape (e.g. [4]) and combinations of these (e.g. [5]) have been used in this context, this comparison focuses on the use of skin colour cues. Skin colour detection provides a useful representation of the extent of the head and hands in each frame as long as the illumination conditions are as expected and the torso and arms are clothed.

History-based representation has been used previously in the form of motion energy and motion history images. In contrast, the history-based representation used in the experiments reported here is computed from the skin detection. This novel representation will be refered to as a *skin history image* (SHI). History images have previously been matched using Hu's moment invariants [1]. Since Hu's invariants resulted in disappointing results on the gesture sequences considered here, several alternative matching algorithms were also evaluated. In particular, central moments, scale-normalised moments and direct image-based matching of history images were used. Significantly reduced error rates were thus achieved.

Several reviews concerned with analysis and recognition of human gesture and motion are available [6,7,8]. Some previous studies have compared recognition engines for gesture recognition using fixed sequences of feature vectors [9]. Others have compared different trajectory-based feature vectors computed from the output of a tracking system [10,11]. The choice of representation used as input to the recognition engine is likely to have a greater effect on performance than the particular choice of recognition algorithm. Furthermore, representations with contrasting properties are likely to give more orthogonal failure modes. The fusion of recognition schemes based on diverse representations is thus likely to result in further reductions in error.

The remainder of this paper is structured as follows. Section 2 describes the skin detection algorithm used. Sections 3 and 4 describe the history-based and trajectory-based recognition schemes. Section 5 reports experimental results and the final section draws conclusions.

2 Skin Detection

Each of the recognition schemes evaluated here used a common preprocessing step to provide a classification of each pixel in each image as skin or non-skin based on its colour and local connectivity. A skin colour probability density function, $p(\mathbf{x})$, was estimated in the form of a histogram [12] from manually cropped skin regions taken under similar illumination conditions. Histograms were estimated in the two-dimensional chromatic space obtained by normalising the red (R) and green (G) components with respect to intensity. Let $C(x, y, t)$ be a chromatic image sequence. A binary image sequence indicating skin coloured pixels, $B(x, y, t)$ can be computed using Equation (1) where T_p is a suitable threshold.

$$B(x, y, t) = \begin{cases} 1 \text{ if } p(C(x, y, t)) > T_p \\ 0 \text{ otherwise} \end{cases} \tag{1}$$

A connected components algorithm was applied to each image in the sequence $B(x, y, t)$. Connected components containing fewer than T_a pixels were removed in order to reduce the effects of noise and enable subsequent processing to focus on the most significant skin-coloured regions. This yielded a binary sequence $S(x, y, t)$ indicating probable skin regions. This is not necessarily the optimal method for segmenting skin regions: many alternative algorithms have been suggested (e.g. [13,14,15,16,17]). It does, however, provide a useful common preprocessing step from which to compute and compare trajectory-based and history-based representations. An example of skin detection is shown in Fig. 1.

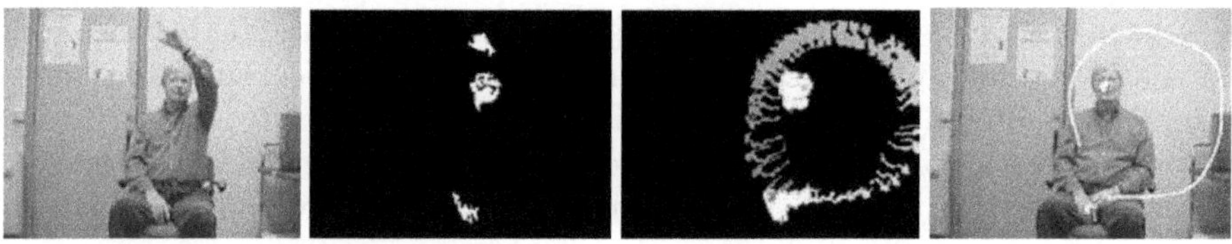

Fig. 1. From left to right: (a) an image from a gesture sequence, (b) the skin regions detected, (c) the skin history image computed from the entire gesture sequence, and (d) the corresponding trajectories.

3 History-Based Recognition

3.1 Skin History Images

In a history image, pixel intensity is a function of the temporal history at that pixel. In particular, a skin history image, H_τ, encodes information about the history of skin colour at each pixel. Somewhat analagously to the motion history image of Bobick and Davis [1], an SHI is defined using a replacement and decay operator:

$$H_\tau(x, y, t) = \begin{cases} \tau & \text{if } S(x, y, t) = 1 \\ \max(0, \Delta) & \text{otherwise} \end{cases} \tag{2}$$

where $\Delta = H_\tau(x, y, t - 1) - 1$. This results in a scalar-valued image in which pixels that are currently skin coloured are brightest, pixels that have not been skin coloured for some time are darker and pixels that have never been skin coloured during the last τ frames are black (zero-valued). An example of a skin history image (SHI) is shown in Fig. 1. Whereas the temporal templates proposed by Bobick and Davis [1] used motion features as components of the templates, an SHI implicitly captures information about the motion of the skin coloured pixels that are of interest here. This motion is well represented by the SHI provided that the sequence does not involve significant motion self-occlusion of skin-coloured regions.

3.2 Recognition

A history image representation summarises a sequence as a single temporal template so that recognition becomes a process of matching templates. An efficient matching algorithm with appropriate invariance properties is needed. Bobick and Davis [18,19,20,21,22] used Hu's seven moment invariants [23] to characterise each history image. Statistical matching was then performed on these invariants. Here, several alternative matching algorithms based on other moment invariants and direct template matching are compared.

Moment Invariants. For the sake of completeness, the invariant moment features used will be defined. The two-dimensional $(p+q)^{th}$ order moments of a discrete image $I(x,y)$ are defined as

$$m_{p,q} = \sum_{x,y} x^p y^q I(x,y) \; p,q = 0,1,2,\ldots \tag{3}$$

These moments are not invariant with respect to translation, rotation or scale. The *central moments* which are translation invariant are defined as

$$\nu_{p,q} = \sum_{x,y} x^p y^q I(x+x_0, y+y_0) \; p,q = 0,1,2,\ldots \tag{4}$$

where (x_0, y_0) are the coordinates of the centroid, given by

$$x_0 = \frac{m_{1,0}}{m_{0,0}} \text{ and } y_0 = \frac{m_{0,1}}{m_{0,0}} \tag{5}$$

Invariance to both translation and scale can be obtained by computing the *scale normalised moments* as

$$\mu_{p,q} = \frac{\nu_{p,q}}{m_{0,0}^{1+(p+q)/2}} \; p,q = 0,1,2,\ldots \tag{6}$$

Hu's moment invariants, originally proposed in 1962 [23] and reformulated by Li [24], exhibit translation, rotation and scale invariance. They are seven functions of the second and third order moments and are given in the Appendix.

Since gestures are oriented consistently (assuming an upright camera and an upright person) rotation invariance is in fact likely to reduce the discriminatory ability of the features. Furthermore, if the distance from the camera to the person is approximately constant then scale invariance can also reduce discrimination. Whether central moments, scale normalised moments or Hu's moment invariants are most effective will therefore depend upon the nature of the gesture sequences. The performance resulting from each of these features sets was evaluated. Similarly to Bobick and Davis' [18] use of Hu's moment invariants, a Mahalanobis distance (based on a diagonal covariance matrix) was used to perform matching.

Normalised Template Matching. Rather than base matching on moment features, it is feasible to perform direct image-based template matching in order to perform recognition. Translation invariance is obtained by translating each template's origin to its centroid (Equation (5)). Invariance to certain amounts of scaling and rotation can be obtained by producing multiple templates that are scaled and rotated versions of the original and using these during matching as well. After this normalisation with respect to one or more of translation, scaling and rotation, templates can be compared directly by pixel-wise comparisons on their overlap. Standard measures for template matching are the mean squared difference (MSD), correlation coefficient (CC) and mean absolute difference (MAD). A nearest neighbour classifier was used to perform recognition based on each of these measures. Here performace using these three measures with translation invariant (centroid normalised) templates is reported.

4 Trajectory-Based Recognition

4.1 Skin Region Trajectories

Several methods that use skin colour as a cue for locating and tracking hands and head have been proposed (see e.g. [14,25,26,27,28]). In general their task is to consistently locate and associate head and hand regions over time. Difficulties arise when the number of objects in the scene varies due for example to occlusion. Grouping errors due to noise and cue ambiguity cause further problems.

Some of the gesture sequences considered here are of one-handed gestures and only a single hand is in the field of view. Other sequences contain both the head and hands in the field of view, especially in the case of two-handed gestures.

In the case of a single hand sequence, the data association problem is trivial since there is only one object, although grouping errors can still give rise to errors. The tracker used here simply locates and tracks the largest connected component in $S(x, y, t)$. In the case of head-hand sequences, the head and hands were located and identified using heuristics based on their size and initial relative positions. The head was assumed to be visible at all times while the hands were allowed to disappear due to occlusion. The head and hands were tracked using the connected component grouping and time-symmetric matching. A persistence parameter (set to 5 frames) was used to allow tracking with temporary loss of image evidence. Additionally, in order to combat noise and false hand/head assignment, each region was assigned an age attribute that was incremented after every frame. A region was not recognised until it had been successfully tracked for 5 frames [29].

The system partially addresses situations in which, temporarily, a hand cannot be located due to head-hand occlusion, hand-hand occlusion or occlusion by another object. It does this through a combination of interpolation and extrapolation. During occlusion, missing data are estimated using a constant velocity dynamic model. Once the occlusion event has finished and the hand is identified again, missing data are linearly interpolated backwards in time. The system thus revises its estimate of the hand's recent trajectory in the renewed track. At any frame, the best available track estimates are used to compute features for recognition. Interpolated data are used in precedence to extrapolated data.

Previously published experiments have compared seven different translation-invariant feature vectors derived from this tracker's output in terms of recognition accuracy [11]. The most effective used the coordinates of the hand centroid(s) in Cartesian coordinates normalised for translation invariance. This normalisation was performed with respect to the endpoint of the gesture sequence. Example extracted hand trajectories are shown in Fig. 1.

4.2 Recognition

Hidden Markov models (HMMs) and related models have been widely used for recognition of human action and gesture using trajectory-based representation (e.g. [30,31,32,33,34,35,36]). There is a comprehensive literature on hidden Markov models and the algorithms involved in their use, Rabiner's tutorial [37] being among the most cited. HMMs provide dynamic time-warping within a probabilistic framework.

HMMs with left-right topology and shared dummy start and end states were used. In particular, a 5-state model with no skip transitions was used for each gesture. Gaussian hidden states were used, i.e. each hidden state generated normally distributed observations according to its associated mean and covariance matrix. Full covariance matrices were not used because they could not be reliably estimated from the small numbers of examples. Instead, diagonal co-variance matrices were used for each hidden state. HMMs were initialised by repeated Viterbi alignment. This provided initial estimates for the various parameters of the HMM, i.e. the variances associated with each hidden state and the probabilities of making transitions between these states. These initial estimates were then refined using Baum-Welch re-estimation, computing the probability of being in a state at each frame using the forward-backward algorithm. Given initial values, the Baum-Welch algorithm iteratively refines these values so as to maximise the likelihood of the HMM given the example observation sequences. In other words, it provides a way to learn the model from the examples. Recognition was performed using the Viterbi algorithm to estimate maximum likelihood state sequences. The most likely paths through the HMMs for each gesture can be used to decide which, if any, of the gestures occurred in the observed sequence. HTK was used to implement HMM training and recognition [38].

5 Experiments

5.1 Gesture Sequences

Gesture recognition systems typically attempt to recognise different people performing a fixed set of pre-specified gestures, perhaps a small subset of gestures from a sign language for example. An alternative approach explored here is to allow each user to specify his or her own gesture vocabulary. This has the advantages that the gestures are likely to be comfortable for the user to perform and easy for them to remember. Furthermore, it increases accessibility to the technology since even users with relatively severe motor impairment are typically able to define and repeat their own, perhaps idiosyncratic, gestures. The constraint imposed upon the gesture recognition system by this approach is that it must be capable of learning gesture models from only a few examples. This is because each user must supply all the training examples and after more than about ten examples per gesture this process becomes tedious.

Six subjects (A-F) were recorded performing ten examples of each of ten gestures of their own devising. These 600 gesture sequences totalled approximately 30,000 images. Fig. 2 shows the skin history images computed from one example sequence of each of the sixty gestures. Three of the subjects (D-F) had a motor disability. Three of the subjects opted for one-handed gestures and three for at least some two-handed gestures.

5.2 Recognition Results

The examples of each gesture g were allocated at random to two disjoint sets, S_1^g and S_2^g, each consisting of five examples. Recognition rates were estimated as follows. Firstly, models were computed using the sets S_1^g and these models were used to recognise the gestures in S_2^g. Secondly, models were computed using the sets S_2^g and used to recognise the gestures in S_1^g. The recognition rates for these two experiments were then averaged together. The results are summarised in Table 1. They should be interpreted as estimates of the expected recognition performance when five examples of each of ten gestures are available for training the recognition system.

The history-based approach achieved consistently higher recognition accuracy using template matching than when moment features were used. Overall, template matching based on mean absolute difference performed best in terms

Table 1. Recognition rates (%ages) using trajectories with hidden Markov models (HMM) and skin history images with central moments (C-Mom), scale-normalised moments (S-Mom), Hu moments (H-Mom), mean absolute difference (MAD), mean squared difference (MSD) and correlation coefficient (CC).

Gesture Type	Subject	Trajectories	Skin History Images					
		HMM	C-Mom	S-Mom	H-Mom	MAD	MSD	CC
One-handed	A	99	68	55	35	91	88	87
	B	95	58	55	48	96	96	96
	C	85	64	67	42	91	82	78
Two-handed	D	84	49	33	27	70	67	74
	E	69	73	72	48	90	91	77
	F	64	92	90	51	98	100	99
	Mean	82.7	67.3	62	41.8	89.3	87.3	85.2

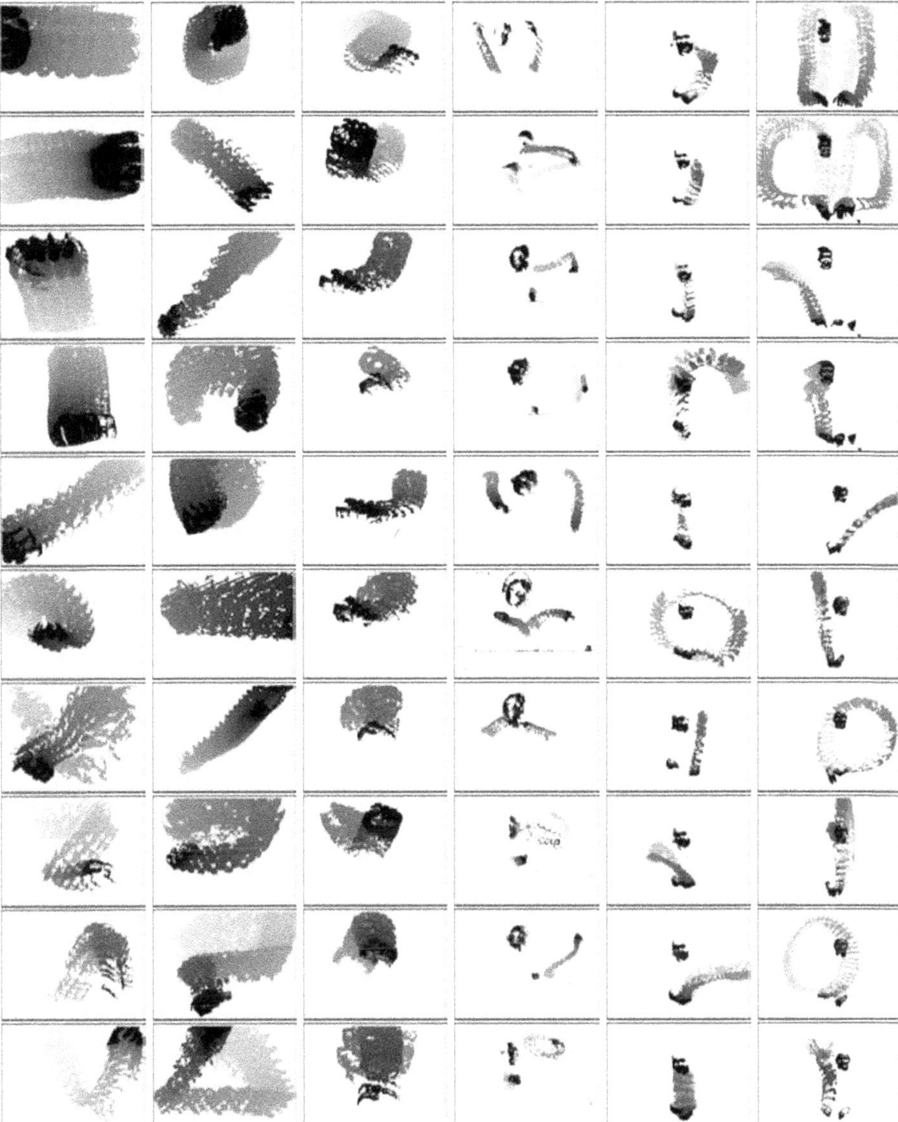

Fig. 2. Skin history images (SHIs) computed from sixty of the gesture sequences. These SHIs have been inverted: the darker a pixel, the more recent the occurence of skin colour. There is one column of images for each of the six subjects. One example of each gesture is shown.

of both computational cost and error rate. The trajectory-based approach using HMMs gave better results than moments with SHIs but did not perform as well on average as template matching of SHIs.

6 Discussion

Trajectory-based representation with HMM recognition can give erroneous results when tracking errors occur. This is more likely when multiple objects (head and hands) are being tracked and can mutually occlude one another. Errors also occur when one gesture's trajectory is similar to all or part of another gesture's trajectory. History-based representation with MAD template matching can give recognition errors when the history representation is inadequate due to motion self-occlusion or when skin history images of gestures are similar.

Nearest neighbour template matching is an efficient and effective method for the application considered here in which small sets of user-defined gestures must be recognised based on small training data sets. It would, however, scale poorly to large data sets in terms of computational cost. In such cases, a more efficient matching strategy based on prototype templates or eigenimages, for example, could be adopted.

Great care was taken to test the implementation of the moment features in order to verify their relatively poor performance. Comparing the three sets of moment features, central moments gave the lowest error rates, followed by scale-normalised moments and finally Hu moments. This can be understood in terms of the invariance properties of these feature sets. In the gesture recognition task investigated here, the person is oriented towards the camera at an approximately fixed distance from the camera. As a result, the feature sets that normalise to achieve scale and rotation invariances result in a loss of discriminative ability. For example, given rotation invariance, an upwards movement can easily be confused with a downwards movement.

An analysis of the recognition errors on the entire data sets showed that of the 104 errors made using HMMs and the 64 errors made using MAD SHI matching, only 5 were a result of confusing the same pair of gestures. In other words, the two approaches largely made different errors. This suggests that it should be possible to combine the approaches to further reduce the error rates.

The comparisons reported here were simplified by ignoring the temporal segmentation problem and instead using isolated gestures. Future work could usefully explore the complementary nature of the representations and recognition methods in the context of gesture spotting. The authors are currently investigating the use of a history-based representation capable of representing self-occluding motion.

Acknowledgments

The authors are grateful to Keith Milburn and Stephen Cassels for their contributions to the software used in the experiments reported. They should also like to thank the subjects for their help with the gesture database and in particular the staff and volunteers at the Mackinnon Centre.

A Hu's Moment Invariants

The seven moment invariants defined by Hu [23] are as follows.

$$\psi_1 = \mu_{2,0} + \mu_{0,2} \tag{7}$$

$$\psi_2 = (\mu_{2,0} - \mu_{0,2})^2 + 4\mu_{1,1}^2 \tag{8}$$

$$\psi_3 = (\mu_{3,0} - 3\mu_{1,2})^2 + (3\mu_{2,1} - \mu_{0,3})^2 \tag{9}$$

$$\psi_4 = (\mu_{3,0} + \mu_{1,2})^2 + (\mu_{2,1} + \mu_{0,3})^2 \tag{10}$$

$$\begin{aligned}\psi_5 = {} & (\mu_{3,0} - 3\mu_{1,2})(\mu_{3,0} + \mu_{1,2})[(\mu_{3,0} + \mu_{1,2})^2 \\ & -3(\mu_{2,1} + \mu_{0,3})^2] \\ & +3(\mu_{2,1} - \mu_{0,3})(\mu_{2,1} + \mu_{0,3})[3(\mu_{3,0} + \mu_{1,2})^2 \\ & -(\mu_{2,1} + \mu_{0,3})^2]\end{aligned} \tag{11}$$

$$\begin{aligned}\psi_6 = {} & (\mu_{2,0} - \mu_{0,2})[(\mu_{3,0} + \mu_{1,2})^2 - (\mu_{2,1} + \mu_{0,3})^2] \\ & +4\mu_{1,1}(\mu_{3,0} + \mu_{1,2})(\mu_{2,1} + \mu_{0,3})\end{aligned} \tag{12}$$

$$\begin{aligned}\psi_7 = {} & 3(\mu_{2,1} - \mu_{0,3})(\mu_{3,0} + \mu_{1,2})[(\mu_{3,0} + \mu_{1,2})^2 \\ & -3(\mu_{2,1} + \mu_{0,3})^2] \\ & -(\mu_{3,0} - 3\mu_{1,2})(\mu_{2,1} + \mu_{0,3})[3(\mu_{3,0} + \mu_{1,2})^2 \\ & -(\mu_{2,1} + \mu_{0,3})^2]\end{aligned} \tag{13}$$

References

1. A. Bobick and J. Davis. The recognition of human movement using temporal templates. *IEEE Transactions on Pattern Analysis and Machine Intelligence*, 23(3):257–267, March 2001.
2. S.J. McKenna and S. Gong. Gesture recognition for visually mediated interaction using probabilistic event trajectories. In *British Machine Vision Conference*, pages 498–507, Southampton, England, September 1998.
3. R. Cutler and M. Turk. View-based interpretation of real-time optical flow for gesture recognition. In *IEEE International Conference on Face & Gesture Recognition*, pages 416–421, Nara, Japan, 1998.

4. T. Ahmad, C. J. Taylor, A. Lanitis, and T. F. Cootes. Tracking and recognising hand gestures using statistical shape models. *Images and Vision Computing*, 15(5):345–352, 1997.
5. M.-H. Yang and N. Ahuja. Extracting gestural motion trajectories. In *IEEE International Conference on Face & Gesture Recognition*, pages 10–15, 1998.
6. V.I. Pavlovic, R. Sharma, and T.S. Huang. Visual interpretation of hand gestures for human-computer interaction: A review. *IEEE Transactions on Pattern Analysis and Machine Intelligence*, 19(7):677–695, July 1997.
7. D.M. Gavrila. The visual analysis of human movement: A survey. *Computer Vision and Image Understanding*, 73(1):82–98, January 1999.
8. Y. Wu and T.S. Huang. Vision-based gesture recognition: A review. *Lecture Notes in Artificial Intelligence*, 1999.
9. A. Corradini and H.-M. Gross. Implementation and comparison of three architectures for gesture recognition. In *Proceedings of the IEEE International Conference on Acoustics, Speech, and Signal Processing (ICASSP'2000)*, volume IV, pages 2361–2364, Istanbul (Turkey), June 2000.
10. L. W. Campbell, D. A. Becker, A. Azarbayejani, A. F. Bobick, and A. Pentland. Invariant features for 3-d gesture recognition. In *IEEE International Conference on Face & Gesture Recognition*, pages 157–162, Killington, USA, 1996.
11. K. Morrison and S. J. McKenna. Automatic visual recognition of gestures made by motor-impaired computer users. *Journal of Technology and Disability, Special Issue on Rehabilitation Engineering, In Press*, 2002.
12. M.J. Swain and D.H. Ballard. Color indexing. *International Journal of Computer Vision*, 7(1):11–32, 1991.
13. R. Kjeldsen and J. Kender. Finding skin in color images. In *IEEE International Conference on Face & Gesture Recognition*, pages 312–317, Killington, Vermont, October 1996.
14. Y. Raja, S. J. McKenna, and S. Gong. Tracking and segmenting people in varying lighting conditions using colour. In *IEEE International Conference on Face & Gesture Recognition*, pages 228–233, Nara, Japan, 1998.
15. L. Sigal, S. Sclaroff, and V. Athitos. Estimation and prediction of evolving color distributions for skin segmentation under varying illumination. In *IEEE Conference on Computer Vision and Pattern Recognition*, South Carolina, June 2000.
16. M. Storring, H.J. Andersen, and E. Granum. Skin colour detection under changing lighting conditions. In *7th Symposium on Intelligent Robotic Systems*, Coimbra, Portugal, July 1999.
17. X. Zhu, J. Yang, and A. Waibel. Segmenting hands of arbitrary color. In *IEEE International Conference on Face & Gesture Recognition*, pages 446–453, Grenoble, France, March 2000.
18. A.F. Bobick and J.W. Davis. An appearance-based representation of action. In *International Conference on Pattern Recognition*, Vienna, 1996.
19. A.F. Bobick. Computers seeing action. In *British Machine Vision Conference*, pages 13–22, Edinburgh, Scotland, September 1996.
20. A.F. Bobick and J.W. Davis. Real-time recognition of activity using temporal templates. In *Workshop on Applications of Computer Vision*, Sarasoto, Florida, December 1996.
21. J.W. Davis. Appearance-based motion recognition of human actions. Master's thesis, Massachusetts Institute of Technology, July 1996.
22. J.W. Davis and A.F. Bobick. The representation and recognition of action using temporal templates. In *IEEE Conference on Computer Vision and Pattern Recognition*, 1997.

23. M. Hu. Visual pattern recognition by moment invariants. *IRE Trans. Information Theory*, 8(2), 1962.
24. K. Li. Reforming the theory of invariant moments for pattern recognition. *Pattern Recognition*, 25(7):723–730, 1992.
25. S. Ahmad. A usable real-time 3D hand tracker. In *28th Asilomar Conference on Signals, Systems and Computers*, pages 1257–1261, Pacific Grove, CA, Oct 1994.
26. K. Imagawa, S. Lu, and S. Igi. Color-based hands tracking system for sign language recognition. In *IEEE International Conference on Face & Gesture Recognition*, pages 462–467, Nara, Japan, 1998.
27. M. Isard and A. Blake. Icondensation: Unifying low-level and high-level tracking in a stochastic framework. In *European Conference on Computer Vision*, pages 893–908, 1998.
28. J. Sherrah and S. Gong. Tracking discontinuous motion using Bayesian inference. In *European Conference on Computer Vision*, pages 150–166, Dublin, Ireland, 2000.
29. S. J. McKenna and S. Gong. Tracking faces. In *IEEE International Conference on Face & Gesture Recognition*, Killington, Vermont, USA, October 1996.
30. B.-W. Min, H.-S. Yoon, J. Soh, T. Ohashi, and T. Ejima. Visual recognition of static/dynamic gesture: Gesture-driven editing system. *Journal of Visual Languages and Computing*, 10(3):291–309, June 1999.
31. T. Starner, J. Weaver, and A. Pentland. Real-time American Sign Language recognition using desk and wearable computer based video. *IEEE Transactions on Pattern Analysis and Machine Intelligence*, 20(12), December 1998.
32. A.D. Wilson and A.F. Bobick. Learning visual behaviour for gesture analysis. In *IEEE Symposium on Computer Vision*, Coral Gables, Florida, November 1995.
33. D.A. Becker. Sensei: A real-time recognition, feedback and training system for T'ai Chi gestures. Master's thesis, Massachusetts Institute of Technology, May 1997.
34. T.E. Starner. Visual recognition of American Sign Language using hidden Markov models. Master's thesis, Massachusetts Institute of Technology, February 1995.
35. Y. Iwai, H. Shimizu, and M. Yachida. Real-time context-based gesture recognition using HMM and automaton. In *International Workshop on Recognition, Analysis and Tracking of Faces and Gestures in Real-Time Systems*, Corfu, Greece, September 1999.
36. Y. Nam and K.Y. Wohn. Recognition of space-time hand-gestures using hidden Markov model. In *ACM Symposium on Virtual Reality Software and Technology*, pages 51–58, 1996.
37. L. R. Rabiner. A tutorial on hidden Markov models and selected applications in speech recognition. *Proceedings of the IEEE*, 77(2):257–286, 1989.
38. S. Young, D. Kershaw, J. Odell, D. Ollason, V. Vatlchev, and P. Woodland. *The HTK Book*. Cambridge University Engineering Department, 2000.

Tracking of Real Time Acrobatic Movements by Image Processing

Ryan Cassel and Christophe Collet

Dept. of Communication Homme-Machine groupe Geste & image
LIMSI-CNRS, University of Paris XI, BP 133, 91403 Orsay cedex, France
{ryan.cassel,christophe.collet}@limsi.fr

Abstract. This paper presents the design and evaluation approach of a video camera-based system for tracking and evaluating acrobatic movements. The context of this study is human gesture recognition in trampoline competition performance. Our work builds a model of trampoline movement and conducts efficient real time tracking of the trampolinist in order to recognize and evaluate a competition routine. We describe the prospective architecture of our system, which satisfies constraints of real time image processing. The global project includes three consecutive phases: first, body extraction and tracking in the image sequence, second, body part localization, and last, gesture recognition and quantification according to our model of trampoline movement characterization. This paper describes the first phase, which combines image processing techniques to perform fast and efficient extraction and tracking of the trampolinist's body. An evaluation protocol is presented, as well as some results for this first stage.

1 Introduction

Studies concerning the analysis and evaluation of sport movements are of growing interest for researchers as well as trainers. Researchers want to understand how the body performs sporting movements, whereas trainers want to teach these movements and to improve their realization. Most studies are based on video analysis performed by experts or direct tracking of the body using specific sensors. The use of magnetic or infra-red sensing enables precise measurements with very high accuracy and frequency, but movements are limited and less natural [1]. In this context, the use of a video-based automatic gesture tracking and recognition system appears very helpful to perform this type of analysis [2]. These systems use image processing techniques to extract measurements from the video sequence. But their scope of application are limited movements or simple gestures (walking, dancing, pointing gesture... [3] [4]). Movement characterization represents a major problem. Many studies focus on segmentation of body parts, human modelling and complex systems to translate basic movements [5] [6] [7]. These algorithms could be more efficient if the observed movements were more clearly characterized. Our purpose is to build a single camera-based system, using a general model with few points, to find and track a body in real time. In

A. Camurri and G. Volpe (Eds.): GW 2003, LNAI 2915, pp. 164–171, 2004.

the proposed method, we characterize and track motion in order to recognize complex acrobatic gestures. We choose to apply this study to the recognition and evaluation of trampolining motion. Trampoline offers several complex body gestures, specifically characterized movements, and a taxonomy of these movements. In trampoline training as well as in competition, gestures need to be analyzed in real time. Sporting gesture analysis using real time computer vision has to use computationally inexpensive algorithms, has to prove generic enough for work in various environments without significant parameter tweaking, and comprise automatic start and initialization with minimum necessary knowledge about the observed scene [8]. The architecture of the proposed system can be segmented as follows. First, we detect and track the human body to create a bounding box. In a second step, we identify each body part using a general model (head, body axis and feet see figure 1). Finally, the body configuration is analyzed dynamically to recognize body gestures.

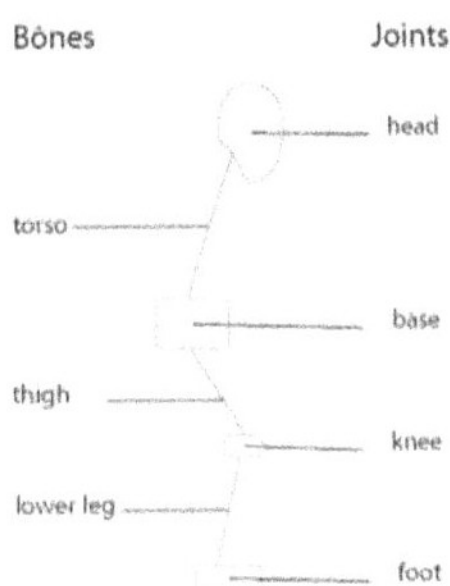

Fig. 1. Model composed of 3 segments and 4 joints.

This paper deals with the characterization of human gestures on a trampoline, then exposes fast tracking algorithms that prepare relevant data for real time recognition. Finally, we present an experimental evaluation of this tracking algorithm.

2 Model of Trampoline Movement Characterization

Trampoline is a sport where the movement is defined to be recognized efficiently. Each elementary mouvement, called an element, is defined by so-called salto (rotation about the transverse axis) and twist (rotation about the longitudinal body axis) quantity. Using the FIG (Fédération Internationale de Gymnastique) numeric system, salto is divided by quarters and twist by halfs. In the *Code of points* [9] used for competition, an element can be represented by an alpha numeric value (for example: "8 0 0 o" is a double back tuck). The first digit describes the number of somersaults, in quarters ($^1/_4$). Subsequent digits represent the distribution and quantity of half twists in each somersault. The shape of the element (called position) is described at the end using an '*o*' or leaving a blank for tucked; '<' for pike and '/' for straight also called layout. In all positions, the feet and legs should be kept together and the feet and toes pointed. Depending on the requirements of the movement, the body should be either tucked, picked or straight (figure 2). The body position is evaluated by measuring angles between different body segments. The most important angles are the angle between lower leg and thigh and the one between thigh and torso. Thus, we need three body segments. To describe segments we use joints [10] for the head, the base, the knees, and the feet. For this study, we use a simplified model (figure 1). The minimum requirements for a particular body shape are defined as follows [9]:

- **Tuck position:** The angle between the upper body and thighs must be equal to or less than 135° and the angle between the thighs and the lower legs must be equal to or less than 135°.
- **Pike position:** The angle between the upper body and thighs must be equal to or less than 135° and the angle between the thighs and the lower legs must be greater than 135°.
- **Layout position:** The angle between the upper body and thighs must be greater than 135°.

Fig. 2. Human body's positions in trampoline.

This *Code of points* allows the judge to differentiate each element. Nevertheless, the judge analyses the trampolinist's routine and adds important information to the notation such as direction and the starting posture (from feet, back...) of the elements. For example, the numeric notation "4 0 o" fails to indicate whether the figure is a backward or a forward somersault. The information we do have is that the figure is a 4 quarters somersault, 0 half twist, in a tuck position. Therefore, the official *Code of points* is insufficient and ambiguous. It needs improvement if it is to be used as a model in an automatic recognition system. We add information about the direction of somersaults (forward or backward) at the beginning of the notation in order to be exhaustive for recognition purposes. A backward tuck somersault becomes "b 4 0 o", whereas a front tuck somersault becomes "f 4 0 o". We don't add information about the starting posture because it can be deduced from the previous figure. All ambiguities are now lifted. Now we can use this extended notation as a model for a recognition system.

While the important interval in a trampoline sequence is the achievement of ten competition elements, the complete sequence can be divided into two important periods and one final important signal. In the initial period, the jumps of the trampolinist are used to achieve good starting conditions (in terms of height and stability). The second and most important period is the segment with the ten competition elements. The final important signal is when the trampolinist stops his movement (stopping is achieved on the trampoline). In order to comply with the international competition rules, the subject has to gain sufficient height. This has the advantage that it effectively leads to discovering the entire background. This information is crucial because an adaptive background will be generated during the tracking procedure.

3 Software Architecture of the Recognition System

To compute a recognition we need the subject images and the first step allows us to extract and track this data. In this article, we develop the tracking part; the subsequent steps (localization of body parts and recognition of body gesture) are still under investigation. The techniques to extract the subject image are successive image subtraction, background generation and motion filter for tracking.

Using the characterization described above, we need to detect, the direction, position, number of somersaults and the number of half twists depending on time. Immediately after capturing this data, the numeric notation can be sent to the judges. A coach can also analyze the starting twist in the somersault for comparison purposes.

4 Fast and Efficient Tracking Algorithm

In our method, image subtraction combined with a thresholding operation are used to detect the most important motions. With each frame, the system generates an updated background image. Because of potential background changes (movements in the audience, light variations, shadow casting...), adaptive background is better than a static background image. However this method has not been evaluated yet.

The tracking algorithm is divided into three modules: a module to extract important motion areas (corresponding to the trampolinist body), a module to automatically generate an adaptive background image, and a module to compute motion quantity. These three modules undergo an initialization phase first. Once the background is generated, these modules run in a continuous processing mode to track the trampolinist and to extract a bounding box that contains the subject from the image sequence

ich com-

is always in the foreground and he is represented
ng pixels. The motion is extracted using a classical
dynamic threshold eliminates noise and highlights

4.2 Filtering Motion

The notion of motion quantity is presented in [11,12]. It is a value which characterizes a quantity of movement in the image, in order to determine the location of the bounding box according to its previous coordinates. For insignificant movements, the value of the motion quantity ($Q(t)$) is near 0; consequently, the system takes coordinates from the previous location of the bounding box. When significant movements are measured, $Q(t)$ is near 1; the location of the bounding box has to move to the new computed location. The advantage of this method is the stability of the bounding box and its computationally inexpensive algorithm.

4.3 Background Generation

Adaptive background generation [11,13] allows the system to perform more efficient motion detection. Its principle is to generate a continuous background image that takes changes into account (light, shadows, audience...). A standard subtraction algorithm (operating between the generated background and the current image) only detects the trampolinist. To generate a continuous background, the system takes an average value of each pixel which is not in the bounding box. An initialization phase allows the system to set up and generate this background.

4.4 Principle of the Tracking System

Background generation is triggered during the initialization phase, and this phase continues until the background image is completed. The tracking system is effective to track the trampolinist and return a valid bounding box. A subtraction image is then computed between the current image and the adaptative background. The result is added to the classic incremental subtraction image, highlighting the subject's body parts as well as the motion areas (typically the subject's image contours).

5 Experimental Results

To verify our proposed method, we tested the system with image sequences for three different trampolinists. The motion of the human body was taken with a Mini DV video camera, which can take 25 frames per second at 720x576 pixels. There is an average of 1700 images per sequence. The first sequence was used to set up the system, the other two were used for testing. The evaluation was done on off-line image sequences.

5.1 Protocol

We developed three software programs to evaluate our method [11]:

The first software is the main program described in this article
putes and returns the bounding box.

The second is an indexing software program to manually add information for each image of the sequence (to determine the coordinates of each body part). We manually labeled the three image sequences: this labeling consists in indexing all visible body parts to identify them and in recording each body part coordinates. We indexed the joints: the head, the base, the two hands, the two knees and the feet.

The last program takes the output of the two previous software programs and performs the evaluation. It computes statistics about all body parts in/out of the bounding box, on a frame by frame basis, and measures the bounding box effectiveness for each video segment.

Fig. 3. Chronogram of a backward somersault (b 4 0 o).

To perform the evaluation, we started the main program to compute the bounding box coordinates. Then, we computed the membership of body parts to the corresponding bounding box with the evaluation program.

5.2 Result

Table 1 presents the result of a normal run of the system, for the entire sequence and for the ten elements of the competition routine. The neutrality of hand movement during the first jumps, as opposed to the 10 elements period, explains the differences between the two periods in table 1. In effect, during the 10 elements the trampolinist performs complex gestures which combine various rotations around the transverse and longitudinal axes. These variations generate variable blur (Figure 3). Motion quantity is more important during the routine and at this point the bounding box is effective.

The setup sequence has been used to develop the system, and unsurprisingly one gets goodresults for this sequence. The test sequence is a beginner tram-

Table 1. Body parts belonging to the bounding box in different parts of the sequence. A: Entire sequence. B: the 10 competition elements.

	setup sequence		test sequence	
Body part	**A**	**B**	**A**	**B**
hands	73 %	70 %	72 %	72 %
head	97 %	96 %	94 %	92 %
base	100 %	100 %	97 %	96 %
knees	99 %	100 %	69 %	97 %
feet	85 %	92 %	59 %	87 %

polinist practising a different routine. Results show that the system is efficient throughout the 10 elements.

The current system currently processes an image in 30 milliseconds, thus reaching realtime video constraints. The remaining bottleneck was bandwidth for data access, as the 720 x 576 resolution prevented us from loading or storing results at video rates with standard PC equipment (fast video access solutions are of course commonly achievable.) Figure 4 shows the bounding box created as part of the evaluation sequence. In this figure the heavy blur on the arms is clearly visible. We can adjust the camera shutter speed and open the iris to achieve better image quality (sharpen images).

Fig. 4. Bounding box computed by the system on a part of the sequence (every 6 frames). (f 1 0 /).

6 Conclusion and Future Works

We have designed a system which allows efficient tracking of a natural sporting practice, i.e. trampoline competitions. The key idea behind our work was to adapt the machine to the athlete, and not the other way around. In particular, the system had to be non-intrusive. We obtained an effective characterization of the movements that allowed us to design a real-time video tracking system. The evaluation part denoted good results in terms of bounding box quality, but jumps of the trampolinist are used to achieve good starting conditions (in terms of height and stability). The second and most important period is the segment with the ten competition elements. The final important signal is when the trampolinist stops his movement (stopping is achieved on the trampoline). In order to comply with the international competition rules, the subject has to gain sufficient height. This has the advantage that it effectively leads to discovering the entire background. This information is crucial because an adaptive background will be generated during the tracking procedure.

3 Software Architecture of the Recognition System

To compute a recognition we need the subject images and the first step allows us to extract and track this data. In this article, we develop the tracking part; the subsequent steps (localization of body parts and recognition of body gesture) are still under investigation. The techniques to extract the subject image are successive image subtraction, background generation and motion filter for tracking.

Using the characterization described above, we need to detect, the direction, position, number of somersaults and the number of half twists depending on time. Immediately after capturing this data, the numeric notation can be sent to the judges. A coach can also analyze the starting twist in the somersault for comparison purposes.

4 Fast and Efficient Tracking Algorithm

In our method, image subtraction combined with a thresholding operation are used to detect the most important motions. With each frame, the system generates an updated background image. Because of potential background changes (movements in the audience, light variations, shadow casting...), adaptive background is better than a static background image. However this method has not been evaluated yet.

The tracking algorithm is divided into three modules: a module to extract important motion areas (corresponding to the trampolinist body), a module to automatically generate an adaptive background image, and a module to compute motion quantity. These three modules undergo an initialization phase first. Once the background is generated, these modules run in a continuous processing mode to track the trampolinist and to extract a bounding box that contains the subject from the image sequence.

4.1 Subject Detection

In this context, the subject is always in the foreground and he is represented by a collection of neighboring pixels. The motion is extracted using a classical image-subtraction method. A dynamic threshold eliminates noise and highlights the main motion [11].

4.2 Filtering Motion

The notion of motion quantity is presented in [11,12]. It is a value which characterizes a quantity of movement in the image, in order to determine the location of the bounding box according to its previous coordinates. For insignificant movements, the value of the motion quantity ($Q(t)$) is near 0; consequently, the system takes coordinates from the previous location of the bounding box. When significant movements are measured, $Q(t)$ is near 1; the location of the bounding box has to move to the new computed location. The advantage of this method is the stability of the bounding box and its computationally inexpensive algorithm.

4.3 Background Generation

Adaptive background generation [11,13] allows the system to perform more efficient motion detection. Its principle is to generate a continuous background image that takes changes into account (light, shadows, audience...). A standard subtraction algorithm (operating between the generated background and the current image) only detects the trampolinist. To generate a continuous background, the system takes an average value of each pixel which is not in the bounding box. An initialization phase allows the system to set up and generate this background.

4.4 Principle of the Tracking System

Background generation is triggered during the initialization phase, and this phase continues until the background image is completed. The tracking system is effective to track the trampolinist and return a valid bounding box. A subtraction image is then computed between the current image and the adaptative background. The result is added to the classic incremental subtraction image, highlighting the subject's body parts as well as the motion areas (typically the subject's image contours).

5 Experimental Results

To verify our proposed method, we tested the system with image sequences for three different trampolinists. The motion of the human body was taken with a Mini DV video camera, which can take 25 frames per second at 720x576 pixels. There is an average of 1700 images per sequence. The first sequence was used to set up the system, the other two were used for testing. The evaluation was done on off-line image sequences.

5.1 Protocol

We developed three software programs to evaluate our method [11]:

The first software is the main program described in this article which computes and returns the bounding box.

this study emphasizes a significant problem regarding image quality, namely acrobatic sports generate fast variable blur on different body parts. Nevertheless, the results proved sufficient to detecting body parts. Future work will include many improvements for tracking and acquisition to allow live processing. Then we plan on implementing automatic segmentation of each body part present in the bounding box. Prior bounding box analysis will significantly reduce the amount of data to be processed at this stage. The last phase will include recognition of real time trampolinist motions based on our characterization model.

References

1. T. Molet, R. Boulic, D.T.: A Real-Time Anatomical Converter for Human Motion Capture. In: Proc. 7h Eurographics Workshop on Animation and SimulationS, Springer-Verlag, Wien (1996)
2. Aggarwal, J., Cai, Q.: Human motion analysis: A review. Computer Vision and Image Understanding: CVIU **73** (1999) 428–440
3. N.R. Howe, M.E. Leventon, W.F.: Bayesian reconstruction of 3-d human motion from single-camera video. Technical Report TR9937-12, ANIPS (1999)
4. Bottino, A., Laurentini, A.: Non-intrusive silhouette based motion capture. In: Proc. of 4th World Multiconference on Systemics, Cybernetics and Informatics, SCI 2000, Orlando (FL) (2000)
5. Lee Campbell, A.B.: Recognition of human body motion using phase space constraints. Fifth International Conference on Computer Vision **309** (1995) 624–630
6. A. Bharatkumar, K. Daigle, M.P.Q.C.J.A.: Lower limb kinematics of human walking with the medial axis transformation. In: Workshop on Motion of Non-Rigid and Articulated Objects, Austin, Texas, USA (1994)
7. M. Yamamoto, T. Kondo, T.Y.K.Y.: Skill Recognition. In: Third IEEE International Conference on Automatic Face and Gesture Recognition. (1998)
8. J. Perš, G. Vučkovič, S. Kovačič, Branko Dežman: A low-cost real-time tracker of live sport events. In: ISPA 2001 Pula, Croatia, University Computing Center, University of Zagreb (2001) 362–365
9. Fédération Internationale de Gymnastique: Code of points. FIG Store, www.fig-gymnastics.com (2001)
10. Leung, M.K., Yang, Y.H.: First Sight: A Human Body Outline Labeling System. In: IEEE Trans. on PAMI. Volume 17. (1995)
11. R. Cassel: Etude sur le suivi et la reconnaissance des mouvements en temps réel d'un trampoliniste par traitement d'images. Master's thesis, École doctorale en informatique de l'Université Paris Sud & LIMSI-CNRS, Orsay (2002)
12. C. Collet, R. Gherbi: Visual perception tools for natural interaction a gaze capture and tracking system. In: IEEE SSIAI'98, Tucson, Arizona, U.S.A (1998) 91–96
13. Haritaoglu, I., Harwood, D., Davis, L.: w^4 s: A real-time system for detecting and tracking people. In: Computer Vision—ECCV. (1998)

A Dynamic Model for Real-Time Tracking of Hands in Bimanual Movements

Atid Shamaie and Alistair Sutherland

Centre for Digital Video Processing, School of Computer Applications
Dublin City University, Dublin 9, Ireland
{ashamaie,alistair}@computing.dcu.ie

Abstract. The problem of hand tracking in the presence of occlusion is addressed. In bimanual movements the hands tend to be synchronised effortlessly. Different aspects of this synchronisation are the basis of our research to track the hands. The spatial synchronisation in bimanual movements is modelled by the position and the temporal synchronisation by the velocity and acceleration of each hand. Based on a dynamic model, we introduce algorithms for occlusion detection and hand tracking.

1 Introduction

Many tasks are performed everyday by the two hands coordinately. Activities where bimanual coordination is important include clapping, opening a wine bottle, typing on a keyboard, eating with knife and fork, drumming, guiding a pilot driving an aircraft to the parking, showing the size of something, etc. Tracking the hands in a bimanual movement is important in order to recognise the meaning of the movement.

Hand tracking and gesture recognition have been widely addressed in the literature [1]. Spatio-temporal hand gesture recognition [2], hidden Markov models for gesture recognition [3], [4], parametric hidden Markov models [5], CONDENSATION algorithm for tracking objects [6], tracking interacting hands using Bayesian networks [7], tracking of articulated structures in disparity maps derived from stereo image sequences [8], tracking of multiple articulated objects in the presence of occlusion in moderately complex scenes [9], representing and recognising human body motion [10], hand tracking for behavior understanding [11] and many other techniques have been used to deal with the problems of tracking and recognition of hand and body gestures.

Hand tracking in bimanual movements is a significant problem due to the presence of the two hands and occlusion. The tracking algorithms in the literature are either time consuming (e.g. references [6], [7]) or have some restrictions (e.g. reference [11]), which cannot be used for general real-time tracking. In this paper, we introduce a new hand tracking algorithm based on a dynamic model and the Kalman filter. Tracking hands in bimanual movements and the neuroscientific phenomenon of bimanual coordination are discussed in Sections 2 and 3 respectively. In Sections 4 and 5 the pre-processing techniques and the proposed hand tracking algorithm are presented. Evaluation of the algorithm is presented in Section 6.

A. Camurri and G. Volpe (Eds.): GW 2003, LNAI 2915, pp. 172–179, 2004.

2 Tracking Hands in Bimanual Movements

In a bimanual movement, when one hand, completely or partially, covers the other hand resuming tracking at the end of occlusion is crucial. We have to understand the hands' behaviour in order to reacquire the hands at the end of an occlusion period. The hands may pass each other, movement types *a*, *c*, *d*, and *h* shown in Fig. 1(a), 1(c), 1(d), and 1(h), or may collide and return in opposite direction, types *b* and *g* presented in Fig. 1(b) and 1(g). In some cases they may not to collide but pause and return in opposite direction, types *e*, *f*, and *g* shown in Fig. 1(e), (f), and (g).

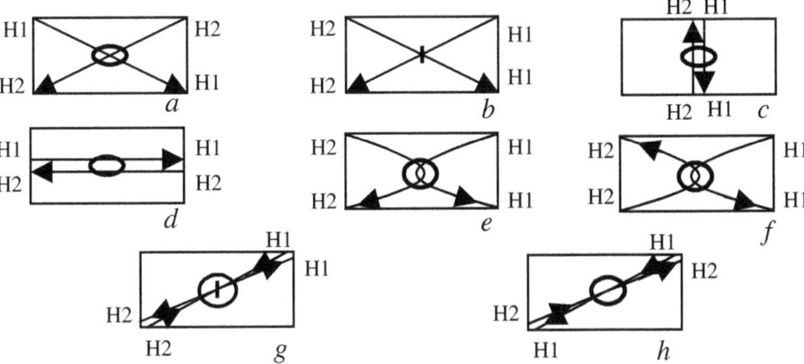

Fig. 1. The path of the hands in the 8 types of bimanual movements. The thick ellipses represent the occlusion areas (*a, c, d, e, f, g and h*), and the small lines represent collision (*b and g*). In the type *g* the hands may either collide or pause and return. This model represents all the rotations of paths including pure horizontal or vertical

3 Bimanual Coordination

In bimanual movements, naturally, there are temporal and spatial synchronisations between the hands [12]. Temporally, when the two hands reach for different goals, they start and end their movements simultaneously [13]. Spatially, we are almost not able to draw a circle and a rectangle by the two hands at the same time [13]. Researchers have presented different anatomical and perceptual explanations for this phenomenon [14], [15]. The temporal synchronisation in bimanual movements causes synchronous hand velocities and simultaneous hand pauses. These pauses help us to track the hands during occlusion. In order to detect the hand pauses we monitor the hand velocities. A well-known experiment called Circle Drawing shows that the two hand velocities are highly synchronised with no phase difference in bimanual movements [16]. This synchronisation is the basis of the algorithm proposed here.

4 Hand Extraction and Pre-processing

In order to extract the hand from the background we use grey-level segmentation and an algorithm called Grassfire [17]. The Grassfire algorithm scans the image from left to right, top to bottom to find connected regions with the same grey values as the hands. The first connected region is labeled number 1, the second is labeled number 2, and so on. However, because of the search manner of Grassfire, in two consecutive images the hands may be labelled interchangeably. The other problem is occlusion. As soon as the hands reach each other the Grassfire algorithm finds a big blob and labels it as a single object. Occlusion detection, and hand tracking and reacquiring are the problems to be addressed in the next section.

5 A Dynamic Model for Occlusion Detection and Tracking

In this section, first we deal with the problem of detecting occlusion and then tracking the hands.

5.1 Occlusion Detection

In order to detect occlusion, for every hand in an image a rectangle is constructed around it. The sides of each rectangle represent the leftmost, rightmost, top and bottom of the hand. By tracking the rectangles, if any intersection is detected between them it can be recognised as an alarm for occlusion. However, it is possible that occlusion happens without any prior intersection (see Fig. 2), and the Grassfire algorithm detects only one region, which is the same as the case where one hand hides behind e.g. body. We must predict future movement of each hand and detect occlusion.

Fig. 2. A rectangle is formed around the hands or the big blob in occlusion. In two consecutive images the hands may reach each other without any prior intersection of the rectangles

5.2 A Dynamic Model

We propose a Kalman filter-based algorithm to track the hands and predict the future position of the rectangles. Every side of a rectangle is modelled by a dynamic model. The position, velocity and acceleration of each side are considered in this model. These parameters are related together based on Kinematic equations of motion [18], Equation 1. The rectangle models make the algorithm independent of the hand shapes.

$$\begin{cases} x_{k+1} = x_k + hv_k + \frac{1}{2}h^2 a_k \\ v_{k+1} = v_k + ha_k \end{cases} . \tag{1}$$

where $h>0$ is the sampling time [18], k is the time index, x is the position, v the velocity and a the acceleration of each side of a rectangle. In the Kalman filter loop [19] the estimation of a state vector representing a rectangle side is updated with the current measurement of the position of the side and its prior estimation calculated in the last iteration of the loop. We use this prior estimation to predict the next position of each side of a rectangle in advance. If, by prediction, there is any intersection between the rectangles of the two hands, an occlusion alarm is set. Therefore, we are able to forecast a hand-hand occlusion before it actually happens.

5.3 Hand Tracking

By defining the centre of the hands as the centres of the associated tracked rectangles and comparing them in consecutive images the problem of mislabelling can be resolved. By using this technique we are able to track the hands correctly even when something else like the body occludes them. It can be done by keeping records of the last position of the hand before occlusion and the position of the other hand in the images. This is a proper technique because when a hand moves behind something like the body or leaves the scene it most probably appears in an area near the last position prior to occlusion.

In order to track the hands in the presence of occlusion we introduce a technique based on the Kalman filter model of section 5.2. As in Section 5.1, as soon as an occlusion is detected a big rectangle around the big blob is formed. We use the dynamic model-based Kalman filtering process of the last section to model the occlusion rectangle. Based on bimanual coordination the velocities of the hands are synchronised and reach zero together. During occlusion, if the vertical sides of the rectangle pause, the velocities of these sides tend to zero. This is recognised as a horizontal pause of the hands. Therefore, they would return horizontally. However, if the hands pass each other we observe a sign change in the velocities of the vertical sides without passing through zero. These are similarly observable in the vertical or diagonal movements of the hands. By capturing the hand-pause during occlusion and comparing the positions of the hands at the end of occlusion, with respect to each other, with their positions prior to occlusion we can conclude the correct position of each hand. We label the sides of the occlusion rectangle with a and b for the horizontal and c and d for the vertical sides. The following model is defined,

$$\begin{cases} V_{v,k} = \sqrt{v_{a,k}^2 + v_{b,k}^2} \\ V_{h,k} = \sqrt{v_{c,k}^2 + v_{d,k}^2} \end{cases} . \tag{2}$$

where $v_{a,k}$, $v_{b,k}$, $v_{c,k}$, and $v_{d,k}$ stand for the velocity of sides a, b, c, and d at time k. Therefore, if V_v or V_h reaches zero (or less than a small threshold ε) a vertical or horizontal pause is detected. For example, if the hands have a movement of type d, see Fig. 1(d), no horizontal pause is detected. Therefore, we conclude that the position of the hands is the opposite of their position prior to occlusion. In Figure 1(g), however, the hands pause or collide and the model detects it. Therefore, the correct positions of the hands at the end of occlusion are the same as before the occlusion. In some of the movements such as types *c* and *d* an unwanted horizontal or vertical pause may be detected during occlusion. On the other hand, in a movement of type a or *e* no vertical pause is detected and we may conclude that the hands have passed each other vertically. We call these the positive synchronisation of the hands as opposed to negative synchronisation in which the hands move in opposite directions (e.g. left and right). The positive synchronisation may cause wrong conclusions by the algorithm. In order to deal with this problem, the standard deviation of the velocity differences (relative velocity) of the horizontal sides, S_v, and vertical sides, S_h, over the occlusion period are employed. If a small standard deviation is observed we base the tracking on detecting the pauses of the other sides of the occlusion rectangle. The tracking algorithm is summarised as follows,

1. *If* S_v *is small, the hands are positively synchronised in vertical direction*
   1.A. *If there is a k such that* $V_{h,k} < \varepsilon$ *then: the hands are horizontally back to their original sides*
   1.B. *Else: the hands horizontally passed each other*
2. *Else: if* S_h *is small, the hands are positively synchronised in horizontal direction*
   2.A. *If there is a k such that* $V_{v,k} < \varepsilon$ *then: the hands are vertically back to their original sides*
   2.B. *Else: the hands vertically passed each other*
3. *Else: if there is a k such that* $V_{h,k} < \varepsilon$ *then: the hands are horizontally back to their original sides*
4. *Else: if there is a k such that* $V_{v,k} < \varepsilon$ *then: the hands are vertically back to their original position*
5. *Else: the hands passed each other*

6 Evaluation

For the sake of brevity, we just look at the dynamic model in tracking and predicting one of the sides of a rectangle. Fig. 3 shows a part of an experiment. The predicted next position, the triangles, at each time is very close to the actual position of the side of the rectangle at the next step, the solid small circles.

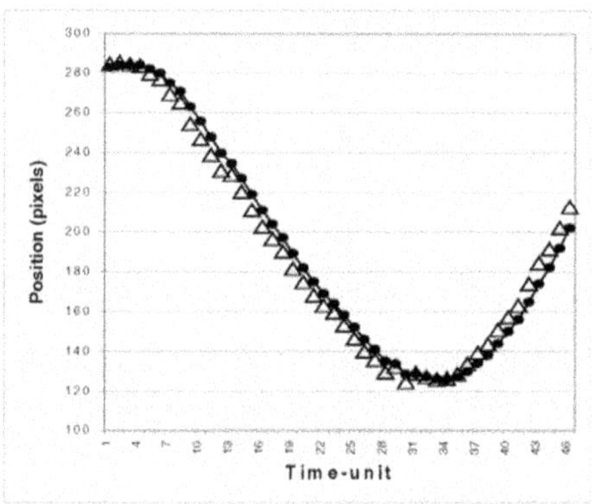

Fig. 3. Prediction by the dynamic model in a hand movement. The small solid circles represent the actual position and the triangles are the predictions one step in advance. Time-unit = 26.6ms

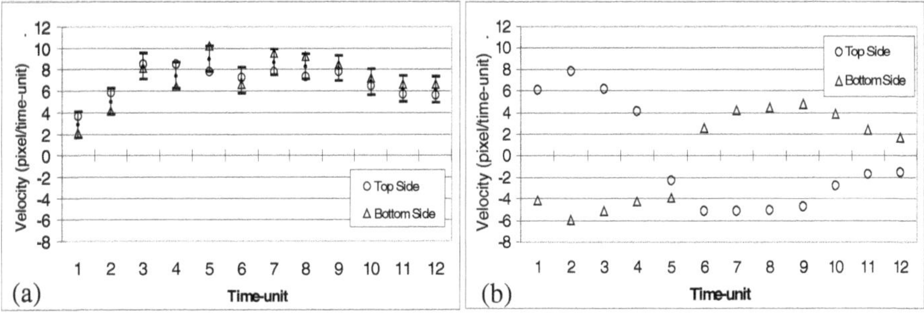

Fig. 4. Relative velocities of the horizontal sides of the occlusion rectangles in the movements of (a) type *e*, and (b) type *h*. Each time-unit is 26.6ms

In Fig. 4(a) the velocities of horizontal sides of the occlusion rectangle for a type *a* movement are shown. In this example, the difference of the velocities at each time frame is less than a small value represented by the vertical lines in the graph. This is captured by a small standard deviation of the relative velocities.

However, the velocities of the sides of the occlusion rectangle in the movements where the hands pass each other in opposite directions (e.g. a type *h* movement) are negatively synchronised, see Fig. 4(b). Large standard deviation in this case enables us to detect the negative synchronisation. A change in the sign of the velocities in this figure is due to the fact that when the hands pass each other they push the sides in the opposite directions. A few images of a movement of type *h* are shown in Fig. 5. For a movement of type *g*, in which the hand collision is detected by the model, the graphs of the occlusion rectangle sides velocities are presented in Fig. 6. The hand collision is detected in the 9th to 11th time frames in which all the velocities reach almost zero.

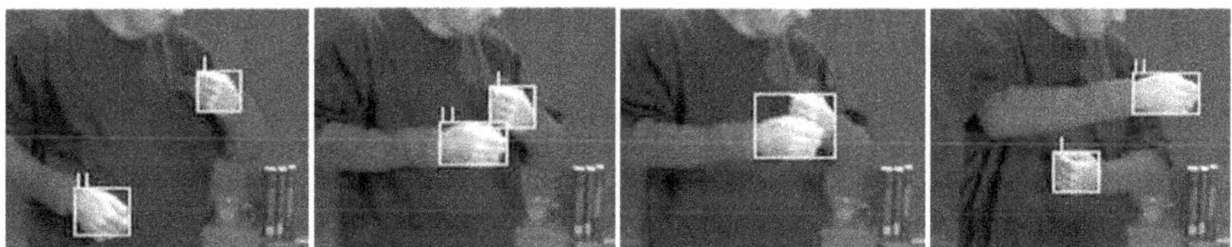

Fig. 5. A hand movement of type *h*. The hands are reacquired correctly at the end of occlusion

In order to measure the performance of the algorithm a corpus of 3500 movement trials, including clapping, signing, etc. performed by one person, was evaluated. The results are presented in Table 1. An important parameter is the processing speed of the algorithm. Using a fast camera working in 120 frames per second on a Pentium II 1 GHz computer the algorithm is able to process 37.5 frames per second in average.

We briefly compare the proposed algorithm and the algorithms reported in the literature. The CONDENSATION algorithm [6] is a time consuming process able to process sometimes less than an image per second [7]. Gong et al. [7] have a Bayesian Network based technique for modeling interactive behaviors able to process 5 frames per second on a Pentium II 330 MHz computer. Their result of 13% error is based on the number of images in their database. The performance reported in Table 1 is event-based in which each event (movement) consists dozens of images.

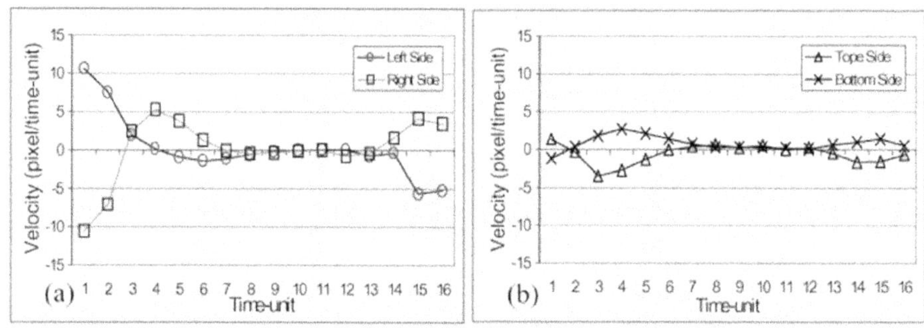

Fig. 6. Velocities of the occlusion rectangle sides. The velocities of the (*a*) vertical sides, (*b*) horizontal sides reach almost zero from 9th to 11th time-unit. Each time-unit is 26.6ms

Table 1. Performance of the proposed tracking algorithm using the dynamic model

Movement Type	# Events (movements)	# Errors	Error Rate (%)
a	400	25	6.25
b	600	106	17.67
c	400	65	16.25
d	500	29	5.8
e	400	41	10.25
f	400	44	11
g	400	17	4.25
h	400	24	6
Total:	3500	Weighted Average:	10.03

The algorithm presented in this paper does not have the restrictions on the hand shape or camera view direction. Therefore, for different angles of view and changing hand shapes during movements it works effectively.

7 Conclusion

An algorithm for tracking the hands in bimanual movements was proposed based on a dynamic model and a neuroscience phenomenon. The dynamic model was employed to track the hands, detect occlusion and recognise the behavior of the hands during occlusion. Based on bimanual coordination the tracking algorithm reacquires the hands at the end of an occlusion period. The proposed algorithm is fast with high performance and independent of changing hand shapes and camera view direction. Therefore, it can be used as a general technique in a wide range of applications.

References

1. Cipolla, R., Pentland, A.: Computer Vision for Human-Machine Interaction. Cambridge University Press (1998)
2. Lin, D.: Spatio-Temporal Hand Gesture Recognition Using Neural Networks. Proc. IEEE World Congress on Computational Intelligence (1998)

3. Starner, T., Pentland, A.: Visual Recognition of American Sign Language Using Hidden Markov Models. Proc. Int'l Workshop on Automatic Face and Gesture Recognition, Zurich, Switzerland (1995)
4. Lee, H., Kim, J.: An HMM-Based Threshold Model Approach for Gesture Recognition. IEEE Trans. Patt. Anal. Mach. Intell., Vol. 21, No. 10 (1999)
5. Wilson, A.D., Bobick, A.: Parametric Hidden Markov Models for Gesture Recognition. IEEE Trans. Patt. Anal. Mach. Intell., Vol. 21, No. 9 (1999)
6. Isard, M., Blake, A.: CONDENSATION - Conditional Density Propagation for Visual Tracking. Intl. J. Computer Vision, Vol. 29 (1998)
7. Gong, S., Ng, J., Sherrah, J.: On the Semantics of Visual Behaviour, Structured Events and Trajectories of Human Action. Image and Vision Computing, Vol. 20 (2002)
8. Jojic, N., Turk, M., Huang, T.: Tracking Self-occluding Articulated Objects in Dense Disparity Maps. Proc. IEEE International Conf. Computer Vision ICCV'99, Kerkyra Greece (1999)
9. Dockstader, S., Tekalp, A.M.: Tracking Multiple Objects in the Presence of Articulated and Occluded Motion. Workshop on Human Motion HUMO'00, Austin Texas (2000)
10. Campbell, L., Bobick, A.: Recognition of Human Body Motion Using Phase Space Constraints. 5th International Conf. Computer Vision, Cambridge Massachusetts (1995)
11. McAllister, G., McKenna, S. J., Ricketts, I. W.: Hand Tracking for Behaviour Understanding. Image and Vision Computing, Vol. 20 (2002)
12. Jackson, G.M., Jackson, S.R., Husain, M., Harvey, M., Kramer, T., Dow, L.: The Coordination of Bimanual Prehension Movements in a Centrally Deafferented Patient. Brain, Vol. 123 (2000)
13. Diedrichsen, J., Hazeltine, E., Kennerley, S., Ivry, R.B.: Moving to Directly Cued Locations Abolishes Spatial Interference During Bimanual Actions. Psychological Science, Vol. 12, No. 6 (2001)
14. Mechsner, F.: Why Are We Particularly Good at Performing Symmetrical Movements. Max-Planck Research (2002)
15. Mechsner, F., Kerzel, D., Knoblich, G., Prinz, W.: Perceptual Basis of Bimanual Coordination. Nature, Vol. 414 (2001)
16. Kennerley, S., Diedrichsen, J., Hazeltine, E., Semjen, A., Ivry, R.B.: Callosotomy Patients Exhibit Temporal Uncoupling During Continuous Bimanual Movements. Nature Neuroscience. Online Publication (2002)
17. Pitas, I.: Digital Image Processing Algorithms, Prentice Hall (1993)
18. Chui, C.K., Chen, G.: Kalman Filtering With Real Time Applications. Springer-Verlag (1999)
19. Brown, R.G., Hwang, P.Y.C.: Introduction to Random Signals and Applied Kalman Filtering. John Wiley and Sons (1997)

Robust Video-Based Recognition of Dynamic Head Gestures in Various Domains – Comparing a Rule-Based and a Stochastic Approach

Gregor McGlaun, Frank Althoff, Manfred Lang, and Gerhard Rigoll

Institute for Human-Machine Communication
Technical University of Munich (TUM)
Arcisstr. 21, 80290 Munich, Germany
{mcglaun,althoff,lang,rigoll}@ei.tum.de

Abstract. This work describes two video-based approaches for detecting and classifying dynamic head-gestures. We compare a simple, fast, and efficient rule-based algorithm with a powerful, robust, and flexible stochastic implementation. In both realizations, the head is localized via a combination of color- and shape-based segmentation. For a continuous feature extraction, the rule-based approach uses a template-matching of the nose bridge. In addition, the stochastic algorithm applies features derived from the optical flow, and classifies them by a set of discrete Hidden Markov Models. The rule-based implementation evaluates the key-feature in a finite state machine. We extensively tested the systems in two different application domains (VR desktop scenario vs. automotive environment). Six different gestures can be classified with an overall recognition rate of 93.7% (rule-based) and 97.3% (stochastic) in the VR (92.6% and 95.5% in the automotive environment, respectively). Both approaches work independently from the image background. Concerning the stochastic concept, further gesture types can easily be implemented.

1 Introduction

The development of user interfaces has become a significant factor in the software design process. Growing functional complexity and mostly restriction to purely tactile interaction devices required extensive learning periods and adaptation by the user to a high degree. To overcome these limitations, various interface types and interaction paradigms have been introduced. Multimodal interfaces currently resemble the latest step in this development. They enable the user to freely choose among multiple input devices, provide essential means to resolve recognition errors of individual components, and thus lead to systems that can be worked with easily, effectively, and above all intuitively[1]. Moreover, besides speech input, the use of gestures provides an interesting alternative for people with certain disabilities. This contribution illustrates the design and the evaluation of a system component for a video-based recognition of dynamic head gestures. The module is to be used as an integral part of an application-invariant multimodal architecture.

A. Camurri and G. Volpe (Eds.): GW 2003, LNAI 2915, pp. 180–197, 2004.

1.1 Application Domains

Our overall research work focuses on the design of a generic platform for developing multimodal interfaces. Currently, the architectural concepts are being used in two different application domains. The first project deals with the development of a multimodal system for interacting with VRML browsers in a virtual-reality (VR) desktop environment[2]. Hence the user can arbitrarily combine conventional tactile devices with special VR hardware. As a key feature, (s)he can interact via paradigms on a semantic higher level, i.e. natural speech as well as dynamic hand or head gestures. The second project concentrates on the design of intuitive and error-robust components of a multimodal interface for controlling various infotainment and communication applications in an automotive field[3]. In both domains, the use of head gestures as an alternative or additional input possibility has proved to be very helpful with regard to increased system acceptance and the resolution of errors in the multimodal setup[4].

1.2 Related Work

Many research groups have contributed significant work in the field of video-based head gesture recognition. In a system developed by Morimoto[5], movements in the facial plane are tracked by evaluating the temporal sequence of image rotations. These parameters are processed by a dynamic vector quantization scheme to form the abstract input symbols of a discrete HMM which can differentiate between four head gestures (*yes, no, maybe* and *hello*). Based on the IBM PupilCam technology, Davis[6] proposed a real-time approach for detecting user acknowledgments. Motion parameters are evaluated in a finite state machine which incorporates individual timing parameters. Using optical flow parameters as primary features, Tang[7] applies a neural network to classify ten different head gestures. The approach is quite robust with regard to different background conditions. Tang obtained an average recognition rate of 89.2% on an SGI workstation processing 30 frames per second.

1.3 System Overview

Our system module for recognizing dynamic head gestures consists of four independent components: loading a single image (*image grabbing*), localizing the head candidates (*segmentation*), calculating movements of key points in the facial plane and in adjacent regions (*continuous feature extraction*), and finally, determining the type of the head gesture (*classification*).

The input image can be a frame of an MPEG stream, an isolated BMP image of a stored sequence, or directly streamed in by a dedicated hardware device (in our case a Video4Linux compatible grabbing card). Afterwards, the position and the size of potential head candidates in the given image are calculated by a color segmentation followed by a series of morphological filters. Additionally, we apply a template matching algorithm to find the nose bridge. These two steps are completed in the preprocessing which is identical for the two approaches.

On the basis of the segmentation result, the search space for the subsequent frames is restricted. Both the position differences of the nose bridge and diverse optical flow parameters are continuously stored in a feature vector. To determine which gesture occurred at which point time, elements of this vector are evaluated by a rule-based and a stochastic approach.

2 Preliminary Analysis

Before designing specific algorithms, we analyzed and categorized different types of natural dynamic head movements and determined the set of recognizable gestures. Hence we could benefit from the extensive video-material we collected in numerous usability experiments in both domains.

2.1 Gesture Vocabulary

In general, the movement of the head can completely be described by a six element vector denoting the three degrees of freedom with regard to translational and rotational movements, respectively. As an important result of a dedicated offline analysis of the video material, we found out that the majority of gestures (96.4%) has exclusively been composed of purely rotational movements. Thus in the approaches presented here, we exclusively consider head gestures that consist of one or a combination of head rotations.

With regard to the reference coordinate system shown in figure 1, six different elementary head gestures could be observed: moving the head *left* and *right* (rotation around the *yaw*-axis), *up* and *down* (rotations around the *pitch*-axis), and bending the head left and right (rotation around the *curl*-axis). Additionally, by combining basic movements, two compound gestures could be identified: head *nodding* and head *shaking*. A detailed analysis of the gesture material revealed that regarding the totality of rotations around the *yaw*-and the *curl*-axis, only 3.6% of the movements were twist gestures. Against the background of our application scenarios, this type of gestures can be neglected without a noticeable loss of system usability.

Concerning the VR desktop scenario, head gestures have mainly been used as alternative input possibility in case the hands of the user were busy with operating certain tactile devices. Moreover, head gestures have been applied

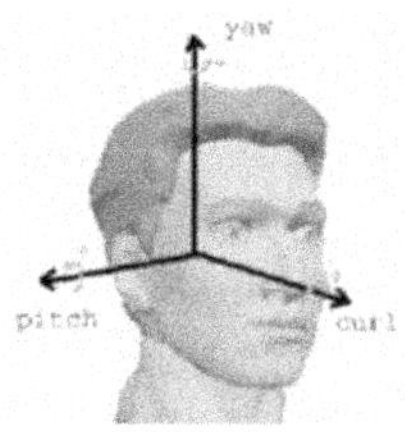

Fig. 1. Rotational axes for the different head movements

unconsciously to emphasize commands given by speech [3][2]. Analyzing the functional meaning of the observed head gestures, the purpose was to specify directions of movements in the virtual world.

Where in the VR application domain, the user can absolutely concentrate on the scene and the respective task, in the automotive environment, the primary task of the user is to drive the car (i.e. to perform a driving task). Operating the multimodal interface is the secondary task. The superposition of both tasks massively biases the workload of the user. In the automotive test scenarios, head gestures have mainly been applied to support yes/no-decisions in a dialog system, e.g., to accept or deny an incoming phone call. Moreover, in selected cases, head gestures were used to skip between individual audio tracks. In noisy fields, like the car, recognition of speech is often error-prone. Moreover, tactile interaction is usually coupled with a set of control glances at the display or special button devices[8]. Hence in special cases, head gestures offer a highly effective input alternative, as both hands can still be used to drive the car.

Since the recognition module is to be implemented in various contexts, we define two sets of possible head gestures. The first set (GS_1) contains all six gestures mentioned above. The vocabulary of the second set (GS_2) is designed to exclusively support user acknowledgment decisions. Thus we reduced it to the gestures head *nodding* and head *shaking*.

2.2 Interaction Time

To obtain quantitative results with regard to the interaction time of the individual gesture types and application scenarios, the video material has partly been segmented manually. For each gesture, 15 samples of twelve users (VR environment) and 15 samples of nine users (automotive environment) have been evaluated. Table 1 summarizes the average length of the gestures in frames and seconds, respectively. Interestingly, the compound gestures (*shake* and *nod*) had a significant smaller execution time in the automotive environment, which per judgment of the subjects, is due to an increased workload in the car (see section 2.1).

Table 1. Head-gesture interaction times in both test domains

	VR desktop		Automotive	
gesture	frames	time[sec]	frames	time[sec]
LEFT	21.75	0.87	23.25	0.93
RIGHT	19.75	0.79	23.50	0.94
UP	15.50	0.62	22.75	0.91
DOWN	17.48	0.70	23.30	0.93
NOD	40.03	1.60	27.25	1.09
SHAKE	39.09	1.56	28.00	1.12
mean	25.58	1.02	24.67	0.99

3 Preprocessing

Before describing the different classification approaches, we briefly compare common techniques and sketch the preliminary steps of the image processing. The result of a successful segmentation process is a rectangle that characterizes the position and the size of potential head candidates in the input image.

3.1 Comparing Head Segmentation Approaches

Based on the excellent overview given in[9], we experimented with various techniques. Since a fundamental requirement of our approach is real-time processing capability, various methods cannot be used due to enormous running time (e.g., Hough transformation and Eigenfaces). Localizing the eyes by checking for user blinks has proved to be insufficient when the head is moved intensely. The system could be initialized by an explicit twinkle without any kind of accompanying head motion, but this assumption would massively decrease the naturalness and usability of the system. To purely use background recognition, the image background would have to be separated from the moving foreground (the head). In this case, the background would have to be static, and the foreground always dynamic, which does not hold for our application domains. Therefore, we propose a color-based segmentation approach, because it is rotation- and scale-invariant, and the calculation is very fast. Moreover, this method does not require any kind of initialization, and has proved to be highly robust with regard to arbitrary motion in the background.

3.2 Color-Based Segmentation

The individual steps of the segmentation process are visualized by the two sequences shown in figure 2. Given in the standard size of 382x288 pixels, the input image is in standard RGB color format, with each channel composed of 8 bit (figure 2(a)). The image is converted into the $YCbCr$ color space by neglecting the luminance (Y)-component in further reflections. Despite the theoretical and experimental findings illustrated in[10] and[11], in this case, the performance of the algorithm is slightly improved, since for reasons of efficiency, we apply just a single Gaussian distribution

$$\mathrm{p}(Cr, Cb) = \exp[-0.5(\boldsymbol{x_i} - \boldsymbol{m})^T C^{-1}(\boldsymbol{x_i} - \boldsymbol{m})]$$

to discriminate between skin color and background. Let $\mathbb{E}$ denote the expectation value, then the mean value $\boldsymbol{m}$ and the covariance matrix C are calculated on the basis of 42 random user skin samples $\boldsymbol{x_i}$ via

$$\boldsymbol{m} = \mathbb{E}\{\boldsymbol{x_i}\} \text{ with } \boldsymbol{x_i} = \begin{pmatrix} Cr \\ Cb \end{pmatrix} \quad \text{and} \quad C = \mathbb{E}\{(\boldsymbol{x_i} - \boldsymbol{m})(\boldsymbol{x_i} - \boldsymbol{m})^T\}.$$

To filter out non skin-color areas, the histogram of the $CbCr$ part of the input image is multiplied with the Gaussian distribution $\mathrm{p}(Cr, Cb)$. The resulting

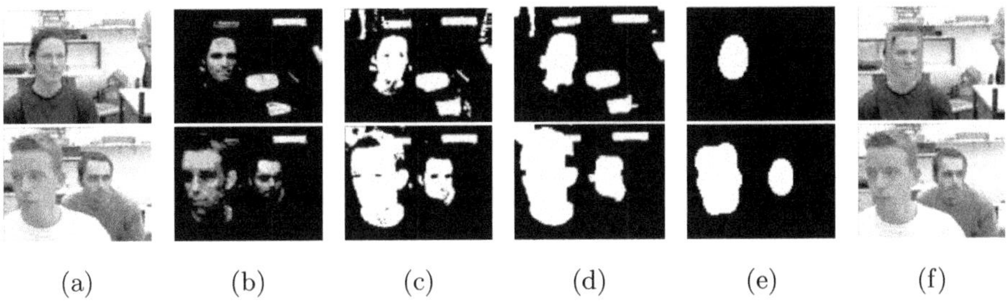

Fig. 2. Individual steps of the segmentation process: the input image given in standard RGB format with a size of 382x288 pixels (a), skin-color information coded in a gray-value image (b), binarized image due to a certain threshold differentiating between potential areas of skin-color and background (c), result of a sequence of morphological filters to improve the segmentation result (d), final closing with a longish ellipse to identify potential head candidates (e), and marking head regions in the original input image (f)

histogram is used to project the color image onto a gray-value image (figure 2(b)), in which each skin color value is represented by a value according to the probability specified by p(Cr, Cb). Afterwards, this gray-value image is binarized differentiating between potential skin colors and background (figure 2(c)). Moreover, we apply a sequence of morphological filters on the binary image. First a *closing* with a small ellipse eliminates small particles that have occurred due to noise. Then an *opening* with a medium-sized rectangle tries to cover dark areas like in the eyes. For each blob, potentially occurring leaks will be filled. These leaks can often be found near to the eyes. As they are not skin-colored, they have a negative influence on the correct segmentation of the whole face region. The result of the filter process is shown in figure 2(d). Finally, a closing with a longish bigger ellipse removes all areas which do not have the correct size (figure 2(e)). By a bounding box R around the best-fitting ellipse, the position of the potential head candidate is specified (figure 2(f)).

3.3 Template Matching

To further improve the quality of the segmentation result, we additionally apply a template matching algorithm. Therefore, a striking, invariable *region of interest* (ROI) in the facial plane has to be identified. A basic requirement for a robust tracking of this ROI should be independence from special faces. Taking the center of the eyes as ROI results in misclassifications, when the user blinks. In this case, the eyes fuse with the rest of the face to one single blob. Moreover, the mouth drops out as a potential ROI, since it changes its form during talking. Therefore, we concentrate on the nose bridge as the key feature. For enlarging the matching criteria, we use a symmetric template including the nose bridge, the area of the eyes, and parts of the eye-brows.

For each of these head candidates, we calculate a measure of how good the template matches the current image region R. This is done by determining the match quality of the template and the input image column by column and row by row. The result of this match depends both on the quality of the template and the special kind of the matching algorithm. We use the standard gray-level correlation

$$c(x,y) = \sum_{(u,v)\in R} t(u,v)b(x+u,y+v),$$

where the template $t(x,y)$ is defined over $\mathbb{R}$ and $b(x,y)$ denotes the input image. We relate the individual gray-values to the medium gray-value and normalize them by their standard deviation. Using the gray-scale correlation instead of the sum of absolute gray-scale differences, changes in the light conditions can easily be handled. If the resulting match value is below a certain confidence measure (by default set to 0.7), the head candidate will not be accepted as a potential position of a head. If more than one candidate exceeds the threshold, the best correlation candidate is taken for further processing. This can be seen in the lower series of images in figure 2, where the right candidate is preferred.

The native segmentation phase is exited, if a head region is found. In subsequent phases, this head region is used for further calculation steps. In case the area gets to small or no blob is found anymore, the search is extended to the complete image. This principle guarantees an integral robust localization of the head and a fast tracking of the head regions in the image.

4 A Bottom-Up Rule-Based Classification

The rule-based approach (RBA) is a simple and fast implementation. Exclusively using one feature for classification, we could achieve considerable high recognition rates under the test conditions described in section 6.

4.1 Continuous Feature Extraction

Based on the template matching outlined in section 3.3, we can establish a local Cartesian coordinate system with its zero point in the lower left corner of the rectangle R (see figure 2(f)). Let j be an integer indexing each frame F of a video sequence. For the j-th frame F_j, let the center of the template be denoted by $\boldsymbol{c}_j$. Referring to the previous frame F_{j-1}, we can express the motion of the nose bridge by the difference vector $\boldsymbol{d}_j = \boldsymbol{c}_j - \boldsymbol{c}_{j-1}$. This vector is transformed into a polar representation using the absolute value $\|\boldsymbol{d}_j\|_2$ and the phase φ. Let $d_{j,1}$ be the x-component and $d_{j,2}$ denote the y-component of $\boldsymbol{d}_j$, then the phase can be calculated via

$$\varphi_j = \begin{cases} 0 & , \text{if } d_{j,1} = 0 \\ \arctan(\frac{d_{j,2}}{d_{j,1}}) & \text{else} \end{cases}$$

Using φ_j and $\|\boldsymbol{d}_j\|_2$, we can specify the direction and the speed of the head motion for each frame. This forms the basis for the rule-based classification algorithm.

4.2 Classification

The head movements are modeled by means of a finite state machine (FSM) containing five motion states (*up*, *down*, *left*, *right*) and a non-motion state (*idle*). By means of the scheme depicted in figure 3, a motion direction represented by φ_j is assigned to a corresponding state of the recognizer. If $\theta = 0°$, the two-

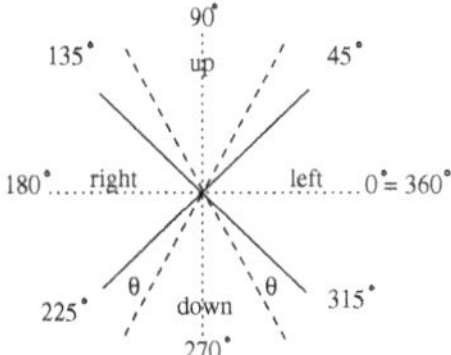

Fig. 3. The mapping scheme for the angle φ consists of four sectors (viewpoint: camera). Their size can be varied by the aperture angle θ

dimensional space is symmetrically partitioned into four motion sectors (from the viewpoint of the camera). In test runs, we varied the partition types by applying different values for θ. A detailed description is presented in section 6.

With each gesture being represented by a certain series of motion and non-motion states, we can categorize the considered head gestures by their number of temporally sequent direction changes of the head motion. Table 2 shows the number and the type of direction changes for classification. Consequently, there is a set of valid and invalid state transitions for each gesture (see figure 4).

Table 2. Classification scheme for different head gestures (HGs) according to the type and the number of changes in direction (CIDs)

HG \ CID	left→right	right→left	up→down	down→up
NOD	–	–	≥ 1	≥ 1
SHAKE	≥ 1	≥ 1	–	–
UP	–	–	1	–
DOWN	–	–	–	1
LEFT	1	–	–	–
RIGHT	–	1	–	–

Initially, the FSM is in the *idle* state. Once a motion is detected, i.e. there is a change to a motion state, the recognition process is triggered. In a state history, each state is stored with respect to the current frame. If a certain number w of non-motion states is detected (the parameter w was adjusted in the evaluation period, see section 6), the system automatically starts to classify the state sequence. For this purpose, the state history is clustered: first we mark all state changes (i.e. transition states A to B with A $\neq$ B). The type and the number of identical states between two state changes are determined. If the number of

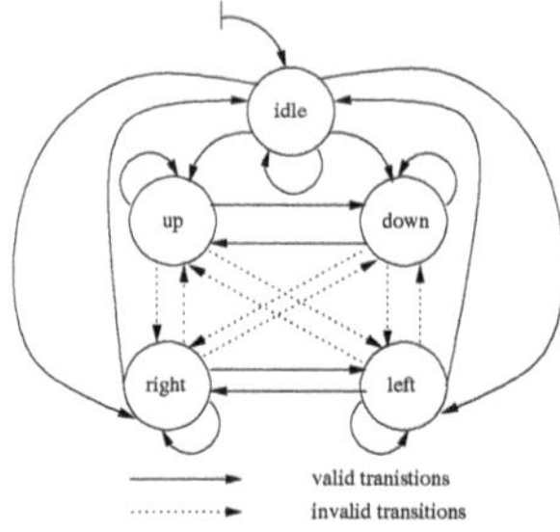

Fig. 4. Overview over the different state transitions in RBA

identical states between two state changes is less or equal two, these states are erased from the state history. Given the state history presented in figure 5, the *up* states in frames 6 and 7, as well as the *down* state in frame 8 will be erased by this procedure. Thus we try to cope small outliers caused by inaccuracies of

state	-	left	left	left	left	left	up	up	down	left	left	left	left	left	left	left	left	left	left ...
frame	0	1	2	3	4	5	6	7	8	9	10	11	12	13	14	15	16	17	18 ...

Fig. 5. Exemplary excerpt of the state history showing a set of *up* and *down* states within a motion to the *left*

the movements. After this step, the motion history is checked for invalid state transitions. If all transitions are valid, the statistics of the recognized direction types and transitions are evaluated applying table 2 to obtain the resulting gesture. On the other hand, if there are invalid state transitions (e.g., a set of *left* states followed by *up* states), the recognition result is mapped to *unknown*.

4.3 Spotting

In the current approach, only a prototypical spotting algorithm is implemented. Hence, we assume that gestures can be separated by a sequence w of *idle* states. w must be larger than the number of idle states that appear, when the head goes through the inflection points within a gesture. In our test sets, there has been a maximum of three idle frames at the inflection points (see section 6.2). If the gestures follow each other too fast, the RBA system is not able to distinguish between them. As soon as any kind of movement is detected, the recognition process is (re-)initialized. In current work, the FSM is being revised for a more efficient spotting.

5 A Top-Down Stochastic Classification

5.1 Continuous Feature Extraction

The tracking module calculates the spacio-temporal movements of head candidates in the image sequences and provides the basic data for the subsequent classification process. Concerning the stochastic approach (STA), we apply a hybrid combination of the Averaged Optical Flow (AOF) and the continuous template matching of the nose bridge. Hence, the template matching is used to estimate the position of the nose bridge in the tracked face region. The optical flow calculates motion vectors of certain areas of interest in subsequent images. The approach tries to find solutions to the known flow equation $\nabla I \cdot \boldsymbol{v} + I_t = 0$. Hence, $I = I(x, y, t)$ denotes the luminance, which depends of the local coordinates x, y, and the time t. Moreover, $\boldsymbol{v} = (\frac{dx}{dt}; \frac{dy}{dt})^T$ represents the vectored velocity of the head movement. For calculating $\boldsymbol{v}$, the standard Lucas-Kanade algorithm[12] is used. For reasons of system performance, we apply this local method instead of techniques operating on the whole image (e.g., the *Horn-Schunk* algorithm). In common implementations, the AOF is usually computed over a rectangle containing the whole head. Yet, we have found out that the bounding box around the head region in itself is sometimes not sufficient for adequate classification results. Concerning rotations of the head in the image plane (*yaw*- and *pitch*-axis), the resulting bounding box does not change significantly. This especially holds for segmentation results in which, for example, the bounding box comprises areas of the chest. As can be seen in figure 6, the bounding box enlarges to the area of the chest. A nod of this user could not

Fig. 6. The result of this skin-color segmentation process is a bounding box that is bigger than the primary head region and thus could, for example, not be used to classify *nod* gestures (left picture). This was a direct result from the first closing with an ellipse in the binary image (right picture)

be detected, because the total movement is completely enclosed in the primary rectangle. Thus the result of the segmentation is only used to restrict the search area for the extraction of the features.

We apply the AOF technique to detect rotational movements around the nose bridge. Using the bounding box of the head, which results from the segmentation process, too much information from the background might be included in the calculation of the rectangles. This adulterates the results, if the bounding box covers a very large field and there is too much motion in the background. In our approach, we use the position of the nose bridge as an approximation for an element on the vertical symmetry axis of the face. Thus we are able to separate the face into a right and a left half. For each half of the face, we determine the AOF separately. Each region is marked with a square (see figure 6). By default, the square size is 40x40 pixels. If the square ranges out of the head region, it is scaled down. Thus the AOF is always calculated within the face region. As an effect of the implementation, we get two competing outputs for the AOF for each side of the face. Concerning the gesture sets GS_1 and GS_2, the AOF of the left and the right side of the face make for almost identical results. Consequently, the two redundant features are supposed to confirm each other.

There was also another motivation for computing the AOF within two separate face regions. Even though bend gestures (around the *curl*-axis) are not part of the evaluated test sets G_1 and G_2, this approach holds strong potential with regard to the recognition of those gestures. In this case, the speed vector of the nose bridge would not be sufficient for a classification. Concerning these *curl*-gestures, the vectors of the optical flow point into opposite directions up- and downwards, respectively, which enables a classification of such gestures.

The nose bridge is used as an origin of the local coordinate system of the rectangles bounding the face halves. In combination with the relative movement of the nose bridge, we are able to distinguish between horizontal movements of the user and head shaking itself. With horizontal movements, the AOF is zero, as the offset generated by the movement is compensated by the offset of the local coordinate system.

As a third feature, we use the difference vector of the nose bridge, just like in RBA (see section 4.1). These three features provide the basis for the classification process of STA to be described subsequently.

5.2 Classification

Modeling head gestures, a fundamental aspect is tolerance of small divergences regarding the temporal run and the duration. In the field of stochastic approaches, Hidden Markov Models very well cope with molding on time variant patterns. In addition, they show a robust behavior on small breaks during a gesture, which are likely to appear when the head moves through the inflection point within a gesture. In the current implementation, we use Discrete Hidden Markov Models (DHMMs) composed of five states for the classification of head gestures. As mentioned in[13], DHMMs in general take more parameters, but the calculation is easier in the recognition process. The generation of the discrete symbols s_1, s_2, and s_3 that are fed into the DHMMs can be split up into two steps. First the optical flow and the arithmetic mean is computed over the regions which are in close vicinity to the nose bridge. Then both vectors as well as the speed vector of the nose bridge are discretized to integers between 0 and 5. Hence symbol 0 represents *no movement.* Symbols 1 to 4 are generated by applying the mapping scheme sketched in figure 3. These three feature symbols are canonically coded into a final symbol, using the known formula $s_1 + 5s_2 + 5^2s_3$. The classifier evaluates the symbol sequences and puts out a probability vector for each DHMM. Finally, the result is returned in terms of an n-best list.

5.3 Spotting

In the current state of development, the recognition process is automatically triggered, when any kind of head movement is detected. For this purpose, the absolute value of the difference vector of the nose bridge (see section 4.1) is evaluated. If two head gestures directly follow one another, a number of five or more idle frames must be detected between these two gestures to separate them. Otherwise, the recognition process continues, which consequently leads to wrong results. The improvement of the segmentation between single gestures is part of current work. Hence we are about to implement a technique proposed by P. Morguet[14], which applies an improved normalized Viterbi algorithm for a continuous observation of the HMM output scores. This approach allows for integrated spotting and classification at a time.

6 Evaluation

The recognition module system has been implemented on an Intel Pentium IV machine with 512KByte cache and 1 GByte memory under the Linux operating system (Kernel 2.4.20). We have evaluated both the time performance and the recognition rates in the various domains. A single input frame is composed of an RGB image with 288x384 pixels.

6.1 Test Environment and Procedure

Both RBA and STA have been evaluated in two different application domains. One test series was run under optimized conditions in the computer-vision laboratory of the institute. We shielded the test environment from glares of the sun, and used a flicker-free light. The scene background was native, consisting of different objects. During the data collection, the test subjects sat on a chair in front of a camera (distance 60cm). They had to interact in different VR desktop scenarios, using head gestures of both test sets GS_1 and GS_2.

In the second test series, we focused to evaluate head gestures under preferably realistic conditions. The test domain was an automotive environment in a driving simulator. Driving the test car in the simulation, the trial participants had to perform head gesture interaction with different in-car infotainment devices. Yet, we did not consider any influences of artificial vibrancies or forces implicated by bumps, curves, or braking. The camera, which had the same sample rate as in the VR desktop environment, was positioned on the dash board over the steering wheel with an approximate distance of 45 cm. To simulate rapidly changing and diffuse light conditions, we shaded the laboratory, and used a set of spotlights.

In both test environments, the gestures have been evaluated in an offline analysis, using captured video sequences. In case subsequent gestures have been made, they were not manually segmented in order to analyze system behavior with respect to the prototypical spotting. For evaluating the recognition performance of the system, three parameters have been chosen: the recognition rate

(RR) measuring the percentage of correctly classified gestures, the false accept rate (FAR) denoting the percentage of misclassified gestures or movements that were misinterpreted as gestures, and the false reject rate (FRR) describing gestures that have erroneously not been accepted as valid.

6.2 Rule-Based Approach

We used a total of 153 video sequences of ten different test subjects, and 120 sequences of eight subjects in the automotive environment. During the implementation of RBA, we found out that in the regions of the inflection point of the head, a certain set of idle frames can appear. In the point of inflection, the motion of the head and thus the absolute value $\|\boldsymbol{d}\|_2$ is so small that the system does not detect any movement. In some cases, this was misinterpreted as a completion of the gesture, and two motion sequences which are actually associated were disjoined. On the other hand, RBA uses a sequence of idle frames for a temporal segmentation of the gestures (see section 4.3). With a too large value, subsequent gestures could not satisfactorily be separated (and consequently not be recognized), unless there was an accordingly larger break between the gestures. Thus, we tried to find a suitable threshold w at which the system assumes a gesture has been completed. As can be seen in table 3, a good performance is reached for $w = 5$. The reason is that the breaks at the inflection points within a gesture varied between one and three idle frames. Between subsequent gestures, there has been an averaged number of 4.7 idle frames. The recognition rate gets worse for $w \geq 6$, as now in most cases, the subsequent gesture can no longer be separated. Results in the automotive domain did not significantly differ from this realization.

Table 3. Performance of RBA for different values of w concerning the test set GS_1 (47 sequences, VR desktop environment)

w	1	2	3	4	5	6	7
RR	33.5	52.8	80.6	90.5	96.3	86.8	75.8
FAR	57.6	32.1	11.8	0.3	0.2	5.7	14.8
FRR	8.9	15.1	7.6	9.2	3.5	7.6	9.4

In some scenarios, the gestures have not been made very exactly. Evaluating motion histories of horizontal head movements, it was remarkable that for a short instant (1-2 frames), some test subjects made a motion which the system classified as a vertical movement. In 18% of all test sets, we have observed this motion sequence short before or after the head ran through its inflection point. On the other hand, an according phenomenon has only occurred in 2% of the evaluated vertical head movements. As mentioned in section 4.2, small outliers can be erased from the state history. To further improve system behavior in this regard, we enlarged the aperture of the horizontal mapping sectors by varying the angle θ (see figure 3 in section 4.2) and studied the effect on the recognition performance. Regarding gesture set GS_1, we have got the recognition rates depicted in figure 7. This chart shows an explicit maximum of RR with a coeval

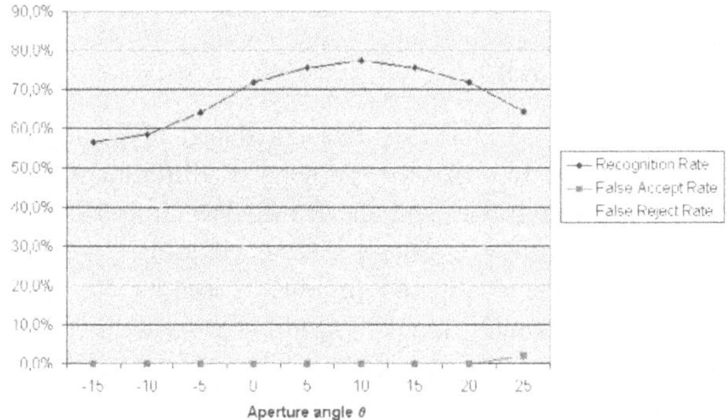

Fig. 7. Performance of RBA for different values of θ (test set GS_1, 27 sequences, VR desktop environment)

minimization of FRR for $\theta = 10°$. With other values of θ, either the horizontal or the vertical sectors get too small. The evaluation of θ in the automotive domain confirmed these results.

Using the optimized parameter settings mentioned above, the recognition performance for both gesture sets (GS_1 and GS_2) dependent on the different domains are presented in table 4. Concerning GS_1 and calculated over both domains, in 38,4% of all error cases, there was a confusion of *shake* with *left* or *right*, or vice versa (29,7% confusion between *nod* with *up* or *down*). Thus expectedly, the system showed a better RR for the reduced set GS_2, where this kind of misinterpretation was a priori impossible.

Table 4. Characteristic rates of RBA in both domains

	VR desktop		Automotive	
Gesture set	GS_1	GS_2	GS_1	GS_2
RR	92.0	95.2	91.2	94.0
FAR	6.5	1.1	2.3	4.7
FRR	1.5	3.7	6.5	1.3

Considering all types of gestures, the RR is better in the VR desktop scenarios than in the automotive environment, where head movements often were less distinct. This particularly happened in cases the subjects did not have a frontal view into the camera. In 20 evaluated test sequences, the head of the test participant was initially rotated by approximately 40°. Hence, RBA had major problems in correctly classifying the gestures. Although the template matching worked well, in a large number of frames, the movement vector $\boldsymbol{d}$ of the nose bridge was close to zero, which was a straight consequence of the distortion of the head movement. Thus a large set of idle states was detected, and consequently, the gesture was erroneously rated complete.

6.3 Stochastic Approach

The training corpus for the DHMMs has consisted of 32 selected symbol sequences. It contained gestures of four persons of different skin colors and one person wearing glasses. We have used the Baum-Welch method for the training. The data for test and training has been strictly disjoint.

STA has intensely been evaluated in both domains. To get a usable basis of comparison, we have exactly fed the same sequences into the STA system. In tables 5 and 6, the recognition results can be seen. Similar to RBA, in both domains, there has been a strong affinity between direction related gestures (*up*, *down*, *nod*, and *left*, *right*, *shake*, respectively). This effect has been aggravated, when the gestures were made very quickly. Then the resulting symbol sequence corresponding to the gesture has contained too few elements, so no good match for an DHMM has been found. Particularly, we achieved very good recognition rates for the reduced set G_2 because of the training corpus containing a great variety of gestures of different durations.

In some cases, blinking or even moving the pupils have had a negative impact on the computation of the AOF, which has consequently lead to misclassifica-

Table 5. Recognition rates of the STA approach with regard to gesture set GS_1 in the VR desktop environment (left table) and in the automotive environment (right table). In the first column, G stands for the actual head gesture, and in the first row, H denotes the HMM modeling this head gesture

G \ H	Up	Down	Left	Right	Shake	Nod
Up	**96.3**	0.4	0.1	0.1	0.6	2.5
Down	0.5	**96.1**	0.2	0.2	0.2	2.8
Left	0.2	0.1	**98.0**	0.8	0.8	0.1
Right	0.1	0.1	0.5	**96.6**	1.9	0.8
Shake	0.1	0.3	1.4	1.0	**97.0**	0.2
Nod	1.3	2.5	0.1	0.3	0.2	**95.6**

G \ H	Up	Down	Left	Right	Shake	Nod
Up	**95.2**	1.2	0.3	0.3	0.2	2.8
Down	1.9	**94.5**	0.4	0.3	0.1	2.8
Left	0.2	0.6	**95.0**	2.2	1.1	0.9
Right	0.5	0.7	1.2	**94.2**	3.1	0.3
Shake	0.3	0.3	2.2	2.5	**93.9**	0.8
Nod	1.5	3.0	0.5	0.2	0.6	**94.2**

Table 6. Recognition rates of the STA approach with regard to gesture set GS_2 in the VR desktop environment (left table) and in the automotive environment (right table). In the first column, G stands for the actual head gesture, and in the first row, H denotes the HMM modeling this head gesture

G \ H	Shake	Nod
Shake	**98.2**	2.2
Nod	1.8	**97.8**

G \ H	Shake	Nod
Shake	**96.8**	3.9
Nod	3.2	**96.1**

tions. Moreover, we have observed that the AOF is more likely to be error-prone to bad light conditions than the template matching algorithm and the feature extracted from it.

With regard to inexact head movements, which were discussed in section 6.2, STA has shown a very robust behavior. Concerning the test set in which the head of the subject was initially rotated by 40°, in 73.2% of all cases the gesture has been classified correctly.

6.4 Comparative Discussion

Each of the discussed implementations offers individual advantages due to different points of view. RBA is a fast implementation which, considering its simplicity, has very good recognition results in the reduced gesture set GS_2. Thus in both domains, it is predestinated for low-cost implementations or the use in dialogs with decision questions. As it hardly takes processing power, an application in a low CPU resource environment, like the automobile, appears to be very interesting. The individual rules of RBA are hard-coded in an implicit knowledge base, thus it is strictly limited to the given gesture vocabulary. At any time, STA can be trained offline with arbitrary additional sets of gesture models of different domains. An extension of RBA to other gesture types is rather expensive, as the FSM has to be completely revised and updated. In this context, the tracking of only a single feature might be problematic in some applications. For example, gestures that are generated by rotations around the *curl*-axis (which we excluded from our test set) can hardly be recognized by RBA, since during *curl*-rotations, the position of the nose bridge hardly changes. Hence the architecture of STA has great potential for an easy extension of the vocabulary, as we separately evaluate the optical flow in the left and right part of the face (see section 5.1).

The segmentation algorithm was absolutely stable concerning moving objects in the background or scenarios with more than one potential head candidate. In the VR field, the template matching algorithm worked extremely robust. In 98.9% of all test sets, the nose bridge has been found correctly. Both the RBA and the STA system were mainly developed in the VR environment. Using the same template in the car, the rates for the matching have been slightly worse, as the template matching algorithm is not scale-invariant with respect to larger distance changes in z-direction (depth dimension). Moreover, the difficult light conditions in the automotive environment contributed to an aggravation of the RR. In 97.4% of all automotive test sets, the template matching algorithm has been localized.

Regarding person independence, both approaches are extremely robust against different skin color types, persons wearing glasses, ear- or nose-jewelry. Yet, both systems have major difficulties categorizing head gestures of persons with strong hair-growth covering the nose-bridge or subjects having a full beard. In this case, either the head localization or the template matching algorithm, which forms the basis for the feature extraction, does no longer work properly. Moreover, the optical flow delivers too many diametrically opposed or divergent direction vectors which leads to unemployable results, especially in the automotive environment, where difficult light conditions negatively contribute to this effect. Hence STA detected direction changes which were actually not made. This lead to the fact that gestures, like *left* or *right* were wrongly interpreted as *shake*.

If test subjects do not sit directly in front of the camera, but have their head slightly turned, STA is again more stable. Hence the optical flow of one half of the face still delivers a movement direction. From the viewpoint of the camera, the motion of the nose bridge is no longer recognizable. Thus the difference vector $\boldsymbol{d}$ (key feature of RBA) is close to zero, and consequently, the system detects idle frames. RBA is more error-prone to inexplicit and indistinct gestures than STA. In the current implementation, RBA has only a set of rigid rules by which the system is able to overcome smaller inaccuracies in the head movements (see section 4.2). Individual nuances of motion phases can hardly be covered unless massively blowing up the code book of the rules. The latter, in fact, would noticeably deteriorate system performance. On the other hand, STA is highly adaptable to both specific conditions and individual users. It has better recognition results than RBA, if gestures are made very quickly or clipped. In this regard, the implementation again benefits from the flexibility of DHMMs to time variant patterns and the broad corpus by which it has been trained.

7 Ongoing and Future Work

The systems presented here are in an intermediate state of development. As mentioned above, especially the HMM approach can be enhanced with regard to recognizing further sets of head gestures. Hence we especially concentrate on gestures generated by rotations around the *curl*-axis.

As the head gesture recognition unit is to be used as part of a multimodal system, two ways of processing the recognizer output are researched. In a current approach, the head gesture recognition unit is to be coupled with a natural speech recognizer[15], using an early feature fusion. This allows for further improvement of the overall recognition rates and benefits from the fact that many user inputs (especially confirmation and negation) are temporally overlapping[16].

In a Late Semantic Fusion approach based on a client-server architecture[3], the outputs of the recognizers are combined in a central integration unit. Applying context knowledge, the integrator can dynamically vary the vocabulary of the head gesture recognizer via a socket-based communication. E.g., if a yes-no answer is expected in a dialog, the system could instruct the recognizer to load configuration GS_2, as other input does not make sense in this context. By this, we expect a significant improvement of the recognition rate and the performance.

8 Conclusions

Head gestures offer strong potential for an intuitive, efficient, and robust human-machine communication. They are an easy and helpful input unit, especially in environments, where tactile interaction is difficult or error-prone (like in the automobile). We discussed two differently motivated approaches. The strongly limited rule-based implementation allows for satisfactory categorization of head gestures. It is predestinated for the evaluation of yes-no dialogs in environments, where CPU-resources are low. On the other hand, the HMM-oriented stochastic approach has excellent means to robustly recognize even inaccurate head movements, and can easily be enhanced for recognizing further types of gestures.

References

1. Oviatt, S.: Multimodal interface research: A science without borders. Proc. of the 6th Int. Conf. on Spoken Language Processing (ICSLP) (2000)
2. Althoff, F., et al.: Using multimodal interaction to navigate in arbitrary virtual worlds. In WS on Perceptive User Interfaces (PUI 01) (2001)
3. McGlaun, G., et al.: A new approach for the integration of multimodal input based on late semantic fusion. In Proc. of USEWARE 2002 (2002)
4. Althoff, F., et al.: Experimental evaluation of user errors at the skill-based level in an automotive environment. Proc. of CHI '02 (2002)
5. Morimoto, C., et al.: Recognition of head gestures using hidden markov models. Proc. of IEEE Int. Conf. on Pattern Recognition (1996)
6. Davis, J., et al.: A perceptual user interface for recognizing head gesture acknowledgements. In WS on Perceptive User Interfaces (PUI 01) (2001)
7. Tang, J., et al.: A head gesture recognition algorithm. In Proc. of the 3rd Int. Conf. on Multimodal Interface (2000)
8. McGlaun, G., et al.: A generic operation concept for an ergonomic speech mmi under fixed constraints in the automotive environment. In Proc. of HCI 2001 (2001)
9. Yang, M., et al.: Detecting faces in images: A survey. In IEEE Transactions on Pattern Analysis and Machine Intelligence (PAMI) **24** (2002) 35–58
10. Albiol, A., et al.: Optimum color spaces for skin detection. In: Proc. of ICIP '02. (2002)
11. Shin, M., et al.: Does color space transformation make any difference on skin detection? In: Proc of IEEE Workshop on App. of Computer Vision '02. (2002)
12. Barron, J., et al.: Performance of optical flow techniques. IJCV **12:1** (1994) 43–77
13. Rabiner, L.: A tutorial on hidden markov models and selected applications in speech recognition. In: Proceedings of the IEEE. Volume 77:11. (1989) 257–285
14. Morguet, P., et al.: Spotting dynamic hand gestures in video image sequences using hidden markov models. Proc. of ICIP 99 (1998) 193–197
15. Schuller, B., et al.: Navigating in virtual worlds via natural speech. In: 9.th Int. Conf. on HCI '01. (2001)
16. Althoff, F., et al.: Combining multiple input modalities for VR navigation - A user study. In: 9.th Int. Conf. on HCI '01. (2001)

Remote Vision-Based Multi-type Gesture Interaction

Christian Brockmann and Heinrich Müller

Informatik VII (Computer Graphics)
University of Dortmund
D-44221 Dortmund, Germany
{brockman,mueller}@ls7.cs.uni-dortmund.de
http://ls7-www.cs.uni-dortmund.de

Abstract. Gestures offer a possibility of interaction with technical systems if other communication channels are excluded, for instance because of distance, noise, or usage for other purposes. However, gestures as the only mode of interaction lead to the problem of deciding whether a posture or motion of the user is indeed a gesture, in particular if commands are issued just from time to time. In this contribution, we overcome this problem by combining different gesture types. The types we use are static hand gestures based on hand postures, dynamic hand gestures based on hand motions, and pointing gestures based on hand or arm location. The gestures are acquired by computer-vision. In the case of remote interaction a difficulty is that some gesture types require a global view of the interaction space while others need local observation, like e.g. hand postures. We present a solution in which a camera with computer-controlled pan, tilt, and zoom is controlled by information captured by this camera, as well as by information captured by static cameras which survey the complete interaction space.

1 Introduction

Computer-vision-based gesture recognition as a mode of interaction with technical systems has found increasing interest in the past few years [10,4]. The advantage of computer vision is that usually less efforts than for other sensors are necessary in order to bring the users into a state in which they can start with interaction. A difficulty with computer vision is that a reliable image analysis is hard to achieve in natural environments with not too severe restrictions concerning e.g. illumination.

A common application of gestures as a way of interaction is as one of several modes in multi-type approaches to interaction [5,8,13]. But also the stand-alone application of gestures is of interest if other modes are not available or considerably restricted, for instance speech in noisy environments. Another example is the interaction with a presentation environment. In this case interaction concerns switching to the next or previous slide, or interaction with an application program which is subject of explanation in the presentation. In this case the

A. Camurri and G. Volpe (Eds.): GW 2003, LNAI 2915, pp. 198–209, 2004.

channel of speech is occupied for the talk, and other modes have been taken for the interaction with the presentation system. One possibility is gestures.

Gestures as a stand-alone mode lead to the problem of deciding whether a posture or motion of the user is indeed meant as a gesture. If multiple modes are available the coincidence of possibly redundant events on several channals can be used as confirmation that the input has been intended. However, in the case of just one mode this sort of time-parallel events or redundancy has to be replaced with other types of confirmation. In the case of gesture input, possibilities are *location-based constraints* and *time-sequential contraints*. An example of a location-based constraint is that a posture has to occur at a certain location in the interaction space in order to be accepted as a gesture. An example of a time-sequential contraint is that not just a single posture but a well-defined sequence of postures has to occur in order to be accepted as a gesture.

The idea presented in this paper is to improve the reliability of gesture-based interaction by additionally combining different gesture types. The types we use are *static hand gestures* based on hand postures, *dynamic hand gestures* based on hand motions, and *pointing gestures* based on hand or arm location. These gesture types are used in parallel or sequentially, similar to the different modes in a multimodal interaction. In a presentation environment, for example, a cursor might be moved to a certain item on screen in the pointing gesture mode, and then an action associated with the item might be activated by a static hand gesture. Static hand gestures might also be used to enter or to leave the dynamic hand gesture mode, that is a dynamic hand gesture is embedded between a starting and a terminating static hand gesture.

The computer-vision-based implementation of a multi-type gesture environment is not straightforward, in particular if the interaction space is not restricted to a small area, like e.g. in a projection-based presentation environment. A particular problem are the hand postures related to static hand gestures which have to be visible in the images acquired by cameras at a size which allows to distinguish between different types of postures. On the other hand, the system needs to have a global view of the interaction space in order to understand motion or pointing gestures. We resolve this difficulty by using several cameras, and in particular one camera with computer-controlled pan, tilt, and zoom. We present a general framework of vision- and gesture-based interaction which can be adapted to concrete application. As a concrete application we use interaction with application programs presented on a projection wall.

Figure 1 shows the concrete interaction environment. In this scenario, cameras observe a user in an interaction space in front of a display. The display presents the application being subject of interaction. It provides a feedback to the input performed by gestures.

The survey on vision-based human motion capturing by Moeslund [10] gives a quite comprehensive collection of existing systems related to vision-based interaction. The number of vision-based systems which include pointing is relatively small.

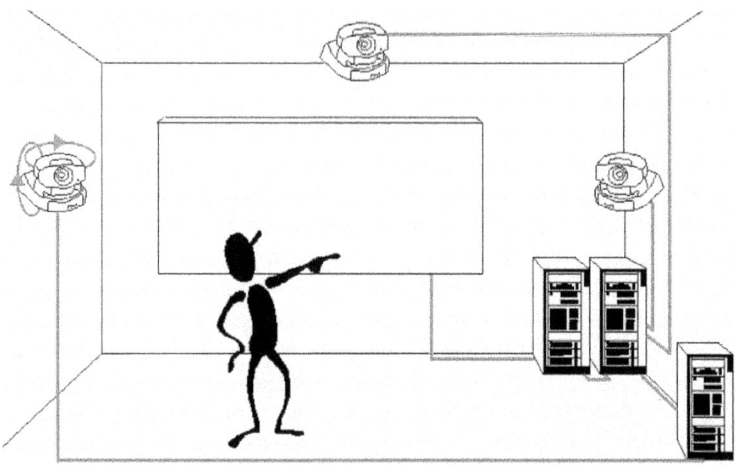

Fig. 1. Computer-vision based interaction in front of a back projection wall.

In the *Visualization Space* by Lucente et al. [8], the pointing direction is determined. Furthermore both hands are captured and their distance is determined. With an additional spoken command "Make this big!" the size of an object presented on a projection screen is changed according to the distance of the hands.

In the *Smart Room* by Wren et al. [13,14] the user is online displayed on a projection wall. Additionally, virtual objects are shown. The user can "touch" the objects, by positioning himself so that he virtually points at them. By speech input, the user can select and move the virtual objects.

In the system of Hoch [2] the user can select, move, and delete objects shown on a backprojection screen by pointing. The commands are activated by speech input.

All the systems mention up to now use speech as an additional input type. Furthermore, they mainly use global pointing gestures. In the ARGUS concept [3], pointing and static hand gestures have been combined in order to interact with devices in a room. The hand and the head of the user are captured by computer-controlled motion cameras. In contrast to the ARGUS concept, we identify different gesture types which can be combined more flexibly. Furthermore, we increase the reliability of gesture recognition by using data of the interacting object (the hand) which come from different sources, from the global observation of the interaction space and from the local observation of the object by a motion camera. ARGUS just relies on data from local tracking.

Chapter 2 outlines the general framework of application into which the multi-type gesture interaction concept is embedded. Chapter 3 is devoted to computer-vision-based gesture recognition. A particular emphasis is on recognition of static hand gestures which requires tracking of the hand by the computer-controlled motion camera. In chapter 4 results of an implementation are presented.

2 A General Framework

Our framework of interaction consists of a sequence of interaction spaces with mappings between them. The first interaction space of the sequence is the *real, physical interaction space* of the user. The last interaction space of the sequence is defined by the *application interface* of the application program which is subject of interaction. In-between we have two further interaction spaces, the *virtual interaction space* and the *abstract interaction space.*

The system may maintain a model of the interaction environment and the relevant parts or aspects of the user. The model is called *virtual interaction space.* Examples of relevant parts of a user are the hand tip or hand, the (fore)arm, the head, or, more comprehensively, a kinematic chain describing the upper body. The virtual interaction space has parameters which define the interface to the real interaction space. Examples of parameters are a 3d-point describing the location of a hand in space, a line describing the direction of the arm, the location and orientation of a coordinate frame in space giving the location and orientation of the head, and a set of points describing the spatial locations of the hands and the head.

The *abstract interaction space* is a place-holder for a real application. It may be identical to the virtual interaction space. One application of the abstract interaction space is indirect interaction. For example, the user may control some sort of avatar like a marionette. The reason is that motion capturing might not be precise enough in order to map the user's pose one-to-one onto the computer-internal virtual actor. Furthermore, the possibilities of a virtual actor might exceed the requirements of the task of interaction. Like the virtual interaction space, the abstract interaction space offers an interface of parameters for its control.

For this paper, we assume that the virtual and the abstract interaction space are identical. It consists of items which correspond to the different gesture modes. We explain this in the following for six gesture modes, point-selecting pointing gestures, projection-based pointing gestures, arm pointing gestures, static hand gestures, and dynamic hand gestures.

A *point-selecting pointing gesture* in the real interaction space consists in moving the hand to the point being the goal of pointing. In the virtual/abstract interaction space it consists of a corresponding point in a fixed region in space. The fixed region is mapped one-to-one of a region in the real interaction space and defines a sensitive region. Sensitive region means that the hand is accepted as a point-selecting pointing gesture only if it is within the region.

A *projection-based pointing gesture* allows to select a point on a plane region in space by moving the hand in a spatial sensitive region. The plane region is one of the faces of the sensitive region. The point on the plane region is associated to the location of the hand by a projection which maps the spatial sensitive region onto the plane region. In the virtual/abstract interaction space, the spatial sensitive region is given in parameter representation $\mathbf{f} : Q \to I\!R^3$ where Q is the unit cube, so that plane region pointed at corresponds to the face defined by $\mathbf{f}(u, v, 0)$, $(u, v) \in [0, 1]^2$. Let $\mathbf{f}(u^*, v*, w*)$ be a gesture point in the abstract interaction space. Then its *associated pointing direction* is defined by the vector from $\mathbf{f}(u^*, v*, w*)$ to $\mathbf{f}(u^*, v*, 0)$ which is another item of the virtual/abstract interaction space. A further item is the pointing goal which is the point $\mathbf{f}(u^*, v*, 0)$. The corresponding pointing direction in the real interaction space is obtained by the mapping between the real and the virtual/abstract interaction space.

An *arm pointing gesture* in the real interaction space is defined by the location of the lower arm in space, combined with a plane region in space which is subject of pointing. The corresponding items of the virtual/abstract interaction space are a plane region R in space and a line L. The intersection of L and R is the pointing goal. The mapping between the real and the virtual/abstract interaction space assigns L to a line along the lower arm, and R to plane region, like e.g. a projection wall.

A further type of pointing gesture is the *head/hand pointing gesture*, see e.g. [3]. In this case the pointing line is determined by connecting a reference point of the head with a reference point of the hand. We do not further use this gesture in the following.

A *dynamic hand gesture* is a curve drawn by moving the hand in the real interaction space. A curve is recognized as a gesture if it has certain features. Different gestures have different features. In the virtual/abstract interaction space, the items are the same as for the pointing gestures. This approach leads to two types of dynamic hand gestures, *spatial dynamic hand gestures* and *projected dynamic hand gestures*. The first version results if the items of point-selecting pointing are used, the second version corresponds to projection-based pointing or arm pointing. In this case the curve drawn by the pointing goal is taken as input of gesture recognition.

A *static hand gesture* in the real interaction space is defined by a posture of the hand. A hand posture is characterized by the deformation of the hand and bendings of the fingers. A hand posture is recognized as a gesture if it has certain features [3]. For instance, the gestures shown in Figure 2, left and middle, can be distinguished by the number of outstretched fingers. The items of the virtual/abstract interaction are a spatial sensitive region, a point in space, and a plane contour. The plane contour corresponds to the hand in the real interaction space observed by a camera. The point corresponds to the location of the hand in the real interaction space. The contour is only relevant for gesture analysis if the point is in the sensitive region and does not move. These two constraints are used as a trigger for entering or leaving a phase of static hand gesture input.

3 Gesture Recognition by Computer-Vision

The body parts of the user to be captured by cameras in order to implement the gesture types of the preceding chapter are a hand and a lower arm. With exception of the static hand gestures no particular requirements on the size of the objects in the captured images have to be taken into consideration. This property makes these gestures immediately suited for larger interaction spaces. It

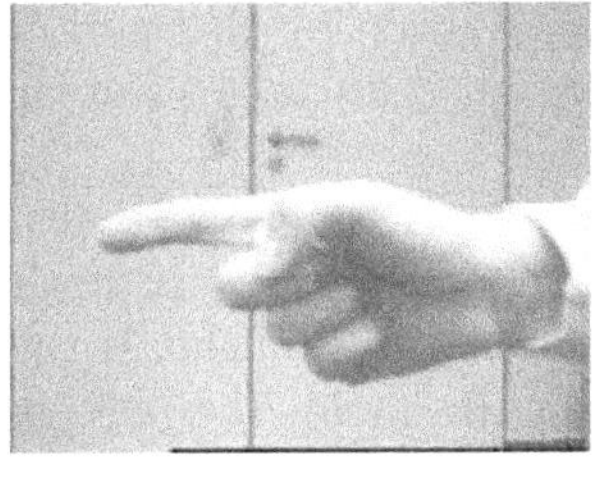
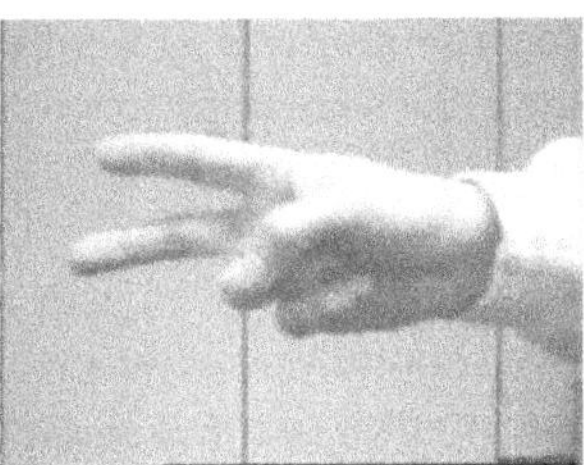
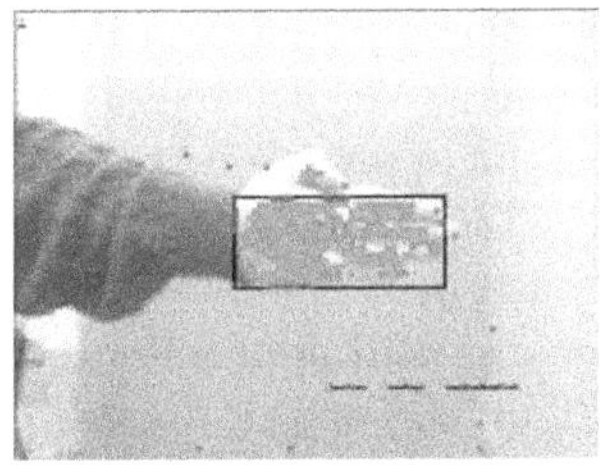

Fig. 2. Examples of static hand gestures and, in the right picture, the result of hand segmentation for hand tracking.

is usually sufficient to use two or more static cameras which cover the interaction space so that the hand and lower arm are visible when a relevant gesture is performed by the user. For example, in the case of interaction with a projection wall it is sufficient to cover the region in front of the wall from the top or the side. The reason is that it is no severe restriction for the user to demand that the pointing arm or hand is the body part closest to the projection wall.

In the case of static hand gestures and larger interaction spaces the number of cameras required to acquire images which show the hand at a reasonable size might become considerable. For that reason we use at least one additional camera with computer-controlled pan, tilt, and zoom, which can be adapted to the current location of the hand. In the scenario of interaction with a projection wall we use one camera of this type which is located at the side or the bottom of the region in front of the projection wall. The user has to orient the hand so that its flat side is in parallel to the projection plane of the camera.

From the images provided by the two or more static cameras, the location of the lower pointing arm and the hand can be determined. We omit this procedure here and refer to [6,7] for a description. In the following we focus on extensions necessary for the types of static and dynamic hand gestures.

3.1 Static Hand Gesture Recognition

In order to capture images of significant quality the hand has to be tracked by the computer-controlled motion camera. For static hand gesture recognition in the image taken by the motion camera we use the Cyclops system. For a description of Cyclops we refer to [3]. In the following we concentrate ourselves on tracking of the hand.

The tracking process consists of several modes: the search mode, the observing mode, and the tracking mode. The mode used depends on the contents of the images taken by the motion camera. If the hand is completely seen in the images and does not change its location significantly if the camera is not moved, the tracking process is kept in the observing mode. The tracking mode is entered if the hand changes its location. If the hand is not in the image, the search mode is initiated. If the hand hand is found, the process switches to the the tracking mode.

This approach is based on the analysis of the images taken by the motion camera. We use region-growing for segmentation, based on color tables similar to the approach described by [12] (Figure 2).

The *tracking mode* works as follows. At every location of the camera, two consecutive images are taken. The regions of the hand are detected in both images and approximated by a bounding rectangle in each of the image. If the difference of the bounding rectangles exceeds a certain threshold, the process stays in the tracking mode. Otherwise it changes into the *observing mode.* If the hand is not present in the second image, the search mode is entered.

If indeed a hand motion is recognized, the motion speed is estimated. A time interval and the next camera position are determined from this information. They have the property that the object should be completely in the image taken by the camera in this position at the end of the time interval. The camera is moved to that position with the required speed. At the new position, the procedure is iterated.

The details are as follows. The location of the object and of the camera are described in polar coordinates (pan angle, tilt angle, and distance) with respect to the optical center of the camera. We are only interested in the two angular components. In the case of the object they yield a line between the camera center and a reference point of the object. In the case of the camera location, they describe the current direction of the optical axis of the camera. Ideally, both locations should be identical. Let $\mathbf{o}_i$ and $\mathbf{o}'_i$ be the two consecutive object locations taken in the current camera position $\mathbf{k}_i$ at times t_i and t'_i. The estimated speed of the object is $\overline{\omega}_i^o := (\mathbf{o}'_i - \mathbf{o}_i)/(t'_i - t_i)$. Let $\overline{\mathbf{o}}_{i+1} := \mathbf{o}'_i + \overline{\omega}_i^o(t_{i+1} - t'_i)$ be the estimated location of the object at a yet unknown time t_{i+1}. Assuming $\mathbf{k}_{i+1} = \overline{\mathbf{o}}_{i+1}$ we have $\overline{\omega}_i^k := (\mathbf{k}_{i+1} - \mathbf{k}_i)/(t_{i+1} - t'_i) = (\overline{\mathbf{o}}_{i+1} - \mathbf{k}_i)/(t_{i+1} - t'_i) = \overline{\omega}_i^o + (\mathbf{o}'_i - \mathbf{k}_i)/(t_{i+1} - t'_i)$. The not yet fixed t_{i+1} is chosen so that the camera is able to reach the goal position $\mathbf{k}_{i+1} = \mathbf{k}_i + \overline{\omega}_i^k(t_{i+1} - t'_i)$ before t_{i+1}.

Alternatively, Kalman filtering might be used, as it has been proposed e.g. for ARGUS [3]. However, the simpler approach just outlined satisfies our requirements.

We have two possible sources of the data about the locations of the hand, $\mathbf{o}_i$ and $\mathbf{o}'_i$, the static cameras and the motion camera. The locations are transformed from their coordinate systems into the polar coordinates used in the motion calculation. The mathematical calculation is corrected by lookup-tables which are interactively initialized in a calibration phase before starting the system. The reason is to compensate deviations caused by camera distortion and measurement errors concerning the positions of the camera. If the location provided by the static cameras is used we call the tracking mode *global*, otherwise *local.*

If data about the position of the hand are neither available from the static cameras nor from the dynamic camera, the process enters the *search mode.* The search mode consists of three phases. In the first phase, the dynamic camera remains unchanged and waits for the appearance of the hand. If the hand does not appear within a given number of frames, the second phase is entered. In the second phase the camera zooms out step by step, in the hope that the hand appears in the extended field of view. If the hand is not found, the third phase is started which consists in resetting the camera to a pre-defined home position, and waiting there for appearance of the hand either in the image of this camera or in the images of the global cameras.

In the preceding description, we have given some intuitive hints concerning the application and change of the different modes. In the system, the decision of the appropriate mode is controlled by a function with decision variables as input and a decision value as output. The state variables are boolean *local_motion*, boolean *global_motion*, boolean *object_detected_locally*, boolean *object_detected_globally*, boolean *same_object*, boolean *close_in_image*, boolean *close_in_space*, int *local_mode_priority*, and int *global_mode_priority*. The decision values are *null_mode*, *local_mode*, *global_mode*, and *search_mode*. The decision function is evaluated for every frame, based on the updated values of the decision variables. The resulting value activates the corresponding mode.

The decision between the local and the global mode depends on the variables *local_mode_priority* and *global_mode_priority*. If *local_mode_priority* > *global_mode_priority*, the local mode is used, otherwise the global mode. The variables are updated dependent on the current situation. Their values are chosen so that the local mode is preferred. The variable *global_mode_priority* is only increased if the troubles in the local mode can be expected, for instance if the hand comes close of the boarder of the image of the dynamic camera.

Up to now, we have ignored the adaptation of the focus of the motion camera. The goal of zoom adaptation is to keep the size of the hand in the image sufficiently large, but not too large in order that the tracking process can be executed. Because of space restrictions we cannot describe the details here. In principle zoom control works analogously to location tracking.

3.2 Motion Gesture Recognition

The input of the motion gesture process is a sequence of two-dimensional points. These points are calculated using the images of the static cameras, analogously to pointing. The curve defined by the sequence of points is input of the motion gesture recognition process. We use the *Gesture Design Tool* (*GDT*) for motion gesture recognition. A description of GDT is given in [15].

A difficulty may arise if the sequence of points delivered by the image analysis process is of low density. This happens if the user moves the hand or arm fast compared to the frame rate achieved by the process of image analysis. In order to overcome this problem a continuous curve approximating the point sequence is determined. We use B-spline curves for this purpose [1]. From the continuous B-spline curve, a sequence of points is sampled which fulfill the requirements of GDT.

The B-spline curve uses the point sequence as control polygon. The quality of approximation of the control polygon depends on the degree of the B-splines. For a low degree, the curve follows the control polygon rather directly. At a

Fig. 3. Examples of B-spline approximations of sample points of dynamic hand gestures, with degree 5 (left) and 10 (right).

higher B-spline degree the approximation quality is less, but erroneous points are smoothed out. A degree of 5 has shown a reasonable effect (Figure 3).

4 Results

We have implemented the approach described in this paper in an adaptation to the projection-wall scenario. The system allows to move the cursor of an application in the projection-based pointing mode. All effects associated by the application program to a cursor motion can be achieved in this manner. A "mouse click" is performed by a static hand gesture which is issued with the static hand at the position which has broad the cursor to the location where the mouse click has to take place. Furthermore, motion gestures can be used instead of a static hand gesture. In this case, a special static hand gesture brings the system into the dynamic gesture mode. The dynamic gesture is terminated by performing another static hand gesture with the unmoved hand. The use of static and dynamic hand gestures extend the number of intuitive gestures available to the user.

The implemented system consists of three modules: the *global camera tracking module*, the *motion camera tracking and control module*, and the *Cyclops module* for static hand gesture recognition. Dynamic hand gesture recognition is part of the global camera tracking module. These modules run as separate processes which themselves consist of different threads. The three modules communicate by remote procedure call (RPC). This allows the execution of the processes on different computers connected by a network. The timings presented in the following have been taken on a Dual Pentium 1100 MHz PC hosting the motion camera tracking module and Cyclops gesture recognition, and a Dual Celeron 2400 Mhz PC for global camera tracking. The PCs have been equipped with 0.5 GByte RAM. A 100-GByte-Ethernet has been used for communication. Image acquisition has been performed by Matrox Meteor II frame grabbing boards. A Sony EVI-D31 camera [9] has served as the computer-controlled motion camera. The Sony camera has a build-in tracking which is able to follow an initially shown object. This lead to the idea of using this tracking ability for local tracking. However, although it works surprisingly well, it was not sufficient reliable for our purposes. Thus the own local tracking procedure has been implemented.

Fig. 4. The environment used for experimental evaluation of the implemented system.

The software has been implemented under Windows NT in Visual C++. Image processing partly uses the Intel image processing library IPL. For implementation of remote procedure calls, Corba [11] has been used.

The evaluation of the performance of the implemented systems is based on the analysis of special tasks to be performed by the user and which are typical for the system. A difficulty is that the results depend on the environment in which the system is installed. In our test environment, daylight could enter through windows, and the lighting of the room has been switched on (Figure 4). The latter is sufficient for the system, and light from outside does not disturb significantly if not too strong cast shadows occur in the images of the camera. The test task for analysis of the *pointing mode* has been to move the cursor into a region of 6×6 cm on the 1.8×2.4 m backprojection screen. The user has been placed at a distance of about 1 to 2 m from the screen. It turned out that the spatial position of the hand could be correctly determined with 98.8-100%. The amount depends in particular on the stability of the illumination of the environment. From the spatial position, the location of the cursor could be correctly determined by projection-based pointing with 97.3%. This means, if the user tries to hold the cursor in the 6×6 cm region, 97.3% of all calculated cursor positions have been in this square. The main reason of the somewhat worse result in comparison to hand location is noise to which the calculation of the pointing direction is particular sensitive. The system has delivered about 10 locations and pointing directions per second.

Evaluation of the *static hand gesture* has been split in several parts, performance of hand image segmentation, hand tracking performance, and performance of gesture recognition by Cyclops. Local image processing did achieve a correct *segmentation of the hand* with 97,3%, at a frame rate of about 10-20 frames per second, dependent on the size of the hand region in the scene. The additional overhead has reduced the frame rate of image processing to 6-8 frames per second. However, because of technical restrictions outside the influence of our system, the number of tracking steps per second may be considerably less, as we found out by analyzing the data obtained from the following two test tasks.

The first task has been changing the distance of the hand to the camera without horizontal or vertical shift. It turned out that the camera needs 0.4-2 s for a zoom operation. For slow motions, the zoom adapts in a stop-and-go manner which is slower than re-zooming for fast hand motions where about 1 s is necessary in order show the hand again with reasonable size in the image of the motion camera.

The second task consisted in horizontal and vertical motions at a fixed distance from the motion camera. For fast hand motions the camera did need about 1.4 s in order to reach a new location. For slow hand motions, the camera followed the hand by stop-and-go, and found the hand after about 0.6 again.

Static hand gesture recognition by Cyclops has achieved a processing rate of about 14 gestures per second. However, in the worst case the user has to wait for 0.5-2.5 s until a gesture is recognized by the system. The reason is the high update time of the camera, as explained before. For four different hand gestures, about 92% of the gesture recognition results are correct. According to our experience, up to four *dynamic hand gestures* could be reliably recognized by the gesture design tool GDT in our environment. The image processing system has to yield about 8 cursor positions per second in order to have sufficient data points for curve interpolation. Otherwise, in particular sharp bends might be smoothed out causing classification errors. Since the data points are not processed before the end of the gesture motion defined by the second static hand gesture, it takes about 1.8 s until the application can start with execution of the related action.

In summary, the results show that the interaction speed and the reliability of the approach are already acceptable for interaction, although it is desirable to increase speed. The main bottleneck in this respect is the motion camera which might be replaced with a more suitable one. Increasing performance of PC hardware in the future will also contribute to making the interaction more fluent.

References

1. Farin, G.: Curves ans surfaces for computer aided geometric design: a practical guide. Morgan Kaufmann Publisher, 2001
2. Hoch, M.: Intuitive Interface (in German). PhD Thesis, Department of Computer Science, University of Dortmund (1999)
3. Kohler, M.: New Contributions to Vision-Based Human-Computer Interaction in Local and Global Environments. PhD Thesis, Department of Computer Science, University of Dortmund (1999). available from http://ls7-www.cs.uni-dortmund.de

4. Markus Kohler, Vision Based Hand Gesture Recognition Systems, http://ls7-www.cs.uni-dortmund.de/research/gesture/
5. Latoschik, M., Wachsmuth, I.: Exploiting Distant Pointing Gestures for Object Selection in a Virtual Environment. Wachsmuth, I., Fröhlich, M. (eds.): Gesture and Sign Language in Human-Computer Interaction (pp 185-196). Berlin: Springer (LNAI 1371), 1998.
6. Leubner, Ch. and Brockmann, Ch. and Müller, H.: Computer-vision-based Human-Computer Interaction with a Back Projection Wall Using Arm Gestures, in: Proceedings of 27th Euromicro Conference, Warsaw, IEEE Press, 2001
7. Leubner, Ch.: A Framework for Segmentation and Contour Approximation in Computer-Vision Systems, PhD Thesis, Department of Computer Science, University of Dortmund (2002). available from http://ls7-www.cs.uni-dortmund.de
8. Lucente, M. and Zwart, G.J. and George, A.D.: Visualization Space: A Testbed for Deviceless Multimodal User Interface. IBM Research, Intelligent Environments Symposium, American Assoc. for Artificial Intelligence
9. Moeslund, T. B.: Technical Report: Protocol used to control the EVI D31 Sony tracking camera, Laboratory of Image Analysis at Aalborg University, Denmark 1997, http://tbm@vision.auc.dk
10. Moeslund, T. B., Granum, E.: A Survey of Computer Vision-Based Human Motion Capture. In: Computer Vision and Image Understanding: CVIU, Vol. 81 (2001) 231–268.
11. Mowbray, J., Zahavi, R.: The Essential CORBA. John Wiley and Sons (1995)
12. Schröter, S.: Automatic Calibration of Colour Lookup-Tables for Image Segmentation, Proc. 3D Image Analysis and Synthesis, Infix-Verlag (1997), available from http://ls7-www.cs.uni-dortmund.de
13. Wren, C.R. and Sparacino, F. and Azarbayejani, A.J. and Darrell, T.J. and Starner, T.E. and Kotani, A. and Chao, C.M. and Hlavac, M. and Russell, K.B. and Pentland, A.P.: Perceptive Spaces for Performance and Entertainment: Untethered Interaction using Computer Vision and Audition. Applied Artificial Intelligence (1997) 267–284
14. Wren, C. and Azarbayejani, A. and Darrell, T. and Pentland, A.: Pfinder: Real-Time Tracking of the Human Body. IEEE Transactions on Pattern Analysis and Machine Intelligence (1997) 780–785
15. Long, A.C.Jr.:Quill: A Gesture Design Tool for Pen-based User Interface. University of Viginia, University of California at Berkeley (1996).

Model-Based Motion Filtering for Improving Arm Gesture Recognition Performance

Greg S. Schmidt[1] and Donald H. House[2]

[1] ITT Industries at the Virtual Reality Laboratory, Naval Research Laboratory
Washington, DC, USA
schmidt@ait.nrl.navy.mil
[2] Visualization Laboratory, College of Architecture, Texas A&M University
College Station, TX, USA
house@viz.tamu.edu

Abstract. We describe a model-based motion filtering process that, when applied to human arm motion data, leads to improved arm gesture recognition. Arm movements can be viewed as responses to muscle actuations that are guided by responses of the nervous system. Our motion filtering method makes strides towards capturing this structure by integrating a dynamic model with a control system for the arm. We hypothesize that embedding human performance knowledge into the processing of arm movements will lead to better recognition performance. We present details for the design of our filter, our evaluation of the filter from both expert-user and multiple-user pilot studies. Our results show that the filter has a positive impact on recognition performance for arm gestures.

1 Introduction

Gesture recognition techniques have been studied extensively in recent years because of their potential for application in user interfaces. It has long been a goal to apply the "natural" communication means that humans employ with each other to the interfaces of computers. People commonly use arm and hand gestures, ranging from simple actions of "pointing" to more complex gestures that express their feelings and enhance communication. Having the ability to recognize arm gestures by computer would create many possibilities to improve application interfaces, especially those requiring difficult data manipulations (e.g., 3D transformations). Pointing operations would certainly be an effective means to infer directional information such as where to move an object in a computer environment. To date no method has been found for arm gesture recognition that is both very accurate and extendable to broad sets of gestures. Typical approaches (e.g., HMMs, neural networks) have focused on applying analytical methods for breaking down motion sequences and recognizing patterns.

The human model-based approach takes into consideration that while a person is making gestures, the resulting motions and poses are played out by a known, rather than an unknown, process. The gestures can be viewed as responses of a skeletal frame to muscle actuations that are made in response to

A. Camurri and G. Volpe (Eds.): GW 2003, LNAI 2915, pp. 210–230, 2004.

control signals originating in the nervous system. The structure of the skeleton, joints, and musculature, is well known and well studied. The neural control systems that actuate the muscles are becoming better understood. With a solid model of human dynamics and control, much of the analytical heuristic guesswork might be eliminated. The arm is a good subject for testing model-based approaches because it is an articulated structure with well understood musculature and fairly large inertias that must have a significant effect on gesture performance.

We have designed a motion adaptation filter for enhancing the signal leading to the gesture recognizer that integrates both physical and control models of human gesture. Our technique uses two motion filters: one augmented with a "learned" parametric gesture sequence and control system, and the other unaugmented. Our method for incorporating process knowledge – the model and its dynamics – is the extended Kalman filter, though any process estimation filter could be used that can handle non-linearities. The squared difference between the outputs of both filters is computed and normalized, giving a score that can be used by the recognition system.

Our working hypothesis is that the motion adaptation filter will improve the unknown signal's quality enough to improve or simplify the recognition process. We tested the hypothesis by integrating the filter with a simple template gesture recognition system, although our filter can be integrated with any standard type of gesture recognition system. To determine the impact that our filter has on arm-movement recognition performance, we tested the system with an expert user performing multiple sets of gestures and with a multiple-user pilot study.

2 Related Work

Here we briefly describe the most common recognition methods and previous related work utilizing human model-based approaches. More complete details can be found in surveys by Watson [1], Aggarwal and Cai [2], Pavlovic et al. [3] and our technical report [4].

2.1 Overview of Recognition Methodologies

The common methodologies that have been used for motion and gesture recognition are: (1) template matching [1], (2) feature-based [1], (3) statistical [5], [6] and (4) multimodal probabilistic combination [7]. By far the most popular recognition methods are feature based neural networks (e.g., [8], [9], [10]) and statistical hidden Markov models (HMMs) (e.g., [11], [12], [13]). Each approach has drawbacks that either affect performance or limit usability. One of the major drawbacks is that most depend on user-specific training and parameter tuning.

The template approach compares the unclassified input sequence with a set of predefined template patterns. The algorithm requires preliminary work to generate a set of gesture patterns, and usually has poor performance due to the difficulty of spatially and temporally aligning the input with the template patterns [1].

The neural network approach typically uses a pre-determined set of common discriminating features, estimates covariances during a training process, and uses a discriminator (e.g., the classic linear discriminator [14]) to classify gestures. The drawback of this method is that features are manually selected and time-consuming training is involved [1].

The HMM method is a variant of a finite state machine characterized by a set of states, a set of observation symbols for each state, and probability distributions for state transitions, observation symbols and initial states [5]. The major drawbacks of the HMMs are: (1) they require a set of training gestures to generate the state transition network and tune parameters; (2) they make the assumption that successive observed operations are independent, which is typically not the case with human motion [15].

In a multimodal recognition process, two or more human senses are captured and/or two or more capturing technologies are combined. The multiple inputs are processed by a classifier, which rates the set of possible output patterns with a value based upon the likelihood of a match. The set of probabilities for each input are then combined in a manner to be able to select the most likely pattern. Many groups have explored combining speech and gesture (e.g., Cohen et al. [7], Vo and Waibel [16]).

2.2 Methods Utilizing Human Model-Based Approaches

Human model-based approaches integrate a model of human motion, typically approximated as a dynamic process and control system, into the process of filtering motion capture data of human movements. Such a model-based approach seems to have first appeared in Pentland and Horowitz [17]. Model-based approaches to motion generation for animation have been utilized by Zordan and Hodgins [18], Metaxas [19] and others. Wren and Pentland [20] applied dynamics to a 3D skeletal model for a tracking application. They applied 2D measurements from image features and combined them with the extended Kalman filter to drive the 3D model. Their resulting tracking system was able to tolerate temporary image occlusions and the presence of multiple people in the tracked area. In more recent work [21] they explored the notion that people utilize muscles to actively shape purposeful motion. In earlier work [22], we explored the use of a simple particle model for arm motion recognition performance.

3 Background

Here we give the background for methods that we utilized and integrated in the design of our filter.

3.1 Extended Kalman Filter

The extended Kalman filter (EKF) [23] estimates both the time sequence of states of an input data stream and a statistical model of that data stream. The EKF differs from the standard Kalman filter [24] in that it can be used to estimate a process that is non-linear and/or handle a measurement relationship to the process that is non-linear. The EKF can be augmented by a dynamic model of the system being tracked, and knowledge of the reliability of this model. Simply described, the filter is a set of time update equations that estimate the next state vector, current error covariance and the Kalman gain. The Kalman gain affects the weighting of measurement data versus the control model in determining the next state vector estimate. If the dynamic model is left out or is unreliable, the Kalman gain is high and the filter simply smoothes the input data.

The EKF's prediction equations may be written

$$\begin{aligned} \mathbf{x}_{i+1}^{-} &= f(\mathbf{x}_i, \mathbf{u}_i, 0) \\ P_{i+1}^{-} &= A_i P_i A_i^T + W_i Q_i W_i^T, \end{aligned} \tag{1}$$

where f estimates the *a priori* state vector $\mathbf{x}_{i+1}^{-}$, as a function of the current state vector $\mathbf{x}_i$, and the process model vector $\mathbf{u}_i$ at the current time step. P_i and P_{i+1}^{-} are the current and *a priori* estimated error covariances, Q_i is the process model error covariance, A and W are the Jacobians of f with respect to the state $\mathbf{x}$ and a vector of random variables $\mathbf{w}$.

The filter's update equations may be written

$$\begin{aligned} K_i &= P_i^- H_i^T (H_i P_i^- H_i^T + V_i R_i V_i^T)^{-1} \\ \mathbf{x}_i &= \mathbf{x}_i^- + K_i(\mathbf{z}_i - h(\mathbf{x}_i^-, 0)) \\ P_i &= (I - K_i H_i) P_i^-, \end{aligned} \tag{2}$$

where K_i is the current Kalman gain matrix, $\mathbf{v}$ is a vector of random variables, h relates the state vector to the measurement vector $\mathbf{z}_i$, R_i is the measurement error covariance, and H and V are the Jacobians of h with respect to $\mathbf{x}$ and $\mathbf{v}$.

3.2 Lagrangian Formulation for Dynamics

The Lagrangian formulation for dynamics is particularly appropriate for articulated systems. The Lagrangian

$$L(\mathbf{q}, \dot{\mathbf{q}}) = E_k(\mathbf{q}, \dot{\mathbf{q}}) - E_p(\mathbf{q}) \tag{3}$$

is the difference between the kinetic energy E_k and potential energy E_p of the system as a function of state $\mathbf{q}$. The state is a set of generalized joint coordinates and its rate $\dot{\mathbf{q}}$ is a set of related velocities. The Lagrangian formulation for the dynamics of a system is

$$\frac{d}{dt}\frac{\partial L}{\partial \dot{q}_i} - \frac{\partial L}{\partial q_i} = \tau_i, \; i = 1, ..., m, \tag{4}$$

where τ is the set of externally applied or nonconservative forces and torques [25].

Solutions to Equation 4 can be found in closed form, which are more efficient and readily parameterizable than the open form derivations generated by the Featherstone algorithm [26], which is a very efficient rendition of the Newton-Euler approach to dynamics [27]. On the other hand, the open form derivations do have the advantage that they can be easily extended to handle large sets of joint-space configurations.

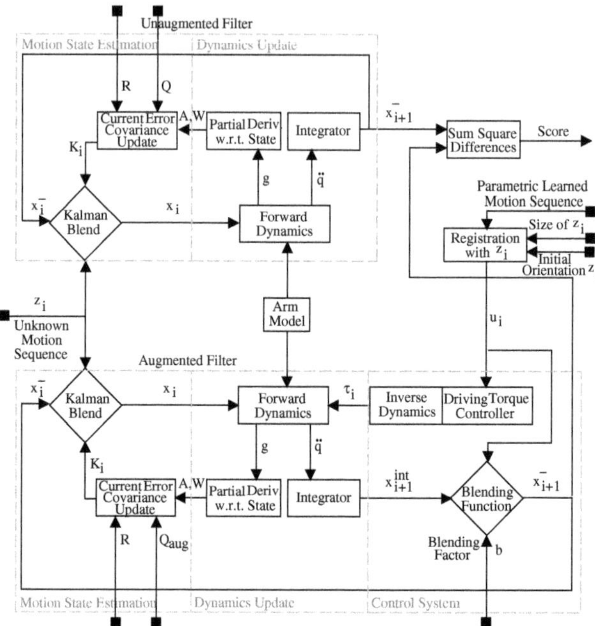

Fig. 1. Motion Adaptation Filter

4 Motion Adaptation Filter

The design of our model-based motion adaptation filter is shown in Figure 1. Its two extended Kalman filters each contain a model of the human arm and its dynamics. Only one is augmented with a model of a control system acting on the arm. The input unknown motion sequence is passed through each filter, compared and a score is computed, which is used as output for the motion adaptation filter.

The unaugmented filter simply smoothes the input motion sequence. Since it contains a control system, the augmented filter attempts to influence the raw input motion sequence to follow a learned motion sequence. We illustrate this notion in Figure 2 by showing five different motion sequences (arc, line, wave, circle and angle) as influenced by a control system generating an arc. Each sequence starts on the right side and proceeds towards the left. The darkest grey line indicates the "influencing" arc sequence, the lightest grey is the input sequence, and the mid-grey is the output sequence. The images show the degree of influence that the arc controller has on each of the input sequences. The degree of this influence is determined by the Kalman gain.

The unaugmented and augmented filters both contain units for motion state estimation and dynamics update. The state estimation unit blends the input motion sequence with the current state vector and passes the data to the dynamics update process. There, forward dynamics are performed on the state

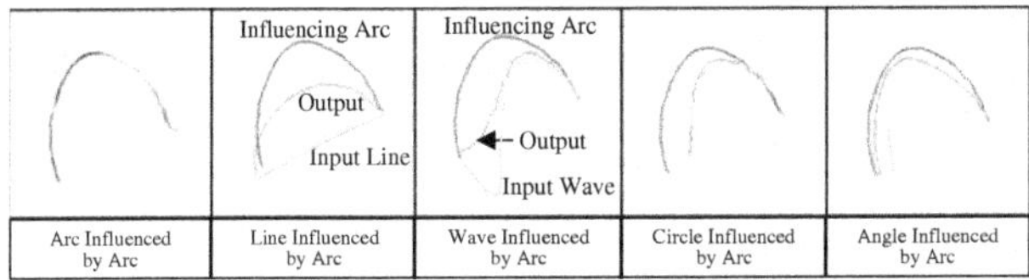

Fig. 2. Five Gestures Influenced by an Arc Motion Sequence

vector producing angular accelerations. These are numerically integrated generating the next state vector. The next state vector is fed back into the system at the Kalman blend and sent to be compared with the output from the augmented filter. The Kalman gain is updated from the current error covariance which is subsequently updated by data from the dynamics update process.

The augmented filter's control system is composed of a driving torque controller and a blending function. Torques used by the controller are derived from the parametric learned motion sequence and model and applied to the forward dynamics of the system. After numerical integration, an intermediate state vector is passed to the blending function where it is mixed with the aligned and parameterized learned motion sequence producing the next state vector. The motivation behind the augmented filter is that if the input motion sequence matches closely to the learned motion sequence (e.g., in Figure 2 the arc in arc module), then the resulting trajectory should be very similar to the input. Thus the trajectories output by the unaugmented and augmented filters will be nearly identical, and the output score will be small. However, if the input motion sequence is dissimilar (e.g., in Figure 2 the line in arc module) to the learned sequence, the trajectories will differ greatly and likewise the score will be large.

4.1 Arm Model

A dynamic articulated model of a human arm is integrated into the filter. The arm model consists of a 3-DOF shoulder joint, a 1-DOF elbow joint and cylinder linkages between the shoulder and elbow, and between the elbow and wrist. The model is shown in Figure 3. We ignore the wrist twist in the lower arm. We also capture the three degrees of freedom for the torso, which is used to produce a relative coordinate system for the arm. The three degrees of freedom from the torso are eliminated after the coordinate transformation takes place between the torso and shoulder.

The position of the wrist and elbow can be determined by using the kinematics equations of motion for the arm model. The equations are parameterized using joint angles for each degree of freedom of the joints in the model. They are

$$\begin{aligned} \chi_E &= (-l_U S_\theta C_\phi, -l_U S_\theta S_\phi, -l_U C_\theta)^T, \\ \chi_W &= R_z(\phi) R_y(\theta) (-l_L S_\rho C_\alpha, -l_L S_\rho S_\alpha, -l_L C_\rho)^T, \end{aligned} \tag{5}$$

where χ_E and χ_W are the positions of the elbow and wrist, respectively, l_U and l_L are the corresponding lengths of the upper and lower arm, $R_z(\phi)$ and $R_y(\theta)$ are rotation matrices about the respective axes z and y, and S and C are sines and cosines of angles of rotation θ, ϕ, α and ρ.

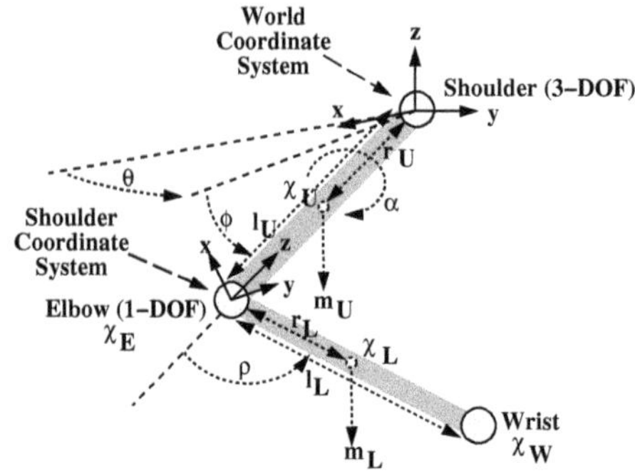

Fig. 3. Articulated Arm Model

4.2 Motion State Estimation

Motion state estimation is used to predict the state vector at the next time step for the current state of measured input, dynamic model and statistical models of the measured and control systems. The statistics for the measurement process and control system are in the form of error covariance matrices and are predetermined using training and measurements from the user workspace. They are used by the EKF along with data from the dynamics update process to determine the current Kalman gain.

The Kalman gain is critical for state estimation in the system and requires knowledge from the dynamics and measurement processes. These data include the four (8x8)-Jacobian matrices A, W, H and V from Equations 1 and 2, which relate the process and measurement system's state vectors to the current state vector. The analytic equations for the elements of these matrices are predetermined and their values updated as the filter operates. They are

$$A = \begin{bmatrix} 1 & t \\ t\frac{\partial g}{\partial \mathbf{q}} & 1 + t\frac{\partial g}{\partial \dot{\mathbf{q}}} \end{bmatrix}, \quad W = \begin{bmatrix} 1 & t \\ t\frac{\partial g}{\partial \mathbf{w}_1} & 1 + t\frac{\partial g}{\partial \mathbf{w}_2} \end{bmatrix},$$

and $H = V = \mathbf{I}$ where $\mathbf{I}$ is the 8x8-identity matrix. The matrices A and W are updated by taking the partial derivatives with respect to the current state vector of their respective complete forward dynamics equation g. The augmented and unaugmented filters have different formulations. The formulation for the augmented filter is

$$\begin{aligned} g(\mathbf{q}, \dot{\mathbf{q}}, \mathbf{w}_1, \mathbf{w}_2) = B'^{-1}[\tfrac{1}{2}(\dot{\mathbf{q}} + \mathbf{w}_2)^T \tfrac{\partial}{\partial \mathbf{q}}[B'](\dot{\mathbf{q}} + \mathbf{w}_2) - \\ \dot{B}'(\dot{q} + \mathbf{w}_2) + \tau(\mathbf{q}^m, \dot{\mathbf{q}}^m)], \end{aligned} \tag{6}$$

and for the unaugmented filter is

$$\begin{aligned} g(\mathbf{q}, \dot{\mathbf{q}}, \mathbf{w}_1, \mathbf{w}_2) = B'^{-1}[\tfrac{1}{2}(\dot{\mathbf{q}} + \mathbf{w}_2)^T \tfrac{\partial}{\partial \mathbf{q}}[B'](\dot{\mathbf{q}} + \mathbf{w}_2) - \\ \dot{B}'(\dot{\mathbf{q}} + \mathbf{w}_2)], \end{aligned} \tag{7}$$

where $\mathbf{w}_1$ and $\mathbf{w}_2$ are vectors of random variables representing "white" noise with zero mean and constant variance associated with the process model's state vector and velocities, respectively. B and $\dot{B}$ are the inertia matrices defined in

Section 4.3 composed of members from the state vector $\mathbf{q}$ and angular velocities $\dot{\mathbf{q}}$. B' and $\dot{B}'$ are similar matrices to B and $\dot{B}$ but wherever an element of $\mathbf{q}$ and $\dot{\mathbf{q}}$ appears, the appropriate random variable from the vectors $\mathbf{w}_1$ or $\mathbf{w}_2$ is added to that member. For example, if θ appears in an element of matrix B, then in B' it is replaced by $\theta + w_{11}$, the first element in the vector $\mathbf{w}_1$, since θ is the first element in $\mathbf{q}$.

4.3 Dynamics Update

The dynamics update process provides parameter updates for motion state estimation and the control system. It takes the current state of the system and the arm model (and a set of torques for the augmented filter), and performs forward dynamics to produce the parameter update functions g (described in Section 4.2) and the angular accelerations $\ddot{q}$. Our experiments showed that Euler numerical integration [28] was adequate for updating the next state vector using the accelerations.

The forward dynamics equation for the 4-DOF articulated arm model generates the angular accelerations and is used to derive the complete forward dynamics equations (Equations 6 and 7). In order to derive these equations, the masses, lengths and moments of inertia of the arm segments are needed. Each arm segment is represented by a thin cylinder rotating about its endpoint. The center of mass for each cylinder is estimated using data from a study on anthropometric parameters for the human body in [29]. The data gives estimations for the segmental center of mass (COM) locations expressed in percentages of the segment lengths. These are measured from the proximal end of the segments. The moment of inertia for each segment is computed by combining the inertia tensor of the representative cylinder body and inertial component associated with the shift of its COM to the endpoint. The inertial components associated with the shift of the COM are

$$\begin{aligned} \chi_U &= (-r_U S_\theta C_\phi, -r_U S_\theta S_\phi, -r_U C_\theta)^T, \\ \chi_L &= R_z(\phi) R_y(\theta)(-r_L S_\rho C_\alpha, -r_L S_\rho S_\alpha, -r_L C_\rho)^T, \end{aligned} \tag{8}$$

where χ_U and χ_L are the positions in Cartesian world space of the estimated COMs of the upper and lower arm, respectively, and r_U and r_L are the corresponding radial distances from the shoulder and elbow, respectively. Time derivatives are taken to get the angular velocities at the estimated COMs of the arm segments. These are

$$\dot{\chi}_i = J_i \dot{\mathbf{q}}, \ i = \{U, L\} \tag{9}$$

where the Jacobian matrices $J_U = \frac{\partial \chi_U}{\partial q}$ and $J_L = \frac{\partial \chi_L}{\partial q}$, and $\dot{q} = (\dot{\theta}, \dot{\phi}, \dot{\alpha}, \dot{\rho})^T$. The inertial components are

$$\begin{aligned} I_U &= m_U J_U^T J_U + Ibody_U, \\ I_L &= m_L J_L^T J_L + Ibody_L, \end{aligned} \tag{10}$$

where I_U and I_L are the inertial components of the upper and lower arm, respectively, m_U and m_L are the estimated masses of the arm segments, and $Ibody_U$ and $Ibody_L$ are diagonal matrices representing the thin cylinder body inertias about each parameterized of the axes θ, ϕ, α and ρ. The elements in $Ibody_U$ and $Ibody_L$ are determined by converting the cylinder's Euclidean coordinates to spherical coordinates.

The angular velocities and inertias are used to compute the kinetic energy

$$E_k = \frac{1}{2}\dot{\mathbf{q}}^T B\dot{\mathbf{q}}, \tag{11}$$

where $B = I_U + I_L$. The potential energy is given as

$$\begin{aligned} E_p = &-m_U g r_U C_t \\ &-m_L g[l_U C_t - r_L S_r C_a S_t + r_L C_t C_r], \end{aligned} \tag{12}$$

where g is the gravitational constant. The two energy terms are used for the Lagrangian, L, of Equations 3 and 4. The dynamics equations are computed and solved for angular acceleration

$$\ddot{q} = B^{-1}[\tfrac{1}{2}\dot{q}^T \tfrac{\partial}{\partial q}[B]\dot{q} - \dot{B}\dot{q} + \tau], \tag{13}$$

where τ is the set of applied torques.

4.4 Control System

Our control system acts as an analogue to the motor nervous system in the human body, influencing how the learned motion sequence acts on the current motion state. It is composed of a driving torque controller and a blending function. The driving torque controller uses data from the learned motion sequence and arm model and performs inverse dynamics, which generates torques for the dynamics update process. The blending function combines the learned motion sequence with an intermediate state vector from the dynamics update process. The degree of its influence is controlled by a fixed predetermined blending factor. The learned motion sequence also remains fixed throughout the iteration of the filter. We see the driving torque controller as analagous to an open-loop predictive control and the blending function as analagous to proprioceptive and sensory feedback. Our control system has similarities to the model reference adaptive control (MRAC) system presented in [30], [31], which incorporates a reference model of a motion sequence, inverts its dynamics and applies the resulting torques in a controlled manner to the input data.

The torques for the driving torque controller are computed using the inverse dynamics torque formulation

$$T(q, \dot{q}) = \tau(q^m, \dot{q}^m) + \tfrac{1}{2}\dot{q}^T \tfrac{\partial}{\partial q} B\dot{q} - \dot{B}\dot{q}. \tag{14}$$

where τ is the vector of applied torques from the controller, and joint angles q^m and angular velocities $\dot{q}^m$ are from the influencing gesture sequence. The joint configurations are transformed so that they correlate with the learned model's joint configurations.

Since there is no feedback in the driving torque controller, the torques can be precomputed. When $T(q, \dot{q})$ is applied to the dynamics it influences the motion of the model to follow a trajectory analogous to the influencing sequence. However, it is not necessarily strongly influencing the raw motion data to move towards the learned motion sequence. The strength of the influence is controlled by a scaling parameter k_c that is applied to the Kalman filter's process model error covariance matrix Q. This affects how much the system "trusts" the raw motion data versus the dynamic model. As k_c changes it directly impacts how the reported controller error relates to the measurement error in the system. As a result, the Kalman filter's gain matrix K (Equation 2), stabilizes differently, therefore changing how the Kalman filter weights input motion versus controller influence.

The blending function supplements the driving torque controller by providing more guidance to the state estimation. The driving torque controller provides the dynamics drive for the model, but it does not always provide sufficient guidance. The influencing motion sequence's torques may be nonlinear with respect to the joint configurations, but the tracking system performs blending of joint configurations linearly. Therefore, due to linear blending, small changes in the joint configurations can produce large changes in the dynamics. This directly affects how the driving torque controller performs. The blending function is intended to counteract this effect.

The blending function incorporates the current state of the system with the raw motion data from a learned motion sequence. The raw motion data includes the joint angles and angular velocities. This data is linear with respect to the motion state configurations of the system. The blending function that we use is

$$\mathbf{x}_{i+1} = b(\mathbf{x}_i + \Delta t\dot{\mathbf{x}}_i) + (1-b)\mathbf{x}_i^m, \tag{15}$$

where $\mathbf{x}_i = [q, \dot{q}]^T$, $\dot{\mathbf{x}}_i = [\dot{q}, \ddot{q}]^T$, $\mathbf{x}_i^m = [q^m, \dot{q}^m]^T$, Δt is the current time step, and b is the blending factor.

5 Analysis of Filter

In order to test its effectiveness, we implemented our new filter, selected a difficult–to–discriminate gesture dataset, and ran user studies.

5.1 Design of Test System

We designed a system to test the motion adaptation filter by adapting a simple template-style gesture recognizer. We chose the template recognition system because it is easy to implement and is very easy to understand. However, our filter can work with most standard recognition architectures with some minor modifications (e.g., see notes in Section 7). The template architecture works by comparing the unknown input sequence with each gesture pattern. For our case, the unknown input is passed through a motion adaptation filter associated with each gesture (see Figure 4 for an overview).

Human motion data is brought into the system by a motion tracking unit and segmented by searching for long pauses in the motion sequences. The choice of tracking system is arbitrary, as long it can generate a continuous sequence of motion states. For this architecture, the output is distributed in parallel to N copies of the filter. Each of the filters is custom-tuned for a specific gesture. The output of the filters is a set of scores that are processed by the recognition

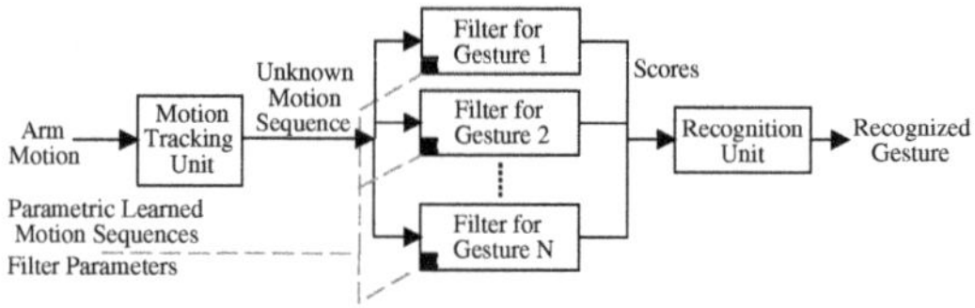

Fig. 4. Test Recognition System Architecture

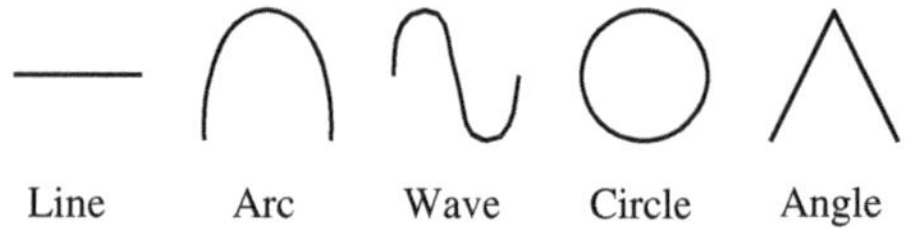

Fig. 5. Wrist-Trajectory Shapes of the Gesture Datasets used for the Expert User Experiments

unit. The scores are the squared differences of the internal unaugmented and augmented filters.

Although our filter can accept tracking data from any motion capturing technology, for purposes of testing we found it convenient to use a magnetic tracking system. There are obviously more accurate input technologies (e.g., acoustic and inertial) and vision systems, but due to occlusion, they do not guarantee a continuous reliable stream of input.

We capture orientations of the lower arm, upper arm, and torso to to retrieve the required four Euler angles. We estimate angular velocities using time difference methods. The set of angles and angular velocities makes up a motion state vector. The sequence of state vectors is sent to the motion state estimation unit.

5.2 Selection of a Hard–to–Discriminate Gesture Dataset

Our first step for analyzing the performance of the filter was to select a set of gestures that are hard to distinguish from each other. The selection criterion was determined by observing trajectories of the wrist for each gesture. The trajectories for the gesture dataset we selected for the introductory experiments are shown in Figure 5. This gesture set has many overlapping features, as can be seen in Figure 6. Two distinct gestures that have overlapping motion segments, especially if they start with the same motion sub-sequence, are more difficult to distinguish than dissimilar nonoverlapping gestures. A properly tuned EKF bases its initial output more on the input data than the dynamic model. But, when it converges to a stable blending state, the dynamics of the system takeover. If two gestures have similar starting trajectories and abruptly change after the dynamics become more dominant, the system will initially fail to discriminate between the two gestures because the derived dynamics of the system are similar. Eventually the mixture of the two dissimilar segments of the gestures will influence and change the system behavior.

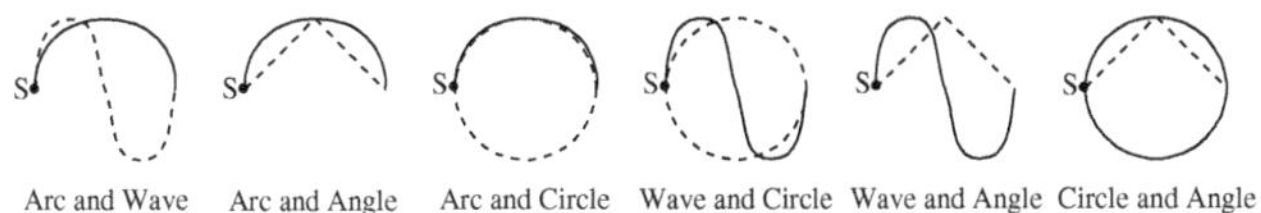

Fig. 6. Overlapping Features Embedded in Gesture Pairs

For our experiments, we also considered the direction in which the motion was performed, thus expanding the five basic shapes to ten. We used combinations of the five basic shapes to generate gesture datasets and test the performance, generalizability and extensability of our approach in four of five expert–user experiments.

5.3 Filter Parameters

Our filter requires a set of parameters that must be predetermined and tuned for individual gestures. The EKF requires error covariance data for the measurement and control processes. The dynamics update requires measurements from the user's arm. Each control system requires a blending constant and a learned motion sequence.

Parameter Determination. To compute the measurement error covariance we affixed three motion tracking receivers in the user workspace to a stationary configuration analogous to that of the right arm. We recorded 1000 samples continuously and computed the error covariance matrix computed using the sampled angles and estimated angular velocities. The measurement covariance matrix needs to be computed once for a given combination of hardware and workspace.

The control process error is computed by using the pre-recorded gesture sequences. A parametric learned motion sequence for each gesture type is selected by determining the closest fitting trajectory to a normal trajectory that is computed from the sample set of gestures. The error matrix is estimated using the mean squared error between the parametric learned motion sequence and the rest of the sequences. The control error needs to be computed for every gesture sequence.

Subject Measurements. Some of the parameters needed for the filters are taken from measurements of the users. The filters require the lengths, radii and masses of the upper and lower arm. These parameters are obtained by combinations of two methods: direct measurements and estimation from anthropometric parameters of the human body. The lengths are determined by either directly measuring the distance between the shoulder and elbow, and elbow and wrist, or estimating them from the height and sex of the user. Estimations of anthropometric parameters are made according to the procedure outlined in Hall [29]. The radii are obtained by measuring the circumferences of the arm segments at the midpoint. The masses for the arm segments are determined as percentages of the whole body mass for males and females.

Parameter Tuning. In order to use the EKF, specific parameters have to be tuned in order to get desirable guidance in the recognition units. One of the parameters that needs tuning is a multiplicative factor k_c used to scale the augmented filter's control error covariance. There is one such scaling factor for each control error covariance matrix. The scaling factor is used to adjust the level of "trust" in the filter by changing the control error with respect to the measurement error. The larger k_c is, the more the filter output depends on the input. The smaller k_c is, the more the filter output depends on the controller and dynamic model. As a result the Kalman gain matrix, essential for the Kalman blend, changes. A similar single parameter is adjusted for the unaugmented filter.

Another parameter to be tuned is the blending factor b. This is applied in the blending function, which performs a blend of the intermediate state vector $\mathbf{x}_{i+1}^{int}$ and the parametric learned motion sequence. This factor is important because it weights how the raw data is blended with the parametric learned motion sequence. The Kalman blend does not directly incorporate knowledge of the parametric learned motion sequence. We used one blending factor for all the gesture types. More details about the choice-of and tuning of these parameters is described in our technical report [4].

An important consideration when selecting the parameters is the degree of alignment of the input gesture with respect to the learned gesture. In the experiments, we ask the users to extend their right arm perpendicular to the chest. The gestures they are asked to perform are then roughly centered around that hand position. Rough alignment and scaling is applied to the parametric learned gesture in addition to the parameterizing that is necessary to perform a matching comparison. This is the registration phase, which can be seen on the right side of the filter diagram in Figure 1. If the parametric learned gesture does not align very well with the gesture it is supposed to accept, it creates a high score for the comparison. This is due to our method for evaluation which compares the augmented and raw input trajectories. If the alignment is extremely bad we could not adjust the k_c parameter to "trust" the model as much. In most cases this is not a problem, but for a difficult dataset to recognize, such as the basic five gestures in Figure 5, some gestures will be improperly classified.

Sensitivity Analysis. If we were to run a full user study on human subjects of widely varying mass and height, it would be important to understand how much of an impact parameter changes have on the dynamics of the system. If it can be shown that the system is relatively insensitive to changes in the parameters then it may be considered to be more generalizable and potentially more powerful. We analyzed the sensitivity of a few of the body parameters (summarized in Schmidt [32]), but did not determine enough meaningful information to make conclusions about the generalizability of our filter.

5.4 Expert User Experiments

We set out to verify the effectiveness of the filter integrated into a gesture recognizer by devising a set of experiments to be performed by an expert user.

These were designed to test the performance of the recognizer with and without our filter. We also wanted to ascertain something about how generalizable and extensable our filter is with respect to different and larger gesture datasets. To accomplish these goals, we ran five experiments. Before beginning, we prerecorded a database of gestures from the user, computed the parameters and learned models, and performed manual parameter tuning.

Accuracy Performance. The purpose of the first experiment was to determine the performance rating of the recognizer integrated with and without our filter. We used the five gestures from Table 1, and recorded 100 samples for each gesture. The gestures were first aligned with the learned motion sequences, then the learned motion sequences were parameterized to match the size of the input sequence. We supplied both the filtered (our method) and unfiltered recognizers with the 500 gestures. The results are given in Table 1.

Table 1. Results of Experiment #1

Arc	Line	Wave	Circle	Angle	Totals
99/100 99%	99/100 99%	100/100 100%	100/100 100%	99/100 99%	Unfiltered Approach 99.4%
98/100 98%	100/100 100%	100/100 100%	100/100 100%	99/100 99%	Our Filtered Approach 99.4%

They show that both methods have an accuracy rating of 99.4%. The fact that both methods produced acceptable results turned out to be only coincidental for the unfiltered approach, which was later shown to be very inconsistent. We analyzed this dataset further and noticed that the gestures were fairly spatially regular with respect to each other. For example, there was not an extensive amount of variation due to alignment, skewing and scaling among the like gestures in this set.

To get a better idea of how our method works, refer back to Figure 2. The arc in the arc module shows the best match between the augmented and the unaugmented (effectively the learned motion sequence) trajectories. The rest of the cases show that the learned arc sequence has a large influence on the data running through the augmented filter which is evident by the output augmented trajectories. This effect pulls the augmented and raw data curves apart. The sequences in Figure 7 illustrate a small set of state transitions from the three arm models used in generating the trajectories for the line and the arc in the arc module. The figures show frames from a 3D simulation of the corresponding schematic 4-DOF arm models. The arm states are very similar for the arc in the arc module, but very different for the line in the arc module.

Generalizability. To test the generalizability of our approach, we ran a second experiment. In the experiment we used the reverse-order wrist trajectories from

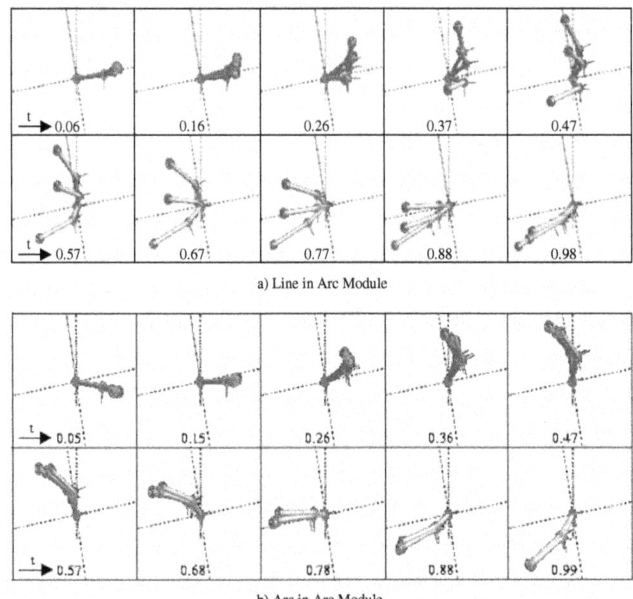

Fig. 7. Arm Model Motion in Time

Table 2. Results of Experiment #2

Arc	Line	Wave	Circle	Angle	Totals
60/100 60%	100/100 100%	78/100 78%	62/100 62%	99/100 99%	Unfiltered Approach 79.8%
98/100 98%	100/100 100%	100/100 100%	100/100 100%	96/100 96%	Our Filtered Approach 98.8%

the gestures used in the first experiment (a completely unique dataset). We recorded 100 samples for each of the five gestures and purposely added noise into the samples to test the robustness of our filter. Then we passed them into the gesture recognizer twice, with and without our filter in the system. The resulting performance ratings are given in Table 2.
In this case, the accuracy of the recognizer integrated with our filter proved to be far superior than without it. The performance rating for our filtered approach is 98.8%, while the unfiltered is 79.8%.

Extensibility. For the third experiment, we examined the extensibility of our approach. To do this, we increased the number of distinct gestures that the recognizer had to distinguish. We used the two sets of gestures from the first two experiments and combine them into one database. Although diagrams make the two gesture sets appear similar, the motions that the human subject has to perform with the arm are totally different. When we performed the same experimental procedure as before, the results show our method has an accuracy rating of 99.1% while the unfiltered approach has a rating of 89.6%. This gives us a good indication that our method is extensable to larger size gesture datasets.

More Generalizability Experiments. At this point we decided to revisit the first experiment with the hope of making it more difficult to distinguish the gestures than before. The goals of the fourth experiment were to show more generalizability with our method. In order to do this, we replaced the line and the wave with a triangle and another form of the arc. The new arc gesture is generated using a bend at the elbow instead of the straight arm motions used for the original arc. By our definition of arm gestures (i.e. movements of the arm that may or may not have any meaningful intent) and our analysis of only the "end-effector" position of the arm at the wrist, we do not make any distinction between the new and old arc gesture since both have identical wrist trajectories. The triangle gesture resembles the angle gesture in the first time steps, but deviates from it near the end. Our assumption was that this choice of gestures would be harder to discriminate. 75 trials were run for each gesture.

The experimental results show that the new gesture set was a bit harder to recognize by both methods. The triangle and bent-arm arc were recognized 90.7% and 86.7%, respectively for the unfiltered approach, and 98.7% and 96.0% for our approach. Our filtered approach showed an overall accuracy rating of 98.1% compared with the unfiltered approach's rating of 95.2%. The results were again encouraging with regard to our method's consistency and accuracy, and also that it generalizes to different gestures quite well.

For our fifth experiment we ran 50 trials with five new gestures, each significantly different from the others. In addition, we decided to make a choice of somewhat natural gestures. The goal of the experiment was to determine if our method works well with gestures that are very easy to distinguish because they are quite distinct and are more natural. Our choices included the "zorro" sign, Catholic cross, salute, wave, and stop gestures. Diagrams of the motions of the wrist and results of the experiment are shown in Table 3.

The results show that our method was 100% accurate on this gesture set, while the unfiltered approach achieved an accuracy rating of 98.4%.

Table 3. Results of Experiment #5

Zorro	Catholic Cross	Waving	Stop	Salute	Totals
50/50 100%	46/50 92%	50/50 100%	50/50 100%	50/50 100%	Unfiltered Approach 98.4%
50/50 100%	50/50 100%	50/50 100%	50/50 100%	50/50 100%	Our Filtered Approach 100%

Discussion. In the experiments, we evaluated the accuracy performance, generalizability and extensability of our filter when integrated in a recognition system. We made steps to ensure that it was difficult to distinguish among gestures by carefully selecting gesture datasets with overlapping motion traits. When compared with the recognizer with no filter attached, our method showed improved recognition performances. Our results from the five experiments show that our method is consistently accurate with rates ranging from 98.1% to 99.4% and extends to multiple gesture datasets. This compares very favorably with the unfiltered method whose accuracy ranged from 79.8% to 99.4%.

6 Pilot Study

We performed a pilot study involving six different subjects, in order to evaluate our model-based approach across different subjects.

6.1 Subject Selection

For the experiment, we selected three males and three females, with varying anatomical proportions. The sex discriminant was desired to accommodate for potential differing mass distributions in the arm between male and female subjects, based on muscle and bone proportions. The proportions we were concerned with were the lengths, radii and masses of the upper and lower right arm. The subjects were selected without regard to ethnicity, age, social or cultural backgrounds. The only screening requirement we had was a visual observation of size proportions in order to assure a subject pool of varying anatomical proportions.

6.2 Subject Measurements

The subjects had body weights ranging from 55 to 87 kg and heights ranging from 1.6 to 1.9 m, giving us a broad spectrum of masses and lengths for the user's arm proportions. The upper arm lengths varied from 28 to 36 cm and the lower arm lengths from 23 to 27 cm. The upper arm radii varied from 3.66 to 5.25 cm and the lower arm radii from 3.18 to 4.38 cm. Trackers were attached using velcro straps at the wrist and near the elbow. A third was affixed with tape to the shoulder.

6.3 Pilot Experiment

In the first subject experiment our goal was to compare the difference between augmenting the recognition process with a model versus not augmenting the process. The subjects were asked to perform 25 trials of each of five different gestures, using the right arm. In between each set of trials for one gesture, the subject was given ample rest time to help avert any fatigue associated with the repetitive motions they were asked to make. We used the same five gestures as illustrated in Table 3, the zorro, Catholic cross, stop, salute and waving gestures.

The results we obtained were measurements of how well each recognition system predicted the correct gesture sequence. The performance rating for the two

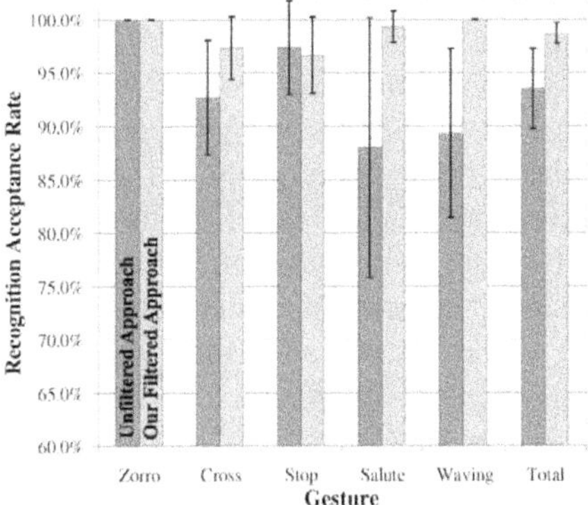

Fig. 8. Comparison of the Unfiltered and Filtered Approaches

methods – the unaugmented and our model-based approach – were computed by averaging the performances for each of five different gestures. The performance for each gesture was computed by averaging the results from each of the six subjects. The histogram chart shown in Figure 8 compares the two sets of data.

The data for each user was analyzed by setting the body parameters for the recognizer to their measurements before running the accuracy tests. The rest of the parameters for the recognizer were individually tuned for each subject. The results for our model-based approach show an overall acceptance rate of 98.7% with standard deviation of 1.0%. The unaugmented approach performed at 93.5% acceptance rate with standard deviation of 3.7%. The high acceptance rate and low variability that our results show give us a fairly good indication that integrating our filter into the recognition process improves recognition accuracy.

A drawback of this experiment is that a significant amount of custom parameter tuning was required for each subject. As a result, we decided to evaluate whether or not our methodology would allow us to reduce the tuning effort required by each experiment. We ran a set of followup experiments to test these ideas. The results were somewhat limited. More details can be found in our technical report [4].

7 Discussion and Conclusions

We have developed a new model-based filter that incorporates a dynamics model, a control system and motion state estimation and applied it to the gesture recognition process. The dynamic model gives us a way to represent the underlying mechanical motion of the human arm. The control system acts as a means to exert control over and provide guidance for the motion applied by the dynamics.

Our filter proved to be effective in improving the performance of the recognition process as shown by our expert-user and pilot user studies. We showed this by comparing an unfiltered recognition process with one augmented with our model-based filter. Our method works acceptably well for hard–to–distinguish gesture sets and even better for very dissimilar sets. The results definitely warrant further user evaluation studies.

Our method does involve a small amount of parameter tuning and training for the error covariances. A lot of the tuning is associated with the registration of the input and learned gestures. Obviously, if the registration problem can be solved, a lot of the tuning can be eliminated. It also might be the case that more sophisticated models for the human motion or a more extensive model of the human body would reduce the need for some of the parameters.

One issue that our work did not address is the differences that may occur with people tracing the same "end-effector" path with different arm and joint configurations. For example, the "bent-arm" arc used in the fourth expert-user experiment has an equivalent wrist trajectory as the "straight-arm" arc had in the first experiments. We analyzed only the wrist trajectories, although we could have additionally analyzed either the elbow or joint configuration trajectories. This in effect increases the size of the gesture alphabet.

We only tested our filter with a template recognition architecture. However, we feel that it can be easily modified for use with a neural network recognizer. By removing the unaugmented sub-filter component the only output would be the augmented filtered sequence. If we setup n filters so that each input to the system produces n output sequences from the filters (for n distinct gesture patterns), each of these outputs will be different amongst themselves but fairly unique for each given input pattern. Then, extracting features from each output sequence which could yield $m \times n$ different features for the neural network. If desired, more features could be added from the raw or unaugmented filtered input sequence. The rest should follow the same as any neural network. The advantage of this (untested) setup would be that the filter could be used to generate many more unique discriminating features. While this is not always an advantage, if the features are good discriminating ones we believe the discriminator should me more powerful.

Based on our evaluation studies, we can conclude that our motion adaptation filter makes a positive contribution to the performance of gesture recognition for arm-based gestures. This seems to imply that a model of human performance can be used to eliminate some of the heuristic guess-work that must be done to make a standard gesture recognizer work.

References

1. R. Watson, "A Survey of Gesture Recognition Techniques," Tech. Rep. TCD-CS-93-11, Department of Computer Science, Trinity College, Cambridge, U.K., July 1993.
2. J.K. Aggarwal and Q. Cai, "Human Motion Analysis: A Review," in *IEEE Non-rigid and Articulated Motion Workshop 1997*, Piscataway, NJ, June 1997, IEEE.
3. V. I. Pavlovic, R. Sharma, and T. S. Huang, "Visual Interpretation of Hand Gestures for Human-Computer Interaction: A Review," *IEEE Transactions on Pattern Analysis and Machine Intelligence*, vol. 19, no. 7, pp. 677–695, July 1997.

4. G. S. Schmidt and D. H. House, "Model-Based Motion Filtering for Improving Arm Gesture Recognition Performance," Tech. Rep. Technical Report, Virtual Reality Laboratory, Naval Research Laboratory, Washington, DC, Sept. 2003.
5. L. Rabiner and B.-H. Juang, *Fundamentals of Speech Recognition*, Old Tappan, NJ: Prentice Hall PTR, 1993.
6. J. Martin, D. Hall, and J. L. Crowley, "Statistical Gesture Recognition through Modelling of Parameter Trajectories," in *Gesture Workshop '99: Gesture-Based Communication in Human-Computer Interaction*, Berlin, Germany, Mar. 1999, Springer-Verlag.
7. P. R. Cohen, D. McGee, S. L. Oviatt, L. Wu, J. Clow, R. King, S. Julier, and L. Rosenblum, "Multimodal Interactions for 2D and 3D Environments," *IEEE Computer Graphics and Applications*, vol. 4, pp. 10–13, July/August 1999.
8. A. D. Wexelblat, "A Feature-Based Approach to Continuous-Gesture Analysis," M.S. thesis, Massachusetts Institute of Technology, May 1994.
9. D. Rubine, "Specifying Gestures by Example," in *ACM SIGGRAPH Computer Graphics Conference Proceedings*, Las Vegas, NV, Aug. 1991.
10. P. D. Gader, J. M. Keller, R. Krishnapuram, J.-H. Chiang, and M. A. Mohamed, "Neural and Fuzzy Methods in Handwriting Recognition," *IEEE Computer*, vol. 30, no. 2, pp. 79–86, Feb. 1997.
11. L. W. Campbell, D. A. Becker, A. Azarbayejani, A. F. Bobick, and A. Pentland, "Invariant Features for 3-D Gesture Recognition," in *Second International Workshop on Face and Gesture Recognition*, Killington, VT, Oct. 1996.
12. G. Herzog and K. Rohr, "Integrating Vision and Language: Towards Automatic Description of Human Movements," in *Proceedings of the 19th Annual German Conference on Artificial Intelligence, KI-95*, Bielefeld, Germany, July 1995.
13. A. D. Wilson and A. Bobick, "Using Configuration States for the Representation and Recognition of Gesture," Tech. Rep. Technical Report No. 308, M.I.T. Media Laboratory, Cambridge, MA, June 1995.
14. R. O. Duda and P. E. Hart, *Pattern Classification and Scene Analysis*, New York, NY: John Wiley & Sons, Inc., 1973.
15. L. R. Rabiner, "A Tutorial on Hidden Markov Models and Selected Applications in Speech Recognition," *Proceedings of the IEEE*, vol. 77, no. 2, pp. 257–286, Feb. 1989.
16. M. T. Vo and A. Waibel, "A Multi-Modal Human-Computer Interface: Combination of Gesture and Speech Recognition," in *Adjunct Proceedings of InterCHI '93*, Apr. 1993.
17. A. Pentland and B. Horowitz, "Recovery of Nonrigid Motion and Structure," *IEEE Transactions of Pattern Analysis and Machine Intelligence*, vol. 13, no. 7, pp. 730–742, 1991.
18. V. B. Zordan and J. K. Hodgins, *Tracking and Modifying Upper-Body Human Motion Data with Dynamic Simulation*, pp. 13–22, Vienna, Austria: Springer-Verlag, Sept. 1999.
19. D. Metaxas, "Articulated Figure Dynamics, Behavior and Control," in *Virtual Humans: Behaviors and Physics, Acting, and Reacting (SIGGRAPH '97 Course Notes)*, Los Angeles, CA, Aug. 1997.
20. C. R. Wren and A. P. Pentland, "Dynamic Models of Human Motion," in *Third IEEE International Workshop on Automatic Face and Gesture Recognition*, Nara, Japan, Apr. 1998.
21. C. R. Wren, B. P. Clarkson, and A. P. Pentland, "Understanding Purposeful Human Motion," in *4th International Workshop on Automatic Face and Gesture Recognition*, Grenoble, France, Mar. 2000.

22. G. S. Schmidt and D. H. House, "Towards Model-Based Gesture Recognition," in *4th International Workshop on Automatic Face and Gesture Recognition*, Grenoble, France, Mar. 2000.
23. G. Welch and G. Bishop, "An Introduction to the Kalman Filter," Tech. Rep. TR 95-041, Department of Computer Science, University of North Carolina at Chapel Hill, Chapel Hill, NC, Dec. 1995.
24. R. E. Kalman, "A New Approach to Linear Filtering and Prediction Problems," *Transactions of the ASME–Journal of Basic Engineering*, vol. 1, no. 2, pp. 34–45, 1960.
25. R. M. Murray, Z. Li, and S. S. Sastry, *A Mathematical Introduction to Robotic Manipulation*, New York, NY: CRC Press LLC, 1993.
26. R. Featherstone, "The Calculation of Robot Dynamics Using Articulated-Body Inertias," *International Journal of Robotics Research*, vol. 2, no. 1, pp. 13–30, 1983.
27. J. J. Craig, *Introduction to Robotics: Mechanics and Control*, Reading, MA: Addison-Wesley Publishing Company, Inc., 1989.
28. W. H. Press, S. A. Teukolsky, W. T. Vetterling, and B. P. Flannery, *Numerical Recipes in C*, New York, NY: Cambridge University Press, 1992.
29. S. J. Hall, *Basic Biomechanics*, St. Louis: Mosby, 1995.
30. I. D. Landau, *Adaptive Control, The Model Reference Approach*, New York, NY: Marcel Dekker, 1979.
31. D. P. Stoten and H. Benchoubane, "Empirical Studies of an MRAC Algorithm with Minimal Control Synthesis," *International Journal of Control*, vol. 51, no. 4, pp. 823–849, 1990.
32. G. S. Schmidt, *Model-Based Gesture Recognition*, Ph.D. thesis, Texas A&M University, Computer Science Dept., Texas A&M University, Dec. 2000.

GesRec3D: A Real-Time Coded Gesture-to-Speech System with Automatic Segmentation and Recognition Thresholding Using Dissimilarity Measures*

Michael P. Craven[1] and K. Mervyn Curtis[2]

[1] University of Technology, Jamaica
School of Engineering, Kingston 6, Jamaica, WI
michael.craven@ieee.org
[2] University of the West Indies
Dept. of Mathematics and Computer Science
Mona Campus, Kingston, Jamaica, WI
mervyn_curtis@ieee.org

Abstract. A complete microcomputer system is described, *GesRec3D*, which facilitates the data acquisition, segmentation, learning, and recognition of 3-Dimensional arm gestures, with application as a Augmentative and Alternative Communication (AAC) aid for people with motor and speech disability. The gesture data is acquired from a Polhemus electro-magnetic tracker system, with sensors attached to the finger, wrist and elbow of one arm. Coded gestures are linked to user-defined text, to be spoken by a text-to-speech engine that is integrated into the system. A segmentation method and an algorithm for classification are presented that includes acceptance/rejection thresholds based on intra-class and inter-class dissimilarity measures. Results of recognition hits, confusion misses and rejection misses are given for two experiments, involving predefined and arbitrary 3D gestures.

1 Background

Gesture recognition is an important addition to Augmentative and Alternative Communication (AAC) technology, as the needs of many disabled people may be better served by consideration of all potential means of their interaction with computers and communication aids, especially when one or more senses or body functions are impaired. With the increased availability of new input devices for virtual reality, computer games, and computer aided design, there is an even greater need for improved gesture recognition. Examples in the literature include extensions of character and speech recognition techniques to 2D and 3D gestures[1,2], methods for recognition of hand gestures for sign language and other applications[3,4,5], direct mapping of gestures to speech parameters[6,7] and replacement of the traditional mouse in software applications by the use of mouse gestures which replace the function of the buttons, or head gestures[8,9]. We have previously used 2D projections of arm movements in the

* This work was funded by grant A/P/0543 to University of Nottingham, School of Electrical and Electronic Engineering, from the UK medical research charity Action Research for the project "Improvement of assessment and the use of communication aids through the quantitative analysis of body movements of people with motor disabilities".

A. Camurri and G. Volpe (Eds.): GW 2003, LNAI 2915, pp. 231–238, 2004.

GesRec gesture-to-speech system[10]. Progress with gesture recognition algorithms has been made with Hidden Markov Models[11] and Time-Delay Radial Basic Function neural networks[12]. Another problem is that of dealing correctly with unintentional gestures. In this paper we incorporate acceptance/rejection criteria into both segmentation and recognition strategies.

2 Method

2.1 Data Acquisition and Segmentation

Real-time gesture information was obtained from a Polhemus 3Space Fastrak six-degrees-of-freedom (6DOF) electro-magnetic tracking system[13], comprising of a transmitter module and 3 sensors placed on the finger, wrist and elbow of one arm interfaced to a P133MHz PC with SB16 sound card supporting the Creative TextAssist text-to-speech engine (see Fig 1). Software *GesRec3D* was designed to perform data acquisition from the tracker by prompting the user for several examples of each gesture in a guided training session. Each different gesture class could be freely associated with a text string (from a default or user-defined list) to be spoken by TextAssist, thus implementing a limited vocabulary gesture-to-speech application. The system was designed to support training and data storage for 30 gesture classes of up to 10 seconds in length at 20 samples/sec. The system also produced a continuous text format time-stamped log of the raw Polhemus gesture data for superimposing on to video footage of users during training and evaluation sessions. Limited visual feedback of the movement was provided to the user by projecting a 2D trace of the gesture and distance from the computer screen represented by the radius of a circle, creating a sensation of 3D movement with a minimum of processing. For initial trials with persons with motor disability, limited stamina reduced the number of gestures trained in one session to between 3 and 5, highlighting the need to keep the number of training examples as small as possible and to allow incremental training. To support this *GesRec3D* allowed training data to be saved and reloaded at any point during the training, for extra gesture classes to be added at any time, and vocabulary corresponding to a gesture to be changed after training if necessary.

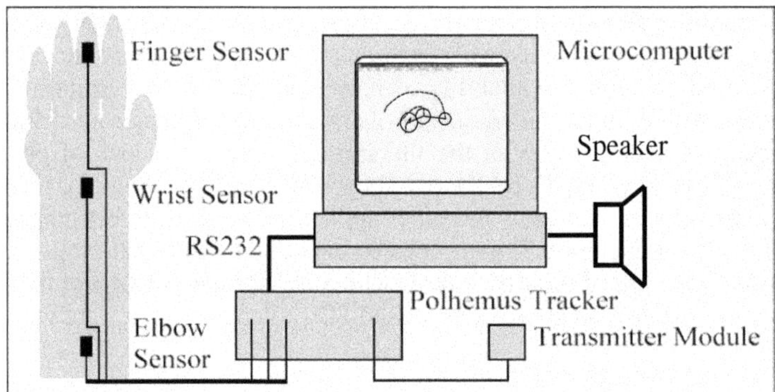

Fig. 1. 3D Gesture-to-speech system using a Polhemus tracker

A generalised D-dimensional gesture or character can be described after segmentation as a sequence of m co-ordinates,

$$G = g_0 g_1 \ldots g_m \tag{1}$$

where $g_i = g_i(X_{i1}, .., X_{iD})$.

The 6DOF data available from the Fastrak consists of both position and orientation values, but the latter were ignored since relative angles change with distance, whereas translation invariance with respect to the transmitter is easily realized. Furthermore, when receivers are placed on a person's body by attaching them to arm and finger bands, these may slip round and cause significant errors in measurement of orientation, whereas the effect of this on position is less of a problem.

A gesture segmentation strategy was devised using five user-adjustable parameters as follows, assuming the user starts in a rest (or minimum movement) position:

1. *Start Gesture Sample Spacing* s_{start} – The system remains in a start state until the distance between samples in any one of the (x,y,z) coordinates is $\geq s_{start}$.
2. *End Gesture Sample Spacing* s_{end} - After the start condition is met, the spacing is increased so that a larger movement is required to continue. If the spacing becomes less than s_{end}, a timed end phase is entered, otherwise the gesture is continued.
3. *Minimum samples* m_{min} - If the end phase is entered before m_{min} samples have been obtained, the recogniser is immediately reset to its starting state, ensuring that short gestures (with $m<m_{min}$) are ignored.
4. *End Gesture Time-out* t_{end} - In the end phase, the s_{end} condition must continue to be met for a time t_{end}, otherwise the timer is reset and the gesture is continued. If the timer expires, the gesture reaches its end state.
5. *Training Delay* t_{delay} - This allows time for the user to return to a rest position during training, as the recogniser is forced to remain in the start state for a time t_{delay}. The parameter is only used in training, so that in normal use the recogniser is always ready for a new gesture.

Note that gestures characterised by 'preparation - stroke - retraction' can have a steady state after the stroke phase is completed which is indistinguishable from an end state. If so, the retraction phase may be ignored, which should not be a problem so long as the stroke phase contains enough information to describe the gesture.

2.2 Dissimilarity Measure

One computationally inexpensive dissimilarity measure between D-dimensional numeric variables uses the city block metric[14]. In order to compare equal length sequences of 3D samples, values are accumulated over m samples and normalized using a scaling factor W. Hence, the dissimilarity measure between two gestures of equal length is given by:

$$d = \frac{W}{m} \sum_{i,j=1}^{m} \left(| x_i - x_j | + | y_i - y_j | + | z_i - z_j | \right) \tag{2}$$

In practice, two gestures will be of different lengths, so either the gestures or the measure must be modified to take account of this. If we are employing time invariance, we can interpolate the shortest gesture to equalise the number of sample and use Equation 2 directly, or use the mismatch in length as a distinguishing factor by the following modification to the measure for two gestures G_a and G_b:

$$d_{ab} = \frac{W}{m_b} \sum_{i,j=1}^{m_a} \left(| x_i - x_j | + | y_i - y_j | + | z_i - z_j | \right) \tag{3}$$

where $m_a > m_b$ and $g_j = (0,0,0)$ for $j > m_b$. Length mismatch is penalised first by comparing the length mismatched part of the longer gesture with zeros, and second by normalising to the smallest length. The measure reduces to Equation 2 when $m_a = m_b$.

2.3 Acceptance Threshold and Recognition

After a training session is completed and the system has acquired enough examples of each gesture class, we can calculate d_{ab} for each pair of gestures. For C gesture classes and n examples of each class, this yields a square $nC \times nC$ dissimilarity matrix. The largest value of d_{ab} is the worst internal (or intra-class) match d_{int}. For consistently made gestures this value should be small, so it gives us a good measure of repeatability. Between a class and each of the other classes the smallest value of d_{ab} is the best external (or inter-class) match d_{ext}, which should preferably be much larger than d_{int} to prevent confusion between classes.

We can now define an acceptance threshold d_{th} between any two classes:

$$d_{th} = \frac{K}{2} \left(d_{\text{int}} + d_{ext} \right) \tag{4}$$

For $K=1$ and $d_{ext} > d_{int}$ this is half way between the worst internal match and best external match and so forms a rejection threshold between non-overlapping classes. However, for very poor matches between classes d_{ext} may be many times greater than d_{int}, making the rejection threshold far greater than necessary. To avoid this situation, an upper bound can be specified for d_{th}. For $d_{ext} < d_{int}$, the rejection threshold is less than d_{int} but as this is between the least similar examples of a class, a match with another more similar example is still possible. If K is decreased, the rejection condition is made stricter, and if increased, it can be made less strict.

To achieve recognition of an unknown gesture, G, that gesture is matched with every gesture in the training set, repeatedly applying Equation 4 to find the winning class with dissimilarity d_{min}. Considering matches between gestures measured using a single sensor, the recognition process is as follows:

1. Find gesture class corresponding to d_{min}
2. If $d_{min} < d_{th}$ select that class, otherwise reject the gesture
3. Perform action linked to the selected gesture class

For multiple sensors the d_{min} and d_{th} are added for each sensor, and the sums compared. This gives an overall rejection condition in the case where all sensors agree. In the case of non-agreement the system chooses the class selected for the finger sensor as that movement is the greatest and most variable between gestures.

3 Experiments and Results

An initial experiment was devised to test the segmentation and thresholding abilities for simple gestures of different sizes and drawing speeds. Users trained the system with three different easily remembered shapes; Circle, Triangle and Square. Each shape had two different sizes, Small and Large, and for each size two speeds, Fast and Slow (see examples in Fig. 2). The training set consisted of a total of 12 gestures, each to be entered 5 times. A vocabulary table was constructed containing text corresponding to each gesture so that the text-to-speech synthesiser would speak the words associated with it e.g. "Small Fast Circle".

Parameters s_{start} and s_{end} were set to defaults 2 mm and 6 mm respectively. The minimum samples parameter m_{min} was set so that a gesture of duration less than 0.5 second would be ignored. The default end gesture time-out t_{end} was set to 0.2 second, and the training delay t_{delay} to 1 second. K was set to 1. In practice most able-bodied users could use the default values without modification to achieve a satisfactory segmentation. However, in preliminary trials with users with motor disabilities e.g. cerebral palsy, it was generally necessary to increase all the segmentation parameters to some extent, to account for continuous involuntary movements.

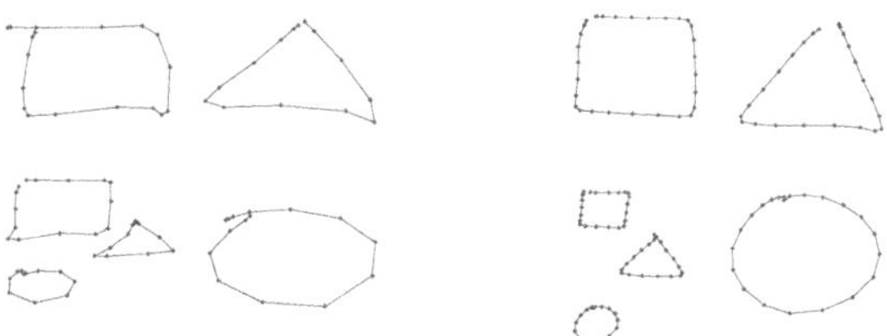

Fig. 2. Examples of Fast (left) and Slow (right) gestures used in the shapes experiment, shown as (x-y) 2D projections of 3D data from the finger sensor

After training, each user was asked to enter each of the training gestures, and also to introduce gestures not in the training set. Fig. 3 shows the recognition results for one able-bodied user testing 50 examples of each gesture class. Recognition hits varied between 82-96% depending on the gesture, and there are in general fewer misses from confusion than rejection. In addition 100 arbitrary gestures were made, of which all but one were rejected. More importantly, movements made by the user moving to the start positions of intended gestures (or retracting from the previous gesture) were all rejected. These results do not include any additional small movements rejected during segmentation, as these are not passed to the recogniser.

Fig. 3 also presents a graph of one row of the dissimilarity matrix computed for the finger sensor, showing the normalized distances between one example of the "Small Fast Circle" (SFC) gesture class with all other gestures in the training set. For each class, the best and worst matches to SFC are given. Within class SFC, the best match is 0, resulting from that gesture being matched to itself. The greatest intra-class dissimilarity for SFC is less than the smallest inter-class dissimilarity (in this case for SFT), indicating that SFC is fairly well separated from the other classes, and that examples of that class have good repeatability. It can be observed that the closest gesture classes to SFC are those with similar size and speed, and that after circles, the better matches are obtained for triangles, and then squares. Training took only 5 minutes for the total of 60 gestures entered. Calculation of the 60×60 dissimilarity matrix took approximately 0.06 seconds per sensor (total 0.17 for the 3 sensors) on the P133MHz, much faster than for time invariant matching calculated using dynamic time warping, which took 7.47 seconds, although the aforementioned linear time-invariant version could be computed in 0.6 seconds.

Shape (Small/Large, Slow/Fast, Circle/Square/Triangle)	**Hits out of 50**	**Confusion Misses** K=1	**Rejection Misses** K=1
SFC	45	2	3
LFC	45	1	4
SSC	44	2	4
LSC	46	2	2
SFS	41	4	5
LFS	43	3	4
SSS	45	3	2
LSS	47	1	2
SFT	44	3	3
LFT	48	1	1
SST	47	1	2
LST	48	1	1

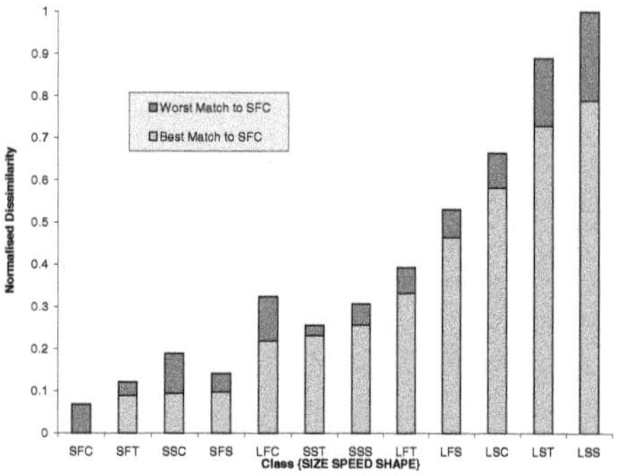

Fig. 3. Table of overall recognition results, and graph of intra- and inter-class dissimilarity measures for a "Small Fast Circle" (SFC) gesture using data from finger sensor.

A second experiment was devised to test the full 3D capability of the system, since in the first experiment the gestures were made in a plane even though all data was processed as 3D. An able-bodied user trained the system with a set of 'greetings' gestures made with one arm. The set of 12 gestures is shown in Fig. 4, together with the recognition results after training on 5 examples and testing with a further 20. The effect of decreasing K by 10% is clearly seen since confusion misses are almost eliminated at the expense of increase in rejection misses (overall recognition rate is slightly reduced). Fig. 4 also shows a row of the dissimilarity matrix corresponding to one of the "Hello" gestures for both the finger and elbow sensors. The rejection threshold for the "Hello" gesture class was computed from the worst intra-class match for "Hello" and the best inter-class match, in this case with a "See you later" gesture. The ambiguity of these two gesture classes is reflected in the confusion or rejection misses in the table. The only other gesture class that resulted in a confusion miss for K=1 was "What is your name", which was also similar to "Hello". Thus the information obtained from the dissimilarity matrix usefully complements the test data.

4 Discussion and Conclusions

GesRec3D was designed to be able to acquire and classify gestures that have been learnt by example, utilising both spatial and temporal characteristics of the gestures and allowing a user to easily trade-off the recognition rate with rejection rate.

Gesture Description	Output Text/Speech	Hits out of 20		Confusion Misses		Rejection Misses	
		K=1	*K*=0.9	*K*=1	*K*=0.9	*K*=1	*K*=0.9
Hand up	"Hello"	18	17	1	0	1	3
Hand up and wave	"Goodbye"	19	19	0	0	1	1
Hand left across body	"How are you"	19	18	0	0	1	2
Hand up & down twice	"Very well"	20	19	0	0	0	1
Hand up & down left diagonal	"Please"	18	18	0	0	2	2
Hand up & down right diagonal	"Thank you"	20	20	0	0	0	0
Point to self	"My name is..."	20	19	0	0	0	1
Point forward	"What is your name"	19	18	1	0	0	2
Point behind	"See you later"	15	15	2	1	3	4
Point from mouth	"Say"	19	19	0	0	1	1
Thumb up	"Okay"	20	20	0	0	0	0
Make a cross shape	"Delete All"	18	18	0	0	2	2

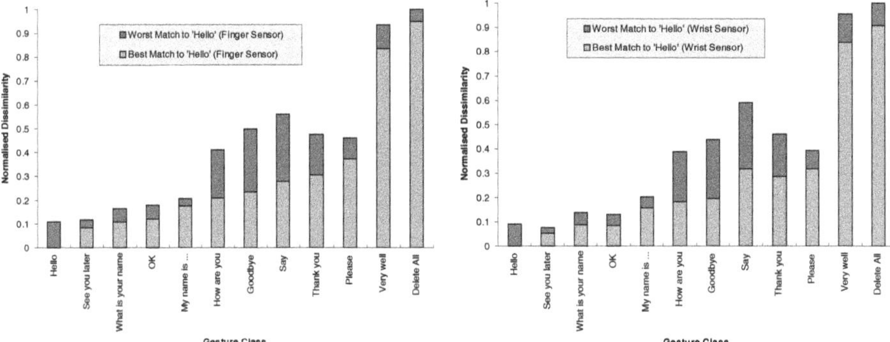

Fig. 4. Results table for greetings, and graphs of intra- and inter-class dissimilarity measures for a "Hello" gesture using data from finger and wrist sensors.

The segmentation method worked well for able-bodied users and also in preliminary trials with disabled users. Some intervention was needed to help the non-technical expert understand the effects of adjusting the segmentation parameters, suggesting the need to simplify or automate this, and it would also be useful to make all of the parameters independent of device characteristics e.g. sampling rate.

Some of the children with motor disability who tried the system were motivated as much by the visual feedback as the speech, one modifying a gesture to produce a more pleasing trace pattern on the computer screen. This motivational aspect could be looked into further.

We have also investigated modifications of the matching algorithms using a variable-width averaging filter that could be used to compensate for tremor. Computation of the dissimilarity matrix is fast so it can be carried out at run-time and recalculated when the filter width is changed, providing the means for a user to quickly compare different filter widths.

The graphical information from the dissimilarity matrices indicates which gestures are consistently made, as well as distances between gesture classes. This information could be processed further and used to provide intelligent feedback to the user in the form of suggestions to repeat or change a particular gesture if it is an outlier in its class or if it is too much like a gesture in a different class. Such an intelligent system could also suggest parameter adjustments to help improve recognition or facilitate automatic adjustment.

Recent work has been reported which also utilises dissimilarity measures. Milios and Petrakis used dynamic programming and dissimilarity cost to compare hand shapes for image retrieval, with favourable comparison to fourier descriptors and moments[15]. Long et al. have investigated creating pen gesture sets with good memorability and learnability by relating these to similarity[16], which would be of importance for persons with cognitive impairment in addition to motor disability.

References

1. Rubine, D.: Specifying Gestures by Example. Computer Graphics, Vol. 25, No. 4 (1991) 329-337.
2. Cairns, A.Y.: Towards the Automatic Recognition of Gesture. PhD Thesis, Uni. of Dundee, Nov. 1993.
3. Harling, P.A., Edwards, A.D.N. (eds.): Progress in Gestural Interaction. Proc. GW'96, Springer-Verlag (1997).
4. Pavlovic, V.I., Sharma, R., Huang, T.S.: Visual Interpretation of Hand Gestures for Human Computer Interaction: A Review. IEEE Trans. Pattern Analysis and Machine Intelligence, Vol. 19, No. 7 (1997) 677-695.
5. Nam, Y., Wohn, K.: Recognition of hand gestures with 3D, non-linear arm movement. Pattern Recognition Letters, Vol. 18, No. 1 (1997) 105-113.
6. Pausch, R., Williams, R.D.: Giving Candy to children: User-tailored input driving an articulator-based speech synthesizer. In Edwards, A.D.N. (ed.): Extra-Ordinary Human-Computer Interaction: interfaces for people with disabilities. Cambridge Series on Human-Computer Interaction 7, Chapter 8, Cambridge University Press (1995) 169-182.
7. Fels, S.S., Hinton, G.E.: Glove-Talk II - A Neural Network Interface which maps Gestures to Parallel Formant Speech Synthesizer Controls. IEEE Trans. Neural Networks, Vol. 8, No. 5 (1997) 977-984.
8. Tew, A.I., Gray, C.J.: A real-time gesture recognizer based on dynamic programming. Journal of Biomedical Engineering, Vol. 15 (1993) 181-187.
9. Keates, S. and Perricos, C.: Gesture as a Means of Computer Access. Communication Matters, Vol. 10, No. 1 (1996) 17-19.
10. Craven, M.P., Curtis, K.M., Hayes-Gill, B.R.,Thursfield, C.D.: A Hybrid Neural Network/Rule-Based Technique for On-Line Gesture and Hand-Written Character Recognition. Proc. IEEE Fourth Intl. Conf. on Electronics, Circuits and Systems, Cairo, Egypt, Vol. 2 (1997) 850-853.
11. Hofmann, F.G., Heyer, P., Hommel, G.: Velocity Profile Based Recognition of Dynamic Gestures with Discrete Hidden Markov Models. In Wachsmuth I., Fröhlich M. (eds.): Gesture and Sign Language in Computer Human Interaction. Lecture Notes in Artificial Intelligence 1371, Proc. GW'97, Springer-Verlag (1998) 81-95.
12. Howell A. J. and Buxton H.: Gesture Recognition for Visually Mediated Interaction. In Braffort A. et al. (eds.). Gesture-Based Communication in Human-Computer Interaction. Lecture Notes in Artificial Intelligence 1739, Proc. GW'99, Springer-Verlag (1999) 141-151.
13. 3Space Fastrak User's Manual. Rev. F, Nov. 1993, Polhemus Inc., Colchester, Vermont, USA.
14. Gordon, A.D.: Classification. Monographs on Applied Probability and Statistics. Chapman and Hall, New York, Chap. 2 (1981) 21.
15. Milios, E., Petrakis, E.G.M.: Shape Retrieval Based on Dynamic Programming. IEEE Trans. Image Processing, Vol. 9, No. 1 (2000) 141-146.
16. Long Jr., A.C., Landay, J.A., Rowe, L.A., Michiels, J.: Visual Similarity of Pen Gestures. Proc. Human Factors in Computing, CHI'00 (2000) 360-367.

Classification of Gesture with Layered Meanings*

Sylvie C.W. Ong and Surendra Ranganath

Department of Electrical and Computer Engineering
National University of Singapore, 4 Engineering Drive 3, Singapore 117576
elesr@nus.edu.sg

Abstract. Automatic sign language recognition research has largely not addressed an integral aspect of sign language communication - grammatical inflections which are conveyed through systematic temporal and spatial movement modifications. We propose to use low-level static and dynamic classifiers, together with Bayesian Networks, to classify gestures that include these inflections layered on top of the basic meaning. With a simulated vocabulary of 6 basic signs and 4 different layered meanings, test data for four test subjects was classified with 84.6% accuracy.

1 Introduction

Automatic sign language recognition is an active research area within gesture recognition research in general. Unlike speech which is sequential in nature, sign languages like ASL (American Sign Language) have parallel channels so that two or more concepts can be expressed simultaneously. These channels of information are the *basic manual sign*, *grammatical modifications* to the manual sign and *nonmanual signals*. Previous research has largely concentrated on recognition of the basic lexical meaning. The focus of this paper is on the important aspect of *layered meanings* in the form of grammatical modifications to the manual sign.

1.1 Layered Meanings: Grammatical Modifications to the Sign

There are 4 basic, independent and simultaneous channels of information which combine to form signs or words. These channels are: a) handshape, b) hand orientation, c) hand movement trajectory shape, and d) overall location of the hands. There are limited sets of categories in each of the 4 channels: e.g. 30 handshapes, 8 hand orientations, 40 movement trajectory shapes and 20 locations.

However, the production of a sign often conveys more than just the basic lexical meaning. The signer can vary the sign in many expressive ways: slowing it down or speeding it up, forming it tightly or expansively, smoothly or abruptly. These systematic *temporal* and *spatial modifications* to a sign's movement convey additional meanings that are layered over the basic sign meaning and which combine to give the complete meaning of the sign gesture [1]. The following examples illustrate this.

* The authors gratefully acknowledge the support of NUS RP No. R-263-000-214-112.

A. Camurri and G. Volpe (Eds.): GW 2003, LNAI 2915, pp. 239–246, 2004.

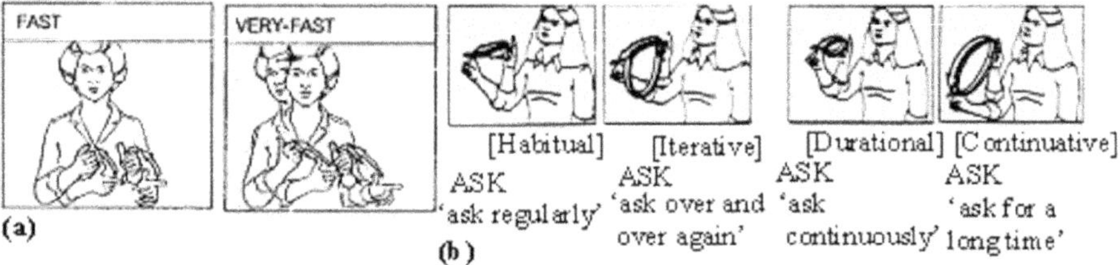

Fig. 1. (a) The sign "FAST" with inflected meaning "very" [2]. (b) The sign "ASK" inflected with various temporal aspects [1]

Example 1. In the inflected (layered) form of the sign, the beginning of the movement is held, followed by a *quick release.* There is also an increase in *spatial extent* of the movement. The added meaning is the adverb "very" (Fig.1(a)).

Example 2. The *movement contour* and *rhythm* of the sign is modified. The sign with layered meaning of "continuously" has a circular movement with an even rhythm, whereas with the layered meaning of "for a long time" the movement is an elongated circle with uneven rhythm (Fig.1(b)).

More than one type of these grammatical modifications can occur concurrently, but not all types of inflections are applicable for any particular sign. For example, we cannot add the adverb "very" to the sign "ASK".

1.2 Analysis of Physical Channels of Signs

The categories of handshape, hand orientation and overall location, can be determined by measuring the appropriate features of the hand at any particular time instant, that is, these features are static. In contrast, for recognition of the movement trajectory shape we would need to know the positional information throughout the sign, ie the features required are dynamic. Most signs involve either the same handshape throughout the sign, or a smooth change from one handshape at the start of the sign to another handshape at the end of the sign. We postulate that for the purpose of recognizing the sign, the dynamics of how the handshape changes from the start to the end is not required.

2 Previous Work in Sign Language Recognition

Hidden Markov models (HMMs) are one of the most successful modelling techniques employed in sign language and gesture recognition (e.g.[3], [4]). In these approaches, only recognition of the basic lexical sign meanings have been addressed. While HMMs may be suitable for classifying movement trajectory shapes, they may not be the most appropriate classifiers for the static channels of handshape, orientation and location. Furthermore, it is not obvious how HMMs could be extended to deal with the complex dependencies between layered

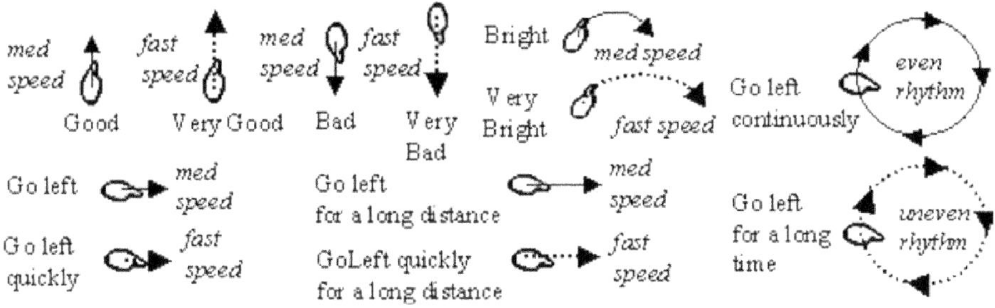

Fig. 2. Possible combinations of **BasicMeaning**, **Intensity**, **Distance**, **Rate** and **Continuance** (*GoRight* and *Dark* gestures are mirror images of *GoLeft* and *Bright* gestures)

meanings and systematic movement modifications. HMMs are designed for absorbing variabilities in the timing, hence any systematic temporal modifications would be discounted.

In [5] changes in the movement direction that indicate the subject and object of a verb are recognized by learning their (Gaussian) probability densities. Average accuracy of 93.4% was obtained for a vocabulary with two basic meanings and three possible subject-object pairs. Braffort[6] classifies inflected signs by taking as input the inflection invariant features of the sign. Accuracy was 92% - 96% for a vocabulary of 7 signs that appear in sentences. An interpreter module is proposed, which extracts layered meanings of the inflected signs by applying a set of rules. These works are limited in that they only deal with a subset of possible spatial variations, with no straightforward extension to modelling systematic speed and timing variations.

3 System Overview

Our proposed approach is to 1) recognize the categories within the 4 basic channels, 2) recognize the categories of systematic temporal and spatial movement modifications, 3) infer the lexical meaning of the sign from inflection invariant features, 4) infer layered meanings of the sign from the systematic movement modifications. Appropriate classifiers are used in steps 1 and 2 according to whether the channel information is categorized by static or dynamic features. We then use a Bayesian Network (BN) to model the dependencies between the gesture information channels, the lexical sign meaning and layered meanings.

3.1 Sign Vocabulary

A sign vocabulary with 6 basic meanings and 4 types of layered meanings (**Intensity**, **Distance**, **Rate** and **Continuance**) was created to yield 20 distinct combined meanings. (Fig.2 and Table 1). The gesture vocabulary was designed to have few ambiguities in the 2D image plane (to keep the image processing simple), while trying to follow the way in which basic meanings and layered meanings are combined in sign language. Hand orientation at start and end of the gesture (**HOrienS**, **HOrienE**), movement trajectory shape (**MShape**) and movement orientation (**MOrien**) determine the 6 basic signs (*GoLeft*, *GoRight*, *Good*, *Bad*, *Bright*, *Dark*). Measuring the hand orientation at only the start and end of the gesture is analogous to how the handshape at only the start and end of gestures are required for recognizing lexical meaning in ASL. Layered meanings are determined by the movement size (**MSize**), speed (**MSpeed**) and **MShape**. Different types of layered meanings are associated with different signs, for example "*GoLeft* + *Very*" does not make any sense. This makes the recognition task more complicated as movement size and speed information must be interpreted differently according to the basic sign meaning.

Table 1. Complete list of sign vocabulary (20 distinct combined meanings)

Artificial vocabulary used in experiments	Basic meaning and layered meaning
Go left	*GoLeft*
Go right	*GoRight*
Good	*Good*
Bad	*Bad*
Bright	*Bright*
Dark	*Dark*
{Go left, Go right} for a long distance	{*GoLeft*, *GoRight*} + *Far*
{Go left, Go right} quickly	{*GoLeft*, *GoRight*} + *Quickly*
{Go left, Go right} quickly for a long distance	{*GoLeft*, *GoRight*} + *Quickly* + *Far*
{Go left, Go right} continuously	{*GoLeft*, *GoRight*} + *Durational*
{Go left, Go right} for a long time	{*GoLeft*, *GoRight*} + *Continuative*
Very {Good, Bad, Bright, Dark}	{*Good*, *Bad*, *Bright*, *Dark*} + *Very*

3.2 Image Processing and Feature Estimation

Image sequences from a PAL digital video camera were manually segmented in time to obtain individual gesture actions. The hand is automatically segmented out in each image by thresholding based on color and motion information. The connected component with the largest area is taken to be the hand. The resultant binary image is then used to obtain the hand centroid, and angle of the axis of least inertia. The following features for each gesture action were then extracted:

- The sine and cosine of the angles of the axis of least inertia in the first and last frames of the gesture. These are used for categorizing **HOrienS** and **HOrienE** respectively.
- The sine and cosine of the angle of the straight line between the hand centroid in the first and last frames of the gesture (for categorizing **MOrien**).
- The length of the straight line between the hand centroid in the first and last frames of the gesture (for categorizing **MSize**).

- The sine and cosine of the change in the angle of hand trajectory in successive image frames. This sequence of features is obtained from all the image frames in the gesture action. These are used for categorizing **MShape**.
- The differential of the hand speed (acceleration) in successive image frames. This sequence of features is obtained from all the image frames in the gesture action. These are used for categorizing **MSpeed**.

4 Bayesian Network for Classifying Basic and Layered Meanings

In our simulations, we implemented the Bayesian Network (BN1) shown in Fig.3(a). We defined query nodes for the basic meaning of the sign and for each of the layered meanings of **Intensity**, **Distance**, **Rate** and **Continuance**. Observed nodes are **HOrienS**, **HOrienE**, **MShape**, **MOrien**, **MSize**, and **MSpeed**. In the following we develop in detail the structure of BN1.

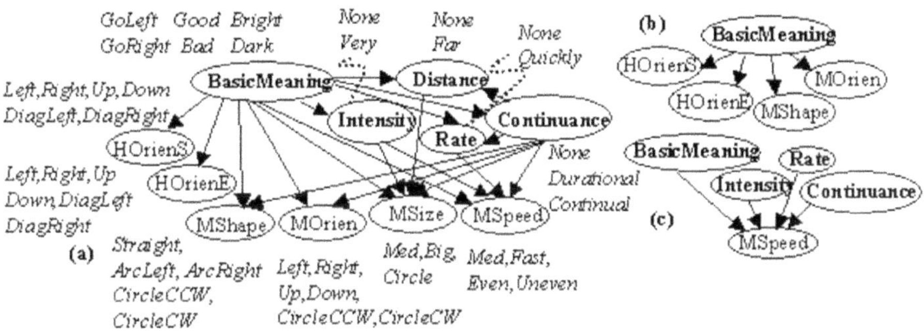

Fig. 3. (a) BN1 models dependencies between sign meanings and gesture parts (node values are in italics). (b) Conditional independence of observation nodes. (c) Temporal modifications to movement encoded in the dependence on layered meanings

In our artificial vocabulary, the basic meaning is derived from hand orientation at start and end of the gesture, the movement shape and movement orientation. Similar to the 4 basic parts of ASL gestures, these four observation nodes are assumed to be independent channels. The conditional independence relationship can be represented by the network in Fig.3(b).

4.1 Dependence of Movement Modifications on Layered Meanings

The dependence of **MSpeed** on **Intensity**, **Rate** and **Continuance** encodes temporal variation in the gesture (Fig.3(c)). For example, for **BasicMeaning** of *GoLeft* without any layering, the movement is fairly slow. However, with the layered meaning of "quickly" the movement speed is increased. And for the layered meanings of "continuously" and "for a long time", the movement has an even and uneven rhythm respectively. The Conditional Probability Table (CPT) for **MSpeed** is a function of its parent nodes, **BasicMeaning**, **Intensity**, **Rate** and **Continuance**. Similarly, movement shape and size variations are encoded in the dependence of **MShape** and **MSize** on their parent nodes.

5 Classifiers for Observation Node Categories

Similar to the basic sign parts in ASL, each observation node in BN1 has a finite number of discrete values. For each node, we build a classifier that categorizes the features extracted in the feature estimation stage (described in Sect.3.2) into an appropriate symbol. Our approach is to learn a parameterized probability density function (pdf) for each category of an observation node. The parameters values, λ_c, are chosen so that the likelihood of training data, $P(X \mid \lambda_c)$ (where X is the set of training data for category c), is maximized. A trained classifier then assigns an input x, to the category which has the highest likelihood.

For nodes **HOrienS**, **HOrienE**, **MSize** and **MOrien**, the discrete symbols are categorized from static features. The pdfs of these features are estimated as mixture of gaussians (with 2 to 20 mixtures), which are trained with the Expectation-Maximization (EM) algorithm. For example, in **MSize** node, 3 categories are defined: a pdf for category *Med* is trained from uninflected gestures, a pdf for category *Big* is trained from gestures that have layered meaning of "very" or "for a long distance", and another pdf for category *Circle* is trained from gestures with layered meaning of "continuously" or "for a long time".

For **MShape** node, we train one HMM for each of its 5 categories using the EM algorithm; training is terminated when the percentage increase in log-likelihood between iterations falls below a threshold. We used a 6-state left-right (Bakis) HMM structure for categories *ArcLeft*, *ArcRight* and *Straight*. *CircleCCW* and *CircleCW* HMMs have an additional loop-back state transition to the first state. The observation nodes of the HMMs have gaussian distributions. The same two HMM topologies above are used for the **MSpeed** node.

Assigning the category that gives the highest likelihood score for a feature value is analogous to inferencing with a simple two node BN structure as in BN2 (Fig.4(a)). The Conditional Probability Distribution (CPD) for **HOrienSFeat** node is $P(\text{HOrienSFeat} \mid \text{HOrienS} = CategoryValue)$ and has the form of a mixture of gaussians. If categories of **HOrienS** are taken to be equiprobable, then the inference process in BN2 which gives the most probable value of **HOrienS** is equivalent to finding the category with highest likelihood for the data, ie.

$$\begin{aligned} &\operatorname*{argmax}_{\text{HOrienS}} P(\text{HOrienS} \mid \text{HOrienSFeat}) \\ &= \operatorname*{argmax}_{\text{HOrienS}} P(\text{HOrienSFeat} \mid \text{HOrienS}) \,. \end{aligned} \tag{1}$$

6 Experimental Results

The dataset was generated from 4 persons (test subjects A, B, C and D), who each performed about 10 repetitions of each of the 20 distinct complete gesture meanings, giving a total of 841 gesture sequences.

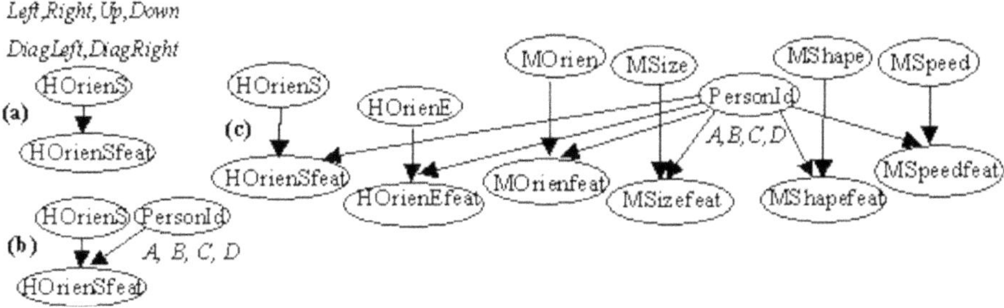

Fig. 4. (a)BN2 for inferring **HOrienS** value. (b)BN3 for inferring **HOrienS** and **PersonId** values. (c) BN4, combined classifier for observation node categories

6.1 Experiment 1 - Individual Modelling of Single Test Subject

For this experiment, we trained the classifiers for observation node categories (as described in Sect.5) on roughly $\frac{2}{3}$ of the gesture sequences obtained from one test subject (e.g. A). We then used the outputs of these trained classifiers (when input features are from the same $\frac{2}{3}$ of gesture sequences above) as the discrete values of the observation nodes in BN1 of Fig.3(a), and thus learned its CPT parameters. In the testing procedure, we used the same trained classifiers to obtain the observation node categories for the remaining $\frac{1}{3}$ of the gesture sequences of the test subject and used the trained BN1 to infer the most probable values for the basic meaning and layered meaning nodes. A test sequence is considered as recognized correctly if all the query node values were inferred correctly. The above procedure was repeated individually on all 4 test subjects. Accuracy results range from 86.8% to 92.5%, with an average accuracy of **90.8%**.

6.2 Experiment 2 - Composite Modelling of Multiple Test Subjects

The methodology was the same as in Experiment 1 with the sole difference being data from all 4 persons was combined for training and testing. The experiment yielded an accuracy of **78.7%** on the (combined) test data. The accuracy dropped as compared to Experiment 1 because when data from all 4 persons is used, the variance of estimated pdfs increases (due to variable distances from the camera and different styles in gesturing) and the pdfs for different categories in an observation node start to overlap. Next we describe a method of characterizing the inter-person variations with a view to improve accuracy.

6.3 Experiment 3 - Combining Individual Modelling of Multiple Test Subjects

We add a node to the BN2 structure to obtain BN3 (Fig.4(b)), where the CPD for **HOrienSFeat** node is $P(\text{HOrienSFeat} \mid \text{HOrienS} = \mathit{CategoryValue}, \text{PersonId} = \mathit{Name})$. Whereas in Experiment 2, we learned the pdf for the **HOrienS** node categories based on data from all 4 test subjects, ie. $P(\text{HOrienSFeat} \mid \text{HOrienS} =$

$CategoryValue$), here we use the pdfs for each individual test subject that was already learned in Experiment 1. In other words, $P(\text{HOrienSFeat} \mid \text{HOrienS} = CategoryValue, \text{PersonId} = A)$, for example, are exactly the same as the pdfs for categories of **HOrienS** that was learned from test subject A in Experiment 1. It is now possible to enter evidence in **HOrienSFeat** node and infer the most probable value of **HOrienS** node as well as that of **PersonId** node.

In line with this idea, we make the **PersonId** node a common node across all the observation nodes and obtain BN4 as shown in Fig.4(c). We then followed the same $\frac{2}{3}$:$\frac{1}{3}$ data split for training and testing as before. We obtained **84.6%** accuracy on the (combined) test data. The identity of the test subject was also inferred from the **PersonId** node in BN4 with an accuracy of **81.6%**.

7 Conclusion and Future Directions

In this paper a basic vocabulary of 6 signs which is combined with layered meanings in 14 different ways was simulated. We presented a Bayesian Network (BN1) to represent 4 different types of layered meanings that modify gesture movements in both the spatial and temporal dimensions. To improve robustness with respect to multiple persons, we developed an additional BN (BN4) to infer the observation node values of BN1. Gesture recognition accuracy results on test data for four test subjects was 84.6%. Future work will deal with continuous gestures and investigate scalability to increased number of test subjects.

References

1. H.Poizner, E.S.Klima, U. Bellugi, R. B. Livingston, "Motion Analysis of Grammatical Processes in a Visual-Gestural Language", N.I.Badler, J.K.Tsotsos (Editors), Motion: Representation and Perception, Elsevier Science Publishing, 1986
2. T.Humphries, C.Padden, T.J.O'Rourke, A Basic Course in American Sign Language, T.J Publishers, 1993
3. B.Bauer, K.-F. Kraiss, "Towards an Automatic Sign Language Recognition System Using Subunits", I. Wachsmuth, T. Sowa (Eds.): Proceedings of GW 2001, London
4. C.Vogler, D.Metaxas, "A Framework for Recognizing the Simultaneous Aspects of American Sign Language", CVIU 81, 358-384, 2001
5. H. Sagawa, M. Takeuchi, "A Method for Analyzing Spatial Relationships Between Words in Sign Language Recogniton", Proceedings International GW 1999
6. A.Braffort, "ARGo: An architecture for sign language recognition and interpretation", Proceedings of GW'96, pgs 17-30, Berlin, New York 1997, Springer

Handshapes and Movements: Multiple-Channel American Sign Language Recognition

Christian Vogler[1] and Dimitris Metaxas[2]

[1] Gallaudet University
christian.vogler@gallaudet.edu
[2] Rutgers University
dnm@cs.rutgers.edu

Abstract. In this paper we present a framework for recognizing American Sign Language (ASL). The main challenges in developing scalable recognition systems are to devise the basic building blocks from which to build up the signs, and to handle simultaneous events, such as signs where both the hand moves and the handshape changes. The latter challenge is particularly thorny, because a naive approach to handling them can quickly result in a combinatorial explosion.
We loosely follow the Movement-Hold model to devise a breakdown of the signs into their constituent phonemes, which provide the fundamental building blocks. We also show how to integrate the handshape into this breakdown, and discuss what handshape representation works best. To handle simultaneous events, we split up the signs into a number of channels that are independent from one another. We validate our framework in experiments with a 22-sign vocabulary and up to three channels.

1 Introduction

Sign languages are the primary mode of communication for many deaf people, just as speech is for hearing people. The rate of progress in the speech recognition field has been impressive in the past decade, with some systems now becoming borderline mainstream. At this moment, the predominant way to interact with a computer is still the keyboard and mouse, but as speech recognition becomes more established, the situation may change.

Such a change would pose major challenges to sign language users, unless we can also advance the field of sign language recognition. Sadly, the current state of the art in sign language recognition research is still lagging far behind speech recognition. One major reason for this disparity is that sign language recognition is much harder than speech recognition. The reason why it is harder can be expressed succinctly in just two words: *simultaneous events*. In speech, we can — on an abstract level — represent every word as a sequence of sounds. In contrast, a major element of sign languages is that several things happen at the same time. For instance, many signs use both hands, which move at the same time. The question is how to capture all the simultaneous events without having to consider every imaginable combination of them. If we had to consider every

A. Camurri and G. Volpe (Eds.): GW 2003, LNAI 2915, pp. 247–258, 2004.

combination, the computational complexity of the task would be prohibitive, as we would quickly run into a combinatorial explosion.

To complicate matters further, sign languages are highly inflected; that is, the appearance of a sign can change according to the subject and the object of the sentence. In addition, there are other processes beside inflection that contribute to a large number of different appearances, such as changing the handshape depending on what type of object is under consideration [1]. The bottom line is that there are too many appearances to model them all explicitly, so it is necessary to cast for more basic building blocks, from which we can build all these appearances. Just like in spoken languages, phonemes take on the role of these basic building blocks. However, it is far from clear how exactly to break down a sign into its constituent phonemes, for two reasons: First, linguistic research into the phonology of signed languages is still in its infancy, overall. Second, it has not been clearly established yet what the computational requirements of recognition systems are, so a breakdown of signs into phonemes must somehow balance linguistic and engineering requirements.

In this paper we present a hidden Markov model (HMM)-based framework for American Sign Language (ASL) recognition that addresses these two challenges. We loosely follow the Movement-Hold phonological model [2] to devise a representation of signs suitable for a recognition system. In contrast to earlier work based on this model [3,4] we now integrate the handshape, as well. We then extend this representation to multiple channels, which capture the simultaneous events in ASL, one in each channel. The key idea to making this approach work is that we assume that the channels are independent from one another. As a consequence, we can recognize the channels independently from one another, and put together combinations of simultaneous events on the fly, which greatly reduces the computational complexity of the recognition task. Although this assumption is unlikely to hold from a theoretical standpoint, the practical experimental results justify it as a reasonable engineering tradeoff.

The rest of this paper is organized as follows: We briefly discuss related work, and then continue with the mainstay of this paper: how to model ASL in a manner that makes it computationally tractable for recognition systems, including how to represent the handshape. Afterward, we briefly discuss HMMs and how they fit into the recognition framework, and conclude with experiments that validate our assumptions.

2 Related Work

This discussion of related work focuses on previous work in sign language recognition. For coverage of gesture recognition, the survey in [5] is an excellent starting point.

C. Wang, W. Gao, and J. Ma described a large-scale HMM-based isolated recognition system for Chinese Sign Language with a very impressive vocabulary size of more than 5000 signs [6]. They used some tricks from speech recognition, such as clustering Gaussian probabilities, and fast matching, to achieve real-time recognition and recognition rates of 95%.

Most work on continuous sign language recognition is based on HMMs. T. Starner and A. Pentland used a view-based approach to ASL recognition with a single camera to extract two-dimensional features as input to HMMs with a 40-word vocabulary and a strongly constrained sentence structure [7]. G. Fang and colleagues proposed an approach to signer-independent continuous recognition of Chinese Sign Language based on an integration of simple recurrent networks (SRNs) and HMMs [8]. They used the SRNs to segment the continuous sentences into individual signs. The recognition rates were 92% over a test data set of 100 sentences with a 208-sign vocabulary.

H. Hienz and colleagues used HMMs to recognize a corpus of German Sign Language [9]. They also experimented with stochastic bigram language models to improve recognition performance. The results of using stochastic grammars largely agreed with the results in [10]. B. Bauer and K.-F. Kraiss from the same group later extended the framework to break down the signs into smaller units. These units were unlike phonemes, however, because they were determined computationally via clustering, instead of being determined linguistically. For this breakdown they achieved an accuracy of 92.5% in isolated sign language recognition experiments [11,12].

R. H. Liang and M. Ouhyoung used HMMs for continuous recognition of Taiwanese Sign Language with a vocabulary of 71–250 signs [13], which they extracted from a Cyberglove in conjunction with a magnetic 3D tracker. They worked with Stokoe's system [14] to detect the handshape, position, and orientation aspects of the running signs. They integrated the handshape, position, orientation, and movement aspects through stochastic parsing and a dynamic programming algorithm at a higher level than the HMMs. The main assumption of their work is that the sign can be represented as a series of postures.

The work described in this paper is an extension of the work done in [3,4]. In this earlier work we proposed an approach to breaking down the signs into phonemes, and devised a framework for recognizing simultaneous aspects of ASL. However, this work was restricted to the movements of the hands and ignored handshape. In this paper we validate the framework further by integrating the handshape into the framework, and extend our phoneme-based modeling approach to ASL to cover the handshape, as well.

3 Modeling ASL

A large part of the difficulty in devising an ASL recognition system is the question of how to represent the language. To keep the complexity of the recognition task small and to ensure that the system is scalable, we need to keep the number of building blocks that constitute the signs small. Likewise, we need to ensure that we can capture the simultaneous events, which happen all the time in signed languages, such as two-handed signs, and handshape changes during hand movements. Doing so without getting bogged down in a combinatorial explosion of such events is nontrivial.

In the following we address how to break down signs into their constituent phonemes, with the idea that the number of phonemes in a language is small.

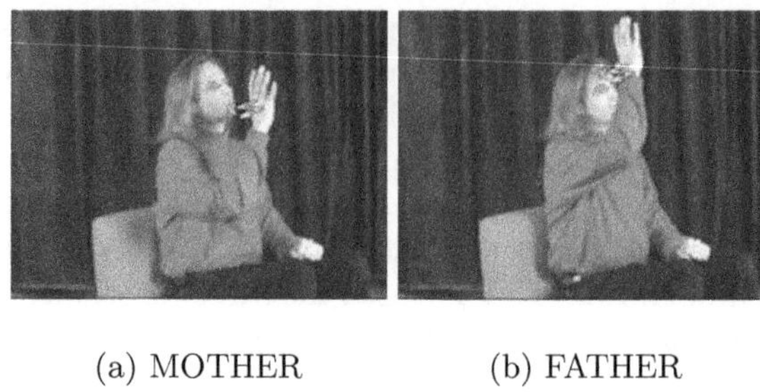

(a) MOTHER (b) FATHER

Fig. 1. Contrast between signs that identifies location as a phoneme in ASL. (a) and (b) differ only in location.

Hence, we can use the phonemes as the basic building blocks for a recognition system. We discuss this breakdown for both the hand movements, and the handshape. In addition, we discuss how to capture simultaneous events in a computationally tractable manner, and how to represent the handshape.

3.1 Phoneme-Based Modeling

A **phoneme** is defined to be the smallest contrastive unit in a language [1]; that is, the smallest unit that can distinguish morphemes (units of meaning) from another. In English, the sounds /*k*/, /æ/, and /*t*/ are examples of phonemes, as can easily be seen by comparing the words "cat" - "hat," "bat" - "bet," and "bet" - "bed." In ASL, the equivalents of phonemes in spoken languages are the various handshapes, locations, orientations and movements.

As an example, consider the location of the hand at the chin in the sign for MOTHER. The arguments that this unit is an example of an ASL phoneme is analogous to the arguments for English: Fig. 1 on page 250 shows that the signs for MOTHER - FATHER differ only in location (chin vs. forehead).

Just like in spoken languages, the *number of phonemes in ASL is limited* and small compared to the number of signs. The exact number is still a matter of debate and depends greatly on the phonological model used. Stokoe's system [14], for instance, identifies 55 units, whereas the Movement-Hold model identifies more than 100 [2].

In this work, we follow the basic ideas of the Movement-Hold model [2]. It is an example of a *segmental model,* in which each sign is broken down into a series of segments. The two major segments in this model are **movements** and **holds.** Movements are defined as those segments during which some aspect of the sign's configuration changes, such as a change in handshape, a hand movement, or a change in hand orientation. Holds are defined as those segments during which all aspects of the sign's configuration remain unchanged; that is, the hands remain stationary for a brief period of time.

Signs are made up of sequences of movements and holds. For example, the sign for MOTHER consists of three movements followed by a hold (Fig. 2 on page 251). Movement segments have features that describe the type of movement

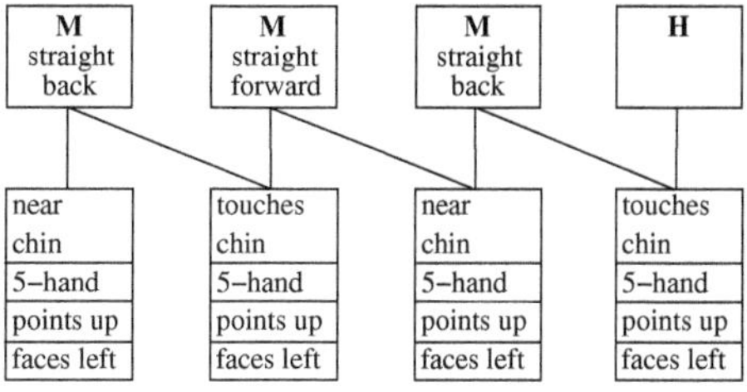

Fig. 2. Schematic description of the sign for MOTHER in the Movement-Hold model. See Fig. 1 to see how the sign is articulated.

(straight, round, sharply angled), as well as the plane and intensity of movement. In addition, attached to each segment is a **bundle of articulatory features** that describe the hand configuration, orientation, and location. Further details on this model and how to map it to HMMs for sign language recognition can be found in [3,4].

There are other segmental models, such as D. Brentari's syllable-based model [15], and further work based on the Movement-Hold model [16]. They differ primarily in what exactly constitutes a segment, but all share a common set of assumptions about the segmental structure of signs. Whether the Movement-Hold model is truly the best choice among the segmental models for ASL recognition systems is an open question that should be resolved in future research.

3.2 Independent Channels

The representation of the sign in Fig. 2 on page 251 has a serious problem that makes it inadequate for a direct application to recognition systems. It occurs when we want to model and recognize the simultaneous aspects of ASL. In particular, the handshape and hand orientation can change while the hand moves. In addition, some signs are two-handed, so both hands must be modeled. Figure 3 on page 252 shows an example of a two-handed sign, during which also multiple aspects of the sign change at the same time. The problem is the sheer number of possible combinations of simultaneous features. Unlike speech, where phonemes occur only in sequence, in ASL they occur both in sequence and in parallel.

To get an idea of the magnitude of the problem that recognition systems face here, it is illuminating to consider the naïve approach first: what about simply tossing all possible feature combinations together, without regard for linguistic constraints and interdependencies? Then the system would have to look at all possible combinations of handshapes, hand orientations, wrist orientations, and locations and movement types of the left and right hands, respectively. This approach leads to a combinatorial explosion, as can easily be seen by multiplying all the numbers of possible respective features. If, for example, we assume that there are 40 distinct handshapes, 8 hand orientations, 8 wrist orientations, and

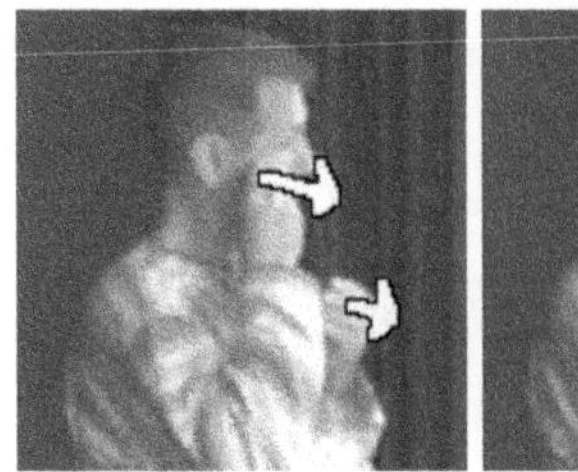

Fig. 3. The sign for INFORMATION demonstrates how several features in ASL change simultaneously. Both hands move, starting at different body locations. Simultaneously, the handshapes change from a flat, closed hand to a cupped open hand during the sign. Source: National Center for Sign Language and Gesture Resources, Boston University (under the direction of C. Neidle and S. Sclaroff). Used with permission.

20 body locations, then the number of possible feature combinations, for both hands together, would be $(40 \times 8 \times 8 \times 20)^2$, which is more than one billion.

The combinatorial explosion stemming from the naïve approach highlights the enormous complexity of modeling the simultaneous aspects of ASL. Modeling all of them *a priori* is infeasible both from a modeling and a computational point of view. From the modeling point of view, it would be impossible to collect enough data for all these combinations in a reasonable time frame. From the computational point of view, attempting to identify the correct models and to match them against the sequence of signs to be recognized would take far too long to be of practical use.

Of course, it would be ludicrous to assume that ASL really exhibits that many combinations, as is evident from the many linguistic constraints, such as handshape constraints [17], and dependencies between handshape, hand orientation, and location (e.g., signs that touch a part of the signer's body with the thumb have only a few orientations that are even physically possible). Unfortunately, the current state of the art in sign language linguistics and recognition makes attempts at enumerating all the valid combinations infeasible.

To make modeling the simultaneous aspects of ASL tractable, it is necessary to decouple the simultaneous events from one another. Instead of attaching bundles of articulatory features to the segments, we break up the features into **channels** that can be viewed as being **independent** from one another. For the purposes of the work presented in this paper, these channels are, one for each hand:

movement channel the channel consisting of the body locations and the movements between the body locations

handshape channel the channel consisting of the handshape

Note that future work on ASL recognition would also have to tackle the hand orientation and facial expressions, possibly in additional channels. These topics, however, are beyond the scope of this paper.

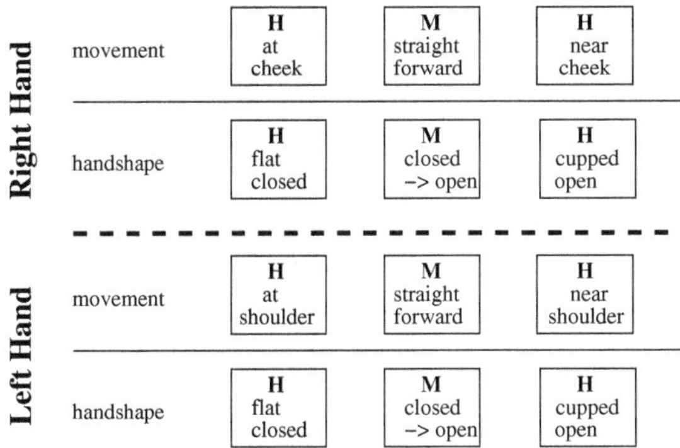

Fig. 4. The sign for INFORMATION, where the different features are modeled in separate channels. Note how several channels change simultaneously. See Figure 3 on page 252 for a picture of this sign.

Figure 4 on page 253 shows how the sign for INFORMATION is represented with the independent channel modeling approach. Note how each channel still contains movements and holds, with the same underlying idea as before: in a movement segment there is a transition from one configuration to another one in the channel, whereas in a hold segment the configuration remains static.

Splitting the feature bundles up into independent channels immediately yields a major reduction in the complexity of the modeling task. It is no longer necessary to consider all possible combinations of phonemes, and how they can interact. Instead, it is enough to model the phonemes in a single channel at a time, and just to look at the phonological and phonetic phenomena in each channel separately. In each channel, the phonemes can be represented by only a small number of different HMMs, which all belong to the same aspect of the sign's configuration, such as the handshape, or hand movement. Combinations of phonemes from different channels are easy to put together on the fly at recognition time, particularly in conjunction with the parallel hidden Markov model recognition framework that we briefly describe in Sec. 4.

The downside of using independent channels is that they entail making a major assumption about the structure of the simultaneous processes in ASL, which in all likelihood is not valid. In essence, these independent channels are a case of an engineering tradeoff, so as to make the recognition problem tractable, versus theoretically correct modeling of ASL. Yet, the experiments in Sec. 5.2 show that modeling ASL in terms of independent channels yields tangible benefits to sign language recognizers.

3.3 Handshape Modeling

Most approaches in the past used joint and abduction angles as features for the hand, whenever these had been available, such as [13]; however, these are very low-level features. The experimental results shown in Sec. 5.1 indicate that these

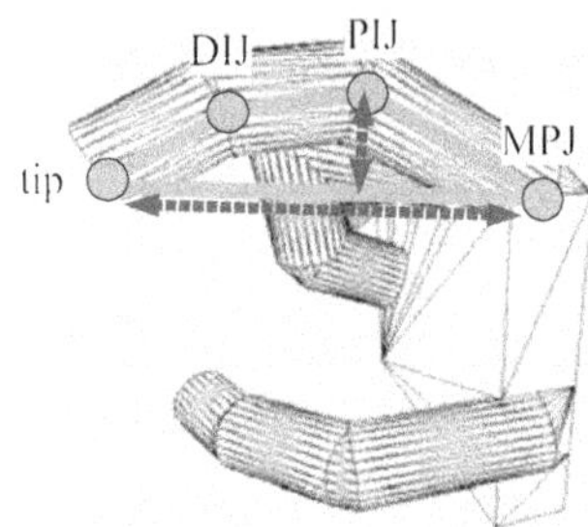

Fig. 5. Measure of the openness of a finger. It depends on the width and height of the quadrilateral described by the sites on the three finger joints and the fingertip.

are not the best choice for recognizing the handshape. Therefore, it makes sense to use a more high-level description of the handshape. For sign languages, in line with Sandler's phonological model of the handshape [18], a representation of the degree of **openness** of a finger seems particularly useful. A finger is open when it is fully extended, and closed when it is fully bent.

For obtaining such a representation, consider the relationship among the fingertip, the metacarpophalangeal joint (MPJ, see Fig. 5), and the degree of openness. If a finger is fully extended, the distance between the tip and the MPJ is maximized. Conversely, if the finger is fully bent, the distance is minimized. In addition, consider connecting the fingertip and the three finger joints into a quadrilateral, as shown in Fig. 5 on page 254, whose base is the line between the tip and the MPJ. The height of the quadrilateral — the distance between the proximal interphalangeal joint (PIJ, see Fig. 5) and the base — is maximized when the finger is fully closed. Conversely, it is minimized when the finger is fully open.

Therefore, the width and the height of the quadrilateral described by a finger are a direct expression of a finger's openness. Note that the MPJ angle only rotates this quadrilateral, but does not affect its dimensions, so the degree of openness is independent of the MPJ angle. Hence, the latter should be part of the feature vector in addition to the width and height measurements. Together with the abduction angles (the spread angles between adjacent fingers), these features all together constitute a somewhat higher-level representation of the hand than the raw joint angles. The experiments in Sec. 5.1 justify this representation.

4 Hidden Markov Models

One of the main challenges in ASL recognition is to capture the variations in the signing of even a single human. In general, humans never perform exactly the same movement twice, even if they intend to. There are always slight variations from one movement to the next one, so a recognition framework must be able to account for them. The most common approach toward handling such variations is to use some kind of statistical model. Hidden Markov models (HMMs) are a type of statistical model well suited for capturing variations. In addition, their state-based nature enables them to describe how a signal changes over time, which is ideal for activity recognition.

HMMs have been used extensively in gesture and sign language recognition in the past, both for whole-sign modeling (one HMM per sign [7]) and phoneme-based modeling (one HMM per phoneme [3]). The phoneme HMMs are chained together to form a single HMM for a sign, and these, in turn, are chained together into a network. The recognition algorithm finds the most probable path through the network and recovers the signs that the path passes through. The parameters of the HMMs are estimated on a training data set, as described in [19].

To handle independent channels, we use parallel HMMs (PaHMMs) as an extension to conventional HMMs. Instead of using only one single network, PaHMMs use one network of HMMs per channel. The recognition algorithm searches all networks in parallel and combines the path probabilities from each path by multiplying them. This multiplication is possible, because in Sec. 3.2 we assume that the channels are independent from one another, and hence the HMM networks are stochastically independent from one another.

The details of mapping phonemes to HMMs are described in [3], and the recognition algorithm for PaHMMs with multiple channels is covered extensively in [4]. We now describe the recognition experiments that validate our approach.

5 Experiments

We ran two types of experiments. The first one was designed to validate our choice of handshape features, and the second one was designed to validate the modeling of the independent channels.

The data set consisted of 499 sentences, between 2 and 7 signs long, and a total of 1604 signs from a 22-sign vocabulary, the details of which can be found in [3]. We collected these data with an Ascension Technologies MotionStar™ system at 60 frames per second. In addition, we collected data from the right hand with a Virtual Technologies Cyberglove™, which records wrist yaw, pitch, and the joint and abduction angles of the fingers, also at 60 frames per second. We split the data set into 400 training sentences and 99 test sentences. No part of the testing data set was used for training the HMMs at any time, and conversely no part of the training data set was used for the recognition experiments.

5.1 Handshape Experiments

To determine the relative merits of using joint angles and measures of finger openness, we ran continuous recognition experiments on only the handshape channel. These experiments were designed to compare the robustness of using raw joint angles versus using the quadrilateral-based representation from Sec. 3.3.

For each feature vector, the experiments varied the number of HMM states and parameters. Because many signs share the same handshape, it is impossible to identify a sign uniquely from the handshape alone. For this reason, the evaluation criterion was the percentage of correctly recognized handshapes, rather

Table 1. Results of continuous handshape feature vector comparisons. μ, σ, Median, Best, and N correspond to the average handshape accuracy, standard deviation, median accuracy, best case, and number of experiments, respectively.

Feature Vector	μ	σ	Median	Best	N
joint angles	83.15%	15.44%	82.66%	98.68%	1912
quadrilateral	95.21%	5.37%	96.83%	99.47%	1956

Table 2. Comparison of conventional HMMs and PaHMMs. The conventional HMMs modeled the strong hand's movement channel, whereas the PaHMMs modeled a combination of multiple channels. H denotes the number of correct signs, D the number of deletion errors, S the number of substitution errors, I the number of insertion errors, and N the total number of signs in the test set.

Type of experiment	Sentence accuracy	Word accuracy	Details
baseline: movement channel right hand, HMM	80.81%	93.27%	H=294, D=3, S=15, I=3, N=312
movement channel both hands, PaHMM	84.85%	94.55%	H=297, D=3, S=12, I=2, N=312
movement channel right hand, hand-shape right hand, PaHMM	88.89%	96.15%	H=302, D=2, S=8, I=2, N=312
all three channels, PaHMM	87.88%	95.51%	H=301, D=1, S=10, I=3, N=312

than the percentage of correctly recognized signs. In addition, whenever the same handshape occurred multiple times in a row, we contracted them into a single handshape. The results, given in Table 1 on page 256, show clearly that the quadrilateral-based description of the handshape is far more robust than the raw joint angles.

5.2 Independent Channel Experiments

We ran four experiments on the 22-sign set to evaluate the recognition accuracy of modeling varying numbers of channels. The first experiment was a baseline experiment with conventional HMMs for just the right hand's movement channel, from earlier work [3]. The second experiment used PaHMMs to capture the movement channels of both hands. The third experiment used PaHMMs to capture the movement and handshape channels of the right hand. The fourth experiment used PaHMMs to capture all three channels.

The results are given in Table 2 on page 256. Of particular note is that using all three channels shows no improvement over just using the movements and handshape from the right hand. We think that the reason is the relatively small size of the data set that we used. Clearly, future work needs to validate our approach with much larger data sets. Yet, overall the results are promising and validate the assumption that in practice channels can be modeled independently from one another.

6 Conclusions and Outlook

The experimental results show that phoneme modeling in conjunction with stochastically independent channels constitutes a promising avenue of research. The integration of the handshape into our recognition framework has provided further evidence for the viability of this modeling approach.

The next step is to validate the framework with larger data sets. It is imperative that the data set comes from native signers in the future, because their articulation of the signs shows characteristics that nonnative signers simply do not exhibit. In addition, future work needs to integrate facial expressions into the framework, and model some of the grammatical processes in sign languages, such as the use of space to denote referents.

Acknowledgments

This work was supported in part by NSF EIA-98-09209, AFOSR F49620-98-1-0434, and NSBRI-NBPF00202.

References

1. Valli, C., Lucas, C.: Linguistics of American Sign Language: An Introduction. Gallaudet University Press, Washington DC (1995)
2. Liddell, S.K., Johnson, R.E.: American Sign Language: The phonological base. Sign Language Studies **64** (1989) 195–277
3. Vogler, C., Metaxas, D.: Toward scalability in ASL recognition: Breaking down signs into phonemes. In Braffort, A., Gherbi, R., Gibet, S., Richardson, J., Teil, D., eds.: Gesture-Based Communication in Human-Computer Interaction. Volume 1739 of Lecture Notes in Artificial Intelligence. Springer (1999) 211–224
4. Vogler, C., Metaxas, D.: A framework for recognizing the simultaneous aspects of American Sign Language. Computer Vision and Image Understanding (2001) 358–384
5. Pavlovic, V., Sharma, R., Huang, T.S.: Visual interpretation of hand gestures for human-computer interaction: a review. IEEE Transactions on Pattern Analysis and Machine Intelligence **19** (1997) 677–695
6. Wang, C., Gao, W., Ma, J.: A real-time large vocabulary recognition system for Chinese Sign Language. In Wachsmuth, I., Sowa, T., eds.: Lecture Notes in Artificial Intelligence. Volume 2298. Springer (2002) 86–95

7. Starner, T., Weaver, J., Pentland, A.: Real-time American Sign Language recognition using desk and wearable computer based video. IEEE Transactions on Pattern Analysis and Machine Intelligence **20** (1998) 1371–1375
8. Fang, G., Gao, W., Chen, X., Wang, C., Ma, J.: Signer-independent continuous sign language recognition based on SRN/HMM. In Wachsmuth, I., Sowa, T., eds.: Gesture and Sign Language in Human-Computer Interaction. International Gesture Workshop. Volume 2298 of Lecture Notes in Artificial Intelligence. Springer (2001) 76–85
9. Hienz, H., Kraiss, K.F., Bauer, B.: Continuous sign language recognition using hidden Markov models. In Tang, Y., ed.: ICMI'99, Hong Kong (1999) IV10–IV15
10. Vogler, C., Metaxas, D.: Adapting hidden Markov models for ASL recognition by using three-dimensional computer vision methods. In: Proceedings of the IEEE International Conference on Systems, Man and Cybernetics, Orlando, FL (1997) 156–161
11. Bauer, B., Kraiss, K.F.: Towards an Automatic Sign Language Recognition System Using Subunits. In Wachsmuth, I., Sowa, T., eds.: Gesture and Sign Language in Human-Computer Interaction. International Gesture Workshop. Volume 2298 of Lecture Notes in Artificial Intelligence. Springer (2001) 64–75
12. Bauer, B., Kraiss, K.F.: Video-Based Sign Recognition using Self-Organizing Subunits. In: International Conference on Pattern Recognition. (2002)
13. Liang, R.H., Ouhyoung, M.: A real-time continuous gesture recognition system for sign language. In: Proceedings of the Third International Conference on Automatic Face and Gesture Recognition, Nara, Japan (1998) 558–565
14. Stokoe, W.C.: Sign Language Structure: An Outline of the Visual Communication System of the American Deaf. Studies in Linguistics: Occasional Papers 8. Linstok Press, Silver Spring, MD (1960) Revised 1978.
15. Brentari, D.: Sign language phonology: ASL. In Goldsmith, J.A., ed.: The Handbook of Phonological Theory. Blackwell Handbooks in Linguistics. Blackwell, Oxford (1995) 615–639
16. Perlmutter, D.: Sonority and syllable structure in American Sign Language. Linguistic Inquiry **23** (1992) 407–442
17. Battison, R. In: Lexical borrowing in American Sign Language. Linstok Press, Silver Spring, MD (1978) 19–58 Reprinted as "Analyzing Signs" in Lucas, C. and Valli, C. Linguistics of American Sign Language, 1995.
18. Sandler, W.: Representing Handshapes. In Edmondson, W.H., Wilbur, R., eds.: International Review of Sign Linguistics. Volume 1. Lawrence Erlbaum Associates, Inc., Mahwah, NJ (1996) 115–158
19. Rabiner, L.R.: A tutorial on Hidden Markov Models and selected applications in speech recognition. Proceedings of the IEEE **77** (1989) 257–286

Hand Postures Recognition in Large–Display VR Environments

Jean-Baptiste de la Rivière and Pascal Guitton

Université Bordeaux 1, LaBRI, INRIA FUTURS, CNRS, ENSEIRB
Bordeaux, France
{leproux,guitton}@labri.fr

Abstract. Large–display environments like Reality Center or Powerwall are recent equipments used in the Virtual Reality (VR) field. In contrast to HMDs or similar displays, they allow several unadorned users to visualize a virtual environment. Bringing interaction possibilities to those displays must not suppress the users' liberty. Thus, devices based on trackers like DataGlove or wand should be forgotten as they oblige users to don such gear. On the contrary, video cameras seem very promising in those environments: their use could range from looking for a laser dot on the display to recovering each user's full body posture. The goal we are considering is to film one's hand in front of a large display in order to recover its posture, which will then be interpreted according to a predefined interaction technique. While most of such systems rely on appearance–based approaches, we have chosen to investigate how far a model–based one could be efficient. This paper presents the first steps of this work, namely the real–time results obtained by using hand silhouette feature and some further conclusions related to working in a large–display VR environment.

1 Introduction

On the one hand, display hardware dedicated to the VR field has evolved from small HMDs attached to the head to large displays supporting comfortable visualization without having to wear any more device than a pair of stereo glasses. On the other hand, optical trackers are beginning to show promising real–time results close to records one could obtain with wands or DataGloves. The goal of our current research is to bring those two technologies together in a single VR system. Optical trackers in a large–display VR environment offer a way to avoid a lot of the drawbacks generally associated to classical input devices. Indeed, users would not anymore need to be linked to the computer, they could walk about in a large area in front of the display with few restrictions. New users could come in and interact without having to look for any piece of hardware. Users would not anymore be obliged to hold any device or tracker when they are not interacting. The users' sense of presence would be enhanced by making them aware that the application always knows in which state they are. Finally people will be able to interact through gestures they are performing in everyday life. For example, one could navigate by moving oneself, select an object via pointing and manipulate it by positioning precisely one's hand and fingers. Since

A. Camurri and G. Volpe (Eds.): GW 2003, LNAI 2915, pp. 259–268, 2004.

tracking the body and hands of all users is a very complex problem, we will only consider hand–based interaction obtained from the input of video cameras set in a large–display VR environment.

Before mapping hand movements into interaction tasks, hand pose must be retrieved from input images. Some previous works have directed their research toward this goal. But most of these attempts usually consider a single specific interaction task and rely on image analysis or database training (appearance–based approaches). Moreover, none has so far been able to precisely compute the fingers configuration necessary to provide careful manipulation of an object held virtually. As model–based tracking algorithms try to match a detailed hand model with the input images, we believe that such an approach in large–display environments would go over such limits. As it is common to argue that model–based algorithms need far more computing power, we investigated how recent PCs could handle these and we developed a system able to operate in near real–time.

The next section presents some of the works which seem the most representative to us, then the next one describes the model–based hand pose recognition system we developed. Finally, its use in a large–display VR environment will be discussed in section 4.

2 Previous Work

2.1 Hand–Based Interaction for Large Displays

When considering large displays, appearance–based approaches are mainly chosen. Leibe *et al.* [1] rely on three cameras and infrared light sources to extract index finger and forearm center features which define deictic postures. However, their specific desk presents special characteristics unavailable in large–display systems. Selection in a CAVE has been implemented by Moeslund *et al.* [2] as they combine single camera optical finger recognition and head tracker data. Precise pointing seems to be possible, but the head tracker has to be avoided when multiple users are present. Powerwalls form the display support of Nölker and Ritter's work [3], where they extract deictic postures in infrared images thanks to neural networks, showing some inaccuracies. Finally, Sato *et al.*'s paper [4] is a recent example of an attempt at instantiating different interaction tasks (manipulation and navigation) in a Reality Center. Triangulation of specific points determines the hand 3D position and orientation, while neural networks classify postures between six basic ones. Tracking precision is limited by the edge extrema and the center of gravity they must compute. Some constraints like dark environment or the user's mobility are not preserved. But results are already very encouraging as most test subjects claim that unadorned hand interaction is far more comfortable than using other devices. The systems Freeman *et al.* [5] have developed, that use image moments to enable body or hand as an input device, again illustrate how simple image analysis algorithms help to build real–time video input. However most such implementations are limited to a basic interaction task, or try to identify a static predefined set of hand poses. Neither are they able to provide enough information to drive, for example, a 21 dof hand model as a DataGlove does.

2.2 Model–Based Systems

On the contrary, model–based approaches seem to provide more precise results at the cost of more computing power as well as occlusion sensitivity. Given a hand model in a starting pose and an input image, a model–based algorithm will make the model gradually converge to a final hand pose. The convergence process is driven by an optimization method which maximizes the correlation between some features measured both in the input image and in the current model pose. The camera number depends on implementation choices, as does each of the algorithm parameter. One of the earliest systems is Digiteyes from Rehg and Kanade [6] where edge (finger axis) and point (finger tips) features are used to drive a 21–degrees–of–freedom (dof) kinematic model thanks to the Levenberg–Marquardt optimization method. Great results were illustrated, and a tracking of 10 Hz was performed on dedicated hardware. The main problems are the need of stereo cameras and the impossibility for one finger to occlude another. Model–based systems from Kameda *et al.* [7] [8] are based on using the entire body silhouette as a feature combined with a hierarchical geometric model. They use a simple prediction algorithm in order to cope with temporary occlusions, thus the system can easily lose track when considering fingers occluded by the palm. Heap and Hogg's system [9] reduces the hand model dof thanks to principal component analysis, then measures model and image similarity by comparing edge distances. Shimada *et al.* [10] work is interesting as the authors adapt their hand model to each new user, but their example restricts to a 3 dof finger moving in a plane. Wu and Huang [11] combine inverse kinematics, genetic–algorithms and least–median–squares in order to track a 21 dof hand with a single camera. However, their results seem no more precise than others, and finger tips occlusion is still a problem.

It appears from the bibliography we established that most propositions are designed to solve a specific problem while ignoring others. So far, no algorithm has been proposed to provide precise, real–time, robust–to–occlusions, background and lighting independent system. More specifically, no real–time system is able to cope with restrictions like low resolution binary images, few cameras and frequent occlusions.

3 Model–Based Video Recognition Algorithm

Therefore we felt the need to develop a real–time model–based hand tracking method intended for a large–display VR environment. This induces some specificities:

1. the room configuration can be controlled such that the hand of interest mostly appears in front of a dark background;
2. users can be far away from the camera, thus fine details such as the white to gray transition we often observe on fingers images won't be available, nor is a large view of one's hand;
3. occlusions may often happen.

From 1, the input images we will use show a white hand in front of a dark background. Easy segmentation provides us with a binary image that respects 2. Point 2 obliges us to deal with low–resolution images. Finally, 2 makes us unable to reliably use image edges and 3 implies we must avoid relying on fingertip features. We are currently using a single camera as our first goal is more to analyze how far our approach is efficient with large–displays induced restrictions rather than to develop a complete system.

3.1 Hand Model and General Optimization Method

The hand model we use is built atop a 1500–triangles hand polygonal model (see figure 1). The palm and each phalanx are made of a single triangle set, therefore we are able to apply specific transformation to each articulation. Since our 3D engine is based on OpenGL, the render call necessary to transform and project the hand model onto the image plane will provide high resolution frame with little computation time. Moreover, useful information such as hand–part bounding boxes or simple collision detection can be added without noticeable computation overhead.

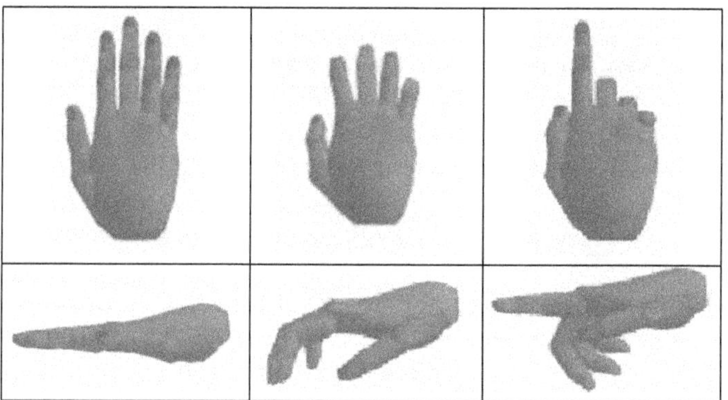

Fig. 1. Upper and side views of different hand model postures.

The model offers 21 dof: 6 describing the hand position and orientation (global parameters), and 3 for each of the pose of each finger (local parameters). Each local parameter can take values within a certain range. For example, the PIP joint — see for example McDonald *et al.* [12] for a brief discussion on hand modeling and anatomy — can vary from 0 to 90 degrees. The last joint, the DIP one, equals two thirds of the PIP joint. All those simplifications and limitations were approved by previous papers and allow to represent natural hand poses.

The optimization method we have implemented so far consists in minimizing the correlation error between the current model pose and the one represented in the input image. The error rate equals the number of different pixels in the projected hand model frame and the input image. Iterative optimization is conducted by considering each parameter in a certain order. For each parameter, the effect of a fixed step incrementation is analysed. The parameter will take this incremented value in the case of a decreased correlation error, otherwise will not be considered anymore.

3.2 Hand Model Initialization

Through the observation of hand silhouette, our system relies heavily on hand shape, which variates from one user to another. Thus measures won't be precise if the hand model is a generic one. So we must adapt the generic model to the hand of every new user. This is done at the beginning of each session where the user is asked to stretch out his fingers while presenting the back of the hand to the camera. Thanks to the dark background, extracting the hand contour from the image is easy. We then apply the same algorithm as Segen and Kumar [13] in order to extract peaks and valleys from it. Linking each finger tip, represented by a peak, to the middle of the two neighboring valleys makes the finger axis appear. The deviation angle from the vertical axis (the middle finger's one) can be used to approximately evaluate the pose of the hand. Using our optimization algorihtm, the palm's dimension (its thickness is linked to its length), then the fingers' radius, then the fingers' length (we suppose the ratio between each phalanx is constant) are evaluated to adapt the hand model to the user (figure 2).

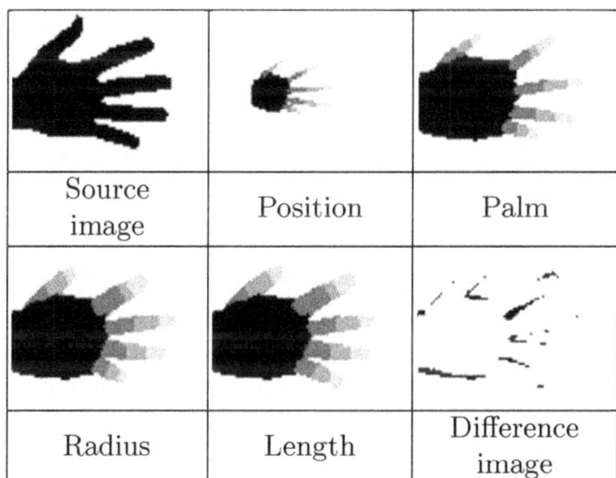

Fig. 2. Source image, parameters evaluations and resulting difference.

3.3 Hand Tracking

Our analysis is stopped and a new one is started when a new image is grabbed. The model's configuration that maximizes the correlation rate is chosen as the starting point of the new analysis. The key idea that makes our simple optimization method work is the sequential search we perform:

1. the hand position in the image is evaluated;
2. its orientation can then be evaluated;
3. local parameters are considered: abduction/adduction angles, first phalanx bending and last bending angle of each finger are evaluated.

Computation in any different order could produce bad hand pose. For example, evaluating any finger's joints will be falsed by a wrong hand position or orientation since the finger's frame of reference will be projected at a wrong pixel. Or last phalanx bending angles must not be considered before we know the position of the second phalanx reference frame, which depends on hand position as well as MCP joint pose.

3.4 Results

Tests were mainly conducted on a standard recent PC: Athlon Xp 2000+ processor, GeForce2 Ti video card, SdRam PC133 memory. The camera is a Philips ToUCam Pro, a webcam whose quality and resolution are highly sufficient when used within the restrictions we imposed. Images are at a 80x60 pixels resolution. We fixed a camera refresh rate of 5 Hz, such that movement speed seems rather natural. Provided the hand movement speed is slow, 10 Hz offer also great results. It is important to notice that all the 21 dof were evaluated in all the tests we did. Since the joint values of the real hand pose aren't available, we will consider the pose is well tracked when real hand silhouette and hand model projection match.

Our hand initialization method works quite well. As expected, we observed that the tracking depends highly on a correct registration: even a slight error in the model adaptation could lead to tracking impossibility. While this stage needs at the moment an operator to decide when to pass to the next adaptation phase, we believe that a totally automated initialization will give the same results. We must also notice that as our system doesn't model the hand wrist, it may lead to too large palm length.

Figure 3 illustrates a hand tracking sequence. It shows that local parameters are well recovered, provided hand position and orientation are correct. As our algorithm just uses a binary image, there are examples where it is impossible to disambiguate two or more fingers' poses. For example, when two fingers cross each other as in figure 4, a hand front view can't show which finger covers the other. Similarly, a side view of an initially flat hand doesn't allow us to be sure of which finger is bending. Quick movements can also make the system lose track. Anyway, it often recovers a correct pose after some more iterations as it will pursue its analysis during the treatment devoted to the next frame. The thumb may be incorrectly estimated under certain viewing angles, but we think this is due to the bad modeling of its joint rotation axes. Global parameters are more a problem. Hand translation in the image plane can be well approximated, as well is hand rotation in this plane. However, translation along the third axis or the two others rotations may be badly estimated. We think this is only due to incorrect registration between the webcam internal parameters and the logical camera ones.

Our future developments involve both simple additions to this algorithm and major rewriting of some parts of the system. First modifications like modeling the hand wrist and modifying some finger's rotation axis will be necessary. We could also add one or more cameras. For example, a second camera with an

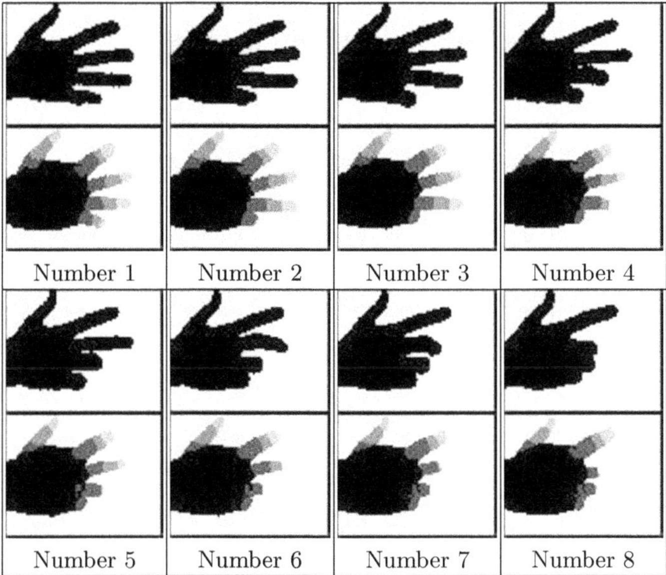

Fig. 3. Bending fingers.

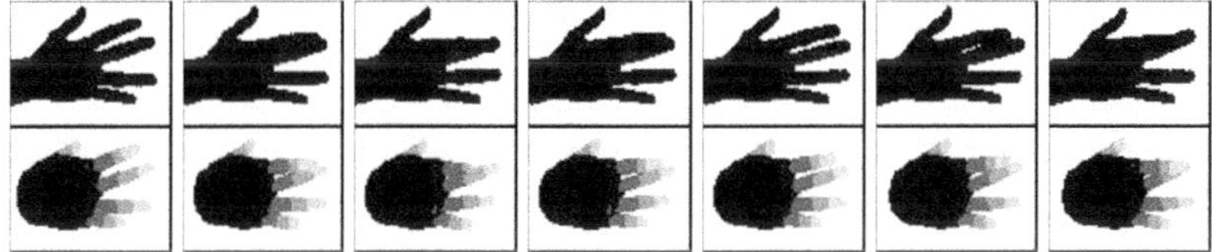

Fig. 4. Crossing two fingers.

upper view of the hand will help to know which finger is bending in the figure 5 case. Otherwise, a single camera and a binary image are not sufficient to prevent the little finger from following the middle one. Besides, adding cameras doesn't necessarily increase the computing power needed. A second camera could be used only when an ambiguous pose is detected, or the system could switch from one camera to the other when the current one doesn't offer the best view of the hand. This is an interesting difference over previous stereo systems: a single camera at a time can be sufficient in order to recover hand configuration, and other cameras could then be switched to or used only when a troublesome hand configuration is detected.

Deeper optimization directions include modifications of the convergence process. We observed that most of the time spent on analyzing an image is dedicated to measuring the correlation rate. As two images are compared, the analysis completion time is linked to their resolution. Reducing it above the 80x60 we use erases details such as different fingers. However we think a multi–resolution approach will work well: a lower resolution image could be generated and compared

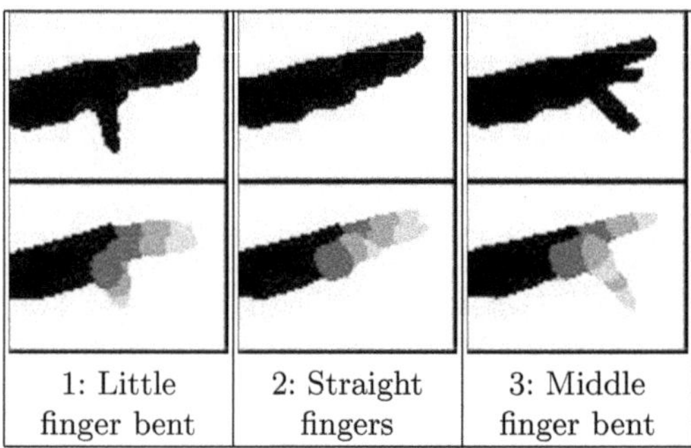

Fig. 5. Side view misregistration.

in order to roughly estimate parameters, while the highest resolution image will lead to finer corrections. To reduce the number of pixels considered, we could as well use only the pixels that are modified by a specific parameter. For example, when we test the last joint of a finger, we just need to update the correlation rate based on values of pixels that belong to this phalanx before and after the new joint value is set. Finally, the bounding boxes will allow to detect the pixels that will be occluded by another part of the hand in order to avoid to test pixels that won't be modified by a particular joint value modification.

However, simple image analysis algorithms used in previous studies must not be forgotten. For example, image moments used like Freeman *et al.* [5] may help to estimate hand global parameters, or quick motion estimation may provide approximation of a hand part movement.

4 Hand Posture Recognition in Front of a Large Display

The large–display VR environment we are experimenting on is a Reality Center. It consists in a 10x3 meters hemicyclindrical wall and 3 high resolution projectors. It sits in a dark room where any light source other than the back–projected wall disturbs the users' immersion. Therefore, video systems must not rely on additional visible light. To our knowledge, most authors use near infrared cameras coupled with such light sources. As the room configuration will never be changed, many cameras can be attached to strategic places. For example, upper and side cameras can help to retreive interesting pointing gestures, like in Leubner *et al.*'s work [14]. Despite the low distance between the user and the wall and the full natural light, their implementation confirms video usability. While an important concern is the potentially large distance between users and cameras, we showed that low resolution binary images still offer enough information to retrieve hand configuration. Hence, another problem will be to develop sufficiently robust algorithms to extract the sub–image containing the hand from the high resolution input.

Once the correct hand pose is retrieved, a proper interaction task may be instantiated. Advantages of our model–based approach is that the hand pose is fully described be each joint angle values. Hence different interaction tasks can be associated to different joint angle values set: pointing may correspond to near 0 index joint values while other fingers are bent, grasping may be mapped to a close hand, and so on. Indeed the pointing interaction task must be associated to the pointing gesture [14] [2], while the target on the wall will be estimated according to hand position and orientation. Object manipulation can be implemented like DataGlove–based manipulations are. For example Kang and Ikeuchi [15] have shown how to segment a grasp gesture in a DataGlove record, and Segen and Kumar [13] have shown how to adapt their hand pose extraction system to simple object manipulation. Examples of navigation are also given by Segen and Kumar [13], or can be found in Freeman *et al.* [5].

5 Conclusion

We described the model–based algorithm we plan to use in a large–display VR environment. The early prototype we developed works in near real–time and, thanks to a detailed hand geometric model, it extracts precise hand pose from hand silhouette binary images. Since it doesn't rely on fingertip or edge features, temporary occlusions are less a trouble than in some previous systems. Moreover, it can already give us some ideas on how it will perform when fully optimized. Then we will be able to study various types of interactions, ranging from selection via pointing to precise manipulation. Finally, we think video in large displays will be fully exploited when multiple body–tracking is added, which is a further step in our research.

Acknowledgements

We would like to thank M. Hosseini for sending us his VRML model. Thanks also to S. Capern, V. Thorel and G. Roque for their participation on the application development, and to J.–J. Bernaulte for his many advices.

References

1. Leibe, B., Starner, T., Ribarsky, W., Wartell, Z., Krum, D., Singletary, B., Hodges, L.: The perceptive workbench: Toward spontaneous and natural interaction in semi–immersive virtual environments. In: IEEE Virtual Reality. (2000) 13–20
2. Moeslund, T., Störring, M., Granum, E.: Vision–based user interface for interacting with a virtual environment. In: DANKOMB. (2000)
3. Nölker, C., Ritter, H.: Illumination independant recognition of deictic arm postures. In: 24th Annual Conference of the IEEE Industrial Electronic Society. (1998) 2006–2011
4. Sato, Y., Saito, M., Koike, H.: Real–time input of 3d hand pose and gestures of a user's hand and its applications for hci. In: Virtual Reality Conference. (2001)
5. Freeman, W., Tanaka, K., Ohta, J., Kyuma, K.: Computer vision for computer games. FG'96 (1996) 100–105

6. Rehg, J., Kanade, T.: Digiteyes: Vision–based hand tracking for human computer interaction. In: Workshop on Motion of Non–Rigid and Articulated Objects. (1994) 16–22
7. Kameda, Y., Minoh, M., Ikeda, K.: Three dimensional pose estimation of an articulated object from its silhouette image. In: Asian Conference on Computer Vision. (1993) 612–615
8. Kameda, Y., Minoh, M., Ikeda, K.: Three dimensional motion estimation of a human body using a difference image sequence. In: Asian Conference on Computer Vision. (1995) 181–185
9. Heap, T., Hogg, D.: Towards 3d hand tracking using a deformable model. In: Conference on Automatic Face and Gesture Recognition. (1996) 140–145
10. Shimada, N., Shirai, Y., Kuno, Y., J.Miura: Hand gesture estimation and model refinment using monocular camera – ambiguity limitation by inequality constraints. In: 3rd conference on Face and Gesture Recognition. (1998) 268–273
11. Wu, Y., Huang, T.: Capturing articulated human hand motion: A divide–and–conquer approach. In: International Conference on Computer Vision. (1999) 606–611
12. McDonald, J., Toro, J., Alkoby, K., Berthiaume, A., Carter, R., Chomwong, P., Christopher, J., Davidson, M., Furst, J., Konie, B., Lancaster, G., Roychoudhuri, L., Sedgwick, E., Tomuro, N., Wolfe, R.: An improved articulated model of the human hand. The Visual Computer **17** (2001) 158–166
13. Segen, J., Kumar, S.: Shadow gestures: 3d hand pose estimation using a single camera. In: IEEE conference on Computer Vision and Pattern Recognition. (1999) 479–485
14. Leubner, C., Brockman, C., Müller, H.: Computer–vision–based human-computer interaction with a back projection wall using arm gestures. Euromicro Conference (2001)
15. Kang, S., Ikeuchi, K.: Toward automatic robot instruction from perception — temporal segmentation of tasks from human hand motion. Transactions on Robotics and Automation **11** (1995)

Developing Task-Specific RBF Hand Gesture Recognition

A. Jonathan Howell, Kingsley Sage, and Hilary Buxton

School of Cognitive and Computing Sciences
University of Sussex, Brighton BN1 9QH, UK

Abstract. In this paper we develop hand gesture learning and recognition techniques to be used in advanced vision applications, such as the ActIPret system for understanding the activities of expert operators for education and training. Radial Basis Function (RBF) networks have been developed for reactive vision tasks and work well, exhibiting fast learning and classification. Specific extensions of our existing work to allow more general 3-D activity analysis reported here are: 1) action-based representation in a hand frame-of-reference by pre-processing of the trajectory data; 2) adaptation of the time-delay RBF network scheme to use this relative velocity information from the 3-D trajectory information in gesture recognition; and 3) development of multi-task support in the classifications by exploiting prototype similarities extracted from different combinations of direction (target tower) and height (target pod) for the hand trajectory.

1 Introduction

Neural network techniques are a powerful, general approach to pattern recognition tasks based on learning, and there are a variety of different methods (for an introduction see [3]). The classical networks do not include a time dimension so they have to be adapted to deal with dynamic scene analysis. Some extended models have internal time like the partially recurrent networks of Elman [6] and Jordan [13]. Others have external time like the time-delay networks described below. Time can be explicitly represented in the architecture at the network level using the connections or can be represented at the neuron level, including the recently developed 'spiking networks'. These model the intrinsic temporal properties of biological neurons, which fire with a pattern of pulses or spikes (for review see [8]). However, these fully dynamic networks have yet to be applied in visual behaviour analysis, although a start has been made [7]. A widely used model is the Time Delay extension of classical Radial Basis Functions (TDRBFs). Networks of this kind have been shown to exhibit rapid training and online processing in tasks such as gesture recognition [10]. We have done some comparative work with Hidden Markov Models (HMM) (see companion paper in this volume): RBF has a lighter computational load, whereas the HMM can learn the data unsupervised and give probabilistic prediction at all timesteps.

Learning in a vision system can be at the level of object models, their movements and actions, and how to control views and processing in the system.

A. Camurri and G. Volpe (Eds.): GW 2003, LNAI 2915, pp. 269–276, 2004.

Our work on appearance-based approaches using RBF nets suggests they are very learnable and robust in comparison with structural approaches for general object categorisation on real-world tasks such as face recognition [9,11]. Natural deformable objects are difficult to specify and so are their movements and actions, so adaptive methods are required. At the heart of a visual learning system is the ability to find the relevant mapping from observable or derivable attributes of image(s) onto the visual categories we require for real-world tasks. In this paper, we show how appearance-based techniques can be extended to 3D gesture recognition, based on velocities recovered from hand trajectories, for the ActIPret system.

The TDRBF model is first described in Section 2. In Sections 3 and 4, the dataset and results from generalisation of the generic gesture models are described. We then go on to consider how robust the recognition is under noise in training and testing trajectory sequences. Extensions of the task-specific processing are described, including the learning of multiple tasks. Finally, in sections 5 and 6, the implications of the work for task control and system integration are then discussed with conclusions and suggestions for further work.

2 Time Delay RBF Network

The RBF network is a two-layer, hybrid learning network [14,15], which combines a supervised layer from the hidden to the output units with an unsupervised layer from the input to the hidden units. The network model is characterised by individual radial Gaussian functions for each hidden unit, which simulate the effect of overlapping and locally tuned receptive fields. Supported by well-developed mathematical theory, the model provides rapid computation and robust generalisation, powerful enough for real-time, real-life tasks [18,19]. The nonlinear decision boundaries of RBF networks make better general function approximations than the hyperplanes created by the multi-layer perceptron (MLP) with sigmoid units [16], and they provide a guaranteed, globally optimal solution via simple, linear optimisation. Another advantage of the RBF network, compared to the MLP, is that it gives low false-positive rates in classification problems as it will not extrapolate beyond its learnt example set. This is because its basis functions cover small localised regions, unlike sigmoidal basis functions which are nonzero over an arbitrarily large region of the input space.

Once training examples have been collected as input-output pairs, with the target class attached to each image, tasks can be learned directly by the system. This type of supervised learning can be seen in mathematical terms as approximating a multivariate function, so that estimations of function values can be made for previously unseen test data where actual values are not known. This process can be undertaken by the RBF network using a linear combination of basis functions, one for every training example, because of the smoothness of the manifold formed by the example views of objects in a space of all possible views of that object [17]. This underlies successful previous work with RBF networks for face recognition from video sequences [11], which uses an RBF centre for each training example, and rapid pseudo-inverse calculation of weights. An important factor in this approach is the flexibility of the RBF network learning approach, which allows formulation of the training in terms of the specific classes of data to be distinguished. For example, extraction of identity, head pose and expression information can be performed separately on the same face training data to learn a computationally cheap RBF classifier for each separate recognition task [5,12].

To extend this research to support *visual interaction*, generic gesture models are developed here for the control of attention in gesture recognition. In previous work a time-delay variant of the Radial Basis Function (TDRBF) network recognised pointing and waving hand gestures in image sequences [10]. This network is created by combining data from a fixed time 'window' into a single vector as input. Characteristic visual evidence is automatically selected during the adaptive learning phase, depending on the task demands. A set of interaction-relevant gestures were modelled and exploited for reactive on-line visual control. These were then interpreted as user intentions for live control of an active camera with adaptive view direction and attentional focus. For ActIPret, some of the ideas for zooming in on activities can still be exploited. Also the gesture recognition is an excellent predictive cue for many of the actions and activities in our ActIPret scenarios. At the earlier levels of processing, but particularly in the gesture recognition, reactive behaviour is important for both camera movement and invoking further 'attentional' processing. The scheme is adapted here to accept 3-D hand trajectories for predictive gesture recognition, using tri-phasic gesture detectors as in previous work on predictive control [12].

3 Gesture Data

The gesture data used for the experiments in this paper was the *Terminal Hand Orientation and Effort Reach Study* Database created by Human Motion Simulation at the Center for Ergonomics, University of Michigan, USA. 3-D hand trajectory data was collected from 22 subjects of varying gender, age, and height. Nineteen of the subjects were right-handed and two were left-handed. 210 target locations and hand orientations were used, giving a total number of 4,410 trials and the 8,820 reach movements.

Four towers were used, from 45° left of the subject to 90° right, each of which had three 'pods' as targets. There is further variation in the targets, as each of the pods has five cubes, each of which can use four hand orientations. For the experiments in this paper, we consider only tower/pod combinations (12 in all). Each trial produced a file of 3-D coordinates for two points (six values each time step) on the subject's hand. For each trial, data was collected at 25Hz for a sequence consisting of five distinct phases:

- Start with hand at a 'home location' on subject's leg, followed by:
- A movement toward the target, which we term *get*;
- A static phase while the hand is at the target;
- A second movement, away from the target, which we term *return*;
- A final static phase at the home location.

Each resulting datafile contained 80–135 timesteps. The 3-D location data was pre-processed by differencing to give relative motion or velocity data.

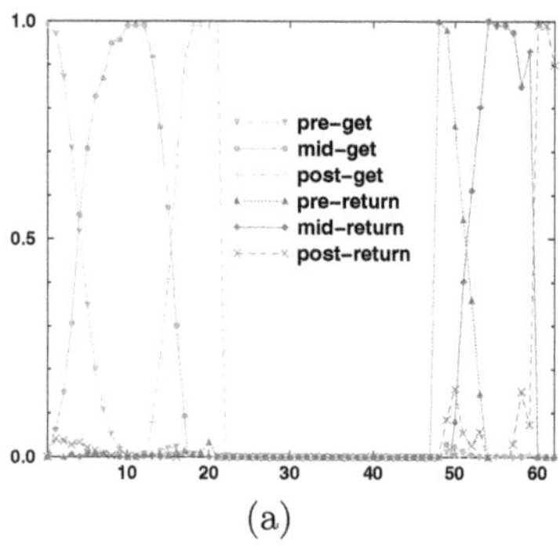

(a)

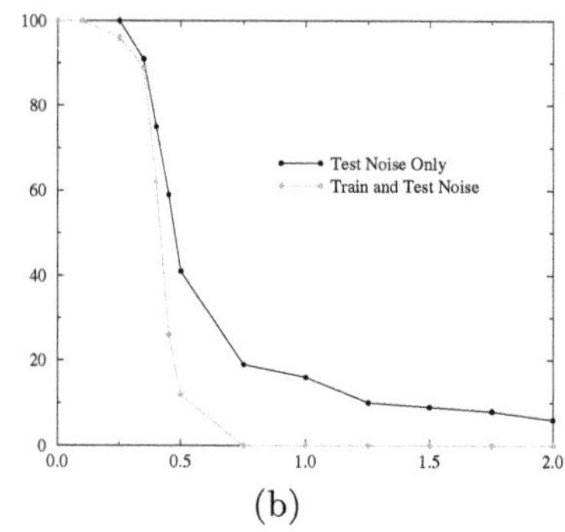

(b)

Fig. 1. Gesture phase classification for a TDRBF network trained and tested with targets in Tower 0 (45° left of subject) (a) tested with a single complete hand trajectory, showing values for output units for each gesture phase class (y-axis) at each time step (x-axis). (b) tested with varying amounts of RMS noise added to the trajectory positions (x-axis, values in cm). The y-axis shows the proportion of test trajectories where gesture phases were correctly interpreted at every time step of the entire trajectory.

4 Method

To train the TDRBF network, training data was segmented automatically according to the level of relative motion within successive time delay segments. The length of these time delays does not affect results particularly as long as it is shorter than the expected gesture phase: in this case, we used a time delay length of six time steps. Based on the definition of the trial data above, we assume two distinct gesture movements are contained in each hand trajectory data file, with static periods in between. We impose three phases within each of these movements: a *pre-phase*, at the start of movement a *mid-phase*, at the midpoint between start and end of movement and a *post-phase*, at the end of movement. Adding an extra class for stasis, or no movement, gives seven classes in all: *pre-, mid- and post-get, pre-, mid- and post-return* and *stasis.*

The three-phase structure for gesture classification is based on previous work [12], where we found that breaking gestures down into smaller parts allowed more reliable recognition as well as supporting prediction. The strategy we developed was to only accept specific plausible sequences of phases as real gestures, eg. the pre-phase needed to be observed before the mid-phase, and confirmed by the post-phase to support appropriate attention frame shifts for visual interaction.

To test the trained TDRBF network, we present successive time-delay vectors over the complete trajectory file, giving a series of outputs representing confidence in each of the six gesture phase classes. Time delay segments with very low levels of relative motion are identified automatically and ignored by the TDRBF network in the test phase, being immediately classified as static.

Parsing Network Output: Our previous work with the HUMOSIM hand trajectory data [4] was able to show RBF methods could effectively learn the

Table 1. Generalisation over hand trajectory angle (around y-axis) for TDRBF networks trained with a range of tower data, from Tower 0 (45° left) to Tower 3 (90° right). The '% Correct' values show the proportion of test trajectories where gesture phases were correctly interpreted at every time step of the entire trajectory.

Training Towers		Test Tower, % Correct			
		0	1	2	3
Single	0	100	66	0	0
	1	100	100	0	0
	2	0	0	94	15
	3	0	0	41	94
Consecutive	0 + 1	100	100	0	0
	2 + 3	0	0	100	94
Alternate	0 + 2	83	83	88	15
	1 + 3	91	94	17	94
All		100	94	100	94

individual gesture phases, for example, see Fig. 1(a) for typical classification. In this example, smooth transitions can be seen between phase classes, and all time steps are correctly classified, even for people and timesteps not included in the training set. We can go on from these results to use these transitions to accurately signal progress through the gesture phases, and devise a metric for assessing how well the network identifies the overall gestures.

The measure for correct classification we use in this paper is that a complete series of valid gesture phase transitions has to be observed during the test output from a whole trajectory, ie. *pre-get* first, followed by *mid-get*, *post-get*, *pre-return*, *mid-return* and *post-return* (with arbitrary static periods before, middle and after). If this exact sequence is observed, the overall classification is deemed correct. Any other transition, eg. *pre-get* to *post-get*, invalidates the classification of the entire sequence. Although this might seem an unduly harsh measure of success, in practise it is quite hard to 'repair' a classification sequence for a test trajectory once incorrect entries have been entered. One strategy which can help is to use an assumption of temporal continuity, where observed transitions are only accepted after consecutive, identical phase classifications, which is effective in excluding transitory mis-classifications.

The advantage of this approach to monitoring the network output is that a complete breakdown of gesture phase start/end positions can be provided for the test trajectory: very useful for an online component of a larger vision system.

5 Results

The experiments presented here are in three phases: the first to determine generalisation characteristics over angle of hand trajectory for the TDRBF network, the second to determine how this generalisation is affected by varying levels of random noise, and the third to develop the training of multiple tasks for the network, such as 'which gesture *and* which tower is the hand aiming for?'

Generalisation over Trajectory Angle: To test generalisation over angle of hand trajectory (around y-axis), we trained and tested the TDRBF network with combinations of data from the four towers (from 45° left to 90° right of the front of the subject), keeping the pod position (x-axis variation) constant. The test set contained trajectories from single towers, but the training data used one of: a single tower, two adjacent towers (eg. 0 and 1), two alternate towers (eg. 0 and 2), or all four towers.

The results for these tests are presented in Table 1. These show that while the networks trained a single tower do not generalise particularly well to other towers, a reasonable performance can be obtained by combining training data from two or more towers.

Adding Noise: The 'Flock of Birds' magnetic sensor used to record hand coordinates for the HUMOSIM hand trajectory data used in this paper is very highly accurate, giving values to a fraction of a mm. In order to simulate less constrained data, such as might be extracted by visual methods, we apply varying levels of random noise to the coordinate values. This altering of the coordinates is not to simulate consistent errors, eg. mis-calibration, where constant offsets will be observed, but transitory errors, eg. due to uncertainty or occlusion, which are common in visual hand tracking.

Noise was added to the 3-D location as random values with a normal distribution with mean zero. The level of noise was determined as an root mean square (RMS) value, for example, a noise level of 1.0cm RMS produced random values between about $\pm$1.2cm. To produce a smoother variation of values, each vector of random values had individual values averaged with its neighbour.

Fig. 1(b) shows how classification performance deteriorates as noise increases. Two test arrangements are shown, each with a separate line on the graph. The first trains the TDRBF network without noise, and tests with varying noise. The second both trains and test with an equal level of noise. The TDRBF network performs slightly better when trained without noise, but overall the limit for useful performance would appear to be around 0.5cm RMS noise (on every axis, every time step).

Multiple Tasks: In this section, we consider how to learn multiple tasks, such as 'which gesture *and* which tower is the hand aiming for?' In previous work, we have shown that separate RBF networks can learn different tasks (face identity, expression, head pose) from the same training data through altering the training signal [5], and that one TDRBF network could learn both gesture and identity by giving different classes to gestures from different individuals [10].

Three tasks can be learnt from the HUMOSIM hand trajectory data:

- *'Which gesture phase?'*, using six gesture phase classes,
- *'Which tower position is the hand aiming for?*, using four position classes (from 45° left to 90° right),
- *'Which pod position is the hand aiming for?*, using three position classes (from 45° above to 45° below).

As an example of combining these tasks, in order to learn both gesture and tower position, we train a network with individual phase classes for each tower.

Table 2. Performance for TDRBF networks trained for multiple tasks: 'Gesture' has six gesture phase classes, 'Tower Position' has four position classes (45° left – 90° right) and 'Pod Position' three (45° above – 45° below). The '% Correct' values show the proportion of test trajectories where combinations of gesture phase, tower and pod positions were correctly interpreted at every time step of the entire trajectory.

Trained Tasks	Classes	Test Tower, % Correct			
		0	1	2	3
Gesture + Tower Position	24	100	100	82	84
Tower + Pod Position	12	100	100	100	100
Gesture + Tower + Pod	72	100	88	82	89

This uses six phases for each of the four towers, 24 classes in all. The results for networks trained on three combinations of these tasks are shown in Table 2, including one trained with all three tasks, which required 72 classes.

Table 2 shows that minimal reduction in performance is observed, compared the the network trained with all towers in Table 1, whilst useful extra information is provided alongside the gesture output.

6 Summary

- The TDRBF network can learn individual gesture phases from 3-D hand trajectories collected from a magnetic sensor.
- An efficient method for parsing network output and measuring correct classification over an entire hand trajectory file has been developed.
- The 3-D coordinate representation limits trajectory angle generalisation due to values moving from one axis to another as the angle is varied, but this can be overcome by explicit training for several target positions.
- Although the magnetic sensor hand trajectory data is very constrained, the trained TDRBF network was shown to be tolerant to a fairly high level of instantaneous random variations in coordinates (around 0.5cm RMS noise on every axis, every time step).
- An efficient method for training the TDRBF network to learn multiple tasks, such as 'which gesture *and* tower is the hand aiming for?' has been shown.

7 Conclusions

We have developed a task-specific Gesture Recognition component and shown that this approach yields promising results, using hybrid learning in the TDRBF. Although the first layer of weights learned during training are unsupervised in the TDRBF, the mapping of class prototypes onto the task-relevant classes needs to be supervised and a seven phase structure was imposed. Further task-specific sub-classes to identify towers, pods and grasp were also defined. Performance on the learning and generalisation tasks was simply supported by rapid weight training in the RBF network. This kind of class-based processing [1,2] has many advantages, including the possibility of learning sufficient information from a single example by exploiting class similarities [20]. The multi-task modelling shown here can be generalised to select any systematic variations known to exist in the dataset as the sub-classes, which can then support activity analysis in the full system [4]. As in the discussion above, there is great potential for task-specific processing using the TDRBF to supply fast, reactive results.

Acknowledgements

The authors gratefully acknowledge the invaluable help provided by the Laboratory for Human Motion Simulation (HUMOSIM) at the University of Michigan, USA in allowing us access to their 'Terminal Hand Orientation and Effort Reach Study, 2000' hand trajectory database; also framework concepts and funding from the EU ActIPret project.

References

1. R. Basri. Recognition by prototypes. *IJ Computer Vision*, 19:147–168, 1996.
2. D. J. Beymer and T. Poggio. Image representations for visual learning. *Science*, 272:1905–1909, 1996.
3. C. M. Bishop. *Neural Networks for Pattern Recognition.* Oxford Univ. Press, 1995.
4. H. Buxton, A. J. Howell, and K. Sage. The role of task control and context in learning to recognise gesture. In *Cognitive Vision Workshop*, Zürich, 2002.
5. S. Duvdevani-Bar, S. Edelman, A. J. Howell, and H. Buxton. A similarity-based method for the generalization of face recognition over pose and expression. In *IEEE Int. Conf. Face Gesture Recognition*, pp. 118–123, Nara, Japan, 1998.
6. J. Elman. Finding structure in time. *Cognitive Science*, 14:179–211, 1990.
7. J. Feng, Y. L. Sun, and H. Buxton. Training the integrate-and-fire model with the Informax Principle II. *IEEE Transactions on Neural Networks*, 14:accepted, 2003.
8. W. Gerstner. Time structure of the activity in neural networks. *Physical Review*, E 51:738–758, 1995.
9. A. J. Howell and H. Buxton. Invariance in radial basis function networks in human face classification. *Neural Processing Letters*, 2:26–30, 1995.
10. A. J. Howell and H. Buxton. Learning gestures for visually mediated interaction. In *British Machine Vision Conference*, Southampton, UK, 1998.
11. A. J. Howell and H. Buxton. Learning identity with radial basis function networks. *Neurocomputing*, 20:15–34, 1998.
12. A. J. Howell and H. Buxton. Time-delay RBF networks for attentional frames in visually mediated interaction. *Neural Processing Letters*, 15:197–211, 2002.
13. M. I. Jordan. Serial order: A parallel, distributed processing approach. In *Advances in Connectionist Theory: Speech.* Lawrence Erlbaum, 1989.
14. J. Moody and C. Darken. Learning with localized receptive fields. In *Proc. 1988 Connectionist Models Summer School*, pp. 133–143, 1988.
15. J. Moody and C. Darken. Fast learning in networks of locally tuned processing units. *Neural Computation*, 1:281–294, 1989.
16. T. Poggio and S. Edelman. A network that learns to recognise three-dimensional objects. *Nature*, 343:263–266, 1990.
17. T. Poggio and F. Girosi. Regularisation algorithms for learning that are equivalent to multilayer networks. *Science*, 247:978–982, 1990.
18. D. A. Pomerleau. ALVINN: An autonomous land vehicle in a neural network. In *NIPS*, vol. 1, pp. 305–313, 1989.
19. M. Rosenblum, Y. Yacoob, and L. D. Davis. Human emotion recognition from motion using a RBF network architecture. *IEEE TNN*, 7:1121–1138, 1996.
20. T. Vetter and T. Poggio. Image synthesis from a single example image. In *ECCV*, pp. 652–659, Cambridge, UK, 1996.

Developing Context Sensitive HMM Gesture Recognition

Kingsley Sage, A. Jonathan Howell, and Hilary Buxton

School of Cognitive and Computing Sciences
University of Sussex, Brighton BN1 9QH, UK

Abstract. We are interested in methods for building cognitive vision systems to understand activities of expert operators for our ActIPret System. Our approach to the gesture recognition required here is to learn the generic models and develop methods for contextual bias of the visual interpretation in the online system. The paper first introduces issues in the development of such flexible and robust gesture learning and recognition, with a brief discussion of related research. Second, the computational model for the Hidden Markov Model (HMM) is described and results with varying amounts of noise in the training and testing phases are given. Third, extensions of this work to allow both top-down bias in the contextual processing and bottom-up augmentation by moment to moment observation of the hand trajectory are described.

1 Introduction

In cognitive science, it is well known that simple moving light displays contain sufficient information for meaningful interpretation of activity, as in the early work of Johansson [12]. Given this human ability, we use hand trajectory data alone for our gesture analysis here. Further, we use a definition of a gesture as a tri-phasic sequence of atomic hand movements as in our earlier work [10]. The essential elements of cognitive vision must be supported here: *memory* organisation of representations for the gestures; *reasoning* about these representations for flexible decisions and actions, including the resolution of ambiguity [17]; *control* of online visual processing for efficient interpretation [19]; and *learning* of both the task-relevant representations and how to use them [6].

Gestures, as above, require matching against their representations in the online system to find the interpretation or model that best explains the observation sequence. These representations have to account for the uncertain and probabilistic nature of gesture instances, including variations in the spatiotemporal evolution of the trajectories. These variations can be handled by techniques such as dynamic time warping in the matching, as in [4,13]. However, the temporal templates required in this approach are subject to the problem of self-occlusion, as well as requiring the whole of the gesture to be completed before it can be recognised. The HMM approach, using the Viterbi algorithm to overcome the problems of variability, is popular as it offers more sophisticated matching for many kinds of time-varying signals [15]. HMMs consist of a series of states, which

A. Camurri and G. Volpe (Eds.): GW 2003, LNAI 2915, pp. 277–287, 2004.

can capture the intrinsic structure of our gestures from a set of training examples. They are further characterised by the probabilistic transitions between the states and the set of probabilities that a particular state gives rise to a particular observation. That is, they are a member of the class of generative models, as we can see from early work [8,16].

HMMs also offer the advantage of unsupervised segmentation of continuous data streams, where the beginning and end is unknown. The Viterbi algorithm, mentioned above, is a kind of dynamic programming algorithm and is used to capture the maximum probability as well as the state sequence. This is of particular importance in sign language interpretation, which follows the lead of Starner and Pentland [18] to emphasise the continuous recognition of gestures [1]. However, the Viterbi algorithm requires calculation of observation probabilities for each state and time step in the Forward-Backward procedure, which is difficult to scale up. New avenues are being explored, based on the condensation algorithm [11], such as the incremental scheme proposed by Black and Jepson [2]. However, in this paper we are concerned with flexibility and robustness to noise, which affect how effective the gesture interpretation can be in a particular context, rather than its efficiency.

For an effective scheme, we need to consider the need to acquire the generic gesture models and contextually augmented versions of them, which can be used in the matching process above. Typically machine learning approaches have required hand labelling of the trajectory data or at least pre-segmentation into classes as in the TDRBF approach [10]. HMMs have an associated learning method, the Baum-Welch algorithm [15], which is a specific variant of the Expectation Maximisation (EM) algorithm [7]. In previous work [8], HMM trajectory prediction from entry regions through intermediate states to the re-fuelling or baggage-handling regions was augmented by updates on the position of vehicles from lower level vision for a known vehicle type. In general, scene context and aspects of the top-down interpretation or bottom-up visual information from moment to moment can be used to augment processing in an HMM without going to a full hierarchical Bayesian network [5]. In our recent work, additional context variables were introduced into the training data, as in [3]. These additional variables cause separate Gaussian components to be generated in feature space such that each context has an independent representation [6]. This work is extended here.

In the following, the HMM model is first formally described in section 2. Then in section 3, some results from the generalisation of the generic gesture models and the state-structure captured are described, together with considerations of how robust the recognition is under noise in training and testing trajectory sequences. In section 4, the extensions of the contextual processing are described, together with preliminary results from top-down contextual bias in the interpretation and on-line augmentation from bottom-up observations. Finally, in sections 5 and 6, the implications of the work for task control and system integration are then discussed with conclusions and suggestions for further work.

2 Hidden Markov Model for Gesture Recognition

A Hidden Markov Model (HMM) is a doubly stochastic process, i.e. there is an underlying stochastic process that is not observable (hidden) but can only be observed through another set of stochastic processes that produce the sequence of observed symbols [15]. The HMM is characterised by a triple $\lambda = (\pi, A, B)$ where A is a square $N * N$ matrix of probabilities for transitions between N discrete hidden states, π is a vector of probabilities describing the initial state of the model (at time $t = 0$) and B is a $N * M$ matrix accounting for the mapping between the N hidden states and the M output (observable) symbols.

There are three general problems we may solve using HMMs. Given a set of observation symbols O and a model λ we can calculate the probability of that sequence $p(O|\lambda)$ (forward evaluation). Given O and λ we can deduce the most likely sequence of hidden states (Viterbi decoding). Finally, and most relevant for what follows, given O we can estimate model parameters λ that maximise the probability of O. The most common form of HMM model parameter estimation is the Baum-Welch algorithm (described in [15]) which is an iterative non-globally optimal procedure for maximum likelihood estimation.

To capture gesture models, we use a continuous output HMM with training observation sequences represented as six-valued vectors (two sets of 3-D hand velocities – see next section) with the observation symbols modelled as 6-component mixture of Gaussian functions. We then vary the number of internal discrete hidden states to explore the underlying dimensionality of the training set (which corresponds approximately to the number of distinct gesture phases) and to demonstrate the ability of the HMM to distinguish the learned gesture from other gestures.

The gesture data used for the experiments in this paper was the *Terminal Hand Orientation and Effort Reach Study* Database created by Human Motion Simulation (HUMOSIM) at the Center for Ergonomics, University of Michigan, USA. 3-D hand trajectory data was collected from 22 subjects of varying gender, age, and height. Nineteen of the subjects were right-handed and two were left-handed. 210 target locations and hand orientations were used, giving a total number of 4,410 trials and the 8,820 reach movements.

This gesture data describes target and task orientated hand trajectories rather than communicative gestures (such as waving and pointing). HUMOSIM tasks represented are limited to the manipulation of targets at a number of positions and heights relative to the user.

Four towers were used in the HUMOSIM hand trajectory data, from 45° left of the subject to 90° right, each of which had three 'pods' as targets. There is further variation in the targets, as each of the pods has five cubes, each of which can use four hand orientations. For the experiments in this paper, we consider only tower/pod combinations (12 in all). Each trial produced a file of 3-D coordinates for two points (six values each time step) on the subject's hand. For each trial, data was collected at 25Hz for a sequence consisting of five distinct phases:

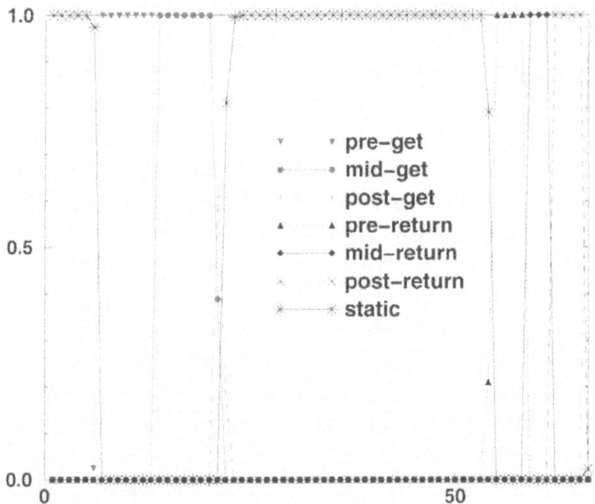

Fig. 1. Gesture phase classification for HMM trained with targets in Tower 0 (45° left of subject), when tested with a single complete hand trajectory also from Tower 0 values for output units for each gesture phase class (y-axis) at each timestep (x-axis). The probability values for each gesture phase correspond to the values associated with the HMM hidden nodes at each timestep.

- Start with a static hand placed at a 'home location':
- A movement toward the target, which we term *get*;
- A static phase while the hand is at the target;
- A second movement, away from the target, which we term *return*;
- A final static phase at the home location.

Each resulting datafile contained 80–135 timesteps. The 3-D location data was pre-processed by differencing it from one time step to the next (relative motion or velocity data).

3 Results

We examined three aspects of HMM performance. We start by demonstrating how transitions between hidden states can be readily visualised facilitating direct comparison with other approaches. We then show how HMMs can generalise the gesture trajectory data, and how that generalisation degrades gracefully in the presence of noise. Section 4 shows how context information can be used to control HMM classifier performance.

We devised a simple technique based on modified Viterbi decoding to facilitate comparison between the transition between the HMM hidden states and six functional gesture phases defined for a comparable TDRBF model ([6]).

Analysis of the fit between the probability of the model parameters given the training data and the number of hidden states shows that the fit reaches an optimal point where low numbers of hidden states are matched against ability to generalise. In our particular task, this point was typically where the HMM had seven hidden states (similar to [14]).

To test the trained HMM we presented complete trajectory files from targets not used for training. Fig. 1 shows the results for an HMM trained with 19 trajectories from a target on Tower 0 (45° left), when tested with another trajectory on the same tower. The seventh hidden state explicitly represents timesteps of minimal motion, interpreted as the 'static' gesture class.

3.1 Generalisation of the Trajectory Data

In the previous section we used the term 'classify' to refer to an analysis of the qualitative transitions between hidden states. In this section we make quantitative comparisons between different HMMs and so use the term classify to refer to a measure of fit between a learned model and a test observation. The usual quantitative measures used for HMMs are the terminal $P(O|\lambda)$ and the log likelihood per symbol *llps*. The measure of model used here is the log_{10} of the mean (non-log) likelihood per observation symbol, or *lmlpos*. This measure varies in the range $[0, -\infty)$ where 0 represents a perfect fit between the model and the testing data at each time step and $-\infty$ represents a zero fit. We use *lmlpos* rather than *llps* as the former represents the arithmetic mean of likelihood per symbol *lps* over a number of testing examples rather than taking an average of a set of log metrics which would constitute a geometric mean.

We wanted to explore the effect of noise on the trajectory data on classifier performance. We assumed that the original trajectory data represented a ground truth. In order to model noise in the data we superimposed independent but identically distributed Gaussian noise on each of the six data dimensions. We generated noise vectors with a given Root Mean Square (RMS) error. The RMS error corresponds to the standard deviation (i.e. square root of the variance). We then smoothed the noise vectors (average of current, previous and next timestep values) to provide a degree of temporal correlation and re-scaled the vectors to a given RMS error and then added these noise vectors to the trajectory data.

We first trained four separate HMMs, one each for trajectory data for each of the four towers with a constant pod setting and no training noise. We preprocessed the training data further slightly by removing timesteps where the sum of the absolute values across the six difference values was less than 1 cm. We then generated testing data by taking sections of the training data and superimposing testing noise at a given RMS level and classified this training data using the learned models. The results obtained using Tower 0 and Tower 1 as testing data are shown in Fig. 2(a) and (b) respectively.

In Fig. 2(a) we see an excellent example of tower generalisation. At testing noise 0.0, we see that the Tower 0 model is, on average, the preferred model with the others models following in tower order at successively lower levels of confidence as measured by *lmlpos*. Similarly, in Fig. 2(b) at testing noise 0.0, we see that the Tower 1 model is, on average, the preferred model with the

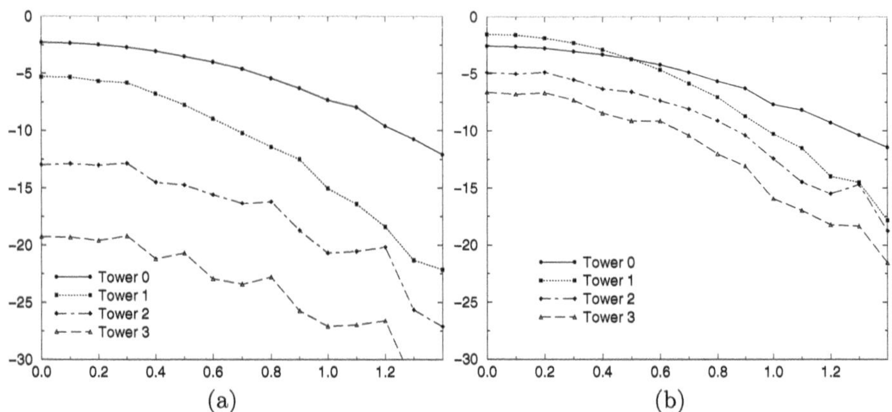

Fig. 2. Level of *lmlpos* fit for hand trajectories using HMM models for Towers 0-3 of as a function of RMS test set noise with test data for (a) Tower 0, (b) Tower 1.

Table 1. Classification rates for HMM models trained with various configurations of towers data when used to classify test towers data with varying amounts of noise.

Training Towers	No Test Noise, % Correct				0.6cm RMS Test Noise, % Correct			
	Tower 0	Tower 1	Tower 2	Tower 3	Tower 0	Tower 1	Tower 2	Tower 3
0	100	0	0	0	100	0	0	0
1	0	100	0	0	72	28	0	0
2	0	0	100	0	0	0	100	0
3	0	0	0	100	0	0	0	100
0 + 1	100	100	0	0	100	100	0	0
2 + 3	0	0	100	100	0	0	100	100

other models following in a logical order (with the tower 3 model being the least preferred).

As an alternative to measuring model fit using *lmlpos*, we can also measure the classification rate. That is, if we classify an individual test trajectory, we get a preferred model (the one that yields the highest *lmlpos*). If that highest value corresponds to the tower associated with the test trajectory then that is a 'correct' classification. For any set of hand trajectories we can therefore calculate a classification rate expressed as the percentage of test trajectories that are correctly associated with their target towers.

Table 1 shows the classification rates achieved with testing data set noise of 0.0 and 0.6cm RMS, both for single and composite tower arrangements. For any given level of test set noise, generalisation is demonstrated as a diagonal classification rate matrix. Off-diagonal elements represent errors, in that the expected model was not the preferred model for some of the trajectory data. 100% classification is seen in all combinations, except Tower 1 with noise, where there is a degeneracy which causes misclassifications. This is shown in more detail in Fig. 2(b). The performance of the Tower 1 model can be seen to deteriorate more quickly than the other models in the presence of testing set noise. The reason for this is that Tower 1 was directly in front of the subjects meaning that the training data exhibits a very low variance along the x-axis. The Gaussian mixture model therefore has a low variance along that axis and so testing examples that deviate significantly from the Gaussian component mean (such as those created in the application of noise to generate training sets) produce a low probability membership estimate. This underlines the need to check for degeneracies in the application of the modelling process to the task.

The problem is easily overcome in a practical system by combining training data for towers 0 and 1 and tower 2 and 3 ([6]).

4 Top-Down and Bottom-Up Context Control

In previous work [8], HMM trajectory prediction from entry regions through intermediate states to the re-fuelling or baggage-handling regions was augmented by updates on the position of vehicles from lower level vision for a known vehicle type. In general, scene context and aspects of the top-down interpretation or bottom-up visual information from moment to moment can be used to augment processing in an HMM without going to a full hierarchical BBN or DBN. In our case, additional context variables could be introduced into the training data (for example, to indicate the target tower) [3]. These additional variables would cause separate Gaussian components to be generated in feature space such that each context would have an independent representation. These context variables are abstract in the sense that there is no difference in implementation between top down and bottom up control.

In order to demonstrate context control using HMMs, we selected four trajectory data sets, one each for the four towers with constant values for pod and cube.

4.1 Using a Single Independent Context Control Variable

For this experiment we augmented the six value vectors generated for relative position with a single context value (a pseudo probability value). This single independent context value represents a gesture-context relationship with two context classes. $context_1$ is the value specified in each vector and $context_2$ is implied as $1 - context_1$. We assume that this context is provided by an external agent (perhaps an object classifier) but for this experiment the training context value is generated directly from a normal distribution about a mean, with a single context value generated for each time step.

We then grouped Towers 0 and 1, and 2 and 3 together and trained 2 composite HMMs using the same seven hidden state structure as before. We then classified the Towers 0 and 1 data using the two models and plotted a measure of model fit as a function of the context value.

For the first test, we set the mean $context_1 = context_2 = 0.5$. The results are shown in Fig. 3(a), the y-axis showing the *lmlpos* value and the x-axis $context_1$.

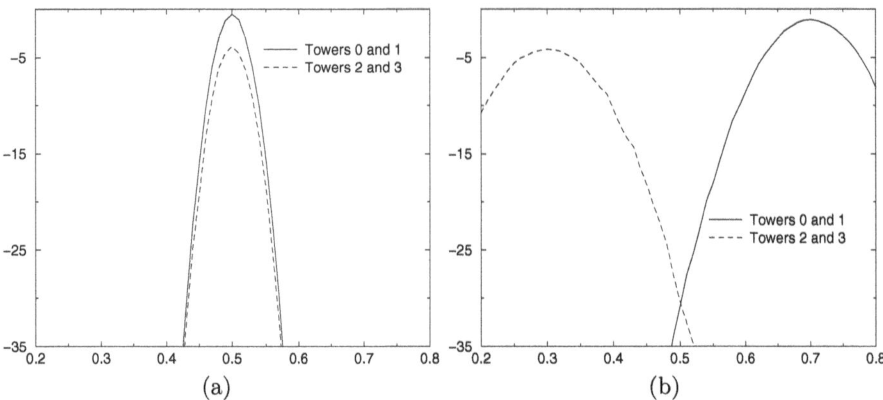

Fig. 3. Classification with HMM of tower 0 and 1 trajectories as a function of context where training context (a) $context_1 = context_2 = 0.5$, (b) $context_1 = 0.7$ and $context_2 = 0.3$.

We see that for all test values of context that the model for Towers 0 and 1 is preferred over the model for Towers 2 and 3 but that the confidence of that fit is maximised where the testing context matches the training context and falls away either side of that value. To see the real value of context control, we then set the mean $context_1 = 0.7$ and $context_2 = 0.3$. The results for this are shown in Fig. 3(b). This time we see that when classifying the Tower 0 and 1 examples, the Towers 0 and 1 model is preferred when the context is around 0.7, but that as the context approaches 0.3, the model for Towers 2 and 3 is preferred, albeit at a lower level of confidence.

4.2 Using Multiple Independent Context Control Variables

For this experiment we augmented the six value vectors generated for relative position with two independent pseudo probabilistic context values $context_1$ and $context_2$. As before, we assume that these contexts are provided by an external agent but for this experiment the training context values are generated directly from a normal distribution about a mean, with two context values generated for each time step. We then used the same towers training grouping as for the previous experiment and classified the Towers 0 and 1 data using the two models and plotted the measure of model fit as a function of the context.

For the first test we trained the Towers 0 and 1 model with a mean $context_1 = 0.7$ and $context_2 = 0.3$. We then simply plotted the Towers 0 and 1 test data as a function of context. The results are shown in Fig. 4(a), the z-axis showing the *lmlpos* value, the x-axis $context_1$ and the y-axis $context_2$. We see that the model fit forms a continuous surface with a peak at the training context values.

For the second test, we retained the previous Towers 0 and 1 model and trained the Towers 2 and 3 model with a mean $context_1 = 0.4$ and $context_2 = 0.6$. We then plotted both models as a functions of context. We then classified

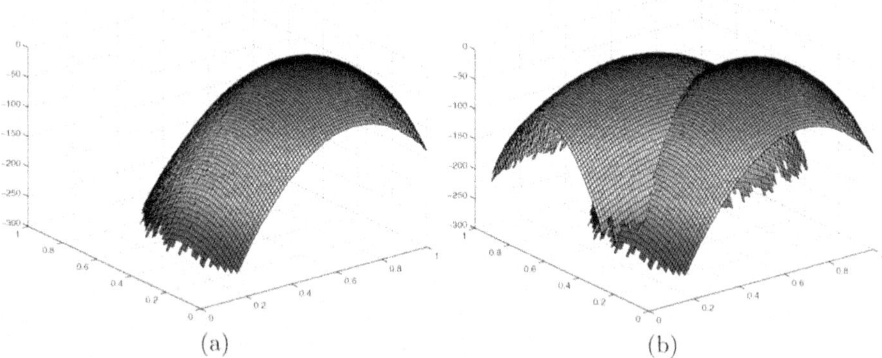

(a) (b)

Fig. 4. Classification with HMM of tower 0 and 1 trajectories as a function of context where (a) Towers 0 and 1 training $context_1 = 0.7$ and $context_2 = 0.3$, (b) Towers 0 and 1 as for (a) and Towers 2 and 3 $context_1 = 0.4$ and $context_2 = 0.6$.

the Towers 0 and 1 test data against both models and the results are shown in Fig. 4(b). We can see that the two surfaces intersect along a classification boundary that defines the values of context at which a switch in model preference takes place. As before, the peak of the Towers 2 and 3 surface (maximum fit) is lower than for the Towers 0 and 1 surface, as it represents a greater degree of generalisation.

5 Summary

We have demonstrated that:

- Modified Viterbi decoding can be used in some circumstances to extract meaning from a HMM forward evaluation trellis in terms of transitions between discrete functional gesture phases, facilitating direct comparison with other model types.
- HMMs are well suited to building gesture models with graceful deterioration in classification performance with increasing parameter distance from the learned model prototype and noise.
- Context control variables can be added at the learning stage to build HMM classifiers that are context sensitive. Such context control can be either top down or bottom up. In either case further context qualifier parameters (such as confidence) could be used to determine model performance when context data is either unavailable of limited quality (e.g. a very early estimate from a predictive cueing process). However there is a trade-off between improvements in performance through context control and the size of the training set.

6 Conclusion

The HMM based learning can discover the temporal structure of the 3D hand gesture trajectories here from data clustering alone. The association of different interpretations with different contexts is also learnt and can allow more effective discrimination boundaries in the online system. Performance on the learning and generalisation tasks were robust to noise and scale well with task complexity, however the training with the Baum-Welch algorithm does not scale so well. The HMM developed here was coded in Matlab, thus it is premature to give computational costs but these will be established in future work. As in the discussion above, there is great potential for contextual processing using the HMM for attentive processing in the ActIPret system.

We have also proposed an approach to task control within the ActIPret system using a Dynamic Decision Network (DDN), e.g.. [9], in the Activity Reasoning Engine. However, we also want distributed control in the lower levels and one way of imposing this is by conditional probability matrices to activate the processing within each lower component, using priority metrics. Initially, it is proposed to hand code utility/task relevance nodes (e.g. watch/ignore) that determine the priority metric. In the longer term, in the context of a complete system, we hope to learn these dynamic dependencies. It may be that we can determine task-relevance automatically in this way, using a uniform Bayesian approach.

Acknowledgements

The authors gratefully acknowledge the invaluable help provided by the Laboratory for Human Motion Simulation (HUMOSIM) at the University of Michigan, USA in allowing us access to their 'Terminal Hand Orientation and Effort Reach Study, 2000' hand trajectory database; also framework concepts and funding from the EU ActIPret project.

References

1. B. Bauer, H. Heinz, and K. Kraiss. Video-based continuous sign language recognition using statistical methods. In *IEEE International Conference on Automatic Face and Gesture Recognition*, pages 440–445, Grenoble, France, 2000.
2. M.J. Black and A. Jepson. A probabilistic framework for matching temporal. In *European Conference on Computer Vision*, pages 343–356, Cambridge, UK, 1996.
3. D. M. Blei and P. J. Moreno. Topic segmentation with an aspect hidden Markov model. In *Proceedings of the 24th International Conference on Research and Development in Information Retrieval (SIGIR 2001)*, pages 343–348, New York, 2001.
4. A. Bobick and J. Davies. The recognition of human movement using temporal templates. *IEEE Transactions on Pattern Analysis and Machine Intelligence*, 23:257–267, 2001.
5. H. Buxton and S. Gong. Visual surveillance in a dynamic and uncertain world. *Artificial Intelligence*, 78:431–459, 1995.

6. H. Buxton, A.J. Howell, and K. Sage. The role of task control and context in learning to recognise gesture. In *Cognitive Vision Workshop*, Zürich, Switzerland, 2002.
7. A. Dempster, N. Laird, and D. Rubin. Maximum likelihood from imcomplete data using the em algorithm. *Journal of the Royal Statistical Society*, 39:185–197, 1977.
8. S. Gong and H. Buxton. On the visual expectations of moving objects: A probabilistic approach with augmented hidden Markov model. In *European Conference on Artificial Intelligence*, pages 781–785, Vienna, Austria, 1992.
9. R. Howarth and H. Buxton. Conceptual descriptions from monitoring and watching image sequences. *Image and Vision Computing*, 18:105–135, 2000.
10. A.J. Howell and H. Buxton. Learning gestures for visually mediated interaction. In *British Machine Vision Conference*, pages 508–517, Southampton, UK, 1998.
11. M. Isard and A. Blake. Contour tracking by stochastic propagation of conditional density. In *European Conference on Computer Vision*, pages 343–356, Cambridge, UK, 1996.
12. G. Johansson. Visual perception of biological motion and a model for its analysis. *Perception and Psychophysics*, 14:201–211, 1973.
13. S. McKenna and S. Gong. Gesture recognition for visually mediated interaction using probabilistic event trajectories. In *British Machine Vision Association*, Southampton, UK, 1998.
14. D. J. Moore, I. A. Essa, and M. H. Hayes. Exploiting human actions and object context for recognition tasks. In *IEEE International Conference on Computer Vision*, pages 80–86, Vancouver, Canada, 1999.
15. L.R. Rabiner. A tutorial on hidden Markov models. *Proceedings of the IEEE*, 77:257–286, 1989.
16. J. Schlenzig, E. Hunter, and R. Jain. Recursive indentification of gesture using Hidden Markov Model. In *Workshop on Applications of Computer Vision*, Sarasota, Florida, 1994.
17. J. Sherrah and S. Gong. Resolving visual uncertainty and occlusion through probabilistic reasoning. In *British Machine Vision Association*, Bristol, UK, 2000.
18. T. Starner and A. Pentland. Real-time american sign language recognition using hidden Markov models. In *International Symposium on Computer Vision*, pages 265–270, Coral Gables, FL, 1995.
19. M. Walter, A. Psarrou, and S. Gong. Data driven model acquistion using minimum description length. In *British Machine Vision Association*, Manchester, UK, 2001.

Database Indexing Methods for 3D Hand Pose Estimation

Vassilis Athitsos and Stan Sclaroff*

Computer Science Department, Boston University
111 Cummington Street, Boston, MA 02215, USA
{athitsos,sclaroff}@cs.bu.edu

Abstract. Estimation of 3D hand pose is useful in many gesture recognition applications, ranging from human-computer interaction to recognition of sign languages. In this paper, 3D hand pose estimation is treated as a database indexing problem. Given an input image of a hand, the most similar images in a large database of hand images are retrieved. The hand pose parameters of the retrieved images are used as estimates for the hand pose in the input image. Lipschitz embeddings are used to map edge images of hands into a Euclidean space. Similarity queries are initially performed in this Euclidean space, to quickly select a small set of candidate matches. These candidate matches are finally ranked using the more computationally expensive chamfer distance. Using Lipschitz embeddings to select likely candidate matches greatly reduces retrieval time over applying the chamfer distance to the entire database, without significant losses in accuracy.

1 Introduction

Automatic estimation of the 3D pose of a human hand can be useful in a wide range of applications. Some examples are human-machine interfaces, automatic recognition of signed languages and gestural communication, and non-intrusive motion capture systems. This paper describes a system that provides estimates of 3D hand pose from a single image. In our approach, hand pose estimation is formulated as an image database indexing problem. The closest matches for an input hand image are retrieved from a large database of synthetic hand images. The ground truth labels of the retrieved matches are used as hand pose estimates for the input.

In [2] we describe the use of Lipschitz embeddings for approximating the chamfer distance, in order to improve retrieval efficiency. With Lipschitz embeddings, the distance between two images can be approximated by looking at the distance between each of those images and a set of reference images. The basic intuition is that, if two images are similar to each other, then their distances to other images will also be similar. In this paper we discuss and evaluate

* This research was supported in part by the National Science Foundation, under grants IIS-0208876, IIS-9912573, and EIA-9809340.

A. Camurri and G. Volpe (Eds.): GW 2003, LNAI 2915, pp. 288–299, 2004.

different methods for choosing reference images, in order to improve overall system accuracy. We then use Lipschitz embeddings in a filter-and-refine retrieval framework, where the approximate chamfer distance is used to quickly identify a small set of candidate matches, and the exact chamfer distance is used to obtain the final ranking of those candidates.

2 Related Work

Computer vision systems that estimate 3D hand pose typically do it in the context of tracking hand pose in a video sequence [7,13,16,17,21]. In the tracking context, the basic assumption is that the system already knows the hand pose in the previous video frame. The goal of the system is to update the hand pose to optimally match the observations in the current frame. Such a tracking framework is insufficient for fully automatic 3D hand pose estimation, because it does not address two problems: estimating hand pose in the first video frame, when no information about previous frames is available, and recovering from errors, when the hand pose for the previous frame was estimated incorrectly.

Solutions to those problems may be provided by methods that estimate hand pose from a single image. A machine learning method for single-image hand pose estimation is described in [14]. In [12] 3D locations of fingers are estimated from a stereo image, and they are used to infer 3D joint angles. In [15] hand pose is estimated from a single image using shadow information and assuming a calibrated light source. Due to the difficulty of obtaining ground truth estimates, none of these approaches reports quantitative results on real images of hands.

Existing 3D hand pose estimation methods typically assume that the hand is cleanly segmented in the input image. Appearance-based methods for hand pose recognition, like [6,11,18,20], can tolerate clutter, but they are limited to estimating 2D hand pose from specific viewpoints.

Our system uses the chamfer distance as a measure of similarity between hand images. The accuracy of the chamfer distance degrades gracefully in the presence of clutter and errors in hand segmentation. The chamfer distance is approximated using Lipschitz embeddings, using an approach similar to the methods described in [5,8,9]. The main novelty in this paper with respect to previous approaches is the formulation and quantitative comparison of methods to choose reference images, in Section 5.

3 Framework for Hand Pose Estimation

We model the hand as an articulated object, consisting of 16 links: the palm and 15 links corresponding to finger parts (Figure 1a). Overall, the values of all joint angles can be specified using a 20-dimensional vector, for which we use the term "hand shape."

The appearance of a hand shape depends on the 3D orientation of the hand. Given a hand shape vector $C_h = (c_1, ..., c_{20})$ and a 3D orientation vector

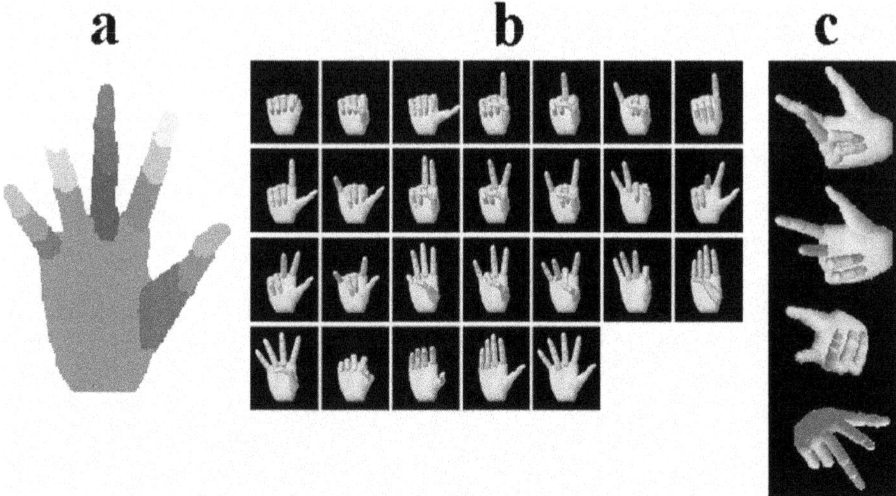

Fig. 1. Synthetic images of hands: a.) The articulated hand model, consisting of 16 links (the palm and 15 finger links). Each link has a different color than its neighbors. b.) The 26 basic shapes used to generate model images in our database. c.) Four different 3D orientations of the same hand shape.

$V_h = (v_1, v_2, v_3)$, we define the hand pose vector P_h to be the 23-dimensional concatenation of C_h and V_h: $P_h = (c_1, ..., c_{20}, v_1, v_2, v_3)$.

Using these definitions, our framework for hand pose estimation can be summarized as follows:

1. Preprocessing step: create a database containing a uniform sampling of all possible views of the hand shapes that we want to recognize. Label each view with the hand pose parameters that generated it.
2. Given an input image, retrieve the database views that are the most similar. Use the parameters of the most similar views as estimates of the hand pose parameters for the input image.

3.1 Database

Our database contains right-hand images of 26 hand shape prototypes (Figure 1b). Each prototype is rendered from 86 different viewpoints (Figure 1c), sampled approximately uniformly from the surface of the viewing sphere. The rendering is done using a hand model and computer graphics [19]. To accommodate rotation-variant similarity measures (like the chamfer distance), 48 images are generated from each viewpoint, giving a total of 4128 different 3D orientations of the hand. Overall, the database includes 107,328 images. We refer to those images using the terms "database images," "model images," or "synthetic images".

4 Approximating the Chamfer Distance

Given an input image, the system has to identify the database images that are the closest to the input. In our system we measure distances between edge images, because edge images tend to be more stable than intensity images with respect to different lighting conditions. The chamfer distance [3] is a well-known method to measure the distance between two edge images. Edge images are represented as sets of points, corresponding to edge pixel locations. Given two edge images, X and Y, the chamfer distance $C(X,Y)$ is:

$$C(X,Y) = \frac{1}{|X|} \sum_{x \in X} \min_{y \in Y} \|x - y\| + \frac{1}{|Y|} \sum_{y \in Y} \min_{x \in X} \|y - x\| \ , \tag{1}$$

where $\|a - b\|$ denotes the Euclidean distance between two pixel locations a and b. $C(X,Y)$ penalizes for points in either edge image that are far from any point in the other edge image. Figure 2 shows an illustration of the chamfer distance.

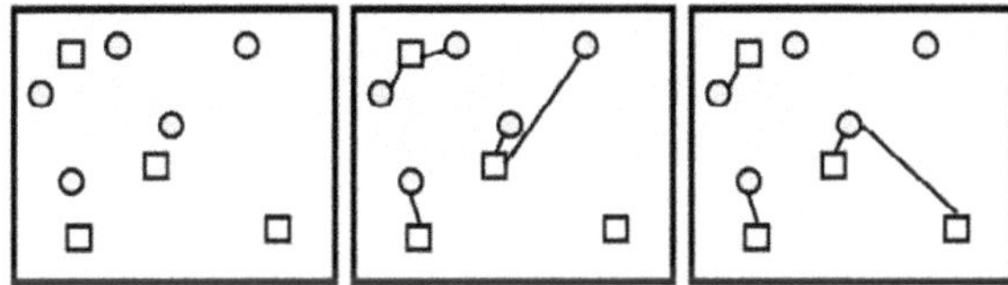

Fig. 2. An example of the chamfer distance. The left image shows two sets of points: a set of circles and a set of squares. The middle image shows a link between each circle and its closest square. The circle-to-square directed chamfer distance is the average distance between a circle and its closest square. The right image shows a link between each square and its closest circle. The square-to-circle chamfer distance is the average distance between a square and its closest circle. The chamfer distance (also known as *undirected chamfer distance*) between squares and circles is the sum of the two directed distances.

4.1 Lipschitz Embeddings

In our application, calculating the chamfer distance between the input image and all database images takes too long (over four minutes) to be used in interactive applications. However, we can obtain an efficient approximation of the chamfer distance by embedding edge images into a Euclidean space.

Embeddings of arbitrary metric spaces into a Euclidean space with an L_p norm have received increased attention in recent years [5,8,9]. Typically the goal is to find a *low-distortion* embedding E of an arbitrary metric space G into a Euclidean space $\Re^k$, i.e. an embedding under which pairwise distances between points in G are preserved with low distortion in $\Re^k$. Such embeddings are useful when it is computationally expensive to evaluate distances in G, and it is more efficient to map points of G into $\Re^k$ and compute their L_p distance in $\Re^k$. A class of embeddings often used in this context are *Lipschitz embeddings* [4,8,9,10]. The basic intuition behind Lipschitz embeddings is that two objects that are close to each other typically have similar distances to all other objects.

An everyday example that illustrates this property is looking at distances between cities. The distance from New York to Boston is about 240 miles, and the distance from New York to Los Angeles is about 2800 miles. Suppose that we did not know these two distances. Furthermore, suppose that someone gave us, for 100 towns spread across the United States, their distances to New York, Boston and Los Angeles. What would that information tell us about the distances from New York to Boston and from New York to Los Angeles?

First we would notice that the distance from each town to New York is always within 240 miles or less of the distance between that town and Boston. On the other hand, there are some towns, like Lincoln, Nebraska, whose distances from Los Angeles and New York are very similar, and some towns, like Sacramento, whose distances to Los Angeles and New York are very different (Sacramento-Los Angeles is 400 miles, Sacramento-New York is 2800 miles). Given these distances, we could deduce that, most likely, New York is a lot closer to Boston than it is to Los Angeles.

This property, that nearby objects have similar distances to all other objects, holds for objects in any space where distances obey the triangle inequality. The chamfer distance does not obey the triangle inequality, but we have found that, in our domain of edge images of hands, only rarely do triples of edge images violate the triangle inequality. This observation allows us to define an efficient approximation of the chamfer distance, for the purposes of identifying similar hand images.

Suppose that we have chosen a *reference set* of k database edge images $R_1, R_2, ..., R_k$. Then, we can define a function E, mapping the space of edge images to the Euclidean space $\Re^k$ as follows:

$$E(G) = (C(G, R_1), C(G, R_2), ..., C(G, R_k)) \ . \tag{2}$$

where C is the chamfer distance, defined in Equation 1, and G is an edge image. The function E is also called an *embedding* of the space of edge images into $\Re^k$, and it is a special case of Lipschitz embeddings [4,10].

We define the *approximate chamfer distance* C' between two edge images A and B to be the L_1 distance between $E(A)$ and $E(B)$:

$$C'(A, B) = \sum_{i=1}^{k} |C(A, R_i) - C(B, R_i)| \ . \tag{3}$$

The actual value of $C'(A, B)$ is not necessarily similar in scale to the value $C(A, B)$. However, $C'(A, B)$ is an approximation of $C(A, B)$ in the sense that, when $C(A, B)$ is much smaller than $C(A, G)$, then we also expect $C'(A, B)$ to be smaller than $C'(A, G)$.

The time complexity of computing the approximate distance C' between an edge image and d database edge images is $O(kn \log n + kd)$, where n is the number of edge pixels in every edge image. On the other hand, computing the chamfer distance C takes $O(dn \log n)$ time. The complexity savings are substantial when k is much smaller than d. In our system it takes more than four minutes to compute the chamfer distances between the input image and all database images. In contrast, for $k = 200$, it takes a fraction of a second to compute the corresponding approximate distances C'. To achieve this speedup we need to precompute, offline, the distances between every database image and every reference image.

5 Choosing Reference Images

In order to define the approximate chamfer distance C' we need to specify a set of k reference images R_i. In this section we discuss methods for selecting reference images among database edge images. The simplest approach is to select reference images randomly, and choose the k that leads to the best retrieval accuracy. The approaches discussed below choose reference images in a more selective way, trying to improve the approximation accuracy of the embedding.

5.1 Minimizing Stress

A natural question to ask is how similar the approximate chamfer distance is to the exact chamfer distance. More generally, given an embedding F from space X with distance D_x to space Y with distance D_y, we can ask how well F preserves distances. Ideally, F would perfectly preserve distances, meaning that for any two objects $x_1, x_2 \in X$, it should hold that $D_x(x_1, x_2) = D_y(F(x_1), F(x_2))$. Unfortunately, there are choices of X, D_x, Y, D_y for which no Euclidean embedding can preserve distances perfectly [8].

Given a pair of objects $x_1, x_2 \in X$, we can measure how well F preserves their distance by defining the *stress* $Q(x_1, x_2, F)$ as

$$Q(x_1, x_2, F) = \frac{D_y(F(x_1), F(x_2)) - D_x(x_1, x_2)}{D_x(x_1, x_2)} . \tag{4}$$

Q measures the amount of change that the embedding has caused to the distance between x_1 and x_2 as a fraction of the original distance $D_x(x_1, x_2)$.

Given m pairs of objects (a_i, b_i), we can evaluate the accuracy of the embedding by computing the overall stress $Q'(F)$ that F causes to those pairs on average:

$$Q'(F) = \frac{\sum_{i=1}^{m} |Q(a_i, b_i, F)|}{m} . \tag{5}$$

Intuitively, in our definition of stress, small changes in the distance between nearby points are as important as large changes in the distance between points that are far from each other. Alternative definitions of stress can be found in the literature, for example in [8].

Suppose that there exists a constant c such that, for any x_1 and x_2, it holds that $D_y(F(x_1,), F(x_2)) = cD_x(x_1, x_2)$. We would like to consider such an embedding to be a zero-stress embedding, because it would maintain all the important structure in the original space X, like nearest neighbors and clusters. However, for high values of c, $Q'(F)$ may be large. In order for $Q'(F)$ to give a meaningful value, we assume that F has been scaled by an appropriate constant, so that $Q'(F)$ is minimized.

Since low-stress embeddings are desirable, a strategy for selecting reference images is to try to pick the ones that minimize stress. We have implemented this strategy in a greedy fashion, picking reference images one by one. We pick the first reference image R_1 to be the database image which, as a single reference image ($k = 1$ in Equation 3), achieves the lowest stress Q', as measured on 50,000 randomly chosen pairs of database images. If we have already chosen i reference images, then the $i + 1$ reference image is chosen to be the one that, when used together with the already chosen reference images, achieves the lowest stress. We stop choosing reference images when the stress stops decreasing significantly.

We pick reference images from a subset of database edge images, consisting of 8944 images (we choose one out of every 12 database images).

5.2 Minimizing Distortion

An alternative to minimizing average stress is minimizing worst-case stress. The term typically used in the literature for worst-case stress is *distortion* [8,10].

In order to define distortion, we first define the scaling $S(x_1, x_2, F)$ that an embedding F causes to the distance between x_1 and x_2 as:

$$S(x_1, x_2, F) = \frac{D_y(F(x_1), F(x_2))}{D_x(x_1, x_2)} . \tag{6}$$

Then, given m pairs of objects (a_i, b_i), we can find the pairs that attain the highest and lowest values of S, $s_{\max}$ and $s_{\min}$ respectively, and we can define the distortion $S'(F)$ as

$$S'(F) = \frac{s_{\max}}{s_{\min}} . \tag{7}$$

If F preserves distances perfectly (or up to scale), then $S'(F) = 1$. It is easy to modify the algorithm outlined in Section 5.1, so that it chooses reference images that minimize distortion, as opposed to stress. At each step, we add to the reference set the image that, combined with the previously chosen reference images, yields the smallest distortion, as measured on a large set of pairs of database edge images.

5.3 Using a Training Set

Another possible criterion for picking reference images is to directly try to maximize retrieval accuracy. The retrieval accuracy attained by different choices of reference images can be measured on a training set of real hand images. To choose reference images that maximize retrieval accuracy, we can again use a modified version of the algorithm described in Section 5.1. When we choose each reference image, we simply choose the one that leads to the best retrieval accuracy on the training set. The next section discusses measures of retrieval accuracy.

Table 1. Accuracy attained by the four different methods of choosing reference images, for different numbers of reference images. The measure of accuracy is the median rank of the highest ranking correct matches retrieved for a set of 426 test images.

# of reference images	4	8	16	32	64	128
random	628	636	527	459	437	463
stress	1009	408	453	343	345	349
distortion	846	570	452	416	477	490
training	916	793	651	492	421	424

In our implementation, we have used 276 images of real hands as the training set for this method. Those images are not part of the database (which only includes synthetic images) and were not included in the test set of 426 real hand images that we used in the experiments described in Section 7.

6 Accuracy Evaluation

To evaluate retrieval accuracy, we use a test set of real images of hands. Each image in this set depicts one of the 26 hand shapes used in generating the database, in an arbitrary 3D orientation. For each test image we manually establish pseudo-ground truth, using the rendering software to identify the hand shape and 3D orientation under which the model hand looks the most similar to the test image. In informal experiments, we found that different human subjects rarely disagreed on the hand shape class, but often disagreed in their estimates of the 3D orientation, by up to 30 degrees. Taking that into account, we consider a database image V to be a *correct match* for a test image I if the hand shapes in V and I are the same, and the 3D hand orientations of V and I differ by less than 30 degrees. Using these criteria, for each test image there are on average 30.4 correct matches in the database. Our measure of retrieval accuracy for a given test image I is the rank of the *highest-ranking correct match*. For example, if, for a given input image, the top 9 database matches are incorrect but the 10th match is correct, then the rank of the highest ranking correct match is 10.

To evaluate retrieval accuracy on a set of test images, we use the median rank of the highest ranking correct match. For example, if we have a test set of 100 images, and the median rank of the highest ranking correct match is 34, then we know that at least 50 of those test images had a correct match of rank at most 34.

Our evaluation method is discussed in more detail in [1].

7 Experiments

We have implemented the four different methods discussed in Section 5. Table 1 shows the accuracy attained by each method, using different numbers of reference images. Accuracy was measured on a test set of 426 images, some of which can be seen in Figure 3. No dramatic improvements in accuracy are achieved by using any of the four methods, but minimizing stress tends to give better results.

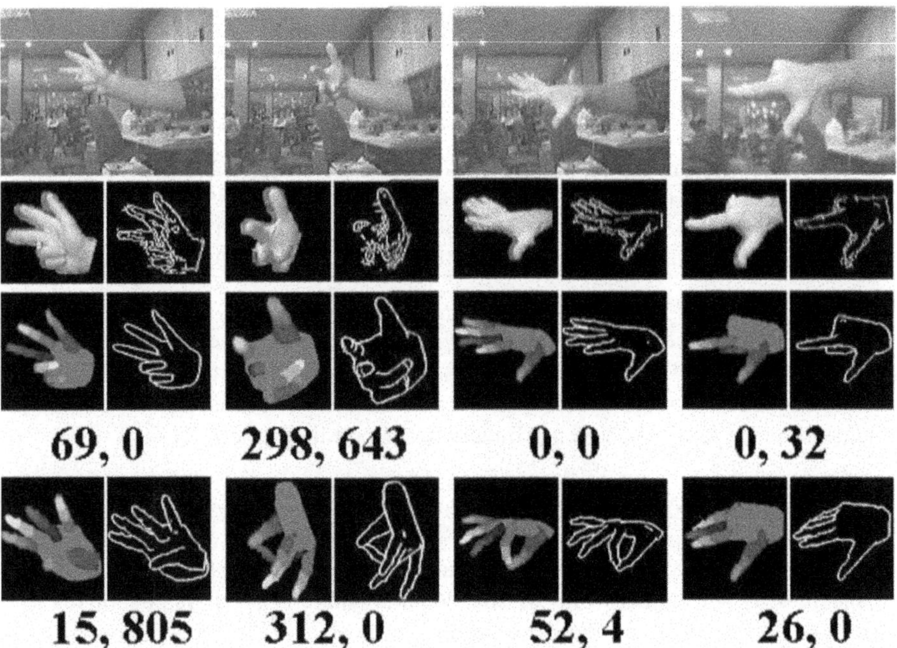

Fig. 3. Examples of input images and results. First row: example input images. Second row: segmented hand images and the corresponding edge images. Third row: examples of correct matches (synthetic hand images and edge images). Fourth row: the ranks of the correct matches using the approximate chamfer distance, and using the combination of the two distances. Fifth row: examples of incorrect matches. Sixth row: ranks of the incorrect matches using the approximate chamfer distance and using the combination of the two distances.

Overall, all four methods give inaccurate rankings; they usually rank hundreds of false matches higher than the highest ranking correct match. On the other hand, the rankings provided by these methods can be used to select a small set of candidates from the database, without losing too many correct matches.

We compared the accuracy of the approximate chamfer distance with that of the exact chamfer distance. For the approximate chamfer distance, using 128 reference images chosen by minimizing stress, the median of the highest correct match is 349, and retrieval takes less than a second. For the exact chamfer distance, the median of the highest ranking correct match is 38, and retrieval takes about five minutes.

The different strengths of the approximate and the exact chamfer distance can be combined in a filter-and-refine retrieval framework. In an experiment, we used the approximate chamfer distance to pick 5,000 candidate matches, and then we applied the chamfer distance to rank those matches. The median of the highest ranking correct match after the second step was 44, and the retrieval time was 15 seconds. We see that by combining the two methods we get significant gains in retrieval efficiency (15 seconds versus 5 minutes), with only a small

Table 2. Stresses and accuracies attained by two different methods of choosing reference images: picking random images (method RAND) and choosing images that minimize stress (method MS). We see that the stress attained by a set of reference images cannot reliably predict the corresponding accuracy.

# of reference images	4	8	16	32	64	128
RAND: stress	.29	.27	.26	.20	.20	.18
RAND: accuracy	628	636	527	459	437	463
MS: stress	.21	.16	.14	.13	.12	.12
MS: accuracy	1009	408	453	343	345	349

Table 3. Comparison of two methods for choosing reference images: choosing randomly (method RAND), and choosing images that minimize stress (method MS). In each trial, 16,32 or 64 reference images were chosen randomly from a set of candidate images, and an equal number of reference images were chosen from the same set of candidates using the method of minimizing stress. Classification accuracy is measured as in Table 1.

Number of reference images:	16	32	64
Number of trials:	26	26	26
Times RAND outperformed MS :	6	2	2
Times MS outperformed RAND:	20	24	24
(Mean, std) of accuracy using RAND:	(621, 170)	(584, 117)	(541, 114)
(Mean, std) of accuracy using MS:	(482, 60)	(438, 54)	(413, 46)

loss in retrieval accuracy (44 versus 38). In [1] and [2] we describe additional similarity measures, that can be used to further improve classification accuracy and retrieval efficiency.

Since minimizing stress seems to give the best classification accuracy, we checked whether stress could reliably predict classification accuracy. The answer turned out to be negative. Table 2 shows the stress and accuracy attained by random picking and by minimizing stress. Using 4 reference images selected by minimizing stress we attain a stress of .21, which is smaller than the stress attained by choosing 4, 8, or 16 reference images randomly. However, the classification accuracy is significantly better using the randomly chosen reference images.

In order to evaluate the degree to which minimizing stress outperforms picking reference images randomly, we ran multiple experiments to compare these two methods. First, we created 26 mutually disjoint sets of candidate reference images. Each of those sets contained 344 images, and consisted of database images generated using only one of the 26 hand shapes. Then, from each set of candidate reference images, and for each value of k among $\{16, 32, 64\}$, we picked two reference sets of size k: a set of images chosen randomly, and a set of images chosen by minimizing stress. Table 3 shows the results. In the majority of the comparisons (68 out of 78), the reference set chosen by minimizing stress outperformed the corresponding reference set of equal size that was chosen randomly from the same set of candidates.

8 Discussion and Future Work

Approximating the chamfer distance using a Lipschitz embedding can be used to significantly speed up retrieval, in a filter-and-refine retrieval framework. However, there are some open questions on how to improve approximation accuracy:

- Is there a fundamental limit to the minimum distortion or stress that can be achieved by the approximate chamfer distance, with respect to the original chamfer distance, regardless of the number and choice of reference images?
- Are there other edge images, that are not included in the database, and that may not even be images of hands, that might be more suitable reference images? How can we construct such images?

Another issue is that the chamfer distance is not a metric: it does not obey the triangle inequality. Minimum-weight bipartite perfect matching is a related metric, that can also be applied to edge images, but at a higher computational cost. It will be interesting to investigate whether the metric properties of bipartite matching lead to better approximation under Lipschitz embeddings.

The chamfer distance assumes that edge images are aligned with respect to translation and scale. Therefore, as a preprocessing step, the hand position and scale must be detected with reasonable accuracy. It is an open question whether we can build edge-based similarity measures that are less dependent on translation and scale alignment, without incurring losses in accuracy and efficiency with respect to the chamfer distance.

We are also interested in integrating our system with a 3D hand tracker, in order to achieve a fully-automated 3D hand pose tracking system.

9 Conclusions

Our system estimates the 3D hand pose of an image by retrieving the most similar images from a large database. A filter-and-refine retrieval framework is applied, in which a Lipschitz-embedding approximation of the chamfer distance is used to quickly identify a small set of candidate matches, and the exact chamfer distance is used to rank those candidates. Combining the approximate and the exact chamfer distance significantly reduces retrieval time, while maintaining most of the retrieval accuracy of the exact chamfer distance. In choosing reference images for the embedding, picking random images yields acceptable results, but minimizing stress leads to the best retrieval accuracy in our experiments.

References

1. V. Athitsos and S. Sclaroff. An appearance-based framework for 3D hand shape classification and camera viewpoint estimation. In *Automatic Face and Gesture Recognition*, pages 45–50, 2002.
2. V. Athitsos and S. Sclaroff. Estimating hand pose from a cluttered image. In *CVPR*, pages 432–439, 2003.

3. H.G. Barrow, J.M. Tenenbaum, R.C. Bolles, and H.C. Wolf. Parametric correspondence and chamfer matching: Two new techniques for image matching. In *IJCAI*, pages 659–663, 1977.
4. J. Bourgain. On Lipschitz embeddings of finite metric spaces in hilbert space. *Israel Journal of Mathematics*, 52:46–52, 1985.
5. C. Faloutsos and K.I. Lin. FastMap: A fast algorithm for indexing, data-mining and visualization of traditional and multimedia datasets. In *ACM SIGMOD International Conference on Management of Data*, pages 163–174, 1995.
6. W.T. Freeman and M. Roth. Computer vision for computer games. In *Automatic Face and Gesture Recognition*, pages 100–105, 1996.
7. T. Heap and D. Hogg. Towards 3D hand tracking using a deformable model. In *Face and Gesture Recognition*, pages 140–145, 1996.
8. G. Hjaltason and H. Samet. Contractive embedding methods for similarity searching in metric spaces. Technical Report TR-4102, Computer Science Department, University of Maryland, 2000.
9. G. Hristescu and M. Farach-Colton. Cluster-preserving embedding of proteins. Technical Report 99-50, Computer Science Department, Rutgers University, 1999.
10. N. Linial, E. London, and Y. Rabinovich. The geometry of graphs and some of its algorithmic applications. In *IEEE Symposium on Foundations of Computer Science*, pages 577–591, 1994.
11. B. Moghaddam and A. Pentland. Probabilistic visual learning for object detection. Technical Report 326, MIT, June 1995.
12. C. Nölker and H. Ritter. Parametrized SOMs for hand posture reconstruction. In *IJCNN*, pages 4139–4144, 2000.
13. J.M. Rehg. *Visual Analysis of High DOF Articulated Objects with Application to Hand Tracking.* PhD thesis, Electrical and Computer Eng., Carnegie Mellon University, 1995.
14. R. Rosales, V. Athitsos, L. Sigal, and S. Sclaroff. 3D hand pose reconstruction using specialized mappings. In *ICCV*, volume 1, pages 378–385, 2001.
15. J. Segen and S. Kumar. Shadow gestures: 3D hand pose estimation using a single camera. In *CVPR*, pages 479–485, 1999.
16. N. Shimada, K. Kimura, and Y. Shirai. Real-time 3-D hand posture estimation based on 2-D appearance retrieval using monocular camera. In *Recognition, Analysis and Tracking of Faces and Gestures in Realtime Systems*, pages 23–30, 2001.
17. B. Stenger, P.R.S. Mendonça, and R. Cipolla. Model based 3D tracking of an articulated hand. In *CVPR*, volume 2, pages 310–315, 2001.
18. J. Triesch and C. von der Malsburg. Robotic gesture recognition. In *Gesture Workshop*, pages 233–244, 1997.
19. Virtual Technologies, Inc., Palo Alto, CA. *VirtualHand Software Library Reference Manual*, August 1998.
20. Y. Wu and T.S. Huang. View-independent recognition of hand postures. In *CVPR*, volume 2, pages 88–94, 2000.
21. Y. Wu, J.Y. Lin, and T.S. Huang. Capturing natural hand articulation. In *ICCV*, volume 2, pages 426–432, 2001.

Experience with and Requirements for a Gesture Description Language for Synthetic Animation

Richard Kennaway

School of Information Systems, University of East Anglia
Norwich, NR4 7TJ, UK
jrk@sys.uea.ac.uk

Abstract. We have created software for automatic synthesis of signing animations from the HamNoSys transcription notation. In this process we have encountered certain shortcomings of the notation. We describe these, and consider how to develop a notation more suited to computer animation.

1 Introduction

Some applications for naturalistic 3D animations require them to be generated in real time. These include 3D chat forums, computer-generated deaf signing, and 3D video games. The large number of possible movements makes it impractical to merely play back pre-composed animations.

In the ViSiCAST project we have used descriptions of signing gestures using HamNoSys, an avatar-independent sign language transcription notation. We have developed software, called Animgen, to synthesize animation data from such descriptions, together with a description of the geometry of the particular avatar. While the basic approach has been successful, it has also shown up some limitations of HamNoSys, and suggested principles for the development of a movement description language purpose-made for animation.

Although this work exists in the context of a project relating to deaf sign languages, this paper is primarily concerned with non-linguistic issues. A description of the role of HamNoSys in the linguistic aspects of the project is given in [7].

2 An Outline of the Visicast System

We have reported on our animation of HamNoSys in [11], and will summarise that here.

The general outline of the Visicast system is given in Figure 1. If the original matter to be signed is English text, it is translated to a representation known as a DRS (Discourse Representation Structure), and the tools of Hierarchical Phrase Structure Grammars are used to generate from it a sequence of signing gestures.

A. Camurri and G. Volpe (Eds.): GW 2003, LNAI 2915, pp. 300–311, 2004.

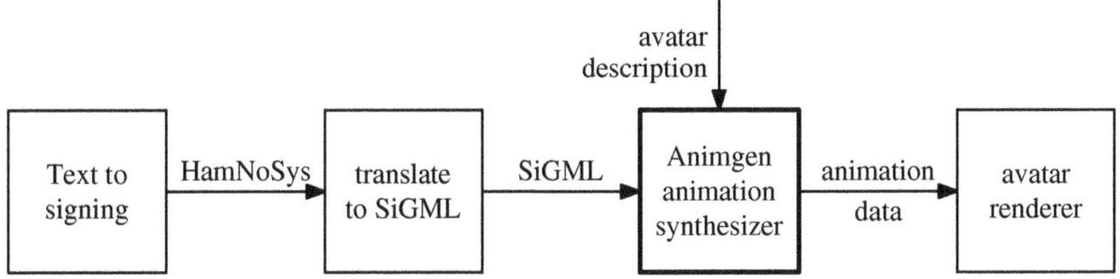

Fig. 1. Block diagram of the generation of synthetic signing animation.

These gestures are described in HamNoSys. This chain of transformations is described in [14], and is represented by the leftmost box of Figure 1.

HamNoSys was developed at the University of Hamburg as a tool for researchers in sign language to make written records of signs [13]. Although not originally designed with computer animation in mind, the ViSiCAST project made use of it as being the only such general-purpose notation available with a substantial body of experience in applying it to multiple sign languages, other notation systems such as Stokoe being specific to particular sign languages. It takes only a minute or two for someone trained in HamNoSys to write a transcription of a sign. This compares very favourably with the time it takes to record signs with motion capture.

As the syntax of HamNoSys is somewhat unwieldy, we designed a version encoded in XML, called SiGML (Signing Gesture Markup Language), and a translator was written from HamNoSys to SiGML. The SiGML representation of a gesture contains exactly the same information as the HamNoSys, but is more amenable to computer processing. As HamNoSys is more widely known, we shall give examples in this paper in terms of HamNoSys.

The next component in the chain is the one we are primarily concerned with in this paper: Animgen, which generates animation from SiGML. After reading the SiGML into its own internal data structures, it endeavours to fill in all the details which the SiGML transcription may have omitted, such as default locations, the duration in seconds of each movement (specified in SiGML merely as fast, slow, or ordinary speed), and so on. For each successive point in time, at intervals of typically 1/25 of a second, Animgen calculates the rotation of each joint of the avatar at that instant. On current desktop machines, Animgen requires about 1 millisecond to calculate each frame of data, i.e. about 2.5% of the available 40 milliseconds for animation at 25 frames per second.

The final component of the chain, the avatar renderer, displays the avatar on the screen in the specified postures at the specified times. For convenience when prototyping, Animgen can also generate output in the form of a VRML file containing the animation data and an avatar in the standard H-anim format[1].

[1] VRML, the Virtual Reality Modelling Language, is an ISO standard defined at `http://www.web3d.org/fs_specifications.htm`. The H-anim standard for a humanoid structure is defined at `http://www.h-anim.org/`.

3 A Brief Description of HamNoSys

HamNoSys is designed according to the following basic principles:

1. *Language-independence.*
   HamNoSys is not specific to any particular sign language; it should be able to record any signing gesture from any sign language. This follows from the original motivation for HamNoSys: to provide a written medium for researchers on sign language to record signs. In linguistic terminology, HamNoSys is phonetic, rather than phonemic.
2. *Record posture and movement, not meaning.*
   The meaning of a gesture is not recorded, only the posture and movement. For example, BSL makes frequent use of its fingerspelling signs to represent other words: the sign for "M" also forms part of the signs for "mother" and "microwave". A gesture can thus mean different things in different contexts, but if it is performed in the same way, the HamNoSys transcription will be the same.
3. *Omit irrelevant information.*
   Only those parts of the posture and movement that are significant in creating the sign are recorded. Most signs are made with the hands and the face. What the elbows and shoulders do is not significant; they should do whatever is natural in order to place the hands in the required places. The elbows and shoulders are therefore not notated for most signs. The placement or movement of the elbow is only recorded when it is a significant component of the gesture, for example in the BSL sign for "Scotland" (Figure 2). Version 4 of HamNoSys allows one to specify that a handshape or direction need only be achieved approximately, its exact form being inessential for the sign.
   To some extent, this is in tension with the previous principle, since which aspects of the gesture are important and which are not, which should be performed exactly and which need only be approximate, are determined by what is a constituent of the gesture in that sign language and what is not. We will, however, later argue that the notion of recording the "meaningful" parts of the gesture arises even for gestures in a non-linguistic context.

Like most signing notations, such as Stokoe [15] and the Stokoe-derived notation used in the BSL dictionary [1], HamNoSys describes signs in terms of hand shape, hand position/orientation, and hand movement (leaving aside exceptional signs involving significant use of other body parts).

There are 12 standard hand shapes in HamNoSys (flat, fist, pointing index finger, etc.), and a set of modifications that can be applied to them, changing the bending of individual fingers or the thumb. Position is specified as a set of named locations on the body or at certain distances from it. There is a repertoire of several hundred such locations. Orientation is specified by "extended finger direction" (hereafter abbreviated to e.f.d.) and palm orientation (p.o.). E.f.d. is the direction the fingers would be pointing if they were straight; alternatively, it can be thought of as the direction of the metacarpal of the middle finger (the immovable finger bone within the palm). It has 26 possible values, being the

Fig. 2. BSL sign for "Scotland".

directions from the centre of a cube to its face centres, edge midpoints, and vertexes; additionally, it can be specified as the direction midway between any two of those 26. Palm orientation is one of eight values, corresponding to the directions from the centre of a square to its edge midpoints and vertexes. They are labelled left, up, right, down, and the four intermediate combinations. These designations have the natural meaning when the e.f.d. is forwards; when the e.f.d. points in other directions a more or less conventional assignment is made of palm orientation names to actual palm orientations.

Movement descriptions can be quite complex. A movement of the hand through space can be straight (in any of the 26 directions), curved (the plane of the curve being oriented in 8 different ways about the axis of movement, similarly to palm orientation), circular, or directed to a specific location. Oscillation of the wrists about three different axes can be described, and a movement called "fingerplay", in which the fingers are waggled as if drumming them on a surface or crumbling something between the fingers and thumb. Movements can be combined sequentially or in parallel, and the hands can perform mirrored movements, parallel movements, or independent movements. The "manner" of a movement can be specified as fast, slow, with a sudden stop, or several other styles. The notation[2] →⌒✱ denotes a large, fast rightward movement with a curve convex upward.

Version 4.0 of HamNoSys has been extended to give substantial coverage of facial expressions. SAMPA codes[2] are used to specify speech-like movements of the mouth (frequently used in signing). There is a set of other facial actions such as movements of the eyebrows, or direction of eyegaze. Movements of the shoulders, and tilting of the body or head are also expressible, together with the synchronisation of these with the manual gestures.

4 Problems with HamNoSys

4.1 Missing Information

Many HamNoSys transcriptions omit information which may be obvious to the human reader, but which are not obvious to a program (because nothing is

[2] Definitions of the HamNoSys symbols used in this paper are given in the appendix.

obvious to a program). In most cases, the missing information can be written explicitly in a more detailed transcription, but some pieces of information are not expressible in HamNoSys at all, and must always be filled in by the reader, human or artificial.

In gestures in which the two hands are placed in some relationship close to one other (what HamNoSys calls a "hand constellation"), there is no way to express the direction from one hand to the other. This must somehow be guessed in every case, but it is difficult to come up with a set of rules which will apply to all cases. In practice, it is usually quite easy to refute any proposed rule by searching through a few dozen randomly chosen entries from the Hamburg corpus of over 3000 HamNoSys transcriptions of DGS signs. In contrast, note that for any particular sign, it is easy for the human reader familiar with HamNoSys to correctly perform it. The problem lies in codifying for computer processing the means by which these judgements are made.

4.2 Extended Finger Direction

The "extended finger direction" of a hand is always physically present, but at least for Dutch sign language, has been found not to be a phonological constituent ([3]). This is not in itself a problem for HamNoSys, which transcribes on the phonetic level, but it does appear difficult even for those trained in HamNoSys to correctly record e.f.d. In the Hamburg corpus of signs, there are several examples for which the direction that has been notated is not the e.f.d., but the direction in which the hand is pointing, which is often different. An example is the DGS sign for "me" (identical to the BSL sign): the right index finger points to the chest or abdomen of the signer. This has sometimes been transcribed as [illegible]. Taken literally (which is the only way a program can take it), this implies the strained posture of Figure 3(a). A correct transcription and performance of the sign is given in Figure 3(b). Contrast the sign for "you", in which the e.f.d. and the direction of pointing coincide (Figure 3(c)).

It is interesting to note that in one introductory textbook on BSL [12], the photographs of signs for "me" and "you/he/she" both show a clear 45 degree bend in the index finger base joint, yet the accompanying line drawings of the handshapes show that joint as being unbent.

4.3 Ambiguity of Gestural Phonetics

There is a significant disanalogy between speech and gesture in the area of phonetics. For a spoken utterance, the only scope for making differing transcriptions lies in decisions about how to classify the continuously variable elements into the available phonetic categories, how precise to make these categories, and what aspects to omit as irrelevant to one's purpose (narrow vs. broad transcription). The different phonetic elements are independent of each other: there is no way to construct, say, a plosive, out of any combination of other elements of the phonetic repertoire. A plosive sound must be notated by one of the symbols for plosives.

Fig. 3. (a) Bad transcription of "me". (b) Good transcription of "me". (c) Good transcription of "you".

This is not at all the case for gesture. There are many geometric elements that can be used to describe a gesture, and every one of them can be constructed out of a combination of a small number of the others. For example, a few geometric elements that one might use are the following:

- direction of the forearm
- e.f.d.
- directions of each finger and thumb bone
- wrist rotation
- bend and splay of the finger and thumb base joints
- bending of the second and third joints of each finger and thumb

Each of these can be defined in terms of others: for example, e.f.d. is determined by wrist rotation and forearm direction; in fact, each of those three can be defined in terms of the other two. Direction of the first bone of a finger is determined by e.f.d. and base joint rotation. And so on. One can arbitrarily pick a basis for gesture space, that is, a selection of geometric elements which are independent of each other, such that every gesture has a unique transcription. However, there does not appear to be any natural choice of such a basis. HamNoSys is one such basis, but as discussed above, some things such as e.f.d. do not appear to be natural choices, at least as regards sign language.

If the aim were simply to give a description of any particular gesture performed on one occasion by a particular person, then any description that accurately reproduced its geometry would do. However, our aim is avatar-independent description, and for that to be possible, the notation must record those aspects of a gesture that would remain the same even if the geometry of the avatar changed. It is necessary to draw a distinction between, for example, pointing to a specific location on the avatar's body, and pointing in a specific direction. The choice of one or other of those geometric elements when transcribing a gesture is a classification of the intention of the gesturer. These intentions are what must be captured by an avatar-independent notation.

The same issue also arises when considering how to perform the "same" sign in different locations. The BSL sign for "shelf" is illustrated in citation form in

Figure 4. "Shelves" can be performed by repeating the sign for "shelf" several times at successive vertical levels. When this is done, it becomes clear that the important direction is that of the straight fingers. When signing "shelf" high up, the hands bend at the finger base joints and the e.f.d. points upwards. The granularity with which HamNoSys can specify e.f.d. is in steps of one quarter of a right angle, and for the finger base joint it is half a right angle. It is thus clear that one cannot accurately produce the desired direction of the fingers at each level by combining values for e.f.d and handshape, even though as continuous variables there would be no problem.

Fig. 4. BSL sign for "shelf".

These considerations apply equally to non-linguistic gesturing. For example, applause is no longer applause if the hands do not contact each other, therefore such contacts must be notated, not a geometry for each arm separately that merely happens to bring the hands in contact for a given avatar.

4.4 Scope

HamNoSys is, by design, limited to the upper body motions required for signing, and in this it has been very successful. Applications for synthetic animation range much more widely, and we wish to have a notation system which could describe the movements required of realistic characters in virtual environments: walking, sitting, standing, manipulating physical objects, conversational gesturing, etc. This is a subject of current research.

5 Iconic and Symbolic Meaning

It is not the business of a gesture notation to represent the symbolic meaning of a sign, and HamNoSys excludes this. It records only what is physically done. The pointing-index-finger handshape is the same whether it is used to mean "that person there" or "the number 1". There is, however, another sort of meaning to be considered, and which HamNoSys verges upon with its principle of representing only the significant aspects of the gesture. For example, most signs involve only the hands and the face. These are the body parts performing meaningful actions, the rest of the body being only the physical vehicle necessary to support the hands and the head.

This concept can be taken further. The most important aspects of signs are not their concrete geometry, but what we might call their "physical intentions" or "iconic meaning". Pointing with the index finger is the intention of the sign for "that person there". The intention is expressed geometrically in the handshape by the following features: the index finger is extended towards the object pointed at; the other fingers and thumb are curled together into a tight or loose fist. The same intention, when directed towards oneself in the sign for "me" is, as we have discussed earlier, performed with a slightly different geometry, with a bent index finger and an e.f.d. that differs from the direction of pointing. It is this intention which should be notated, rather than the specific geometry that encodes it in a particular context.

It is interesting to compare the latter handshape to one found in one of the BSL signs (there are several) for "caravan"[3] (Figure 5).

Fig. 5. BSL sign for "caravan".

The intention of this sign is a mime of the action of towing something: the right hand is the towing hook of the car (upside down), and the left hand is the towing bracket of the caravan. The shape of the right hand in this particular realisation of the sign is almost identical to that of Figure 3(c), but the intention is entirely different: it is not pointing at anything, but hooking into something to pull it. The significant direction associated with the shape is from the inner surface of the index finger towards the wrist. The total range of handshapes that would be correct for the right hand in "caravan" is not identical to the range that would be correct in "me", but there is an overlap.

A gesture notation that recorded these iconic intentions would notate these handshapes differently, although geometrically they might be identical.

[3] In British English, a caravan is a small house on wheels towed behind a car. Citation forms for this sign vary in different references. The picture is based on that given in [1] (sign 537); [12] shows a version with a much more strongly hooked right index finger.

6 Principles for a Gesture Notation

From the above discussion, and our experience thus far with synthesising animations, we arrive at some general principles for a movement notation suitable for this application.

6.1 Intention Is Primary; Geometry Is Secondary

A transcription of a gesture should start from the intentions that the posture and movement are to express, by which we mean those geometric elements of the posture and movement that must be accurately achieved by the avatar and preserved under change of avatar, as distinct from those elements which merely take whatever values they physiologically must in order to achieve the significant elements.

As a concrete example, with any handshape as used in a given context, one can associate one or more significant axes. For a pointing hand, the significant axis is through the pointing finger or fingers; the orientation of the hand about that axis is usually not significant. For the hooked shape in Figure 5, the significant axis is the direction in which the hand pulls. For a fist, any of three different axes might be significant (see Figure 6). To specify the orientation of the hand, the directions of the significant axes should be given, rather than the direction of some fixed part of the hand. Once the direction of the significant axis or axes have been specified, the rest of the geometry should as far as possible be determined automatically from the geometry and physical constraints of the avatar.

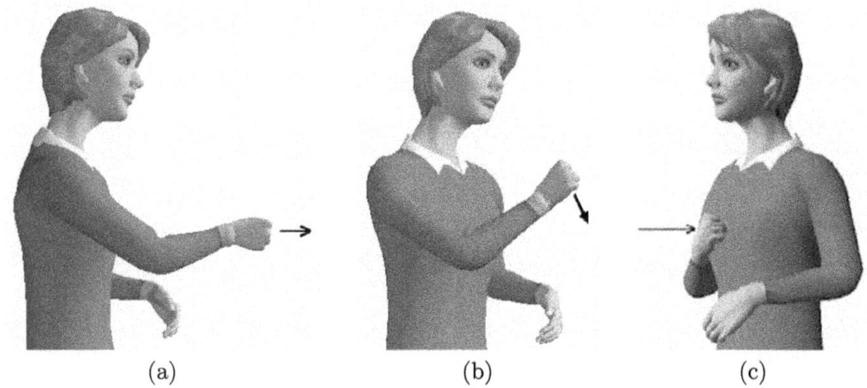

Fig. 6. (a) Axis of punching fist. (b) Axis of hammering action. (c) Axis of tapping chest (BSL sign for "mine").

6.2 Express Geometry so Far as It Cannot Be Deduced from Intention

The human ability to fill in what has been left out in an "obvious" way greatly exceeds that of any piece of software. A practical gesture notation for animation must allow geometry to be explicitly specified in more detail than would be necessary for a human reader of the notation. If the software cannot calculate everything that has been omitted in some piece of notation, or produces an answer that the user finds unsatisfactory, then it must be possible to specify more detail to resolve the difficulty. There is a trade-off here between the complexity of implementing the notation and the effort required by a user of the notation to make a transcription.

6.3 Describe the Avatar

Avatar description is outside the scope of HamNoSys; in fact, no movement notation of which we are aware makes any reference to the individuality of the avatar. However, software which must produce animation data for a particular avatar must at some point be provided with geometric information about the avatar. The information required includes:

1. The positions of all the joints of the avatar when it is placed in some standard pose.
2. The articulation of each joint: whether it operates as a hinge, a ball and socket, etc., and its limits of movement.
3. The positions of all the feature points nameable in the notation – that is, where on the surface of the avatar are such locations as "the centre of the forehead", "the point of the chin", etc. Each feature point must also be associated with the bone which moves the part of the avatar containing that point.
4. Information about aspects of the avatar's "body language": how fast it generally signs, how sudden are the stops which it makes when moving a hand to a target location, etc.
5. The avatar is assumed to be provided with a set of facial deformations, varying amounts of which can be applied to each frame of the animation. A mapping must be given of each facial element of the notation to the facial deformations (or some combination of them) provided for the avatar.

7 Related Work

There are many projects relating to speech synthesis for talking heads, too many to reference here. Their concerns and methods are largely independent of the work described here, which is principally body animation.

VHML (Virtual Human Markup Language) [6] is a programme to devise a notation combining movement synthesis, speech synthesis, emotion, and dialogue, although as yet its more ambitous features have not been implemented. It mainly describes movement at a higher level than we are concerned with.

More directly related are other systems for synthesising animation from movement notations, mostly for deaf signing. These include the research projects GESSYCA ([4]) and SignSynth ([5]), and the commercial systems SigningAvatar (http://www.vcom3d.com) and SignTel (http://www.signtelinc.com). These are all aimed at particular sign languages (French sign language for GESSYCA, and ASL or various forms of signed English for the others).

Zhisheng Huang and others have implemented a low-level animation system based on the H-anim standard structure for a humanoid [9]. As with HamNoSys, the user can specify postures and movements in broad terms, the program choosing the precise numbers. Animation is currently specified at a very low level, in terms of the rotations of individual joints.

For the dance notation Labanotation ([10]) there is the LINTER software ([8]). This generates movement by linear interpolations, using schematic avatars built from ellipsoids. Its purpose is primarily as a teaching aid to demonstrate to dance students what a given piece of Labanotation means, rather than to produce a naturalistic animation.

Acknowledgements

We acknowledge funding from the EU under the Framework V IST Programme (Grant IST-1999-10500). Thomas Hanke, Constanze Schmaling, and Ian Marshall provided many useful comments.

Appendix: Definitions of HamNoSys Symbols Used in the Text

→ Move right. • Large movement. ∩ Bowed upwards. * Fast.

Pointing hand with straight index finger, the other fingers and thumb formed into a fist.

As previous, but with the index finger bent at 90° at the base.

Midway between the two previous shapes.

E.f.d. is outwards. E.f.d. is inwards.

E.f.d. is upwards, inwards, and leftwards.

Palm faces right. Palm faces left.

References

1. British Deaf Association. *Dictionary of British Sign Language.* Faber and Faber, 1992.
2. SAMPA computer readable phonetic alphabet. http://www.phon.ucl.ac.uk/home/sampa/home.htm.
3. Onno Crasborn. *Phonetic implementation of phonological categories in Sign Language of the Netherlands.* PhD thesis, University of Leiden, 2001.
4. S. Gibet and T. Lebourque. High-level specification and animation of communicative gestures. *J. Visual Languages and Computing*, 12:657–687, 2001. On-line at http://www.idealibrary.com.

5. Angus B. Grieve-Smith. Signsynth: A sign language synthesis application using Web3D and Perl. In Ipke Wachsmuth and Timo Sowa, editors, *Gesture and Sign Language in Human-Computer Interaction: International Gesture Workshop GW2001 (LNAI vol.2298*, pages 134–145. Springer, 2001.
6. VHML Working Group. `http://www.vhml.org/`.
7. Thomas Hanke. Hamnosys in a sign language generation context. In Rolf Schulmeister and Heimo Reinitzer, editors, *Progress in sign language research (International Studies on Sign Language and Communication of the Deaf, vol.40)*, pages 249–264, 2002.
8. Don Henderson. LINTER software for animating Labanotation: see `http://www-staff.mcs.uts.edu.au/~don/pubs/led.html`.
9. Zhisheng Huang, Anton Eliëns, and Cees Visser. Implementation of a scripting language for VRML/X3D-based embodied agents. In *Proc. Web3D 2003 Symposium*, pages 91–100, 2003.
10. Ann Hutchinson Guest. *Labanotation: The System of Analyzing and Recording Movement.* Routledge, 1987.
11. Richard Kennaway. Synthetic animation of deaf signing gestures. In *4th International Workshop on Gesture and Sign Language Based Human-Computer Interaction*, volume 2298 of *Lecture Notes in Artificial Intelligence*, pages 146–157, 1999.
12. Richard Magill and Anne Hodgson. *Start To Sign!* RNID, 2000.
13. S. Prillwitz, R. Leven, H. Zienert, T. Hanke, J. Henning, et al. *HamNoSys Version 2.0: Hamburg Notation System for Sign Languages — An Introductory Guide.* International Studies on Sign Language and the Communication of the Deaf, Volume 5. University of Hamburg, 1989. Version 4.0 is documented on the Web at `http://www.sign-lang.uni-hamburg.de/Projekte/HamNoSys/HNS4.0/HNS4.0de/Inhalt.html`.
14. Eva Safar and Ian Marshall. The architecture of an English-text-to-sign-languages translation system. In G. Angelova *et al*, editor, *Recent Advances in Natural Language Processing*, pages 223–228, 2001.
15. William C. Stokoe, Dorothy Casterline, and Carl Croneberg. *A Dictionary of American Sign Language on Linguistic Principles, rev. ed.* Linstok Press, Silver Spring, Maryland, 1976.

The Development of a Computational Notation for Synthesis of Sign and Gesture

Kirsty Crombie Smith and William Edmondson

University of Birmingham, Birmingham B15 2TT, UK
K.J.Crombie-Smith@cs.bham.ac.uk

Abstract. This paper presents a review of four current notation systems used in sign language research.Their properties are discussed with a view to using such systems for synthesising sign with a computer. The evaluation leads to a proposal for a new notational approach, which distinguishes three layers of description in the production of sign. Experimental work is summarised which constrains the synthesis of signs to match the requirements of visual perception. The new notation is described in detail with illustrative example at each of the three layers. The notation is being used in experimental work on sign synthesis and it is envisaged that this work would extend to include synthesis of gesture.

1 Introduction

Since the early 1970s computer scientists have studied methods of generating and recognising speech. However, the recent development of signing avatars and sign recognition techniques[6,11,18] represents the shift of interest to the new area of sign language and computing. The results of this work, offer benefits to the Deaf Community and provide insight into work on gestures. One of the main problems with the current work on signing avatars is their theoretical foundation. Although there are a number of notational systems[1] [1,14,15,19,21,22,23] upon which this work could be based, the results are limited. Their creation is labour intensive, requiring the use of a data glove to capture the sign. The resultant avatars have difficult to follow restricted movements; their vocabulary is limited and additional signs or changes costly. In order to create an accurate and linguistically based simulation of any sign language, there needs to be a suitable underlying body model.

Currently there are a number of existing notational systems used for transcribing sign language. The four discussed here, are those already used as a base for signing synthesis, or which would be easy to parse and use as a base[2]. Each

[1] A notational system is defined as any particular system of characters, symbols, or abbreviated expressions used in art or science, to express briefly technical facts, quantities, etc. Esp., the system of figures, letters, and signs used in arithmetic and algebra to express number, quantity, or operations[25].

[2] One notable exception from this list is Sutton's sign writing[16]. This is as far as we are aware not used as a base for a sign synthesis and its use of symbols and layout on the page makes it more difficult to parse.

A. Camurri and G. Volpe (Eds.): GW 2003, LNAI 2915, pp. 312–323, 2004.

notation was used to transcribe a short piece of video footage of a native deaf signer signing in British Sign Language (BSL). At present, we are concentrating solely on the hands, although we are aware that the facial expression contains as much information about the sign as the hands. There are no claims that the transcriptions are totally correct; but we followed the instructions given to produce the transcription. Next, we examined results that affect the visual perception of signs and the difference that occurs over our visual field, suggesting ways in which this could affect a notational system. Finally following on from this a new notational system is proposed. This three-layer system brings together previous research and creates a new approach to notational systems. It takes the user from a conceptual level through to a realised phonetic level. The three-layer approach is not a novel idea. Tatham[18] proposes a similar three-layer approach to speech production, suggesting that an intermediate layer is necessary to link the high level conceptual to the low level production. It is proposed that such a notational system is the necessary base on which to build effective synthesis of signs and avatar gestures.

The paper is set out in sections. The second section evaluates the four notational systems, concluding with a summary and comparison of the systems. The third section presents information about the visual and perceptual limitations that could affect sign languages. The fourth section proposes a new three-layer notational system, expounding upon each layer. Finally, the fifth section presents conclusions on both the theoretical and practical nature of the system.

2 Sign Language Notational Systems

2.1 Stokoe Notation[14,15,19]

Named after it creator, William Stokoe, this system was created along the same lines as a spoken language notation might be developed. Having discovered that a number of shapes recurred in American sign language (ASL) he decided that one of the parameters was handshape, which he called designator (dez). Following a well-trodden linguistic path, he looked for minimal pairs in order to determine other specific features, defining a further two - place of articulation called tabulation (tab) and action called signation (sig)[14,15,19]. There are then 55 symbols from which the sign can be composed.
Signs can then written:

Tab Dez^{Sig}
Tab Dez ^{SigSig} this means that one action follows another
Tab Dez$^{Sig}_{Sig}$ which means that the actions occur at the same time
Tab Dez Dez^{Sig} two-handed sign, can occur with any combination of "sig's"

For example the sign "make" from the story can be recorded as:

Ø sign performed in the signer's neutral space
A Non-dominant hand in closed fist held below dominant hand
> Palm facing to the dominant side of the body

A Dominant hand in closed fist, held above non-dominant hand
< Palm facing to the non-dominant side of the body
Ͽ Performs circling movement
)(Hands move towards each other
X Hands contact each other
÷ Hands move away from each other again
• Movement is repeated

And in linear form as: ∅A>A<Ͽ)(X÷•
This was the first well-used notational system; it is basic and does not have the extensive descriptors that are available to the other systems. As a system it is easy to understand and use to write down signs, but it has fewer handshapes, positions and movements. It requires the user to 'best fit' features to a sign and lacks finger orientation information. This makes it difficult to define some signs clearly; the handshapes are ambiguous as sometimes one shape being used to fit a number of signs. The movements are vague. For example Ͽ is said to be a circling movement but it gives no idea of the direction, size of the circle, or the plane on which the circling movement occurs. The defined positions around the body are also fuzzy, ⌣ covering all the lower area of the face from the mouth to the chin.

Stokoe provided a good first attempt and it has been the basis for many other notations. However it lacks clear, discerning feature definitions that would enable production of an accurate reproduction of any given sign.

2.2 BSL Dictionary Notation[1]

This notation is used in the BSL-English dictionary it is based upon the Stokoe idea of handshapes (dez), position (tab) and movement (sig) but includes additional information about finger and palm orientation (ori), the hands' relationship to each other (ha) and any contact information. It was designed as a linguistic tool to record the details of each sign on paper.

There are 57 handshapes, grouped into 22 sets. The handshapes are based upon the ASL alphabet with the addition of 8 non-alphabetic characters representing different handshapes. Location of the hands with respect to the body is recorded by 36 different symbols. Palm orientation and finger orientation indicate the orientation of the handshape. The hand arrangement records the relative position of the two hands with respect to each other. Finally the movement of the hands is recorded. The order of all the above varies according to the type of sign that is being transcribed. One handed or single dez signs are tab-dez-ori-ori-sig. Manual tab signs where both hands are involved with a stationary non-dominant hand are: tab-ori-ori- (ha)-dez-ori-ori-sig, the initial tab becoming the non-dominant handshape. Double dez signs or two-handed signs where both hands move are: tab-dez-ori-ori- (ha)-dez-ori-ori-sig. It is important to note that the non-dominant hand is always recorded first in two-handed signs and that palm orientation is recorded before finger orientation[1].

For example the sign 'car' from the story can be recorded as:

Ø Neutral space in front of the body
A closed fist, thumb beside index finger
q T Palm faces up and turned towards the signer
⊥ Fingers face away from signer
A closed fist, thumb beside index finger4
q T Palm faces up and is turned towards the signer
⊥ Fingers face away from signer
(Own notation to separate movement
Alternating movements
N Up and down
Z From side to side
• Repeated movements
) End of movement

And in Linear form as: $\emptyset\mathrm{Aq}\top\perp\mathrm{Aq}\top\perp^{\sim NZ\bullet}$
This notation was fairly easy to understand and use to write down the signs. Once again the BSL dictionary notation uses handshapes and this causes the same problems as above. However, it was designed for use with BSL and most handshapes occurring in BSL can be found. This may cause problems when trying to transcribe other sign languages. There are other small anomalies, the omission how to define the point of contact when other than a fingertip and the direction of the movements other than circular. Adding another symbol to represent them could solve this, but fundamentally the notation is a rich description of the signs.

2.3 SignFont[22,23]

Designed by the linguist Don .E. Newkirk, its aim was to be a literal orthography for ASL, to be able to record fine details needed by linguists, but also to be easy enough for everyday use as a form of written communication[23].

The idea was that it should be reproducible by a keyboard, using the 26 alphabetic characters, ? and the - in the phonemic spelling and punctuation marks for diacritic marks. It attempts to convey all the important linguistic information that is lacking from the Stokoe notation. The descriptive information is fitted into a frame with the small set of symbols meaning that 'a' can be used in three different parts of the word to represent different concepts[23].

Newkirk emphasises that phonemic analysis of ASL is dependent upon a theory of sign structure that defines a common level of phoneme analysis and their interrelationship. He states that "although handshape, place of articulation and movement do figure in phonemic units in ASL, they do not share a common level of analysis (exactly)". He suggests that movement and place of articulation be related in the same way that manner and place of articulation are related in spoken language[22].

The frame is composed of a number of sections:

- The optional prefixes related to the active hands in a sign
- The handshape of the hands
- The contact region if applicable
- The spatial relations between the hands if not predictable
- Movement stem - showing place of articulation and movement type
- Optional suffixes for inflections and variations in number and grammar

For example the sign ‘car’ from the story can be recorded as:

so- Hands move in a contrary movement
a Dominant hand in closed fist
a Non-dominant hand in closed fist
8X Dominant hand located in ipsilateral front of ribcage area.
:X Non-dominant hand located in the contralateral front of the ribcage area
H Hands move in a circular path movement,
D upward and
E downward

And in linear form as: so-aa8X:X HDE
Of all the notational systems I found this was the most difficult one to use and understand. There was limited information about the notational system and problems using the same letters for very different things.

Again, SignFont is restricted by its set of fixed handshapes. It requires the user to find a ‘best fit’ rather than an accurate representation. It lacks any information about the finger orientation, the palm orientation is limited and the local locations are too vague. There is a vast amount of contacting information for different body areas, but some movements are very inadequately recorded. The idea behind the system is good, alphanumeric characters and punctuation means the most people are able to use it to record signs and it would be easy to parse. However it is complex to use and lacks some of the finer details needed to specify signs accurately.

2.4 HamNoSys[20]

HamNoSys was developed about 15 years ago by a group of deaf and hearing people at the University of Hamburg, Germany[20]. It was designed as a linguistics research tool, which could be used to transcribe any sign language in the world. At present there are a number of projects using HamNoSys - ViSiCAST is one such European collaboration, which uses HamNoSys as a basis for a synthetic animation of sign language[8].
HamNoSys is composed of a number of strictly ordered symbols representing the different aspects of the sign.

- The position of the hands with respect to the body
- The dominant hand’s handshape
- The orientation of the dominant hand’s fingers when fully extended

- The orientation of the dominant hand's palm
- The non-dominant hand
- The position of the non-dominant hand if different from the dominant hand.
- The non-dominant hand's handshape
- The orientation of the non-dominant hand's fingers when fully extended
- The orientation of the non-dominant hand's palm
- The movement of the two hands.

For example: The sign "make" from the story in HamNoSys can be written as.

centre of breast line
closed fist thumb extended
extended fingers point 135° perpendicular from body
palm points upwards to perpendicular leftside of body
non-dominant hand
closed fist, thumb crossed over fingers
extended fingers point 225° perpendicular from body
palm points downwards to perpendicular rightside of body
movement in a circle...
contacting...
dominant hand little fingerside and..
non-dominant hand thumbside
indicates the movements repeat

And in linear form as:
The iconic structure of HamNoSys makes it fairly easy to write down the signs. However there are the usual difficulties. HamNoSys uses a set of specific handshapes, making the notation rigid. Similarly when defining movement, there is no strict definition - how far to move, the exact angle of movement or shape of curve. This makes HamNoSys a rich description of the signs, which would require further precision if used as a base for a computational model. R.Kennaway[8] raises these problems when attempting to use HamNoSys as input for a synthetic animation. Commenting on the lack of information about the exact positioning of the arm, the use of concepts such as fast, slow and close too, which need to be more precisely defined for a computer simulation. He attempts to make "precise the fuzzy definitions of HamNoSys components", by specifying arbitrary points based on rough assumption. For example, the 'centre' is defined as being midway between the shoulders, the 'left' is defined as being 0.4m to the left of this midway point and 'to the left of' being a further 0.4m from this 'left' point[8]. This adds the necessary precision but is somewhat arbitary.

Table 1. Comparison of two signs recorded using the four notational systems.

Notational System	*car*	*make*
Stokoe	$\emptyset A>\|A<^{NZ\supset\bullet}$	$\emptyset A>A<^{\supset)(X\div\bullet}$
BSL Dictionary	$\emptyset Aq\top\bot Aq\top\bot^{\sim NZ\bullet}$	$\emptyset A<q\bot A<p\bot^{(?x\bullet)}$
SignFont	so-aa8X:XHDE	a⌣s⌢9ShywLyDE
HamNoSys	[illegible]	[illegible]

2.5 Summary of Notational Systems

The difficulties highlighted show the complexity and non-triviality of the field. The main problem of using these notational systems as a computational base is that they are rich descriptions of the language. Table 1 highlights the similarities of the notational systems; showing that the differences are just the symbols used. A rich description is a good way of transcribing sign languages, but it does not have the level of precision that is needed for a computer simulation. A computational model or computer simulation needs precise definitions as its input.

These problems also apply to any synthesis or notational system for gestures. It might be thought adequate to use rich description for gesture but there are two problems with this assumption. Firstly, it is a mistake to assume that gesture is not systematic; work has shown[7] that natural gesture is systematic and makes use of specific handshape movements. Secondly, regardless of the individual variation between gesturers (which may or may not be more extravagant than between signers) it remains the case that computational synthesis of gesture will require precision of specification in the same degree as that found necessary for signing. The computer has to be told in detail how to wave its hands. Recognition of these notational problems and the links between the fields of gesture and sign language research generate an exciting and positive future for synthetic synthesis.

3 Limitations Due to Vision

Auditory perception limits the sounds of a spoken language and the hearer's understanding of what is being said. Likewise the eyes limit the signs of sign language and the watcher's understanding. One of the limiting factors of human vision is the difference in acuity across the visual field. At the centre of the visual field, acuity is at its highest, it then tails off towards the edges of the field. Visual acuity determines the amount of detail that can be seen. Anstis[24] developed a chart that demonstrates the decreasing visual acuity of the visual field; the letters are scaled from the central fixation point to indicate the diminution of acuity. When viewed with central fixation all letters should appear equally clear.

It was found that about two degrees from the centre acuity was 0.5, at ten degrees from the centre this is decreased to only 0.1[13, quoted in]. This means that if the watcher fixates on the signer's face, they will view the signer's hands with their peripheral vision and a visual acuity of between 0.25 and 0.1[13].

Therefore they are unable to see fine detail of hand movements unless they switch to fixate on them. Research indicates that signers only fixate on the hands when watching fingerspelling. When watching normal signing they concentrate on the mouth and lower half of the face[2,13].

Experiments with peripheral vision have shown that with experience it can be trained to increase performance[4,9,17]. Experienced signers concentrate mainly on the face, unless directed otherwise whilst novice signers are more likely to fixate on the hands. Experimental work examining the amount of detectable difference in finger movement in the peripheral and central vision showed that deaf signers perceived movements differing by more than 6° in central vision and by more than 25° in peripheral vision as different[3].

4 A New Notational System

The creating of the notational system involved a bottom up approach by examining the possible hand and arm movements and then why they did not occur. Goniometry provides the average maximum movements of joint angles[11]. Central and peripheral vision research limits this set further by indicating detectable differences in movements[2,3,13]. This means that this subset of physical possible movements is further reduced into perceivable possible movements.

The aim of the notational system is to provide an accurate transcription of the sign language and then to translate it into input for a computer simulation. The three-layer notational system was named as the Nicene notation after the Nicene Creed; this leads to the names of the layers - thought, word and deed. The first layer is the abstract or 'thought' layer, containing the morphological aspects of the signs. The second layer is the realisable phonemic or 'word' layer, it specifies precise values for the parts of the sign that are necessary for the understanding of the signs. The third and final layer is the realised temporal phonetic or 'deed' layer, this attaches the specified values to a timeline smoothly interpolating between these values, adding default values if not specified.

4.1 Thought

The first layer is the thought layer; it attempts to record the abstract concept of the sign. In the proposed notation the layer is composed of six vectors, two vectors for the hands, two for the arms, one for the face and one for the movement of the sign. The components of the vectors are a rich description of the conceptual ideas. It is at this level that the etymology of the sign is evident. The sign may have iconic properties such as the flatness of the hand representing the flatness of the object or the movement of the sign representing the movement of an object.

The hand vectors records the target hand configurations and any tension in the hand during the sign. The target hand configurations are recorded using the Stokoe notation. Tension in the hands is recorded as '+' otherwise it is not recorded. For example the hand part of the BSL sign 'forget' is recorded as DH/O, 5/. Having been critical of the use of handshapes, this sudden use of Stokoe's notation seems contradictory. However as we are working at the conceptual or thought level, we need to use a descriptive language and following previous research Stokoe's notation is a good base.

The arm vectors contain one target arm configuration and any points of contact. The target arm configuration is the position of the wrist, elbow and shoulder at the initial point of the sign. Contact is whether there is any contact between the hands and/or any other parts of the body. For example the arm part of the BSL sign 'forget' is recorded as DA/arm lifted, elbow bent; finger-tips touching dominant side temple /. The face vector contains all the non-manual features of the sign, such as lip, mouth, tongue, eye, eyebrow, cheeks and nose movements.

The movement vector contains the movement trajectory through the target configurations, information about wiggling, repetition of movement or contact of any parts during the movement and about the manner of the sign, whether the sign is exaggerated and the movements extended or whether they are signing on the sly and the movements are reduced. For example the movement part of the BSL sign 'forget' is recorded as M/ moving forward away from head, conversational manner/.

4.2 Word

The second layer is the word layer; it takes the thought descriptive form and changes the five anatomical vectors into matrices with numerical parameters. One of the major problems encountered when testing the notational systems was the use of hand shapes. It is imprecise and subject to individual interpretation. A way of solving this problem is to break down the handshape to give each finger joint a specification. This makes it highly defined and easily alterable. The values for the parameters for the matrices are found via a look-up table. The visual limitations and experimental results refine these values, but also allow flexibility around the values. The target hand configuration is then recorded in a matrix, with each finger joint angle being documented. The three joints in each finger and thumb are recorded. The top row of the matrix is the distal interphalangeal (DIP) joints of the fingers/thumb. The second row is the proximal interphalangeal (PIP) for the fingers and the metacarpophalangeal (MCP) for the thumb. The third layer is the MCP for the fingers and the carpometacarpal (CMC) for the thumb. Thus a dominant hand closed fist with thumb folded and wrapped across fingers and a non-dominant hand flat palm with thumb extended would be recorded as so:

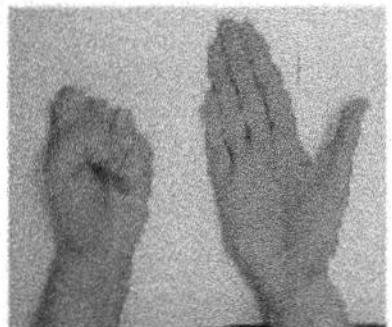

$$\begin{bmatrix} 80 & 90 & 90 & 90 & 90 & 0\,0\,0\,0\,0 \\ 50 & 100 & 100 & 100 & 100 & 0\,0\,0\,0\,0 \\ 70 & 90 & 90 & 90 & 90 & 0\,0\,0\,0\,0 \end{bmatrix}$$

Fig. 1. Dominant left fist and non-dominant right flat hand, thumb extended.

The first number on the top row, first column is the top joint (DIP) of the thumb; set at 80° which is the maximum flexion bend of the joint. The first column of the matrix contains all the thumb joints, set at 80°, 50° and 70° which is the flexion maximum of all the joints meaning the thumb is curled over. The first five columns are the left-hand values, set at the maximum flexion values. Therefore the hand is curled into a fist with the thumb curled over the top of the fingers, the thumb is not positioned under the fingers as they are at maximum flexion bend. The hands are recorded with the dominant hand first with dominant thumb through to little finger followed by the non-dominant hand with non- dominant little finger through to thumb. When the hand configuration changes during the sign then two or more target hand configurations are used, each one being defined in the same manner.

The arm vectors are translated into matrices with the shoulder - 3 angles, elbow - 2 angles and wrist - 2 angles. There is only one target arm configuration for each sign resulting in the movement controlling the position of the arm until the next sign. This underspecification is a feature of the notational system, it allows freedom by specify only what is necessary in the understanding of the sign. The notation avoids any use of the term location and distance, by using velocity and the arm matrices. The former is comprised of a direction vector and a speed; this makes it is a continuous line and does not give a start or end point. The hands are then placed at certain points by the arm matrices.

The movement vector is comprised of a series of movement trajectories through the targets. Unlike the anatomical vectors, the movement vector remains a vector of vectors. It is composed of one or more velocity vectors, depending on the number of target configurations within the sign and the importance of the motion before and after the targets are reached. Velocity is composed of speed and a direction vector. The speed can be predetermined but will be influenced by the manner of the signing and adjective referring to the sign. The direction vector is a three-dimensional vector along which the hand/arm will move. The vector contains information about repetition of the movement, any points of contact and the manner of the sign.

4.3 Deed

The third layer is the deed layer. Based loosely upon Edmondson's ring-bound notebook account of a sign[5]. This brings in the temporal aspects of a sign and therefore creates a dynamic notation. Taking a string of signs, the different targets within the signs are attached to points along the timeline. The movement trajectories link between the targets as shown (fig. 2). Unspecified movement results in computer interpolation between the targets. From the experimental results and vision limitations, we know that movements under 25° are viewed as the same, so the matrix values can be flexible and will be easily alterable to move smoothly along the target trajectory. For each sign, the movement trajectory attempts to reach the target but the speed or style of signing may result in it not being reached completely before moving onto the next target. This simulates everyday signing where signs are not completed but are still understood[2].

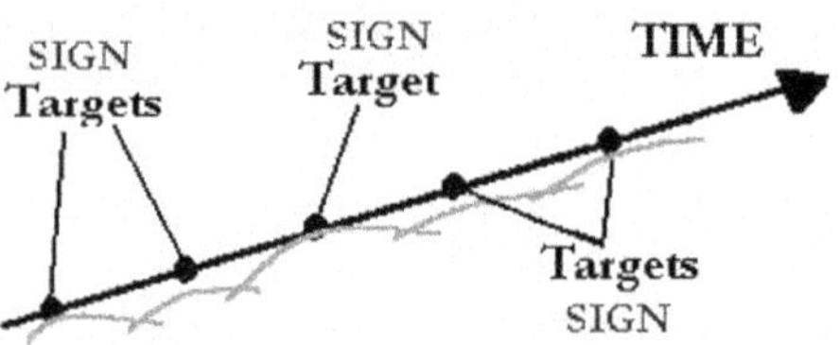

Fig. 2. Deed Layer: - Deed Timeline.

5 Conclusion

5.1 Theorectical Conclusion

In order to create a linguistically informed base for a computational model, we have proposed a new three-layer notation. Unlike previous notations it goes beyond a rich description of the signs to give a realistic realisable notation. The use of targets allows flexibility, the targets do not need to be reached exactly before moving on to the next target. It avoids the problems of using handshapes and location as parameters by defining joint angles and using arm positioning and movement instead. The use of vectors, matrices and angles makes the notation language adaptable and the generality and underspecification of the notation allows for differences between people and merging between strings of signs.

The notations evaluated earlier all provided rich descriptions of signs, suggesting that these are working at a morphological level. However to completely capture the sign and synthetically reproduce it, we also requires information at a phonetic level. This multiple layer approach combines the phonetic and phonological levels. It is similar to the articulatory phonology concept proposed by Browman and Goldstein (1986)[18, quoted in], which unified two models of speech production by using the idea that the two models were different descriptive levels of the same system. However as Tatham[18] points out there are fundamental differences between the two levels, and therefore there needs to be a third level or bridge between the two. Similarly, this new notational system provides this extra level or bridge for sign production, by giving a word layer, which bridges the gap between the conceptual thought layer to the phonetical deed layer. The word layer is constrained by a series of empirical results from experimental, anatomical and visual investigations.

5.2 Practical Conclusion

The next step of the project is to use the nicene notation as a base for a synthesis and create a virtual reality signer. The mathematical nature of the notation will make it easy to parse and implement. Currently underway is a synthesis of BSL using poser and python scripting with the nicene notation as its underlying base. Future work will explore the use of the nicene notation to synthesise natural gesture.

References

1. British Deaf Association.: Dictionary of British Sign Language/English. Faber and Faber, London UK (1992)
2. Crombie Smith, KJW.: MSc Cognitive Science Project 2000 - The Virtual Fingerspeller. Unpublished, University of Birmingham UK (2000)
3. Crombie Smith, KJW.: Thesis Report 4 Unpublished, University of Birmingham UK (2001)
4. Crundall, D.E., Underwood, G.: Effects of experience and processing demands on visual information acquisition in drivers. Ergonomics. **41** (1998) 448–4584.
5. Edmondson, W.: A Notational Basis for Integrated Accounts of Gesture and Speech. In: Messing, L. (ed) Workshop on the Integration of Gesture in Language and Speech, 7-8 October 1996, University of Delaware. (1996), 135–144.
6. Edwards, A.D.: Progress in Sign Language Recognition. In: Proceedings of Gesture Workshop '97 Springer-Verlag Berlin (1997)
7. Kendon,A.: Gestures as illocutionary and discourse structure markers in Southern Italian conversation. Journal of Pragmatics Vol. 23. No. 3. (1995) 247–279
8. Kennaway, R.: Synthetic Animation of Deaf Signing Gestures. In: Wachsmuth, I., Sowa, T. (eds) 4th Workshop on Gesture and Sign Language based Human-Computer Interaction. Lecture Notes in Artifical Intelligence Vol. 2298 (2001)
9. Latham, K., Whitaker, D.: A Comparison of Word Recognition and Reading Performance in Foveal and Peripheral Vision. Vision Research Vol.36. No. 17. (1996) 2665–2674
10. Morris, D., Collet, P., Marsh, P., O'Shaughnessy, M., Cape, J.: Gestures: Their Origins and Distribution. Stein and Day, New York (1979)
11. Norkin, C.C., White, D.J.: Measurement of Joint Motion A Guide to Goniometry. F.A. Davis Company, Philadelphia (1995)
12. Pavlovic, V.I., Shrama, R., Huang, T.S.: Visual Interpretation of Hand Gestures for Human-Computer Interaction: A Review. IEEE Transactions on Pattern Analysis and Machine Intelligence, Vol. 19. No 7 (1997) 677–695
13. Siple, P.: Visual Constraints for Sign Language Communication. Sign Language Studies, **19** (1978) 95–110
14. Stokoe, W., Casterline, D., Croneberg, C.: A Dictionary of American Sign Language on Linguistic Principles. Linstok Press (1976)
15. Stokoe, W.: Sign language Structure. Annual Review of Anthropology, **9** (1980) 365–390
16. Sutton, V.: Lessons in SignWriting: Textbook and Workbook. 2nd edn. The Deaf Action Committee For SignWriting, La Jolla, C.A (1999)
17. Swisher, M.V., Christie, K., Miller, S.: The reception of signs in peripheral vision. Sign Language Studies, **63** (1989) 99–125
18. Tatham, M.: Articulatory Phonology, Task Dynamics and Computation Adequacy. In: Proceedings of the 1st ESCA Tutorial and Research Workshop on Speech Production Modelling. Grenoble: Institut de la Communication Parle, Universit Stendhal (1996) 141–144
19. http://www.signwriting.org/forums/linguistics/ling006.html
20. http://www.sign-lang.uni-hamburg.de/Projects/HamNoSys.html
21. http://members.home.net/dnewkirk/signfont/orthog.htm
22. http://members.home.net/dnewkirk/signfont/charchrt.htm
23. http://members-http-2.rwc1.sfba.home.net/dnewkirk/signfont/orthog.htm
24. http://psy.ucsd.edu/˜sanstis/SABlur.html
25. http://dictionary.reference.com

Gesture in Style

Han Noot and Zsófia Ruttkay

Center for Mathematics and Computer Science
1090 GB Amsterdam, The Netherlands
{Han.Noot,Zsofia.Ruttkay}@cwi.nl

Abstract. GESTYLE is a new markup language to annotate text which has to be spoken by Embodied Conversational Agents (ECA), to prescribe the usage of hand-, head- and facial gestures accompanying the speech in order to augment the communication. The annotation ranges from low level (e.g. perform a specific gesture) to high level (e.g. take turn in a conversation) instructions. On top of that, and central to GESTYLE is the notion of ***style*** which determines the gesture repertoire and the gesturing manner of the ECA. GESTYLE contains constructs to define and dynamically modify style. The low-level tags, prescribing specific gestures to be performed are generated automatically, based on the style definition and the high-level tags. By using GESTYLE, different aspects of gesturing of an ECA can be defined and tailored to the needs of different application situations or user groups.

1 Introduction

1.1 Motivations

Recently a lot of effort has been put into developing so-called embodied conversational agents [5] (ECAs). The believability of ECAs highly depends on their nonverbal communicational skills: the richness of the used modalities and gestures, and the correctness and consistency of choosing and performing a gesture, according to a given situation [10]. Also there is evidence, that the user's response to the ECA depends also on subtle characteristics like ethnicity and personality of the ECA [18, 29].

These observations motivated us to design a framework for the definition of different aspects of style, as manifest in nonverbal modalities. We are interested in how different nonverbal modalities can be used, together or as alternatives, to express some meaning. Hence, through the paper, we use the term **gesture** in a broad sense, covering meaningful signals of all the major nonverbal modalities of facial expressions, eye gaze, head and hand movement alone or in combination. After our previous work of developing a framework to define a subtle, individual facial expressions [24], the focus of our current research [25] is on hand gestures. They are the most noticable of the other modalities, and appropriate to demonstrate stylistic differences.

Different persons, depending on their cultural, social and professional background, and their personality, use different gestures in communication [13, 17]. The difference can be in (not) using specific gestures, preferring some modalities above others (e.g. rather use facial gestures than hand gestures) as well as in the fine details of performing a gesture. The declarative definition of style of an ECA should cover all these

A. Camurri and G. Volpe (Eds.): GW 2003, LNAI 2915, pp. 324–337, 2004.

aspects. Once style is defined, we also need a mechanism to instruct the ECA to act according to this style.

1.2 Related Work

The synthesis of hand gestures [4, 7, 12, 14] and their role in multimodal presentation for different application domains [6, 16] has gained much attention recently. Particularly, there have been XML-based markup languages developed to script multimodal behavior, as MPML [26], VHML [27], APML[8], RRL [21], CML and AML [2], MURML [15], developed for specifying non-verbal behavior for ECAs. Each of these representation languages act either at the discourse and communicative functions level (APML, RRL, CML, MURML) using tags like "belief-relation", "emphasis", "performative", or at the signal level (AML, VHML) with tags like "smile", "turn head left". In each case the semantics of the control tags are given implicitly, expressed in terms of the parameters (MPEG-4 FAP or BAP, muscle contraction, joint angles and the like) used for generating the animation of the expressive facial- or hand gestures.

As far as we know, style has not been addressed in nonverbal communication for ECAs, only considering the style of the used language [30]. But there have been ECAs developed sensitive to social role [23], with personality [20] and emotions [3].

1.3 GESTYLE in a Nutshell

We have designed and implemented a new, XML compliant language called GESTYLE. It can be used to ***define*** style and to instruct the ECA to ***express*** some meaning nonverbally (too). The novelty of GESTYLE is that it deals with the concept of ***style***. For the ECA, its style defines what gestures it "knows", and what are the habits of using these gestures, concerning intended meaning, modalities and subtle characteristics of the gestures. GESTYLE thus allows the usage of high-level meaning tags, which get translated, according to the defined style of the ECA to the low-level gesture tags specifying the appropriate gestures to be performed and may be to some parameter values (like available modalities), see Fig.1.

In most of the cases, an ECA has to produce speech accompanied by nonverbal gestures, hence the markup tags are used to annotate the text to be spoken. The characteristics of the synthetic speech of the ECA are dealt with elsewhere [28] in detail; we sum it up in Chapter 6.2.

GESTYLE is hierarchically organized: At the atomic level there are so-called **basic gestures** (e.g. right-hand beat, nod). Basic gestures can be combined into **composite gestures** (e.g. two-hand beat, right-hand beat and nod) by **gesture expressions.** At the next level, the **meanings** denote the communicative acts (e.g. show happiness, take turn in a conversation) which can be expressed by some gestures. A meaning is mapped to one or more gesture expressions, each specifying an alternative way to convey the same meaning. The mapping of meanings to alternatives of (usually composite) gestures are given as entries of **style dictionaries**. A style dictionary contains a collection of meanings pertinent to a certain style (e.g. a style dictionary for "teacher", "Dutchman" etc.).

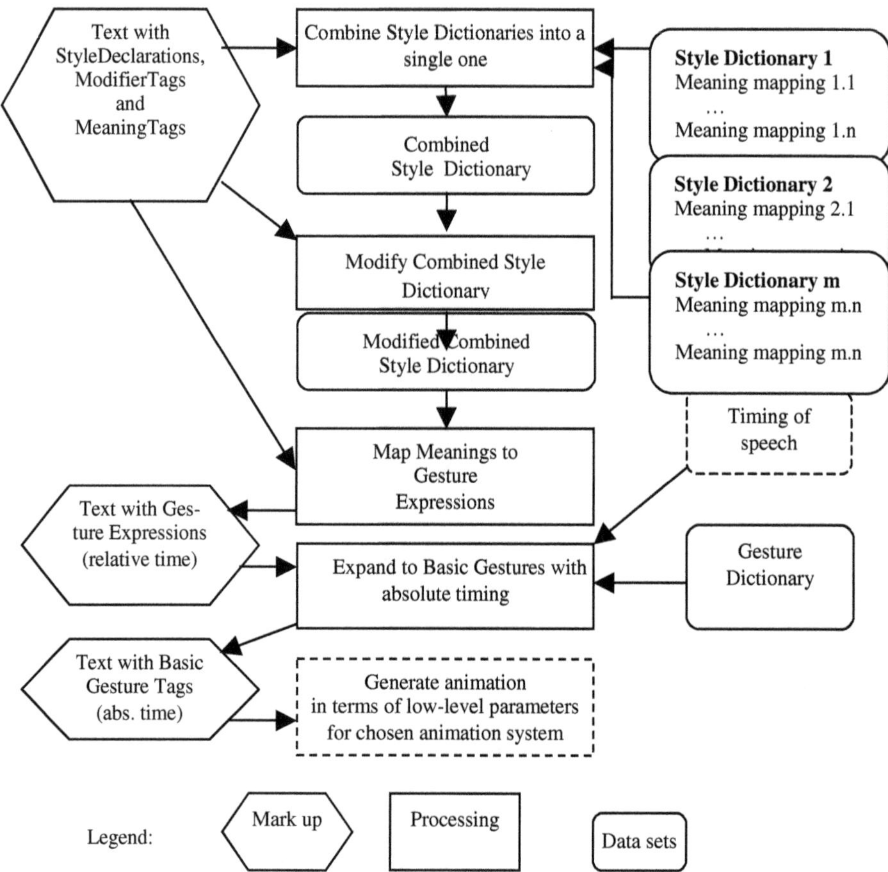

Fig. 1. Stages in the interpretation of text with GESTYLE tags

Separate from this hierarchy GESTYLE supports the **manner definition** specifying motion characteristics of gestures (e.g. whether the motion is smooth or angular) and the **modality usage** specifying preference for the use of certain modalities (e.g. use more/less hand gestures). Finally there is the (static) **style declaration,** which specifies the style of the ECA. A style is declared by specifying a combination of style dictionaries plus optionally a manner definition and a modality usage element. The intended usage of GESTYLE is the exploitation of the power of declared style: a text, marked up with the same meaning tags, can be presented with different gestures, according to the specified style of the ECA.

In the remainder of this paper, we will discuss GESTYLE's elements in detail. When introducing the constructs of GESTYLE, we use BNF notation instead of the lengthier XML notation. The examples are given in XML. The variables and "string values" of the GESTYLE language are given in different font, when referred to in explanatory text.

2 Gestures

A **gesture** is some motion involving one or more of the modalities like face, hands and body, used for the expression of some meaning. In GESTYLE a hierarchical modality model is used. E.g. modality "upper extremities" contains "left upper extremity" and "right upper extremity". The "left upper extremity" contains "left arm" and "left hand" etc. A modality attribute can have as value a set of values from this hierarchy. Furthermore there are predefined sets like "hands" for ("left hand", "right hand").

2.1 Basic Gestures

Basic gestures refer to a single facial feature (eyes, eyebrows, mouth) or a single other modality (right/left arm, hands, ...). Examples of basic gestures are:

eye gesture:	look up, look left, look right,...
head gesture:	head nod, head shake, turn head left,...
hand shape gesture:	hand point, hand fist, hand open, hand one, hand two, ...

From the point of view of GESTYLE, basic gestures are atomic units, uniquely identified by their name. It is up to the "back end" animation system to make sense of them and generate the intended animation.

2.2 Gesture Expressions

Gestures may be defined by **gesture expressions**, built up from basic gestures. For example, to express greeting, one can define compound gestures, like: the sequential execution of "smile" and a "head nod", or the parallel execution of "right arm to right of head" and "open right hand". The syntax for composition is:

```
<gesture_expression> :     <basic_gesture> |
                           <gesture_name> |
                           <gesture_expression> par <gesture_expression> |
                           <gesture_expression> seq <gesture_expression> |
                           repeat (<gesture_expression>, <count>) |
                           (<gesture_expression>)
<gesture_assignment>:      <gesture_name> = <gesture_expression>
<gesture_name>:            An alphanumerical identifier
<count>:                   An integer
```

Gestures are combined into gesture expressions by using the par, seq or repeat operators, to indicate parallel, sequential or repeated execution of the operands.

2.3 Gesture Attributes and Timing of Gestures

In an annotated text basic and composite gestures are indicated by Gesture tags, as in:

```
Do you want <Gesture Name="three" Symmetry ="right"> three </Gesture> or
<Gesture Name="two" Symmetry =left>two tickets ?</Gesture>
```

It is also possible to refer to a gesture expression which is defined "on the fly", by a GestureExpression tag, see below:

```
Well, <GestureExpression MotionManner="gracious"><UseGest Name="look_up"/><PAR/>
<REPEAT Number="3"> <UseGest Name="rub_nose" Symmetry ="right"/> </REPEAT>
I must think ...</GestureExpression>
```

A Gesture or GestureExpression tag may have the following attributes and values:

<intensity>:	***exaggerated | intense | normal | modest | little | none***
<duration>:	***long | normal | short***
<start_time>:	***integer***
<gesture_length>:	***integer***
<noise>:	***smooth | trembling***
<motion_manner>:	***jerky | gracious | sudden_on | sudden_off | sudden_on_off***
<symmetry>:	***lft_more | rght_ more | lft_dimmed | rght_dimmed | left | right | balanced***

These attributes indicate how the gesture's motion is performed, e.g. with "exaggerated" or "normal" intensity, "smooth" or "trembling" noise, etc. If the attributes are not given, some default values are assumed. The start_time, gesture_length and duration attributes are set automatically, based on information from the TTS system based on the position of the opening and closing gesture tags in the text. If the duration is to be given explicitly (qualitatively or quantitatively), XML's "empty element" notation should be used with the duration or gesture_length attribute set, see the following examples:

```
Do you want <Gesture Name="three", gesture_length="1000"/>three tickets?
Do you want <Gesture Name="three", duration="long"/>three tickets?
```

2.4 Gesture Repertoire

All gestures have to be named, listed and defined (if they are not basic) in a **gesture repertoire**. The example below also demonstrates how the semantics of the <PAR/> and <SEQ/> operators can be fine-tuned:

```
<GestureRepertoire>
   <DefGest Name="Nod" GestureLength = "200"/>
   <DefGest Name="Beat" GestureLength = "500" Symmetry="right"/>
      ...
   <DefGest Name="NodAndBeat" gesture_length = "500">
         <UseGest Name="Nod" /><PAR/><UseGest Name="blink"/></DefGest>
   <DefGest Name="NodAndBeat1" gesture_length = "500">
           <UseGest Name="Beat" sub_start_time = "0" /><PAR/>
           <UseGest Name="Nod" sub_start_time="100"/></DefGest>
</GestureRepertoire>
```

3 Usage of Gestures to Express Meaning

3.1 Meaning Tags and Their Mapping to Gestures

Meaning tags are available to annotate the text with communicative functions without specifying what gestures should be used to express them. There are meaning tags to indicate the emotional or cognitive state of the ECA, to emphasize something said, to indicate location, shape or size of an object referred to, to organize the flow of communication by indicating listening or intention of turn taking/giving, etc., as discussed in [22]. From the point of view of the GESTYLE language, all what we assume is that meaning tags are uniquely identified by their name.

A **meaning mapping definition** contains alternative ways of expressing the same meaning by different gestures, each with a certain probability. At runtime these probabilities, taking into account also the fact that some modalities might be in use in a given situation, determine how a meaning is actually expressed. Meaning mappings are defined as elements of style dictionaries.

<meaning_mapping_definition>:	**<combination_mode><emotional_speech>^{opt} (<modifier>^{opt}<gesture_expression><probability>)+**
<combination_mode>:	***dominant* | *combine***
<probability>:	**real**
<modifier>:	**<manner_definition> | <modality_usage> | <manner_definition><modality_usage>**

The core of this definition is that a meaning mapping definition lists one or more gesture expressions, each with an associated probability. Each gesture expression is a way to express the meaning, and the probability indicates the preference for this way of expressing it. The combination mode is used in the process of handling multiple mapping definitions for the meaning from different style dictionaries (see below). The optional modifier follows the syntax and semantics of the modifiers as discussed extensively in Chapter 4. An example of a meaning mapping definition in GESTYLE follows below:

```
<Meaning Name = "emphasize" CombinationMode = "DOMINANT">
<GestureSpec>
    <MannerDefinition intensity="intense"/><UseGest Name="nod_and_beat"/>
    <Probability P="0.7"/>
</GestureSpec>
<GestureSpec>
    <MannerDefinition motion_manner="sudden_on"/><UseGest Name="eyebrow_raise"/>
  <Probability P="0.3"/>
</GestureSpec>
</Meaning>
```

Once the mapping of a meaning is given (in a style dictionary, see below), the Name of the meaning (and certain attributes) can be used to mark up a text, also in a nested way:

```
<Meaning Name=”angry” intensity = “intense”> I have asked you already <Meaning Name= “em-
pasis"> five times </Meaning> to tell the number of tickets you want. </Meaning>
```

3.2 Style Dictionaries

For every aspect of style (e.g. culture, profession, personality) there are different style dictionaries reflecting the difference in gestures used to convey a meaning or the difference in motion characteristics of the same gesture, used by people belonging to different groups from the given aspect. E.g. someone with American culture and someone with Japanese culture, or someone with the profession of brain-surgeon or someone with the profession of woodcutter gestures differently. They may use different gestural signs, their preference for using hand or facial gestures may differ, and their manner of performing gestures too. In a **style dictionary** the gesturing characteristics are given, typical for an individual, professional or cultural group, or people of certain age, sex or personality.

A style dictionary is a collection of meaning mapping definitions (see 3.1). In the example below, given in GESTYLE format, the two dictionaries contain different gestures for expressing emphasis:

```
<StyleDictionary Name = "extrovert">
<Meaning Name = "emphasize" CombinationMode = "DOMINANT">
    <GestureSpec>
        <MannerDefinition intensity="intense"/>
        <UseGest Name="nod_and_beat"/><PAR><UseGest Name="LookAtPerson"/>
        <Probability P="0.7"/>
    </GestureSpec>
    <GestureSpec>
        <MannerDefinition motion_manner="sudden_on"/>
        <UseGest Name="beat"/>
        <Probability P="0.3"/>
    </GestureSpec>
</Meaning>
<Meaning
    ...
</StyleDictionary>

<StyleDictionary Name = "introvert">
<Meaning Name = "emphasize" CombinationMode = "COMBINE">
    <GestureSpec>
        <MannerDefinition intensity="low"/>
        <UseGest Name="eyebrow_raise"/>
        <Probability P="0.7"/>
    </GestureSpec>
    ...
</StyleDictionary>
```

3.3 Style Declaration

The style of an ECA is defined once, and has effect on the entire conversation by the ECA. The style of an ECA is given by the dictionaries for (cultural, professional, age,…) group characteristic of the ECA. These dictionaries may contain conflicting prescriptions for gesture usage, both concerning gestures expressing a given meaning and the manner of gesturing. Hence there should be instructions in the style definition for an ECA for handling these conflicts.

A **style declaration** consists of two parts: the required **style dictionary usage (SDU)** part and the optional **modifier usage (MU)** part, see the syntax below. The style declaration is static, it cannot be changed. This is in accordance with the view that the factors which are decisive in deciding which gestures are to be used by an ECA, do not change during the short time of a conversation. Its syntax is:

```
<style_declaration>:        <style_dictionary_usage><modifier_usage> opt
<style_dictionary_usage>:   (<aspect>=<value> style_dictionary_name)*
                            (aspect=<value> style_dictionary_name <weight>)*
<aspect>:                   culture | gender | profession | ...
<value>:                    string
<weight>:                   real
<modifier_usage>:           <manner_definition> | <modality_usage> |
                            <manner_definition><modality_usage>
```

A style dictionary usage consists of two lists of style dictionaries: a list of dictionaries with associated weights and an ordered list without weights. They define the mapping of a meaning to gestures in the following way:

- The first definition of the meaning encountered in the style dictionaries of the ordered list is used. Hence ordering introduces dominance of meaning definitions.
- If the meaning definition is not found in the dictionaries of the ordered list, it is taken from the weighted list. If it does occur more than once there, definitions are merged on the basis of the weights (see 4.2).

Let's look at an example which illustrates the power of style dictionary usage. In order to have an ECA which gestures according to the style typical of a certain culture, we must have as the first element of the style declaration something like:

<style aspect="culture" dict="Hungarian"/>

If no other dictionaries follow, then our ECA will gesture as a "typical Hungarian". However, if we want to endow the ECA with some personal, idiosyncratic gesturing style too, this should be given in a second dictionary.

<style aspect="individual" dict="indiv_dict_1" />

But because of the ordering of the two dictionaries, in case of conflicts the cultural etiquette will be the one followed, the entries in the personal dictionaries are considered as "extensions" to the ones in the cultural dictionary. The result of merging the entries in the given (ordered and weighted) lists of dictionaries is the so-called combined style dictionary (CSD), with derived definitions for the meanings the ECA can use. Finally, a style declaration can have one manner definition and one modality usage element. When present, they operate on gestures in the combined style dictionary.

3.4 Combining Style Dictionaries

From a style declaration, the resulting **combined style dictionary** (CSD) is produced according to the following procedure:

- Apply all modifiers in meanings in every style dictionary to their gesture expression.
- Form the CSD dictionary according to the followings:
  - Include all meanings from the ordered list of style dictionaries (if not empty). If a meaning occurs only once take that one, otherwise take the one from the style dictionary which is the first one in the sequence containing that meaning.
  - In the weighted list of style dictionaries look for meanings which are not yet included in CSD and which have their dominant attribute set. Include those meanings in CSD. If a specific meaning is declared dominant more than once, just take the first occurrence, ignore the others and warn the user about the conflict.
  - Include all other meanings from the weighted list, provided they are not yet in CSD. If a meaning occurs only once, include it, if it occurs more then once, merge its definitions as follows: Create a new meaning definition by including all the gesture expressions from the meanings to be merged in it. The new

probabilities are calculated by initially giving every gesture expression probability p * w where w is the weight of the style dictionary it came from and p is its probability in that directory and then renormalizing these probabilities by dividing each of them by the sum of all the probabilities.

4 Dynamical Changes to Style

The style of the ECA may change in course of time, due to change in its emotional or physical state, or changes in the situation. E.g. if excited, the ECA tends to perform more expressive gestures, and even the dominance of styles may change. For instance, he may “forget” that he is in a public space where the “public social” style is expected, and will start to use his own personal, informal style. The change of situation may have consequences on modality selection (e.g. hands full, conversation partner is not watching) as well as on the dominance of styles (e.g. private dinner versus business dinner) and even on the motions used in displaying gestures (e.g. smooth when relaxed or angular when agitated).

The (static) style definition is given once, at the beginning of the text which the ECA is supposed to utter. To take care of style changes, the **dynamical modifiers** occur interwoven with the text however, generated either by hand or by some reasoning module. We allow three types of modifiers, for indicating changes in:

- “respecting different styles”,
- usage of modalities, and
- manner characteristics of the gestures.

Loosely speaking, the modifiers change some parameters of the static style declaration and of the meaning definitions in style dictionaries. In general, when a modifier occurs the CSD is recalculated using the given static style declaration, the modifier in question as well as all previously given, still valid modifiers pertinent to other parameters. As a result of a new CSD, the ECA's style has changed.

4.1 Dynamical Modification of Style Dominance

An ECA's gesture repertoire may change according to the situation. E.g. if the listener turns out to be a superior of the speaker, he will probably adjust his style to more polite. But if he gets very angry, he may fall back to his own, less polite style.

In order to handle such situations, GESTYLE allows to swap two elements (style dictionaries) of the <ordered elements> in the static style declaration, or to change the weights of the <weighted elements>. All this can be done by the dominance modifier. In GESTYLE it looks like:

```
<Dominance Modifier dict="StyleDictionaryName", weight="real number"
putbefore="StyleDictionaryName" putafter="StyleDictionaryName"/>
```

The dict attribute is required. It's value is the name of a style dictionary which occurs in the style declaration. By using one of the other attributes, one can change weight of this dictionary or put it in some other place in the <ordered elements> sequence of the style declaration.

4.2 Dynamical Modification of Modality Usage

The available modalities may change in course of a situation. E.g. if the ECA has to hold an object in his right hand, he cannot use it also for gesturing, the left-hand and/or other modalities should take over its gesturing role (e.g when hands full, directional pointing is often done by head among humans). But changes in the environment may require adaptation of modality usage from the ECA. E.g. if the noise level increases, it makes sense to increase the preference for hand and other nonverbal gestures, even if the ECA is an introvert, normally non-gesturing character. The changes in modality usage are indicated by tags of the following syntax, using percentage of the required changes as values for some modalities:

```
<ModalityUsage left_hand="-10%", right_hand="+8%", eyes=".…./>
```

The modalities to be changed are out of the set of values discussed in 2. The combined style dictionary (CSD) is recalculated, according to the required change in the modality usage. Roughly speaking, the probability of using gestures of the given modality is increased (decreased) as required, and the change is compensated by proportional changes in the probabilities of other alternative gestures for a meaning, not using the affected modality.

4.3 Dynamical Modification of Manner

The **manner definition** allows to change the values of attributes for certain gestures in a global way. As some characteristic of gestures like intensity or motion manner may change in the course of time (due to changes e.g. in the physical or emotional state of the ECA), the manner definition will be dynamically recalculated during the conversation to reflect these changes. The effected gestures are the ones which use the modality given in the MannerDefinition. In GESTYLE form:

```
<MannerDefinition modality="hands" intensity=.../>
```

The <MannerDefinition>, if used for dynamical changes, must have its modality attribute set, which can have values like "left_hand", "right_hand", "left_brow", "right_brow" etc. Furthermore it can use the intensity, noise, motion_manner and symmetry attributes with the same semantics and the same values as the corresponding attributes of the <Gesture> element.

5 An Example

The following example shows GESTYLE in operation. The text is borrowed from the award winning Aardman animation [1]. It starts with a style declaration, followed by text marked up with meanings and a gesture.

```
<?xml version="1.0"?>
<!DOCTYPE emotive_text SYSTEM "EmotiveText.dtd">
<aardman_text>
1.  <StyledText>
2.  <StyleDeclaration>
3.      <weighted elements>
4.          <style aspect="social status" dict="simple person" weight = "2"/>
```

```
5.        <style aspect=”culture” dict=”Brazilian”  weight = “2”/>
6.        <style aspect=”gender” dict =”male” weight=”1”/>
7.     </weighted elements>
8.  </StyleDeclaration>
9.  <TextBody>
10. <Meaning Name="sad">
11.     <Meaning Name="start_turn"> Well, </Meaning>
12.     <Meaning Name="thinking">I would like to live in a </Meaning>
13.     <Meaning Name="emphasis"> hot </Meaning> country.  I need the
14.     <Meaning Name="space">space, </Meaning> with
15.     <Meaning Name="wide_location_above"> blue skies, </Meaning>
16.     <Meaning Name="remembering">... that I can see
17.     <Meaning Name="point_location_above">the sun </Meaning> every day,
18. </Meaning>
19. </!-- The speaker becomes excited -->
20.     <MannerDefinition modality=”hands” intensity=+2>
21.       all right, that I have a <Meaning Name="likes">
22.           <Meaning Name="emphasis">nice </Meaning> weather, that  I can just have a
23.           <Meaning Name="emphasis"> nice water, </Meaning>
24.       </Meaning>
25.       <Meaning Name="address_listener">you know, </Meaning>
26.       to <Meaning Name="diving ">dive</Meaning>, to
27. <Meaning Name="swimming "> swim</Meaning>.
28.     </MannerDefinition >
29.     It means a <Meaning Name="emphasis" intensity=”high”> tropical country. </Meaning>
30.     <Meaning Name="give_turn">
31.       <Meaning Name="rejection"> Not in an island, </Meaning>
32.       <Gesture Name="I”m not crazy"> a cold </Gesture> one.
33.     </Meaning>
34. </TextBody>
35. </StyledText>
36.       </aardman_text>
```

The above annotated text has several meaning tags, and a single gesture tag, in line 32. While the final gesturing expressing the indicated meanings is decided on the basis of the style declaration (line 2-8) and the meaning mappings in accordance with the style dictionaries, the (only) explicit gesture tag will result in a specific gesture to be performed.

Note that if the text is “compiled” to one with low-level gesture tags, the result may be different at each compilation. This might sound odd, but reflects the fact that humans do not repeat a sentence and gesture in the same way.

It is indicated that the ECA is telling the story first in a sad mood (line 10-18). Then he becomes excited (line 19), which has an effect on using his hands more for gesturing (line 20).

The gestures he uses are determined by the style declaration, where the ECA is said to be a simple male Brazilian. The possible conflicts in gesturing, due to these categories, are resolved according to the preferences indicated by the weights.

If we want a different character to utter the same text, all what we need to do is to modify some or all of the tags which influence the gesturing. By changing the elements of the style declaration (e.g. changing the culture to Greek, or the gender to female, or the social status to academic) the meaning mappings and the manner of used gestures will be changed. It is also possible to add further elements to the style declaration, to express additional aspects (e.g. personality) of the speaker. By changing the weights, our ECA will gesture more or less according to the specified aspects.

If we change the MannerDefinition in line 20, we can make a character who's speciality is to do more facial expressions when excited.

On the other had, once the dictionaries for a style definition are available, we do not need to worry, not even to know, about the gestures the ECA will perform, we may use exclusively meaning tags. These tags may be automatically generated by the syntactical and semantical analysis of the text to be spoken, or put in by hand (like in the example too).

6 Discussion

6.1 Implementation

A prototype implementation of GESTYLE is available to demonstrate the effectiveness of the concepts underlying GESTYLE, in particular its style aspect. First there is a renderer independent part, implemented in XSL (using the Apache's xalan XSL style sheet processor [31]) , Java and the Flexvoice [32] TTS system. This layer produces a text annotated only with timed basic gestures in XML style. The gestures from this text must be sent to some system capable of displaying them.

We have interfaces to two systems:

- The Chartoon [19] system is suited in particular for the animation of 2-D (cartoon-style) faces which can show lip-sync visual speech. So this system enables us to experiment in particular with GESTYLE's capabilities to address the "modalities" speech and facial expressions.
- The STEP[9] system, a system based on distributed logic programming which is able to control a H-Anim compliant [11] 3D full-body ECAs. This system allows us in the first place to experiment with GESTYLE's capabilities to address "body-language" aspects.

6.2 Integration with Speech Style

GESTYLE also has a "speech style" component which we sum up only here. The idea and hierarchical structure of the speech tags [28] are similar to gesture tags. One can easily incorporate the highest-level tags of the speech markup language, and map meanings to these tags of the speech modality too. E.g. emphasis can be then expressed by speech only, speech and some facial and/or hand gestures, etc. The acoustic and intonation characteristics of the generated speech are the responsibility of the TTS system. It is also possible to extend the concept of gesture repertoire to vocal repertoire, and to define the vocal and intonation style of an ECA.

6.3 Further Steps and Research Issues

A naturally arising issue is to be able to give in a declarative way the effect of possible dynamical changes in the state of the ECA and in the environment. With some extension of GESTYLE, this would allow that the insertion of a tag indicating that the

ECA turns sad, would result in appropriate motion manner and modality usage modifications (slow, limited motions, hand gestures less preferred). The identification of the dynamical situation variables, and their effect on style, are of the real issues.

We have not solved yet the problem of parameterization of gestures with non-GESTYLE parameters. Binding of parameters to locations of the environment (e.g. to be able to make the ECA look at the listener's or of some object's location) would allow some interactive nonverbal behaviour. We are working along this line, experimenting with an ECA in VR environment.

Our framework lacks a model of and feedback from the user. In real-life conversations, this is a major source of "choosing the right style". The user (listener) could be introduced into the GESTYLE framework as a decisive factor for tuning the style.

Last but not least: in order to perform experiments on the power of our approach and on the effect of styled ECAs, one has to design style dictionaries for different aspects. As a first step in this direction, we plan to make a few dictionaries for different styles for ECAs in limited application domains.

References

1. Aardman Studios, Creature Comforts, URL:http://atomfilms.shockwave.com/af/content/atom_221
2. Arafa, Y., Kamyab, K., Kshirsagar, S., Guye-Vuilleme, A., Thalmann, N. "Two Approaches to Scripting Character Animation", *Porc. of the AAMAS Workshop on "Embodied conversational agents – Let's specify and evaluate them!"*, 2002, Bologna.
3. Ball, G., Breese, J. "Emotion and personality in a conversational agent", In: Cassell et al. 2000, pp. 189-219.
4. Cassell, J. "A framework for gesture generation and interpretation" In: Cipolla, R., Pentland, A. (eds.) *Computer Vision for Human-machine Interaction*, Cambridge University Press, 1998.
5. Cassell J., Sullivan J., Prevost S., Churchill E. *Embodied Conversational Agents*, MIT Press, Cambridge, MA. 2000.
6. Cassell, J., Bickmore, T., Billinghurst, M., Campbell, L., Chang, K., Vilhjálmsson, H., Yan, H. "Embodiment in Conversational Interfaces: Rea", *ACM CHI 99 Conference Proceedings*, Pittsburgh, PA, 1999. pp. 520-527.
7. Chi D., Costa M., Zhao L., Badler N. "The EMOTE Model for Effort and Shape", *Proc. of Siggraph*, 2000. pp. 173-182.
8. De Carolis, Carofiglio, Bilvi, M., Pelachaud, C. "APML, a Mark-up Language for Believable Behavior Generation" *Porc. of the AAMAS Workshop on "Embodied conversational agents – Let's specify and evaluate them!"*, 2002, Bologna.
9. Eliens, A., Huang, Z., Visser, C. "A platform for Embodied Conversational Agents based on Distributed Logic Programming", *Porc. of the AAMAS Workshop on "Embodied conversational agents – Let's specify and evaluate them!"*, 2002, Bologna.
10. Gratch, J., Rickel, J., Andre, J., Badler, N., Cassell, J., Petajan, E. "Creating Interactive Virtual Humans: Some Assembly Required", *IEEE Intelligent Systems*, July/August 2002, pp. 54-63.
11. H-anim 2002, Humanoid animation working group: http://www.hanim. org/Specifications/H-Anim1.1/
12. Hartmann, B., Mancini, M., Pelachaud, C. "Formational parameters and adaptive prototype instantiation for MPEG-4 compliant gesture synthesis", *Proc. of Computer Animation 2002*, IEEE Computer Society Press, pp. 111-119.

13. Kendon A. "Human gesture", In: Ingold T. and Gibson K. (eds.) *Tools, Language and Intelligence*, Cambridge University Press. 1993.
14. Kopp, S., Wachsmuth, I. "Planning and motion control in lifelike gesture: a refined approach", *Post-proceedings of Computer Animation 2000*. IEEE Computer Society Press, 2000. pp. 92-97.
15. Krandsted, A., Kopp, S., Wachsmuth, I. "MURML: A Multimodal Utterance Representation Markup Language for Conversational Agents", *Porc. of the AAMAS Workshop on "Embodied conversational agents – Let's specify and evaluate them!"*, 2002, Bologna.
16. Lester, J., Voerman, J., Towns, S., Callaway, C. "Deictic believability: Coordinated gesture, locomotion and speech in lifelike pedagogical agents", *Applied AI*, Vol. 13. No. 4/5. 1999. pp. 383-414.
17. McNeill D., *Hand and Mind: What Gestures Reveal about Thought*. The University of Chicago Press. 1991.
18. Nass C., Isbister K., Lee E-J. "Truth is beauty: Researching embodied conversational agents," In: Cassell et al. 2000. pp. 374-402.
19. Noot H., Ruttkay Zs. *CharToon 2.0 Manual*, CWI Report INS-R0004, 2000. Amsterdam.
20. Perlin K. "Real time responsive animation with personality", *IEEE Transactions on Visualization and Computer Graphics*, Vol. 1. No. 1. 1995.
21. Piwek, P., Krenn, B. Schröder, M. Grice, M., Baumann, S. Pirker, H. "RRL: A Rich Representation Language for the Description of Agent Behaviour in NECA". *Proceedings of the AAMAS workshop on "Embodied conversational agents - let's specify and evaluate them!* ", Bologna, Italy. 2002.
22. Poggi I. "Mind Markers", In: Mueller C. and Posner R. (eds): *The Semantics and Pragmatics of Everyday Gestures*, Berlin Verlag Arno Spitz, 2001.
23. Prendinger H., Ishizuka M. "Social role awareness in animated agents", *Proc. of Autonomous Agents Conference*, 270-277, Montreal, Canada. 2001.
24. Ruttkay, Zs. "Constraint-based facial animation", *Int. Journal of Constraints*, 2001. Vol. 6. pp. 85-113.
25. Ruttkay Zs., Pelachaud, C., Poggi, I., Noot H. "Excercises of Syle for Virtual Humans", In: L. Canamero, R. Aylett eds (forthcoming 2004), Animating Expressive Characters for Social Interactions. John Benjamins Publishing Co., Advances in Consciousness Research Series.
26. Tsutsui, T. Saeyor, S., Ishizuka, M. "MPML: A Multimodal Presentation Markup Language with Character Agent Control Functions", *Proc.(CD-ROM) WebNet 2000 World Conf. on the WWW and Internet*, San Antonio, Texas. 2000.
27. Virtual Human Markup Language (VHML) http://www.vhml.org
28. Van Moppes, V. *Improving the quality of synthesized speech through mark-up of input text with emotions*, Master Thesis, VU, Amsterdam, 2002.
29. Walker, J., Sproull, L., Subramani, R. "Using a human face in an interface", *Proc. of CHI'94*, pp. 85-91. 1994.
30. Walker, M., Cahn, J., Whittaker, S. "Improvising linguistic style: Social and affective bases for agent personality", *Proc. of Autonomous Agents Conference*. 1997.
31. http://www.apache.org/
32. http://www.flexvoice.com/

Gestural Mind Markers in ECAs

Isabella Poggi[1], Catherine Pelachaud[2], and E. Magno Caldognetto[3]

[1] Dipartimento di Scienze dell'Educazione, Università Roma Tre
poggi@uniroma3.it
[2] LINC, Paragraphe, IUT de Montreuil - Université de Paris 8
c.pelachaud@iut.univ-paris8.fr
[3] Istituto di Fonetica e Dialettologia, CNR - Padova
magno@csrf.pd.cnr.it

Abstract. We aim at creating Embodied Conversational Agents (ECAs) able to communicate multimodally with a user or with other ECAs. In this paper we focus on the Gestural Mind Markers, that is, those gestures that convey information on the Speaker's Mind; we present the ANVIL-SCORE, a tool to analyze and classify multimodal data that is a semantically augmented version of Kipp's ANVIL [1]. Thanks to an analysis through the ANVIL-SCORE of a set Gestural Mind Markers taken from a corpus of video-taped data, we classify gestures both on the level of the signal and of the meaning; finally we show how they can be implemented in an ECA System, and how they can be integrated with facial and bodily communication.

1 Introduction

In the works aimed at constructing Embodied Conversational Agents that make communicative gestures, the gestures produced are usually classified as deictics, iconics, beats, metaphorics, emblems, affect displays or adaptors, thus following two of the most famous typologies of gestures, by Ekman and Friesen [2] and McNeill [3]. These typologies distinguish gestures as to their direct or indirect similarity to the referent (iconic and metaphoric), or to their quasi-linguistic status (emblems), or their making reference to spatial contextual information (deictic), or their function in scanning the syntactic structure of the sentence, or their mentioning particular semantic contents (affect displays). These are all quite different criteria of classification, and only the last one takes the meaning of the gesture into account. Our aim in this paper is to show how gestures can be generated in an Embodied Agent starting from the meanings the Agent has to convey. We focus on a particular subset of gestures that share a particular type of meaning: gestures informing on the Speaker's Mind.

In the work of analyzing everyday gestures, some scholars ([4,5]) have specifically focused on some gestures that do not have referential meanings, but have an illocutionary or discourse marker function. Others [6] distinguish three basic kinds of information that we can convey by any communicative signal - words, sentences, prosody and intonation, gestures, gaze, facial expression, posture, body movement. A speaker (or any sender of a communicative message)

A. Camurri and G. Volpe (Eds.): GW 2003, LNAI 2915, pp. 338–349, 2004.

in communicating may provide information about the World, one's Identity, or one's Mind. Information on the world concerns the concrete and abstract entities and events of the world outside the speaker (objects, persons, organisms, events, their place and time); Information on the Speaker's Identity concerns his/her age, sex, personality, culture roots; while Information on the Speaker's Mind concerns the Speaker's mental states: his/her goals, beliefs and emotions. These kinds of information may be conveyed in verbal and nonverbal systems of communication by means of specific signals called Mind Markers, more specifically, Belief Markers, Goal Markers and Emotion Markers. Poggi [6] proposed a taxonomy of Mind Markers that proved useful in order to classify signals in various modalities, showing that also facial and gaze signals bear information on the Speaker's beliefs, goals and emotions [7].

In this paper we focus on the Gestural Mind Markers, that is, those gestures that convey information on the Speaker's Mind; we present the ANVIL-SCORE, a tool to analyze and classify multimodal data that is a semantically augmented version [8] of Kipp's ANVIL [1]. Thanks to an analysis of a set Gestural Mind Markers taken from a corpus of video-taped data carried on through the ANVIL-SCORE, and to the use of a set of parameters to describe gestures both on the level of the signal and of the meaning, we finally show how Gestural Mind Markers can be implemented in an Embodied Conversational Agent System[1]. In particular, we show how the analysis of video corpus provides ways to establish the correspondence between meaning and signal and allow us to generate an animation given as in input a text enhanced with communicative information.

2 State of the Art

ECAs are receiving more and more attention not only in academic world but also in industry. Several systems have been developed embedded ECAs in different applications. To name a few, they may be pedagogical agents [9], web agents [10], kiosk presenter [11], medical councelor [12]. To reach believability and naturalness as well as to engage users, agents should exhibit a variety of communicative and emotional behaviors. GestureJack was one of the first attempt to create ECAs. Cassell et al. [13] animate two conversational agents dialoguing with each others by automatically generating facial expression, gaze and hand gestures synchronized with speech. Communicative gestures were classified following McNeill's taxonomy into iconic gestures, metaphorics, deictics and beats. The gestures were specified along three parts: hand shape, wrist, and arm position. Each of these parts is defined by specific parameters and is controlled by its own engine. Gestures are stored in a library in their parameterized symbolic representation. The speed and any temporal values (preparation phase, stroke, and relaxation phase) of a gesture are instantiated to be synchronized with the speech. Carmen's Bright IDEAS [14] is an interactive drama where characters exhibit gestures based on their emotional states and personality traits. Through

[1] We would like to thank Bjoern Hartmann and Maurizio Mancini for their indispensable input during the development of Gesture Engine and Planner.

a feedback mechanism a gesture made by of a character may modulate her affective state. When several items of information arise from the same body part, a mechanism is used to select which body part will display which information while maintaining consistency of the emotional state. Cassell and her colleagues have proposed several ECAs' settings. REA, the real estate agent [15], is an interactive agent able to converse with a user in real-time. REA exhibits refined interactional behaviors such as gestures for feedback or turn-taking functions. Cassell and Stone [16] designed a multi-modal manager whose role is to supervise the distribution of behaviors across the several channels (verbal, head, hand, face, body and gaze).

Several attempts have been done toward the creation of synthetic agents able to sign. These systems are based on Sign Languages and use a symbolic representation of gesture. Lebourque and Gibet [17] use a sign-language derived coding scheme with an inverse-kinematics-based dynamics model for gestures. The authors developed an imperative language to describe the compositionality of a gesture (succession of elementary gesture or parallelism of gesture action. The language specifies also the temporal characteristics of a gesture composition. The generation of gesture animation is done using an inversion control model called sensori-motor model. Kennaway [18] uses a higher level definition of signs such as the HamNoSys [19] transcription to automatically synthesize signs animation. The input to the system is a plain text that is then represented by its semantic representation to be further decomposed into signing gestures. As most systems dealing with gesture of avatars, a sign is represented by three entities: hand shape, wrist orientation and arm position. Each single sign is defined as a static position of the hands and/or arms and is represented by values of each body joints involved. To go from one sign to the next, the system computes the trajectory of each joint using a biologically-based approach in which each joint is modelled as a control system. These control systems are responsible to reach and/or maintain required properties.

Only few works have tackled the problem of modelling the expressiveness of gesture [20,21]. In particular, EMOTE [20] implemented the Laban annotation scheme for dance to change through a set of parameters the way a gesture looks like depending on values such as the strength of a gesture, its tempo. EMOTE works as a post-filter after a gesture animation as been computed.

3 An ECA That Makes Gestures

What are the steps required to construct an ECA able to make gestures? Such a system requires at least the following modules:

1. a plan generator, that conceives of a communicative goal and generates a tree whose leaves are the single meanings to convey;
2. the mode-specific communication systems, that is, the set of lexical, phonological and syntactic rules that form the communication systems in the different modalities. Syntax proper is typical only of verbal language and sign language; but also for other systems, like face, gaze, gesture or posture both

a lexicon and a "phonology" can be found [6]: with lexicon defined as the set of correspondences between signals and meanings, and phonology as the set of sub-lexical elements that combined simultaneously or in sequence generate all possible signals in a lexicon;

3. an inter-modal manager, that decides how to dispatch the different meanings to convey in the different modalities, by choosing the signals from the mode-specific communicative systems and allocating them temporally, synchronizing them or putting them in sequence.

In this work we do not deal with the plan generator module (see [12]) nor with the inter-modal manager that still needs to be developed. In Section 4, we illustrate the phonology of gestures, that is the parameters of gesture production that we adopt in our ECA. In Section 5, we illustrate a subset of the lexicon of gestures: the Gestural Mind Markers. In Section 6, we present a tool for the analysis of video data that can be used to find out and analyze Gestures, in particular to build our lexicon. Finally in Section 7, we provide a sketch of the inter-modal manager module.

4 Mode-Specific Phonology. Parameters of Gestures

We have developed a gesture specification language as a high level scripting language for hand-arm gestures based on a functional separation of arm position, wrist orientation and hand shape [22]. The gestures are specified as a sequence of key-frames, representing different positions of the gestures (such as preparation phase, stroke, hold, and retraction [3]). Each of the gesture parameters has its own definition scheme. Arm position is parameterized using McNeill's system of concentric squares centred on the actor[3]. We use HamNoSys [19] to describe wrist orientation and hand shape determination. Each gesture definition is stored is a library. Tools have been built to create gestures through a user friendly interface. A default timing value is assigned to each gesture. But this value serves only as a suggestion to the gesture planner; the exact timing is computed exactly as to be synchronized with speech.

5 Mode-Specific Lexicon. Gestural Mind Markers

The gestures we aim at simulating in our ECA are Gestural Mind Markers, that is, those gesture that provide information on the Speaker's Mind - on his/her beliefs, goals and emotions. But how can we write down a lexicon of Gestural Mind Markers? To this goal, two different strategies, top-down and bottom-up, can be combined: the top-down strategy is to start from a taxonomy of possible meanings, namely different types of Information on the Speaker's Mind, and then try to figure what gestures convey those meanings; the bottom-up strategy is to analyze a corpus of videotaped data and single out the gestures that correspond to the meanings hypothesized. In this section we show how gestures can be found through the top-down strategy. In section 6, we look at how they can be found in empirical data with a bottom-up strategy. Through information obtained by both strategies we can create our gestural lexicon. The examples given throughout both sections (5 and 6) are taken by careful analysis of real multimodal data.

The information on the Speaker's Mind can be distinguished into three classes, information on the Speaker's Beliefs, Goals and Emotions according a cognitive model of Mind and Social interaction [23] based on the notion of Goals and Beliefs. Let us see what gestures provide Information on the Speaker's Beliefs, Goals and Emotions[2].

5.1 Belief Markers

Among the Gestural Markers that inform on the Speaker's Beliefs we distinguish two kinds of information: Certainty Information and Metacognitive Information.

Certainty. While communicating we can provide information about the degree of certainty of the beliefs we are mentioning. Some Mind Markers (words, gestures, gaze...) express certainty, others uncertainty, others finally utterly deny, that is, they say that "certainly not". The "palm up open hand" [5] means that what we are saying is obvious, self-evident. But this meaning can also be communicated by opening hands with palms up, a gesture that iconically reminds an opening flower, which means "this is visible to everybody". One more gesture that shows self-confidence of the speaker is the "precise pick", thumb and index touching and almost squeezed to each other: it means "I am precise and exact in what I am saying". The Speaker is not only sure of what he's saying, but he knows it with precision. A typical gesture expressing uncertainty is the shrugging of the shoulder, that tells "I am not sure of this " but also "I don't care about this so much (so my uncertainty is not serious)". Another expression is to show "empty hands while lowering the forearms". Two gestures of negation are the extended index finger, palm to Hearer, moved left-right. It means "I think this is not true" (=No), but, according to greater or lesser amplitude of the movement, it is a stronger or feebler negation. Another negation, but with a more assertive attitude, is the open hand with fingers close, palm down, that cuts the air fast and strong. This means: "definitely not", that is: "this is not so, and I do not want this to be questioned".

Metacognitive Information. A second kind of Gestural Belief Marker provide metacognitive information: they inform on the source of the beliefs the Speaker is mentioning, or on the processes of though s/he is performing at the moment.

[2] For many of these gestures we presume, on the basis of systematic obstervations, that they are also used by other cultures, with some modulations (e.g. the writing direction, left to right or right to left, may influence the temporal representation of past and future events [24]) while maintaining the same meaning; but of course, this presumption cannot be proved before dictionaries of gestures of many different cultures are written down (for some attemps in this field see [25,5,26]).

For instance, we snap thumb and index finger as we are trying to retrieve some belief from our long-term memory; we move curve index and middle fingers of both hands up and down to mean "quote", that is, to warn that what we are saying is not ours but others' responsibility.

5.2 Goal Markers

Gestures that inform on the Speaker's Goals are the following:

Performative. Many gestures inform on the goal of a sentence, that is on its performative, or else about the whole meaning of a sentence, including both its performative and its propositional content. Some gestures express performatives with the general goal of providing information, and with different degrees of certainty[3]. The horizontal ring (thumb and index forming a ring, with palm down) moved up and down means "I strongly assert, I peremptorily assert, I am completely sure of what I am asserting, and commit myself to defend this assertion". A gesture which may be used both as a strong assertion and a warning is the extended index finger, palm to left, rotating up and down on wrist (the same analyzed by [24], that means "I assert, and I hold that it is convenient for you to believe it (worse for you if you don't)". Instead, to move forward the right hand curve open, with palm to Speaker and oblique forearm is used to assert in a more tolerant way, by showing oneself willing to argument what one asserts: it means "I assert, but I could even argue for this: I am sure of this and I am sure also of the arguments for this". Other gestures have a performative different from information. Hand up, palm to left, with index finger up is a request for attention; the Calbris gesture above can also be used as a reproach. In Italy, but not in other cultures, the "purse-hand" (hand with all fingertips touching, palm up) ([25,26]) is an interrogative gesture.

Topic – Comment. Through gestures, the Speaker often also marks what is the give, taken-for-granted part of the sentence (the topic) and what is the new important one (the comment). Topic and Comment are especially marked by one parameter of gestures, direction of movement: during the topic, the hand is up, during the comment it drops down; and this holds whatever the hand-shape, that is, whatever the type of gesture performed; in such a way that, possibly, the meaning "this is the topic" or "this is the comment" can overlap with the specific meaning of the gesture.

Meta-discursive. Often the Speaker provides meta-discursive information on the discourse s/he is delivering, in that s/he tries to make clear what are the logical relationships among sentences in his/her discourse. For example, in the

[3] As shown in [7] the performative of a sentence, which claims the sentence specific communicative goal, often contain an information on the Speaker's degree of certainty in claiming that goal.

verbal modality we use adverbs as 'afterwards', 'beforehand' to state a temporal relation between mentioned events, and conjunctions like 'because' or 'but' to state a link of cause-effect (belief X allows one to infer belief Y) or contrast (belief X would lead to infer a belief that is different or opposite to belief Y). We may use a different intonation, or perform a posture shift, or, verbally, we use expressions like "by the way...", or "apart from this...." as we start a digression in our discourse.

These relationships among parts of our discourse can also be expressed by gestures, that we call, in fact, meta-discursive gestures. A Meta-discursive Gesture is numbering on fingers to list the points of a plan or different examples of the same class, just like numbering paragraphs. Symmetrical and rhythmical gestures, for example dropping hands palm up down alternatively, like the plates of a balance, is an analogue of syntactic parallelism or of words like "on the one hand...", "on the other hand....". Finally, in narratives but also in argumentative and explanatory texts, locating discourse characters or topics at some points in space, and then pointing at them is a way to set links among parts of one's discourse, similar to saying: "I now come back to this topic" or "now I come to talk about this character".

Meta-conversational Gestures. With gestures, as well as in other modalities, we can also communicate our goals relative to the management of conversation and face-to-face interaction: namely, the goals of turn-taking and back-channelling. To ask for speaking turn, we raise our hand or just raise our index finger, depending on whether we are in a more formal or informal setting. As we want to hold the floor because we have not finished but we are still thinking and planning our sentence, we can raise our hand, palm to Hearer, which means "wait (do not take up the turn, I am not finished)". As we have finished, we "offer" the Interlocutor to take up the turn, with our hand palm up moving towards the Speaker like in handing some concrete object.

Gestures for back-channel are, on the contrary, quite rare: at most we can use the gesture of negation seen above (extended index oscillating left-right) to tell we do not believe or agree with what our interlocutor is saying.

5.3 Emotion Gestures

Emotions are best expressed, generally, by facial expression; yet, also some gestures are devoted to convey affective states. By raising fists up we show elation for some achievement or victory; we cover our face with hands in shame, and take our head or pull our hair in despair. More frequently, though, it is not a specific gesture that expresses some emotion, but some parameters in the production of non-affective gestures. Typically, speed and tension of movements leaks anxiety, smooth movements witness serenity.

6 How to Analyze and Find out Gestural Mind Markers. The ANVIL-SCORE

In this section we show how gestures to fill into gestural lexicon can be found out in empirical data through a bottom up strategy.

6.1 The Musical Score of Multimodal Communication

In order to find out and classify gestures in empirical data, various methods have been used ([4,3]). Magno Caldognetto and Poggi ([8]) have proposed the "musical score" of multimodal communication, a procedure where signals in two or more modalities are transcribed, analysed and classified. The "musical score" starts by a metaphor that views multimodal communication as a concert where different instruments (voice, hands, face, body) play together; so the researcher's job is to write down, just as in a musical score proper, the signals produced by the different instruments at the same time. In a classical "musical score", signals delivered in five different modalities are reported on parallel lines:

v. verbal modality (the words and sentences uttered);
p. prosodic modality (speech rhythm, pauses, intensity, stress, intonation);
g. gestural modality (movements of the hands, arms and shoulders);
f. facial modality (head and eye movements, gaze, smile and other facial expressions);
b. bodily modality, (trunk and leg movements, body posture, orientation and movements in space).

For each communicative item in each modality five levels of analysis can be provided:

SD. signal description: the surface (acoustic or visual) features of the movement, gesture, gaze, or vocal element at issue are described.
ST. signal type: an item is classified according to some typology (for example, symbolic gesture, deictic gaze...);
MD. meaning description: a verbal formulation is provided of the meaning attributed to each communicative item (e.g., raising the right hand is glossed like: "just wait, be careful").
MT. meaning type: each communicative item is classified in terms of a semantic typology, that distinguishes Information on the World, on the Speaker's Identity, and on the Speaker's Mind.
F. function: each signal is also marked as to its function, that is, the semantic relationship it holds against another parallel signal. The function of a signal X with respect to a signal Y may be one of repetition, if X provides the same meaning as Y; addition, as it adds different but congruent information; substitution, as X says something which is not communicated in the other modality; contradiction, if X says something opposite to Y, and finally, independence, as X and Y are simultaneous but belonging to different communicative plans.

A relevant aspect of the score [8] is that the levels of analysis concerning meaning and function mention and classify not only the literal meaning but also the indirect meaning of each item. For example a frown, that means "I do not understand" at the literal meaning level, at the indirect meaning level may mean "I do not agree with you". And attributing two different meanings (literal and indirect) to the signal under analysis will imply also two different analyses at the level of the meaning type and of the signal function. The "musical score" has been used, so far, in the analysis of kind of multimodal data taken from TV-talk shows, political discourses, teacher-students' interaction, orchestra, concert and rehearsal, dramatic and comic movies, and theatre plays [27,28,29].

6.2 ANVIL

Several tools exist for transcribing and analyzing multimodal data through an automatic system: for example, "Media Tagger"; "Observer"; "Com-Trans" [30]. A particularly usable and friendly tool, for its qualities of robustness, flexibility and ease of use, is ANVIL by Kipp ([1]). ANVIL is a research tool where temporally parallel information is encoded through an annotation scheme that can be freely defined by the User. It is completely written in Java and can run on any platform, its file are based on XML, so they can be read by various Internet Browsers. Video files can be segmented by marking begin and end of fragments, and can be annotated on multiple layers called tracks. All track elements contain attribute-value pairs to be specified by the user.

6.3 The ANVIL-SCORE

We implemented the score onto ANVIL. For each visual and auditory modality, a menu was created for the five levels of analysis above. On the signal side, for the analysis of gesture we inserted option menus with the formational parameters and respective values proposed by HamNoSys; for gaze signals the parameters and values proposed by [29]. The use of PRAAT software already present in ANVIL was augmented: pitch and intensity curves were endowed with scales of values for the quantitative analysis of acoustic, prosodic, intonational properties of fragments, while also adding the TOBI system for phonetic segmentation and tagging, a layer for IPA transcription and segmentation into syllables; this allows one to quantify phonetic features of speech like duration variations depending on different speaking styles, focus stressing and so on, as well as to single out the co-production of some types of gestures, like beats, with speech sub-lexical units like syllables. Once the analysis at all levels is carried out, the ANVIL-SCORE makes available both the comparative evaluation of the meanings conveyed by all signals and the quantification of temporal relationships among the different units singled out within the different signals. These data are used to build a precise lexicon in which to each meaning one or more gestures are associated. The analysis allows one to establish such correspondence between meaning and signal.

7 The Computation of Gestural Mind Markers in an ECA

In previous work [12], we have developed a dialog manager that not only plans discourse moves but also provides information on the co-occuring nonverbal behaviors. To ensure synchronism between the verbal and nonverbal streams, we are defining an XML language specification APML (Affective Presentation Markup Language) that includes nonverbal communicative acts [12] and intonation tags. The output of the discourse planner is an utterance tagged with nonverbal information. An example of such a file is:

```
<performative type="inform">
<theme belief-relation="gen-spec" affect="sorry-for">
I'm sorry to <emphasis x-pitchaccent="LplusHstar"> tell </emphasis>
you <boundary type="LH"/> </theme>
<rheme> that you have been
<emphasis x-pitchaccent="Hstar"> diagnosed </emphasis>
as <emphasis x-pitchaccent="Hstar"> suffering </emphasis> from a
<emphasis x-pitchaccent="Hstar" adjectival="small"> mild </emphasis>
<emphasis x-pitchaccent="Hstar"> form </emphasis> of what we call
<emphasis x-pitchaccent="Hstar"> angina </emphasis>
<emphasis x-pitchaccent="Hstar"> pectoris.</emphasis>
<boundary type="LL"/></rheme></performative>
```

The system is integrated with Festival [31], a speech synthesizer that produces an audio file and decomposes the text into a list of phonemes with their duration. This temporal information is used to synchronize the gesture with the audio stream. Gesture Engine parses the XML file and determines all the tags that get instantiated by mapping the communicative functions specified by the tags with the corresponding gesture [22]. This mapping is specified by the lexicon which has been built during the analysis of video corpus using the ANVIL-SCORE technique. The gesture planner is responsible to instantiate all these gestures according to temporal and contextual constraints (e.g. coarticulation between gestures). We implemented McNeill' s axiom stating that the stroke of a gesture will most probably occur on the stressed syllables or slightly precede it. The other phases of a gesture (preparation phase, retraction...) are then rescheduled appropriately. Gestures do not add to each other except with beat [3]. We defined the concept of stroke expansion that will repeat partially the stroke of a gesture: the repetition is done through the arm movement while keeping the same hand shape as defined at the stroke. This way we model the combination of a beat with other gestures. The output of the gesture planner is a list of joint angles following the format of MPEG-4 BAP frames and a BAP player displays the animation.

8 Conclusion

In this paper we have presented what we defined Gestural Mind Markers and how they may be embedded in the computation of Agent's nonverbal behavior.

We have also presented a tool, ANVIL, with which one may annotate verbal and nonverbal information on different levels. Finally we discuss our classification scheme of gestures both on the level of the signal and of the meaning; finally we have shown how they can be implemented in an ECA System.

References

1. Kipp, M.: From human gesture to synthetic action. In: workshop "Multimodal Communication and Context in Embodied Agents", the Fifth International Conference on Autonomous Agents, Montreal (2001)
2. Ekman, P., Friesen, W.: The repertoire of nonverbal behavior: Categories, origins, usage, and coding. Semiotica **1** (1969)
3. McNeill, D.: Hand and Mind: What Gestures Reveal about Thought. University of Chicago (1992)
4. Kendon, A.: Gestures as illocutionary and discourse structure markers in southern italian conversation. Journal of Pragmatics **23** (1995) 247–279
5. Mueller, C.: Conventional gestures in speech pauses. In C.Mueller, R.Posner, eds.: The Semantics and Pragmatics of Everyday Gestures. Berlin Verlag Arno Spitz, Berlin (2002)
6. Poggi, I.: Mind markers. In M. Rector, I. Poggi, N.T., ed.: Gestures. Meaning and use. University Fernando Pessoa Press, Oporto, Portugal (2002)
7. Poggi, I., Pelachaud, C.: Facial performative in a conversational system. In J. Cassell, J. Sullivan, S.P., Churchill, E., eds.: Embodied Conversational Characters. MITpress, Cambridge, MA (2000)
8. Poggi, I., Caldognetto, E.M.: A score for the analysis of gestures in multimodal communication. In L.Messing, ed.: Proceedings of the Workshop on the Integration of Gesture and Language in Speech, Applied Science and Engineering Laboratories, Newark and Wilmington, Del. (1996) 235–244
9. Johnson, W., Rickel, J., Lester, J.: Animated pedagogical agents: Face-to-face interaction in interactive learning environments. To appear in International Journal of Artificial Intelligence in Education (2000)
10. André, E., Rist, T., Mueller, J.: Webpersona: A lifelike presentation agent for the World-Wide Web. knowledge-Based Systems **11** (1998)
11. Waters, K., Rehg, J., Loughlin, M., Kang, S., Terzopoulos, D.: Visual sensing of humans for active public interfaces. Technical Report Technical Report CRL 96/5, Cambridge Research Laboratory, Digital Equipment Corporation (1996)
12. Pelachaud, C., Carofiglio, V., Carolis, B.D., de Rosis, F., Poggi, I.: Embodied contextual agent in information delivering application. In: First International Joint Conference on Autonomous Agents & Multi-Agent Systems (AAMAS), Bologna, Italy (2002)
13. Cassell, J., Pelachaud, C., Badler, N., Steedman, M., Achorn, B., Becket, T., Douville, B., Prevost, S., Stone, M.: Animated conversation: Rule-based generation of facial expression, gesture and spoken intonation for multiple conversational agents. In: Computer Graphics Proceedings, Annual Conference Series, ACM SIGGRAPH (1994) 413–420
14. Marsella, S., Johnson, W., LaBore, K.: Interactive pedagogical drama. In: Proceedings of the 4th International Conference on Autonomous Agents, Barcelona, Spain (2000) 301–308

15. Cassell, J., Bickmore, J., Billinghurst, M., Campbell, L., Chang, K., Vilhjálmsson, H., Yan, H.: Embodiment in conversational interfaces: Rea. In: CHI'99, Pittsburgh, PA (1999) 520–527
16. Cassell, J., Stone, M.: Living hand and mouth. Psychological theories about speech and gestures in interactive dialogue systems. In: AAAI99 Fall Symposium on Psychological Models of Communication in Collaborative Systems. (1999)
17. Lebourque, T., Gibet, S.: High level specification and control of communication gestures: the GESSYCA system. In: Computer Animation'99, IEEE Computer Society (1999) 24–35
18. Kennaway, R.: Synthetic animation of deaf signing gestures. In: Proceedings of International Gesture Workshop '01, London (2001)
19. Prillwitz, S., Leven, R., Zienert, H., Hanke, T., Henning, J.: Hamburg notation system for sign languages: An introductory guide. In: International Studies on Sign Language and Communication of the Deaf. Volume 5. Signum Press, Hamburg, Germany (1989)
20. Chi, D.M., Costa, M., Zhao, L., Badler, N.I.: The EMOTE model for effort and shape. In Akeley, K., ed.: Siggraph 2000, Computer Graphics Proceedings, ACM Press / ACM SIGGRAPH / Addison Wesley Longman (2000) 173–182
21. Perlin, K., Goldberg, A.: Improv: A system for interactive actors in virtual worlds. In: Computer Graphics Proceedings, Annual Conference Series, ACM SIGGRAPH (1996) 205–216
22. Hartmann, B., Mancini, M., Pelachaud, C.: Formational parameters and adaptive prototype instantiation for MPEG-4 compliant gesture synthesis. In: Computer Animation'02, Geneva, Switzerland, IEEE Computer Society Press (2002) 111–119
23. Conte, R., Castelfranchi, C.: Cognitive and Social Action. University College, London (1995)
24. Calbris, G.: The semiotics of French gestures. University Press, Bloomington: Indiana (1990)
25. Morris, D.: Manwatching. Cape, London (1977)
26. Poggi, I.: Towards the alphabet and the lexicon of gesture, gaze and touch. In Bouissac, P., ed.: Multimodality of Human Communication. Theories, problems and applications. Virtual Symposium. (2002)
27. Poggi, I., Magno-Caldognetto, E.: The score of multimodal communication and the analysis of political discourse. Technical report, Quaderni dell'Istituto di Fonetica e Dialettologia del CNR, Padova (1999)
28. Poggi, I.: The lexicon of conductor's face. In McKevitt, P., Nualláin, S.O., Mulvihill, C., eds.: Language, Vision and Music. John Benjamins Publishing Company, Amsterdam/Philadelphia (2002)
29. Poggi, I., Pelachaud, C., de Rosis, F.: Eye communication in a conversational 3D synthetic agent. AI Communications **13** (2000) 169–181
30. Ingenhoff, D., Schmidt, H.: Com-trans: A multimedia tool for scientific transcriptions and analysis of communication. In M. Rector, I. Poggi, N.T., ed.: Gestures. Meaning and use. University Fernando Pessoa Press, Oporto, Portugal (2002)
31. Taylor, P., Black, A., Caley, R.: The architecture of the Festival Speech Synthesis System. In: Proceedings of the Third ESCA Workshop on Speech Synthesis. (1998) 147–151

Audio Based Real-Time Speech Animation of Embodied Conversational Agents

Mario Malcangi[1] and Raffaele de Tintis[2]

[1] DICo – Dipartimento di Informatica e Comunicazione, Università degli Studi di Milano
Via Comelico 39, 20135 Milano, Italy
malcangi@dico.unimi.it
[2] DSPengineering, Via Burigozzo 8, 20122 Milano, Italy
rdt@dspeng.com

Abstract. A framework dedicated to embodied agents facial animation based on speech analysis in presence of background noise is described. Target application areas are entertainment and mobile visual communication. This novel approach derives from the speech signal all the necessary information needed to drive 3-D facial models. Using both digital signal processing and soft computing (fuzzy logic and neural networks) methodologies, a very flexible and low-cost solution for the extraction of lips and facial-related information has been implemented. The main advantage of the speech-based approach is that it is not invasive, as speech is captured by means of a microphone and there is no physical contact with the subject (no use of magnetic sensors or optical markers). This gives additional flexibility to the application in that more applicability derives, if compared to other methodologies. First a speech-based lip driver system was developed in order to synchronize speech to lip movements, then the methodology was extended to some important facial movements so that a face-synching system could be modeled. The developed system is speaker and language independent, so also neural network training operations are not required.

Introduction

Audio based technologies for the implementation of single components integrated in speech animation systems are known and well described in literature. However two more steps must be taken. The first consists in the realization of effective real-time systems for phonemic classification and audio features extraction, dedicated to speech animation. The second step will be the development of technologies dedicated not only to studio productions but also embeddable in systems for entertainment and visual mobile communication [1].

Embodied virtual agents utilization in game industry, in mobile communication and in novel applications like spoken messages readers/viewers, do not allow lip-sync and facial modelling to be based on optic or magnetic technologies. Calibration and markers setting operations are also highly time consuming in most studio production stages. For these applications real-time speech animation is more effective. Moreover it can be performed with different levels of accuracy also on low cost platforms.

A professional speech animation system needs complex processing, as several analysis and identification techniques need to be applied. Basically, a short-time Fou-

A. Camurri and G. Volpe (Eds.): GW 2003, LNAI 2915, pp. 350–360, 2004.

rier analysis can be helpful [2], however, an accurate modelling system needs to extract more features than just a frequency spectrum. Pitch, zero-crossing rate and energy dynamics are key information for correct mouth posture estimation and facial modelling.

An important processing step is the standard coding of lip postures and real-time driving of a 3-D model (continuous processing).

However, a key subsystem is the phonemic classifier, as the most difficult task is to dynamically classify a speech frame as a viseme. Phonemes are part of basic speech information directly related to mouth, lips and tongue positions during the production of utterances, so the core of a speech-based lips-synching solution is a robust phonemes recognition system.

Many techniques have been applied for this task. Among them, soft-computing based methodologies (fuzzy logic and neural networks), proved more robust and efficient. Furthermore, neural networks work optimally as phoneme classifiers. For this task, a neural network must be fed by an "intelligent" segmentation system, able to distinguish between a real speech signal (related to lip movement) and speech signal absence. Basic study of speech production shows us that signal absence is not an indication of speech absence, so a classical amplitude-level based detector is not applicable. A Text-To-Speech (TTS) processor can support the neural network classifier if the alphabetical transcription of the utterances is available [1][5]. The transcription of the phonemes can be compared to the neural-network phoneme classification of the same utterances, and perform an error correction on the classification.

The System Framework

Speech is captured by means of a microphone and converted to digital format by means of an analog-to-digital converter. Then it is sent to the computer running the speech processing algorithms. The speech is segmented into short-time windows, using an overlapping technique to avoid missing information between adjacent analysis frames. Noise has to be estimated and modelled in order to help the speech processor to enhance the speech signal and hide noise. At analysis time, Linear Predictive Coding (LPC) is applied for speech production modelling and pitch estimation. In order to improve correct identification of speech absence during utterance, a fuzzy logic based end-point detector has been developed. A fuzzy logic processor dynamically evaluates the speech signal features extracted during analysis. As training can be driven by human experience, more sophisticated discrimination capability can be reached. Moreover, a neural network classifier has been modelled in order to process windowed and analysed speech frames at its input layer.

The network has been trained on a large database containing the phonemes needed to recognize the defined phonemic classes. After training, the network performs speaker-independent classification on unlimited vocabularies. A neural network is a static classifier. Thus when a transition occurs between two different phonemes it generates an undefined classification. This unidentified classification, coded as "interpolation between two mouth positions", is regarded as important information when transmitted to the 3D model to be animated.

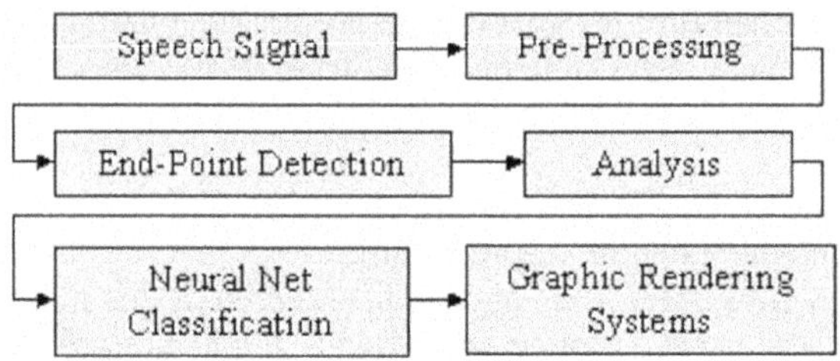

Fig. 1. The LipSync automation framework.

Speech Data Analysis

First, signal offset is removed, then, normalization occurs by means of an AGC (Automatic Gain Control) algorithm. After windowing, a speech signal pre-emphasis operation is applied using high-pass filtering to remove the DC component and very low frequencies. LPC (Levinson-Durbin) analysis is then computed.

The neural network is fed, frame by frame, by the following speech data:

- Zero-crossing rate
- Total signal energy (RMS)
- 12 z-transformed LPC coefficients

The use of multidimensional analysis data vectors is necessary because single data distributions overlap between phonemic classes. Speech data analysis are computed every 20 ms both in time and frequency domain. In the implemented framework animation data playback can be performed at rates in the range 1-50 frames per second. Low-pass filtering is applied to analysis data in order to reduce speech analysis frame rate to animation frame rate.

The Fuzzy Logic Engine

Speech end-point detection is a key task in speech recognition systems. A pattern matching subsystem has to be fed only by speech information, so it is very important to identify end-points of speech utterances. Noise modelling must be considered an important feature when coming to entertainment and visual mobile communication in that audio can be captured in presence of background noise. Especially when our challenge is to move these technologies from studio productions to real-life communication systems, this task cannot be solved by means of a traditional amplitude level-based Voice Activity Detector (VAD) [10]. A speech end-point detector must be able to separate speech frames from speech absent frames. Moreover, it is necessary to compute a general signal model representing noisy frames without utterance. Comparing input signal parameters to the noise model, the system must be able to avoid incorrect activations of the speech classification process. A simple model of background noise is represented in our framework by the following parameters:

- Q_N = Average noise energy
- Z_N = Average noise zero-crossing rate
- P_N = Average noise spectral power inside the speech frequency range 100-4000 Hz.

In order to model background noise, these parameters are computed at initialisation time or periodically if the noise is not stationary. The following parameters are computed at run-time for speech information modelling:

- $Q_S(t)$ = Time domain signal energy
- $Z_S(t)$ = Zero-crossing rate
- $P_S(t)$ = Spectral power within the range 100-4000 Hz (speech frequency range)
- S(t) = Period of continuous "non-speech" coding collected at current time
- PDim(t) = Period of a valid speech frame
- DP(t) = Ratio between word energy and energy computed at actual frame
- PDist(t) = Period measured between last valid speech frame and previous frame.

Speech end-point evaluation is computed by means of a fuzzy logic engine evaluating, frame by frame, the following input parameters:

- Input[0] = $Q_S(t) / Q_N$
- Input[1] = $Z_S(t) / Z_N$
- Input[2] = $P_S(t) / P_N$
- Input[3] = S(t)
- Input[4] = PDim(t)
- Input[5] = DP(t)
- Input[6] = PDist(t)

The Neural Network Engine

Two neural networks (back propagation architecture) have been used for phonemes classification. These receive coded speech features at their input layers and forward neural signals to hidden layers. Hidden layers embed all necessary information for phoneme classification learned at training-time.

The output layers report the classification degree for each phoneme, then, the best-classified one is evaluated by a confirmation logic (correlated when available with the phonetic transcription). In order to train the neural networks, a large multi-speaker database was used (TIMIT). The implemented architecture is shown in Fig.2:

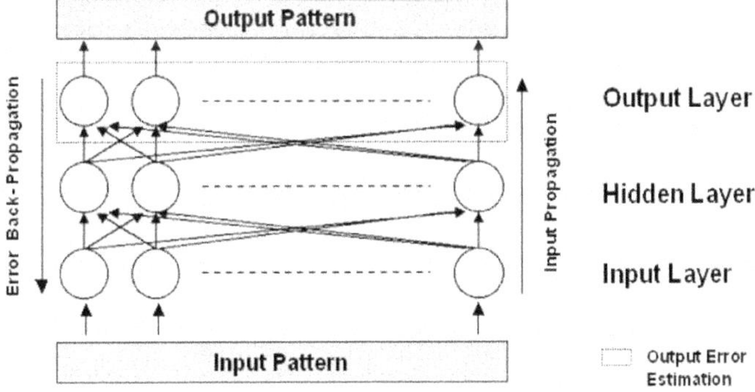

Fig. 2. The Error Back-Propagation Network.

Input layer is fed by 14 parameter values: zero crossing rate, signal energy and 12 z-transformed LPC coefficients. Hidden layer dimension, was chosen according to the following formula:

$$h = k/10*(m+n)$$

h = Hidden layer dimension, k = Number of templates in the training set, m = Output layer dimension, n = Input layer dimension.

The classic sigmoidal transfer function was adopted:

$$f(z) = (1+e^{-z})^{-1}.$$

When trained, the networks are able to recognize speech events on unlimited vocabularies. Two different neural networks have been trained: the first targeted for vowel recognition, and the second targeted for consonant recognition. The use of two small-specialized neural networks instead of one larger network, proved to occupy less memory and also to enhance performance. Response from the voiced/unvoiced decision computed by LPC analysis is used for network selection.

The Lip-Synching System

The phonemic detection system based on two specialized neural networks has been developed to identify the speaker's lips and tongue postures during utterance. In each analysis frame, the identified phoneme is coded and transmitted to a 2-D/3-D modelling system by MIDI interface (live animation) or by file passing (non real-time mode).

Once the user specifies the gender of the speaker, the system is able to carry out speaker independent coding on unlimited vocabularies.

When coming to live communication, the system can be connected to other external devices through MIDI interface. The user is therefore not forced to choose a specific 2-D/3-D modelling environment, moreover, lip-synching data can be easily transmitted to different systems and platforms. It is also possible to exploit all the visual and editing features of any MIDI data viewer (sequencers, etc.) for lip-synch data viewing/processing. Furthermore, it is possible to add audio and video effects, which can be triggered by the recognized events and consequently be synchronized with the speech flow. This synchronization might be especially useful when it comes to multimedia applications where it can be integrated with audio/video MIDI systems.

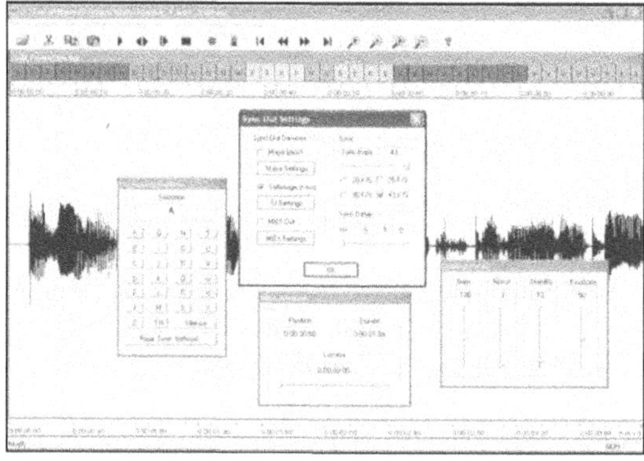

Fig. 3. The LipSync 2.0 main panel.

Amplitude Controlled Facial Movements

Amplitude level in speech flows is not stationary.

Unvoiced phonemes can have lengths of a few milliseconds and present much lower energy than voiced phonemes. In normal speech flows, this results in fast high amplitude changes.

In order to follow amplitude variations the average magnitude is computed. If N is the window length, the average magnitude function is defined as follows:

$$M(t) = \Sigma_n |s(n)| \qquad n = 0,\dots,N$$

Speech volume can be used to control two different components of facial modelling. The first one is mouth opening strength. Energy dynamics used to modulate the amplitude of the lips opening strength, results in more natural movements. Continuous modulation always produces different instances of the same phoneme, in that the mouth shape corresponding to different occurrences of the same phoneme will always be different, similar to what happens in real-life mouth movements.

Also facial modifications depending on emotions can be automated by volume tracking. When volume is high, these modifications are:

- Facial muscles become stretched
- Eyebrows tend to frown
- Forehead tends to wrinkle
- Nostrils tend to extend

The avatar model should embed speech energy as a variable parameter to control the above aspects so that related facial movements can be automated.

Lip Related Events and Emotional Related Events

Here phonemic classification is presented in a simpler form than in the classic speech-to-text transcription. It is not necessary to recognize all of the different phonemes in a chosen language, only the smaller set which corresponds to the set of visemes. In all natural languages, some spoken phoneme have different spectral content mainly due to different tongue positions inside the mouth, also if their corresponding lip position is the same or very similar [12]. Moreover, in some cases differences in tongue position are slight or not relevant for face animation.

The lip related events recognized by Lip*Sync* are the following:

- Speech signal amplitude (RMS)
- No-speech frames
- Vowels
- Consonants

Vowels are important events to be recognized for lip synchronization because they present average lengths longer (up to 4/5 times) than other phonemes. For these reasons they are individually recognized as [a], [e], [i/y as in "*youth*"], [o], [u]". Consonants are grouped in 7 classes corresponding to similar lip and tongue positions: (r), (b, m, p), (v, f, th), (d, l, n, t), (s, z), (ch, g, j, sh), (c, k, g) as shown in Tab.1.

Table 1. Visemes classes corresponding to non vowel phonemes.

r	as in "*free*"			
b,m,p	b sound	m sound	p sound	
v, f, th	v sound	f sound	th as in "*thin*"	
d, l, n, t	d as in "*dime*"	l as in "*leaf*"	n as in "*nine*"	t as in "*time*"
s, z	s as in "*see*"	z as in "*zebra*"		
ch, g, j, sh	ch as in "*chip*"	g as in "*gentle*"	j as in "*jam*"	sh as in "*ship*"
c, k, g	c as in "*cat*"	k as in *keep*"	g as in "*go*"	

Phonemes Animation

Several models have been proposed for speech animation, each one requiring different complexity levels and computational costs [4].

The proposed model is based on a simplification of the Nitchie lip reading model [5][6] based on 18 different visemes. A viseme is one visually distinguishable speech posture involving lips, tongue and teeth. In our model 12 different visemes are employed. Some of these visemes were derived from the 18 included in the original Nitchie model, others were derived from modifications necessary for reduction.

In Fig.4 it is shown the viseme corresponding to vowel "*e*".

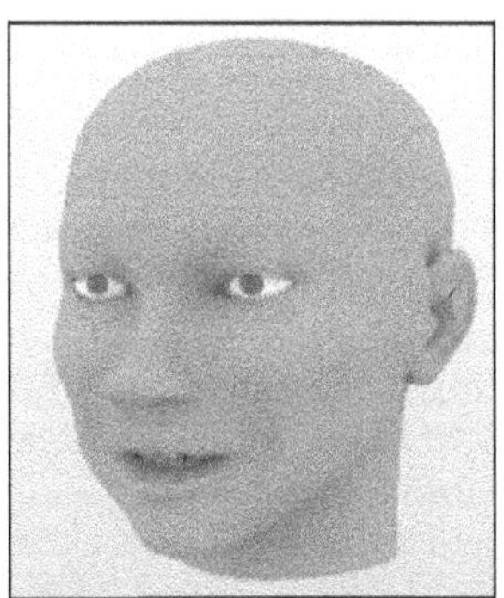

Fig. 4. Viseme "E" by Carlo Macchiavello (DB-Line) for DSPengineering.

Each viseme is associated to a class containing one or more phonemes. The current phoneme at each analysis frame is computed by means of the neural classifier. Therefore a timed phoneme sequence is presented at the end of the analysis/classification step.

Coarticulation

Speech is not realistically animated by means of phonemes recognition alone. A model for coarticulation must also be adopted. In our system we implemented a simplification of the Cohen and Massaro model for coarticulation [7], based on Lofqvist's work on speech gestures [8]. Simplification was necessary in order to achieve real-time animation. The Cohen and Massaro model avoids impulsive transitions between phonemes while preserving speech dependent timing characteristics during coarticulation. At each analysis frame the recognized phoneme is mapped into a set of facial control parameters that will be used during the phoneme segment. The phoneme segment is the time location in the utterance where the phoneme presents its influence. Generally it will be a multiple of the analysis frame. In order to compute actual parameters, we must introduce two functions:

Real-Time Dominance

$$RTD_{sp}(t) = \alpha_{sp} e^{-(\theta sp\ \tau)^{\wedge}c} \quad \tau >= \tau_{SA},\ 0 \text{ otherwise} \qquad \tau_{SA} = t - t_A$$

RTD_{sp} is the real-time dominance function for parameter P in segment S.

α_{sp} is the magnitude of RTD_{sp}.,τ is the time distance from phoneme activation, t_A is the phoneme activation time, θp and C are the control parameters for the exponential function.

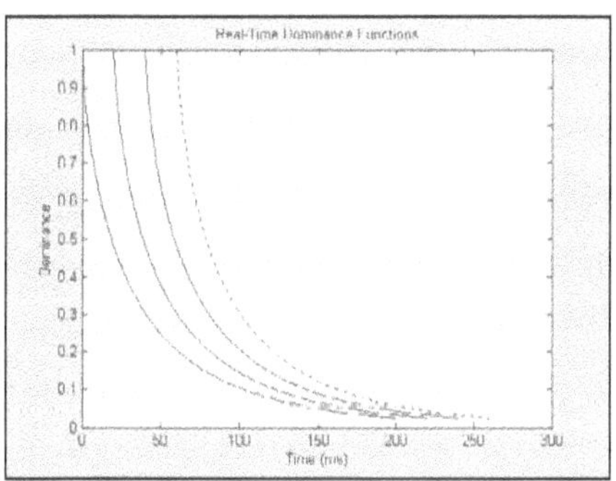

Fig. 5. Real-time dominance functions of 4 adjacent phoneme segments assuming α_{sp}=1, θ_{sp} =0.09, C=0.7.

The amplitude of the real-time dominance function is controlled by the α_{sp} parameter. The θ_{sp} and C parameters control its shape.

Real-Time Blending

Blending is applied to the dominance functions of each parameter in order to compute final parameter values. In our model the real-time blending function is defined as follows:

$$RTF_p(t) = \Sigma_n (D_{sp}(t) T_{sp}) / \Sigma_s D_{sp}(t)$$

n = 1,..,N and N is the number of active phoneme segments at frame t. A phoneme segment is active when its dominance function is non-zero.

Emotional Related Events

In order to improve facial modelling, some emotional aspects can be estimated using speech analysis.

Anger, for example, presents high average pitch with large fluctuations. Also volume is high on average and presents large fluctuations.
In the implemented system, the computed emotional related events are:

- Average Loudness (L_A)
- Loudness Fluctuations Rate and Intensity (L_{FR}, L_{FI})
- Average Pitch (P_A)
- Pitch Fluctuations Rate and Intensity (P_{FR}, P_{FI})
- Pauses Length (S_L)

An estimation scheme for anger and sadness can be estimated as shown in Tab.2.

Table 2. Anger/Sadness Estimation Scheme.

	L_A	L_{FR}	L_{FI}	P_A	P_{FR}	P_{FI}	S_L
Anger	High	High	High	High	High	High	Low
Sadness	Low	Low	Low	Low	Low	Low	High

Both emotions and intonation produce variations of pitch. Accurate pitch estimation, however, is not necessary, and less computational intensive related parameters could be used. Average zero-crossing rate and average zero-crossing rate fluctuations are important variables that can be computed. Zero-crossing rate is a very rough measure of pitch in wideband signals, but is always correlated to pitch in voiced frames. Analysis studies [11] show that the mean short-time average value for 10 ms analysis frames is 14 for voiced phonemes and 49 for unvoiced phonemes. It is possible to track zero-crossing rate only on voiced frames.

In our model, voiced frames are assumed to be only those frames with zero-crossing rate lower than 25 and presenting energy values not lower than half the average loudness. This reduces errors due to zero-crossing rate overlapping between voiced and unvoiced distributions. Low pass filtering is applied in order to provide smooth zero-crossing rate envelope tracking.

Pauses Length Estimation

When estimating pause length in emotional analysis, the speech/silence identification problem is presented in a different form than in the similar problem of speech recognition. The first major difference is that it is not necessary to recognize silent frames between words from silent frames inside words. Both kinds of pauses share the same semantic significance. For example, sadness is characterized by long pauses inside words as well as between words. However pause estimation cannot be solved by means of a traditional amplitude level voice activity detector (VAD), as commonly done in speech recognition applications. It is necessary to have a model representing noisy frames without utterance. Comparing input signal parameters to the noise model, the system must be able to avoid incorrect classification of low level speech frames as silent frames. The model of background noise used for pauses estimation was described in the paragraph "*The fuzzy logic engine*".

Cheeck Tension Tracking

Another information concerning the mouth posture can be extracted when adopting spectral analysis techniques.

The mouth acts as a resonating cavity reinforcing sound waves produced by vocal cords at certain frequencies. According to the source-filter model of speech production, mouth movements dynamically modify the filter response.

It is possible to obtain important information about the mouth and related cheek posture using spectral analysis. Cheek tension is possible when the zygomaticus major and the risorius muscles located at the corner of the mouth are tightened [9]. In this posture the angle of the mouth is pulled laterally as shown in Fig.6b.

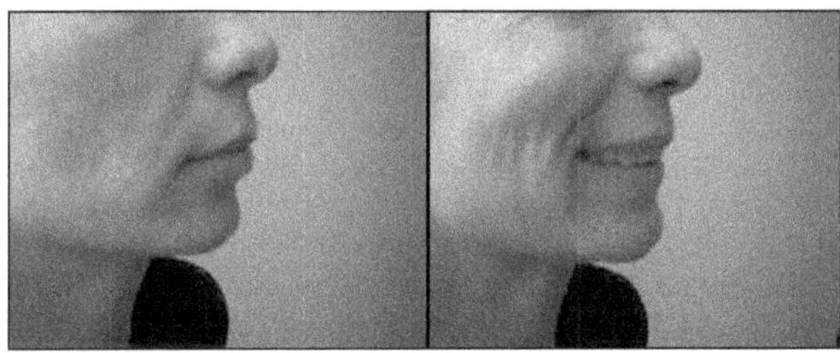

Fig. 6a/6b. Normal cheek posture (6a) and cheek posture corresponding to a tension of the muscles located at the corners of the mouth (6b).

When the mouth is assuming the posture in Fig.6b, a low pass action of the vocal tract filters speech utterance, producing the results shown in Fig.7. Spectral energy at frequencies higher than 2000 Hz is attenuated.

If F_N is the Nyquist frequency, then cheeck tension can be estimated as:

$$T(n) = G_T \Sigma_f \, 20\log_{10}(E_n(f)) \qquad f = 2.5 \text{ KHz},..,F_N$$

Where $E_n(f)$ is the energy at frequency f, at time n and G_T is a scale coefficient.

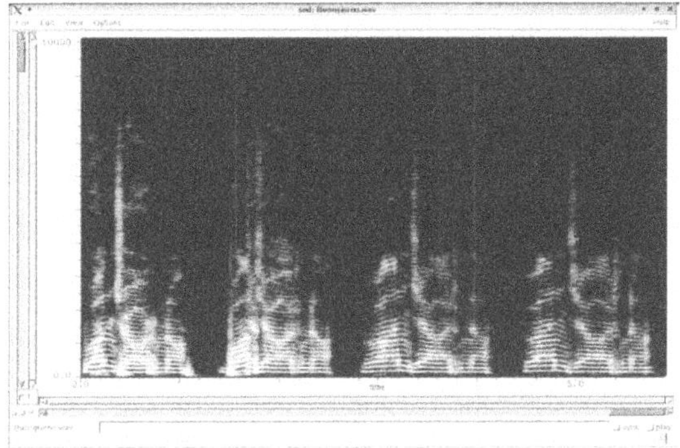

Fig. 7. Four instances of the word "buongiorno" pronounced with an increasing tension of the muscles at the corner of the mouth.

References

1. M. Malcangi: "*A Soft-Computing approach to fit a speech recognition system on a single-chip*", 2002 International Workshop System-on-Chip for Real-Time Applications Proceedings, Banff, Canada, July 6-7, 2002.
2. M. Malcangi, R. de Tintis, "*LipSync: A Real-Time System for Virtual Characters Lip-Synching*", XIII Colloquium on Musical Informatics Proceedings, L'Aquila, Italy, 2000
3. M.Malcangi, R. de Tintis, "*Sincronizzazione Labiale e Modellazione Facciale in Tempo Reale per l'Animazione di Personaggi Virtuali*", II Convegno Tecnico Scientifico di MIMOS, Proceedings, Torino, October 28-29, 2002
4. I.Poggi, C. Pelachaud, "*Performative Facial Expressions in Animated Faces*", in Embodied Conversational Agents, MIT Press, 2000
5. F.I.Parke, K.Waters, "*Speech Synchronized Animation*" in Computer Facial Animation, A K Peters, Ltd., 1996.
6. E.B. Nitchie, "*How to Read Lips For Fun and Profit*", Hawthorne Books, New York, 1979.
7. M. Cohen and D. Massaro, "*Modeling co articulation in synthetic visual speech*", N.M. Thalmann editors, Models and Techniques in Computer Animation. Springer-Verlag, Tokyo, 1993.
8. A.Löfquist, "*Speech as audible gestures*", In W.J. Hardcastle and A. Marchal editors, Speech Production and Speech Modeling, Kluwer Academic Publishers, Dordrecht, 1990.
9. F.I.Parke, K.Waters, "*Anatomy of the Face, Head, and Neck*" in "Computer Facial Animation", A K Peters, Ltd., 1996.
10. J.C. Junqua, B. Mak, B. Reaves, "*A robust algorithm for word boundary detection in presence of noise*", IEEE Trans. Speech and Audio Processing, Vol. 2, No. 3, July 1994.
11. Y. Cao, S. Sridharan, M. Moody, "*Voiced/Unvoiced/Silence Classification of Noisy Speech in Real Time Audio Signal Processing*", 5th Australian Regional Convention, April, 1995, Sydney, (AES Preprint N. 4045)
12. J.A. Markowitz, "*The Data of Speech Recognition*" in Using Speech Recognition, Prentice Hall, 1996

Neo Euclide: A Low-Cost System for Performance Animation and Puppetry

Samuele Vacchi[1], Giovanni Civati[1], Daniele Marini[2], and Alessandro Rizzi[1]

[1] Dept. of Information Technology, University of Milan, Italy
[2] Dept. of Information and Communication, University of Milan, Italy

Abstract. This paper presents a low-cost flexible Performance Animation system for gesture generation and mapping, easy to use and general purpose, focusing on the most ancient and classical idea of animation: Puppetry. A system designed for generic puppetry, and not for a special purpose that can be easily adapted to different scenarios and budgets. For this reason we chose consumer and mainstream technologies, common graphic libraries, PC graphic cards and cheap motion-capture equipment allowing the user to insert movies and sounds integrated with a three-dimensional scene.

1 Introduction

Performance Animation is a Computer Science branch studying real-time 3D model animation. Here are the steps to be performed for each video frame during Performance Animation:

- collection of all motion device data
- data application to a 3D digital scene
- digital image rendering.

The first step is the so-called motion capture, i.e. the sampling and recording of the animator's movements. The animation quality depends on the correspondence between these data and every single element of the scene. Most animators use procedural expressions and predefined animations to reduce their job complexity. This is a deeply studied research field [1,2]. In Performance Animation a great amount of movements allows the animator to make the character really expressive and look more natural [3,4]. In this context, the interpretation of the animator's gesture and their mapping as the character's expressions can remarkably simplify the animation process [5]. The character can become autonomous by means of physical, technical and artificial intelligence simulations or simple geometrical relations. The scene rendering is the step that requires more computational power and it depends on the complexity of the scene. People who create characters for Performance Animation have to cope with the image quality, the character expressiveness and the scene structure simplicity for the animation.

Performance Animation differs substantially from the traditional animation techniques like the keyframe animation, where the animator moves every character's single part separately to obtain a gesture. This traditional technique

A. Camurri and G. Volpe (Eds.): GW 2003, LNAI 2915, pp. 361–368, 2004.

allows the animator to get a precise result, but requires a lot of work. On the contrary Performance Animation makes it possible to realize animations more quickly, moving every character's part simultaneously [6]. The real-time rendering of the scene during animation generates an immediate feedback permitting the animator to synchronise his own physical movements to the virtual ones in the scene. During a sequence creation he can even use Performance Animation as a framework for the animation itself and then touch it up with sharper techniques. Moreover, a motion capture mechanism replaces mathematical interpolation curves with a real movement sampling. During a live performance the character - guided by the animator - can directly interact with the public, as if he was alive. Thanks to "Neo Euclide", our new Performance Animation system, the animator can see the public through a camera and the character can talk and interact with people. The natural interaction between a virtual character and a real person is useful to study people's reactions before such virtual interface. Moreover, if we connect movement detection sensors covering a sufficiently wide area to the system it is possible to create 3D real-time interactive environments [7].

The next section presents an overview of the Performance Animation state of the art and an analysis of the available products. Further on the "Neo Euclide" system is presented, and its new features are explained in detail.

2 Developments in Animation

Before the use of real-time 3D graphic, extreme puppeters and special effect geniuses used analogical and digital motion capture devices to remotely control mechanical creatures. These mechanical creatures were called remote-control animatronics. An Animatronic (Ani-ma-tron-ik) is a robotic puppet. This term was coined by Walt Disney Imagineering Company in 1960 to describe its moving creatures. "Jim Henson Creature Shop" [8,9,10] creations have been used in some well-known movies as "Babe", "George of the jungle", "Dr Dolittle" and "Lost in Space". In 1980 "Jim Henson creature Shop" created the first animatronic control system, known as Henson Performance Control System (HPCS) [11]. Thanks to HPCS, animators could control many activation points through a combination of manual controls. In 1986, Jim Henson, Michael Frith and other members of the "Jim Henson Production" understood the potentialities of real-time computer graphics that they conceived as the natural extension of remote-control animatronics; so mechanical creatures were replaced by digital ones. At that time the only computers capable of applying real-time rendering were very expensive flight simulators. Hence, the first concepts were created by "Digital Productions" only in wire-frame. After a short time "InterPro 32C", the first workstation capable of performing real-time shading was produced. In 1988 the first live performance took place at Siggraph: "Mike the talking head" by DeGraf and Wahrman [12], followed by "Waldo C.Graphic" by Henson and PDI at the "Jim Henson Hour" [13]. "MIT Media Lab" has always worked on the edge of Performance Animation technology development, improving its own software more and more. Since its birth (Paris 1989) it has created 30 characters ("Nickelodeon", "U.K.'s Bert", "the Fish and Elvis", "Pepe the cricket", "The Adventures of Pinocchio and Cleo"). "Seagull" made its first appearance at Siggraph Digital Bayou in 1996 as part of the "Smart Spaces" of MIT MediaLab. It is a kind of Performance Animation based on a computer vision device called "Smart Desk" developed by the "Vision and Modelling Group" in the "Mit Media Lab". This system uses a special device able to recognize the hand gestures. The animator's naked hand movements are captured by a camera. This image is then translated into a 3D gesture by matching it to a set of low-definition bi-dimensional sample images and the gesture applied to the character. Using the same system, Luxomatic made a winning demonstration of human movements applied to a non-human character: "Luxo Jr." [14]. In 1999 Matthew Brand presented at Siggraph an alternative approach to motion capture using audio signals as an input [15].

3 The Proposed System: "Neo Euclide"

Historically, Performance Animation has been based on dedicated and closed systems, i.e. expensive devices to give special inputs and super computers to perform rendering. Now, with the coming of the actual 3D graphic accelerators and hardware abstraction layers it is possible to achieve great results using cheaper appliances.

To perform motion-capture we use low-cost devices like data-gloves and MIDI instruments. Data-gloves can work with different technologies: optical fibre bending sensors like General Reality 5th Glove, resistive bending sensors like Immersion Cyberglove, flex and abduction-adduction sensors like Humanware Humanglove. The price and performance of the gloves can vary widely. So far supported controls have been standard devices (mouse, keyboards and joystick), data-gloves, MIDI instruments and software data generators (DataGen). The MIDI protocol is fully supported, thus the animator can use any device or software producing compatible messages, like a musical keyboard or a MIDI file. So far, the MIDI features have met any need of interaction and registration of data.

3D scenes can be realized by using commercial modelling tools for which an integrated file exporter has been developed: Avid Softimage—3D and Discreet 3DStudioMax. Our system maintains the hierarchical relationships defined during the modelling phase, thus it is able to control articulated objects like structured bones, improving the flexibility of control for skinned animation. This feature is fundamental in the creation of complex animations with few controls and to maintain the body parts correctly positioned for the anthropomorphic puppet control. Another way to smoothly deform a mesh representing the model skin is by means of the Shape animation technique; but, since it is necessary to save the exact position of the vertices in every key-frame, it is memory consuming, less versatile and animation keys must be limited in number. However in some cases, shape animation can be a suitable solution. Being able to support both methods, Neo Euclide allows the modeller to choose between bone and shape animation. We created a multipurpose Performance Animation system both in the hardware used for the rendering and in the input devices which can differ in every session. "Neo Euclide" is composed of a connection editor and of a full-screen performance player. The editor allows the user to insert 3D models, to integrate movies,and sounds, and to easily connect any physical sensor to any virtual element (Fig. 1). We apologize for the presence of Italian terms. They refer to some model elements in the 3D scene that can be linked to the desired device sensors. The parameters of these links can be inserted using the "Animation Params Setup" input section which is displayed on the left bottom area of the interface. The list of the active links is given on the right bottom section. The player, described in the next section, is used for live animation and loads different sets of models in runtime.

Fig. 1. A screen shot of "Neo Euclide" editor

4 Using "Neo Euclide"

The whole scene must be defined in a modelling software tool for which an exporter has previously been developed and integrated within the modeller. As for the exporter, the "plug in" way is necessary because of the system target. Since Neo Euclide is a sort of "puppet manager", it can be considered the last step in the puppet production. The puppet consists of several coupled files, binary model files (.ddd), audio files (All DirectMusic supported formats), movie files (All DirectShow supported formats), and of a text file (.neo) containing the relations between the previous ones. The model files are protected against piracy, modification and reuse, so the proprietary format file (.ddd) keeps the whole source from being touched. Once the modelling and animation structure is completed the scene is ready. At that point the "puppeteer" must translate and codify his work with the exporter which translates the geometry into some objects compatible with the graphic engine of the Neo Euclide system. The exporter generates a .ddd file containing the model, the texture references, the animations, the relations with the bones and everything relevant to the scene created with the modelling software. Then the puppeteer has to deal with the interface of "Neo Euclide Editor". This software program allows the animator to connect the sensors of the chosen devices to any element of the modelled scene and to define its movements and set their limits by using a visual interface. A connected sensor can modify the position of a point associated to an element in the scene. So the puppeteer can both choose the Human Interface Devices to be used and define how their sensors must work in the scene.

We have developed a sensor connection by means of multipliers. If a sensor is connected to a second sensor, it can control the intensity of its interaction with the scene. This association is called multiplier link. For example a MIDI slider can change the data interpretation of a given sensor connected to an object rotation in order that if the MIDI slider is in position 0, the sensor can rotate the object from -90 to 90 degrees, while if the MIDI slider is in position 127 the sensor can rotate the object from -180 to 180 degrees. Any sensor can be used in any connection and in any multimedia 3D scene. The underlying technology makes the system widely customizable hence adjustable to the features of a particular scene or to a particular device set.

"Neo Euclide Editor" has many functions that help the puppeteer in "wiring" his puppet. First he has to load the model in the .ddd format. Then he can load a previously saved .neo file containing all the relations between the elements and the sensor, or simply create a new empty one. After the model has been loaded, the Editor interface summarizes the elements in the scene that can be connected to a sensor. Any sensor can control more than one element, but two different sensors cannot control the same element. The sensor connection to the scene's elements can be modified by the animator so that he can decide in any moment how each sensor can influence each of the elements in the scene. Each sensor is set up during a calibration phase assigning different values to the minimum, intermediate and maximum positions (Fig. 2). A finger rest position does not always correspond to the middle position of the connected data-glove sensor; moreover, the animator's hand does not always reach the sensor extension limits. Thus the calibration phase of the sensor has been introduced to help the animator to use the devices and to avoid uncomfortable or painful positions.

Moreover, during the editing phase the animator can decide to what extent each sensor must change the object status in the 3D scene. It is often useful to link large movements in the scene to short movements of the sensor, and it is also suitable to set the rest position near to the minimum or maximum point. Setting up an entire model can be very laborious, so some functions as "copy and paste"

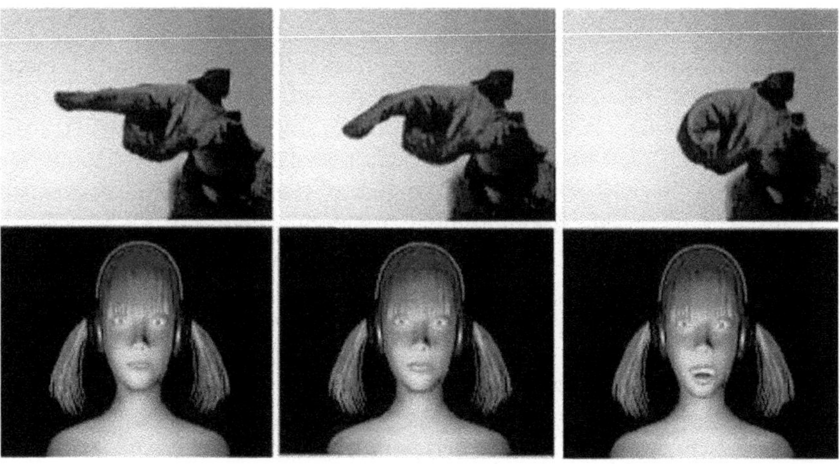

Fig. 2. Minimum, medium and maximum positions

have been added to avoid repeating the same things over and over. When all the connections have been made the puppet is totally "wired up" but not fine-tuned yet. Using the Navigator and the Run features of "Neo Euclide Editor" the puppeteer can find out any irregularity in the connections and then tune them by readjusting the sensors inside the Editor. But he can even find errors in the model (i.e. elements or meshes not properly joined), in the animation (i.e. a bone badly placed that alters the geometry making it useless) or simply try to make the character's movements more natural. One of the man's major limits is the ability to control each part of his body independently, such as the fingers of his hand. To overcome these huge limits "Neo Euclide" provides automatic instruments to control some secondary or repeating movements thus allowing the animator not to focus on the animation background details. Thanks to "Neo Euclide Player", the system live section, the puppeteer can animate characters in the full-screen (and full-performance) mode where more characters can be used in real-time, making it possible to switch from one to another simply by pressing a key.

"Neo Euclide Player" permits to create a Performance Animation in a remote mode trough an IP connection or a telephone call. Moreover, using a local area network, this feature allows one single animator to use more computers as rendering clients and give performances on more displays at a time (Fig. 3).

5 Uses and Tests

Up to now "Neo Euclide" has been interfaced with "Eyesweb" [16] - a software program for input data transfer and management - to manage multiple show points from a single input station. We are also working to interface the system with "Lipsync" [17] - a software program for the synthesis of facial expressions

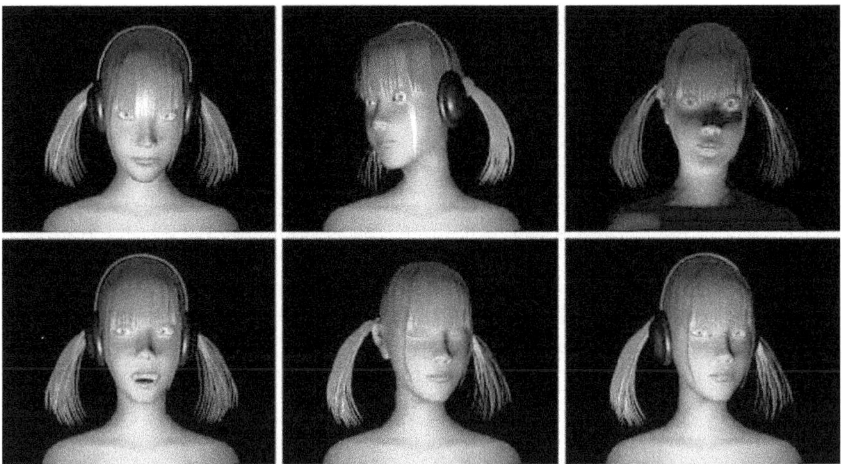

Fig. 3. A series of screen shots of "Neo Euclide" player

from the voice audio signal - for the lip movement automation. The MIDI standard has been used to interface the two software systems, which is at present the major means of communication between third party programs and "Neo Euclide" opening to any form of interaction and giving the system the opportunity to attain a higher level of independency from the human puppeteer.

The system is in use at the "Citta' della Scienza" Museum [18] in Naples for the animation of the museum guide called "Bit". This installation has been created by "Studio Azzurro Produzioni S.R.L" in Milan [7]; it consists of 5 locations, where the character interacts with the public, and a control room, where the animator can decide the location to animate.

6 Conclusions

After describing the state of the art of Performance animation "Neo Euclide" system has been presented. This new approach:

- requires a low-cost hardware;
- is general-purpose;
- enables comfortable live performances;
- makes it possible to communicate with other software programs.

"Neo Euclide" works with all video hardware and input devices supported by DirectX hardware abstraction layer and some other input devices such as datagloves and MIDI instruments. Hence the animator can choose the best configuration for any situation or budget. The system can employ models crated using the most common modelling tools through dedicated plug-ins able to export 3D scenes to a custom file format. Other software programs can be interfaced via the MIDI protocol to "Neo Euclide".

References

1. Hyun Joon Shin, Jehee Lee, Sung Yong Shin, Michael Gleicher: Computer puppetry: An importance-based approach. ACM Transactions on Graphics (TOG) April 2001, Volume 20 Issue 2.
2. Nadia Magnenat Thalmann , Daniel Thalmann. Computer animation: Computer animation. ACM Computing Surveys (CSUR) March 1996, Volume 28 Issue 1.
3. David J. Sturman: Computer Puppetry. IEEE Computer graphics and application. Jenuary/February 1998.
4. M.Brand: Shadow Puppetry. int. Conf. on Computer Vision, ICCV '99, 1999.
5. Francesca Barrientos: Continuous control of avatar gesture. Proceedings of the 2000 ACM workshops on Multimedia November 2000.
6. V.Banquey and L.Juppé: The use of Real-Time Performance Animation in the Production Process. Motion Capture in Practice. ACM Siggraph 97 Course Notes, ACM Press, New York, 1997.
7. http://www.studioazzurro.com/
8. Finch, Christopher, and Charles S. Finch: Jim Henson: The Works: The Art, the Magic, the Imagination. New York: Random House, 1993.
9. St. Pierre, Stephanie: The Story of Jim Henson: Creator of the Muppets. N.p.: Gareth Stevens, 1997.
10. http://www.creatureshop.com/
11. Bacon, Matt: No Strings Attached: The Inside Story of Jim Henson's Creature Shop. New York: MacMillan, 1997.
12. T.Ezzat, T.Poggio: Miketalk: A talking facial display on morphing visemes. In Proc. Computer animation Conference, June 1998.
13. G.Walters: The Story of Waldo C.Graphics. 3D Character Animation by computer, ACM Siggraph 89 Course Notes, ACM Press, New York 1989,pp.65-79.
14. Pixar: Luxo Jr. (film), 1986
15. Brand, M.E.: Voice Puppetry. ACM SIGGRAPH, ISBN: 0-201-48560-5, pps 21-28, August 1999
16. A.Camurri, P.Coletta, M.Peri, M.Ricchetti, A.Ricci, R.Trocca, G.Volpe: A real-time platform for interactive performance. Proc. ICMC-2000, Berlin
17. M. Malcangi, R. de Tintis: LipSync 1.0: A System for Real-Time Virtual Characters Lip-Synching and Facial Modeling. XIII Colloquium on Musical Informatics CIM 2000, pp 216-219, L'Aquila, 2000
18. http://www.cittadellascienza.it/

Gesture Desk – An Integrated Multi-modal Gestural Workplace for Sonification

Thomas Hermann, Thomas Henning, and Helge Ritter

Neuroinformatics Group
Faculty of Technology, Bielefeld University, D-33501 Bielefeld, Germany
{thermann,thenning,helge}@techfak.uni-bielefeld.de

Abstract. This paper presents the *gesture desk*, a new platform for a human-computer interface at a regular computer workplace. It extends classical input devices like keyboard and mouse by arm and hand gestures, without the need to use any inconvenient accessories like data gloves or markers. A central element is a "gesture box" containing two infrared cameras and a color camera which is positioned under a glass desk. Arm and hand motions are tracked in three dimensions. A synchronizer board has been developed to provide an active glare-free IR-illumination for robust body and hand tracking. As a first application, we demonstrate interactive real-time browsing and querying of *auditory self-organizing maps* (AuSOMs). An AuSOM is a combined visual and auditory presentation of high-dimensional data sets. Moving the hand above the desk surface allows to select neurons on the map and to manipulate how they contribute to data sonification. Each neuron is associated with a prototype vector in high-dimensional space, so that a set of 2D-topologically ordered feature maps is queried simultaneously. The level of detail is selected by hand altitude over the table surface, allowing to emphasize or deemphasize neurons on the map.

1 Introduction

Gestural Human-Computer Interaction has still not become a natural means of communication with a machine. While in face-to-face communication between humans, gestures are ubiquitously used to emphasize or disambiguate utterances, they are rarely used to determine precisely an action or referenced object. They rather support an action either by using body gestures or mimics.

The existence of sign languages and non-ambiguous gestures, however, shows, that gestures may be used even beyond the range of their usual occurrences in human-human interaction [1]. For instance in the context of musical conducting, gestures play an important role for communication between the conductor and the orchestra and provide many different types of information either explicitly or implicitly.

Similar modes of communication are still absent in human-computer interaction. Especially in the field of *exploratory data analysis* [2] which aims at providing researchers with techniques to inspect high-dimensional data and to

A. Camurri and G. Volpe (Eds.): GW 2003, LNAI 2915, pp. 369–379, 2004.

enable them to discern patterns or regularities in data, there is a great need for techniques to interact with data presentations. During the past decades mainly visualization was used for exploring data. Now, more and more researchers consider auditory displays to represent high-dimensional data. Such auditory data presentations are called *sonifications* [3]. In contrast to visualizations, which may also be static, sonifications are intrinsically dynamic since sound always evolves in time. Such information displays thus pose special demands on the human-computer interface that shall support interactive sonification, like real-time responsiveness and multi-dimensionality of control [4].

In this paper, we present a new gestural system that allows to use arm and hand gestures at a standard computer workplace. The interface extends the modalities of human-machine communication without restraining other well-established interfaces like the keyboard or mouse. The interface operates purely from visual recognition of the arms and hands, so that there is no need for extra markers or special gloves in order to use gestures. An illumination-independent visual recognition is ensured by an infrared strobe which is synchronized to the frame rate of the cameras. Using multiple cameras allows to infer the configuration of the upper limbs if they stay within a 3D-volume above the desk surface. The interface is designed so that all components are housed in a small T-shaped box with an integrated vision processor, so that it can easily be transported and used in different locations. The interface can also be adjusted to be used without a table, for instance in front of a projector display or an 'intelligent wall'.

Several applications are targeted with our gesture box: firstly, it is used to extend the human-computer interfaces in a standard computer workplace. In particular, we aim at applications in the field of exploratory data analysis and data mining. Secondly, the gesture desk will be used to study grasping strategies as well as object manipulation by human hands, a research effort in the context of our cognitive robotics group, where intelligent grasping techniques for robot hands are being developed.

The application focused in this paper is interactive browsing of high-dimensional data by gestural control of an *auditory map* [5]. For that purpose, the new technique of *auditory self-organizing maps* (AuSOMs) is introduced here. A 2D-map is adapted in a high-dimensional data space by using the Kohonen algorithm, resulting in a *self-organizing map* [6]. The hand's height above the desk surface is used to select the level of detail for browsing the map. The focus can be continuously controlled between accessing individual neurons on the map and accessing averages over a large neighborhood on the map. Such gestural controls are then used for conducting data sonifications which are rendered in real-time.

The paper is structured as follows: first the setup of the gesture desk is presented. Section 3 presents the currently applied tracking algorithm used to follow moving hands. Section 4 introduces the technique of auditory maps to browse high-dimensional data by means of interactive sonifications and in particular the AuSOM. Section 5 provides sound examples for such interactive sonifications. The paper ends with a discussion and prospects for future work.

2 System Overview

The design of the gesture desk was chosen to meet the following requirements that arise from prospected utility and usage scenarios:

- **Portability:** the gesture desk should be a transportable unit which can easily be used in different rooms with no or minor need for adjustment or adaptation of the hardware setup. Portability limits the maximum size and weight of the interface box.
- **Non-intrusiveness:** it is required that no restrictions are made to potential users. Any accessories like fingertip markers or data gloves are inconvenient. As a consequence, a computer-vision based system is the only practical choice.
- **Illumination-independence:** the gesture desk has to be able to be operated at different illumination conditions. This can be accomplished by active illumination of the hands. As the illumination has to be glare-free, infrared light is used here.
- **Interaction volume:** using gestures in a standard computer workspace, the full volume in front of a seated user, delimited by the screen and the desk shall be available for gestural control. However, for practical reasons, we limit the interaction area to 70×50 cm on top of the desk, as will be illustrated below.
- **Spatial resolution:** motion of the arms/hands shall be analyzed in a 3D volume on top of the desk. This demands multiple cameras in order to capture different views of the user to evaluate the z-coordinate (height over desk surface). Spatial resolution scales with the difference in viewing angle, which depends on the distance between the cameras in the box. However, large camera distances conflict with the demand for limited size.
- **Multiple hands/multiple users:** we aim at an interface that is able to analyze two-arm gestures rather than the motion of a single arm. Furthermore, we are interested in collaborative gestures, performed by two communicating users. However, such usage scenarios are compatible with our vision-based approach and just demand for suitable algorithms.

Beginning with the obvious conclusions from the demands listed above, the gesture desk was designed by rapid prototyping in a ray-tracing environment. Using a CAD-model proved extremely helpful in considering and tuning the setup, determining viewing angles, adjustment of the cameras, and the arrangement of additional optical elements like mirrors or filters. Furthermore, modern ray-tracing programs like *POVRay*[1] allow to compute pictures including all relevant physical effects, like shadows, glares, reflections, attenuation, and so forth, so that the simulations effectively supported the convergence of the design process. Figure 1 shows a raytraced prototype design, rendered with POVRay.

It can be seen in Figure 1, that the interface is a T-shaped box, positioned below the glass desk. The views from below the table are particularly advantageous, since the palms are often oriented downwards, so that the fingers are

[1] See www.povray.org

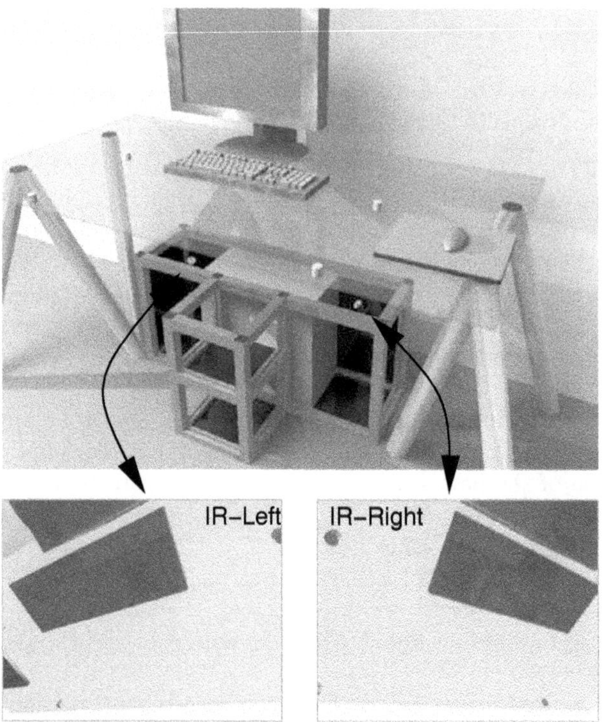

Fig. 1. Model of the gesture desk, obtained by raytracing of a 3D-model. The plots below show views from the perspective of the infrared cameras. The small cylinders are located on the desk at the borders of the intended interaction volume.

better visible from below and occlusions are reduced from this angle. Two IR-cameras are located on the wings of the 'T'. They capture the scene through IR bandpass-filters. The filters limit the camera sensitivity to the invisible infrared spectral range, in which actively controlled illumination is provided by infrared LED cluster lamps (IR-LEDs), which are currently assembled. At the moment we use Pulnix TM-765E cameras with f = 8 mm lenses, offering an opening angle of 55 degrees. Our cameras can be operated with external video-synchronization and are sensitive in the infrared up to 1000 nm. Schott IR-low-pass filters (ν_c = 875 nm) are mounted to limit the sensitivity to the used IR-illumination described below. To facilitate arm/hand detection, the IR-LED lamps will be flashed at half the video rate, so that the difference between successive camera images allows to isolate the IR-illuminated view, independent of other illumination in the infrared. Since the IR-LED intensity decays rapidly, the lamps mainly illuminate the hands/arms and reflected light from the ceiling can be neglected and is easily removed by a simple thresholding operation. The video rate as well as the processing time, however, limits the responsiveness of gestural interaction.

The symmetric alignment of the IR-cameras and the large camera distance of about 60 cm to typical hand positions allows high accuracy for deriving the z-coordinate for two corresponding 2D-points (x_1, y_1) and (x_2, y_2) in the camera images. The resolution depends on the capture resolution and on the distance. For precisely located objects it is about 3 mm when using a resolution of 384×288 pixels.

A third camera, recording a full RGB-color image of the hand will be mounted on the base of the 'T' and serve for two purposes: firstly, the color information helps to segment the skin from the background and thus to follow hands more accurately around the position indicated from the IR-cameras; secondly, it provides an additional view, which is useful in case of occlusions. Thirdly, this camera can be operated in opposite phase to the IR cameras, allowing to increase the effective frame rate by a factor of two.

The size of the T-shaped interface box was chosen from considering the need of space for mounting the cameras and by considering portability: integrated in the box is a Linux/Pentium 4 computer with frame grabber hardware (Matrox Meteor).

The interface box was constructed from system elements (BOSCH Assembly Technologies [7]), which allow flexible reconfiguration and adaption of the setup to changing needs. Figure 2 shows a photograph of the current version of the gesture box.

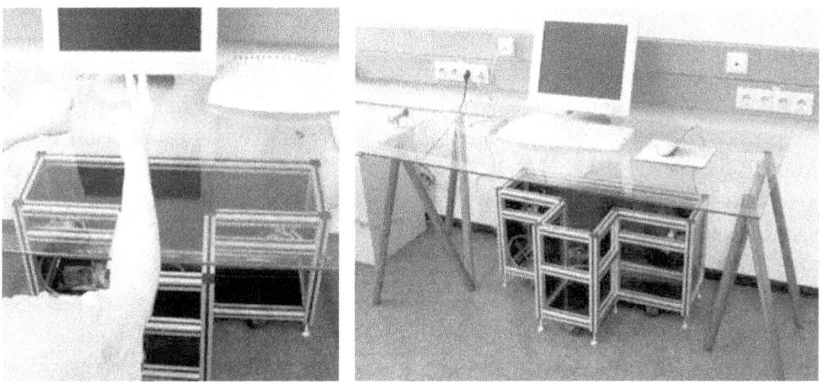

Fig. 2. Photos of the gesture desk.

3 Tracking Human Hands on the Gesture Desk

For interpreting the camera images correctly w.r.t. the user's gestural actions, it is required that the computer generates (or updates) an internal representation of the user at each time step. This can be accomplished for instance by a body model, which can be implemented by means of a stick figure with given element lengths and joint angle ranges [8]. A complete model of the user, however, has to include the structure of the hand with many degrees of freedom. The advantage

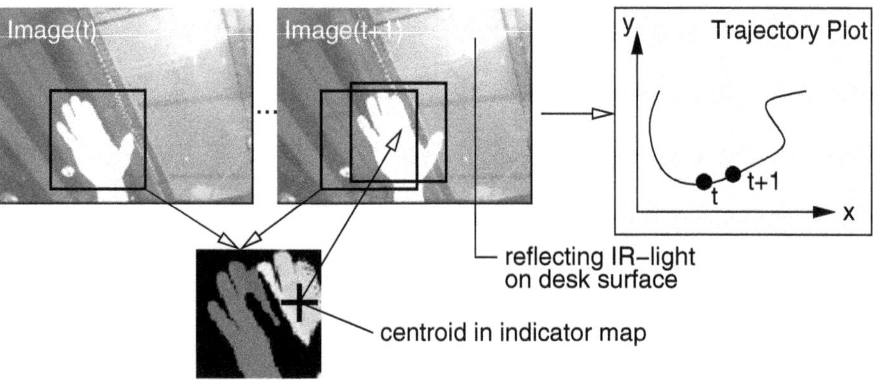

Fig. 3. Illustration of the tracking technique. The captured IR-camera images and the difference between successive frames are shown. The plot on the right shows the obtained results as a trajectory.

of using a model is that it enables us to make use of explicit knowledge about the domain, like e.g. that the bone lengths usually do not change during a session or that posture changes in successive frames are expected to be small. The tracking technique that we intend to use is *holistic tracking* as introduced in [9]. The model configuration, given by a vector of joint angles will be updated by random steps in the joint angle space, accepting proposed moves if they reduce an error measure computed from both the recorded images and rendered images using virtual cameras in model space. The setup of this tracking is still ongoing and will be reported elsewhere. We just started with a rather simple tracking, that uses the difference of successive images to update the estimation for hand coordinates. Practically this is achieved by shifting the hand coordinate vector towards the locally weighted mean expectation of movement by computing the motion indicator image

$$\boldsymbol{D}(\mathbf{x}) = \epsilon|\boldsymbol{T}_{t+1}(\mathbf{x}) - \boldsymbol{T}_t(\mathbf{x})| \cdot \boldsymbol{T}_{t+1}(\mathbf{x})K(\mathbf{x} - \mathbf{x}_t) \tag{1}$$

where $\mathbf{x}_t$ is the estimated hand coordinate vector in image $\boldsymbol{T}_t$ and $K(\cdot)$ is a kernel function centered at the origin. Then the estimate $\mathbf{x}_{t+1}$ is computed by using the centroid

$$\mathbf{x}_{t+1} = \frac{\langle \boldsymbol{D}(\mathbf{x})\mathbf{x}\rangle_{\mathbf{x}}}{\langle \boldsymbol{D}(\mathbf{x})\rangle_{\mathbf{x}}} \,. \tag{2}$$

This algorithm tracks the hand position quite accurately, if an illuminated hand moves slowly enough in front of a darker background. Figure 3 shows some images captured from the right IR-camera and a typical trajectory plot obtained from gestural interaction with one hand.

4 Self-organizing Auditory Maps

The strength of gestures is their high expressivity and multi-dimensionality. Assuming 5 joint angles for one arm (three degrees of freedom for the shoulder plus one for elbow and hand wrist) and 10 independent joint angles for the hand (about two per finger), an arm motion specifies a trajectory in a 15-dimensional configuration space. The following application presents a technique for using multi-dimensional control for interfacing with high-dimensional data presentations using *auditory self-organizing maps* (AuSOMs). Auditory maps [5] are visualized maps, that have attached to each location in representation space (map space) a high-dimensional data vector that is presented acoustically. However, parts of the map can also be presented visually in the map, e.g. by using spatially resolved color or texture. Whereas the dimensionality of visual representations is limited (e.g. the eye is only sensitive to three color channels like red, green and blue (RGB)) the auditory system is able to distinct and process a much higher number of frequencies in parallel at the same time. This motivates to use sound as a means to represent the high-dimensional data vector attached to a map. Such acoustic representations of data are called *sonifications* and are a rather new technique in the context of exploratory data analysis [3].

While auditory maps were already considered in [5,10], *self-organizing maps* are so far not used in combination with sonification. Self-organizing maps are neural networks that adapt a (usually 2D) grid of neurons so that neurons nearby on the map are activated by stimuli or data vectors that are nearby in data space. As a result, the SOM provides a low-dimensional non-linear representation of the data. Interpreting the neuron weight vectors as positions in data space, the map can be be imagined as a flexible 2D surface unfolded in the high-dimensional data space so that the neurons are close to the data. Although the SOM algorithm is given by a heuristic learning rule, it shows qualitatively a similar behavior as principal surfaces [11]. Self-organizing maps have been applied in many areas including clustering, control, visualization or data compression [12]. Figure 4 illustrates the relation between map space and data space.

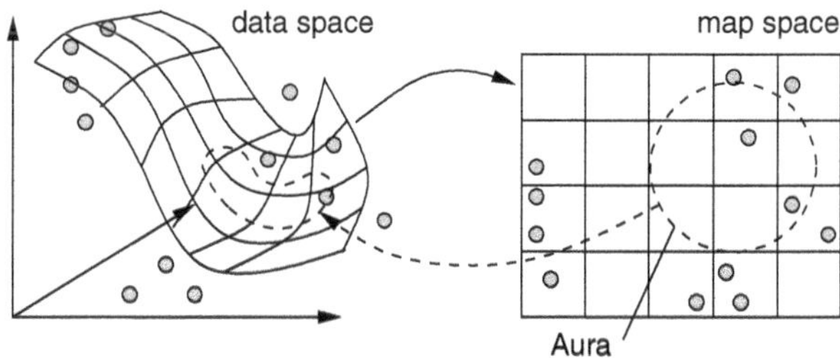

Fig. 4. Illustration of the relation between the AuSOM map space and data space. Neurons within the aura correspond to locations in data space on a 2d-manifold.

While the map visualization is easily accessed by just inspecting the map, it is unclear what would be an intuitive way to access the locally attached sonifications. The most direct way would be to click on a neuron to trigger playback of the localized sonification. However, this allows only a sequential access. A very intuitive technique to facilitate browsing auditory maps was proposed by

Fernström et al. [10] with the idea of an *aura*. An aura is a two-dimensional field in the map space in which acoustic entities may contribute to the perceived sound. Playback of auditory information is triggered when a data point enters the aura; sound level and orientation in the listening space are related to its relative position to the aura center on the map.

The AuSOM brings the ideas of auditory maps and aura together with the new and generic approach of SOM sonification and a gestural interface. Hand movements on the gesture desk are used to navigate the aura on a SOM visualization in an intuitive manner: altitude of the hand over the desk surface is translated into aura size. Together with the motion parallel to the surface this allows continuous control of focus and location. Since the type of hand posture so far remains unused, it may be chosen for selecting dimensions to be sonified. For this purpose we intend to integrate an ANN-based subsystem developed in our group for hand posture recognition, presented in [13]. In this way, the sonification can be controlled with one hand (usually the left arm) so that the right hand remains free for controlling the mouse and keyboard. Figure 5 shows our SOM visualization. A selected feature component of interest is color-mapped. Alternatively, different color channels can be used for up to three features. However, within the auditory map, all features are used.

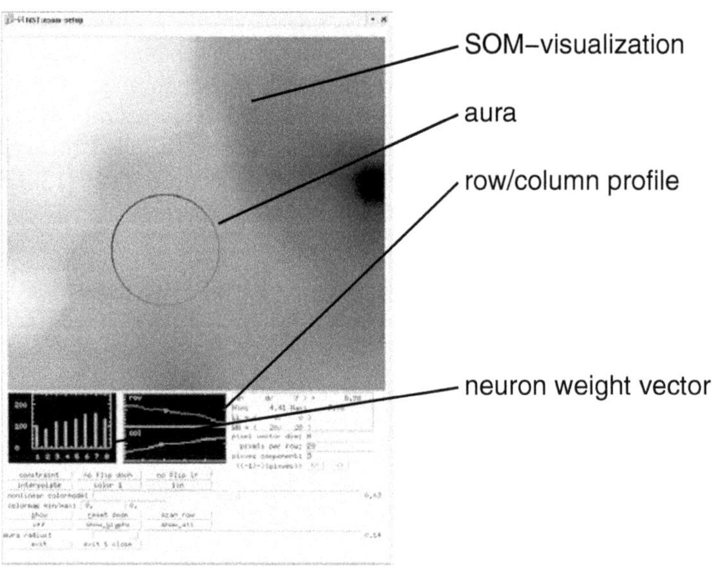

Fig. 5. Visualization of the SOM with Neo/NST [14]. The visualization shows attribute 3 (petal width) of the Iris dataset using a color mapping.

5 Results and Sound Examples

Figure 5 shows a SOM visualization for the Iris data set [15], a classical benchmark data set for cluster analysis. The dataset consists of 150 records in 4D plus a class label. The attributes are the sepal length, sepal width, petal length and petal width of 150 plants that cluster in three groups, 50 each. On the screenshot, map color is an interpolated color mapping from the 3rd component of the neuron map. The other attributes of the data set, however, are difficult to be visualized at the same time. They can be queried with gestural controls and are presented in the sonification. Sepal length, sepal width and petal length determine parameters of the sound.

Many different approaches are possible to represent the aura content. One strategy is to associate a sound element to each neuron. A neuron can be described by its weight vector and/or the data in the environment to its weight vector in data space. In this case, the sonification will be the mix of all neuron sound patterns superimposed in an "acoustically ecologic" way, for instance assuming that neurons having a larger distance to the aura center contribute with a softer sound. In addition, a spatial localization of the neuron sounds in the listening space is appropriate. Alternatively, the aura sound can be imagined as consisting of a superposition of as many auditory streams as there are features. Locally weighted observables (i.e. kernel regression or nearest neighbor statistics) may be used to estimate interpolated feature values at the aura center. Obviously, the aura size then corresponds to the kernel width.

For the example of gestural interaction with AuSOMs, here the latter approach was taken, leading to location-dependent acoustic textures by adding a set of d FM-generators [16] with sinusoidal amplitude modulation and index modulation to represent features. Left/right-panning allows to determine the feature gradient.

In addition to this stationary sound texture, event-driven sound elements, similar to 'geiger tick' sounds will be used to announce that data points enter or leave the aura. Raising or lowering the hand above the desk surface then allows to scan the local environment to any point of interest and thus provides "insight" into the local density distribution by attending the tick sounds.

Sound example S1 exemplifies interaction with the auditory map using the Iris dataset as a pedagogic example. A spectrogram of the sonification is shown in Figure 6. The wave-file can be found on our web site [17]. It is difficult to convey

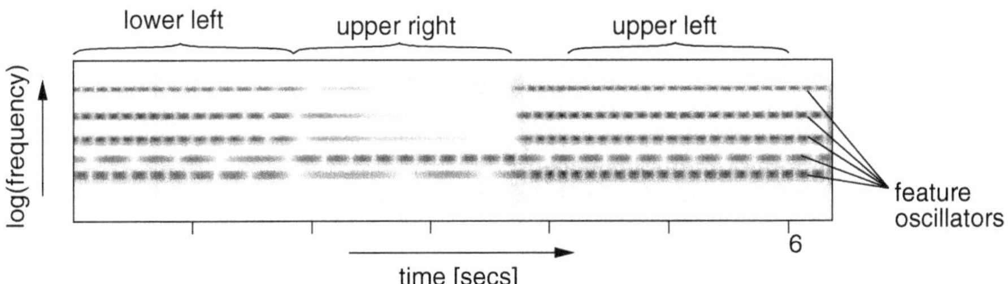

Fig. 6. Sound example: spectrogram of a sonification (STFT) of browsing the Iris data set. The region in the map is indicated above. The rhythmical pattern changes with the location on the map.

in a diagram or even a wave-file the experience of using the display since its strength arises from the direct interaction between user actions and the acoustic "re-actions". Listening to the sound without performing the actions in real-time therefore is not able to fully demonstrate the utility of the technique.

The degree of interaction while exploring high-dimensional data is expected to have strong impact on the time required to get insight in structures hidden in the data. For an evaluation, this factor has to be assessed more closely by psychophysical experiments. Such experiments may be considered after the display has completely evolved and been optimized further.

6 Conclusion

Arm gestures and hand postures provide an attractive interface for controlling dynamic and interactive data displays. Auditory displays are particularly suited for such control, since sound is an intrinsically dynamic medium. As humans are used to have their actions related to an acoustic feedback of their environment, the presented connection between gestural control and sonification is close-by.

In this paper, an interface for the use of hand motions to control auditory displays has been presented. This paper describes our system and presents first examples of real-time gestural control of sound in the context of sonification.

The presented interface box combines several attractive features concerning non-intrusiveness, robustness, portability, flexibility and responsiveness. For a first application of the gesture desk, the new technique of auditory self-organizing maps (AuSOMs) has been introduced and a gestural control interface has been designed and implemented.

The gesture desk is in an early stage, and especially the tracking has to be improved severely. Aside from this, the framework is offering many possibilities for further evolution. Concerning the human-computer interface, we currently extend the interface to include object manipulation as a means to manipulate virtual entities, which leads us to a versatile *tangible computing* platform with especially sonification as a new output channel.

Acknowledgement

Thanks to Oliver Lieske who built the sync-board.

References

1. International Gesture Workshop, GW 2001, *Gestures and Sign Languages in Human-Computer Interaction*, Lecture Notes in Artificial Intelligence, London, 4 2001. Springer.
2. J. W. Tukey, *Exploratory Data Analysis*, Addison-Wesley, 1977.
3. G. Kramer, Ed., *Auditory Display - Sonification, Audification, and Auditory Interfaces*. Addison-Wesley, 1994.

4. T. Hermann, J. Krause, and H. Ritter, "Real-time control of sonification models with an audio-haptic interface," in *Proc. of the Int. Conf. on Auditory Display*, R. Nakatsu and H. Kawahara, Eds. Int. Community for Auditory Display, 2002, pp. 82–86, Int. Community for Auditory Display, accepted.
5. A. L. Papp III, M M. Blattner and E. P. Glinert, "Sonic enhancement of two-dimensional graphics displays," in *Auditory Display*, G. Kramer, Ed. ICAD, 1994, pp. 447–470, Addison-Wesley.
6. T. Kohonen, "Self-organized formation of topologically correct feature maps," *Biological Cybernetics*, vol. 43, pp. 56–69, 1982.
7. "Linear motion and assembly technologies," `http://www.boschrexroth.com/BoschRexroth/business_units/brl/en/produkte/profilschienen_fuehrungen/index.jsp`.
8. M. Grosso, R. Quach, E. Otani, J. Zhao, S. Wei, P. Ho, J. Lu, and N. Badler, "Anthropometry for computer graphics human figures," Tech. Rep. MS-CIS-87-71, University of Pennsylvania, Dept. of Computer and Information Science, Philadelphia, PA, 1987.
9. C. Lange, T. Hermann, and H. Ritter, "Holistic body tracking for gestural interfaces," in this volume. International Gesture Workshop, 2003
10. M. Fernström and C. McNamara, "After direct manipulation - direct sonification," in *Proc. ICAD '98*. 1998, British Computer Society.
11. V. Cherkassky and F. Mulier, "Self-organizing networks for nonparametric regression," in *From Statistics to Neural Networks*, 1994, pp. 188–212.
12. T. Kohonen, *Self-Organizing maps*, Springer Series in Information Sciences Vol. 30. Springer, Berlin, Heidelberg, New York, third edition, 2001.
13. C. Nölker and H. Ritter, "Visual recognition of continuous hand postures," *IEEE Transactions on Neural Networks, Special Issue Multimedia*, vol. 13, no. 4, pp. 983–994, July 2002.
14. H. Ritter, "The graphical simulation toolkit Neo/NST," `http://www.techfak.uni-bielefeld.de/ags/ni/projects/simulation_and_visual/neo/neo_e.html`, 2000.
15. R. A. Fisher, "UCI repository of maschine learning databases," `ftp://ftp.ics.uci.edu/pub/machine-learning-databases/iris`, 1999.
16. J. Chowning, "The synthesis of complex spectra by means of frequency modulation," *Journal of the Audio Engineering Society*, vol. 21, no. 7, pp. 526–534, 1973.
17. T. Hermann, "Sonification for exploratory data analysis – demonstrations and sound examples," `http://www.techfak.uni-bielefeld.de/~thermann/projects/index.html`, 2002.

Gesture Frame – A Screen Navigation System for Interactive Multimedia Kiosks

Yinlin Li, Christoph Groenegress, Wolfgang Strauss, and Monika Fleischmann

Media Art & Research Studies, Fraunhofer Institute for Media Communication (IMK)
Schloss Birlinghoven, 53754 Sankt-Augustin, Germany
{yinlin.li,groenegress,strauss,fleischmann}@imk.fhg.de
http://imk.fraunhofer.de/mars

Abstract. In this article we present the gesture frame, a system based on quasi-electrostatic field sensing. The system captures the arm gestures of the user and translates pointing gestures into screen coordinates and selection command, which become a gesture-based, hands-free interface for browsing and searching multimedia archives of an information kiosk in public spaces. The interface is intuitive and body-centered, and the playful interaction allows visitors to experience a new and magical means to communicate with computers. The system can be placed on or behind any surface and can be used as a user interface in conjunction with any display device.

1 Introduction

The mouse and keyboard have been the standard input devices for human computer interaction (HCI) since the birth of the PC, which provided the basis for the standard WIMP (Windows, Icons, Mouse, Pull-down menus) interface. Recent advances in HCI, however, have expressed the need to move away from this approach, and rather adopt more traditional (or so-called human-centered) interaction and communication techniques. The emphasis is placed on building computer interfaces that emulate the way people interact with each other, so that, in essence, computers become smarter and easier to use.

The gesture frame interface is such an effort that puts the human user at the centre of the interaction. It is an attempt at hiding the internal soft- and hardware architecture from the user, but maintaining a high degree of flexibility and usability. It reverses the situation that humans need to adapt to computers: the computer adapts to the human user.

2 Related Works

The most commonly used technologies for gesture-based interfaces include data gloves, computer vision techniques and various other sensing devices, notably infrared. The data glove is expensive and also requires users to wear it, so it is not suitable for use in an unconstrained environment. Other non-contact interfaces are based on computer vision techniques and often use some kind of model of the human body (or

A. Camurri and G. Volpe (Eds.): GW 2003, LNAI 2915, pp. 380–385, 2004.

parts of it) [1] [5] in order to enable interaction. In other methods, markers are attached to the body [2]. Computer vision systems need to be calibrated and have a relatively low update rate (approx. 30Hz) compared to other techniques. They are also sensitive to external conditions such as lighting.

Similar attempts based on electric field sensing have been carried out by Smith et al. [4]. They demonstrate the capabilities of the technology in a number of installations such as the *Brain Opera* [3]. However, the interface requires calibration for different users and has not been used as an interface for screen navigation [6].

3 Gesture Analyses

The use of body gestures provides us with a unique way of expressing needs and desires in a non-verbal way. For example, infants who haven't learned to speak yet, express themselves via pointing at things.

Even when we have learned a language it is impossible for us to reach everything by touching it. Objects, which can be seen at a distance, can't be grasped but the distance can be overcome plainly by pointing at them. Pointing at an object immediately turns one's focus to it and can thus clarify our intentions.

In fact, arm gestures are a very natural and efficient way of emphasizing one's focus of attention. For pointing gestures, an action begins by raising the arm, then moving it until the hand points at the desired object or direction. In order to clearly express focus, the arm should remain in the same position for a short time. Finally, the end of this action is expressed by dropping one's arm.

From this assumption, we can infer that, in order to be able to process pointing gestures, we need to be able to interpret at least four states: raising one's arm, positioning of the arm, focus, and dropping the arm.

Comparing this to screen navigation, these actions correspond to cursor movement and (mouse) click. By identifying the above four signals, gesture-based screen interaction becomes possible. The screen cursor can be controlled by arm movement and selection of an item is represented by an idle position. Raising one's arm generally enables these two actions, while dropping it disabled them.

4 Gesture Frame

In order to capture the arm gesture and control the cursor of the computer, a gesture frame sensor system was implemented. The system consists of a frame of antennas (Fig.2), a signal processing electronic part and a computer that all parts are connected to.

The gesture frame is based on the following principle. It is widely known that the human body can radiate (or reflect) energy in the form of heat, infrared waves, electromagnetic power and others. Especially, the electromagnetic field is most closely related to our body, since it may be caused by biochemical effects in the cells, friction of clothes, space electric field induction or coupled from a power cable. This is why sometimes people may feel shocked by body electricity (e.g. when you take off your wool sweater). Indeed, the human body is surrounded by an electromagnetic field more or less at all time, as can be seen in Fig.1 (left).

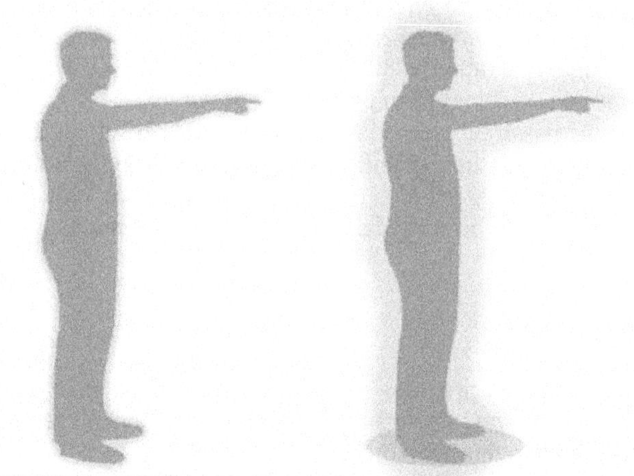

Fig. 1. Natural (left) and enhanced (right) electromagnetic field around human body

Unfortunately, the natural electromagnetic field around the human body is extremely weak and difficult to deal with for human computer interaction, whereas artificially created fields are easier to control.

When the body is immersed in an electromagnetic field, it will become a medium or path for the field and extends to the surrounding environment as illustrated in right of Fig1. When the user steps on the plate, a low frequency (about 60 KHz) weak electric field is coupled into the body. In fact, the human body field or energy is enhanced in this way to invisibly extend the measurable size of the body.

Actually, the gesture frame is used to sense this field to achieve the orientation and movement of user arm or hand. As in Fig.2, the gesture frame consists of four separate antennas (indicated by a, b, c, d, respectively), which will capture the corresponding electric field strength around the user arm or hand. For each direction in the x, y coordinate, there is an antenna pairs used. One of the antennas in the pairs is utilized for reference, by which the environment interference could be removed with the assistance of the special algorithm. Since the quasi-electrostatic field decrease in strength rapidly with distance, when the arm is raised the main factors in the measured signal comes from the arm. During arm pointing, the arm poses a gesture and different parts of arm get a different proximity to the four antennas. So from the overall information of the four antennas, the pointing direction and status is possible to extract with some custom algorithm. Then the position of the arm or hand is computed using a user body property (height, shoe impedance, etc.) adaptive algorithm, which allows the interface to work naturally even without prior calibration. Users can therefore control the cursor on the screen by simple pointing gestures.

Objects can be selected by pointing at them for a short period of time. Alternatively users can select items by clicking their fingers. A microphone that is connected to the PC measures the sound signals in the environment, and analyses them for spectral characteristics basing on Fast Fourier Transforms (FFT) that only correspond to the sound of a finger click.

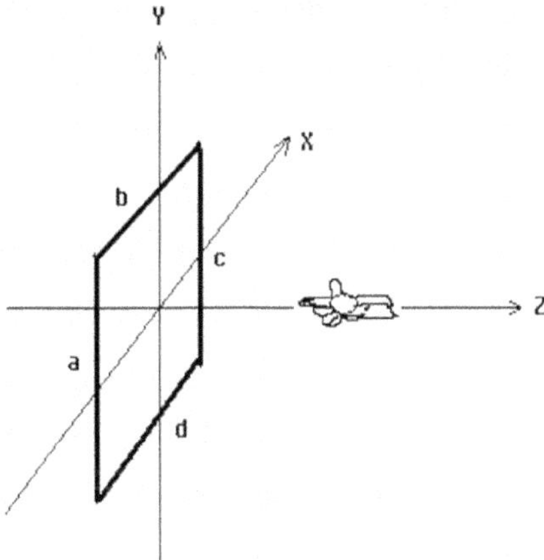

Fig. 2. The gesture frame model for the sensor

Fig. 3. Whole setup of the Info-Jukebox

The cursor control is initiated by raising the arm and terminated by dropping it. All of the information is captured by the frame system.

The antenna of the gesture frame is made of thin metal stick or film. It can be attached to or hidden behind any surface and used with any display device to provide a means for screen navigation.

5 Interactive Multimedia Kiosks

The gesture frame system has been successfully used as a human computer interface (HCI) in our Info-Jukebox, as shown in Fig.3.

The Info-Jukebox plays on the traditional *Wurlitzer* music box, one of the first interactive automatic entertainers. The cubic form of the installation ranges back to Mario Bellini's *Brionvega Black ST 201* TV set.

Fig. 4. The Info-Jukebox with gesture frame

The Info-Jukebox is an information kiosk for browsing and searching multimedia archives in public spaces. As shown in Fig.4, multimedia video clips are represented by images in the graphical user interface. In the centre, there is a multimedia player window, which will play the selected video. If the user drops his arm, the video will run until the end. Furthermore, any video can be viewed in full-screen mode by selecting a dedicated icon in the GUI.

The Info-Jukebox is physically built from a set of Plexiglas boxes that can be stacked on top of each other. A projector placed on the floor inside the box is directed upward and the projection is reflected by a mirror held at an angle of 45° at the top of the Info-Jukebox, towards one side of the upper box to produce a projection. It also has built-in speakers and a microphone.

With the gesture frame system inbuilt, it provides an intuitive body-centered interface for controlling a cursor on the screen in a natural and playful way. This makes the system accessible and easy to use for everyone. The disappearing computing architecture hides hardware components from the user and thus simplifies the interaction. The sensors employed translate pointing gestures into screen coordinates and items can be selected by holding this position for some time – this interface doesn't require to be calibrated for different users or environments. The desired information (e.g. text, video) is then presented on the navigation space as well as on a large projection screen to ensure that the Info-Jukebox can be installed in large public paces.

The Info-Jukebox is a playful interface that allows visitors to experience a new and magical way of communicating with computers. This may attract a much greater audience (e.g. children) than comparable technologies.

6 Conclusions and Future Work

The Info-Jukebox was first shown in public at the media arts exhibition Emoção Art.ficial in São Paulo, Brazil, between 11 August and 13 October 2002. An estimated 8000 visitors per week saw the installation during this time. Since users don't need to touch a device, and although initially, the projection screen was mistaken for a touch screen, none of the equipment was damaged. This demonstrates the robustness of the system towards mass usage.

From our observation, visitors quickly adapted to the new interface and enjoyed the playful experience of interaction and also the content presented, which were short video clips about previous work done at the MARS Exploratory Media Lab.

In future work, we will also investigate whether the technology can be used to determine the exact pose of the user's hand. This would offer additional interaction techniques and application scenarios. For instance, the system could be used to automatically translate sign language into text or speech.

References

1. J. Crowley, F. Berard, J. Coutaz.: Finger Tracking as an Input Device for Augmented Reality. In Proc. Int'l Workshop Automatic Face Gesture Recognition, 1995, pp. 195-200.
2. K. Dorfmüller-Ulhaas, D. Schmalstieg: Finger Tracking for Interaction in Augmented Environments. Proceedings ISAR'01, Oct. 2001.
3. T. Machover, *Brain Opera*. In Memesis: The Future of Evolution. Ars Electronica Editions, Linz, Austria, 1996.
4. JA Paradiso, K. Hsiao, J. Strickon , J. Lifton, A. Adler.: Sensor Systems for Interactive Surfaces. IBM Systems Journal Vol. 39(3&4), 2000.
5. J. Rehg, T. Kanade.: Digiteyes: Vision-based hand tracking for Human-Computer Interaction. Proc. of the IEEE Workshop of Motion on Non-Rigid and Articulated Objects, Austin, Texas, Nov. 1994, , pp. 16-22.
6. J. Smith, T. White, C. Dodge, D. Allport, J. Paradiso, N. Gershenfeld.: Electric Field Sensing for Graphical Interfaces. IEEE Computer Graphics and Applications, Vol. 18, No. 3, May-June 1998, pp. 54-60.

Intuitive Manipulation of a Haptic Monitor for the Gestural Human-Computer Interaction

Hidefumi Moritani, Yuki Kawai, and Hideyuki Sawada

Faculty of Engineering, Kagawa University
2217-20, Hayashi-cho, Takamatsu-city, Kagawa, 761-0396, Japan
sawada@eng.kagawa-u.ac.jp
http://www.eng.kagawa-u.ac.jp/~sawada/index_e.html

Abstract. A display device called intuition-driven monitor will be introduced. The device has been developed by combining a LCD, a flexible arm suspending the display, angle sensors and a CCD camera, and is directly manipulated by a user with his direct operations by hands, eye-gaze and facial expressions. A user is able to explore virtual space and manipulate virtual environment with gestures and the sense of haptics.

1 Introduction

Humans are able to communicate with each other by using not only verbal media but also the five senses effectively using their body parts. Information transmitted through non-verbal media directly affects our emotions and feelings, and especially gesture plays an important role for the emotional human communication. With the widespread availability of computers which have been used for the calculation and information processing, they are now used as an extensive tool for the communication and creative activities. The development of Graphical User Interface (GUI) has made the computer familiar to the general public, but the user's inputs to the computer are mainly conducted by using a mouse and a keyboard, which is far from the way we use in the human to human communication. If a computer is able to understand what the human requests with his non-verbal means, and also to present an answer appealing to human mind and emotions, a new communication system will be realized.

We are surrounded by various computer graphics (CGs) and images generated by a computer with the development of the image processing technology, however, there still exists bothersome manipulations in handing them especially for beginners and elderly people, since the operation to the virtual object is indirect and the operation itself is difficult and complicated. This paper introduces a new human-interface device, which can be used for the direct manipulations of a CG and Virtual Reality (VR) space.

A display device called intuition-driven monitor has been developed by combining a liquid crystal display (LCD), a flexible arm, angle sensors and a CCD camera, and an application system realizing a gestural human-computer interaction is proposed in this paper. A user is able to look a virtual 3D object into the display from an arbitrary direction by directly manipulating the device at his will. The system also accepts user's intuitive operations of the monitor based on the recognition algorithms of motion and facial expressions, with which the user is able to transmit his intention to the

A. Camurri and G. Volpe (Eds.): GW 2003, LNAI 2915, pp. 386–398, 2004.

virtual object using the gestural action and haptics. The system was evaluated by questionnaires to present a new human-interface to be employed not only in the CG handling and computerized designing, but also in the new haptic and gestural communication for elderly persons and physically challenged who have difficulties in using the conventional interface devices.

2 Backgrounds of Haptic and Gesture Studies

2.1 Haptic Devices

Several haptic devices have been introduced so far to display realtime haptic and touch feeling by combining 3D virtual images. SPIDAR [1] is a wire controlled haptic device, with which a user feels haptics in a finger sack. PHANToM [2], which was developed by SensAble Technologies, is equipped with a stylus pen to apply haptics against its manipulation.

By combining a 3D display with the haptic devices above, a user is able to touch or manipulate a 3D virtual object, and explore in a 3D virtual space. In the system the virtual object and space have to be synchronized with the haptics, but the algorithm to associate user's manipulation with object motion for the natural interaction is still hard to be realized.

2.2 Recognition of Gesture and Facial Expressions

Many attempts for recognizing gestures have been reported so far [3]-[5], part of which were applied to realize realtime recognition of sign-languages. A gesture has to be measured by some sensors first, and the obtained data are processed in the computer. Measurement of human gestures has been studied by mainly two approaches: one is to use image processing techniques, and the other is to employ wearable sensing devices.

Image processing techniques are actively applied to the realtime motion analysis by restricting the measurement condition, and let the performer be free from wearing sensing devices. A universal algorithm for the realtime motion analysis is, however, difficult to be made up because of the occlusion problem and the low spatio-temporal resolution. For the recognition of facial expressions, image processing seems the only technique. By restricting the attention area in a face with a marker or glasses with a colored frame to reduce the computational time, a new interface system to assist the user's inputs has been proposed [6][7].

In the latter approaches, a dataglove and a position sensor are widely applied to the gesture recognition. By distributing ten bend sensors along the five finger parts of the glove, the dataglove measures the bending angles of finger joints. The position sensor is able to sense its three dimensional position and its posture.

We have been studying gesture recognition works by the two approaches mentioned above, and found that the important emotional information presented in human gestures seems to appear in the forces applied to the body, although most of the existing works introducing the analysis of gestures treat the hand figure or the position of the body. In our former studies we have paid attention to emotional feelings presented in gestures, and have constructed a gesture recognition system reacting to emotions by using compact 3D accelerometers to measure force patterns [8]-[10]. In this research we noted the manipulating motion of the intuition-driven monitor, and have tried to extract the user's intention and feelings from the gestural patterns obtained by the device.

3 Intuition-Driven Monitor

The intuition-driven monitor is a monitor device, which has been developed to accept the user's haptic operations with his hands [11]. A LCD is suspended by a flexible arm with three joints as shown in Figure 1. The joint angles are measured by angle sensors (Omron absolute rotary encoder, E6CP-AG5C), which are used for the realtime calculation of three-dimensional position and posture of the display. The display is moved to and stayed still at any position and posture by the user's haptic manipulations. A CCD camera fixed on the display inputs the user's face images, and an eye-gaze and facial expressions are recognized for the intuitive manipulations.

Figure 2 shows the pictures of a user manipulating the device. With the device, a user is able to look CG objects in virtual 3D space by his direct manipulation. This device gives visual feedback reacting to the user's haptic manipulation. An image-rendering algorithm is presented in the following chapter.

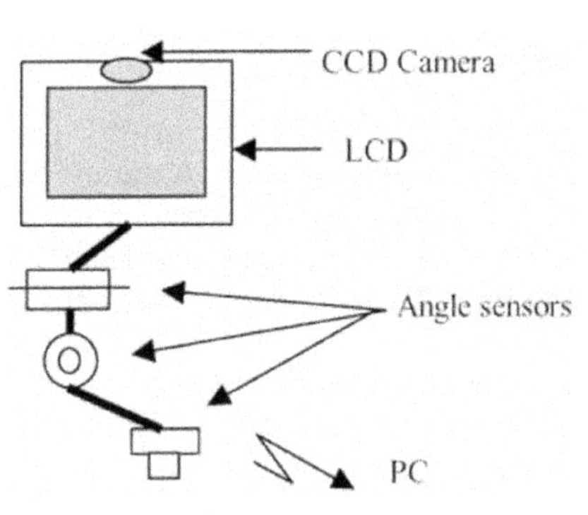

Fig. 1. Intuition-driven monitor

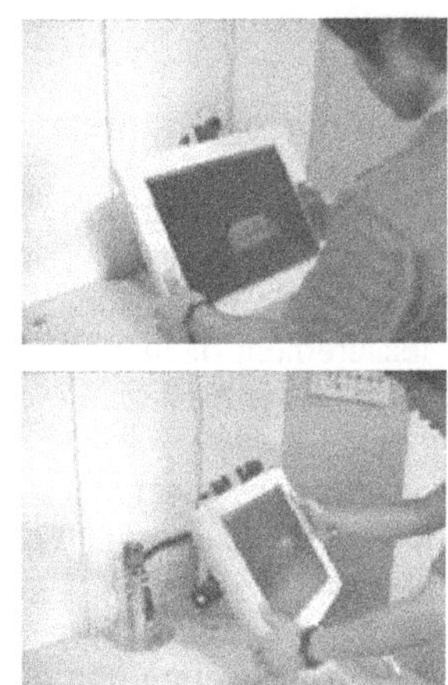

Fig. 2. Manipulation of the device

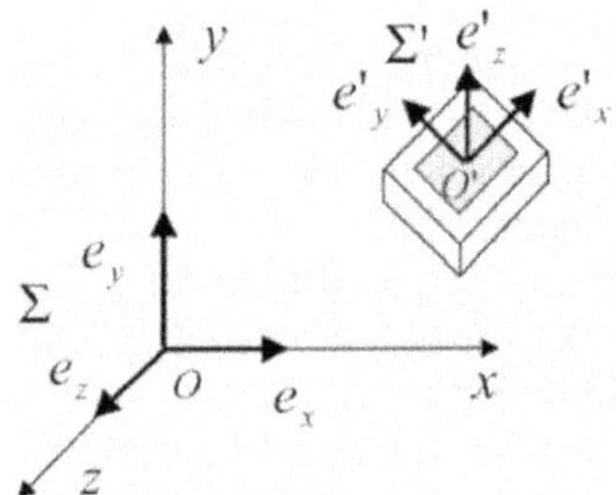

Fig. 3. Relation between world and monitor coordinate system

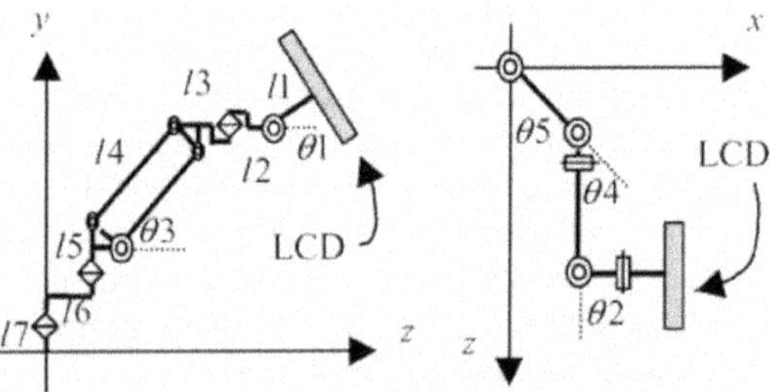

Fig. 4. Coordinate system of monitor

4 Direct Operation of 3D Object

Let the world coordinate system be set as Σ =(O; $\boldsymbol{e}_x$, $\boldsymbol{e}_y$, $\boldsymbol{e}_z$), where the monitor device is established. Figure 3 shows the relation between the world coordinate and monitor coordinate system.

By defining the joint angles and lengths of each part of the arm as shown in Figure 4, the coordinate of the LCD display center (x, y, z) and the surface vector (f_x, f_y, f_z) can be calculated as follows.

$$\begin{bmatrix} x \\ y \\ z \end{bmatrix} = \begin{bmatrix} 0 \\ l_7 \\ 0 \end{bmatrix} + \begin{bmatrix} l_6 \sin\theta_5 \\ 0 \\ l_6 \cos\theta_5 \end{bmatrix} + \begin{bmatrix} 0 \\ l_5 \\ 0 \end{bmatrix} + \begin{bmatrix} l_4 \cos\theta_3 \sin(\theta_5+\theta_4) \\ l_4 \sin\theta_3 \\ l_4 \cos\theta_3 \cos(\theta_5+\theta_4) \end{bmatrix} + \begin{bmatrix} l_3 \sin(\theta_5+\theta_4) \\ 0 \\ l_3 \cos(\theta_5+\theta_4) \end{bmatrix}$$
$$+ \begin{bmatrix} l_2 \sin(\theta_5+\theta_4+\theta_2) \\ 0 \\ l_2 \cos(\theta_5+\theta_4+\theta_2) \end{bmatrix} + \begin{bmatrix} l_1 \cos\theta_1 \sin(\theta_5+\theta_4+\theta_2) \\ l_1 \sin\theta_1 \\ l_1 \cos\theta_1 \cos(\theta_5+\theta_4+\theta_2) \end{bmatrix}, \tag{1}$$

$$\begin{bmatrix} f_x \\ f_y \\ f_z \end{bmatrix} = \begin{bmatrix} \cos\theta_1 \sin(\theta_5+\theta_4+\theta_2) \\ \sin\theta_1 \\ \cos\theta_1 \cos(\theta_5+\theta_4+\theta_2) \end{bmatrix}. \tag{2}$$

The projection of the virtual 3D space to be displayed in the monitor is calculated by the inner product computation.

The distance between the origin of the world coordinate system and the position of display is not considered due to the vertical projection, we could add the zooming function by reflecting the size of the projected image with the length l calculated as

$$l = \sqrt{x^2 + y^2 + z^2}. \tag{3}$$

Direct operation system was constructed by applying the algorithm of image rendering. With the system, a user is able to look a 3D object in a virtual space from an arbitrary direction according to his direct operation of monitor. For example, when a user moves the monitor up, he is able to look over the object from the upper position.

5 Logical Operation Based on Motion Recognition

Humans are able to transmit emotion and intention by effectively using gestures, and intensively communicate with each other by employing the touch feelings and physical contacts. We have paid attention to the motion of the monitor driven by user's manipulations, and tried to extract his tacit intention and emotion given to the monitor.

5.1 Extraction of Velocity Components from Position and Posture

The velocity component (v_x', v_y', v_z') derived from the motion and posture of the monitor is used here for the motion recognition, since the velocity information is considered to be reflected into the motion features.

5.2 Algorithm of Motion Recognition

The motion features are extracted from the following three two-dimensional vectors in order to obtain the intuitive characteristics of motion.

$$\boldsymbol{v}_{xy}' = (v_x', v_y'),\ \boldsymbol{v}_{yz}' = (v_y', v_z'),\ \boldsymbol{v}_{zx}' = (v_z', v_x') \quad (4)$$

Three kinds of characteristic parameters shown as *a) - c)* below are extracted from the sequence of each set of projection vectors in the *x-y, y-z* and *z-x* planes to achieve the realtime motion recognition [11].

a) Characteristics of motion size
b) Characteristics of motion direction [6]
c) Characteristics of rotational direction

Motion recognition is executed along the following three procedures.

1) Detection of start point and Estimation of motion candidate
When a user moves the monitor, the value of the motion size parameter starts increasing. With the observation of this parameter, the start point of the motion can be detected and the recognition is executed. Each parameter value is calculated and the motion type is estimated as a candidate by using the standard values, which are determined in advance by experiments.

2) Determination of motion direction
When a shift motion is done, the direction parameter shows a localized peak at a particular direction. With a shake motion, two localized peaks will appear with the difference of 180 degrees. When a rotation motion is given, the parameter values are broad distributed along the angle axis. The direction of the shift and shake motions is determined by referring to the angular localization.

3) Determination of rotational direction
When the rotation motion is estimated in the procedure above, the rotation plane is extracted and the rotating direction in the plane is determined.

5.3 Experimental Results of Motion Recognition

We conducted an experiment of the recognition for 11 simple motions, which is shown in Figure 5. In the experiment, the sampling rate was set to 20 Hz. The recognition was executed every 1/20 seconds by using 10 sampled data. A subject repeated the 11 gestures 20 times each. 100% recognition was achieved for almost all the motions, except for the up shift. Due to the mechanism of the monitor arm, the limit of upward-motion area restricted the user's motion, and the weight of the display disturbed the manipulations.

5.4 Virtual Object Manipulation

Virtual object manipulation system was constructed by applying the motion recognition algorithm. The system estimates human intentions in actions by detecting the beginning of the human motions, to autonomously support the human-computer interaction. In the system, the 11 motions were associated with the particular commands for CG manipulation. Examples of the relation between the motion and object operation is shown in Table 1. For example, when a user lightly pushes the right side of the monitor, the system extracts the right rotational motion and shows the user the backside of the object by turning it from the right. A user was able to operate the virtual 3D object by the haptic manipulation to the device.

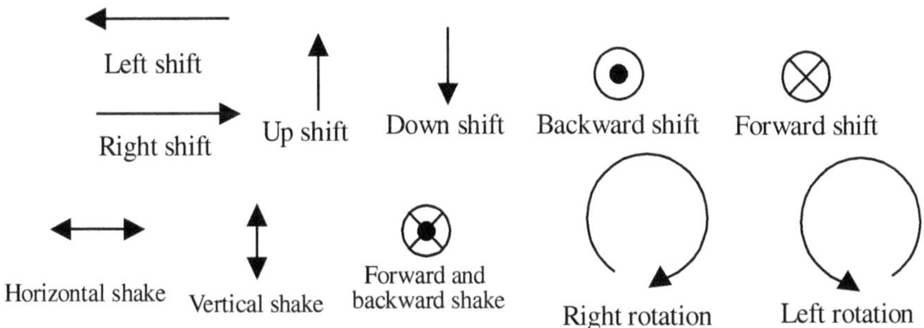

Fig. 5. Monitor motions

Table 1. Examples of object operation

Monitor motion	Object operation
Horizontal shift	Horizontal rotation
Vertical shift	Vertical rotation
Forward / backward shift	Scaling up / down
Vertical shake	Undo vertical rotation
Horizontal shake	Undo horizontal rot
Forward& backward shake	Undo scaling up / down
Left / right rotation	Mode switch between Direct mode and Logical operation mode

6 Recognition of Gaze and Facial Expression for Object Manipulation

The motion recognition enables a user to roughly manipulate a virtual object in the monitor. In this chapter the recognition of eye-gaze and facial expression is introduced for the intuitive manipulation.

6.1 Acquisition of Individual Standard Face Model

The recognition of gaze and facial expression is executed by referring to an individual standard face model, which describes and stores the neutral shape and location of parts in a face area such as an eye, eyebrow, nose and mouth of individuals. In this study, the standard model consists of two files; one is a face model which stores the information of face parts and is used for the recognition of facial expressions, and the other is an eyeball model which describes the size and shape of an eyeball for the eye-gaze estimation. The deformation of face parts is measured by referring to the standard models, and is used for the interactive manipulation of virtual objects displayed in the LCD.

Face parts areas are extracted first from face images obtained from the CCD camera to construct the standard face model by using the image processing algorithms described below. To avoid the head motion, the subject's head is fixed by the calibration device shown in Figure 6.

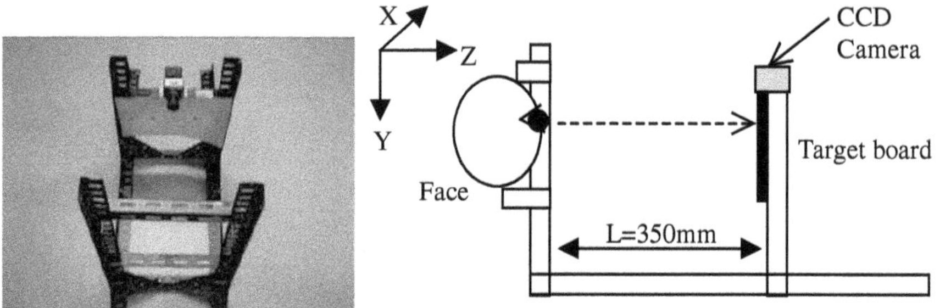

Fig. 6. Calibration device

6.2 Iris Extraction Based on Face Feature Points

The input image is transformed into YUV image, and skin color area is extracted first. After binarizing the image, the face area is determined by the X- and Y-axis projection. Here, no inclination nor rotation of the face is assumed, and face parts are approximated by applying the search mask to the face area. The mask has the information of expected locations of face parts to restrict the searching area within the skin color area. Figure 7 shows the result of the face area detection.

Next, the eye area is binarized to extract iris by the X- and Y-axis projection, since the iris is approximated as a circular shape. The iris center is also estimated by using the projection data. Then the iris size and center position are compared with the standard face model. If the difference is larger than a threshold value, the recognition process is repeated from the face area detection. Examples of the iris extraction are shown in Figure 8 and 9.

Input Image

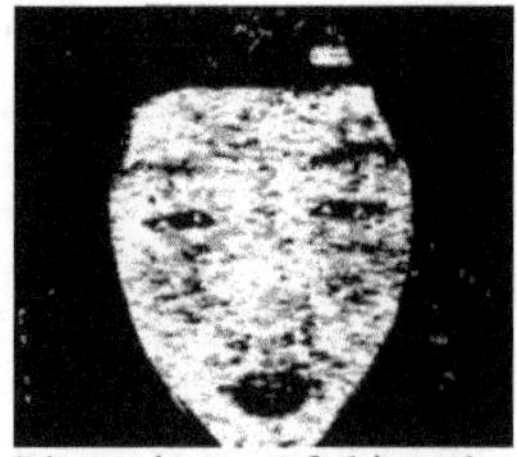

Binary image of skin color

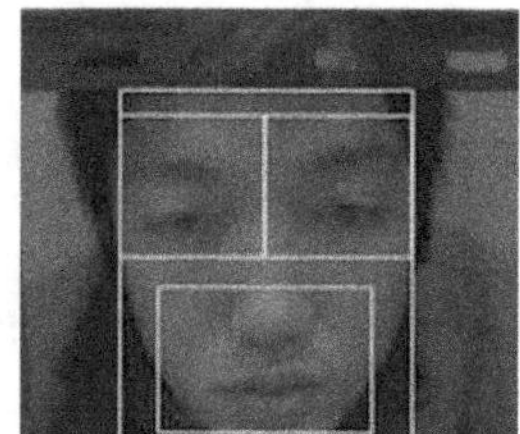

Search Mask Application

Fig. 7. Extraction of face and eye area

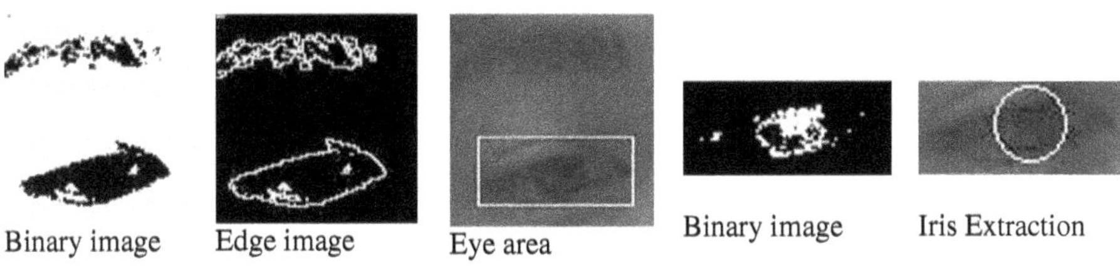

Fig. 8. Extraction of eye area and iris

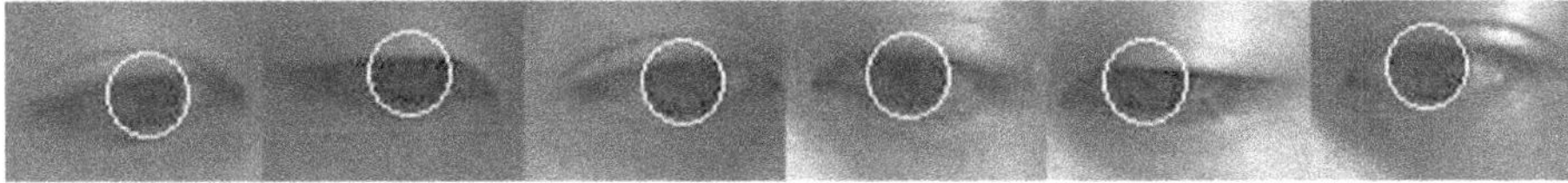

Fig. 9. Results of iris extraction

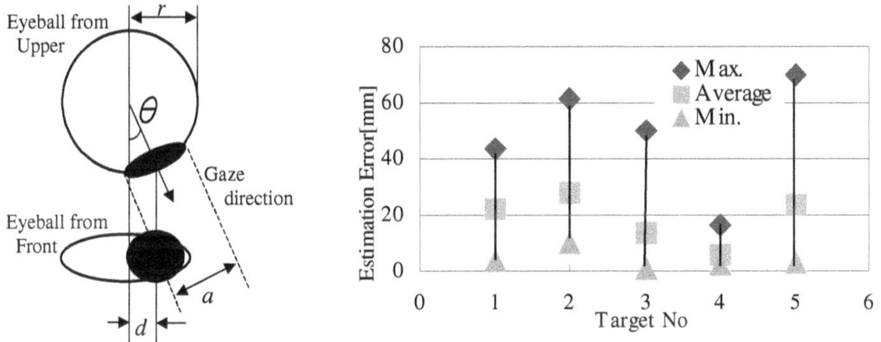

Fig. 10. Gaze estimation by eyeball

Fig. 11. Results of gaze estimation

6.3 Eye-Gaze Estimation

Gaze direction is estimated by using the eyeball model shown in Figure 10. The rotation angle θ of an eyeball is calculated as

$$\theta = \sin^{-1} \frac{d}{a} \tag{5}$$

by using an iris size a and the offset of an iris center d.

We conducted an experiment of the gaze estimation by using a target board with five gazing points arranged at 60mm distance, which was set under the camera. First, a subject gazed at the four corners and the center of the board for the calibration. Three subjects gazed at the points 1-5 in the numerical order, which was repeated 10 times. As shown in Figure 11, gaze direction was estimated with the accuracy of 30mm. The mis-detection of iris extraction caused the decline of the accuracy, and the improvement of the extraction algorithm will contribute to the gaze estimation.

6.4 Recognition of Facial Expressions

In the human communication, facial expression can be recognized by perceiving the motion of facial parts. In this study we are trying to recognize facial expressions based on the measurements of the parts deformations. By referring to the individual face standard model, the deformation of facial parts is detected as the displacements of each part.

The eyebrow area is extracted by applying X- and Y-axis projection to the edge image in the eye area shown in Figure 8. By applying noise elimination and morphological filtering, an eyebrow is extracted as a pruning image as shown in Figure 12. Then the inner, center and end points (P1-P3) of an eyebrow are detected as the feature points as shown in Figure 13. Motion of eyebrow is measured by tracking the displacements of the three feature points.

Fig. 12. Process of eyebrow extraction

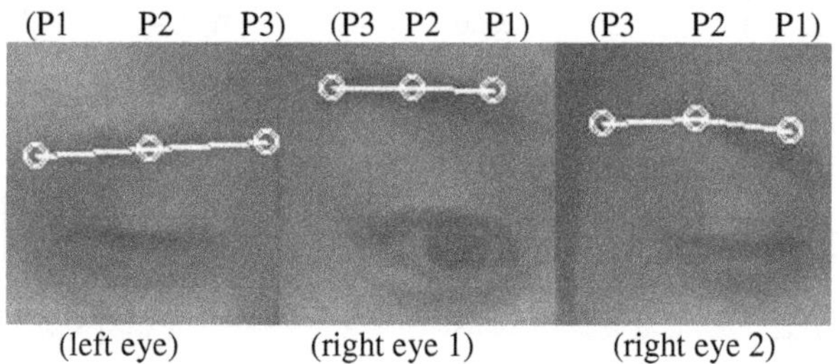

Fig. 13. Feature extraction of eyebrow

Mouth area is detected by finding the lip color in the lower area of a face. The extracted area is binarized with a predetermined threshold value. After the noise elimination and morphological filtering, extracted clusters are labeled in the pixel size order. By examining the clusters from upper and lower in the area referring to the pixel size, upper and lower lips are determined as shown in Figure 14. Figure 15 shows several results of the mouth detection.

6.5 Measurement of Facial Expressions

When a user gives a facial expression, the deformations of facial parts are extracted. Experimental results of the measurement are shown in Table 2 (a) and (b), when a subject raised his eyebrows and opened a mouth, respectively. Figure 16 shows the extraction of facial parts for the two facial expressions above. When a user raised his eyebrow, the displacements of right and left eyebrow increased, which were well extracted by the image processing technique. In opening a mouth, displacements concerning the mouth changed, while other displacements were not presented remarkably.

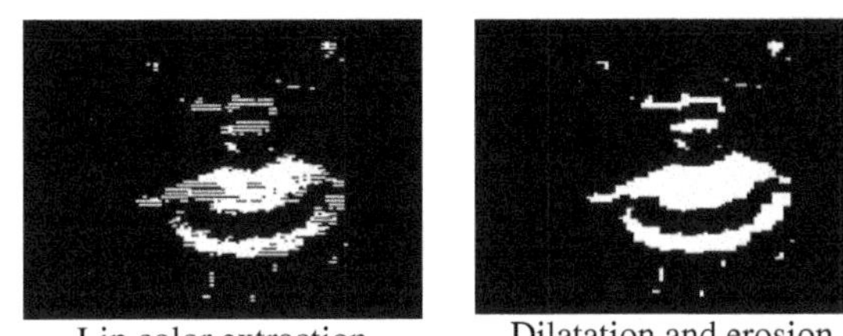

Fig. 14. Process of lip extraction

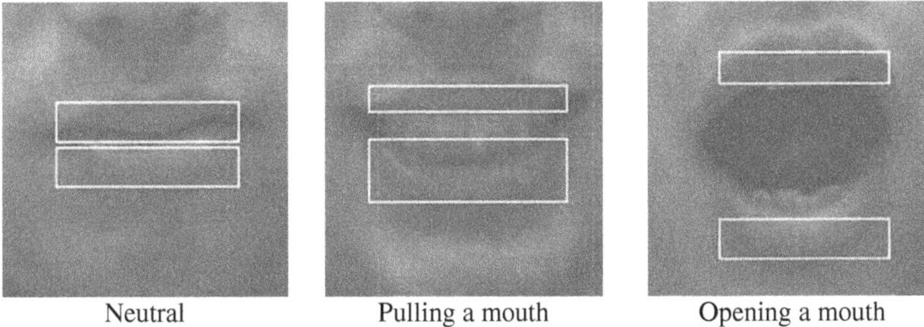

Fig. 15. Results of mouth extraction

Table 2. (a) Displacement of face parts (Eyebrow up)

Feature point	Displacements in pixel
Right eyebrow, P1 (X1, Y1)	(-1.0, 16.8)
Right eyebrow, P2 (X2, Y2)	(1.0, 18.6)
Right eyebrow, P3 (X3, Y3)	(4.0, 19.6)
Left eyebrow, P1 (X1, Y1)	(2.0, 14.6)
Left eyebrow, P2 (X2, Y2)	(-3.0, 14.6)
Left eyebrow, P3 (X3, Y3)	(-7.0, 12.6)
Height of right eye	0.0
Height of left eye	3.0
Amount of mouth opening	1.0
Height of upper lip	4.0
Length of upper lip	0.0
Height of lower lip	4.0
Length of lower lip	2.0

By associating the deformation of facial parts with the facial expressions, we are currently constructing a system to understand the user's intention based on the motion of eye-gaze, face parts and facial expressions.

Table 2. (b) Displacement of face parts (Mouth open)

Feature point	Displacements in pixel
Right eyebrow, P1 (X1, Y1)	(12.0, 3.3)
Right eyebrow, P2 (X2, Y2)	(7.5, 2.1)
Right eyebrow, P3 (X3, Y3)	(3.0, 5.1)
Left eyebrow, P1 (X1, Y1)	(-3.0, 3.1)
Left eyebrow, P2 (X2, Y2)	(-6.5, 9.1)
Left eyebrow, P3 (X3, Y3)	(-11.0, 10.1)
Height of right eye	1.0
Height of left eye	0.0
Amount of mouth opening	61.0
Height of upper lip	19.0
Length of upper lip	63.0
Height of lower lip	19.0
Length of lower lip	0.0

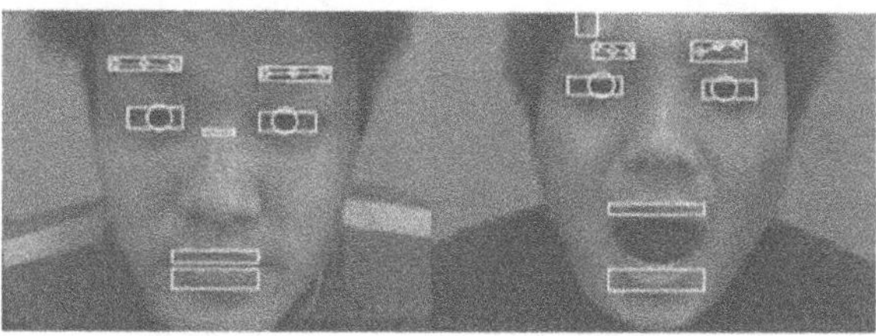

(a)Raise eyebrow (b) Open mouth

Fig. 16. Extraction of face parts

7 Virtual Object Manipulation by Motion, Gaze and Face

The recognition of gaze and facial expressions was installed in the intuition-driven monitor to introduce a new operation system of a computer by combining with the haptics. In the system, extracted gaze and facial expressions were associated with operation commands for CG and VR space manipulation as listed in Table 3, while motions given to the monitor by a user were related to the object manipulation commands shown in Table 2. With the system, a user was able to multi-modally manipulate, and interactively communicate with a virtual object in the display by intuitively employing gestures, haptics, gaze and facial expressions.

An experiment was conducted to 9 users for the evaluation of the system. In the experiment, a virtual 3D sofa was initially placed at the center of the display, which was moved by user's manipulations at his own will using head motions, facial expressions and haptic actions. After the use of the system, a questionnaire was conducted for the evaluation from the viewpoints of usefulness, availability and interests. Table 4 shows the results of the questionnaire.

The monitor device was evaluated almost favorably. Especially, most of the users found the interests and availability of the device, and evaluated positively. On the other hand, there were several opinions to point out the difficulties in manipulating the object based on the recognition of motion and facial expressions. The association of user's action with CG outputs should be further examined in the future system.

Table 3. Object manipulation by head motion and facial expressions

Actions	Object operation
Horizontal shift	Horizontal rotation
Vertical shift	Vertical rotation
Forward / backward shift	Scaling up / down
Eyebrow Up	Move up
Eyebrow Down	Move down
Frowning	Undo previous operation
Mouth Open	Expand vertically
Mouth pulling	Expand horizontally
Mouth pushing	Move forward
Gaze	Attention point

Table 4. System evaluation by questionnaires

	5(good)	4	3	2	1(bad)
Reaction of object motion	1	4	2	2	0
Easiness of operation	1	4	3	1	0
Satisfaction of manipulation	1	2	2	4	0
Usefulness	1	4	3	1	0
Interest	6	2	1	0	0
Availability and Usability	3	4	2	0	0

8 Conclusions

This paper introduced a new monitor device, which can be operated by the user's direct manipulations using haptics, gaze and facial expressions. We experimentally constructed a new operation system based on haptics and face, which was evaluated by the questionnaires. A user was able to directly manipulate a virtual space or an object with his hands, gaze and facial expressions. In the manipulation of CG object and VR space, the system was evaluated favorably comparing with the use of the conventional devices such as a mouse and a keyboard. There were several assessments to point out the difficulties in the logical operations based on the motion recognition. We have to further study the association algorithm of the haptic manipulation with the expression of emotion and intention. The improvement of the accuracy of gaze recognition, together with the robust recognition of face and facial expression against head motion, will be the future challenge for the development of the new interface device.

We are now working to construct a new communication device for the physically challenged. A patient with cerebral palsy, for example, will be able to operate a computer on a wheel chair with his facial expression and direct actions to the display. With the expansion of communication capacity, the media which directly affect our emotions will be effectively utilized together with the audio and images.

Acknowledgments

This research project was conducted as a part of the "Domestic Study for the International Joint Research Program into Intelligent Manufacturing System" commissioned by IMS Promotion Center.

References

1. M. Sato, Y. Hirata and H.Kawaharada, "Space Interface Device for Artificial Reality - SPIDAR-", IEICE, D-II, vol.J74-D-II, no.7, pp.887-894, July, 1991
2. T. M. Massie and J. K. Salisbury, "The PHANToM haptic interface: a device for probing virtual objects", Proc. ASME Dynamic Systems and Control Division, DSC-vol.55-1, pp.295-301, 1994.
3. T. Starner and A. Pentland, "Real-Time American Sign Language Recognition from Video Using Hidden Markov Models", Proc. of ISCV'95, 1995
4. J. Kim, W. Jang, and Z. Bien: "A Dynamic Gesture Recognition System for the Korean Sign Language (KSL)", IEEE Trans. on Systems, Man and Cybernetics Part B:Cybernetics, Vol.26, No.2, April, 1996
5. H. Sagawa, M. Takeuchi, M. Ohki: "Description and Recognition Methods for Sign Language Based on Gesture Components", 1997 Int'l Conference on Intelligent User Interface , pp.97-104, 1997
6. T. Takegami and T. Gotoh, "Vision-Based Algorithm for Eye Movement Detection Using Corneal Reflection and Iris Contour", IEICE, D-I, vol.J82-D-I, no.10, pp.1295-1303, July, 1991
7. T. Ohno, N. Mukawa, A. Yoshikawa, "An Eye Tracking System Based on Eye Ball Model -Toward Realization of Gaze Controlled Input Device-", IPSJ Technical Report 2001-HI-93, pp.47-54, 2001
8. H. Sawada and S. Hashimoto, "Gesture Recognition Using an Acceleration Sensor and Its Application to Musical Performance Control", Trans. Electronics and Communications, Vol.80, No.5, pp. 9-17, 1997
9. H. Sawada and S. Hashimoto, "A Haptic Device Driven by Grasping Force for Hand Gesture Tele-Communication", Proc. of ASME Dynamic Systems and Control Division, pp.437-444, 1999
10. H. Sawada and S. Hashimoto, "Gesture-Sensitive Interface for Human-Machine Interaction", Proc. of International Conference on Quality Control by Artificial Vision QCAV'99, 1999
11. Yuki Kawai, Hidehumi Moritani and Hideyuki Sawada, "Intuition-driven monitor: a monitor device driven by user's haptic manipulation", Proc. of IEEE International Conference on Systems, Man and Cybernetics, MIPR2, 2002

Gesturing with Tangible Interfaces for Mixed Reality

José Miguel Salles Dias, Pedro Santos, and Rafael Bastos

ADETTI/ISCTE, Associação para o Desenvolvimento das Telecomunicações
e Técnicas de Informática, Edifício ISCTE, 1600-082 Lisboa
{Miguel.Dias,Pedro.Santos,Rafael.Bastos}@adetti.iscte.pt
http:// www.adetti.pt

Abstract. This work reports a Tangible Mixed Reality system that can be applied to interactive visualisation scenarios in diverse human-assisted operations, such as in training, troubleshooting and maintenance tasks of real equipments, or in product design scenarios in various sectors: Architecture, Automotive or Aerospace. With the system, the user is able to intuitively interact with an augmented version of real equipment, in normal working settings, where she can observe 3D virtual objects (in the VRML 97 format) registered to the real ones. Totally sensor-less Tangible Interfaces (Paddle and Magic Ring), are used to aid interaction and visualisation tasks in the mixed environment. By means of Tangible Interfaces gesturing recognition, it is possible to activate menus, browse and choose menu items or pick, move, rotate and scale 3D virtual objects, within the user's real working area or transport the user from Augmented Reality to a fully Virtual Environment and back.

1 Introduction

With our work, we are aiming to provide the user with innovative Mixed Reality technology, applicable in training, human-assisted real-time visualisation of simulation data, where the fusion of the reality with different information sources is mandatory, and in industrial product design operations. Within these environments, the user can seamlessly evolve from a real working context, such as operating specific equipment, into an augmented reality version of it, where virtual objects are correctly superimposed (registered) onto real ones. This set-up will enhance the perception of the reality and will provide a metaphor for the fusion of the real situation with context relevant information, coming from different sources. Depending on the context, related information to the equipment in fault could be displayed and registered, such as 3D animated models, detailed specifications or more general hypermedia information. Upon user request and using an intuitive interface, based on gesture detection of Tangible Interfaces, this environment could also be turned into a fully 3D Virtual Reality one, thus providing a complete Mixed Reality experience. This could give the user a very close perception of, for example, a specific operational unit with a malfunction, supporting a vivid tutorial session on the troubleshooting of the noticed fault, while she is concentrated in handling that task in the field. That is, the augmentation of the reality introduced by our system, would not add a cognitive seam in the visualisation process and would not distract the user from the task at hand. In training scenarios, creating a technological environment where a user could experience and test different

A. Camurri and G. Volpe (Eds.): GW 2003, LNAI 2915, pp. 399–408, 2004.

equipments, as fully and as closely to the reality as possible, through an easy and intuitive way based on gestures, could be something very rewarding and revolutionary for these users. In synthesis, in this paper we address the appropriateness and viability of Tangible Interfaces and Mixed Reality technologies, for the enhanced visualisation of simulation data.

The paper is organised as follows: in section 2, we provide a background and state-of-the-art in the issues of Augmented Reality, Mixed Reality and Tangible Interfaces. In section 3, we present our modular system functions. Section 4 covers the issues of Tangible User Interfaces. Section 5 details the hardware and software of the developed prototype platforms, which was subjected to preliminary technical tests. Finally, in section 6, conclusions and future directions of research are given.

2 Background and State-Of-The-Art

Augmented Reality (or AR) systems and technologies were introduced in 1992 by Caudel and Mizell [3], in the context of a pilot project, where they were used to simplify an industrial manufacturing process in a Boeing airplane factory. In general these systems provide the means for "intuitive information presentation, which enhances the perceiver's situational awareness and cognitive perception of the real world" [4]. This enhancement is achieved by placing virtual objects or information cues into the real world, which is made possible by performing "virtual camera calibration", that is, by computing the virtual camera parameters that match the position and orientation of the observer of the real scene. With this technique, "virtual" objects can then be registered in relation to "real" objects, which means that these objects can be seen in the same position and orientation of other "real" objects of the scene, as perceived by the user. This is usually done using optical or video see-through head mounted displays and tracking devices, linked to either standalone computers with 3D graphics capabilities, or mobile wearable computers. Video see-through AR is where virtual images are overlaid on live video of the real world. A possible alternative is optical see-through AR, where computer graphics are overlaid directly on a view of the real world. Optical see-through augmented reality has more complex camera calibration and registration requirements.

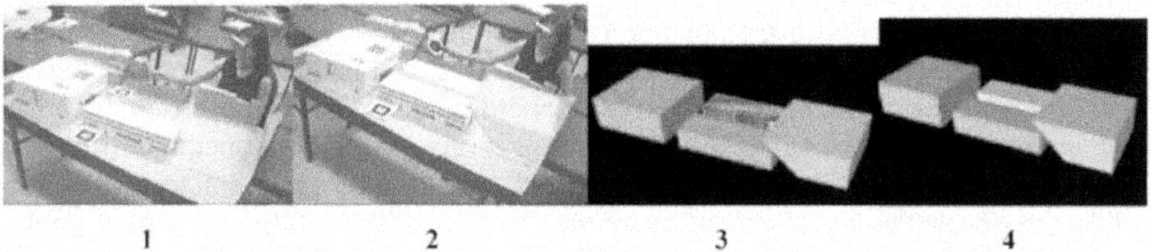

Fig. 1. The Mixed Reality paradigm by examples, from left to right: 1 - RE, Real Environment; 2 - AR, Augmented Reality ; 3 - AV – Augmented Virtuality; 4 - VE – Virtual Environment.

According to Azuma [5], AR "...1) combines real and virtual environments; 2) is interactive in real-time; 3) is registered in 3D". We can conclude that AR is a challenging multidisciplinary field and a particularly promising new user interface paradigm, integrating computer graphics, computer vision, positional and orientation tracking technologies, wearable computer architectures, psychology, artificial intelligence, ergonomics and others. In view of this integration framework and associated complexity, Milgram and Herman [6], have proposed a new taxonomy that supplements the definition of Augmented Reality, by introducing the concepts of Augmented Virtuality (AV) and Mixed Reality (MR). They argue that Real Environments (RE) and Virtual Environments (VE) are, in fact, two poles of the Reality-Virtuality Continuum, being RE the left pole and VE, the right pole (see Fig. 1). REs include sample data acquired and digitised from real scenarios, such as image, video (Fig 1 – 1), ultra-sound, X-ray, laser range and light intensity data and others, whereas VEs, refer to computer models of 3D scenarios that can be rendered in real time (Fig 1 – 4). AV includes 3D scenarios that are supplemented by the inclusion of sample data acquired and digitised from real scenarios, through for example, texture mapping techniques (Fig 1 – 3). Mixed Reality is thus the overall framework that includes the continuum transitions from RE, to AR, passing through AV and towards VE.

On the user interaction side of the equation within immersive Mixed Reality environments, where the user experiences a "visual augmentation" of the reality using, for example, a video see-through head-mounted display, standard input devices such as keyboards or mice are useless, since they distract the user from the task at hand, thus creating a severe cognitive seam within the interaction process. On the other hand, traditional input devices used in virtual environments, such as the data glove or a 3D mouse with 6 degrees of freedom, introduce undesirable complexity in the tracking technology, or add "strange" gadgets, to the user's workspace, with whom he's not daily accustomed. To face this problem, Kato [7] proposes Tangible Interfaces, as a new approach for the design of Augmented Reality interactions. According to the author, Tangible Interfaces, "are those in which 1) each virtual object is registered to a (tangible) physical object; and 2) the user interacts with virtual objects by manipulating the corresponding tangible object". Tangible Interfaces are described in the literature as being intuitive, since physical object manipulations are mapped to virtual object operations. If the mapping is one-to-one, we classify the interface as a space-multiplexed one. A time-multiplexed interface is the one where a physical object may correspond to different functions, at different points in time.

Since 1996, AR and its applications, have also been researched by a group of Fhg-IGD[1], in areas like repair and maintenance of complex facilities, interior and exterior architecture, as well as in medical scenarios, such as needle biopsy and minimal invasive treatment, combining Computed Tomography (CT), Magnetic Resonance (MR) and Ultrasound (U) imaging, with the real scene, enabling new means of interaction of the physician with the patient [8]. More recently, ARVIKA [9], a large initiative funded by the German Ministry of Education and Research, is developing Augmented Reality technology and applications in the areas of product development, production and service in the automotive and aerospace industries, for power and processing plants and for machine tools and production machinery. This initiative includes some of the worlds largest European and global players in the automotive and aerospace industries. Some of the on-going projects include: "Localization of components in industrial environments"; "Protocolling and annotation to assist recurring inspections and troubleshooting of equipments"; and "AR supported simplification of cable loom assembly for the Eurofighter military combat aircraft". ARVIKA efforts are focused in mobile use of AR in industrial applications, involving the fusion of real and virtual

[1] FHG-IGD, Fraunhofer Institute for Computer Graphics IGD, www.igd.fhg.de

information, the delivery of such information as a function of context and multimodal input/output, including Speech, Tangible Interfaces and Hands-Free operations. The general problem of satisfactory user tracking and object registration is being investigated, using both fiducial markers placed on the environment and marker-less tracking.

3 System Architecture

Our system provides a Tangible Time-Multiplexed Mixed-Reality system, and adopts a broader definition of Tangible Interfaces, in the sense that virtual objects are registered to real ones, such as a P*addle*, a *Magic Ring* or square pieces of cards with markers, as in [7], [11] or [12], but we add novel uses for them, since they are also physical means of interaction between the user and the system, that will trigger the functionalities of the platform, by the way of tangible interface gesture detection. With this system, a user such as an architect can intuitively interact with a real scale model of the design, in her usual working table, where she can observe an enhanced version of the scale model (see Fig. 1), with 3D virtual objects registered to the real ones, as long as the video camera mounted on her video see-though glasses, is "seeing" a fiducial marker. To deploy this visualisation paradigm, two modules comprise our proposed system: an authoring tool, **Mix It**, and a run-time visualization tool, the **AR Viewer**. Mix It, is a pre-processing tool required to configure the Mixed Reality environment, which is responsible for associating 3D objects to markers, so that virtual shapes can be registered and superimposed over well-known 2D fiducial patterns (which are also produced by the tool). The AR Viewer tool adopts the metaphor of the Magic Book described in the literature [11], where a user can look at an ordinary paper book with fiducial markers printed on the pages and observe, through video or optical see-through glasses, and notice virtual objects registered over the markers (see Fig. 4). The AR Viewer is based in ArToolkit [10], a C/Open GL-based open source library that uses accurate vision based tracking methods to determine the virtual camera viewpoint information through the detection of fiducial markers. In fact, upon detection of a specific marker, ArToolkit provides the programmer with a complete 3D visualization transformation matrix, from the virtual camera coordinate reference frame to the local reference frame associated to the marker. Since the virtual and real camera coordinates are the same, the programmer can precisely superimpose the image of a virtual object onto the real world, using OpenGL, resulting in an Augmented Reality effect. In higher level, Mix IT and AR Viewer, are base on MX Toolkit [14], an object-oriented programming Toolkit developed by our team and oriented to the mixed reality applications developer. MX Toolkit is defined at a somewhat higher abstraction level than the ArToolkit software layer, by hiding from the programmer, low level implementation details and facilitating AR/MR object-oriented programming. MX Toolkit is an SDK written in C++ which uses extensively the ArToolkit library, for all matters regarding marker-based tracking, but also has a simple dialog with Microsoft Foundation Classes and other standards and third party file formats, such as Open VRML, 3D Studio or Open SceneGraph[2].

[2] www.openscenegraph.org

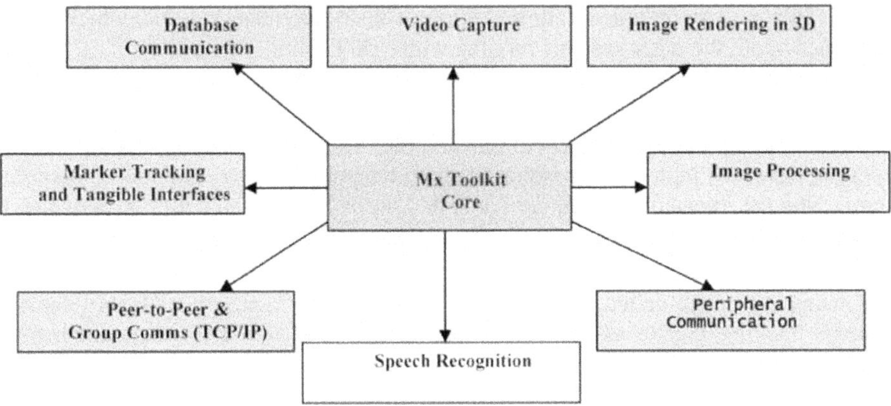

Fig. 2. System Architecture

The MX Toolkit comprises eight functionally independent modules (the Speech module is under development), communicating with each other through the main system core (Fig. 2):

Core System: This module provides an efficient mixed reality programming environment, supporting applications, scenes and sounds plug-in management, that are controlled by a set of three galleries: *Application Gallery* (Mx Toolkit applications, such as Mix It and AR Viewer, are developed as DLL plug-ins, that can be built and later loaded, started, updated and terminated at run-time by the Core Module), *Shape Gallery* (allows the system to load DLL Shape Plug-ins – 3DS and VRML 97 3D file formats are currently supported) and *Sound Gallery* (supports Sound Engine platforms, such as Open Audio Library and Microsoft Direct Sound and also contains loaded Sound File Plug-ins, such as Windows Wave and MPEG Layer 3). The Core contains also a set of base class descriptors that can be used by external plug-in applications, such as the Abstract Augmented Reality Object, Augmented Reality Markers, Abstract Shape and Sound Plug-ins, Tangible Interfaces, Magic Books and even specific Hardware Sensors and Hardware Interfaces. This module provides all that is needed for all the other modules to work perfectly in a higher abstraction layer, without the need of concerning which application has been started, which plug-in has been loaded or even which scene is being rendered.

Peer-to-Peer Communication: This module can serve applications to stream data or communicate in a higher abstraction level, hiding the application from the TCP/IP layer and communication protocol.

Peripheral Communication: This module allows the system to communicate with the Wearable System hardware and with other specific hardware by a serial communication port.

Database Communication: This module provides a set of methods to enable database communication. It accesses data through a Data Access Object (DAO) based on the Microsoft Jet database engine. This engine provides the access to data, including through ODBC drivers, via a specific database engine. It also supports Data Definition Language (DDL) operations, such as adding tables and other modifying operations. This module intends to allow the use of distributed data objects, which can be obtained by all the other systems running with MX Toolkit.

Video Capture: This module allows the system to acquire images from any WDM (Windows Device Manager) or VFW (Video for Windows) compatible capturing device, like cameras, VCRs, DVD players, etc. The user can select the input video device, the video input video resolution and the output window resolution, possibility correcting the image rendering, vertically and horizontally, which will be delivered to the Rendering Module.

Marker Tracking and Tangible Interfaces: This module is a DLL with an ArToolkit wrapping object called MX AR Toolkit. It provides a set of methods related to marker tracking, creates associations between 3D shapes and 2D markers and handles Tangible Interfaces, placing the programming user at a higher (object-oriented) level of abstraction.

Image Processing: One of the features of this component is the ability of applying image filters in a single pass, or in various passes with a given sequence, such as: Flip Image, Brighten Image, Adaptive Contrast, Threshold Image and Adaptive Image Enhance. Another feature is the compression of live streamed video. It uses any type of compression compatible with the Windows Video Compression Manager.

3D Rendering: Objects are rendered by this module independently of their geometry and topology. When creating an object to be rendered, it's geometrical and topological structures must be defined as well as it's rendering methods (currently using the OpenGL API). This module also features a set of utilities like Menus, Menu Bars and Text display methods, allowing the user to create, in a simple way, an Augmented Graphical User Interface (AGUI). The AGUI is recognized by the Core, and can be controlled by a Tangible Interface just like a simple mouse cursor.

4 Tangible User Interfaces

Users generally require real-time user interaction in Mixed Reality. Having this in mind, we have developed Tangible Interfaces as intuitive as possible and we have come up with a series of tools, similar to the ones found in [11] or [12], which are suitable for our tangible interfaces requirements: The *Paddle* [14] (Fig. 3) and the *Magic Ring* (see Fig. 4) and they all have a specific marker attached. As a visual aid, when this marker is recognized by the system, a virtual paddle (Fig. 3) or virtual blue circle (Fig. 5) will be displayed on top of it. The *Magic Ring* (a small marker attached to a finger, by means of a ring) is used in several interaction tasks, such as object picking, moving and dropping, object scaling and rotation, menu manipulation, menu items browsing and selection, and for all various types of commands given to the system. This is an alternative approach to the one found in [2], that uses a sensor-based tracking "mixed-pen" metaphor, for this type of user interaction.

One of the basic Tangible Interfaces supported, is based in finger gesture tracking by computer vision means. Using a *Magic Ring* on a finger, the software is able to recognize and track its position and orientation. Typically, we use a ring in the right and in the left thumbs. The ARToolkit library provides us, in real time, with the spatial evolution of the 3D coordinates of the centre of the visible markers superimposed onto these rings, relatively to the camera reference frame. From this kinematics law,

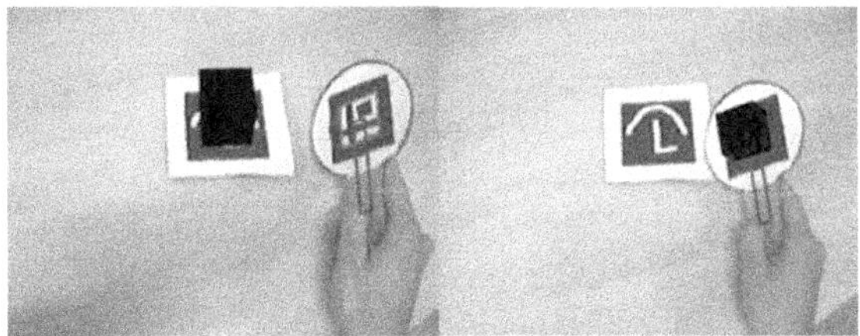

Fig. 3. (Left) A Tangible Interaction that will succeed: the *Paddle* is initially empty, and the marker has a registered 3D object. (Right): The object is transferred from the marker to the *Paddle* in real time.

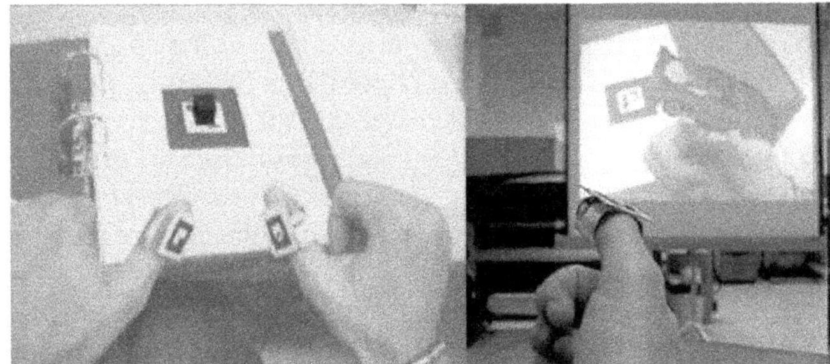

Fig. 4. (Left) Manipulating *Magic Rings*, a new type of Tangible Interface, within the context of a *Magic Book.* (Right) Picking an object with the finger using a *Magic Ring.*

we can estimate the finger's tip 3D coordinates trajectory, which can be used as an input for different kinds of geometric transformations. One of the possibilities is, for example, to use the finger to pick and drop any virtual object placed on a marker. Additionally, we can also project these same 3D coordinates to known 2D coordinates of the visualization window, enabling the use the Magic Ring gesturing just like a mouse cursor, and opening the possibility to provide user interaction with custom made "augmented" menus, buttons, windows, etc.

Using the finger's tip estimated 3D coordinates, we can determine its Cartesian distance to any marker centre that contains an object. When this value is below a threshold, the user can switch (pick or drop) the virtual object to (or from) the marker on his finger. She will feel like she is picking and dropping objects to and from her own finger. It is then possible for her to have a closer look and inspect the object on her finger (Fig. 4 Right).

We have also designed a simple graphical interface based on Menus, which the user can interact with, using the *Magic Rings*. These custom menus are drawn in 2D and have a similar look and feel as ones available with the Microsoft Windows® operating systems. It is possible to activate menus, browse and select menu items. The interaction is simple and intuitive. A menu is activated when the user presses the marker in her left thumb using her right thumb; it feels just like clicking a button except that she is using her fingers. When this action is performed a menu is activated and displayed next to the left thumb. It is then tracked to this finger (marker) so that when she moves it, the menu will follow. The user is then able to use her right thumb to scroll the menu items. This is done by simply moving her finger along her transversal direction (corresponding to the screen *yy*' axis) so that her transversal coordinates ('*y*' coordinates) match the same '*y*' screen coordinates of the corresponding menu item. The visual result of this is like using a mouse cursor to scroll/browse through a menu (Fig. 5 Left). Finally, the user can now select a menu item. For this, she just moves her right thumb (her special "mouse cursor") on top of the menu item she chooses. This item will then be highlight, blink for a brief period of time and its associated menu function will then be executed, which could well be a nested menu. After the menu option is selected, any kind of system action can be associated to it and invoked. This introduces us a wide variety of possible operations.

Magic Rings (and fingers) gesturing can also be used to manipulate geometrically the virtual objects. These can be translated, rotated, and scaled. Geometrical operations are available from the menu described earlier. Each one of these modelling transformations has a special processing routine. However, they all require the previous definition of the principal axis (*xx´*, *yy´*or *zz´*), that will be used as a parameter for the operation. This is done by initially positioning the fingers along the principal axis, the user wishes to choose (it should be noted that all transformations operate on the camera's absolute coordinate system). Left and right thumb on the left and right edge of the screen, will choose the *xx*' axis; left and right thumb on the top and bottom edge, will choose the *yy*' axis; and left thumb close to the camera with the right thumb far away, will choose the *zz*' axis. Once the axis is chosen any of the three main object transformations can be performed. In order to do this, we use the 3D distance vector between both fingers. The translation transformation is straightforward. If both fingers are far apart, the object will start moving to the right. If they are closer, it will move to the left. If they are near each other, within a certain tolerance, the translation will be reset. As mentioned, all these operations are performed relatively to the axis that was previously defined.

Fig. 5. (Left) Popping and Browsing with a menu using two *Magic Rings*. (Centre) Using finger gesticulation to rotate a 3D shape superimposed onto a Magic Book. (Right) Using finger gesticulation to scale a 3D shape superimposed onto the Magic Book.

The scaling transformation is similar. By moving both fingers apart from each other, the object will become larger. If they get closer, it will shrink (Fig. 5 Right). By moving them right next to each other, the scaling will also reset.

In order to rotate the object a very intuitive method is used. The user just has to perform a circular movement in relation to the selected axis; for example, to rotate along the *yy*' axis, the movement of the Tangible Interfaces is just like turning a car wheel in front of the user (Fig. 5 Centre).

5 System Configuration

The typical hardware and software platforms required by our system, are as follows:

1. Video See-Through Head Mounted Display: Olympus Eye-trek FMD 700, Multimedia Glasses (800x600 pixel), with a wireless video input link with the Base Station Computer and Micro Cam wireless ultra miniature video camera from Swann Security;
2. Wearable Unit: Jacket equipped with bidirectional wireless video link and batteries;
3. Base Station Computer:
   - Hardware - CPU: HP Pentium IV 2.5GHZ; RAM: 1G byte; Graphics card: NVIDIA GFORCE 4 65 Mbyte;
   - Software - MS Visual C++ 6.0 enterprise edition; ArToolkit 2.5.2; Video Input - Direct X 8.1; Graphics - Open GL and Open VRML;
   - Indoor Tracking method - Computer vision-based approach (ArToolkit) with sparsely placed fiducial markers.

6 Conclusions and Future Directions

This system presented in this paper describes a general Tangible Mixed Reality platform, developed using an object-oriented Mixed Reality Toolkit (MX Toolkit) that can be applied in a viable way, in interactive visualisation scenarios for training, troubleshooting and maintenance tasks, or in industrial product design. With the aid of the system and its future enhancement, these real-life scenarios can be performed by users in an increasingly autonomous way, and concern diverse industrial contexts. The modular system functions were presented and several issues relevant for a Mixed Reality application were raised, namely, system architecture, virtual camera tracking and gesturing of Tangible Interfaces.

Several future directions can be envisaged for this kind of system, towards the enhancement of the new paradigm of Tangible Mixed Reality for Interactive Visualisation, starting with structured usability testing and evaluation, by a panel of users, to provide feedback for the improvement of system features.

Concerning the system architecture, enhancements could be made in the mobility and the cooperative support of the system, to increase the sense of mixed reality, that is, of seamless transition between real, augmented and virtual environments both in standalone and collaborative working scenarios. In fact, as a future evolution, we would support, multiple collaborators (such as in [1] or [2]), where discussion meetings and collaborative working sessions could take place amongst local and remote users, immersed on different collaborative environment modalities over the Internet: real, augmented or virtual. As concluded by preliminary technical tests to the system, we need to develop better camera tracking and handle the virtual to real occlusion problem. New tangible interfaces would also be "invented", for specific use cases, such as a *Magic Pen*, similar to a normal pen, able to provide accuracy in pointing and picking, within mixed reality design scenarios. Hybrid indoor virtual camera tracking would also be developed, using a combination of vision-based approaches (both marker-based, as in ArToolkit, and marker-less), ultra-sound sensors positioned along the workspace area, and accelerometers located on the Wearable Unit. This approach could be a possible solution for the accurate registration problem, enabling, for example, the user to walk freely within a certain working area, while experiencing augmented or virtual (mixed) worlds. The use of two cameras (stereo) and the enhancement of filtering techniques applied to the different sources of tracking signals (using the Kalman filter), could also improve the accurate registration of virtual to real objects, by better control of the distortion errors.

Acknowledgements

The authors would like to thank Luis Monteiro and Rui Silvestre for the collaboration in the development of the system and Arq. Nancy Diniz for the authoring of VR models.

References

1. Dias, Cooperative Work Support And Automatic Design Verification In Architecture And Building Construction, eSM@RT 2002 , University of Salford, United Kingdom, 19 - 21 November 2002.
2. Grasset, R., et al., "MARE: Multiuser Augmented Reality Environment on table setup", SIGGRAPH 2002,Conf. Abstract. And Applications, pp 213, 2002
3. Caudel, T., Mizell, D., "Augmented Reality: An Application of Heads-up Display Technology to Manual Manufacturing Processes", Proc. Hawaaii International Conference on Systems Sciences, Maui, Hawaii, IEEE press, pp 659-669, January 1992.
4. Behringer, R., et al, editors, Augmented Reality, Placing Artificial Objects in Real Scenes, Proceedings of 1st International workshop on Augmented Reality - 1998, A. K. Peters ed., pp xi-xx, 1999.
5. Azuma, R. T., "A survey of augmented reality", in Presence: Teleoperators and Virtual Environments, 6, 355-385, 1997
6. Milgram, P., Herman, C. J., "A Taxonomy of Real and Virtual World Display Integration", in Mixed Reality, Merging Real and Virtual Environments, Ohmshda & Springer-Verlag, pp 5-30, 1999
7. Kato, H., Billinghurst, M., Poupyrev, I., "Tangible Augmented Reality", in Augmented Reality: the Interface is Everywhere, SIGGRAPH 2001 Course Notes 27, 2001
8. Reiners D., Stricker, D., Klinker, G. "Augmented Reality: Applications", Computer Graphik Topics, reports on Computer Graphics, 4/98 Vol 10, pp 36-38.
9. Friedrich W. "ARVIKA – Augmented Reality for Development, Production and Service", Prooceedings of the ISMAR 2002, IEEE and ACM International Symposium on Mixed and Augmented Reality, Darmstad, pp 3-4, 30th Sept-1 Oct, 2002
10. Kato, H., "Developing Applications with ARToolkit", SIGGRAPH 2001 Course Notes 27, 2001.
11. Billinghurst, M., Kato, H., Poupyrev, I., "The MagicBook: A Transitional AR Interface", in Augmented Reality: the Interface is Everywhere, SIGGRAPH 2001 Course Notes 27, 2001
12. T. Kawashima, K. Imamoto, H. Kato, K. Tachibana, M. Billinghurst, "Magic Paddle: A Tangible Augmented Reality Interface for Object, Manipulation", Proc. on ISMR2001, pp.194-195, 2001
13. Dias, J.M.S., Santos, P., e tal, "Tangible Interaction for Conceptual Architectural Design", "ART02, First IEEE International Augmented Reality Toolkit Workshop", ISMAR 2002, IGD, Darmstad, Germany, September 2002
14. Dias, J.M.S., Santos, P., e tal, "Developing and Authoring Mixed Reality with MX Toolkit", "ART03, Second IEEE International Augmented Reality Toolkit Workshop", ISMAR 2003, Tokio, Japan, October 2003

A Procedure for Developing Intuitive and Ergonomic Gesture Interfaces for HCI

Michael Nielsen, Moritz Störring, Thomas B. Moeslund, and Erik Granum

Aalborg University, Laboratory of Computer Vision and Media Technology
Niels Jernes Vej 14, DK-9220 Aalborg, Denmark
{mnielsen,mst,tbm,eg}@cvmt.dk

Abstract. Many disciplines of multimedia and communication go towards ubiquitous computing and hand-free- and no-touch interaction with computers. Application domains in this direction involve virtual reality, augmented reality, wearable computing, and smart spaces, where gesturing is a possible method of interaction. This paper presents some important issues in choosing the set of gestures for the interface from a user-centred view such as the learning rate, ergonomics, and intuition. A procedure is proposed which includes those issues in the selection of gestures, and to test the resulting set of gestures. The procedure is tested and demonstrated on an example application with a small test group. The procedure is concluded to be useful for finding a basis for the choice of gestures. The importance of tailoring the gesture vocabulary for the user group was also shown.

1 Introduction

Much work has been conducted in the investigation and development of natural interaction interfaces, including gesture interfaces [1][2][3][4][5][6][7]. Science fiction literature and movies also dream up gesture interfaces, for example the movies Johnny Mnemonic (1995), Final Fantasy (2001), and Minority Report (2002). Furthermore, gesture interfaces are applied to solve problems with people with physical disabilities [8].

It is important to remember that a gesture interface is to be seen as complementing or an alternative to existing interface techniques, such as the old desktop paradigm. Other examples are the new alternatives to the mouse, such as ergonomic trackballs, mouse pens, and the iGesture Pad [9]. They can all navigate a Windows interface with the mouse cursor just as well or better than the mouse, while they may be more or less useless when it comes to fast computer games, such as 3D shooters and Airplane Simulators.

When developing a gesture interface, the objective should not be "to make a generic gesture interface". A gesture interface is not universally the best interface for any application. The objective is "to develop a more efficient interface" for a given application.

This can be illustrated by the following example. An interface is desired for artistic modelling of a sculpture. An artist is hired for the job. The artist may be given a mouse and a keyboard for a CAD program. The result is perfect to the smallest detail in regard to accuracy of the lines, because it is possible to set coordinates explicitly.

A. Camurri and G. Volpe (Eds.): GW 2003, LNAI 2915, pp. 409–420, 2004.

However, these tools may not be well suited to convey the creativity of the artist. If the artist is instead provided with a gesture interface in which a virtual kind of clay model can be altered by touching and squeezing it, it will not be accurate in terms of coordinates and straight lines, but it might be aesthetically closer to the artist's vision. Thus, the choice of interface is to be related to the desired outcome of the application.

Consequently, the first step is the analysis of which kind of interface is most suitable for this task. This might lead to the conclusion that a gesture interface is the type that should be developed.

The focus in this paper is the next step; to design this hand-gesture interface and to find the specific gestures that make this specific interface for this specific application most efficient.

The set of gestures in an interface is called the "gesture vocabulary". This should not be confused with a general non-verbal communication dictionary. There are several ways of labelling gestures. This paper uses the taxonomy presented by Justine Cassell [1].

Section 2 investigates the foundation of gestures and gives an understanding of the gesture domain. Section 3 proposes a procedure for finding and testing gestures for a gesture interface. Section 4 presents the executed test of the procedure. Section 5 concludes the work.

2 Choosing Gestures

This section will motivate the need for the proposed procedure. There are two approaches [22] of choosing the gestures; the technical based approach and the human based approach.

The technical approach of choosing gestures is to choose a set of gestures which is simple to recognise. It starts with an idea for a method that can recognise some certain gestures. Like an example at the authors' department, where the method counts the number of extended fingers. Once this gesture vocabulary has been established, the next step is to apply them to an application. The problem with this technical approach is that some gestures are stressing or impossible to perform to some people. Furthermore, the functionalities and the gestures are illogically mapped.

An important question to ask is if the cultural dependence is a problem. Conventional international interfaces are generally in English, but most software is available with selectable national language packages, and some nations have different keyboard layouts. In a gesture interface this can be translated into selectable gesture sets, if it should become a problem that an emblem [1] is illogic to another culture. Furthermore, if a culturally dependent gesture is used, this does not necessarily mean that it is utterly illogic for other cultures to learn them if presented with them.

2.1 Human Based Gesture Vocabulary

The human based gesture approach investigates the people who are going to use the interface. Wizard-of-Oz experiments have proven valuable in the development of gestures [10]. The experiments simulate the response of the system by having a person respond to the user commands. This approach tests a developed interface.

Gesture research [1] shows that there is no such thing as a universal gesture vocabulary, so a good gesture vocabulary may only match one specific application and user group. Developers need to make it easy for the users to use their systems. Otherwise, the users will choose the work of the competitors. The human based principles should make the gestures:

- Easy to perform and remember
- Intuitive
- Metaphorically and iconically logical towards functionality
- Ergonomic; not physically stressing when used often

This means that the gesture vocabulary must be tailored for the specific task. Of course, it would still be wise to keep in mind that they should be possible to recognize unambiguously by the system.

In order to achieve these principles it is necessary to take usability theory, and biomechanics/ergonomics. See [22] for further details. The work of Jakob Nielsen [23] on usability gives a good overview. Research on usability focuses on five main principles [11][12][13]:

Learnability	The time and effort required to reach a specific level of use performance.
Efficiency	Steady-state performance of expert users.
Memorability	Ease of system intermittently for casual users.
Errors	Error rate for minor and catastrophic errors.
Coverage	The amount of operators discovered vs. the total operators.

Furthermore, Nielsen suggests a set of heuristics [13] which facilitates these principles:

1. Use simple and natural dialogue
2. Speak the user's language
3. Minimize user memory load
4. Be consistent
5. Provide feedback
6. Provide clearly marked exits
7. Provide shortcuts
8. Provide good error messages
9. Prevent errors

Biomechanics and ergonomics [14][15][18][19][20] tell about constraints in postures and the usage of the gestures, such as avoiding to stay in static positions, and moving joints too far from their neutral positions. There are constraining relationships between individual joints within fingers and between neighbouring fingers. These constraints are different in people.

Wrist movement can have adverse effects on comfort as well as the external- and internal force. Experiments have shown that the entire body posture is important to be aware of, even when dealing with hand gestures. This is because it affects the elbow and wrist postures, which again affects the force needed to set the finger postures [17].

The ergonomics show that it is important to make the recognition algorithms tolerant to de-stressing movements, which allows the user to avoid staying fixed in e.g. a static "residue" or "pointing" gesture. Tolerance for deviations in gestures is desirable when implementing gesture interfaces, also because of varying hand shapes and posture performance.

3 Approach to Finding Gestures

Section 2 outlined the importance of choosing a logical and ergonomic gesture vocabulary and the parameters that can be tuned to achieve that. This section presents a procedure to find an appropriate gesture vocabulary for a given application.

In order to ensure intuitive and logical mapping, the first step is an investigation into the interfaces of known applications is conducted to identify the needed functionalities.

In the development of interfaces scenarios have proven valuable [21] to define the context, functionalities, and investigate the user and problem domain.

A tool in this approach is to examine human-to-human non-verbal communication in these scenarios by preparing scripts. Testees will be taken through the scenarios such that they will communicate the same things to a person as they would communicate to the computer application.

Points 1 and 2 of the nine usability heuristics from section 2.1 support the view that the gestures must be chosen by looking at natural gesturing, but also show that the testees must be part of the designated user group.

Two approaches of this investigation are at hand; bottom-up and top-down. Bottom-up takes functions and finds matching gestures, while the top-down presents gestures and finds which functions are logically matched with those. Another tool that is needed is a benchmark to measure the goodness of gestures by the principles that are valued in the human-based approach.

3.1 Procedure to Finding Gestures

This section describes the proposed procedure and benchmark when developing a gesture interface. In section 4 an example of execution will be shown in order to test and improve the procedure, as the development of such a procedure and benchmark is an iterative process.

3.1.1 Step A. Find the Functions

Find the functions needed by the application and which the gestures will have to communicate. Keep in mind the user interface of existing similar applications of standard interfaces (e.g. if the new application is an architectural design application, 3D Studio, MicroStation, CAD, etc. would be relevant).

Keep the gesture vocabulary at a minimum, e.g. with use of context menus or spatial zones (the same gesture activates different things depending on context).

3.1.2 Step B. User Tests – Collect Gestures from User Domain

The goal is to find the gestures that represent the functions found in step A. This is done through experiments with people by taking them through scenarios under camera surveillance where they communicate the above functions, which they would otherwise communicate to the computer, e.g. to the "operator" (i.e. the person who conducts the experiment) or another testee.

It is important to design the experiments on a way that the testees use gestures in a natural way, especially when conducting the tests with technically minded people. Otherwise, there is the risk that they will still think in terms of interfaces and algorithms. If it is desired to write a scenario with a technical interface aspect, it can be performed as a Wizard-of-Oz experiment [3][10], which tests not only the gesturing, but also the design of the entire interface, including the feedback from the system and the sequencing in the interfacing.

The number of people that are required for this investigation depends on how broad the user group is, and how diverse the results of the test are.

3.1.3 Step C. Analysis – Extract Gesture Vocabulary

The video recorded data is evaluated to extract the gestures that the testees used in their interaction.

Note and capture the frames with the commonly used gestures, and note how consistently the different testees use them. Note if they are used only as static postures or if the dynamics play an important part in the interpretation of the gesture.

The theory in section 2 should be taken into account in the selection of gestures:

- Evaluate internal force caused by posture
  - Deviation from neutral position
  - Outer limits
  - Forces from inter-joint relations
- Evaluate frequency and duration of that gesture
- Consider effect on wrist from wrist and finger posture

See section 4 step C how this is done in praxis. Furthermore, note that the selection should not be strictly limited to the recordings. It is meant to be an inspiration.

3.1.4 Step D. Test – Benchmark the Chosen Gesture Vocabulary

The final step is to test the resulting gesture vocabulary. This might lead to changes in the gesture vocabulary. The test has three parts. The following is to be tested in the benchmark: Semantic interpretation, generalisation, intuitivity, memory, learning rate, and stress. The lowest score is best.

Test 1: Guess the Function

Give the testee a list of functions. Present the gestures and ask the person to guess the functions. Gestures that depend on context must be presented in context. Score = errors divided by number of gestures

Test 2: Memory

Give the gesture vocabulary to the testee, who will then try the gestures to make sure they are understood.

Present a slideshow of names of functions in a swift pace, 2 seconds per function. The testee must perform them correctly while the name is displayed. The order should be logical towards sequences in the application. Restart the slideshow at every mistake, and show the gesture vocabulary to the testee between each retry. Continue until they are all correct. Score = number of restarts.

Test 3: Stress
This is a subjective evaluation of ergonomics. Present the list with a sequence of the gestures. The testee must perform the sequence X times, where X times the size of gesture vocabulary equals 200. Between each gesture go back to neutral hand position Note how stressing they are. Make space for comments to illuminate if it was certain gestures that gave stress.

Use the following score list for each gesture and overall for the sequence: 1) No problem. 2) Mildly Tiring/Stressing. 3) Tiring/Stressing. 4) Very annoying. 5) Impossible

The benchmark can be used to compare two gesture vocabularies, but test 2 is only comparable if the vocabularies are of the same size. If testing a single vocabulary, reasonable success criteria must be stated. These aims depend on the gesture vocabulary at hand. See section 4 step D how this can be done in praxis. It can also be used to compare different user profiles and test cultural dependences.

4 Human-Based Experiment

This section demonstrates and tests how to use the procedure, and the theory that is presented in sections 2.1 through 3.1.

The test case for testing the approach is an architectural design application. The application enables the user to place virtual 3D objects on the table, moving them, and changing style settings on them. The key functions of a simple design interface are: Activate menu, select, select all, insert, move, scale, rotate, delete, yes/confirm, no/undo, and copy-paste. In order to cover conscious and subconscious top-down investigation three scenarios are chosen for the user tests, which are outlined below:

- ***Scenario I: The Pub Visit***
  - Noisy environment
  - Verbal communication prevented
  - Spontaneous and forced gesturing
- ***Scenario II: Planning of Furnishing***
  - Collaboration through verbal communication
  - Spontaneous gesturing
- ***Scenario III: Simulated Furnishing***
  - Directing through gestures
  - Conscious gesturing

Scenario I simulated a pub visit, where similar messages are being conveyed to the bartender in a noisy environment, where gesturing is necessary. The remaining scenarios were based on the principle that a floor plan is to be furnished with templates of furniture. In the first scenario two testees are verbally discussing how they want to furnish the room. In those discussions they will use some spontaneous gestures, mainly deictic and propositional. Scenario 3 is similar to a wizard of oz experiment, where a testee directs an operator through gestures alone, being aware of which functions are available. Paper and scissors are available for the operator to simulate scaling and copying. The testees used in the scenarios were engineers.

Fig. 1. Scenario II-III from stationary camera (left) and head-mounted camera (right).

The camera setup for all scenarios is that a stationary camera, records the testee including audio. The testee is equipped with a head-mounted camera on headphones, see Figure 1. The number of testees is limited to 5-7 in this test of the procedure.

4.1 Analysis – Extract Gesture Vocabulary

Once the scenarios were done, the gestures used were observed and counted for each function.

The gesture variation and frequency were noted. It was also noted whether the information in the gesture is static and dynamic. Sometimes the information in a dynamic gesture is actually static. Then the gestures were evaluated in terms of ergonomics, functionality and recognition. The gestures found in the video material should be seen as an inspiration, but the choice is not limited to those. The result for move will be discussed below.

Table 1 shows the result of the move gesture from scenario III. The full results are available in [22]. The gestures resulting from the analysis are presented in Figure 2.

Table 1. Results – Move. S = Static, D = Dynamic, N = Frequency of particular gesture.

Function	F	Gesture	S/D	N
Move	12	1. "Put-that-there"	D	4
		2. Wave it in the desired direction, stop with confirm or palm up like "halt".	D	3
		3. Wave it in the direction, rely on "snap to grid" to stop movement.	D	5

Move Gesture: There were variations of *move* gestures. In the pub scenario they were characterized by the fact that there were two bottles that needed to be moved aside, hence, the "open gate" and "birdie flapping wings" gestures. These can be broken down to waving the hand one way for one bottle and then the other way for the other bottle. This leaves only two versions of the move gesture: "put-that-there" and "wave

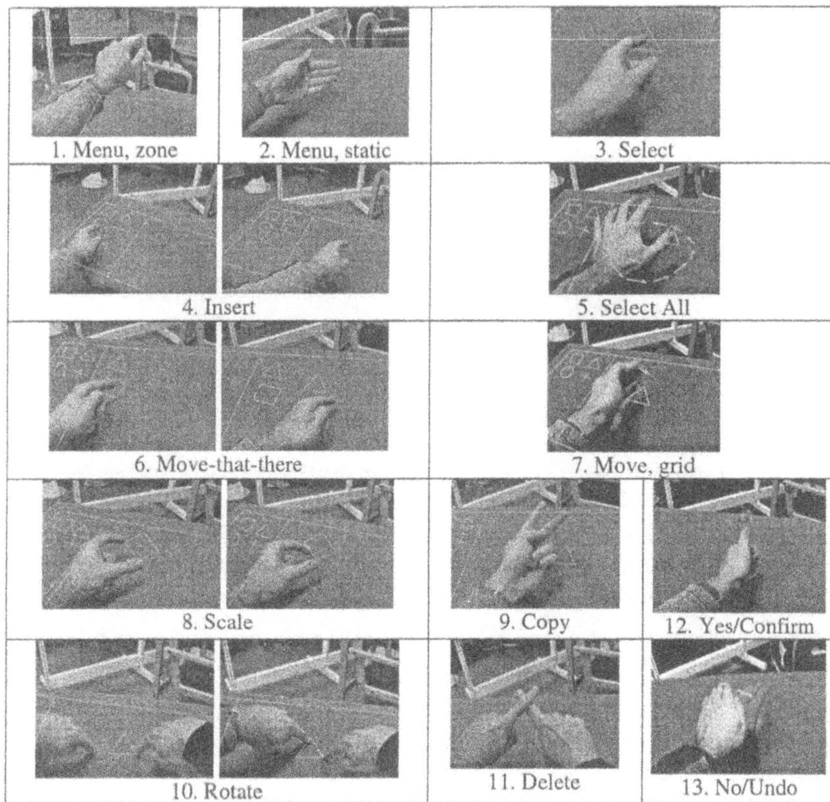

Fig. 2. Resulting gestures. The small light arrows indicate movement.

in the desired direction". Notable is that the first was used mainly when moving an object far, while the latter was used to move it slightly to a wall or the middle between two walls. It seems natural to implement both, and the waving gesture moves one tick at a time in a "snap to grid"-feature. The gesture is not mistaken for "select all" or "no/undo", because the palm faces sideways, instead of downwards.

4.2 Step D. Benchmark

The benchmark was done with 3 test groups; 8 engineers, 5 architects, and 11 engineer students.

In benchmark test 1 the "menu, using zone" is removed, because its context is hard to illustrate without doing a Wizard-of-Oz experiment. This leaves 12 gestures to be guessed, and it is expected that people will get up to 2-3 errors: The menu gesture is not very logical and the no/undo and delete gestures are interchangeable.

For test 2 it is a rather big vocabulary to learn, and the slideshow is performed at a speed of 2 seconds. It is expected that people will need 3 retries.

The stress in test 3 is expected to be mildly tiring, because it is laborious to perform 200 static and dynamic gestures in a row without resting. The results of the

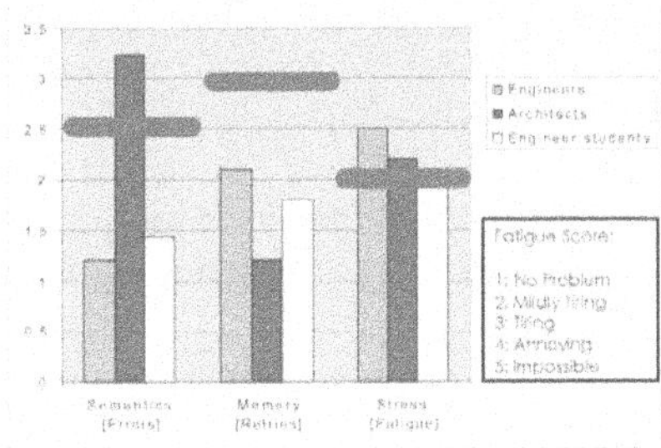

Fig. 3. Benchmark results. Comparison between 3 test groups. The horizontal lines denote the expected results. It shows that the engineer groups scored better in the semantic test, while architects scored better in the memory test.

benchmark are found in figure 3. It is interesting that the two engineer groups performed similarly, and notably different from the architect group.

In test 1 the problems for the engineer groups were mainly those that were expected, but "Move, using grid" and "no/undo" got mixed up as well. The architects did not perform well and explained that they could not follow the logic in the iconic symbolism. This supports the notion of cultural dependence and that the user groups must be chosen carefully.

Test 2 showed surprisingly that it was generally easier to remember this large vocabulary, especially for the architects. Their spatial intelligence and practice with visual objects seem to give them an advantage.

Half of the testees found the gesturing to be more tiring than expected. The mean is just between mildly tiring and tiring. The question is where the subjective threshold is between the categories. Individual stress assessments are presented in table 2.

Table 2. Individual Gesture Stress scores. Highlighted results are commented in the text.

Gesture	Avg.Score	Variance
Rotate	***1.88***	***1.27***
No/undo	***2.13***	***1.27***
Select	1.13	0.13
Copy	***2.13***	***2.41***
Move, grid	***1.75***	***0.79***
Scale	1.25	0.21
Menu	1.38	0.27
Select All	1.5	0.57
Delete	1.5	0.57
Yes/Confirm	1.5	0.21
Move, Insert	***1.63***	***1.13***

Several testees found it laborious to use two hands in general. For rotation this is a worthwhile trade off for the precise rotation control given by using both hands like this. For deletion it is deliberate in order to prevent spontaneous deletion of objects.

The gesture no/undo was given either 1 or 4 by the testees. The stress on those who gave it 4 came from producing the movement with radial- and ulnar deviation in the wrist with the forearm muscles. The correct method is to do the motion with the entire forearm and elbow. It may be necessary to convert the gesture into a static gesture; to simply hold the palm out.

Concerning copy: Stress comes from doing selection with a pronated forearm. The result is that the hand must be supinated rather far, and the testees who found it stressing did it as far as the motion limit. "Move, using grid" is similarly dependent of flexing/extending the wrist or using the entire forearm, or just the fingers' TCP joints to do the waving.

Move and Insert was found laborious because it was in two steps and can be a long movement. Obviously, this depends on how far the object is to be moved. It is especially stressing when the hand has to cross the body axis. The distance of the gesturing from the body also has impact on the physical fatigue.

The stress benchmark clearly proves the importance of clear instruction how to perform the gestures, and to be aware of the entire body posture when using gesture interfaces.

5 Conclusions

A procedure to find gestures based on human factors is presented and tested. While the traditional technology-based approach is technically solvable, it leads to an awkward gesture vocabulary without intuitive mapping towards functionality, and a system which works under strictly pre-defined conditions.

The human-based approach and procedure described in section 3 was tested and lead to an easy-to-use gesture vocabulary. It was fast for the testees to learn and remember it. However, it is rather time consuming, and the scenarios must be carefully written. This time is well spent, if it is a matter of the future users using the application or preferring another application, because it is too stressing or slow to use.

It was shown in the test that user profile is relevant when choosing a gesture vocabulary, because the gestures extracted from engineers performed best with engineers.

The experiments also revealed that gesturing concerns more than just a hand posture or movement. It affects a greater part of the body, biomechanically speaking. It is important to analyse and instruct the user in the execution of the gestures and the posture of the entire upper body.

Usability heuristic 4, to be consistent, is a tricky when dealing with gesturing. There are no platform standards to be consistent with. Being consistent towards nonverbal communication is desirable, but most gesturing is spontaneous. This means that people are not aware of the gestures they use. Test scenario III showed an interesting aspect, though. Despite the fact that the testees chose their gestures consciously, they were not consistent in their choices. The same person would use 2-3 different gestures for the same instruction. That gives the developer of a gesture interface some degree of flexibility in choosing the gesture for a function.

5.1 Future Work

Further testing and tweaking is necessary, increasing the number of testees for better generalization and cultural coverage. Benchmarking a single gesture vocabulary requires goals, which can be hard to predefine. The benchmark needs to be tested by comparing different gesture vocabularies.

The computer vision recognition of the human-based gesture vocabulary is hard to solve technically, and the question stands how this will be solved. With the aid of vast corpora the technology may be driven towards robust solutions. The use of shared resources and data sets to encourage the development of complex processing and recognition systems has been very successful in the speech analysis and recognition field. Applying this in gesture recognition might help to produce robust solutions, which is the aim of the current FG-Net project.

Acknowledgements

This research is in part funded by the ARTHUR project under the European Commission's IST program (IST-2000-28559) and the FG-Net project under the European Commission's IST program (IST-2000-26434). This support is gratefully acknowledged. The authors would also like to thank the participants of the experiments.

References

1. Justine Cassell, "A Framework For Gesture Generation and Interpretation" in Cipolla, R. and Pentland, A. (eds.), Computer Vision in Human-Machine Interaction, pp. 191-215. New York: Cambridge University Press, 1998
2. W.T.Freeman and C.D.Weissman, "Television Control By Hand Gestures" from IEEE Intl. Wksp on Automatic Face and Gesture Recognition, June 1995.
3. C. Hummels, P.J. Stapers, "Meaningful Gestures for Human Computer Interaction: Beyond Hand Postures", Proceedings of the 3rd International Conference on Automatic Face &Gesture Recognition (FG'98), Nara, Japan, April 14-16. IEEE Computer Society Press, Los Alamitos, CA. 591-596, 1998.
4. T. Moeslund, M. Stoerring, E. Granum, "A Natural Interface to a Virtual Environment through Computer Vision-estimated Pointing Gestures", In I. Wachsmuth and T. Sowa (Eds.),GW2001 Springer LNAI 2298, pages 59-63, 2002.
5. Patrizio Paggio and Bradley Music, "Linguistic Interaction in Staging – A Language Engineering View" in L. Qvortrup (ed.) Virtual Interaction: Interaction in/with Virtual Inhabited 3D Worlds, 2000
6. S. Steininger, B. Lindemann, T. Paetzold, "Labeling of Gestures in SmartKom – The Coding System" in I. Wachsmuth and T. Sowa (eds.) GW 2001, LNAI 2298, pp 215-227, 2002
7. Norbert A. Streitz et al, "Roomware: Towards the Next Generation of Human-Computer Interaction Based on an Integrated Design of Real and Virtual Worlds", German National Research Center for Information Technology, Integrated Publication and Information Systems Institute, Germany, 2001
8. Simeon Keates, Peter Robinson, "The Use of Gestures in Multimodal Input", University of Cambridge, Proceedings of ACM SIGCAPH ASSETS 98 35-42., 1998
9. Fingerworks, "iGesture Pad", http://www.fingerworks.com/igesture.html
10. Nicole Beringer, "Evoking Gestures in SmartKom – Design of the Graphical User Interface" in I. Wachsmuth and T. Sowa (eds.) GW 2001, LNAI 2298, pp 228-240, 2002
11. Marcello Federico, "Usability Evaluation of a Spoken Data-Entry Interface", ITC-Irst Centro per la Ricera Scientifica e Technologica, 1999
12. Nigel Bevan, Ian Curson, "Methods for Measuring Usability", Proceedings of the sixth IFIP conference on human-computer interaction, Sydney, Australia, 1997.
13. Jakob Nielsen, "The Usability Engineering Life Cycle", IEEE, 1992

14. J. Lin, Ying Wu, T.S.Huang, "Modeling the Constraints of Human Hand Motion", Proc. 5th Annual Federated Laboratory Symposium(ARL2001), Maryland, 2001.
15. Jintae Lee and Tosiyasu Kunjii, "Model-Based Analysis of Hand Posture", University of Aizu, IEEE, 1995
16. Charles Eaton MD, "Electronic Textbook on Hand Surgery", http://www.eatonhand.com/, 1997
17. Keir, Bach, Rempel, "Effects of Finger Posture on Carpal Tunnel Pressure During Wrist Motion", Division of Occupational Medicine, U.C.S.F., 1998
18. Chris Grant, "Ten Things You Should Know about Hand and Wrist Pain", F-One Ergonomics, Ann Arbor, Michigan.
19. G. Shaw, A. Hedge, "The Effect of Keyboard and Mouse Placement on Shoulder Muscle Activity and Wrist posture", CU Ergo, Cornell University.
20. A. Hedge, T. M. Muss, M. Barrero, "Comparative Study of Two Computer Mouse Designs", Cornell University, 1999
21. Wolfgang Dzida and Regine Freitag, "Making Use of Scenarios for Validating Analysis and Design", IEEE, 1998
22. Michael Nielsen, Thomas Moeslund, Moritz Störring, Erik Granum, "A Procedure For Developing Intuitive And Ergonomic Gesture Interfaces For Man-Machine Interaction", Technical Report CVMT 03-01, ISSN 1601-3646, http://www.cvmt.dk/~mnielsen, 2003
23. Jakob Nielsen, http://www.useit.com/

Evaluating Multimodal Interaction Patterns in Various Application Scenarios

Frank Althoff, Gregor McGlaun, Manfred Lang, and Gerhard Rigoll

Institute for Human-Machine Communication
Technical University of Munich (TUM)
Arcisstr. 21, 80290 Munich, Germany
{althoff,mcglaun,lang,rigoll}@ei.tum.de

Abstract. In this work, we present the results of a comparative user study evaluating multimodal user interactions with regard to two different operation scenarios: a desktop Virtual-Reality application (DVA) and an automotive infotainment application (AIA). Besides classical tactile input devices, like touch-screen and key-console, the systems can be controlled by natural speech as well as by hand and head gestures. Concerning both domains, we have found out that experts tend to use tactile devices, but normal users and beginners prefer combinations of more advanced input possibilities. Complementary actions most often occurred in DVA, whereas in AIA, the use of redundant input clearly dominates the set of multimodal interactions. Concerning time relations, the individual interaction length of speech and gesture-based input was below 1.5 seconds on the average and staggered intermodal overlapping occurred most often. Additionally, we could find out that the test users try to stay within a chosen interaction form. With regard to the overall subjective user experiences, the interfaces were rated very positively.

1 Introduction

Parallel to the rapid development of computer systems the design of comfortable, robust, and intuitive user interfaces (UIs) has undergone significant changes, too, leading to various generations of advanced human-machine interfaces. The class of *multimodal interfaces* currently resembles the latest step in this development. Providing multidimensional input possibilities and employing innovative audio-visual feedback strategies, these types of interfaces facilitate flexible and intuitive access to the complex functionality of today's technical systems[1][2]. Moreover, multimodal systems offer an increased level of error-robustness, since they integrate redundant information shared between the individual input modalities[3]. Concerning the design of interactive multimodal systems, the fundamental problem consists in effectively combining the individual input modalities to interpret the primary intention of the user (*multimodal integration*). Thereby, the system has to cope with the evaluation of varying interaction patterns with regard to both the semantic content and the time relations of the individual information entities. According to the basic taxonomy developed in [4], the interfaces in this work operate on a late semantic level of synergistic information fusion.

A. Camurri and G. Volpe (Eds.): GW 2003, LNAI 2915, pp. 421–435, 2004.

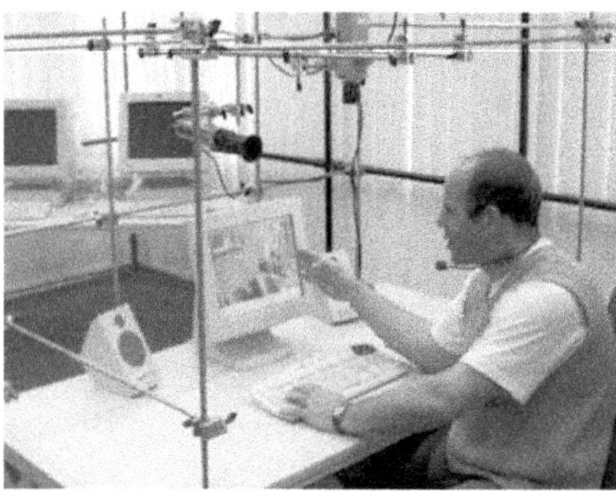

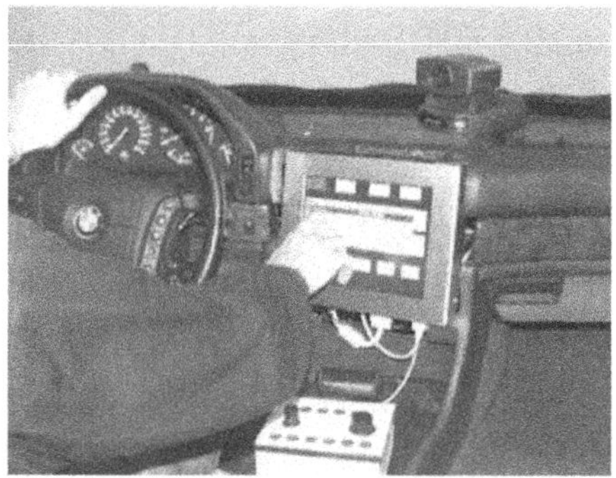

Fig. 1. Multimedia test environment for the DVA (left) and the AIA (right) scenario

1.1 Application Domains

In this contribution, we present selected results from a universal usability study evaluating prototypical multimodal interfaces with regard to two different scenarios: controlling a VRML browser in a native desktop Virtual-Reality application (DVA) and operating various audio and communication devices in an automotive infotainment application (AIA). The characteristics of the individual domains are extensively discussed in section 3. A first impression of the specific test environments can be taken from figure 1. Thereby, the user can freely choose among different input channels: conventional tactile interaction, natural speech utterances as well as dynamic head and hand gestures. In the DVA scenario, the user can absolutely concentrate on the tasks in the virtual scene, whereas in the automotive environment, the user additionally has to perform in a driving task. In this setup, operating the multimodal interface is the secondary task only.

1.2 Related Work

The group of Oviatt reports on results of an empirical study of people interacting with a bimodal pen- and speech based interface for planning real-estate issues[3]. Unimodal commands given by speech clearly dominated the distribution of interaction patterns (63.5%), followed by command combinations (19.0%), and isolated pen-gestures (17.5%). Contradicting their initial expectations, multimodal draw-and-speak commands were used most often (86.0%), subdivided in simultaneous (42.0%), sequential (32.0%) and compound interactions (12.0%). Concerning intermodal time relations, written input was significantly more likely to precede speech. Detailed analysis revealed that the multimodal interactions occurred within a maximum time zone of four seconds.

Cohen evaluated multimodal time relations in a computer mediated system for battle planning[5]. Astonishingly, the quota of multimodal commands made up more than two thirds (69%) of all interactions which clearly contradicts the prior study. In direct analogy to Oviatt's results, gestural input mostly preceded speech (82%). Sequential interactions occurred less often (11%).

2 General Experimental Setup

This section describes the general parts of the test setup that are identical for both domains (DVA and AIA), including the overall goals, the available input modalities, the test methodology, and the framework for the test procedures.

2.1 Study Background

The primary goal of our usability studies is to evaluate which modalities, and modality combinations, respectively, are preferred with regard to the particular application scenarios and the individual operation tasks at hand. We want to determine to which extent the overall user intention is distributed among complementary, redundant, and competing information streams of the available input modalities. By studying the individual modality transitions, prototypical multimodal interaction patterns of different user classes will be worked out. Additionally, we are interested in analyzing the time relations, i.e. the length of the individual interactions and the specific temporal overlapping. On the basis of these results we are planning to derive some fundamental requirements for a user-centered development of a generic multimodal system architecture.

2.2 Input Modalities

To communicate with the target applications, our interfaces provide a wide range of interaction paradigms that can be classified into tactile-based input, speech-based input as well as gesture-based input. Thereby, the individual input devices are designed in a way to support the full set of functionalities if technically possible, i.e. a priori they are not restricted to device-specific interaction forms.

Concerning tactile interactions, our interfaces support input by a conventional touch-screen and a domain specific key-console, which is a standard keyboard in DVA and a special key-console in AIA. By introducing more advanced interaction styles, such as the use of speech and gestures as well as combinations of various input modalities, our interfaces provide a more natural and flexible form of human-machine communication. Speech allows direct interaction without losing eye-focus on the scenario by glancing at the specific input devices. Gestures often support speech in interpersonal communication. In various domains, e.g. when dealing with spatial problems, information can be communicated easier and even more precisely using gestures instead of describing certain circumstances by speech[6]. Moreover, gesture-based input represents an interesting alternative in noisy environments or for people with certain disabilities.

To benefit from the advantages of the individual modalities, in our experimental setup the user can arbitrarily choose among five different input channels: conventional tactile input by **t**ouch-screen (T) or **k**ey-console (K) as well as semantically higher level input by **s**peech (S) and dynamic **h**and (H) and h**e**ad gestures (E). Theoretically, the combinations form a bimodal interaction space of ten possible modality combinations (TK, TH, TE, TS, KH, KE, KS, HE, HS, ES), not regarding any order of usage. Concerning speech input, both natural spontaneous speech utterances and command speech is supported.

2.3 Test Methodology

The functionalities of the test interfaces are partly realized according to the *Wizard-of-Oz* test paradigm[7]. In contrast to tactile interactions (touch-screen and key-console), that are directly transcribed by the system, the recognition of the semantic higher-level modalities (speech, hand and head gestures) is simulated by a human person supervising the test-subjects via audio- and video-signals. With regard to speech, an open-microphone metaphor[8] guarantees an optimal degree of naturalness and flexibility since the utterances are segmented automatically. The so-called *wizard* interprets the user's intention and generates the appropriate system commands, which are routed back to the interface to trigger the intended functionality. Thereby, the wizard is instructed to be extremely cooperative. In case of ambiguous user interactions, the input is to be interpreted at best in the current system context. For exchanging information between the individual modules of the system we have developed a special communication architecture based on an extended context-free grammar formalism[9]. As the grammar completely describes the interaction vocabulary of the underlying application on an abstract symbolic level, it facilitates the representation of both domain- and device independent multimodal information contents.

2.4 Test Plan

First, the test subjects have to fill out an initial questionnaire. Hence standard data and specific previous knowledge of the users with regard to the application domain is ascertained. For pre-classifying the individual subjects, we apply a weighted evaluation scheme that divides the users into three distinct clusters: **b**eginners (B), **n**ormal users (N), and **e**xperts (E). Afterwards, the test subjects are learning the functionality of the interface in an interactive training period together with the wizard, mainly by employing tactile interaction. At the same time, the use of the other modalities and potential modality combinations are motivated. Although the test subjects are allowed to use their own vocabulary, a basic set of meaningful dynamic hand and head gestures is introduced [10].

A full test consists of two phases. In the first part, consisting of four separate blocks, the participants have to use prescribed modality combinations (TK, TS, HS, ES), each to solve identical operation tasks. The second phase exposes a much more complex operation task, but the test subjects are now allowed to combine all of the available input devices. After each part, the usability of the current interaction paradigm has to be rated according to a six-point semantic differential scale with regard to several adjectives. Additionally, the test users can state universal remarks and discuss upcoming problems with the wizard.

3 Domain-Specific Setup

Concerning both application scenarios, special preparations and adjustments have been made, which are described subsequently. Thereby, in each case, we explain the software prototype itself, the specific test environment, and finally discuss the individual tasks which the users are exposed to during the test runs.

3.1 Desktop VR Browser

Test System. The first application is based on a multimodal front-end to the standard functionality of a common VRML browser[11]. In the test setup, we solely concentrate on the aspects of navigation. As we apply a first-person-view, the user can directly experience what a virtual avatar would see, thereby covering the full spectrum of continuous movements. Changing the field of view is equal to modifying the location and orientation of a central scene camera.

In VRML, both objects and any kind of interactions are defined with reference to a fixed world coordinate system (*wcs*). Navigating in this scene is equal to transforming an avatar centered coordinate system (*acs*) within this system. Mathematically, this can be described by a homogeneous transformation operation $p_{new} = T_{4x4} \cdot p_{old}$, covering both translational and rotational components.

With respect to the local *acs* shown on the left side of figure 2, six degrees of freedom can be identified. In the following, the names for the particular command clusters are given in parentheses. Concerning translational movements, the user can change the position along the z-axis, moving forward and backward (TFB), along the x-axis, moving left and right (TLR), and along the y-axis, moving up and down (TUD). Concerning rotational movements, turning the field of view left and right around the y-axis is called *yaw* (RLR), rotating up and down around the x-axis is called *pitch* (RUD) and a twisting move around the optical axis of the virtual scene camera (z-axis) is called *roll* (RRO).

Test Environment. The user study is carried out at the usability laboratory of our institute[8]. This laboratory consists of two rooms. The test subjects are located in a dedicated test room that is equipped with multiple, freely adjustable cameras and microphones. Separated from this area by a semi permeable mirror, the control room serves for recording and analyzing the individual user interactions. To carry out reproducible test runs with identical boundary conditions and to decrease the cognitive workload of the wizard, we have developed a special software suit[12] simplifying the management of various system parameters, semi-automatically announcing the operation tasks at specified points of time, and logging all kind of transactions on a millisecond basis.

User Tasks. In the first phase, the test users have to navigate through a kind of tunnel (see figure 2), mainly by employing translational and rotational movements (TFB, TLR, RLR). At the end of tunnel, they find a text string written on the wall. The test persons have to change their view in a way that the text becomes clearly readable in a horizontal position. This movement involves a rotation around the optical axis of the virtual camera (RRO). Finally, by the far end of the tunnel, there is a box located on the floor. The task is to look into the box which involves a combination of translational movements in the image plane and the horizontal plane as well as up/down rotations (TUD, TFB, RUD). In the second phase, the test subjects have to navigate through a curved series of archways. Thereby, they have to apply the full spectrum of movements which they have learned in the first four modality specific training blocks.

Fig. 2. Avatar centered coordinate system (left) and two screen-shots of the VRML scenario for evaluating the navigation tasks, showing the tunnel of the first phase (middle) and a fraction of the curved series of arch-ways of the second test part (right)

3.2 Automotive Audio- and Communication Services

Test System. The second application scenario deals with a multimodal front-end for controlling various audio devices as well as standard telecommunication units [13]. The player module provides well-known CD-player functionalities (*play, pause, stop, skip, etc.*). In radio mode, the user can switch between 25 different predefined radio stations. The telephone functions are restricted to basic call handling of predefined address-book entries. Moreover, the volume of the audio signal can be adjusted in a separate mode. As shown on the right-hand side of figure 1, the interface can be operated by the same class of input devices like the DVA, only differing in a specially designed key-console. As the central design element, the interface provides a list containing individual items that can vertically be scrolled through by means of two buttons on the right. Above the list, four buttons provide direct access to the individual modes of the application (MP3, radio, telephone, and control). In addition, the area beneath the list contains context specific buttons varying from three to five buttons in the specific modes as well as a feedback line. The design of the key-console is organized in direct analogy to the layout of the buttons on the touch-screen.

Test Environment. The user study is carried out at a usability laboratory that has specially been adapted to evaluate multimodal user interfaces in automotive environments[8]. To simulate realistic conditions in non-field studies, the lab provides a simple driving simulator, consisting of a specially prepared BMW limousine. Using steering wheel, gas and break pedals, the subjects have to control a 3D-driving task, which is projected on a white wall in front of the car[14]. Thus, they experience the driving scenario from a natural in-car perspective and can better anticipate the roadway. The individual parameters of the simulation can fully be controlled, e.g. the degree of the curves, day- or night sight conditions, speed regulations, obstacles, or passing cars. Besides touch-screen and key console, the car is equipped with a number of microphones and cameras to supervise the test subjects. The audio- and video signals from inside the car are transferred to a separated control room that serves for recording and analyzing user interactions with the test interface and the driving performance.

Table 1. Distribution of the command structure (left) and the proportion of unimodal and multimodal system interactions (right) in DVA for all user groups **b**eginners (B), **n**ormal users (N), and **e**xperts (E) as well as the average mean value (M) for all users

DVA	B	N	E	M
full command	58.2	73.6	72.6	69.5
partial command	41.8	26.4	27.4	30.5

DVA	B	N	E	M
unimodal	73.8	82.1	81.5	79.8
multimodal	26.2	17.9	18.5	20.2

User Tasks. In direct analogy to the DVA scenario, the user test in the automotive environment consists of two phases. Thereby, the test subjects are exposed to a wide variety of tasks that can be subdivided into five command clusters: player commands (PLY) for starting, stopping and pausing the currently selected track as well as skipping in the play-list, radio commands (RAD), telephone commands (TEL), mode-spanning list commands (LIS) for scrolling in the list display and selecting individual entries and, finally, universal control commands (CTL) for adjusting sound parameters or selecting various operation modes.

Concerning the modality specific training phase of the first four blocks, the test subjects have to accomplish 16 different operation tasks that are uniformly distributed among the various command clusters. To keep the test subjects from devoting most of their attention to control the test interface, they have to perform in a driving task simultaneously. In the second part, the subjects have to fulfill 23 operation tasks on the background of a slightly more difficult driving task and, additionally, they are distracted by changing boundary conditions like an increased frequency of curves, speed limits, and obstacles on the road.

4 Results Desktop VR Application (DVA)

A total of 40 persons participated in the usability tests (14 female and 26 male), with 11 beginners, 20 normal computer users, and nine experts. The average age of the users was 28.8 years. Besides many engineering students, people of different education and profession took part in the tests. Since the second test block symbolizes the core, non-restricted multimodal test conditions, we especially concentrate on evaluating the data of this part in the following subsections.

4.1 Command Structure

The distribution of command types is shown on the left side of table 6. The average number of all system interactions in the second part is 237.4, varying from 85 to 679 (σ=115.33). Strongly related to the navigation tasks that have been superimposed on the subjects, as expected, the set of translational forward/backward movements (TFB) have been used most often, making up more than the half of all commands. With 16.0% on the average, the class of left/right rotations (RLR) provides the second-best frequented type of system interactions.

Concentrating on the semantic content, an isolated system command is composed of a *functional part*, i.e. indicating the special kind of navigation movement

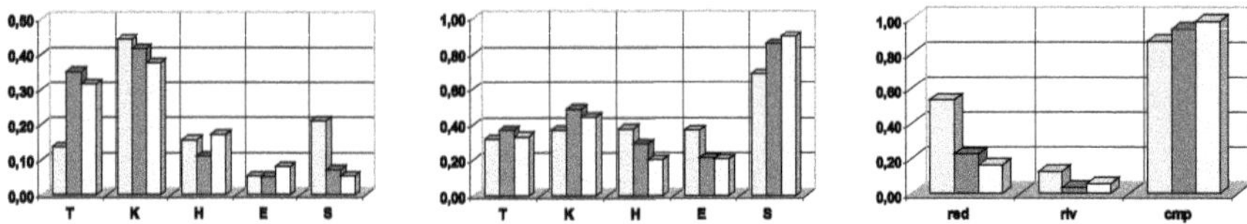

Fig. 3. Distribution of unimodal (left) and multimodal (middle) user interactions with regard to the individual modalities in DVA. The right diagram shows the distribution of multimodal information parts (red=redundant, riv=rivaling, cmp=complementary) in DVA. Concerning each diagram, the left column (green) stands for beginners, the middle column (purple) for normal users and the right column (yellow) for experts

(translation or rotation) and a and *parameter value* qualifying the direction of the movement (forward, backward, left, right, up and down). A user interaction can either consist of both components (*full command*) or only one single slot (*partial command*). The left side of table 1 contains group specific details.

4.2 Use of Modalities

The distribution of unimodal system commands is visualized in the left diagram of figure 3. Obviously, all user groups favor keyboard for unimodal interactions (B=44.5%, N=41.7%, E=37.7%). For next best choice, experts and normal users clearly prefer touch screen (N=35.1%, E=31.7%), whereas beginners tend to employ speech (20.9%), closely followed by hand gestures (15.7%).

As the navigation tasks were quite simple, unimodal interaction clearly overruled multimodal interaction. The respective quota for the individual user groups (B,N,E) and the average mean value (M) is listed on the right side of table 1. Yet, detailed analysis clearly prooves that with growing complexity, the use of multimodal interaction increases. Although only applied in about one fifth of all interactions, combined multimodal commands symbolize the core interaction style, as they were particularly used to change navigation contexts. For all groups, the use of speech clearly dominates the distribution of multimodal interactions (see middle of figure 3). When combining multiple input modalities, especially beginners favored gestures and speech. The other two groups strongly combined speech for mode setting with tactile devices to indicate directions.

4.3 Multimodal Interaction

The distribution of redundant (red), rival (riv), and complementary (cmp) interactions is shown in the right diagram of figure 3. For all groups of users, complementary actions occurrs most often (B=86.9%, N=93.9%, E=98.3%). In only 12.5% of all complementary actions, more than two modalities are applied. Real multimodal commands (showing no intramodal dependencies) appears in 67.3% of combined interactions. Especially beginners seem to apply redundant interactions (53,2%) more than twice as much in comparison to normal users

Table 2. Distribution of relative modality transitions (RMT) in DVA (left) and AIA (right) from source modality mod_s to target modality mod_t, specified in % relative to all transitions of a given source modality, self transitions are marked in bold letters

DVA	T_t	K_t	H_t	E_t	S_t
T_s	**63.79**	12.61	2.59	2.50	12.20
K_s	22.48	**60.52**	5.22	4.65	11.48
H_s	7.84	7.94	**52.41**	7.65	32.57
E_s	9.23	21.00	21.56	**35.10**	33.05
S_s	16.25	31.64	23.07	13.75	**46.49**

AIA	T_t	K_t	H_t	E_t	S_t
T_s	**38.01**	18.77	7.53	2.32	35.44
K_s	16.73	**47.47**	9.20	2.74	23.97
H_s	17.69	24.45	**4.17**	2.07	48.14
E_s	16.67	4.17	14.58	**0.00**	67.36
S_s	20.49	8.59	7.10	1.52	**60.48**

(22.4%). These results also emphasize the observation that beginners show complementary behavior coupled with redundancy to a high degree.

The effectiveness of combined user interactions can be measured as the number of performed transactions per time (TpT). Experts and normal users work most efficient when combining touch screen with keyboard (1.04 / 0.95 TpT) or speech (0.54/0.47 TpT). As an outstanding result, we obtained that in part three of the first block (SH), beginners get even higher scores than the other two groups (0.30 compared to 0.27 and 0.23 TpT, respectively). Purely tactile interaction (TK) is still most time efficient, but concerning the other combination scenarios, all groups of test subjects work significantly more effective ($p < 0.01$) in the second block with free modality combination. In this regard, normal users nearly perform 32% better than experts (0.80 vs. 0.61 TpT).

4.4 Modality Transitions

Concerning the transitions between the individual modalities, we have examined the relative modality transitions (RMT), defined as the percentage of transitions with respect to a fixed source modality $mod_s \in \{T_s, K_s, H_s, E_s, S_s\}$ to the potential target modalities $mod_t \in \{T_t, K_t, H_t, E_t, S_t\}$. The results for the DVA are shown on the left side of table 2 as an average mean value for all user groups. As in the case of redundant multimodal interactions several modalities contribute to a single system command, selective rows sum up to a value higher than 100%.

The results clearly confirm the primary expectations, that users tend to stick to tactile interactions much stronger than to speech or gestures. This interaction behavior can be observed for all user groups. Especially after an interaction with a head gesture, the modality is changed in most cases. Analyzing the average modality specific retention period ($AMRP$), which is defined by the number of self transitions divided by the total number of transitions to other modalities, the observations above are worked out even more clearly ($AMRP_T = 4.69$, $AMRP_K = 10.13$, $AMRP_H = 2.02$, $AMRP_E = 0.71$, and $AMRP_S = 5.42$).

4.5 Time Relations

The left side of table 3 summarizes the medium interaction times for the semantically higher level modalities speech, hand and head gestures in DVA. For

Table 3. Average interaction times in seconds for semantic higher-level input by speech utterances, as well as by hand and head gestures in DVA (left) and AIA (right)

DVA	B	N	E	M
speech	0.99	0.90	1.06	0.96
hand gesture	1.02	0.99	1.32	1.08
head gesture	1.15	1.15	1.31	1.17

AIA	B	N	E	M
speech	0.87	0.87	1.10	0.94
hand gesture	0.90	0.90	1.20	1.08
head gesture	1.98	1.98	1.73	1.49

Table 4. Distribution of time relations in DVA (left) and AIA (right), subdivided in staggered, nested, and sequential interactions according to the scheme given in [3]

DVA	B	N	E	M
staggered	37.08	69.16	46.43	55.16
sequential	7.03	8.43	7.14	7.79
nested	55.89	22.41	46.43	37.05

AIA	B	N	E	M
staggered	50.00	66.67	50.00	43.75
sequential	50.00	0.00	12.50	39.06
nested	0.00	33.33	37.50	17.19

all groups of users, in the case of speech the shortest interaction times could be observed. Astonishingly, expert users exposed significant longer interaction times compared to beginners and normal users.

With reference to the scheme for analyzing intermodal time relations described by Oviatt[3], multimodal interactions are classified into *sequential*, *staggered*, and *nested* interactions. Assume, we have two interactions I_1 and I_2 lasting from time-stamp t_{1s} to t_{1e} and t_{2s} to t_{2e}, respectively (with $t_{1s} < t_{1e}$, $t_{2s} < t_{2e}$ and $t_{1s} < t_{2s}$). Then we speak of a sequential action, if $t_{2s} > t_{1e}$, a staggered action, if $t_{2s} < t_{1e}$ and $t_{1e} < t_{2e}$, and a nested action, if $t_{2e} < t_{1e}$.

The different user groups exhibit massively varying interaction patterns. While beginner and experts mainly use nested interactions with one modality completely enclosing the other, normal users tend to prefer staggered interactions. For each group, purely sequential interactions have been applied rarely. Finally, analyzing the interaction time by separately regarding only unimodal and multimodal interactions, respectively, we did not find any significant differences in the lengths of the individual interactions.

4.6 Subjective User Experiences

As an overall result, analyzing the questionnaires reveals good accordance with the measured values discussed above. Experts and normal users rate touch-screen in combination with speech best, whereas beginners state to prefer speech in combination with hand gestures. Interestingly, head gestures have been rated very bad, which contradicts the measured values. In fact, combined with speech, head movements make up at least 20.0% of all combined interactions. Concerning the remarks of the closing questionnaire users have asked for advanced navigation features, i.e. they want the system to continuously react on head and hand movements. Moreover subjects have demanded to phrase browser commands applying context knowledge of the current navigation situation, e.g. “go to the wall” or “turn the view until the arch-way is in a horizontal position”.

Table 5. Distribution of unimodal (left) and multimodal (right) interactions in AIA

AIA	T	K	H	E	S
B	24.98	31.09	3.49	0.96	39.49
N	38.69	41.14	0.00	0.13	20.04
E	36.21	34.92	4.81	0.43	23.63
M	31.87	34.43	2.77	0.93	30.00

AIA	T	K	H	E	S
B	0.00	0.00	50.00	0.00	50.00
N	0.00	0.00	33.33	16.67	50.00
E	0.00	0.00	25.00	25.00	50.00
M	0.00	0.00	33.33	16.67	50.00

Table 6. Distribution of the command types for DVA (left) and AIA (right), listed in % for the individual user groups (B,N,E) and the average mean value (M) for all users

DVA	TFB	TLR	TUD	RRO	RLR	RUD
B	50.7	8.9	8.4	5.5	16.8	9.5
N	51.4	10.1	4.6	5.2	16.5	12.1
E	52.4	10.3	6.4	8.7	13.9	8.4
M	51.4	9.8	6.1	6.1	16.0	10.6

AIA	PLY	RAD	TEL	LIS	CTL
B	18.6	4.0	16.1	31.1	30.1
N	19.8	4.3	17.2	36.6	22.1
E	20.9	4.2	17.0	35.0	24.3
M	20.0	4.3	17.0	34.8	24.3

5 Results Automotive Infotainment Application (AIA)

A total of 28 persons participated in the second usability test (five female, 23 male). The participants are grouped in eight beginners, 13 normal computer users and seven experts. The average age of the test users was nearly 29 years. An intersection of five participants have taken part in both usability studies. Just like the DVA szenario, the evaluation of the test data mainly concentrates on the analysis of the second block.

5.1 Command Structure

The distribution of the command types is shown on the right side in table 6. Again, the results are strongly related to the specific tasks in the test. Thereby, the individual users mostly differed in the number of list commands (LIS) and control commands (CTL), because some test subjects changed volume parameters several time during the test run. The average number of all system interactions (ASI) in the second block is 48.50 with a standard deviation $\sigma = 9.98$. Concerning the semantic content of an isolated system command, we exclusively find full commands in the AIA.

5.2 Use of Modalities

Although the test subjects have been allowed to use the full spectrum of input devices, a detailed analysis of the audio-visual material offers an unambiguous tendency towards a concentration on two devices. For most of the users, this has been the combination touch-screen and speech which is supported by the data on the left in table 5 showing the distribution of unimodal interactions and on the right in table 5 containing the distribution of multimodal interactions.

Regarding all test subjects, in total 51 multimodal interactions have been observed. On the background of 1358 transcribed system interactions, this corresponds to an overall multimodal quota of only 4.2%. This result contradicts to our expectations, but can be explained by the fundamental differences in the experimental setups. The tactile devices have not been used in combination with speech and gestures at all, which is an important difference compared to the results in DVA. Concerning the distribution of multimodal information, redundant components make up 85.71% of all multimodal interactions. Since rivaling interactions have not been observed, the complementary parts cover the remaining 14.29%. As the total number of multimodal interactions is very small and only two test users showed more than two multimodal interactions, no significant differences between the individual user groups can be identified. The underlying test material does not provide a sufficiant basis for statistically valuable arguments.

5.3 Modality Transitions

The average *RMT*s for the automotive scenario are shown on the right in table 2. In contrast to the DVA, self-transitions do not symbolize the primary form of modality changes. Concerning hand gestures, the users change to speech instead of continuing purely gesture-based interaction. If head gestures are applied, none of the test subjects uses them for a second time in a row.

5.4 Time Relations

The right side of table 3 summarizes the medium interaction times for the semantically higher level modalities. According to the interaction times, speech offers the fastest access, closely followed by hand gestures. With regard to the head gestures, we find significantly longer interaction times, compared to DVA. The observation that experts show longer interaction times can be confirmed in AIA. In direct analogy to the results in the DVA scenario, the analysis of the interaction times in the unimodal and multimodal case does not reveal any significant differences. The different user groups again showed strongly varying interaction patterns documented on the right in table 4. While beginner and experts mainly use nested interactions with one modality completely enclosing the other, normal users tend to prefer staggered interactions. For each group, purely sequential interactions have been applied rarely.

5.5 Subjective User Experiences

Compared to the prescribed modality combinations in the first block, the system offering the full functionality obtaines significantly better ratings with regard to various usability criteria. Only the combination of speech and touch-screen was rated better concerning the quality of effective usage.

Natural speech has clearly been preferred for almost all system functionalities. While the key-console has obtaines best ratings for scrolling in the list and

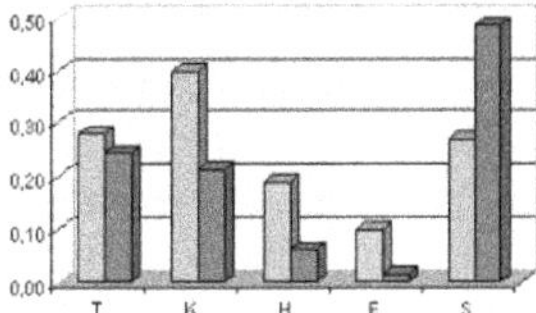

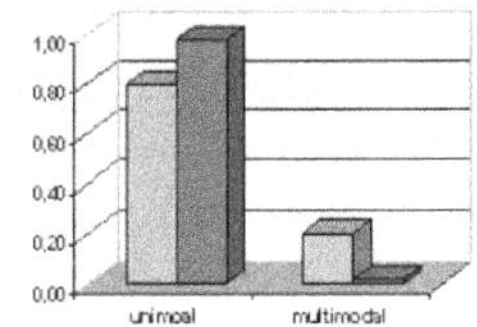

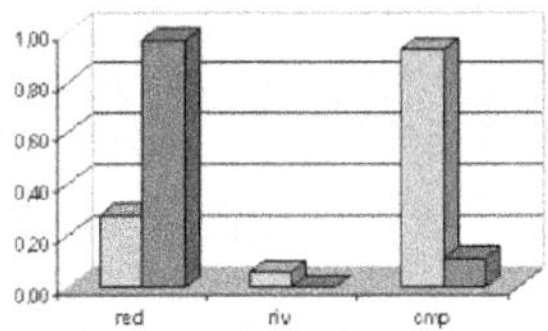

Fig. 4. Comparing DVA and AIA: the distribution of the individual modalities (left), the proportion of unimodal and multimodal commands (middle) and the distribution of multimodal information parts (right); concerning each diagram, the left column (blue) represents the DVA scenario and the right column (purple) the AIA domain

adjusting the volume, the touch-screen is chosen most often to skip between individual tracks in a play list. Head gestures represent an interesting special case. With eight of the test subjects favoring them as the primary input modality for yes/no decisions, like in accepting or denying an incoming phone call, the other users totally dislike this input form. When applying speech, the test subjects make extensive use of natural speech utterances, that are mainly applied for complex system functions involving context knowledge of the application domain (e.g. directly saying "play radio station *ABC*" instead of scrolling in the list and selecting the appropriate entry). Moreover, the test users expect the system to understand combined commands, like "go to the last entry".

6 Comparative Discussion

Although the two application domains cannot be compared directly due to massively varying boundary conditions, certain characteristics of multimodal interaction patterns can be worked out. Concerning the general distribution of the individual input modalities, speech clearly dominates the use of the semantic higher-level modalities in the automotive environment. The results of the direct comparison are shown in the left diagram of figure 4. In the automotive setup, head and hand gestures have been used very rarely. This partly results from the fact that speech has been recognized on a basis of 100% due to the simulated Wizard-of-Oz recognition module and a highly tolerant wizard.

Comparing multimodal and unimodal interactions, the DVA exposes a much higher quota of combined interactions in general (more than 20% in DVA and only 2.1% in AIA). The ratio is visualized in the middle diagram of figure 4. While experienced users tend to focus on standard tactile devices, beginners prefer speech and gestures and combine modalities more often. Especially beginners show complementary interactions accompanied by simultaneous redundant information. Regarding the distribution of multimodal information (shown on the right in figure 4) we have determined an increased level of redundant interactions in DVA compared to more complementary interactions in AIA.

A detailed analysis of the audio-visual data material clearly reveales that the lengths of the interactions by the semantical higher-level modalities speech, head and hand gestures stay within a maximum time-period of 1.5 seconds. Concerning the intermodal time relations, staggered interactions are used in most cases. With reference to the modality transitions we have found out that once adapted to a specific modality, the test users try to stay within the chosen interaction form. This especially holds for the tactile devices and less for head-gestures. Concerning selected functionalities like yes/no decisions head-gestures represent the preferred form of input, at least for about one fourth of all users in the test trials. Analysing the closing questionaires with reference to several usability criteria, the full multimodal interaction paradigm has been rated significantly better compared to the individual bimodal combinations.

7 Conclusion and Future Work

In this work, we have presented the results of a comprehensive evaluation on multimodal system interaction regarding five input modalities and two different application scenarios: a desktop Virtual-Reality browser and an automotive infotainment application. The individual multimodal interfaces have been compared with regard to command clusters, the use of modalities, multimodal combinations, modality transitions, time relations and subjective user experiences.

Currently, we are working on running detailed statistical tests on the data material, especially evaluating the results with regard to specific tasks and potential user errors that may always occur during the interaction. For the nearest future, we plan to integrate the results of this study as empirical data in the design of a generic integration architecture for multimodal interactive systems.

References

1. Oviatt, S.L.: Multimodal interface research: A science without borders. Proc. of the 6th Int. Conf. on Spoken Language Processing (ICSLP) (2000)
2. Cheyer, A., Julia, L.: Designing, developing and evaluating multimodal applications. In: WS on Pen/Voice Interfaces (CHI 99). (1999)
3. Oviatt, S.L., et al.: Integration and synchronization of input modes during multimodal human-computer interaction. Proc. of the 6th ICSLP (2000)
4. Nigay, L., Coutaz, J.: A Design Space for Multimodal Systems: Concurrent Processing and Data Fusion. In: Proc. of INTERCHI '93, ACM Press (1993) 172–178
5. Cohen, P., et al.: Multimodal interaction during multiparty dialogues: Initial results. Proc. of 4th IEEE Int. Conf. on Multimodal Interfaces (2002)
6. Sowa, T.: Coverbal iconic gestures for object descriptions in virtual environments: An empirical study. Post-Proc. of Int. Conf on Gestures: Meaning and Use (2000)
7. Nielsen, J.: Usability Engineering. Morgan Kaufmann Publishers Inc. (1993)
8. Neuss, R.: Usability Engineering als Ansatz zum Multimodalen Mensch-Maschine-Dialog. PhD thesis, Technical University of Munich (2001)
9. McGlaun, G., et al.: A new approach for the integration of multimodal input based on late semantic fusion. In Proc. of USEWARE 2002 (2002)
10. Zobl, M., et al.: A usability-study on hand-gesture controlled operation of in-car devices. Proc. of 9th Int. Conf. on HCI (2001)

11. Althoff, F., et al.: A generic approach for interfacing VRML browsers to various input devices. Proc. of ACM Web3D Symposium (2001) 67–74
12. Schuller, B., Lang, M., et al.: Towards automation of usability studies. Proc. of IEEE Int. Conf. on Systems, Man and Cybernetics (SMC02) (2002)
13. Althoff, F., Geiss, K., et al.: Experimental evaluation of user errors at the skill-based level in an automotive environment. Proc. of CHI 02 (2002)
14. McGlaun, G., Althoff, F., Lang, M.: A new technique for adjusting distraction moments in multitasking non-field usability tests. Proc. of CHI 02 (2002)

Imitation Games with an Artificial Agent: From Mimicking to Understanding Shape-Related Iconic Gestures

Stefan Kopp, Timo Sowa, and Ipke Wachsmuth

Artificial Intelligence Group
Faculty of Technology, University of Bielefeld
D-33594 Bielefeld, Germany
{skopp,tsowa,ipke}@techfak.uni-bielefeld.de

Abstract. We describe an anthropomorphic agent that is engaged in an imitation game with the human user. In imitating natural gestures demonstrated by the user, the agent brings together gesture recognition and synthesis on two levels of representation. On the mimicking level, the essential form features of the meaning-bearing gesture phase (stroke) are extracted and reproduced by the agent. Meaning-based imitation requires extracting the semantic content of such gestures and re-expressing it with possibly alternative gestural forms. Based on a compositional semantics for shape-related iconic gestures, we present first steps towards this higher-level gesture imitation in a restricted domain.

1 Introduction

Intuitive and natural communication with a computer is a primary research goal in human-computer interaction. This vision includes the usage of all communicative modalities, e.g., speech, gesture, gaze, and intonation, and has led to extensive work on processing a user's multimodal input as well as on creating natural utterances with humanoid agents. To address these problems with regard to gesture, we employ a scenario in which the human user is engaged in an imitation game with an anthropomorphic agent, *Max*. The human user meets Max in a virtual environment where he is visualized in human size. The agent's task is to immediately *imitate* any gesture that has been demonstrated by the user.

Imitation tasks are of particular interest as this capability can be considered a key competence for communicative behavior in artificial agents. Just like in infant development of communicative skills, two important steps towards this competence would be the following: First, the agent's capability to perceive the various behaviors in his opposite's utterance and to mimic them in a consistent way (*mimicking-level*). Second, and higher-level, to understand the meaning of the perceived utterance and re-express its content with his own communicative means, i.e., in his own words and with his own gestures (*meaning-level*).

Our previous work was directed to processing multimodal utterances of the user and to synthesizing multimodal responses of Max, both including coverbal

A. Camurri and G. Volpe (Eds.): GW 2003, LNAI 2915, pp. 436–447, 2004.

gestures [13,7]. This contribution describes how the developed systems can be combined to enable the gesture imitation game on both aforementioned levels (see Fig. 1 for an overview):

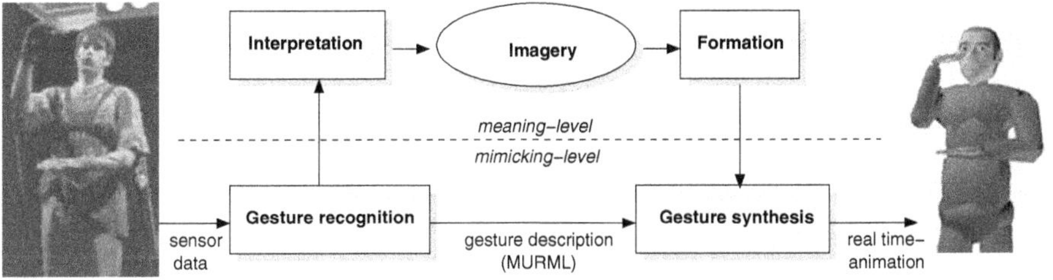

Fig. 1. Levels of gesture imitation (bottom-up: form-based and meaning-based)

On the mimicking level, Max employs a body-centered representation of the gesture as an interface between his recognition and production systems. Imitation therefore includes formally describing a gesture's meaningful (stroke) phase in terms of its mandatory spatiotemporal features which transcends the direct transfer of low-level body configuration parameters like in motion capture. This kind of gesture imitation has been successfully realized for a certain range of gestures and is described in more detail in Section 3. Beyond mimicking, a recognized gesture can be conceptualized on the meaning level yielding a modality-independent representation of its content (idea unit). From this representation a gestural imitation can be generated that preserves the original communicative idea but may very well result in different realizations, e.g., dependent on the availability of expressive resources. For a domain limited to object shape descriptions by iconic gestures, we present a spatial representation for a gesture's imaginal content in Section 4. First steps towards automatically building such representations, i.e., interpreting gestures, as well as forming particular gestures for them are described.

2 Related Work

In spite of its significance for the cognitively plausible development of human-computer communication, imitation scenarios have not been adopted in previous systems and especially not so with respect to gestures. There is a large body of research on gesture recognition viewed as pattern classification. Systems based on this paradigm segment the input data stream from the sensing device and consider gestures as atomic pieces of information that can be mapped one-to-one on some application-dependent meaning. Popular computer vision methods include training-based approaches like Hidden Markov Models and Artificial Neural Networks, as well as explicit feature-based methods [16]. Multimodal approaches that include gesture and speech additionally consider the context-dependency of gesture semantics. Usually, some form of multimodal grammar is employed to unify gesture and speech tokens in a common complex of meaning [4]. A semantic aspect which is particularly important in natural gestures is iconicity. However, most current systems do not provide any means to model gestural images explicitly based on their inner structure. One noteworthy exception is the ICONIC system that maps object descriptions with coverbal gestures on possible referents based on an explicit comparison of form features and their spatial configuration [15].

Similar to most recognition approaches, gesture generation in conversational agents (e.g. [12,1]) usually relies on a fixed one-to-one mapping from communicative intent to predefined animations that are drawn from static libraries on the basis of specific heuristics. Although the animations can be parametrized to a certain extent or concatenated to form more complex movements, this approach obviously does not resemble a real "transformation" of meaning into gesture. Cassell et al. [2] present a system for planning multimodal utterances from a grammar which describes coverbal gestures declaratively in terms of their discourse function, semantics, and synchrony with speech. However, gesture production again does not associate semantic features with particular gesture features (i.e., handshape, orientation, movement) that would constitute a literally context-dependent gesture (cf. [2, p. 175]). A fully automatic gesture creation was targeted by only few researchers. Gibet et al. [3] apply generic error-correcting controllers for generating sign language from script-like notations. Matarić et al. [10] stress the problem of determining appropriate control strategies and propose the combined application of different controllers for simulating upper limb movements. For Max, we emphasize the accurate and reliable reproduction of spatiotemporal gesture properties. To this end, motor control is planned directly from required form properties and realized by means of model-based animation.

3 Mimicking: Form-Based Imitation

By gesture mimicking we mean the reproduction of the *essential* form properties of a demonstrated gesture by an articulated agent. This kind of imitation should be independent from the agent's body properties (e.g., measures, proportions, level of articulation) and, furthermore, should not need to take subsidiary movement features into account. As depicted in Fig. 1, mimicking therefore includes (1) recognizing gestural movements from sensory input, (2) extracting form features of the gesture stroke and specifying them in relation to the gesturer's body, and (3) synthesizing a complete gesture animation that reproduces these features in its stroke phase. This section describes the methods developed for all three stages and their combination in Max in order to enable real-time gesture mimicking.

3.1 Feature-Based Representation of Gesture Form

A gesture's form features are described by a subset of MURML, a markup language for specifying multimodal utterances for communicative agents [7].

MURML defines a hand/arm configuration in terms of three features: (1) the location of the wrist, (2) the shape of the hand, and (3) the orientation of the wrist, compositionally described by the extended finger orientation/direction and the normal vector of the palm (palm orientation). Feature values (except for handshape) can be defined either numerically or symbolically using augmented HamNoSys [11] descriptions. Handshape is compositionally described by the overall handshape and additional symbols denoting the flexion of various fingers.

A gesture is described in MURML by specifying its stroke phase that is considered as an arbitrarily complex combination of sub-movements within the three features, e.g., moving the hand up while keeping a fist. To state the relationships between such features, simultaneity, posteriority, repetition, and symmetry of sub-movements can be denoted by specific MURML elements constituting a constraint tree for the gesture (see Figure 2 for an example).

```
<constraints>
  <parallel>
    <symmetrical dominant=“right_arm” symmetry=“SymMST”
      center=“0 0 0 0 0 15.0”>
      <parallel>
        <static slot=“HandShape” value=“BSflat”/>
        <static slot=“ExtFingerOrientation” value=“DirAL”/>
        <static slot=“HandLocation” value=“LocChin
          LocCCenterRight LocNorm”/>
      </parallel>
    </symmetrical>
    <static slot=“PalmOrientation” value=“DirD” scope=“left_arm” />
    <static slot=“PalmOrientation” value=“DirD” scope=“right_arm” />
  </parallel>
</constraints>
```

Fig. 2. Example specification of a static two-handed, symmetrical gesture

Each feature is defined over a certain period of time to be either (1) static, i.e., a postural feature held before retraction, or (2) dynamic, i.e., a significant sub-movement fluently connected with adjacent movement phases. For complex trajectories, dynamic constraints are made up of segments, which can be further differentiated for hand location constraints either as linear or curvilinear.

Like in HamNoSys, symmetric two-handed gestures are defined in terms of the movement of the dominant hand and the type of symmetry obeyed by the following hand. We define eight different symmetries made up of combinations of mirror symmetries w.r.t. the frontal, transversal, and sagittal body planes (“SymMST” in Figure 2 denotes mirror symmetries w.r.t. the sagittal and the transversal plane). Regardless of the symmetry condition, handshapes are identical in both hands and the wrist orientation vectors are always switched in transversal direction (left-right). Exceptions from this rule can be described explicitly by combining respective movement constraints with the symmetrical node (as in Figure 2 for palm orientation).

3.2 Gesture Recognition and Feature Extraction

The gesture recognition stage transforms sensory data into a MURML form representation (Fig. 3). We employ a 6DOF tracking system and data-gloves to capture hand motion as well as posture information. Data from the devices is processed by a chain of software modules which are tightly integrated in the immersive virtual reality environment [9]. The modules compute form and movement features of MURML as well as cues for gesture segmentation. A specialized segmentation module processes such cues to divide the data stream into gesture phases based on the approach by Kita et al. [5]. A movement interval, including hand motion and posture changes, is segmented at points where an abrupt change of the movement direction occurs and the velocity profile significantly changes. An alternation of direction includes the transition between movement and holds. For each phase, a form description frame is created that includes the relevant features. The resulting frame sequence is searched for typical profiles that indicate a gesture phrase, for example, a phase in which the hand rises, followed by a hold, and then a lowering phase, is regarded as a *preparation-stroke-retraction* phrase. The hold in the middle would then be tagged as the meaningful phase and encoded in MURML.

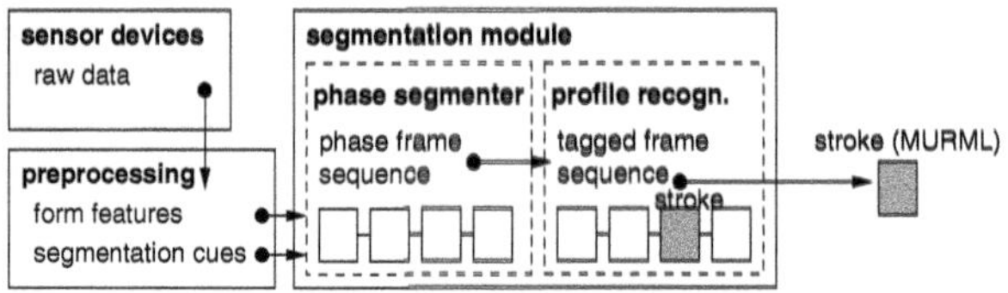

Fig. 3. Stages of the recognition process

3.3 Gesture Synthesis

On the gesture synthesis stage, Max is able to create and execute gesture animations from MURML descriptions in real-time. An underlying kinematic skeleton for the agent was defined comprising 103 DOF in 57 joints, all subject to realistic joint limits. This articulated body is driven by a hierarchical gesture generation model, shown in Figure 4, that includes two stages: (1) high-level gesture planning and (2) motor planning. During gesture planning (see [6]), the expressive phase of a gesture is defined by setting up a fully qualified set of movement constraints. This stage optionally includes selecting an abstract gesture template from a lexicon, allocating body parts, expanding two-handed symmetrical gestures, resolving deictic references, and defining the timing of the stroke phase. During lower-level motor planning (described in [7]), a solution is sought to control movements of the agent's upper limbs that satisfy the constraints at disposal. A kinematic model of human hand-arm movement is employed that is based on findings from human movement science and neurophysiology. Each limb's motion is kinematically controlled by a motor program that concurrently employs low-level controllers (local motor programs; LMPs). LMPs animate sub-movements, i.e., within a limited set of DOFs and over a designated period of time, by employing suitable motion generation methods. During planning, specialized motor control modules instantiate and prepare LMPs and subjoin them to the motor program(s). Our system provides modules for the hand, the wrist, the arm, as well as the neck and the face of the agent. Depending on body feedback during execution, blending of single gesture phases emerges from self-activation of the LMPs as well as the transfer of activation between them and their predecessors or successors, respectively.

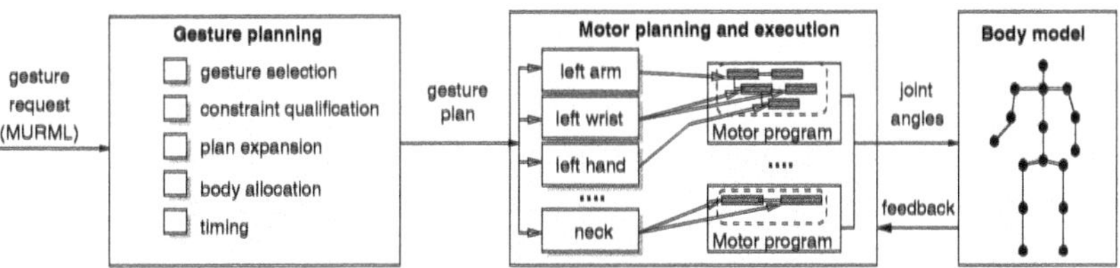

Fig. 4. Overview of the gesture generation model

Gesture recognition and synthesis have been connected by way of transferring the essential form features of a gesture encoded in MURML. That way, Max is able to mimic gestures in real-time standing face-to-face to the user (see Fig. 5 for examples). The recognition capabilities of the agent are currently limited to meaningful hold phases or turning points combined with arbitrary handshapes (e.g., as in pointing gestures). Dynamic movements and especially curvilinear trajectories pose particular problems for gesture segmentation as well as feature extraction and are subject of ongoing work.

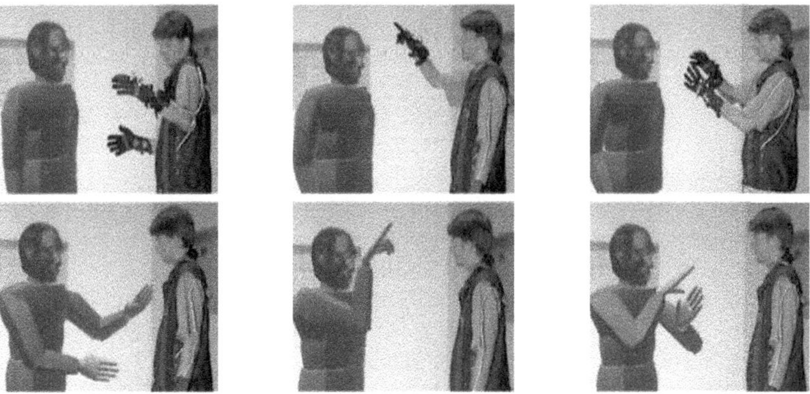

Fig. 5. Form-based gesture imitation: The form of a demonstrated gesture (upper picture) is mimicked by Max (lower picture)

4 Understanding: Meaning-Based Imitation

The recognition and generation systems described so far realize a first-level abstraction of upper limb movements to their essential form features (cf. Fig. 1). On this basis, we can approach meaning-based gesture imitation by deriving the idea unit behind the gesture from its form features (interpretation), formally representing this semantics, and re-expressing it in possibly alternative gestures (formation). To this end, plausible "sense-preserving" transformations between gesture morphology and meaning are needed. This section, first, describes a spatial representation for the semantics of iconic gestures for a domain limited to object shape descriptions. Experimentally derived, heuristic rules are presented for the mapping between this representation of gesture meaning and the feature-based descriptions of gesture form. Finally, first steps towards implementing this mapping in both directions, i.e., interpreting as well as forming shape-related iconic gestures, are described.

4.1 Imagistic Representation of Object Shape

We conducted an empirical study to unveil the semantic features of shape and to determine the mapping between form and meaning of gestures in an object description task [14]. We observed that most gestures reflect an abstract image of their object which represents its extent in different spatial dimensions. We introduced the term *dimensional gestures* for this particular class. Such gestures are often reduced to convey just one or two dimensions, a phenomenon that we call *dimensional underspecification.* Following the object's structure, gestural descriptions mostly decompose objects into simple geometric shapes that are described successively. Sometimes such descriptions contain an abstract sketch of the whole object before going into details. Successive dimensional gestures tend to coherently retain the spatial relations between the objects they represent. Groups of them may form complex elusive images in gesture space that reflect the qualitative arrangement of objects and their parts. For example, the main body of a riddled bar introduced by an iconic gesture may serve as a frame of reference for gestures indicating the position of the holes. Therefore, the spatial representation should cover larger semantic units spanning several gestures to allow for analyzing or synthesizing spatial coherence. We have chosen a structured, 3D representation called *imagistic description tree (IDT)* to model these properties. Each node represents an object's or part's basic spatial proportions. The approach is derived from a semantic representation schema for dimensional adjectives [8][1]. An *object schema* consists of up to three orthogonal axes describing the object's extent. An *integrated axis* covers more than one dimension. A 2D-integrated axis can be regarded as the diameter of some object with a roundish cross-cut, and a 3D-integrated axis as the diameter of a sphere.

[1] The original implementation as a graph structure [13] allowed an arbitrary number of axes and spatial relations. It was modified to be compatible with Lang's more restricted object schemas [8] which simplifies the recognition process.

Axis proportions and "meanings" can be qualitatively specified by the following attributes:

max defines the perceptually most salient axis which is commonly associated with the object's length. It is always disintegrated.
sub defines an integrated or disintegrated axis which is perceptually less salient. It is associated with the object's thickness, its material, or substance.
dist defines an interior extent, e.g., of non-material "parts" like holes.

Each axis' extent may be specified quantitatively with a length. To integrate verbal information, each schema contains names for the part it defines, e.g. "head" and "shank" for a screw. The tree structure models a part-of relation together with the spatial relation of a child node relative to its parent specified by a homogeneous transformation matrix. Thus it is possible to represent decomposition and spatial coherence. Fig. 6 shows an IDT for a stylized screw. It contains an underspecified schema for the whole object as root node as well as part schemas for the "head", the "shank", and the "slot" as a part of the head. The letters a, b, and c mark the spatial dimensions. Integrated axes are marked with parentheses, e.g. $(b \quad c)$. Attributes and quantitative values are listed below the axes.

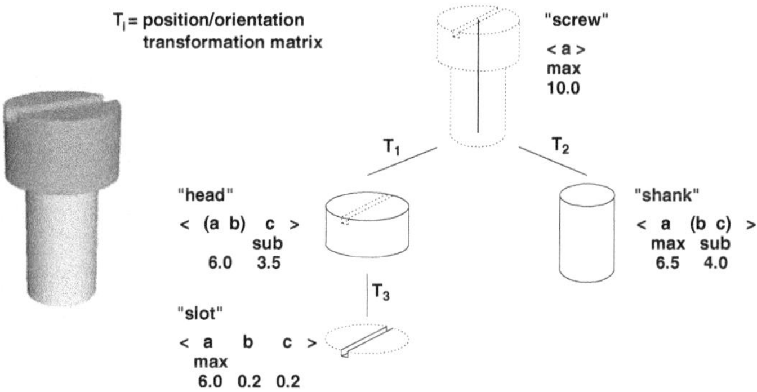

Fig. 6. Imagistic description tree for a stylized screw

4.2 The Mapping between Form and Meaning

The gesture interpretation and formation stages concern the mutual conversion between a MURML form description and the semantic layer represented as an IDT. Indications for this mapping were obtained from the empirical study. It provides information about the form features used to gesturally encode spatial axes. Table 1 illustrates the combination frequencies of spatial features and form features in a corpus of 383 gestures judged as iconic. Note that the sum over all cells of the table exceeds 383 since several features may be present in a single gesture. The first column shows the number of gestural expressions of linear axes, i.e. length, breadth, or width, the second one of the diameter of objects with a circular cross-cut. The third column lists cases in which a round shape, e.g. a hole, is indicated. The last two columns refer to indications of rounded corners or edges and the hexagonal shape of one of the stimulus objects. Axis, diameter, and round shape properties can be modeled with the imagistic description approach, whereas the model provides no means to describe the latter two. This weakness is acceptable since it affects only a small portion of the semantic object properties indicated by gestures (less than 3% of all descriptions).

Table 1. Frequency of gesture form attributes expressing geometrical attributes

	linear	diameter	round	r. edge/corner	hexagonal
movement	166	27	50	9	3
distance	87	40			
hand aperture	55	16			
palm orientation	15				
curved/round handshape			45		
index finger direction	1				

Generally, the relation between gesture form and meaning is a many-to-many mapping. However, Tab. 1 shows that a rather concise set of – still not unambiguous – heuristic rules can be derived if a compositional, feature-based approach is used on both the form- and the meaning-level. These rules are listed in Tab. 2.

Table 2. Rules for the conversion of form- and meaning-based representations

#	form feature	axis type	axis orientation	axis degree
1	linear movement	disintegrated	orientation of movement segment	length of segment
2	circular movement	2D-integrated	movement plane	diameter of the circle
3	two-handed static posture, palms facing each other, flat handshape	disintegrated	difference segment between palms	distance between palms
4	two-handed static posture, palms facing each other, rounded handshape	2D-integrated	plane by difference vector between palms and extended finger orientation	distance between palms
5	precision-grip posture (thumb and other fingers facing each other)	disintegrated	vector between thumb tip and finger tip closest to thumb	hand aperture
6	flat hand (one-handed gesture)	disintegrated	extended finger orientation	(undefined)

Complex images emerge either from the parallel use of features in a single gesture, or from their sequential expression in successive gestures. Since in the first case simultaneous form features must not occupy the same motor resources, the elementary mappings from Tab. 2 are composable in the following ways:

- 1 + 3: linear movement, two-handed symmetrical posture, flat hands
- 1+4: linear movement, two-handed symmetrical posture, rounded handshape
- 1 + 5: linear movement, precision-grip
- 3 + 5: two-handed symmetrical posture, precision-grip

Other combinations seem possible, but have not been observed in our corpus. Sequential arrangements of features, i.e., the distribution of an object schema across more than one gesture phrase, appear when incompatible form features are employed. An example is the description of a cube with three two-handed gestures of type 3, indicating successively its width, height, and length.

4.3 First Implementation Steps

The realization of meaning-based gesture imitation is an ongoing challenge in our lab. However, the imagistic shape representation provides an already operational basis for formalizing a gesture's imaginal content and the heuristic rules offer hints on how gestural form features can be associated. First steps towards utilizing these rules to automatically build an imagistic description tree from given gesture descriptions in MURML (interpretation) as well as to transform such a tree into MURML definitions (formation) have been taken. We expect that their combination will enable Max to recognize the image behind a sequence of iconic gestures and to create a different gestural depiction on his own.

Gesture Interpretation. For gesture interpretation the rules from Tab. 2 are basically implemented "from left to right". If a suitable form feature occurs in the MURML description, the corresponding axis type, its orientation and degree are inserted into the imagistic model. There are several possibilities for insertion depending on the feature arrangement strategy. Axes concurrently recognized, i.e. in a single dimensional gesture, always belong to one object schema. An axis expressed in sequence to another either completes the current object schema, or it opens up a new one. Furthermore, the algorithm has to decide where spatial coherence ends and a new gestural image begins. In its current state, the system assumes the beginning of a new image description if the hands return to a rest position after performing several gestures.

Gesture Formation. Starting from an imagistic description tree, gesture formation must cope with sequencing gestures that – in combination – are to express multiple object schemas with possibly multiple object features. Regarding this problem on a higher level, we assume that an object is described from its general spatial properties to more specific ones. This strategy resembles a depth-first traversal of the imagistic description tree which, in addition, increases the spatial coherence in elaborating an object schema by describing its descendant schemas (e.g., the slot of the screw in Fig. 6 appears in relation to the head). For each object schema, a gestural expression is formed by iterating through its axes (from the dominant to the smaller ones), determining form features for each axis, and combining them if possible in accord to the aforementioned composition rules. Form features are selected according to the heuristic rules in Tab. 2. The ambiguity of this choice can be partially resolved based on the degree of the axis (e.g., feature 5 is selected for an axis of small degree rather than feature 1 or 3). In case feature selection is still ambiguous, the choice is done by chance. For each selected form feature, the corresponding movement constraints in MURML are created and adapted to the particular properties of the axis, e.g., hand aperture to axis degree. If the movement constraints of two or more axes cannot be combined due to conflicting consumption of body resources, separate gestures are instantiated as children of a sequence node in the MURML tree. All gestures formed for single object schemas are added into a single utterance, i.e. a single gesture unit, for the entire description tree. Currently, the composability of features of different axes is ignored during feature selection.

5 Conclusion

We have presented an approach for enabling artificial agents to imitate in a immediate, game-like fashion natural gestures demonstrated by a human user. The imitation scenario demands the connection of gesture recognition and synthesis methods. We propose two levels of gesture imitation, where representations of different degrees of abstraction are employed: On the mimicking-level, a gestural body movement of the user is reduced to the essential form features of its meaningful phase. These features proved successful for form-based gesture imitation when appropriate models are employed for both gesture recognition and synthesis. Gesture mimicking is demonstrable – so far limited to static gestures – in a real-time imitation game with Max. Building on the form-level abstraction, we further presented novel steps towards processing the meaning of iconic gestures that depict geometrical objects. A spatial representation for the semantics of such gestures was described along with experimentally derived rules that formalize the ambiguous mapping between form and meaning in an implementable way. Realizing this mapping in both directions is subject of ongoing work. In future work, we intend to include speech in the meaning-based imitation process. This would, for example allow the user to refer to an object using one modality (e.g., saying "bolt") and getting it re-expressed by Max using the other modality (e.g., confirming the bolt's shape with iconic gestures).

References

1. J. Cassell, T. Bickmore, M. Billinghurst, L. Campbell, K. Chang, H. Vilhjalmsoon, and H. Yan. Embodiment on conversational interfaces: Rea. In *CHI'99 Conference Proceedings*, pages 520–527. ACM, 1999.
2. J. Cassell, M. Stone, and H. Yan. Coordination and context-dependence in the generation of embodied conversation. In *Proceedings of the International Natural Language Generation Conference*, pages 171–178, Mitzpe Ramon, Israel, June 2000.
3. S. Gibet, T. Lebourque, and P. Marteau. High-level specification and animation of communicative gestures. *Journal of Visual Languages and Computing*, 12(6):657–687, 2001.

4. M. Johnston. Multimodal unification-based grammars. Technical Report WS-98-09, AAAI Press, Menlo Park (CA), 1998.
5. S. Kita, I. van Gijn, and H. van der Hulst. Movement phases in signs and co-speech gestures, and their transcription by human coders. In I. Wachsmuth and M. Fröhlich, editors, *Gesture and Sign Language in Human-Computer Interaction: Proceedings of Gesture Workshop '97*, LNAI 1371, pages 23–36, Berlin, 1998. Springer-Verlag.
6. S. Kopp and I. Wachsmuth. A knowledge-based approach for lifelike gesture animation. In W. Horn, editor, *ECAI 2000 Proceedings of the 14th European Conference on Artificial Intelligence*, pages 661–667, Amsterdam, 2000. IOS Press.
7. S. Kopp and I. Wachsmuth. Model-based animation of coverbal gesture. In *Proc. of Computer Animation 2002*, pages 252–257, Los Alamitos, CA, 2002. IEEE Computer Society Press.
8. E. Lang. The semantics of dimensional designation of spatial objects. In M. Bierwisch and E. Lang, editors, *Dimensional Adjectives: Grammatical Structure and Conceptual Interpretation*, pages 263–417. Springer, Berlin, Heidelberg, New York, 1989.
9. M. E. Latoschik. A general framework for multimodal interaction in virtual reality systems: PrOSA. In *VR2001 workshop proceedings: The Future of VR and AR Interfaces: Multi-modal, Humanoid, Adaptive and Intelligent*, 2001. in press.
10. M. Matarić, V. Zordan, and M. Williamson. Making complex articulated agents dance. *Autonomous Agents and Multi-Agent Systems*, 2(1):23–44, July 1999.
11. S. Prillwitz, R. Leven, H. Zienert, T. Hamke, and J. Henning. *HamNoSys Version 2.0: Hamburg Notation System for Sign Languages: An Introductory Guide*, volume 5 of *International Studies on Sign Language and Communication of the Deaf*. Signum Press, Hamburg, Germany, 1989.
12. J. Rickel and W. Johnson. Animated agents for procedural training in virtual reality: Perception, cognition, and motor control. *Applied Artificial Intelligence*, 13:343–382, 1999.
13. T. Sowa and I. Wachsmuth. Interpretation of shape-related iconic gestures in virtual environments. In I. Wachsmuth and T. Sowa, editors, *Gesture and Sign Language in Human-Computer Interaction*, LNAI 2298, pages 21–33, Berlin, 2002. Springer-Verlag.
14. T. Sowa and I. Wachsmuth. Coverbal Iconic Gestures for Object Descriptions in Virtual Environments: An Empirical Study. In M. Rector, I. Poggi, and N. Trigo, editors, *Proceedings of the Conference "Gestures. Meaning and Use."*, pages 365–376, Porto, Portugal, 2003. Edições Universidade Fernando Pessoa.
15. C. J. Sparrell and D. B. Koons. Interpretation of coverbal depictive gestures. In *AAAI Spring Symposium Series: Intelligent Multi-Media Multi-Modal Systems*, pages 8–12. Stanford University, March 1994.
16. Y. Wu and T. S. Huang. Vision-based gesture recognition: A review. In A. Braffort, R. Gherbi, S. Gibet, J. Richardson, and D. Teil, editors, *Gesture-Based Communication in Human-Computer Interaction (Proceedings of the Gesture Workshop 1999)*, Lecture Notes in Artificial Intelligence (1739), pages 103–115, Berlin, 1999. Springer-Verlag.

Gesture Components for Natural Interaction with In-Car Devices

Martin Zobl, Ralf Nieschulz, Michael Geiger,
Manfred Lang, and Gerhard Rigoll

Institute for Human-Machine Communication
Munich University of Technology, D-80290 München, Germany
{zobl,nieschulz,geiger,lang,rigoll}@ei.tum.de
http://www.mmk.ei.tum.de

Abstract. The integration of more and more functionality into the human machine interface (HMI) of vehicles increases the complexity of device handling. Thus optimal use of different human sensory channels is an approach to simplify the interaction with in-car devices. This way the user convenience increases as much as distraction decreases. In this paper the gesture part of a multimodal system is described. It consists of a gesture optimized user interface, a real time gesture recognition system and an adaptive help system for gesture input. The components were developed in course of extensive usability studies. The so built HMI allows intuitive, effective and assisted operation of infotainment in-car devices, like radio, CD, telephone and navigation system, with handposes and dynamic hand gestures.

1 Introduction

In [1] a comprehensive survey of existing gesture recognition systems is given. The most important area of application in the past was sign language recognition [2]. Due to fast technical evolution with increasing complexity of the HMI and a broad variety of application possibilities, applications in the technical domain have become more important in the last years. Examples are controlling the computer desktop environment [3,4,5] and presentations [6] as well as operating multimedia systems [7]. Especially in the car domain new HMI solutions have been in focus of interest [8,9] to reduce distraction effects and to simplify the usage. In this environment strict constraints limit the possibilities of user interface design. A drivers primary task always is controlling the car. This task should not be interfered by other tasks, like controlling a HMI. So only short time slots can be used for interaction between the user and the HMI. Additionally feedback possibilities are very limited, because displays are not placed in the primary view of the user. In usability studies, gesture controlled operation of infotainment in-car devices proved to be intuitive, effective [10,11] and less distracting than haptical user input with knobs and buttons [12].

For this reason the development of a gesture operated HMI is worthwhile. To lower one's inhibition threshold of this new operating type, an automatic,

A. Camurri and G. Volpe (Eds.): GW 2003, LNAI 2915, pp. 448–459, 2004.

adaptive help system to provide unobtrusive assistance for gestural operation is a reasonable completion. Regarding human and machine as an overall system, a more stable overall system behavior is achieved casually. Of course the presented components concerning gestures are part of a multimodal system, as some functions like a selection out of long lists are better performed with speech.

In the following section a short introduction to the whole system is given. Accordingly the single components are presented. At the end, results are discussed and an outlook about future work is given.

2 Overview

In figure 1 the gesture components and their relationship is shown. The user interface (see section 4) is driven by the performed gestures. These are recognized by a gesture recognition system (see section 5). Additionally the associated confidence measures and timestamps of the recognized gestures are sent for use with the adaptive help system (see section 6). The help system gets information about

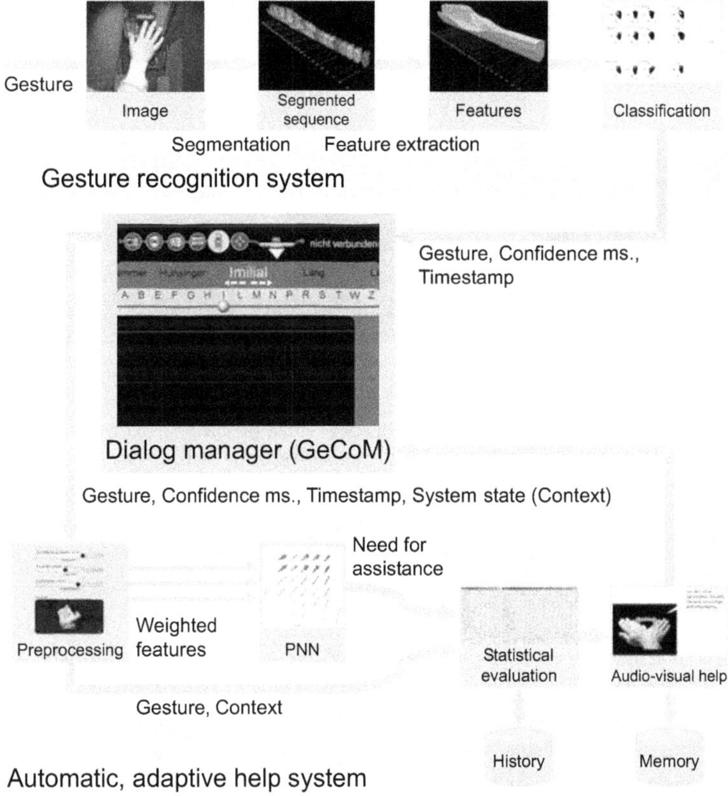

Fig. 1. System Overview

the performed gestures with confidences and timestamps as long as information about the state of the user interface. With these features the need for help and type of help is calculated and audio visual help is presented in the user interface when necessary.

3 Gesture Inventory

The used gesture inventory is fitted to the findings in usability studies [10,11] which makes is suitable to a mean user. In figure 2, examples out of the gesture inventory are shown. There are eleven gesture classes of dynamic hand gestures (some containing several equivalent gestures) and four hand poses. Dynamic hand gestures are used for indirect manipulation (discrete control steps). Hand poses can be applied for different tasks. Two examples out of the handposes are discussed here. With the hand pose 'open' the dynamic gesture recognizer is activated and then is waiting for dynamic gesture input. An activation mechanism is necessary, because some of the gestures out of the inventory are as common (e.g. 'to the left', 'to the right') that they could be used casually by the driver while talking to other persons inside the car. The hand pose 'grab' is applied for direct manipulation. This direct manipulation allows the user to control functions that are inconvenient to handle with single dynamic gestures like adjusting the music volume or moving a navigation map in 3D [13].

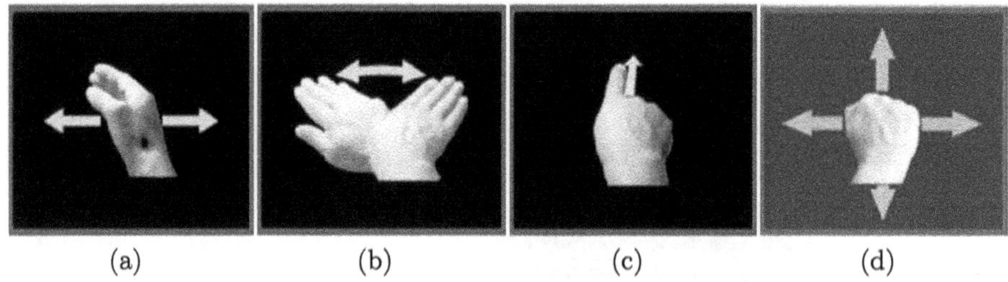

(a) (b) (c) (d)

Fig. 2. Examples out of the gesture inventory with possible directions: 'wave to the left/right' (a) to change to the previous/next function, 'wipe' (b) to stop a system action, 'point' (c) to confirm and 'grab' (d) for direct manipulation of e.g. the volume

4 User Interface

As a result of usability studies, we developed a Gesture Controlled Man-Machine Interface (GeCoM) [12]. It was evaluated in the course of several usability investigations (Wizard-of-Oz methodology) in our driving simulator. By iterative re-design, the interface was optimized for gestural control. The implemented functional range consists of typical devices of automotive infotainment systems like radio, CD, phone and navigation. The HMI is displayed over a 10" TFT display mounted in the mid console.

The probably most important task for composition of GeCoM is its the visual representation. Especially when performing kinemimic gestures, the user follows the alignment of the displayed elements without exception. Horizontal elements are exclusively controlled with horizontal movements, whereas vertical structures are controlled with vertical movements (see fig. 3). Beyond it, a strong correlation

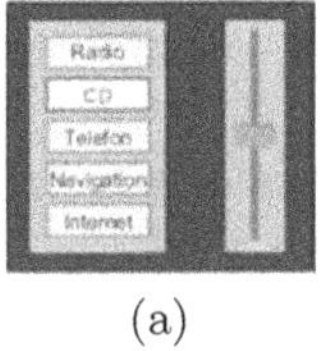

(a)

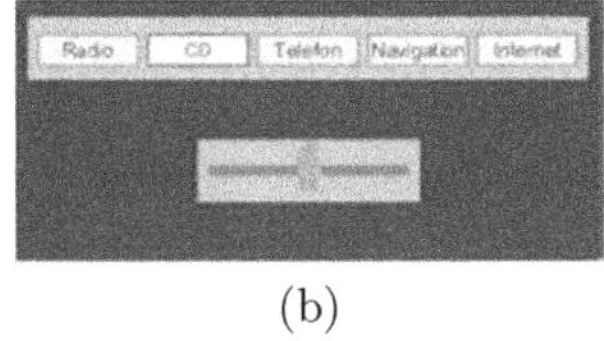

(b)

Fig. 3. Vertical (a) and horizontal alignment (b) of menu points with visual presentation for indirect (left) and direct (right) manipulation

between the user's behavior exists even when no interface is displayed at all. A large number of subjects use for example horizontal gestures to the right in the sense of 'next function' and horizontal gestures to the left in the sense of 'previous function'. Accordingly up and down movements are used to raise or lower a control variable (e.g. volume).

Being aware of this, a horizontal aligned primary interaction structure with selectable menu points and a vertical aligned secondary structure for controlling the volume was implemented (see fig. 4). To reconsider the relation between the gesture and the system reaction, state changes are smoothly animated. The active device is represented by a self-explanatory pictogram. The displayed information is reduced to a minimum to allow the user an instantaneous recognition of the system state. The described visual attributes support the user in building a correct system model, which is a precondition for controlling without averting the gaze off the road. In addition, acoustical feedback in form of beeps and speech is given with every system reaction.

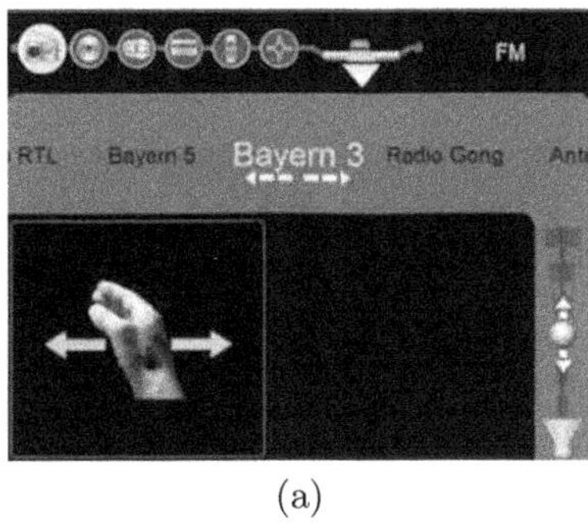

(a)

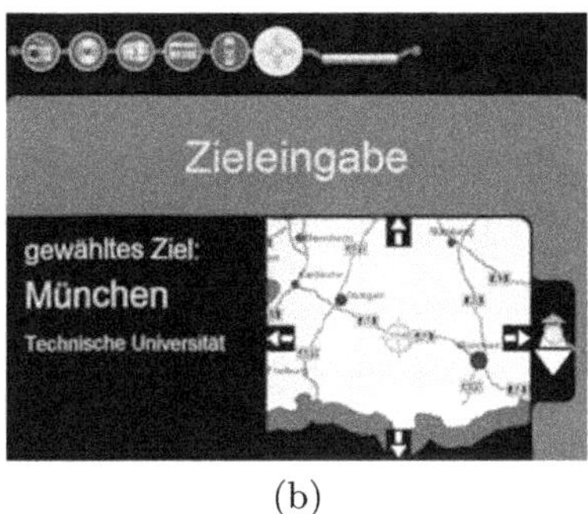

(b)

Fig. 4. GeCoM in radio (a) and navigation mode (b). In (a) a help screen is displayed to assist the user in changing the radio station

5 Gesture Recognition

5.1 Feature Extraction

For image acquisition, a standard CCD camera is mounted at the roof with its field of vision centered to the mid console. This is the area where most gestures were performed by test subjects in usability studies. As proposed in [9] the camera is equipped with a daylight filter and the scene is illuminated by NIR LEDs (950nm) to achieve independence from ambient light as well as to prevent the driver from being disturbed. Fields are grabbed with 25fps at a resolution of 384*144 to avoid *frame comb* that would destroy the features in case of fast hand movements. For spatial segmentation, it is assumed that the hand is a large object that does not belong to the background and is very bright because of the NIR illumination. Thus, on the original image background subtraction is performed to remove pixels not belonging to the hand. The so processed image is then multiplied with the gray values of the original image to consider the brightness. The resulting image is thresholded at an adaptive level T. At time step n, with the original image $I_n[x,y]$ and the background image $B_n[x,y]$, the hand mask $\widetilde{I}[x,y]_n$ can be written as follows.

$$\widetilde{I}_n[x,y] = \begin{cases} 1 \; \forall \; I_n[x,y] \cdot |I_n[x,y] - B_n[x,y]| \geq T \\ 0 \text{ otherwise} \end{cases} \tag{1}$$

Small objects are removed with cleaning operators. The background image is updated in a sliding mean window with every region that does not belong to the hand, to adapt to background and ambient light changes. Figure 5 illustrates the used segmentation cues and their combination.

After segmentation, a modified *forearm filter* based on [14] is applied to remove the forearm's influence on the features. Moment based features like area, center of mass (trajectory) and Hu's moments [15] (handform) are calculated from the segmented image.

5.2 Recognition Performance

A feature vector is formed for every image. It consists of features that are necessary for the respective task (v. tab. 1).

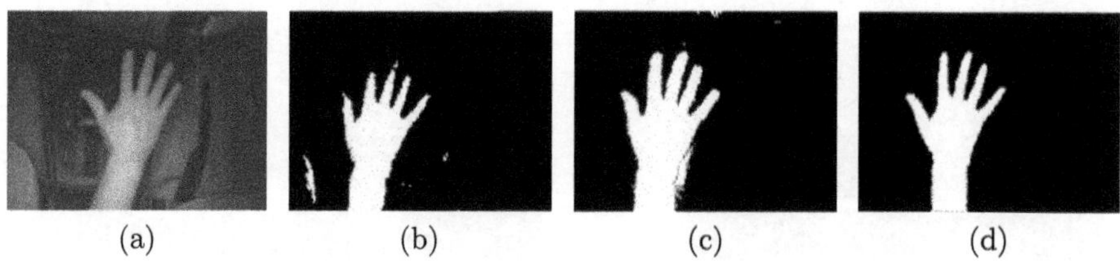

(a) (b) (c) (d)

Fig. 5. Cues for hand segmentation: The grabbed image (a), when only thresholded (b) or background subtracted (c). Combination of background subtraction and thresholding (d)

Table 1. Features used for the different tasks. A: area, C: center of mass, HU: Hu's moments

	$\sqrt{A}$	ΔA	C	ΔC	HU
hand pose recognition	-	-	-	-	+
dynamic gesture recog.	-	+	-	+	+
direct manipulation	+	-	+	-	-

Hand Pose Recognition. Since the form of the hand is independent of area, position and hand rotation, Hu's moments are used for hand pose description. For classification, the Mahalanobis-Distance between the actual feature vector and every class representing prototype (previously trained) is calculated. To avoid a system reaction on casual hand poses, the distances are smoothed by a sliding window filter. Additionally a trash model is introduced. The reciprocal values (*scores*) of the smoothed distances are finally transformed into confidence measures as described in section 5.4.

Recognition of Dynamic Gestures. In dynamic gestures also the form of the hand as well as the relative trajectory data contains relevant information. Not only one vector, but a vector stream here has to be classified. In the first stage, the vectors containing the gesture are cut out from the vector stream with a *movement detection* that uses the derivatives of the movement features (area, center of mass). In the second stage the cut feature vector sequence is fed to Hidden Markov Models (HMMs) [16]. Here semi-continuous HMMs are used because of their low quantity of parameters and smooth vector quantization. The Viterbi search through the models delivers a score for every model (representing a gesture) given a feature vector sequence. These scores are transformed into confidence measures as described in section 5.4, too.

5.3 Results

The recognition results are preliminary results for offline recognition with datasets from one person.
For the evaluation of the hand pose recognition 500 datasets per class were collected. 350 datasets were used to train the prototypes and 150 datasets to test the recognition performance. In figure 6 the recognition rate over the feature vector dimension is shown. With increasing the accuracy of the hand pose description, the recognition result is increasing. Some poses ('grab', 'open hand') already show very good recognition rates (95%) with low feature dimensions. The other poses (e.g. 'hitchhiker left', 'hitchhiker right') are very similar with respect to the Hu's moments (rotation invariance) and can only be separated in higher feature dimensions. To achieve accurate results using the described methods, the forearm filter proved as a precondition. The so achieved recognition results nearly reach those using pictures with manually removed forearm segments. The evaluation of the dynamic gesture recognition system was done

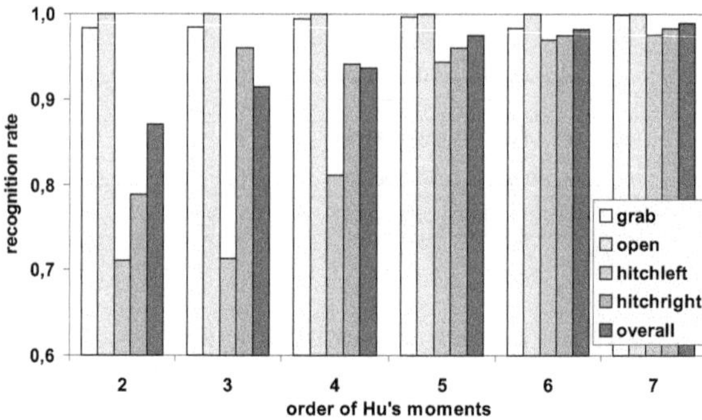

Fig. 6. Recognition rates for four handposes depending on the order of Hu's moments for building the feature vector. Single hand pose results are shown as long as the overall recognition rate

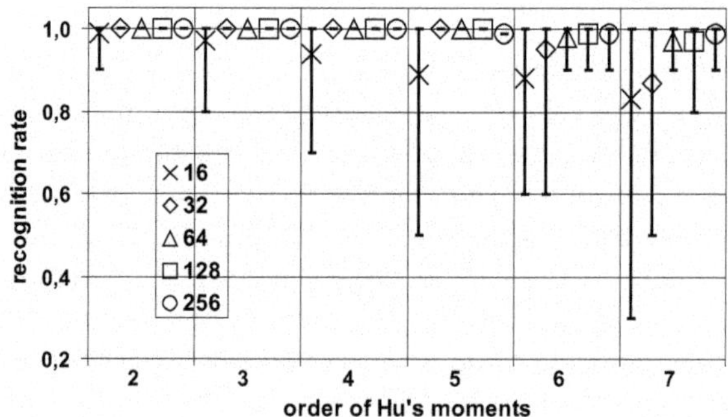

Fig. 7. Average recognition rates for 11 dynamic gesture classes depending on the order of Hu's moments for building the feature vector. The codebook size of the semi continuous HMMs is given as parameter between 16 and 256. The error bars show the rate of the worst and best recognized gesture class

with 20 datasets per gesture. 13 sets were used to train the HMMs and seven to test the recognition. Since the duration of certain gestures is sometimes as short as seven frames, the HMMs consist of seven states. Given a simple forward structure, not more than seven states can be used. In figure 7 the results of different feature and HMM configurations is given. They already show a very high recognition rate at low feature and codebook dimensions. The low feature dimension means, that a lot of the gestures out of the vocabulary could be recognized using only relative trajectory data and the low codebook dimension, that the used features cluster very well in the feature space.

The recognition results demonstrate, that the described gesture recognition system works very well, for both hand pose and dynamic gesture recognition, when adapted to a single user.

5.4 Confidence Measure

A Maximum-Likelihood decision about the hand pose or dynamic gesture based only on the best match is relatively uncertain. A measure is needed to show how safe the decision for the best match is - regarding the output of every model given a vector or a vector sequence. Further this measure should spread between zero and one to resemble a probability. With the number of existing gesture classes N and class i delivering the best match, the measure

$$c_i = \frac{score_i}{\sum_{j \in N} score_j} \tag{2}$$

fits to our demands and delivers good results with the described classifiers. When the best score is high and the other scores are low then $c \to 1$. When every score is equal then $c = \frac{1}{N}$. Now for every gesture class a threshold is defined above which the recognition is accepted. Below this threshold it is rejected. This becomes necessary because some gestures are relative similar to others, while other gestures are totally different. This would lead to an always low confidence measure for similar gestures. False rejection and acceptance levels have not been tested so far with the presented confidence measure, because of the lack of multiple user data.

6 Adaptive Help System

The adaptive help system is implemented in a 2-stage methodology. The first stage is a neural network based classification that determines if a user needs help while performing a certain task. This stage works automatically if desired, which is the default mode. Alternatively a user is able to request a help information manually. In the second stage a postprocessing based on statistics determines which help this user actually needs in the given context (q.v. [17,18]).

6.1 Need of Assistance

For every gesture the user performs, the following data is send from the gesture recognition system to the adaptive help system, in order to infer the user's *need of assistance*: the gesture type (e.g. 'right') the appropriate confidence measure as described in section 5.4 and the gestures start and ending time. This input is then preprocessed to adapt it to a user's gestural behavior. In short, all features are weighted with memory functions regarding all past gestures of this person. The preprocessed feature vector now provides information about the user adapted quality of a gesture by its weighted confidence measure, as well as the user adapted execution duration and cognition time (q.v. [18]).

The feature vector is then used as input to a neural network, which supplies the statement, whether a user needs assistance, or not, at that time. The neural network is built as a probabilistic neural network (PNN) based on radial basis functions (RBFs). About 2000 gestures out of a test series about gestural operation of in-car devices (q.v. sec. 4) were used as training corpus. First, the optimal positions of the neurons of the PNN in its feature space are determined, applying a LVQ-algorithm (linear vector quantization) to the training material. That way an effective, lean and powerful neural network design is obtained. Build on that the PNN is trained to classify a users *need of assistance* with the mentioned training corpus.

The performance of this classifier was tested using about another 1000 gestures from the study. With further consideration of the operating context the recognition rate of the neural network is 96% and the error rate 4%. As can be seen in figure 8 the recognition rate of the case, that the user actually doesn't need help, is 98%, while the rate of the other case, where the user needs assistance, is only 81%.

6.2 Help Content

If *need of assistance* is detected in the first stage of the help system or if a user demands for help explicitly, the help content is determined in the second stage. Therefore the current context of the HMI and a users operation history is taken into account. The following information is gathered: which gestures have been used in what context at what time in a correct respectively false manner by this user so far, and which help content has been provided to this user in what context at what time so far. Out of this data a weight is calculated for every separate help content and for every help type (that is to represent cognitive coherences between related help contents) using memory functions.

A bayesian network, which contains the description of the whole help corpus, is continuously adapted by means of these weights. After the adaptation of the network, it is able to infer the statistically most probable help content. The help content thus calculated is then audio-visually presented to the user via GeCoM

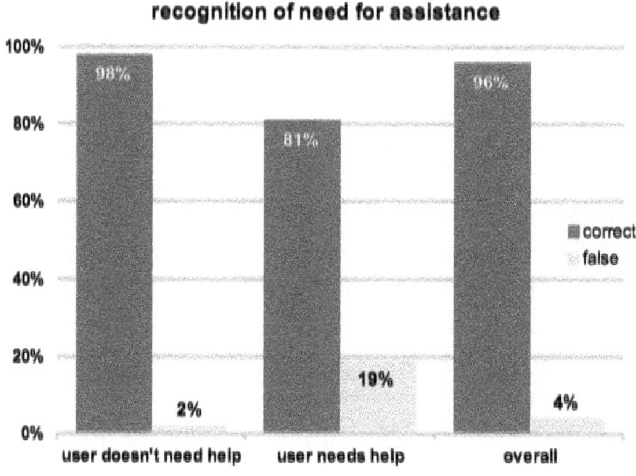

Fig. 8. Recognition rate of the probabilistic neural network used in the first stage of the help system

(v. figure 4) [17,18]. If the provided information strikes the user as insufficient or wrong, he can request further assistance.

As results of a usability study regarding gestural operation of in-car devices combined with the presented help system show (v. figure 9), the system had to provide 1.35 help contents on average for satisfaction of the users. This is a significant enhancement compared to conventional online help systems. Usually one time-consuming has to search through a more or less extensive menu structure, which is possibly shortened by the current context. The study has also shown, that even if a user does not require any help actually, the provided information is useful most of the time nevertheless.

7 Summary and Outlook

In this paper a system of gesture components for a natural interaction with in-car devices was presented. It was shown, that consequent user centered re-design coupled with implementation of new techniques enhance the operation of the HMI. By the use of an integrated adaptive help system the whole gesture operated HMI obviously gains convenience. In particular the learning procedure is significantly accelerated. Moreover an earlier overcome of a persons inhibition threshold in using gestures is achieved.

Future work will be an online evaluation of the system with different subjects to get an overall result. Nevertheless, gestural operation should be part of a multimodal system in which the user is allowed to control every functionality with the optimal or familiar modality (haptics, speech, gestures). The so build HMI will enable the user to handle complex multimedia systems like in-car devices in an intuitive and effective way while driving a car.

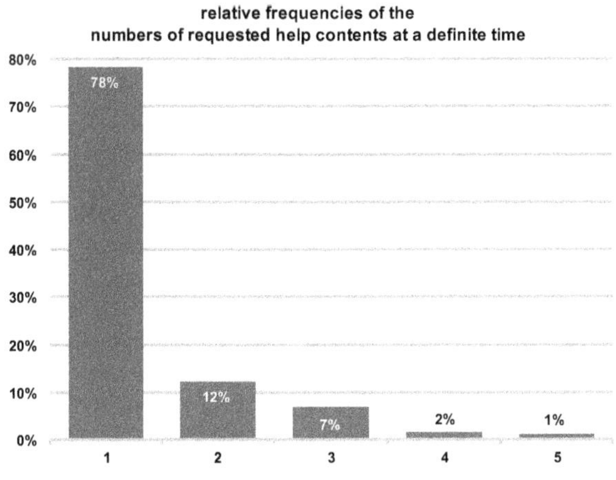

Fig. 9. Performance of the second stage of the help system: users had to request 1.35 help contents on average to achieve appropriate help

References

1. Pavlovic, V., Sharma, R., Huang, T.: Visual interpretation of hand gestures for human-computer interaction. IEEE Transactions on Pattern Analysis and Machine Intelligence **19.7** (1997) 677–695
2. Hienz, H., Kraiss, K., Bauer, B.: Continuous sign language recognition using hidden markov models. In: Proceedings, 2nd Int. Conference on Multimodal Interfaces, Hong Kong, China, 1999. (1999) IV10–IV15
3. Althoff, F., McGlaun, G., Schuller, B., Morguet, P., Lang, M.: Using multimodal interaction to navigate in arbitrary virtual vrml worlds. In: Proceedings, PUI 2001 Workshop on Perceptive User Interfaces, Orlando, Florida, USA, November 15-16, 2001, Association for Computing Machinery, ACM Digital Library: www.acm.org/uist/uist2001. CD-ROM (2001)
4. Sato, Y., Kobayashi, Y.: Fast tracking of hands and fingertips in infrared images for augmented desk interface. In: Proceedings, 4th Int. Conference on Automatic Face and Gesture Recognition, Grenoble, France, 2000. (2000) 462–467
5. Morguet, P., Lang, M.: Comparison of approaches to continuous hand gesture recognition for a visual dialog system. In: Proceedings, ICASP 1999 Int. Concef-erence on Acoustics and Signal Processing, Phoenix, Arizona, USA, March 15-19, 1999, IEEE (1999) 3549–3552
6. Hardenberg, C., Bérard, F.: Bare-hand human-computer interaction. In: Proceedings, PUI 2001 Workshop on Perceptive User Interfaces, Orlando, Florida, USA, November 15-16, 2001, Association for Computing Machinery, ACM Digital Library: www.acm.org/uist/uist2001. CD-ROM (2001)
7. Jestertek Inc. Homepage. (www.jestertek.com)
8. Klarreich, E.: No more fumbling in the car. In: nature, Glasgow, Great Britain, November, 2001, British Association for the Advancement of Science, Nature News Service (2001)
9. Akyol, S., Canzler, U., Bengler, K., Hahn, W.: Gesture control for use in automobiles. In: Proceedings, MVA 2000 Workshop on Machine Vision Applications, Tokyo, Japan, November 28-30, 2000, IAPR, ISBN 4-901122-00-2 (2000) 28–30
10. Zobl, M., Geiger, M., Morguet, P., Nieschulz, R., Lang, M.: Gesture-based control of in-car devices. In: VDI-Berichte 1678: USEWARE 2002 Mensch-Maschine-Kommunikation/Design, GMA Fachtagung USEWARE 2002, Darmstadt, Germany, June 11-12, 2002, Düsseldorf, VDI, VDI-Verlag (2002) 305–309
11. Zobl, M., Geiger, M., Bengler, K., Lang, M.: A usability study on hand gesture controlled operation of in-car devices. In: Abridged Proceedings, HCI 2001 9th Int. Conference on Human Machine Interaction, New Orleans, Louisiana, USA, August 5-10, 2001, New Jersey, Lawrence Erlbaum Ass. (2001) 166–168
12. Geiger, M., Zobl, M., Bengler, K., Lang, M.: Intermodal differences in distraction effects while controlling automotive user interfaces. In: Proceedings Vol. 1: Usability Evaluation and Interface Design , HCI 2001 9th Int. Conference on Human Machine Interaction, New Orleans, Louisiana, USA, August 5-10, 2001, New Jersey, Lawrence Erlbaum Ass. (2001) 263–267
13. Geiger, M., Nieschulz, R., Zobl, M., Lang, M.: Gesture-based control concept for in-car devicess. In: VDI-Berichte 1678: USEWARE 2002 Mensch-Maschine-Kommunikation/Design, GMA Fachtagung USEWARE 2002, Darmstadt, Germany, June 11-12, 2002, Düsseldorf, VDI, VDI-Verlag (2002) 299–303
14. Broekl-Fox, U.: Untersuchung neuer, gestenbasierter Verfahren für die 3D-Interaktion. PhD thesis. Shaker Publishing (1995)

15. Hu, M.: Visual pattern recognition by moment invariants. IRE Transactions on Information Theory **IT8** (1962) 179–187
16. Rabiner, L.R.: A tutorial on hidden markov models and selected applications in speech recognition. Proceedings of the IEEE **77** (1989) 257–286
17. Nieschulz, R., Geiger, M., Zobl, M., Lang, M.: Need for assistance in automotive gestural interaction. In: VDI-Berichte 1678: USEWARE 2002 Mensch-Maschine-Kommunikation/Design, GMA Fachtagung USEWARE 2002, Darmstadt, Germany, June 11-12, 2002, Düsseldorf, VDI, VDI-Verlag (2002) 293–297
18. Nieschulz, R., Geiger, M., Bengler, K., Lang, M.: An automatic, adaptive help system to support gestural operation of an automotive mmi. In: Proceedings Vol. 1: Usability Evaluation and Interface Design , HCI 2001 9th Int. Conference on Human Machine Interaction, New Orleans, Louisiana, USA, August 5-10, 2001, New Jersey, Lawrence Erlbaum Ass. (2001) 272–276

Analysis of Expressive Gesture: The EyesWeb Expressive Gesture Processing Library

Antonio Camurri, Barbara Mazzarino, and Gualtiero Volpe

InfoMus Lab, DIST – University of Genova
Viale Causa 13, I-16145 Genova, Italy
{Antonio.Camurri,Barbara.Mazzarino,Gualtiero.Volpe}@unige.it
http://infomus.dist.unige.it

Abstract. This paper presents some results of a research work concerning algorithms and computational models for real-time analysis of expressive gesture in full-body human movement. As a main concrete result of our research work, we present a collection of algorithms and related software modules for the EyesWeb open architecture (freely available from www.eyesweb.org). These software modules, collected in the EyesWeb Expressive Gesture Processing Library, have been used in real scenarios and applications, mainly in the fields of performing arts, therapy and rehabilitation, museum interactive installations, and other immersive augmented reality and cooperative virtual environment applications. The work has been carried out at DIST - InfoMus Lab in the framework of the EU IST Project MEGA (Multisensory Expressive Gesture Applications, www.megaproject.org).

1 Introduction

Our research is focused on the design of multimodal interfaces involving full-body human interaction, explicitly considering and enabling the communication of non-verbal expressive, emotional content. The general objective is to improve state of the art in immersive, experience-centric mixed reality and virtual environment applications. Computational models of expressiveness in human gestures can contribute to new paradigms for the design of interactive systems, improved presence and physicality in the interaction [1]. Main research directions include (i) multimodal analysis and classification of expressive gestures in musical signals and human movement, (ii) real-time generation and post-processing of audio and visual content depending on the output of the analysis, (iii) study of the interaction mechanisms and mapping strategies enabling the results of the (multimodal) analysis to be employed (transformed) in the process of automatic generation of audio and visual content, and possibly of behavior of mobile robots (e.g. a moving scenery on stage, a robot for museums) [2,3,4].

In this paper we focus on the first aspect. In particular, we address algorithms and computational models for the extraction of a collection of expressive features from human movement in real-time.

Dance has been chosen as a particular test-bed for our research since our particular interest in interactive systems for performing art and since dance can be considered as a main artistic expression of human movement.

A. Camurri and G. Volpe (Eds.): GW 2003, LNAI 2915, pp. 460–467, 2004.

The generation of a particular output (e.g., sound, color, images) can directly depend on low-level motion features (e.g., position of a dancer on the stage, speed of the detected motion), or can be the result of the application of a number of decision rules considering the context, the history of the performance, the information about the classified expressive intention of a dancer, e.g., in term of basic emotions (joy, grief, fear, anger), of expressive qualities (e.g. fluent/rigid, light/heavy), and ideally in term of the "tension" in the artistic performance. A layered approach [2] has been proposed to model these aspects that we named "expressive gesture". This approach models expressive gesture from low-level physical measures (e.g., in the case of human movement: position, speed, acceleration of body parts) up to descriptors of overall (motion) features (e.g., fluency, directness, impulsiveness).

Models and algorithms are here presented with reference to a concrete output of the research: the EyesWeb Expressive Gesture Processing Library, a collection of software modules for the EyesWeb open software platform (distributed for free at www.eyesweb.org). This library has been developed in the three-year EU IST MEGA project. MEGA is centered on the modeling and communication of expressive and emotional content in non-verbal interaction by multi-sensory interfaces in shared interactive Mixed Reality environments (www.megaproject.org).

2 The EyesWeb Expressive Gesture Processing Library

The *EyesWeb Expressive Gesture Processing Library* includes a collection of software modules and patches (interconnections of modules) in three main sub-libraries:

- *The EyesWeb Motion Analysis Library*: a collection of modules for real-time motion tracking and extraction of movement cues from human full-body motion. It is based on one or more videocameras and other sensor systems.
- *The EyesWeb Space Analysis Library*: a collection of modules for analysis of occupation of 2D (real as well as virtual) spaces. If from the one hand this sub-library can be used to extract low-level motion cues (e.g., how much time a dancer occupied a given position on the stage), on the other hand it can also be used to carry out analyses of gesture in semantic, abstract spaces.
- *The EyesWeb Trajectory Analysis Library*: a collection of modules for extraction of features from trajectories in 2D (real as well as virtual) spaces. These spaces may again be either physical spaces or semantic and expressive spaces.

2.1 The EyesWeb Motion Analysis Library

The EyesWeb Motion Analysis Library applies computer vision, statistical, and signal processing techniques to extract expressive cues from human full-body movement.

A first task consists in individuating and tracking motion in the incoming images from one or more videocameras. Background subtraction techniques can be used to segment the body silhouette. Given a silhouette, algorithms based on searching for body centroids and on optical flow based techniques (e.g., the Lucas and Kanade tracking algorithm [5]) are available.

For example, an algorithm has been developed to segment the body silhouette in sub-regions using spatio-temporal projection patterns (see [6] for an example of how such patterns are employed for gait analysis). This algorithm also provides a way to compute more robustly the position of the body center of gravity and sub-regions in the silhouette (see Figure 1a). Software modules for extracting silhouette's contour and computing its convex hull are also available (see Figure 1b).

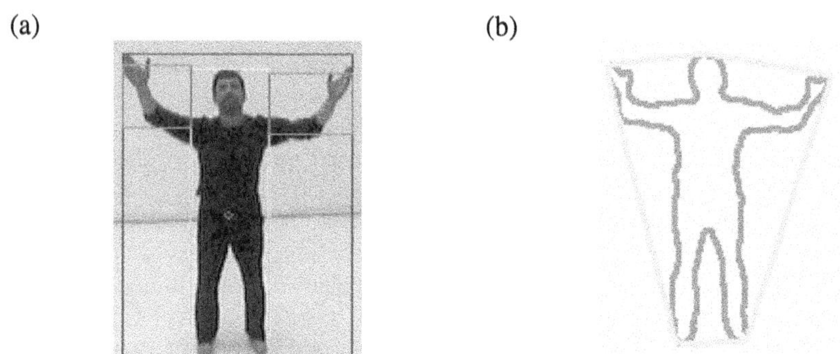

Fig. 1. (a) Sub-regions of the body silhouette and body center of gravity; (b) contour and convex hull of the body silhouette.

Starting from body silhouettes and tracking information a collection of expressive parameters is extracted. Three of them are described in the following.

- *Quantity of Motion* (QoM), i.e., the amount of detected movement. It is based on the Silhouette Motion Images. A Silhouette Motion Image (SMI) is an image carrying information about variations of the silhouette shape and position in the last few frames. SMIs are inspired to motion-energy images (MEI) and motion-history images (MHI) [7]. They differ from MEIs in the fact that the silhouette in the last (more recent) frame is removed from the output image: in such a way only motion is considered while the current posture is skipped. QoM is computed as the area (i.e., number of pixels) of a SMI. It can be considered as an overall measure of the amount of detected motion, involving velocity and force. Algorithms are provided to compute both the overall QoM and the QoM internal to the body silhouette.

- *Silhouette shape/orientation of body parts.* It is based on an analogy between image moments and mechanical moments: in this perspective, the three central moments of second order build the components of the inertial tensor of the rotation of the silhouette around its center of gravity: this allows to compute the axes (corresponding to the main inertial axes of the silhouette) of an ellipse that can be considered as an approximation of the silhouette: orientation of the axes is related to the orientation of the body [8]. Figure 2 shows the ellipse calculated on a reference dance fragment. By applying the extraction of the ellipse to different body parts, other information can be obtained. For example, by considering the main axis of the ellipses associated to the head and to the torso of the dancer, it can be possible to obtain an estimate of the directional changes in face and torso, a cue that psychologists consider important for communicating expressive intention (see for example [9]).

- *Contraction Index* (CI), a measure, ranging from 0 to 1, of how the dancer's body uses the space surrounding it. It is related to Laban's "personal space"(see [10][11]). It can be calculated in two different ways: (i) considering as contraction index the eccentricity of the ellipse obtained as described above, (ii) using a technique related to the bounding region, i.e., the minimum rectangle surrounding the dancer's body: the algorithm compares the area covered by this rectangle with the area currently covered by the silhouette. Intuitively, if the limbs are fully stretched and not lying along the body, this component of the CI will be low, while, if the limbs are kept tightly nearby the body, it will be high (near to 1).

Fig. 2. Silhouette shape and orientation. The ellipse approximates the silhouette; its axes give an approximation of the silhouette's orientation.

The EyesWeb Motion Analysis Library also includes blocks and patches extracting measures related to the temporal dynamics of movement. A main issue is the segmentation of movement in pause and motion phases. A motion phase can be associated to a dance phrase and considered as a gesture. A pause phase can be associated to a posture and considered as a gesture as well. For example, in a related work [12] the QoM measure has been used to perform the segmentation between pause and motion phases. In fact, QoM is related to the overall amount of motion and its evolution in time can be seen as a sequence of bell-shaped curves (*motion bells*). In order to segment motion, a list of these motion bells has been extracted and their features (e.g., peak value and duration) computed. Then, an empirical threshold has been defined: the dancer was considered to be moving if the area of the motion image (i.e., the QoM) was greater than 2.5% of the total area of the silhouette.

Several movement cues can be measured after segmenting motion in motion and pause phases: for example, blocks are available for calculating durations of pause and motion phases and inter-onset intervals as the time interval between the beginning of two subsequent motion phases. Furthermore, descriptive statistics of values of extracted cues can be computed on motion phases: for example, it is possible to calculate the sample mean and variance of the QoM during a motion phase.

2.2 The EyesWeb Space Analysis Library

The EyesWeb Space Analysis Library is based on a model considering a collection of discrete potential functions defined on a 2D space [13]. The space is divided into active cells forming a grid. A point moving in the space is considered and tracked. Three main kinds of potential functions are considered: (i) potential functions *not* depending on the current position of the tracked point, (ii) potential functions depending on the current position of the tracked point, (iii) potential functions depending on the definition of regions inside the space.

Objects and subjects in the space can be modeled by time-varying potentials. For example, a point moving in a 2D space (e.g., corresponding to a stage) can be associated to a dancer. Objects (such as fixed scenery or lights) can be modeled with potential functions independent from the position of the tracked object: notice that "independent from the position of the tracked object" does not mean time-invariant. The trajectory of a dancer with respect to such a potential function can be studied in order to identify relationships between movement and scenery. The dancer himself can be modeled as a bell-shaped potential moving around the space by using the second kind of potential functions. Interactions between potentials can be used to model interactions between (real or virtual) objects and subjects in the space.

Regions in the space can also be defined. For example, it is possible that some regions exist on a stage in which the presence of movement is more meaningful than in other regions. A certain number of "meaningful" regions (i.e., regions on which a particular focus is placed) can be defined and cues can be measured on them (e.g., how much time a dancer occupied a given region).

This metaphor can be applied both to real spaces (e.g., scenery and actors on a stage, the dancer's General Space as described in [11]) and to virtual, semantic, expressive spaces (e.g., a space of parameters where gestures are represented as trajectories): for example, if, from the one hand, the tracked point is a dancer on a stage, a measure of the time duration along which the dancer was in the scope of a given light can be obtained; on the other hand, if the tracked point represents a position in a semantic, expressive space where regions corresponds to basic emotions, the time duration along which a given emotion has been recognized can also be obtained.

The EyesWeb Space Analysis Library implements the model and includes blocks allowing the definition of interacting discrete potentials on 2D spaces, the definition of regions, and the extraction of cues (such as, for example, the occupation rates of regions in the space). For example, Figure 3 shows the occupation rates calculated on a rectangular space divided into 25 cells. The intensity (saturation) of the color for each cell is directly proportional to the occupation rate of the cell.

2.3 The EyesWeb Trajectory Analysis Library

The EyesWeb Trajectory Analysis Library contains a collection of blocks and patches for extraction of features from trajectories in 2D (real or virtual) spaces. It complements the EyesWeb Space Analysis Library and it can be used in conjunction with the EyesWeb Motion Analysis Library.

Blocks can deal with lot of trajectories at the same time, for example the trajectories of the body joints (e.g., head, hands, and feet tracked by means of color tracking techniques – occlusions are not dealt with at this stage) or the trajectories of the points tracked using the Lucas-Kanade feature tracker available in the Motion Analysis sub-library.

Features that can be extracted include geometric and kinematics measures.

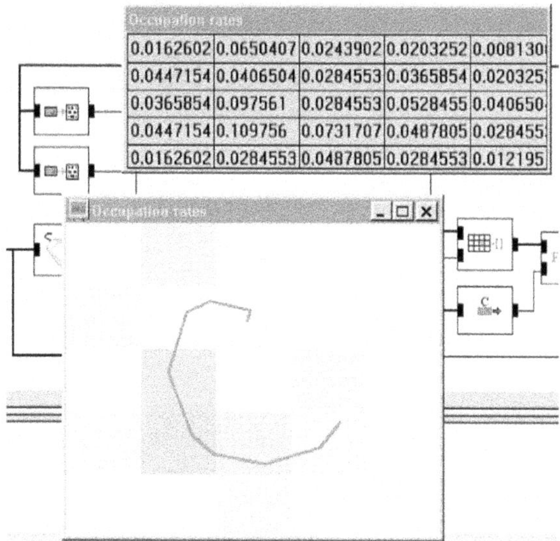

Fig. 3. Occupation rates calculated with the EyesWeb Space Analysis Library for a trajectory in a 2D space divided into 25 cells. The displayed trajectory refers to the last 25 frames (i.e., 1 s), but the occupations rates are calculated for the whole trajectory since the start of the gesture.

Examples of geometric features are the length of a trajectory, its direction and its *Directness Index* (DI). The Directness Index is a measure of how much a trajectory is direct or flexible. In the Laban's Theory of Effort [10] it is related to the Space dimension. In the current implementation the DI is computed as the ratio between the length of the straight line connecting the first and last point of a given trajectory and the sum of the lengths of each segment constituting the given trajectory. Therefore, the more it is near to one, the more direct is the trajectory (i.e., the trajectory is "near" to the straight line).

The available kinematical measures are velocity, acceleration, and curvature. Their instantaneous values are calculated on each input trajectory. Numeric derivatives can be computed using both the symmetric and the asymmetric backward methods (the user can select the one he/she prefers). Acceleration is available both in the usual x and y components and in the normal-tangent components.

Descriptive statistic measures can also be computed:

(i) *Along time*: for example, average and peak values calculated either on running windows or on all the samples between two subsequent commands (e.g., the average velocity of the hand of a dancer during a given motion phase)

(ii) *Among trajectories*: for example, average velocity of groups of trajectories available at the same time (e.g., the average instantaneous velocity of all the tracked points located on the arm of a dancer).

As in the case of the EyesWeb Space Analysis Library, trajectories can be real trajectories coming from tracking algorithms in the real world (e.g., the trajectory of the head of a dancer tracked using a tracker included in the EyesWeb Motion Analysis Library) or trajectories in virtual, semantic spaces (e.g., a trajectory representing a gesture in a semantic, expressive space).

The extracted measures can be used as input for clustering algorithms in order to group trajectories having similar features. In the physical space this approach can be used to idntify points moving in a similar way (e.g., points associated to the same limb in the case of the Lucas-Kanade feature tracker). In a semantic space whose axes might be for example some of the expressive cues discussed above, the approach could allow grouping similar gestures, or gestures communicating the same expressive intention. Further developments and experiments in these direction are presented in a forthcoming paper.

3 Evaluation and Validation of Expressive Cues

Some of the algorithms for the extraction of expressive cues included in the EyesWeb Motion Analysis Library have been recently validated through a collection of perceptual experiments.

For example, in an experiment on segmentation of dance performances in pause and motion phases, spectators were asked to segment dance fragments in pause and motion phases (corresponding to a gesture or to a part of it). Two different dance fragments were used in the experiment, characterized by hard and smooth movement. Preliminary results evidenced the main effect of the expressive qualities (hard vs. smooth) in the perceived segmentation. Results were compared with automatic segmentation performed by the developed algorithms. The algorithms generally revealed to be more sensible than humans since they could identify motion and pause phase that humans were not able to distinguish.

In another experiment, subjects were asked to indicate through continuous measurement how much energy they perceive in a dance fragment and how much contraction they perceive in the dancer body. Results (available in a forthcoming paper) are compared with the automatically measured Quantity of Motion and Contraction Index cues.

4 Conclusion

The EyesWeb Expressive Gesture Processing Library has been employed in a number of artistic events (list and description of performances available at the EU IST MEGA project website www.megaproject.org), and in therapy and rehabilitation [14].
This library consists of a distinct and separate add-on with respect to the EyesWeb open software platform and includes some of the research and development carried out during the three-year EU IST Project MEGA.

Novel algorithms and related software modules for the EyesWeb Expressive Gesture Processing Library are currently under development, including for example refined motion tracking (e.g. with multiple cameras), extraction of new cues, machine-learning techniques for higher-level gesture analysis.

Acknowledgements

We thank Matteo Ricchetti and Riccardo Trocca for discussions and their concrete contributes to this project. We also thank the other members of the EyesWeb staff, and in particular Paolo Coletta, Massimiliano Peri, and Andrea Ricci.

This work has been partially supported by the EU – IST Project MEGA (Multisensory Expressive Gesture Applications) and by the National CNR Project CNRG0024AF "Metodi di analisi dell'espressività nel movimento umano per applicazioni in Virtual Environment".

References

1. Camurri A., Mazzarino B., Ricchetti M., Timmers R., Volpe G. (2004), "Multimodal analysis of expressive gesture in music and dance performances", in A. Camurri, G. Volpe (Eds.), "Gesture-based Communication in Human-Computer Interaction", LNAI 2915, Springer Verlag, 2004.
2. Camurri, A., De Poli G., Leman M. "MEGASE - A Multisensory Expressive Gesture Applications System Environment for Artistic Performances", Proc. Intl. Conf. CAST01, GMD, St Augustin-Bonn, pp.59-62, 2001.
3. Camurri, A., Coglio, A. "An Architecture for Emotional Agents". IEEE MULTIMEDIA, 5(4):24-33, Oct-Dec 1998.
4. Camurri, A., Ferrentino, P. "Interactive Environments for Music and Multimedia. ACM MULTIMEDIA SYSTEMS, 7:32-47, Special issue on *Audio and Multimedia*, January 1999, ACM-Springer.
5. Lucas B., Kanade T., "An iterative image registration technique with an application to stereo vision" in Proceedings of the International Joint Conference on Artificial Intelligence, 1981.
6. Liu Y., Collins R., Tsin Y., "Gait Sequence Analysis using Frieze Patterns" European Conference on Computer Vision, Copenhagen, May 2002, pp.657-671.
7. Bobick, A.F., Davis J., "The Recognition of Human Movement Using Temporal Templates", in IEEE Transactions on Pattern Analysis and Machine Intelligence, 23(3): 257-267, 2001.
8. Kilian J., "Simple Image Analysis by Moments" OpenCV library documentation, 2001.
9. Boone, R. T., Cunningham, J. G., "Children's decoding of emotion in expressive body movement: The development of cue attunement" Developmental Psychology, 34, 1007-1016, 1998
10. Laban, R., Lawrence F.C., "Effort", Macdonald & Evans Ltd. London, 1947.
11. Laban, R., "Modern Educational Dance" Macdonald & Evans Ltd. London, 1963.
12. Camurri A., Lagerlöf I., Volpe G., "Recognizing Emotion from Dance Movement: Comparison of Spectator Recognition and Automated Techniques", International Journal of Human-Computer Studies, Elsevier Science, in press.
13. Camurri A., Mazzarino B., Trocca R., Volpe G. "Real-Time Analysis of Expressive Cues in Human Movement." Proc. Intl. Conf. CAST01, GMD, St Augustin-Bonn, pp. 63-68, 2001.
14. Camurri A., Mazzarino B., Volpe G., Morasso P., Priano F., Re C., "Application of multimedia techniques in the physical rehabilitation of Parkinson's patients", Journal of Visualization and Computer Animation (In Press).

Performance Gestures of Musicians: What Structural and Emotional Information Do They Convey?

Bradley W. Vines[1], Marcelo M. Wanderley[2], Carol L. Krumhansl[3], Regina L. Nuzzo[1], and Daniel J. Levitin[1,2]

[1] Department of Psychology, McGill University, Montreal, Qc, Canada
[2] Faculty of Music, McGill University, Montreal, Qc, Canada
[3] Department of Psychology, Cornell University, Ithaca, NY, USA

Abstract. This paper investigates how expressive gestures of a professional clarinetist contribute to the perception of structure and affect in musical performance. The thirty musically trained subjects saw, heard, or both saw and heard the performance. All subjects made the same judgments including a real-time judgment of phrasing, which targeted the experience of structure, and a real-time judgment of tension, which targeted emotional experience.
In addition to standard statistical methods, techniques in the field of Functional Data Analysis were used to interpret the data. These new techniques model data drawn from continuous processes and explore the hidden structures of the data as they change over time.
Three main findings add to our knowledge of gesture and movement in music: 1) The visual component carries much of the same structural information as the audio. 2) Gestures elongate the sense of phrasing during a pause in the sound and certain gestures cue the beginning of a new phrase. 3) The importance of visual information to the experience of tension changes with certain structural features in the sound. When loudness, pitch height, and note density are relatively low, the effect of removing the visual component is to decrease the experience of tension.

1 Introduction

The visual experience of a musical performance can play an important role in our appreciation and perception of music. Many of us spend considerable time and money to see live performances rather than simply listening to CDs , which offer repeatable listening and higher sound quality. The research presented in this paper investigated what the visual information in a musical performance contributes to an observer's sensory experience. We sought to reveal the relations between sensory modalities (auditory and visual) in conveying structural and affective information.

Past research has shown that the movements of musicians are closely related to the piece being performed. Delalande [4] investigated the movements of Glen Gould and found that they were not haphazard, but reflected structural characteristics of the music. Interestingly, Gould's gestural behavior at the piano changed upon moving into the studio. This shows that, consciously or unconsciously, the movements of musicians can be influenced by the audience, whether through feedback or communicative intention of the performer.

A. Camurri and G. Volpe (Eds.): GW 2003, LNAI 2915, pp. 468–478, 2004.

Davidson [3] found that the expressive intentions of musical performers were carried most accurately by their movements. She used a point-light display to present recorded performances of classical musicians to subjects in her study. The performers were instructed to perform in one of three ways: in a deadpan manner (without expressivity), in a standard manner (as if performing to a public audience), and in an exaggerated manner (with exaggerated expressivity). Subjects rated each performer's intended level of expressivity. Those subjects who only saw the video identified the different levels most accurately. Subjects who were denied the visual information performed more poorly. This study showed that not only is the visual aspect of a performance not superfluous, it carries information about expressive intention with greater resolution than the auditory component.

It has been shown that, in a ballet performance, the visual modality can convey much of the same structural and emotional information as the auditory modality does. Krumhansl and Schenck [12] used a choreographed work by Ballanchine to investigate the relations between sensory modalities in ballet. The first group of subjects both heard the sound and saw the dance. The other two groups either only heard the sound or only saw the dance, with sound removed. Subjects made four different judgments in real time: identifying section ends, identifying new ideas, a continuous judgment of tension, and a continuous judgments of the amount of emotion. The judgments were similar across modalities, especially in the coincidence of section ends, new ideas and regions of tension. Krumhansl and Schenck showed that stimulation of completely different modalities may lead to similar experiences and they paved the way for similar investigations involving continuous measures and cross-modal comparisons.

Research conducted by Wanderley [20] showed that the movements of clarinetists are consistent across performances of the same piece and that they are not essential to the physical performance of the instrument. Wanderley used an Optotrak device to track locations on clarinetists' bodies and instruments over time. Even though the performers were unaware of their movements for the most part, they repeated them from one performance of the same piece to another. Like Davidson, Wanderley instructed his musicians to use particular manners of performance. One instruction was to remain as still as possible. All four clarinetists were able to execute the pieces accurately, even in the absence of expressive movements. This shows that some of the clarinetist's movements are not essential to the physical execution of the piece, and that they may have other functions.

Wanderley's research is being used to improve the realism of synthesized musical instruments [18] [19]. By taking into account the changing relations between a virtual microphone and an electronic instrument, it is possible to model spectral fluctuations that are present in acoustic clarinet performances.

The research presented in this paper employed the multi-modal approach [3] [12] and real-time judgments [12] to investigate a musical performance. Relations between the audio and visual modalities are explored in terms of the structural and emotional information they convey. A continuous judgment of tension was used to observe the experience of emotion and a continuous judgment of phrasing targeted the experience of structure.

The continuous tension judgment, pioneered by Nielsen [16], has been shown to be correlated with continuous judgments of dominant emotions as well as a variety of physiological measures [11]. Krumhansl and Schenck [12] found that subjects' judgments of tension are similar to their judgments of the amount of emotion. The tension judgment is sensitive to changes in a performance [6], and it depends on a wide variety of structural, harmonic, and rhythmic features in the music [16] [14] [6] [10] [12]. This measure is consistent across age groups, musical skill levels, and levels of familiarity with the stimulus music [7] [8] [9] [10]. It is an informative and consistent measure.

The continuous phrasing judgment was exploratory, in that it had never been used in the same form before. However, similar real-time judgments have been used with success [2] [5] [10] [11]. In these studies, beginnings or endings of musical ideas or sections were marked as the performances were presented. In the present investigation, the shape of the phrase was included as well. Phrasing is a structural feature. A musical phrase is analogous to a complete idea in speech [1]. A judgment of phrasing captures the sense of form, as opposed to content.

We used new statistical techniques in Functional Data Analysis [17] to reveal changes in the effect of having either audio or visual information removed from a subject's experience. Traditional statistics have some limitations when they are used with data that are sampled over time. Traditional methods produce one-dimensional descriptions that are incapable of revealing changes over time. For example, correlations and regression models return single numbers to summarize the relations between entire data sets. In the experiment presented here, judgments were performed over a time span of 80 seconds, which encompassed a total of 800 data points per subject. Subjects were responding to a musical piece with great variation in dynamics, expressive movements, and harmony. It would have been an oversimplification to reduce all of the information gathered to a one-dimensional description of the relations across treatment groups.

Functional Data Analysis, however, yields solutions that are themselves functions of time. These new statistical techniques treat data as mathematical functions. So, it is possible to ask questions like "When during the performance does removing the visual component have a strong impact on the tension judgment, as compared to the audio plus visual experience?" We only used these techniques with the tension data because the phrasing analysis did not require functional tools, like smoothing and registration. In particular, registration would have eliminated the fine temporal differences that were important to this investigation. For the data collected here, functional techniques were most useful for identifying global trends in the tension judgments.

This paper is part of a larger investigation involving multiple performers and multiple manners of execution. We will concentrate on a standard performance of one clarinetist here.

2 Method

2.1 Stimuli

The stimuli consisted of a performance by a professional clarinetist of Stravinsky's second piece for solo clarinet. The performer played the piece as if presenting to a public audience. The recording was originally created for an investigation mentioned above [20].

Fig. 1. A screen shot of the stimuli video used in the experiment, from [20]

We chose the Stravinsky piece for three reasons: 1) It is an unaccompanied piece, so the performer's movements and sound were not influenced by another instrument. 2) The piece is rhythmically free; it has no underlying pulse or meter. Clarinetists tend to entrain their movements to the underlying pulse when there is a consistent meter [20]. In the Stravinsky piece, the musicians were free to move expressively and idiosyncratically. 3) This music is standard repertoire for advanced clarinetists around the world. This makes replication and cross-cultural comparisons accessible to future work.

2.2 Subjects

Thirty subjects participated in the experiment. All of them had at least five years of musical training. This criterion ensured that subjects had a developed ear and an understanding of basic terms in music, like "phrasing." Also, research with music has shown that the judgments of musicians are similar to the judgments of non-musicians, but with less noise [5] [10]. This means that research with musician subjects tends to give a clearer image of the musical process.

Using a Between-Subjects design, the subjects were randomly divided into three equally sized treatment groups. The first group experienced the performance with both audio and visual information intact. The second group heard the performance with the visual component removed, and the last group saw the performance with the audio removed.

The performance was shown with digital-video quality (25 frames per second) on a G4 desktop Macintosh.

2.3 Tasks

All subjects performed the same real-time tasks, including a continuous judgment of tension and a continuous judgment of phrasing. Both judgments were made using one track on a Peavy 1600X slider. Subjects moved the slider up and down along a track as the performance was presented. The location of the slider was sampled once every 100 milliseconds. Continuous judgments reveal a subject's present mental state more accurately than retrospective judgments, which are subject to memory errors.

Tension: These are the exact instructions that subjects read before performing the task:

> - Use the full range of the slider to express the TENSION you experience in the performance. Move the slider upward as the tension increases and downward as the tension decreases.

Phrasing: Here are the exact instructions read by each subject:

> - Use the full range of the slider to express the PHRASING you experience in the performance. Move the slider upward as a phrase is entered and downward as a phrase is exited. The slider should be near the top in the middle of a phrase and near the bottom between phrases.

3 Results

3.1 The Tension Data

The effects of having visual or audio information removed from a subject's experience changed over time, as revealed by Functional Data Analysis.

Figure 2 shows the fitted curves for each of the treatment conditions. These functions are essentially an average of the subjects' judgments in each condition, after taking into account their unique reaction times and the range of slider that they used. The curves have been smoothed to eliminate high frequency noise in the data.

When we applied a linear model to the data functions[1], the coefficients shown in Figure 3 emerged. The dotted line shows the effect of having the audio removed and the dashed line shows the effect of having the visual component removed. When either line is above the $y = 0$ axis, the effect of being in that particular treatment group is to increase the judgment of tension in comparison to the average judgment in the audio plus visual condition.

The graph of the functional coefficients drew our attention to the region from about 35 to 65 seconds. During this period of time, the effect of removing sound remained strongly and consistently positive. The effect of removing the visual component was correspondingly negative for most of this temporal region. The corresponding section in the performance encompasses the middle section in the piece. During this section,

[1] The following linear model was used:

$$Y = U + B1(t)[ifminusaudio] + B2(t)[ifminusvideo] \quad (1)$$

where U is the audio plus visual function, and $B1(t)$ and $B2(t)$ are coefficients that change with time.

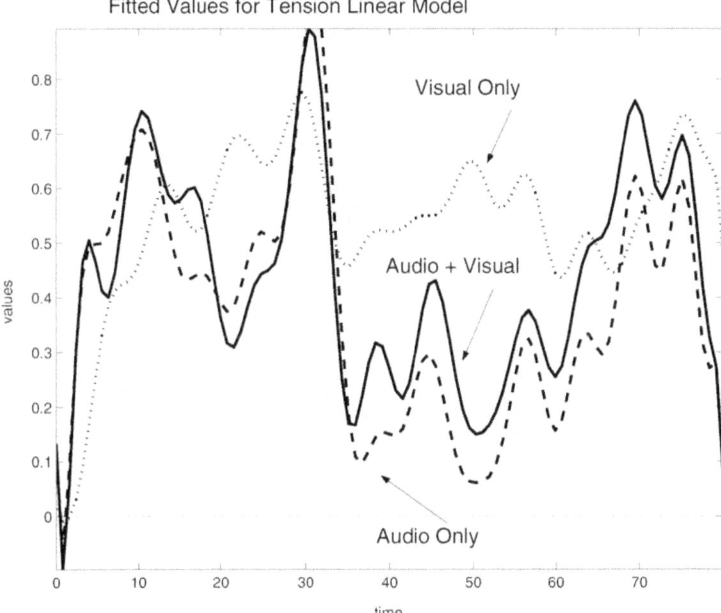

Fig. 2. The fitted curves for each treatment group after registering, scaling and smoothing. Registering takes into account varying reaction times across subjects. It is possible that two subjects, who are responding to the same physical event, might give responses at different points in time, due to variations in their reaction times. Registering, also known as *Time Warping*, takes this possibility into account by aligning major peaks and troughs in the judgments. Scaling corrects for the different spans of the slider that subjects use, and smoothing irons out the high frequency wobbles in the curves

the dynamics decreased dramatically, from mezzo forte to pianissimo, the note density decreased from 16th and 32nd notes to 8th notes, and the pitch height decreased as well. From this, we can see that the importance of visual information to the typical tension judgment was associated with loudness, note density, and pitch height.

3.2 Phrasing Data

As mentioned above, we did not use functional techniques to analyze the phrasing data. The phrasing judgment is not a measure of magnitude, like the tension judgment, but a measure of structural shape, so the use of a regression analysis would not have been appropriate. Also, the fine temporal differences between groups, which were of particular interest to this study, would have been eliminated by registration and potentially lost if the data were smoothed. Therefore, only traditional statistical tools were employed with the phrasing data.

Structural Content of the Performance Gestures. The raw phrasing averages for the three treatment groups, shown in Figure 4, tell a very different story from the tension averages.

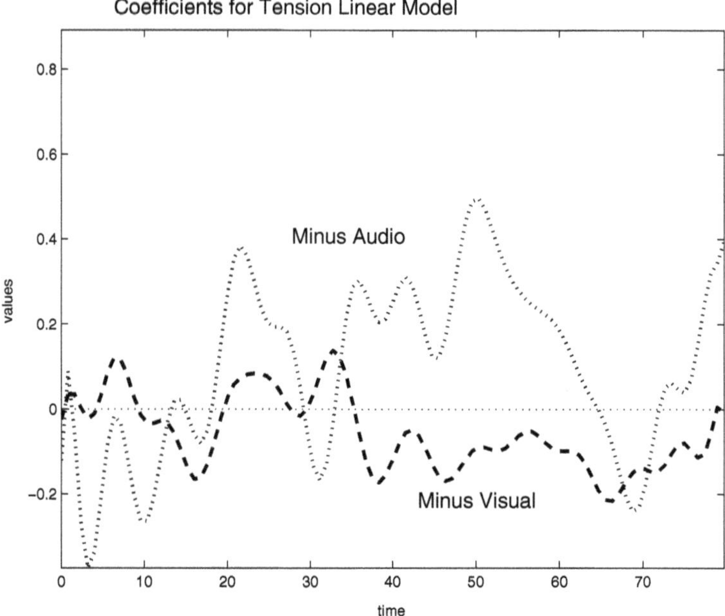

Fig. 3. A graph of the coefficients for two treatment groups over time. These are products of new statistical methods, *Functional Data Analysis*, which treat data as functions of time. The dashed line shows the effect of being in a group for which the auditory component was removed. The dotted line shows the effect of being in the group for which the visual component was removed. Values above the $y = 0$ line represent an effective increase in the judgment of tension

There is a striking similarity between the judgments for all three groups, in spite of the fact that the Audio-only group and the Visual-only group had no overlap in stimulus material. Subjects in the Audio-only group had all of the visual component removed. Subjects in the Visual-only group had all the auditory component removed. Yet their judgments show that both sensory modalities expressed very similar phrasing information. The magnitude of judgments varied from group to group, but the troughs and peaks which mark the temporal boundaries of each phrase align consistently. These data show that the visual component of the musical performance also conveyed the structural content of the piece.

The Effect of Gestures during the Major Transition. Figure 5 shows a detail of the only major transition between sections. During this transition, a fermata ends the first section and there is a pause in sound. The clarinetist takes a breath before entering the new section.

The zoomed-in region of the raw data averages shows that the Visual-only group was slow to recognize the end of the preceding phrase and the Audio-only group was slow to recognize the beginning of the new phrase. The visual component had an important effect on the sense of phrasing in this segment.

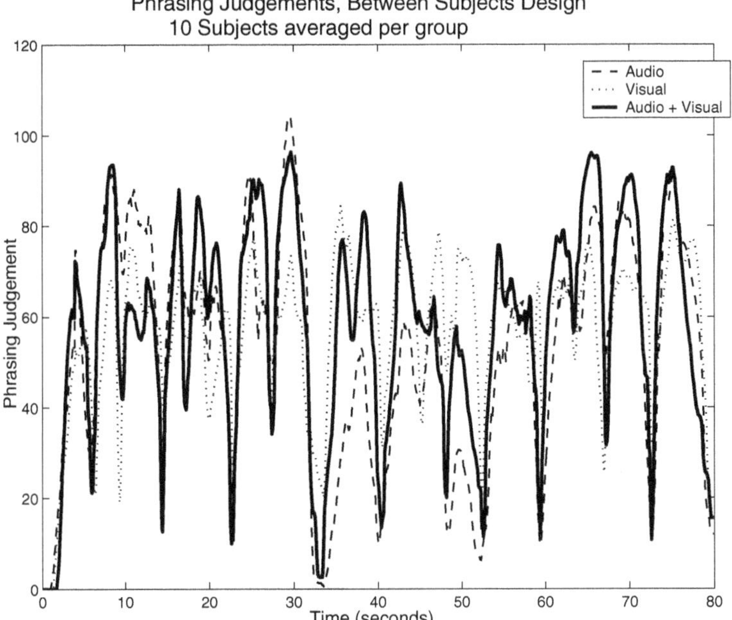

Fig. 4. Graphs of phrasing judgments. Judgments of the ten subjects from each treatment group were averaged to create these lines. The coincidence of troughs and peaks across treatment conditions shows that the visual aspect of the performance is also carrying structural information about the piece

The performer ended the fermata with a strong movement of his body. His left hand raised from the clarinet and then slowly descended during the silent rest. We hypothesize that gestural movement during the pause extended the sensation of the phrase for the Visual-only group. These subjects did not have the benefit of hearing the note come to a clear and concise end. The sound was important for recognizing the conclusion of the phrase and the visual information served to elongate the experience. The phrase-end was extended for subjects in the Audio+Visual group as well, though not as dramatically.

Before the new phrase began, the performer made certain movements in anticipation of the sound. He took a deep breath, raised the clarinet and brought it back down in a swooping motion before initiating the sound at the bottom of his arc. Without these visual cues, the Audio-only group could not anticipate the onset of sound. Subjects in the Audio-only group had a sense of phrasing that lagged behind the other two groups who were privy to the movement cues that anticipated the coming sound. The visual information was important for engaging the experience of a new phrase.

There are corresponding phenomena in speech to those found here in music. Preparation of the vocal articulators begins before the speech sound is initiated [13]. This visual cue helps an observer to anticipate the onset of a new speech sound and gives some information about what that sound will be. Also, breathing cues are used by people engaged in conversation to help in timing their exchange [15]. In a musical situation, certain movements cue the beginning of a new phrase, including breath and body gesture.

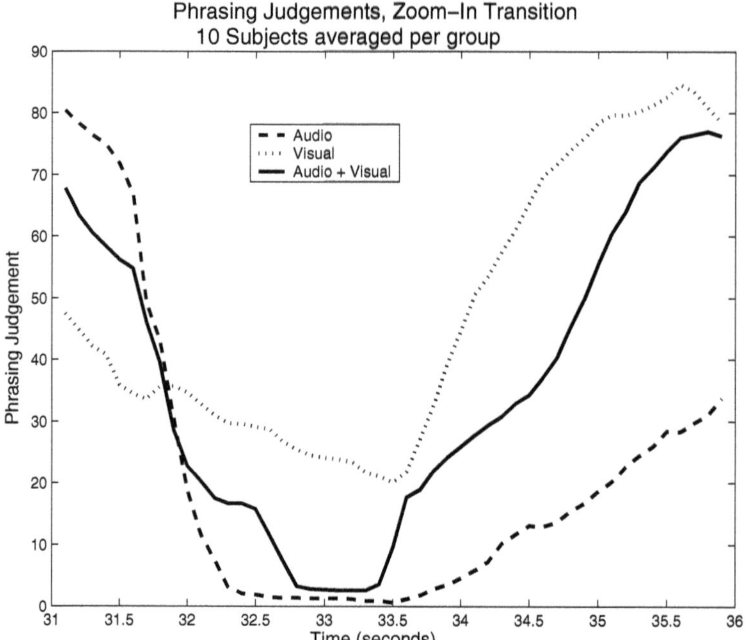

Fig. 5. A zoom-in on the transition between musical sections. The Visual-only (*dotted line*) is slowest to recognize the end of the phrase and the Audio-only (*dashed line*) group is slowest to recognize the beginning of the new phrase

We hypothesize that for important transitions that involve a pause in the sound, visual information affects an observer's experience by extending the sensation of the phrase being concluded, and by cuing the beginning of the new phrase by means of particular gestures.

4 Conclusion

We found Functional Data Analysis methods to be very useful for revealing the relations between modalities as they changed over time. These statistical techniques are important tools for the fields of gesture, music, and emotion research. They reveal the hidden structures of data and how those structures evolve. Functional techniques are useful for analyzing continuous judgment data as well as measures of gestures and movements themselves (i.e. Optotrak data).

Using Functional Data Analysis, we have observed that the importance of the visual component to the typical tension judgment was dependent upon the loudness, note density, and pitch height in sound. When the note density was low, the dynamics were soft, and the pitch height was low, the effect of removing the visual component was to decrease the judgment of tension.

The visual modality was shown to carry much of the same structural information as the auditory modality, as indicated by similarities in the phrasing judgments across presentation conditions. Despite the fact that the Audio-only group and the Visual-only group had no physical overlap in their stimuli, their judgments of phrasing showed precise synchrony in the onsets and conclusions of phrases.

During the most important transition in the piece, where a pause in sound occurs, the clarinetist's gestures had a marked effect on the sense of phrasing. The group that was denied auditory information showed a lag in its recognition of the phrase ending because body movements continue during the pause. The movements elongate the sense of phrasing. There is no such ambiguity in the audio component. When the note ends, there is only silence to clearly mark the phrase end. The sense of phrasing was extended for the Audio+Visual group, though not as dramatically as it was for the Visual-only group. During the major transition, gestures served to cue the beginning of a new phrase. Without visual information, the sense of phrasing lagged behind after the long pause in sound. The Audio-only group did not experience the gestures that cued the beginning of the new phrase, including a substantial breath and a swooping motion of the clarinet.

This research augments our understanding of multi-modal relations in a musical performance and sheds light upon the important involvement of performance gestures in the perception of music.

Acknowledgments

We would like to thank the performers Oskar Ramspek and Lars Wouters for participating in this research. Thanks also to the Free University Amsterdam (Peter Beek), NICI Nijmegen (Peter Desain) and Ircam-Centre Pompidou Paris for collaboration. The following research assistants were instrumental in collecting data and in analyzing the video: Nora Hussein, Sawsan M'birkou, and Eve-Marie Quintin.

This work was supported by grants from VRQ (Valorisation Recherche Québec), NSERC (National Science and Engineering Research Council), CFI (Canadian Foundation for Innovation) to Daniel J. Levitin and from FQRNT (Fonds Québecois de Recherche sur la Nature et les Technologies) and McGill Individual New Researcher to Marcelo M. Wanderley.

References

1. Aiello, R. Music and Language: Parallels and Contrasts. In R. Aiello and J. Sloboda (Eds.) *Music Perceptions*, pages 40-63. New York: Oxford University Press, 1994.
2. Clarke, E. F. and Krumhansl, C. L. Perceiving Musical Time. *Music Perception*, 7:213-252, 1990.
3. Davidson, J. Visual Perception of Performance Manner in the Movements of Solo Musicians. *Psychology of Music* 21: 103 - 113, 1993.
4. Delalande, F. La Gestique de Gould. In *Glen Gould Pluriel*, pages 85-111. Louse Courteau, editrice, inc., 1988.
5. Deliège, I. and El Ahmade, A. Mechanisms for Cue Extraction in Musical Groupings: A Study of Perception on *Sequenza VI* for Viola Solo by Luciano Berio. *Psychology of Music*, 18:18-44, 1990.
6. Fredrickson, W. E. A Comparison of Perceived Musical Tension and Aesthetic Response. *Psychology of Music* 23: 81-87, 1995.

7. Fredrickson, W. E. Elementary, Middle, and High School Student Perceptions of Tension in Music. *Journal of Research in Music Education* 45(4): 626-635, 1997.
8. Fredrickson, W. E. Effect of Musical Performance on Perception of Tension in Gustav Holst's First Suite in E-flat. *Journal of Research in Music Education* 47(1): 44-52, 1999.
9. Fredrickson, W. E. Perception of Tension in Music: Musicians versus Nonmusicians. *Journal of Music Therapy* 37(1): 40-50, 2000.
10. Krumhansl, C.L. A Perceptual Analysis of Mozart's Piano Sonata K. 282: Segmentation, Tension, and Musical Ideas. *Music Perception* 13(3): 401-432, 1996.
11. Krumhansl, C. L. An Exploratory Study of Musical Emotions and Psychophysiology. *Canadian Journal of Experimental Psychology* 51(4): 336-352, 1997.
12. Krumhansl, C. L. and Schenck, D.L. Can dance reflect the structural and expressive qualities of music? A perceptual experiment on Balanchine's choreography of Mozart's Divertimento No. 15. *Musicae Scientiae* 1(Spring): 63-85, 1997.
13. Levelt, W. J. M. *Speaking: From Intention to Articulation.* Cambridge, Massachusetts: MIT Press, 1989.
14. Madsen, C. K. and Fredrickson, W. E. The Experience of Musical Tension: A Replication of Nielsen's Research Using the Continuous Response Digital Interface. *Journal of Music Therapy* 30(1): 46-63, 1993.
15. McFarland, D.H. Respiratory Markers of Conversational Interaction. *Journal of Speech, Language, and Hearing Research* 44(1): 128-143, 2001.
16. Nielsen, F.V. *Oplevelse af misikalsk spending* (The experience of musical tension). Copenhagen: Akademisk Forlag, 1983.
17. Ramsay, J.O. and Silverman, B.W. *Functional Data Analysis.* New York: Springer-Verlag, 1997.
18. Wanderley, M. M. Non-Obvious Performer Gestures in Instrumental Music. In A. Braffort, R. Gherbi, S. Gibet, J. Richardson, and D. Teil (eds.) *Gesture-Based Communication in Human-Computer Interaction.* Berlin, Heidelberg: Springer Verlag, pages 37-48, 1999.
19. Wanderley, M. M. and Depalle, P. Gesturally Controlled Digital Audio Effects. In *Proceedings of the COST-6 Conference on Digital Audio Effects (DAFx-01).* Limerick, Ireland, pages 165-169, 2001.
20. Wanderley, M. M. Quantitative Analysis of Non-Obvious Performer Gestures. In I. Wachsmuth and T. Sowa (eds.) *Gesture and Sign Language in Human-Computer Interaction.* Berlin, Heidelberg: Springer Verlag, pages 241-253, 2002.

Expressiveness of Musician's Body Movements in Performances on Marimba

Sofia Dahl and Anders Friberg

Dept. of Speech, Music and Hearing
KTH, Royal Institute of Technology
SE-100 44 Stockholm, Sweden
{sofia,andersf}@speech.kth.se

Abstract. To explore to what extent emotional intentions can be conveyed through musicians' movements, video recordings were made of a marimba player performing the same piece with the intentions Happy, Sad, Angry and Fearful. 20 subjects were presented video clips, without sound, and asked to rate both the perceived emotional content as well as the movement qualities. The video clips were presented in different conditions, showing the player to different extent. The observers' ratings for the intended emotions confirmed that the intentions Happiness, Sadness and Anger were well communicated, while Fear was not. Identification of the intended emotion was only slightly influenced by the viewing condition. The movement ratings indicated that there were cues that the observers used to distinguish between intentions, similar to cues found for audio signals in music performance.

1 Introduction

Music has an intimate relationship with movement in several different aspects. First of all, all sounds on traditional acoustic instruments are produced by human motion. Some characteristics of this motion will inevitably be reflected in the resulting tones.

Musicians move also their bodies in a way that is not directly related to the production of notes. Wanderley [1] refers to these other performer movements as *ancillary, accompanist* or *non-obvious* movements. We prefer to think of it as a kind of *body language* since, as we will see below, it serves several important functions in music performance. It seems reasonable to assume that some of the expressivity in the music is reflected in these movements. However, the body movements may also be used for more explicit communication. Davidson and Correia [2] suggests four aspects that influence the body language in musical performances: (1) Communication with co-performers, (2) individual interpretations of the narrative or expressive/emotional elements of the music, (3) the performer's own experiences and behaviors, and (4) the aim to interact and entertain an audience. To separate the influence of each of the aspects suggested by Davidson and Correia on a specific movement may not be possible, but by concentrating on solo performances without an audience, (2) and (3) above may

A. Camurri and G. Volpe (Eds.): GW 2003, LNAI 2915, pp. 479–486, 2004.

be the dominating aspects and the more extra-musical influences (1) and (4) would be minimized.

It is now well documented that a viewer can perceive expressive nuances from a musician's body language only. Davidson has made several studies on expressive movements in musical performance relating the overall perceived expressiveness to musicians' movements (e.g. [3][4][5]). It was found that subjects were about equally successful in identifying the expressive intent in piano or violin performances, regardless of whether they were allowed to only listen, only watch or both watch and listen [3]. Musically naive subjects actually performed better when only watching, compared to the other conditions [6]. In a similar study, focusing on emotional expression, Sörgjerd [7] found that subjects were more successful in identifying the emotions Happiness, Sadness, Anger and Fear, than the emotions Solemnity and Tenderness.

An interesting comparison can be done between the studies mentioned and how musical expressiveness is encoded and decoded using only the sound. In analysis of music performances Gabrielsson and Juslin [8][9] found that there are a number of cues (such as tempo, sound level etc) that listeners utilize when discriminating between different emotional expression performances. For example, a Happy performance is characterized by a fast mean tempo, high sound level, staccato articulation, and fast tone attacks, while a Sad performance is characterized by a slow tempo, low sound level, legato articulation and slow tone attacks. It seems reasonable to assume that the body movements in the performances contain cues corresponding to those appearing in the audio signal.

In this study the objective was to explore both the communication of more specific expressive intentions, and whether this communication can be described in terms of motion cues (such as fast - slow, abrupt - smooth etc.), cues similar to those appearing when listening to music performances. A number of different aspects of musicians' body movements have been identified above. We assume that in this investigation the body movement of the player mainly consists of (1) movements for the direct sound production on the instrument, and (2) natural expressive movements not primarily intended to convey visual information to the audience or to fellow musicians.

The questions for this study were the following:

1. How good is the overall communication of each intended emotion?
2. Are there any differences depending on intended emotion, or what part of the player the observers see?
3. How can perceived emotions be classified in terms of movement cues?

2 Recording

A professional percussionist was asked to prepare a piece for marimba with four different expressive intentions: Anger, Happiness, Sadness and Fear. The piece chosen was a practice piece from a study book by Morris Goldenberg: "Melodic study in sixteens". This piece was found to be of a suitable duration and of rather "neutral" emotional character, allowing for the different interpretations.

The recording was carried out using a digital video camera (SONY DCR-VX1000E). The experimenter checked that the player was clearly in view and made the camera ready for recording, but was not present in the room during the recording. The player performed each intention twice with a short break between each performance.

3 Experiment

Stimuli. The original video recordings were presented to the observers in different *viewing conditions*, showing the player in the image to a varying degree. Four viewing conditions were used; *full* (showing the full image), *nohands* (the player's hands not visible), *torso* (player's hands and head not visible) and *head* (only the player's head visible).

Figure 1 shows an example of a frame with the four viewing conditions. The original video files were edited using a freeware video editing software (Virtual Dub). To remove facial expression a threshold filter of 19 % was used, transforming the color image to a strict black and white image (without gray scales). The four conditions were then cut out from the original full scale image, using a cropping filter. Based on the original eight video recordings a total of 32 (4 emotions x 2 repetitions x 4 conditions) video clips were generated.

Subjects and Method. Twenty (10 male and 10 female) subjects participated in the experiment, mostly students and researchers at the department. The subjects did not receive any compensation for their participation.

Subjects were asked to rate the emotional content for each video clip on a scale from 0 (nothing) to 6 (very much), for the four emotions Fear, Anger, Happiness and Sadness. The subjects were also asked to mark how they perceived the movements. The ratings of movement cues were carried out using bipolar scales. The scales for movement ratings were amount of movement (no movement - large movements), speed (fast - slow), fluency (jerky - smooth) and the distribution of movements (uneven - even).

The 32 video clips were shown on a PC and rated individually. Each clip could be viewed as many times as the subject liked, but subjects could not go back to rate the previous one.

Fig. 1. Original (far left) and filtered video images exemplifying the four viewing conditions used in the test: full, nohands, head, and torso.

4 Results and Discussion

Emotion Ratings. In Fig. 2 the mean ratings for each of the intended emotions and the viewing conditions can be seen. Each panel shows the mean ratings for the four emotions averaged across 20 subjects and the two performances of each intended emotion. The Sad intention was the most successfully identified, followed by Angry and Happy. The occasional confusion of Anger with Happiness and vice versa indicate that these two expressions might have some features in common. The ratings for intention Fear, however, seems to be evenly spread across the four available emotions.

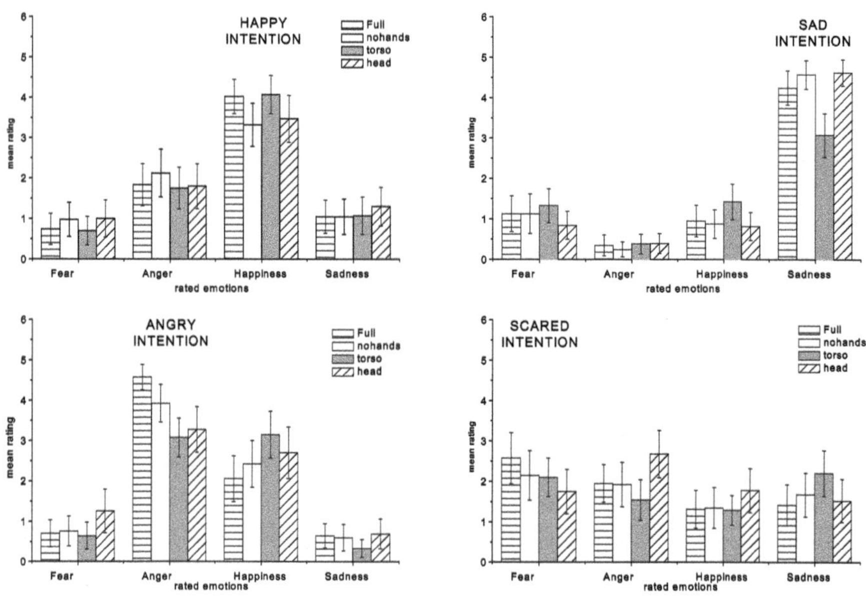

Fig. 2. Ratings for the four intended emotions and viewing conditions. Each panel shows the mean ratings for the four emotions averaged across 20 subjects and the two performances of each intended emotion. The pattern of the bars show the four viewing conditions: full (horizontally striped), nohands (white), torso (grey), and head (diagonally striped). The error bars indicate 95 % confidence intervals. As seen in the panels the Happy (top left panel), Sad (top right) and Angry (bottom left) performances receive ratings in correspondence to the intention, while Scared (bottom right) hardly was recognized at all.

The influence of the different viewing conditions on the ratings is surprisingly small, but some interaction effects with the intended emotion can be observed. For the Sad intention all the conditions where the head is visible (full, nohands, and head) receive high ratings for Sadness (means from 4.3 to 4.6 in Fig. 2), while torso rates much lower (mean 3.1). For Anger, the full condition receives the highest Anger ratings, while the conditions torso and head seem less successful in conveying the intention.

By transforming the ratings into forced choice responses, the subjects' identification of the intended emotions were calculated. In doing this, only the ratings where the intended emotion received the highest rating were considered as "correct". Responses where several emotions were rated equally high were considered as incorrect. The percentage of correct responses are shown in Table 1. The pattern of these values corresponds well to the mean ratings across the performances shown in Fig. 2.

The percentage correct responses also relates well to comparisons with other studies. Subjects in this study performed equally well, or better in terms of percentage correct identifications (c.f. [10][11][12]).

Table 1. Correct identification of the intended emotions in percent for the four viewing conditions, averaged across the two performances for each intention. The values were calculated as the portion of ratings where the intended emotion received the highest rating. The viewing condition receiving the most correct identifications for a specific intention is shown in bold.

	full	nohands	torso	head
Happiness	68	50	**73**	56
Sadness	80	80	53	**95**
Anger	**85**	60	38	45
Fear	**35**	23	23	10

Movement Cues. Figure 3 shows the mean ratings for movement cues for each intended emotion. The different movement cues; amount of movement (none - large), speed (fast - slow), fluency (jerky - smooth) and movement distribution (uneven - even), received different ratings depending on whether the intended expression was Happy, Sad, Angry, or Scared. Note that high ratings correspond to large amounts of movement, slow speed, smooth fluency, and even distribution, while low ratings correspond to small amounts of movement, fast speed, jerky fluency, and uneven distribution.

The intentions Happiness and Anger obtained similar rating patterns. Both Anger and Happiness seem to display large movements, but the Angry performances are somewhat faster and jerkier compared to the Happy performances. In contrast, the ratings for the Sad performances display small, slow, smooth and even movements. The ratings for Fear are less clear-cut, but tend to be somewhat small, fast, and jerky. A similar pattern was found when investigating how the subjects related the emotions to the movement cues. The correlation between the rated emotions and the ratings of movement cues is shown in Table 2. According to the table, Anger is associated with large, fast, uneven, and jerky movements; Happy with large and somewhat fast movements, Sadness with small, slow, even and smooth movements, and Fear with somewhat small, jerky and uneven movements. However, since the communication of Fear failed, its characterization is questionable.

Differences in cue ratings for different viewing conditions were, in general, small. For the intentions Happy and Sad and partly for Anger, the cue ratings

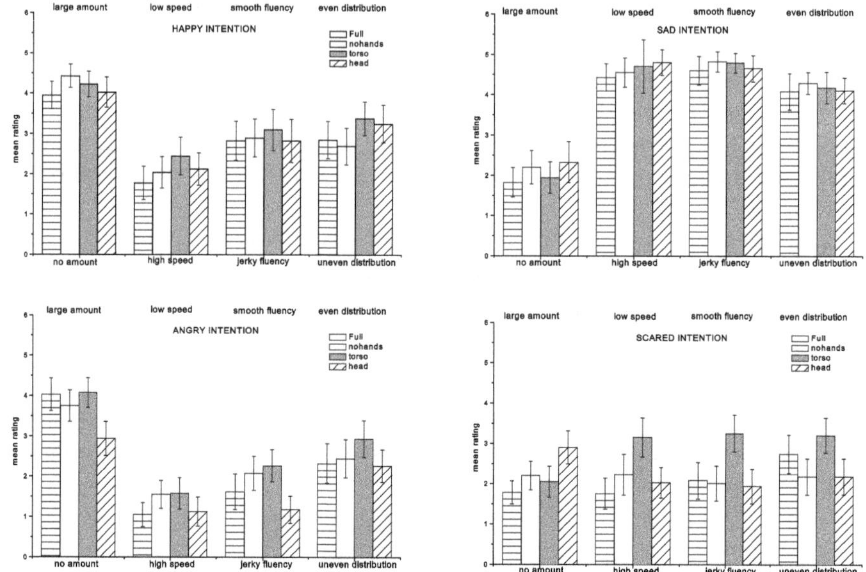

Fig. 3. Ratings for movement cues for each intended emotion and viewing condition. Each panel shows the mean markings for the four emotions averaged across 20 subjects and the two performances of each intended emotion. The pattern of the bars show the four viewing conditions: full (horizontally striped), nohands (white), torso (grey), and head (diagonally striped). The error bars indicate 95 % confidence intervals.

Table 2. Correlations between rated emotions and rated movement cues. All correlations, except between Fear and speed, were statistically significant ($p < 0.01, N = 603$).

	amount	speed	fluency	distrib.
Anger	0.31	-0.48	-0.54	-0.44
Happiness	0.40	-0.27	-0.15	-0.12
Sadness	0.32	0.60	0.50	0.38
Fear	-0.24	-0.01	-0.13	-0.11

Table 3. Intercorrelations between the movement cues. All correlations were statistically significant ($p < 0.01, N = 617$).

	amount	speed	fluency	distrib.
amount	-			
speed	-0.26	-		
fluency	-0.19	0.62	-	
distrib.	-0.12	0.44	0.58	-

are closely clustered. Again, the head seems to play a special role. When a rating stands out from the other viewing conditions it is either for the head or for the torso. Since the latter is the only condition where the head is not visible, it can in fact also be related to the head's movements. Also Davidson [4] found that the head was important for the observers to discriminate between expressive performances, while the hands were not.

In order to check the independence of the different cues the intercorrelations were calculated, see Table 3. As expected, they are all somewhat correlated with values ranging from -0.26 to 0.62. The amount of movement seems to be relatively independent since the intercorrelations with the other cues are rather small. Speed, Fluency and Distribution all show relatively medium intercorrelations.

5 Conclusions

The communication of the four intended emotions were successful, with the exception for Fear. The most successfully conveyed intention seems to be Sadness. For this intention it was also evident that the head provided important cues for correctly identifying the intention. The viewing conditions where the head was not visible (torso) got much lower ratings than did the other conditions. Possible explanations could be that there is a specific cue from the player occurring for this intention, visible in the head only, that observers have learned to recognize.

The movement ratings indicate that there was less amount of movement for Sadness and Fear than for Anger and Happiness; lower speed and more smooth and even movements for Sadness than for Happiness and Fear, which in turn had lower speed with more smooth and even movements than Anger. The movement ratings indicate that there are cues in expressive movements that bear strong resemblance to the audio cues used in expressive music performances. In music performance Sadness is typically characterized by slow tempo, low sound level and legato articulation, while Anger manifests itself through high sound level, fast tempo and abrupt sound onsets. The connection between movement speed and musical tempo seem rather obvious, but also the similarities between amount of movement and sound level, or fluency and articulation, seem clear. Further research could reveal whether these cues are the same for other performances and instruments.

Acknowledgements

The authors would like to thank Alison Eddington for the marimba performances and all persons participating as subjects in the viewing test.

This work was supported by the European Union (MEGA - Multisensory Expressive Gesture Applications, IST-1999-20410; http://www.megaproject.org/).

References

1. Wanderley, M. M., "Quantitative Analysis of Non-Obvious Performer Gestures", In Wachsmuth, I. and Sowa, T. (Eds.) Gesture and sign language in Human-Computer Interaction, Springer Verlag (2002) 241–253.

2. Davidson, J. W., Correia, J. S., "Body movement" In Parncutt, R., McPherson, G. E. (Eds.) The science and psychology of music performance. Creative strategies for teaching and learning. Oxford University Press (2002) 237–250.
3. Davidson, J. W.,"Visual perception and performance manner in the movements of solo musicians", Psychology of Music, **21** (1993) 103–113.
4. Davidson, J. W.,"What type of information is conveyed in the body movements of solo musician performers?", Journal of Human Movement Studies, **6** (1994) 279–301.
5. Clarke, E. F., Davidson, J. W., "The body in performance", In Thomas, W. (Ed.) Composition-performance-reception. Aldershot, Ashgate, (1998), 74–92.
6. Davidson, J. W., "What does the visual information contained in music performances offer the observer? Some preliminary thoughts", In Steinberg, R. (Ed.) Music and the mind machine: Psychophysiology and psychopathology of the sense of music, Heidelberg: Springer (1995) 105–114.
7. Sörgjerd, M., "Auditory and visual recognition of emotional expression in performances of music", Unpublished thesis, Uppsala University, Dep of Psychology, Uppsala Sweden (2000).
8. Gabrielsson, A., and Juslin, P. N., "Emotional expression in music performance: Between the performer's intention and the listener's experience", Psychology of Music, **24** (1996) 68–91.
9. Juslin, P. N., "Communicating emotion in music performance: A review and theoretical framework", In Music and Emotion. Oxford Unviersity Press (2001) 309–337. Journal of Experimental Psychology: Human Perception and Performance, **26(6)** (2000) 1797-1813.
10. Walk, R. D, Homan, C. P., "Emotion and dance in dynamic light displays represented in dance", Bulletin of Psychonomic Society **22** (1984) 437–440.
11. Dittrich, W. H., Troscianko, T., Lea, S. E., and Morgan, D., "Perception of emotion from dynamic point-light displays represented in dance", Perception **6** (1996) 727–738.
12. Camurri, A., Lagerlöf, I., Volpe, G., "Recognizing emotion from dance movements: Comparisons of spectator recognition and automated techniques", International Journal of Human-Computer Studies **59** (2003), 213–225.

Expressive Bowing on a Virtual String Instrument

Jean-Loup Florens

ACROE-ICA
INPG – 46 Av. Félix Viallet 38000, Grenoble - France
florens@imag.fr

Abstract. The physical model and its real-time computing with gesture feedback interfaces provide powerful means for making new playable and musically interesting instrumental synthesis process. Bowed strings models can be designed and built with these tools. Like the real bow instruments, they present a great sensitivity of the gesture dynamics. Beyond the musical interest of these synthesis process, the tuning possibilities of the gesture interface and the general context of the modular simulation system provide new means for evaluating and understanding some of the complex gesture interaction features that characterize the bowing action.

1 Introduction

The context of this work is a research program that aims generally at creating an "instrumental relation" between musicians and computer synthesis process. The main research axes are the followings:

1. The physical model formalism definition and conceptualization: based on the mass/interaction physics, the CORDIS-ANIMA system [5] provides a very general mean of designing instrument models.
2. Experimental and theoretical works on physical models, among which bowed string, reed instrument plucked string and percussion instruments [16], [9].
3. Computer architectures, specific hardware and software for interactive and real-time physical model simulation [11].
4. Force feedback devices designed for the gesture interaction [4].
5. User graphical interfaces that include modelling, compositional and analysis tools.

In the context of physical modelling, it is possible to create interactive synthesis that presents interesting gesture sensitivity in a similar way than real instruments. By gesture sensitivity of the instrument we mean that a wide range of different behaviours may be induced by a subtle or tiny variations of the gesture. This property is significant in the case of sustained-oscillation instruments and especially melodic instruments like monophonic wind instruments and bowed strings. In these instruments the sound evolution is closely linked to the gesture and even in its short time determination, it depends on the action or behaviour of the instrumentalist. It is well known that the player can radically change the timbral properties of a sustained instrument sound. However this inter-dependence between player and timbral properties has never been clearly explained so far.

A. Camurri and G. Volpe (Eds.): GW 2003, LNAI 2915, pp. 487–496, 2004.

Our general hypothesis [3], [13] is that the instrumental gesture, especially in the case of excitation gestures, must not be reduced to a simple control model, a data flow from the player to the instrument. Thus the observable gesture movements and forces are rather the consequence of the interaction between the two mechanical systems: the instrument and the hand of the player. In these conditions the instrumental gesture has to be considered as a component of a *closed loop* system.

The physical model and interactive simulation context are powerful means to investigate such systems. Firstly, whereas in the case of real instruments, even elementary measurements are not possible in playing situations, in the case of interactive simulation all the internal data of the instrument, in particular the gesture signal, may be recorded in real time.

Secondly, in order to emphasise some "hidden" components of the gesture and bring them at a perceptible level, it is possible to re-scale some parts of the virtual instrument. We principally applied this method to reveal the effect of the oscillating state of the instrument on the gesture force feedback.

Finally we point out that the conditions of the simulation lead to simplify the problem and often to exhibit the minimal model sufficient to obtain the researched property.

The objectives of the presented work are not only the analysis of the gesture interaction in a pure knowledge goal but mainly the musical synthesis by the means of new playable and "gesture sensitive" instruments families.

In the following we present a gesture sensitive virtual instrument made from a bowed string interactive physical model. In a first part are shown works related to real-time and interactive instrumental synthesis, the second and third parts describe the bowing model and the experimental set-up, while in the two last parts are presented the the experimental results and discussions on bowing gestures.

2 Related Works

Several real-time implementations of sustained sound instruments have been made since 1982 [21], [22] and [7]. They are based on wave-guide techniques, particularly efficient for real-time implementation. To our knowledge, they have never been used with a real-time gesture force feedback interaction. On the contrary, interesting works on hybrid wind instrument and hybrid bowed string instrument provide a real interactive gesture control [2], [14]. In 1985, we introduced a first real-time bowed string simulation based on the particle-interaction system we had designed. This instrument allowed a gesture control of pressure and sliding by an especially designed device [9]. The force-feedback gesture interaction was introduced later in 1990, in the same mass-interaction context with a force feedback keyboard [4]. This interactive simulation has proved that it is possible to obtain a very sensitive virtual instrument even with an elementary model [10]. Recently new bowing-dedicated devices have been designed at CCRMA [18]. They use a classical rotational servomotor combined with a capstan system.

3 Physical Modeling Context

Our physical modelling framework gathers objects into a physical system whose internal evolution law can be computed in an explicit and deterministic way. These objects can be combined thanks to their connection points that act as dual physical signal input-output pairs. The main difference compared to other physical model approaches and musical synthesis tools is at the modeling level: the user is never concerned by the data flow manipulation but only by the physical objects assembling operations. The modelling encoding and its subsequent simulation algorithmic system are founded on the inertia and interaction duality (named *particle system*).

The minimal elementary components from which a general physical model can be built are: the <MAT> element (typically the punctual inertia), and the <LIA> element or interaction element that generates the axial interaction force between the two <MAT> it is connected with. All these components are provided with adjustable constants (physical parameters) that belong to the 4 categories: inertia for the MAT, stiffness, viscosity and length for the LIA.

In addition to these basic components, special modules are created to model specific properties in a non-expensive way. One of these contains the control of the friction coefficient necessary in the bow/string model. The gesture interface may be seen as a set of specific <MAT> elements linked to the simulated objects by using the normal object composition rules. The displacement space is usually limited to one dimension in the context of sound synthesis. This situation implies that neither shape nor other geometrical properties are represented, but it allows as a counterpart an high efficiency when modelling the significant and essential dynamic properties of the instruments.

4 The Bowed String Instrument

Among the sustained-oscillation instruments model, the bowed string presents several interest: it is a completely mechanical system and its representation is easier compared to the aero-acoustical models of the usual wind instruments [12],[14]. The bow behaves like a *tool* that can be handled all along the time of a playing session. In this case the pertinent movements that have to be taken in account are deduced from the analysis of the tool/task interaction, i.e. the bow/string interaction and the number of independent axis (or degrees of freedom) of the gesture interface will never exceed 6. This is an important simplification in comparison to some direct handled instruments in which the hand/object contact is not permanent and where the instrument presents an important number of degrees of freedom at its hand interface (ex.: hand struck, membranes or other vibrating structures, keyboards…).

The left hand interaction that sets the length of the active part of the string by stopping it, cannot be identically reproduced in a virtual instrument system because it would need a non-finite degrees of freedom gesture interface. We have overcome this difficulty by introducing the principle of an intermediate object that interacts like a finger with the virtual string. In this case only a few number of degrees of freedom gesture interface is necessary.

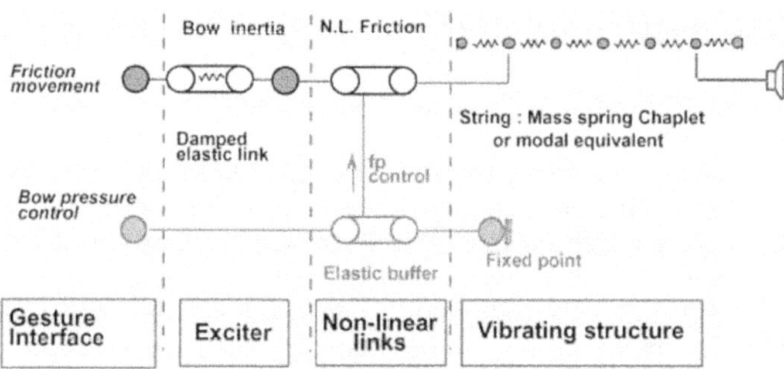

Fig. 1. The 3 mains computed parts (Exciter, NL Link and Vibrating Structure) and the Gesture interface of the virtual bowed string instrument. Sring length control by the left hand is not represented.

4.1 The Model

Using the Cordis modelling encoding the bowed string is made of 3 main elements (Fig.1): the bow module (Exciter block), the bow/string interaction (Non-linear links block) and a double string module (Vibrating structure block). In addition and apart to the computed parts of the model we will firstly consider the gesture interface whose configuration determines the gesture morphology of the instrument.

4.2 The Gesture Interface

The gesture interface provides the force feedback coupling with the virtual bow. In the minimal model, this coupling concerns only the two main minimal motions of a bow : the friction transversal motion and the pressure control. In order to bow multiple string-instrument we have used an horizontal joystick (Fig..2a). whose three axis movements in a vertical plane are coupled to the simulation.

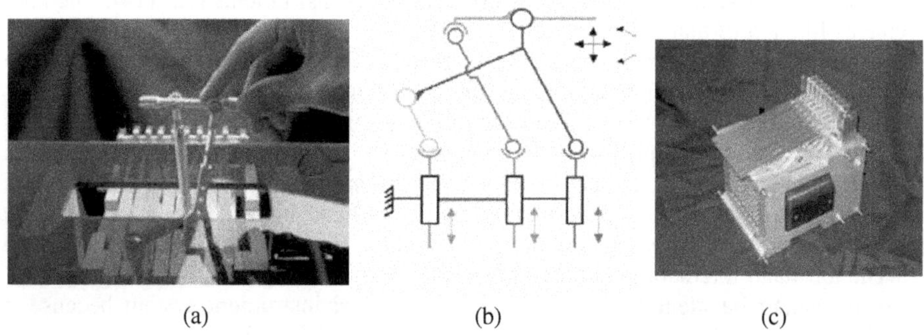

Fig. 2. The 3 degrees of freedom bowing force feedback interface (a) and its cinematic scheme (b) showing the relation between the manipulated part and the 3 parallel actuator (c) The actuator/sensor base shown without the horizontal joystick.

This device, like a real bow, combines 3 functional movements:

1) The horizontal movement that corresponds to the friction movement and that is common to both strings.
2) The vertical movement that controls the bow pressure.
3) The rotational movement (its axis is orthogonal to the 2 previous) in conjunction with the second movement allows to select the string or bow multiple strings with a balanced pressure.

Compared to real bowing we have neglected many other motion axes, in particular the ability to vary the hair width, or the distance of the bowing point from the bridge. In addition, the stick bowing differs from the usual bowing by the lower amplitude of the friction motion.

The handled device is a little aluminium stick. It is linked to the actuator and sensor system by means of a cinematic transformer that converts the 3 movements of the bowing into 3 parallel axis movements of the actuator (Fig. 2b).

The actuator and sensor system is a part of a modular tabletop system (Fig. 2c) that has been specially designed for the gesture force feedback interfaces. The same actuator can be equipped with various cinematic transformers that provide different morphological manipulators (2D or 3D joysticks, 6D ball, keyboard etc.)

The device is made of a staking of flat electro-dynamic actuators that share the same excitation magnetic circuit whose coil currents are controlled from the force signals produced by the real-time simulation. This is an iron-less structure that allows very intensive transient forces with a good linearity and wide bandwidth[1].

Each actuator coil is equipped with a high precision inductive position sensor from which the position and velocity signals are fed back to the simulation.

In this system, the mechanical frictions at low charge are minimized by the vertical orientation of the actuators axis, the weight of the moving parts being directly balanced by the active electromagnetic forces.

4.3 The Bow

The part so called "bow" is an intermediate mass between the gesture interface and the strings. It is linked on one side by a visco-elastic link to the interface and on the other side to the strings by the non-linear friction module. Because of the 1D representation, the two axis of this part that correspond to each of the two dimensions of the gesture, are made of two distinct <MAT> / <LIA> links (Fig.1). The tunable parameters of this element are:

- the stiffness and damping of the link between this inertia and the gesture interface
- the scaling parameters of the link with the force feedback gesture interface. These concern independently the two axis forces and the two axis displacements.

4.4 The Virtual Strings

The basic model of the string is a chaplet composed of 25 to 60 masses linked by visco-elastic elements. Its ends are attached to high inertia damped oscillators that

[1] Maximum Peak force: 200N. Force setup time: 0,1ms.Total displacement: 20mm.

behave as bridges. These bridges can serve as sound outputs or can be linked to other parts of the instrument.

Because of its non-harmonic natural spectrum, the discrete homogeneous chaplet produces slower attacks than a harmonic string. To overcome this difficulty we can use in place of the chaplet, its equivalent modal model. The modelling formalism CORDIS-ANIMA allows building a standard modal model as made of a set of mass-spring cells and special coupling modules that provide the strictly equivalent <MAT> points of the chaplet as described in [5] and [8]. The re-tuning in this case consists in directly adjusting these modal oscillators parameter while using the same modal deforms.

4.5 Bow-String Interaction

The specificity of the bowed string instruments is mainly due to the particular properties of the bow/string interaction: sharpness of a specific dry friction and wide sensitivity of friction effect to bow pressure.

Recent related works on bowed string synthesis take into account some hysteretis properties of dry friction [20], in the aim of getting a more accurate representation of the rosin effect.

In the present simulation we use only the memory-less model of rosin friction (Fig. 3). This minimal model is sufficient to provide the stick-slip effect and the usual behaviours of the bowed string. Within it, friction forces are linked to the sliding velocity by a non-linear function and to the pressure by a proportional law.

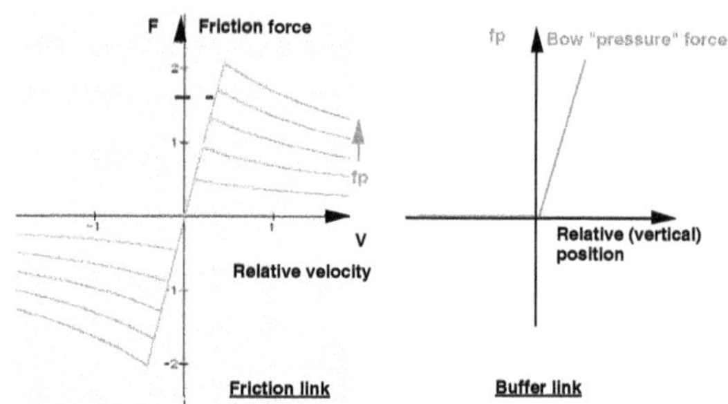

Fig. 3. The two components of the bow/string interaction module.

This model has been implemented in a special double <LIA> module, which also takes into account the bow pressure component of the interaction. In this module this bow pressure interaction model is an elastic buffer whose force is used as the control parameter of the friction part. The use of such a "quadripole" element avoids explicit signal flow manipulation being thus compatible with the physical basic formalism. One can check that this module is strictly dissipative so it can be used as an independent physical component.

4.6 The String Pitches Control and Left-Hand Play

The pitch control is based on the principle of the stopped string like on a real instrument. The pitch variation is obtained by stopping the string at a chosen point along its length. If we use a modal equivalent of the string instead of the direct finite mass spring model the stopping point position can be continuously set along the string. The stopping action is not equivalent to a simpler method that would consist in controlling physical parameters like inertia or stiffness. This last kind of control introduces non-consistent energy. On the contrary, the stopping method preserves the integrity of the string as a permanent and invariant element. This invariance is revealed, for example, by the residual oscillation of the dead part of the string, and the ability to obtain a harmonic oscillation by releasing the stopping pressure.

5 Implementation

The bowed string model has been implemented on a SGI workstation specially adapted for the physical model interactive simulation. It is equipped with specific hardware: the gesture interface system, an audio interface system, and clock generation devices.

The software environment consists in an open library of physical modules and a kernel that assumes all real-time synchronisation and communication functions. This software takes advantage of the multi-processor architecture by dedicating one processor to the system management whereas all of the others perform the real time computations in a special reserved mode [11].

The specificity of the bowed string model that are the sharpness of the non linear part and the need to provide an efficient gesture coupling have led us to use various computing rates for the different parts of the model.

6 Experimentation and Results

If we try to compare this instrument to a real one, a first observation is that the space of playing is narrower. That concerns the pitch space, the bowing space and the dynamic of the possible and pertinent bow pressure variations.

As explained, the pitch space limitation is due to the finite number of modes.

The bowing space is limited to about 15 cm because of the mechanical size of the interface that has been designed more for hand and digital manipulations than for arm and body gestures. The space of possible pressure and bow speed variations is mainly limited by the computation frequency that determines the stability limits of the string bow interaction.

However, inside the limits of this playing space the resemblance is striking, and it is possible to obtain interesting phrasing and timbre variation.

Compared to previous works on the same topics, the main improvements concern the ability to use a 'sharper' bow/string interaction model while preserving the stability of the computation. This allows higher bow pressures, wider pitch tuning area and higher string damping. In the same way the stick/slip effect is still efficient at the very low bow speeds. This is interesting to obtain realistic attacks and detached playing.

The designed model presents other interests that could not be found in real instruments: it is possible to vary the scaling factors of the gesture interface force and displacement without changing the acoustical and other properties of the strings.

Among these various changes it is possible to increase or decrease the equivalent inertia and stiffness of the string (as projected throw the gestures axis) while preserving its tuning and the size of the bowing space. The incidence of this string "re- adjusted" on the bowing gesture has been experimented: the most realistic and easy to play situation corresponds to the "light" strings that provide a tiny but non-null friction force. A quasi-null friction force provides a less interesting feeling mainly at the transitions of the bowing speed (transitions to rest state and attacks).

The "heavy" strings provide high friction force feedback with several unusual but clearly identifiable effects (Fig. 4):

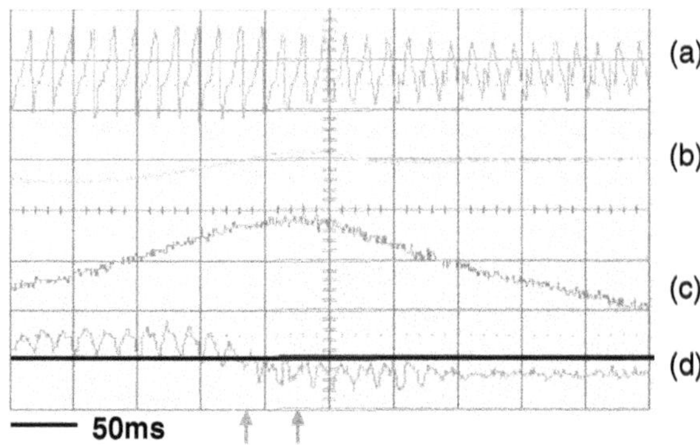

Fig. 4. String oscillation (a). Bow pressure (b). Bow position (c). Bow friction force (d). The player does back and forward movements keeping the sound continuity. A bow pulling effect can be observed: the inversion of friction force takes place 50 ms before the inversion of bow position. The (d) curve reveals also the pulsed component as a bow force feedback.

a) We can observe a low frequency force component that consists in a higher resistance at the attack if the string is bowed from its rest state. This reaction force releases as soon as the oscillation starts. If the player holds back the bow after a steady state oscillation phase he can feel the pulling effect (Fig. 4c and 4d). This observation shows that the bowing friction force may be influenced by the internal dynamic state of the string and that these effects may be perceptible.
b) Another effect if the string is tuned at a low frequency (up to 150 Hz) is that the pulsed component of the friction force is strongly driven back to the hand. This last situation exists in the case of the real bowing [1]. It shows that the hand may be closely coupled to the vibrating system as it does in some hand percussion instruments.
c) In the case of very heavy strings or if the oscillation is constrained, we can observe an oscillation at the equivalent bow mass level that can be transmitted to the hand itself if the hand is released as a kind of "chalk on the blackboard" effect. This oscillation may coexist with the oscillation of the string, and if the bow pressure is correctly adjusted, it produces a high frequency amplitude modulation of the sound.

Some of these phenomena point out clearly the perceived effects from the traditional bowed string instruments and their importance for the sound control. Other effects, non-perceptible but crucial on the traditional instruments can be pointed out and measured. A third category of effects includes the new ones, non-relevant on the traditional instruments can provide the appearance of new play techniques in the instrumental synthesis field.

It is interesting to notice that these different phenomena constitute a first base for the qualification of the instrument feedback effect and, consequently, for the different types of gesture actions that appear from these properties.

Indeed we can distinguish:

1) The low frequency effect where the instrument feedback induces a constraint against the global gesture movement - a) case- that affects the slow shape of the sound. In this case the player may interact and compose with this constraint in an active manner, for example at the attacks control or when he has to invert the sense of bowing.
2) The high frequency effects where the hand of the player is coupled to some of the audio frequency oscillating parts of the instrument. The player may only interact at a passive level (for instance by varying his finger or hand stiffness) to induce some timbral variations.
3) The mean frequency effects where the hand of the player constitutes with some parts of the instrument a sub-audio but fast oscillator. It also affects the shape of the sound but the player can only control the phenomenon at a passive level (by varying his finger equivalent stiffness or inertia.

7 Conclusion

This model and its interactive implementation allow many investigations concerning bowed string sound synthesis and the bowing gesture. Its high efficiency enlarges the field of possible complexity and higher pitch frequencies for the real time interactive simulations.

The high bandwidth of the gesture interface channels has provided in the case of force feedback coupling a more precise and sensitive interaction between the instrumentalist's hand and the vibrating string. This is interesting in the case of live synthesis but also for the musical studio creation in which one may use either sequences of real playing or artificial gesture composition.

It also provides a powerful experimentation tool on the instrumental gesture that concerns especially the high bandwidth coupling. Indeed, thanks to ability to tune the gesture coupling scale factors, some interesting tenuous effects can be revealed and enhanced. All these results open a new way in for the musical creation and technical research in the context of virtual instruments.

References

1. Askenfelt, A., Jansson, E.V. :1992 " On Vibration Sensation and Finger Touch in Stringed Instrument Playing", Music Perception, Spring 1992, Vol 9, N°3 pp. 311-350
2. Boutillon, X., Guerard, J. : 1995"Hybrid Synthesis ", International Symposium on Musical Acoustics Proc., Société Francaise d'Acoustique, Paris, pp. 439-445.

3. Cadoz, C. : 1994 "Le geste canal de communication homme-machine. La communication instrumentale", Science Informatiques, Numéro spécial IHM, 1994, pp 31-61.
4. Cadoz, C., Lisowski, L., Florens, J.L : 1990 "Modular Feedback Keyboard", Computer Music Journal, MIT Press, Vol. 14, N°2, 1990.
5. Cadoz, C., Luciani, A., Florens, J.L. : 1993 "CORDIS-ANIMA : a Modeling and Simulation System for Sound and Image Synthesis - The General Formalism", Computer Music Journal, MIT press, Vol 17-1, spring 1993.
6. Caussé, R. : 1992 "Mise au point des archets numériques. Utilisation pour l'étude de la corde frottée", Thèse d'Etat, Université du Maine, 1992.
7. Cook, P. : 1992 "A meta-wind-instrument physical model", International Computer Music Proc., Conference, San Jose, 1992, pp. 273-276.
8. Djoharian, P. : 1993 "Modèles pour la synthèse modale", Colloque International sur les Modèles Physiques, Grenoble, Septembre 1990, Ed. Maison des Sciences de l'Homme, Paris, 1993.
9. Florens, J.L., Cadoz C., Luciani, A. 1986 "Optimized Real Time simulation of objects for music synthesis and animated images synthesis "International Music Conference Proc., International Computer Music Association., pp. 65-70.
10. Florens, J.L., Cadoz, C. : 1990 "Modèle et simulation en temps réel de corde frottée",1er Congrès Français d'Acoustique, Editions de Physique Paris 1990, C2-1990, pp C2-873-876.
11. Florens, J.L. :1998 "A real-Time Workstation for Physical model of multi-sensorial and gesturally controlled instrument", Proceedings of ICMC98., ICMA San Frnacisco 1998 pp. 518-26.
12. Florens, J.L., Germond, J. : 1999 "Reed Instruments modular representation and their interactive real time simulations " , Proceedings of ICMC99., ICMA San Francisco 1999 pp. 291-294.
13. Gibet, S. : 1987 "Codage, représentation et traitement du geste instrumental", Thèse INPG, INPG Grenoble, 1987.
14. Guerard, J. : 1998 "Modélisation et Simulation expérimentale de systèmes acoustiques. Application aux instruments de musique." Thèse de doctorat, Université de Paris VI, 1998.
15. Incerti, E. : 1996 "Synthesis and Analysis tools with Physical Modelling: An Environment for Musical Sounds Production", International Computer Music Conference 1996.
16. Incerti, E. : 1996 "Synthèse de sons par modélisation physique de structures vibrantes. Application à la creation musicale par ordinateur". Thèse INPG Grenoble 1996.
17. McIntyre, Schumacher, Woodhouse : 1981 " Aperiodicity in bowed string motion " Acustica, Vol. 49 (1981) pp. 13 –32.
18. Nichols, C. : 2002 "The vBow : A Four Degrees of Freedom Haptic Musical Controller Human-Computer Interface", ICMC 2002 Proc., pp. 522-5525, ICMA San Francisco, 2002
19. Ramstein, C. : 1991 "Analyse, représentation et traitement du geste instrumental", Thèse INPG spec Informatique, Grenoble 1991.
20. Serafin, S.,Vergez, C., Rodet, X. : 1999 "Friction And Application to Real-time Physical Modeling of a Violin", ICMC 99 Proc., International Computer Music Association, pp. 216-219.
21. Smith, J.O. : 1986 " Efficient Simulation of the Reed-Bore and Bow-String Mechanisms" International Music Conference Proc., International Computer Music Association, pp.275-280.
22. Smith, J.O. : 1982 "Synthesis of bowed strings", International Music Conference Proc., International Computer Music Association.
23. Wanderley : 1999 "Non-Obvious Performer Gestures in Instrumental Music", In Gesture-Based Communication in Human-Computer interaction. International Gesture Workshop, GW'99 Proc., Springer 1999.

Recognition of Musical Gestures in Known Pieces and in Improvisations

Damien Cirotteau, Giovanni De Poli, Luca Mion, Alvise Vidolin, and Patrick Zanon

CSC - DEI, University of Padua
Via Gradenigo 6/a, 35131 Padova, Italy
cirotteau@csc.unipd.it
{depoli,randy,vidolin,patrick}@dei.unipd.it
http://www.dei.unipd.it/ricerca/csc/

Abstract. Understanding the content in musical gestures is an ambitious issue in scientific environment. Several studies demonstrated how different expressive intentions can be conveyed by a musical performance and correctly recognized by the listeners: several models for the synthesis can also be found in the literature. In this paper we draw an overview of the studies which have been done at the Center of Computational Sonology (CSC) during the last year on automatic recognition of musical gestures. These studies can be grouped in two main branches: analysis with the score knowledge and analysis without. A brief description of the implementations and validations is presented.

Keywords: Gestural communication; Gestural perception and production; Analysis, Segmentation and Synthesis of Gestures.

1 Introduction

Traditionally, gestures have been intended as body movements that convey some kind of information [1]. This information can refer both to real world objects, and/or to the affective/emotional domain. We are interested on the latter case mainly, but with a generalization: a huge amount of theoretical and empirical works try to draw an explicit relation between physical motion and music [2]. Humanistic theories, which refer to the role that gestures have in communicating expressiveness [3], tried to extend the definition of gesture to include the "musical gestures", which are supposed to share the same kind of rules or spatial/temporal patterns to convey the expressive information [4]. For example, in [5] investigations have been made to find out if there is a common pattern among final ritard timing patterns and stopping runner timing patterns. In [6] there is no explicit relation with the locomotion, but expressive timing patterns were analyzed to investigate their relation with phrase boundaries. Thus, musical gestures as to be intended as another communication channel of affective or emotional content, that the artists can use to communicate their intentions. In fact, it has been proven that music can be a communication mean between

A. Camurri and G. Volpe (Eds.): GW 2003, LNAI 2915, pp. 497–508, 2004.

performer and listener [7]. There is a plethora of ways in which this could happen. Musicians can use the melody or the harmony to this aim, but there is something else too. Even in the case of a given piece, the performer can convey his emotions using other strategies. Tensions are not only related to melody and harmony, but they can also be enhanced or decreased by interacting with the structure of the piece, by stretching the timing or modifying the intensity in "sensible" positions [8]. There is indeed a general agreement among performers and audience on this kind of communication [9]. Thus, several models for the synthesis of expressive performances have been proposed [10] [11]. These models were developed on the basis of deep analyzes of the musical material, while the automatic analysis of expressive performances is quite recent [12] [13]. Using automation such as Markov Chains and Hidden Markov Models (HMM) yielded to another research stream. Their use in music is quite old: the main application field was the automatic music generation. Xenakis was a pioneer in the use of Markov chains. He used them to calculate clouds of sounds in *Analogiques* A (1958) or glissandi in *Syrmos* (1959) [14]. Interesting automatons based on Markov chains were created by Barbaud to generate tonal music [15]. On the analysis side, different kinds of experiments were realized with HMMs. Depalle and al. in [16] presented a sinusoidal partial tracking method for additive synthesis of sound, done by a purely combinatorial HMM. An important work on machine learning musical style recognition has been done by Dannenberg et al. in [17]. They showed that high-level understanding of musical performance, like style recognition, is highly beneficial from a machine learning approach.

In this paper we deal with the automatic expressive analysis tools for musical performances developed at CSC in the last year and with collaboration with the Austrian Research Institute for Artificial Intelligence (ÖFAI) on machine learning techniques for automatic performer recognition. These methods can be grouped in two main branches: in the first the score knowledge is required, and in the second the analysis has been intended on musical improvisations. The paper is organized as follow: in the next section a brief description of the methods used is presented. Its first subsection is devoted to recall previous results that were used in the present work. In the second subsection the data used in the experiments is briefly described. The third section describes the analysis method that requires the score knowledge, and in the following section we describe how we overcame to this limitation. The fifth section is devoted to some validation and results.

2 Analysis Methodology

In our studies we used two approaches for the analysis: the analysis by measurements and the analysis by synthesis. The former helped us to clarify some basic strategies used by musicians in order to communicate their expressiveness. This allowed implementing a model for the synthesis. In this way it was possible both to test the reliability of what we learned, and also to take the first steps towards the automatic analysis. In fact, the perceptual tests on the expressive synthetic performances allowed to refine the synthesis model and to identify the relationships between the sonologic parameters and some of the expressive labels we used. Thus, it was possible to implement an application able to analyze musical performances essentially based on the synthesis model.These methods were applied on well-known western classical pieces. In order to verify this hypothesis, we conducted another experiment on improvisations by both some pianists and non-musicians in order to infer an analysis model able to work without the score knowledge. Then we tested the model on the data available.

2.1 Previous Works and Collaboration

The analysis models we realized are based on two previous studies that were carried out at CSC [21]. In the first a synthesis model turned out, and in the second several analyzes were carried out on a set of musical improvisations. The synthesis model was described in [10] and it can synthesize an expressive performance by transforming a *neutral* one (i.e. a literal human performance of the score without any expressive intention or stylistic choice), referencing to a given score. The transformation is carried out taking into account how listeners organize expressive performances in their mind (see figure 1). By the perceptual test, a "Perceptual Parametric Space" (PPS) was obtained, in which the expressive labels were placed. It was found that the two axis of the space are closely related to physical acoustic quantities, respectively the *kinetics* (tempo and legato values) of the music (bright vs. dark), and the *energy* (loudness) of the sound (soft vs. hard). Thus, the micro deviations of acoustic quantities are computed by transforming those that are already present in the neutral performance. The transformations are applied to the various acoustic quantities (tempo, legato, and intensity) by means of two sets of coefficients named *K-coefficients* and *M-coefficients* : a K-coefficient changes the average values of an acoustic quantity, and the respective M-coefficient is used to scale the deviations of the actual values of the same parameter from the average. In this way, each expressive intention can be represented by a set of 6 parameters and the continuous morphing of expressive performances in the PPS can be realized by changing of the set of K and M-coefficients. The analysis of musical gestures can take advantage from a collaboration with the ÖFAI, in which machine learning techniques were used to answer the question whether a computer can learn to identify famous performers (pianists) based on their style of playing. Musical improvisations were investigated at CSC: in a previous work [18], piano improvisations by different performers were recorded and analyzed; performances were inspired by a set of adjectives and the analysis yielded several hypotheses on adjectives' character, validated by human judgment on a perceptual test and on a factor analysis. The results incited us to investigate on improvisations' feature, and we carried out further analysis in order to discover how to build a Bayesian network for the automatic recognition of performers' expressive intentions.

2.2 The Data Used in the Experiments

In our experiments two sets of data were used. For the analysis with the score knowledge, we used several interpretations of the "Sonata in C major" K.545

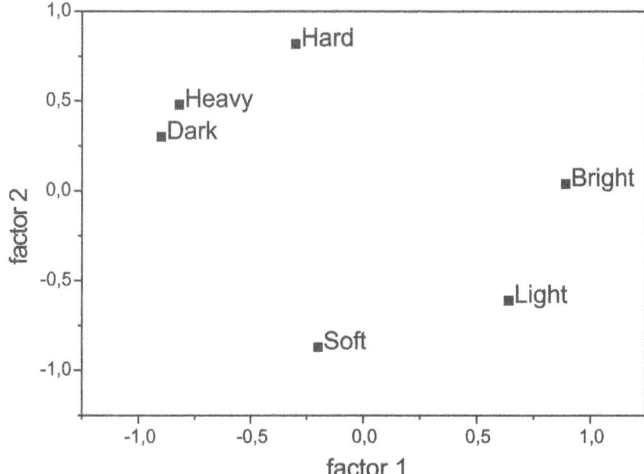

Fig. 1. "Perceptual Parametric Space" (PPS) obtained by data analysis performed on perceptual test. The first factor (75.2%) is related to the kinetics of music (tempo and legato); the second factor is related to the energy of the sound (loudness).

by W.A. Mozart. Four pianists were invited to play according to 5 expressive intentions: natural, hard, soft, heavy and light. In the case of the improvisation we used a set of piano improvisations. Six performers were invited to improvise on a digital piano according to eight expressive intentions suggested by means of groups of adjectives. The eight groups are: 1. (SLA) slashing, impetuous, resolute; 2. (HEA) Heavy, Hard, Rigid; 3. (HOP) Hopping, Galloping, Springing; 4. (VAC) Vacuous, Hesitant, Tired; 5. (BOL) Bold, Torrential, Unbridled; 6. (HOL) Hollow, Solemn, Obscure; 7. (FLU) Fluid, Fluent, Fleetly; 8. (TEN) Tender, Sweet, Simple. Performers could choose a note but they could not play any melody (i.e. they had to improvise without changing the pitch). The experiment had been planned in four phases, in order to progressively limit the musical means available to the performer.

3 Analysis Using the Score Knowledge

We made the implementation of the analysis model using EyesWeb, a product of the Music and Informatics Lab of the University of Genoa [19]. It turned out to be a graphical environment planned for the processing of multimedia data streams and the creation of audio/video interactive applications. In our work we developed a number of new blocks that implement dedicated functions and we connected them in a patch for the real time analysis of a performance. Figure 2 shows the patch that analyzes the pieces using the score knowledge (Expressive Analyzer). The system can be divided into three different parts: the *Neutral Analyzer*, the *Real Time Analyzer* and the *Expressiveness Recognizer*. The Neutral Analyzer sub-patch is the set of modules located in the upper left rectangle of the patch in figure 2. It is dedicated to the computation of the profiles of the sonologic parameters (tempo, articulation and intensity) related to the neutral performance. The Real Time Analyzer sub-patch is the set of modules that lies below the Neutral Analyzer. This block achieves the same computations to those accomplished by the previous sub-patch. The computations of the expressive quantities tempo, legato and key velocity, are in this case relative to each sound event of the expressive performance that is received as a real time stream of MIDI events. No average is computed in this case. The final sub-patch, on the right of the picture, is the Expressiveness Recognizer. It performs two separate tasks: the computation of the K and M-coefficients and the expressive labelling. A lot of time was also spent tuning the system and the values were then corrected by hand in order to increase the accuracy of the analysis.

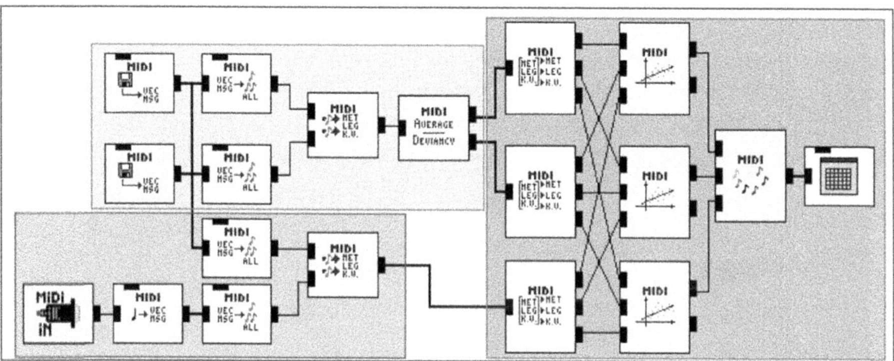

Fig. 2. The three parts composing the Expressive Analyzer: the Neutral Analyzer, the Real Time Analyzer and the Expressiveness Recognizer.

4 Analysis without the Score Knowledge

To overcome the limitation imposed by the knowledge of the score, a simple patch developed with EyesWeb was developed, using some results of the previous study [8] on the main relevant sonologic parameters. The patch tries to label in real time the expressive content of an expressive improvisation using simple statistical analysis of the relevant perceptual sonologic parameters (notes per second, loudness and legato). For example, one of the rules is the following:

```
If KeyVelocity > 85 and
   Legato > 0.7 and
   NotePerSecond < 3 then Heavy
```

It should be noted that the pitch was not taken into account and the threshold values were tuned by hand on the basis of some improvisations played by the Ing. Antonio Rod‘a (a researcher of the CSC). This simple but quite robust work suggested to us to use more sophisticated statistical techniques in order to analyze real time improvisations. A set of improvisations were then recorded and analyzed to infer both a Bayesian network and a set of HMMs able to give as output the probability that the input performance is played according to an expressive intention.

4.1 Bayesian Analyzer

The general structure of the patch that realizes the Bayesian networks is shown in figure 3. The design of this structure comes from the preliminary analysis of a set of piano improvisations [18]. Six performances were available, but we chose only the Basilicati's ones based on his higher bent to interpretation. We made a perceptual test, mean values' analysis, a factor analysis on expressive profiles and a note-by-note analysis. In the perceptual test, we asked listeners to describe qualitatively the expressive content of the improvisations. The analysis had the purpose of understanding how similar or different the expressive performances were perceived by listeners and to determine in how many dimensions listeners discriminate the performances. Extracted factors have been associated to the sonologic parameters that better explain each dimension. These parameters

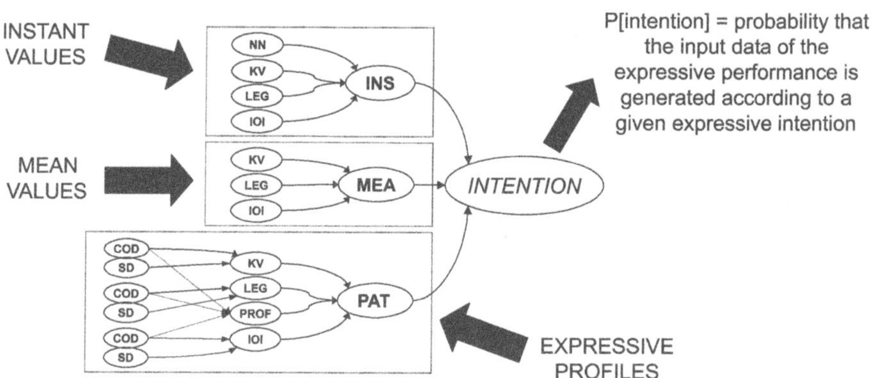

Fig. 3. The Bayesian network structure. It's possible to see the three main categories of cues used (in the dotted rectangles): the instant values, the mean values, and the pattern. Marginal nodes (on the left) are inferred firstly. Each node conditions its descendant nodes until node intention, which value is the probability that input performance is played with a given expressive intention.

were respectively: Pitch (P), Note Number (NN), Key Velocity (KV), Legato (LEG) and Inter Onset Interval (IOI). In the case of the phase 1, we obtained 2 significant factors (see figure 4). The linear combination of these two factors yields a bi-dimensional space where each axis represents a factor. For example, along the horizontal axis, the Fluid, Hopping, and Bold intentions show the lowest scores, while the Heavy and Hollow intentions show the highest values. Considering that the Fluid intention was played with a fast tempo, and that the

Hollow was played with a slow tempo, we can reasonably associate this axis to tempo parameter. The same reasoning has to be done for the other axis regarding the intensity parameter. Then, the mean values' analysis and the ANOVA test revealed which intentions show highest and lowest significance of the parameters. On the basis of a previous work [6], we made a factor analysis on expressive pro-

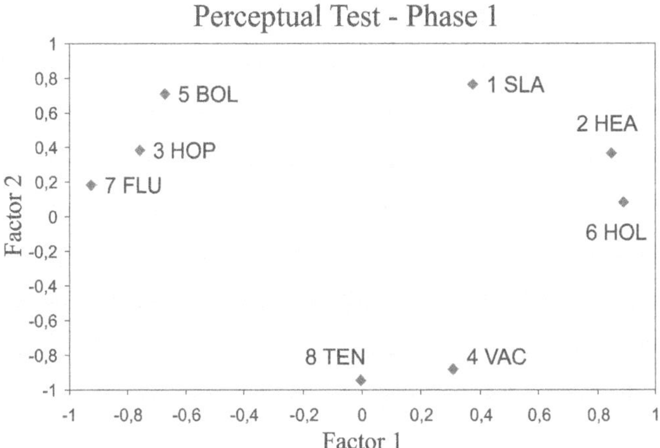

Fig. 4. Factor analysis on perceptual test on phase 1. Factor 1 opposes performances 3, 5 and 7, on one extremity, with performances 2 and 6 on the other, clearly indicating a style characterized by the Tempo parameter (fast performances 3, 5 and 7, vs. slow ones 2 and 6). Factor 2 opposes performances 1 and 5 with performances 4 and 8, defining a style characterized by the Intensity parameter (high volume of performances 1 and 5, vs. low volume of per. 4 and 8).

files for each of the parameters. This analysis determined in how many directions the musician discriminates the performances in terms of patterns of a particular sonologic parameter. Finally, a note-by-note analysis showed the presence of several relationships among the parameters' profiles. For example, in the case of the hopping performance, this analysis revealed that the intensity and the articulation profiles are closely proportional. On the basis of the previous analysis, we organized the topology of the Bayesian Networks (see figure 3), and each of them is intended to recognize a given expressive intention. In the upper side of each network, the sonologic parameters (Pitch, KV, LEG and IOI) are evaluated by their instant values. In the second part, mean values are taken into account while the third part is devoted to evaluating if the input data contains some relevant patterns which can be used to recognize the intention. By probability distributions which rule the inner probabilities we can achieve the probability of node INTENTION; one can compute the final probability as follows:

$$P[intention] = \sum_{cue} P[intention|cue]P[cue] \tag{1}$$

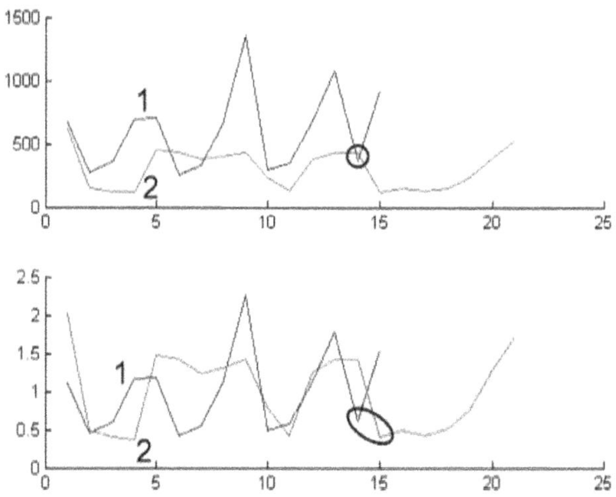

Fig. 5. Comparison of the IOI of two improvisations from the slashing intention. The first graph represents the absolute values, and the second one represents the values relative to the average. We notice that in the first case a long IOI of the profile 2 is aggregated with a short IOI of the profile 1. In the second case two relatively short IOI are merged in the same state.

4.2 Hidden Markov Model Approach

In [17], machine learning musical style recognition has been done. However, the authors concentrated on only one performer. Our study intends to model the expressive intentions of different pianists. We want to answer the question whether improvisations from different performers expressing a similar intention share a common structure. Previous work [18] shows a good consistence in the set of improvisations. Each of the eight intentions was modelled by a single HMM with few states (typically 8) and continuous output with Gaussian distribution. Then data is classified according those different models. Experiments with absolute data show us that two IOIs from different improvisations can be confused and aggregated into the same state, leading to wrong context evaluation (see figure 5), especially for improvisations with very different tempi. As shown in the figure a relatively short IOI in a low tempo improvisation is considered similar to a relatively long IOI in an high tempo improvisation, although their meaning is very different in their own context. As a solution for this issue, relative data have been used (all data is scaled by the mean of the IOIs).

5 Validation

5.1 Expressive Analyzer

The model has been tuned and tested with the 16 expressive performances introduced in section 1.2 (neutral performances were excluded). After the tuning

Table 1. Percentage of correct classified notes for each piece and performer. The performances with less than 50% of correct classification are underlined.

Intention	Pianist A	Pianist B	Pianist C	Pianist D
Light	52%	45%	75%	29%
Hard	54%	43%	33%	45%
Heavy	69%	78%	27%	86%
Soft	53%	61%	68%	89%

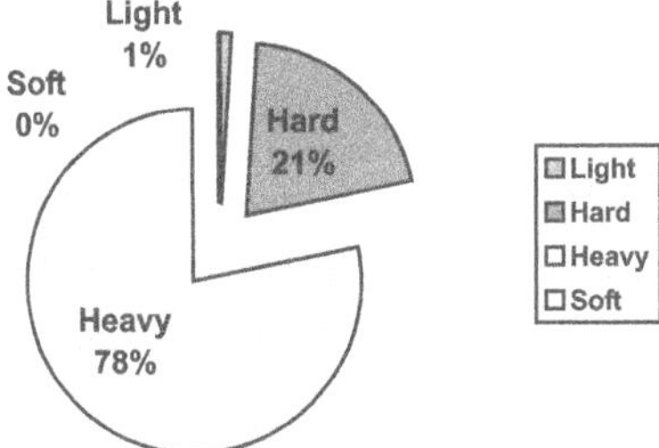

Fig. 6. Recognition graph for the heavy performance played by the pianist B. 78% of the event is correctly recognized.

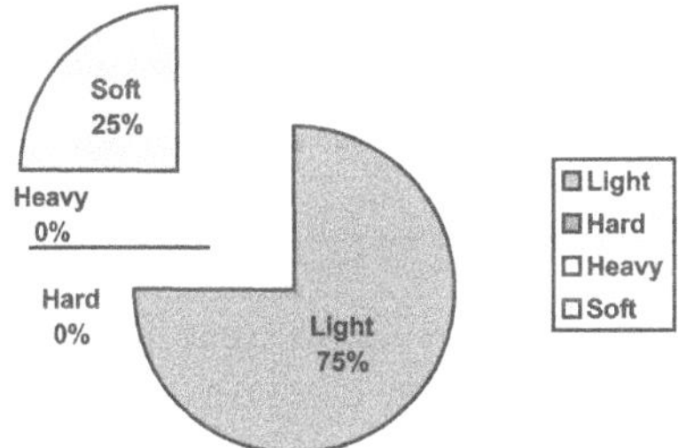

Fig. 7. Recognition graph for the light performance played by the pianist C. 75% of the event is correctly recognized.

process, the system was tested and the results are presented in table 1. The table shows the percentage of correct classified notes for each piece and performer. The performances with less than 50% of correct classification are underlined.

The results were in general quite good, even if there is a certain degree of misunderstanding for some pianists (C and D) and for some expressive intentions (Light and Hard). For the pianists B and C, a more detailed insight is given in figure 6 and figure 7. In the first one, it is possible to see that the recognition of the Heavy performance is very good, even if there is a number of notes that were classified as Hard. In the second figure, the confusion was made among Light and Soft performances.

5.2 Bayesian Analyzer

Each network was tested with the whole set of Basilicati's performances. Table 2 shows the results. The computation has been carried out by a Matlab Toolbox for Bayesian Networks [20], which yields the probability of node intention after having properly assigned both the conditional probabilities of inner nodes and the rules for the marginal ones. As shown, most of the networks give higher probability (gray cells) when they are subjected to the data used for their training. Hollow and Fluid networks give the highest value of probability to the corresponding performances; Vacuous and Tender networks confuse the input data, giving higher probability to other intentions (circled cells). We noticed that intentions confused in perceptual test (as mean and factor analysis revealed) caused difficulties in assigning decision rules in their networks; thus, those intentions are recognized with difficulty. For example, we can see that Vacuous and Tender networks give low reliability to their recognitions indeed. This is an interesting result: it underlines that these Bayesian networks' behavior is similar to human perception.

Table 2. Mean probabilities given by Bayesian networks using the eight performances as input: the cell (x, y) contains the mean P value given by network x subjected to performance y; the values on the diagonal represents the mean values given by networks subjected to the performances they were trained with.

Networks \ Input Data	SLA	HEA	HOP	VAC	BOL	HOL	FLU	TEN
SLA	0,70	0,46	0,64	0,49	0,54	0,35	0,52	0,48
HEA	0,36	0,77	0,21	0,25	0,34	0,13	0,21	0,28
HOP	0,68	0,76	0,77	0,48	0,67	0,50	0,72	0,67
VAC	0,34	0,20	0,27	0,41	0,21	0,48	0,40	0,54
BOL	0,63	0,52	0,58	0,08	0,69	0,39	0,61	0,31
HOL	0,35	0,48	0,25	0,69	0,36	0,89	0,29	0,25
FLU	0,59	0,39	0,58	0,42	0,57	0,49	0,83	0,59
TEN	0,44	0,49	0,37	0,26	0,40	0,29	0,56	0,52

5.3 Hidden Markov Model Approach

As for the Bayesian Analyzer, computations as been carried out with the Bayesian Network Toolbox for Matlab. Good results have been obtained when data to be classified is part of the training set. The right intention is recognized in almost every case especially for professional pianists. New models with all but one improvisations have been constructed to know if the HMM was modelling a group of casual improvisations or, as we want, a particular intention. We measured the performances of the models by cross validation: models were trained with 5 of the 6 pianists and then the remaining one was classified. Results give us a casual classification with a relatively equal probability for all the models in both absolute and relative data case. For all the intentions, only one or two improvisations are correctly classified and the probability is not significantly higher for the correct intention than for the other ones.

6 Conclusions

An overview of three expressive analysis methods was presented. The methods present a satisfactory behavior if used with a suitable tuning of the parameters. Further improvements of the models are necessary. In the case of score knowledge, a more detailed insight of the results has to be done, in order to underline where the system fails and why. For the Bayesian network approach, further works are necessary to find other intentions' features in terms of pattern and relations between the parameters' profiles, which showed to be a very important aspect. The HMM approach taken alone revealed that direct modelling fails to recognize correctly a given intention when tested on material not used for training. Once those "expressive" patterns are extracted, perceptual tests have to be conducted in order to map accurately a given expression with a set of patterns.

Acknowledgements

This research was supported by the EC project IST-1999-20410 MEGA and by the EC project HPRN-CT-2000-00115 MOSART.

References

1. Wanderley, M., Battier, M.:Trends in Gestural Control of Music (Edition électronique). IRCAM, Paris (2000).
2. Shove, P., Repp, B.: Musical motion and performance: Theoretical and empirical perspectives. In J. Rink (Ed.), The practice of performance. Cambridge, U.K.: Cambridge University Press (1995), 55-83.
3. Coker, W.:Music and Meaning: A theoretical Introduction to Musical Aesthetics. The Free Press, New York (1972).
4. Camurri, A., De Poli, G., Leman, M., Volpe, G.: A Multi-layered Conceptual Framework for Expressive Gesture Applications. Proceedings of the MOSART Workshop on Current Research Directions in Computer Music, Barcelona (2001), 29-34.
5. Friberg, A., Sundberg, J.: Does music performance allude to locomotion? A model of final ritardandi derived from measurements of stopping runners. J. Acoust. Soc. Amer., vol. 105, no. 3 (1999), 1469-1484.
6. Repp, B.: Patterns of expressive timing in performances of a Beethoven minuet by nineteen pianists. Journal of Acoustical Society of America 88(2), (1990), 622-641.
7. P. N. Juslin: Communicating emotion in music performance: a review and theoretical framework, in P. N. Juslin & J. A. Sloboda (ed), Music and emotion. Theory and research, Oxford University Press (2001), 279-309.

8. De Poli, G., Rodà, A., Vidolin, A.: Note-by-note Analysis of the Influence of Expressive Intentions and Musical Structure in Violin Performance. Journal of New Music Research 27(3), (1998), 293-321.
9. Canazza, S., De Poli, G., Rodà, A., Vidolin, A.: An abstract control space for communication of sensory expressive intentions in music performance, Journal of the New Music Research (2002) (accepted for publication).
10. Canazza, S., De Poli, G., Drioli, C., Rodà, A., Vidolin, A.: Audio Morphing Different Expressive Intentions for Multimedia Systems IEEE Multimedia 7(3), (2000), 79-83.
11. Friberg, A., Frydén, L., Bodin, L., Sundberg, J.: Performance Rules for Computer-Controlled Contemporary Keyboard Music. Computer Music Journal 15(2), (1991), 49-55.
12. Canazza, S., De Poli, G., Rodà, A., Soleni, G. Zanon, P.: Real time analysis of expressive contents in piano performances, Proc. International Computer Music Conference, Göteborg (2002), 414-418.
13. Friberg, A., Schoonderwaldt, E., Juslin, P., Bresin, R.: Automatic Real-Time Extraction of Musical Expression, Proc. International Computer Music Conference, Göteborg (2002), 365-367.
14. Chemillier, M.: Générateurs musicaux et singularités. Proceedings of the JIM 99 Journées d'Informatique Musicale (1999), CNET-CEMAMu, Issy-les-Moulineaux, 167-177.
15. Chemillier, M.: Grammaires, automates et musique. J-P. Briot, F. Pachet (ed.), Informatique musicale, Traité IC2, Hermès, Paris (2002).
16. Depalle, Ph., Garcia, G., Rodet, X.: Tracking of partials for additive sound synthesis using Hidden Markov Models. Proceedings of the IEEE-ICASSP, Mineapolis (1993), 225-228.
17. Dannenberg, R., Thom, B., Watson, D.: A Machine Learning Approach to Musical Style Recognition, in Proceedings of the International Computer Music Conference, San Francisco (1997), 344-347.
18. Bonini, F., Rodà, A.: Expressive content analysis of musical gesture: an experiment on piano improvisation. Workshop on Current Research Directions in Computer Music, Barcelona (2001).
19. Camurri, A., Coletta, P., Peri, M., Ricchetti, M., Ricci, A., Trocca, R., Volpe, G.: A real-time platform for interactive performance, Proc. ICMC-2000, Berlin (2000), 374-379.
20. Murphy, K.: The Bayes Net Toolbox for Matlab, in Computing Science and Staistics (2001), vol. 33.
21. CSC's home page: http://www.dei.unipd.it/ricerca/csc/

Design and Use of Some New Digital Musical Instruments

Daniel Arfib, Jean-Michel Couturier, and Loïc Kessous

LMA-CNRS
31, chemin Joseph Aiguier, 13402 Marseille Cedex 20
{arfib,couturier,kessous}@lma.cnrs-mrs.fr

Abstract. This article presents some facts about the use of gesture in computer music, more specifically in home made instruments dedicated to performance on stage. We first give some theoretical and practical ideas to design an instrument, in the following areas: the sound, the gesture and the mapping. Then, we introduce three examples of digital instruments we have created, focusing on their design and their musical use.

1 Introduction

Creating a digital musical instrument is complex and some skills and methods can help the designer. During our research project about creative gesture in computer music, we have designed some particular instruments, now largely described elsewhere [2] [3] [4] [12] [13] [17]; this article introduces our global approach to design digital musical instruments.

In a first section, we describe our way "from sound to gesture" by giving some theoretical and practical ideas to design an instrument in the sound, the gesture and the mapping areas. In a second section, we describe the design and the use of three digital instruments we have created, the "Voicer", the Scanned Synthesis Synthesizer, and the Photosonic Emulator.

2 Theoretical and Practical Ideas to Design an Instrument

2.1 Ingredients for Sound Space Exploration

To create a digital musical instrument, two different options are possible; the first one is to conceive the instrument from gesture to sound, in other words to sonify a gesture, or a gestural fact. Concerning the second option, creative people such as composers usually start from the algorithms, explore their possibilities, imagine their expressive language and associated gestures, and only after choose the adequate peripherals. The definition of a sonic space and its exploration is equivalent to build an "inverse chain": the creative imagination of sound induces the determination of the instrumental play, and so induces adapted gesture and peripherals that support them. We try to be close to this idea.

A. Camurri and G. Volpe (Eds.): GW 2003, LNAI 2915, pp. 509–518, 2004.

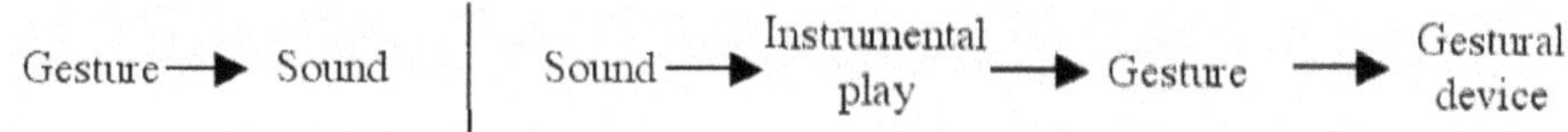

Fig. 1. Regular (on the left) and inverse (on the right) chain between gesture and sound.

Gesture can intervene at different levels. At the global composition level, gesture drives the "macroform", the global structure of a piece; at the sequence level, the sequences of notes are driven by gesture; at the 'notes' level, decision or selection gestures trigger events (abrupt changes in parameters); at the 'curves' level: modulation gesture drive curves (microforms) which are related to sound parameters; at the microscopic level, timbre is controlled by statistic or stochastic processes of micro events; finally, at the quantum level, clicks or dirac impulses are directly controlled. Our choice is to work at the level of notes and curves. This way is in continuity with a long work on synthesis models that use curves and triggering events. On the other hand, our work on gesture has led us to define selection, decision and modulation gestures, a natural way to control such events and curves.

Finally, design choices depend upon three elements: sound, gesture, instrumental play, which respectively correspond to the synthesis methods, the choice of peripherals and the type of mapping. The choice of a synthesis method or a digital audio effect is crucial in the design because it indicates the gesture metaphors. Gestural devices imply an ergonomic dimension that conditions the gesture. The choice of a mapping is the key point to obtain a musical instrument that one can learn and play: it transforms the information of the gestural device to the synthesis parameters but moreover it gives some coherence in the link between what we hear and what we do.

2.2 About Sound

2.2.1 Definition of a Sonic Domain

In this path from sound to gesture, the first question is: what type of sound or what type of music does one want to play; what are the limits one imposes? These decisions will lead to the choice of a synthesis method and give an idea of the type of sensors that can do what is needed or not.

Sounds can be classified according to their means of producing, but also according to the impact they have on perception [24]. These sound typologies are often dichotic, and it is very interesting to put a name on what kind of sounds/music we want in terms of these typologies. As a matter of example, the separation between harmonic/inharmonic sounds is natural and a musical choice must rely on such categories. However, such a division is only a subclass of the noisy/timbral dichotomy, on the right side of this branch.

The determination of how the sound evolution will be treated is a matter of choice and complementarity. If the playing style is melodic, pitch must be in some way a part of the focus of the instrument with its different ways to control it (continuous or not). If sound timbre is the main focus, one must find the way to describe the expressiveness that one require and how it can be brought out.

2.2.2 Synthesis Methods

Synthetic sounds have fascinated the pioneers of computer music, who tended to find sounds that could sound atypical but quite musical. A good source to discover the computer music sounds are books such as the Csound book [6] or Miranda's inspiring one [22], records such as the Wergo series (including JC Risset's catalog [27]) and web sites where one can find patches that are compilable [15].

In wavetable synthesis, a wavetable is defined, and it is possible to read it with a variable index and to produce a periodic sound. The timbre of the sound obtained is fixed. The addition of jitter (small variations of random noise) or vibrato (a slow sinusoid) on the drive of frequency can make the sound alive [27].

Additive synthesis consists in adding partials having frequency and amplitude envelopes. Analysis techniques can also derive harmonic envelopes, such as the heterodyne filter [6] [23] or SMS.

In substractive synthesis, a source-filter model is used, where the source is usually coming from a simple synthesis (waveform synthesis with regular shapes such as square, sawtooth, triangle, etc or noise) and the evolution of the sound comes from the filter. This method is successful because one recognizes the voice formants (peaks in the spectrum due to vocal tract resonances in speech). Analog synthesisers make a general use of filters and silent instruments (silent cello, violin, piano) use banks of resonant filter to simulate usual and unusual harmony boards [19] [26].

Inititiating the FM synthesis, John Chowning [11] demonstrated that two oscillators associated in a modulation frequency scheme give rise to ray spectra in which partials vary with the modulation index. Non-linear distortion also named waveshaping is another modulative synthesis which has been worked out independently by D. Arfib and M. Lebrun [1] [18]. Distorting a sinusoid through a waveshaping function creates a harmonic spectrum. This spectrum evolves with the input amplitude of the sinusoid and gives an easy entry point for gestural control [2].

Granular synthesis consists in adding grains in order to obtain granular sounds [28]. The two most important parameters for the sound are the position of the grains and their shape. These grains can be replications of a mother-grain or a sample of recorded sound, dilated or compressed in time. In granular synthesis, many control functions are at a macrocontrol level, like synchronicity or random injection [29].

2.2.3 Digital Audio Effects

The limit between synthesis and transformation is very thin: for example, in a vocal synthesis with formants, one can replace the first part (source synthesis) by the reading of a natural sound and keep the filtering action and its control, making this way an electronic equivalent of the talk box [4]. Transformation techniques have been classified this way in the DAFx book [38]: filters, delays, modulators and demodulators, nonlinear processing, spatial effects, time-segment processing, time-frequency processing, source-filter processing and spectral processing. One naturally finds the filtering and distortion (but here applied to sounds that are not sine waves), diverse granulation styles, time compression/expansion and purely spectral transformations using analysis-synthesis methods. The matter of controlling effects with gesture can be found in [32] and [30]; it is also possible to make instruments where the heart is a digital effect. Adaptive effects use a feature extraction to give or modify control parameters, or even the mapping of the effect [33].

2.3 About Gesture

2.3.1 Think Different about Gesture

Working with digital sound and gesture is efficient if we can keep a symbolic link between the act and the resulting sound. This symbolism can be unfolded in two levels: the act itself as a function, and the movement as an expressive gesture.

As far as musical play is concerned, two strategies can be taken. In the first one, one can imitate the musician's play movements on traditional instruments: as an example, using the two hands on a guitar for pitch and trigger induces the notion of bimanuality, which is fruitful in the design of digital instruments. In the second attitude, one explores the universal symbolism of gesture, and discovers the intention behind a gesture and tries to extract it in a sensitive way.

Gestures must have a dynamic appearance compatible with human possibilities in terms of space and speed, and allow to touch the limits that one requires for the sonic domain; gesture sensors by themselves have idiosyncrasies, like the heaviness of some equipment or the need for a specific light environment for cameras.

Musical or expressive general gestures have been classified by some authors. As an example,three functions for the "gestural channel" have been defined by Cadoz [9], [10]: semiotic, ergotic, and epistemic. See also [14].

2.3.2 Sensor Typology

The typology of sensors has been largely discussed in the field of Human Computer Interaction and even in the field of sound control. Paradiso [25] makes an historic and practical view of controllers; Wanderley [37] gives a survey of different methodologies for the conception of gestural interfaces and an evaluation of some alternative interfaces. Some classifications as equipped/non-equipped, continuous/discrete provide a great help in the conception stage of an instrument.

Sensors that are usable in gesture controlled musical instruments are of three types. Sensors that imitate acoustic ones, such as breath controller or keyboard, allow to sense expert gestures that the performer makes. These sensors can control the same acoustic changes as the original instruments. As an example, a keyboard is used to control pitch and amplitude in most commercial synthesisers. These sensors can also manipulate other exotic parameters, and this is more specifically powerful for spectral processing. Hybrid controllers allow to play acoustic instrumental sounds and they also have other controls to modify other parameters. Alternate controllers are specifically made for new instruments or diverted from other non-musical applications. They range from as simple as linear or circular potentiometers or buttons, to video cameras and force feedback sensor. All of them enable musicians to step in new modes of artistic expression.

2.4 About Mapping

Mapping binds the gesture to the sound, connecting the gesture data and the synthesis parameters. Constituting a bridge between the action and the perception, the mapping represents the essence of a digital instrument. Several approaches have been used [16] [36] [37]; we have developed a strategy at LMA that we explain in details in [5]. This strategy is based on a multilayer mapping using perceptual spaces. We have defined three layers above two perceptual spaces. These layers are: from sound perceptual space to synthesis parameters, from gesture data to gesture perceptual space and between the two perceptual spaces.

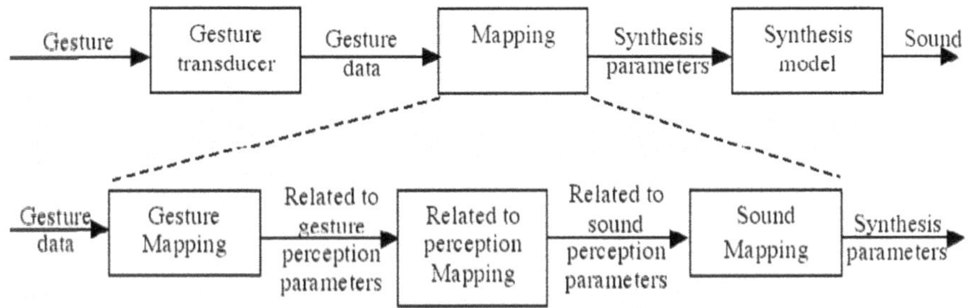

Fig. 2. The Mapping Chain can be divided in several steps with perceptual spaces.

The aim of this structure is having a higher flexibility and modularity in the realisation of a musical instrument: the definition of high-level parameters from gesture data and from sound synthesis parameters is realized upstream, and the mapping between the two perceptual spaces becomes very simple.

Independently of this multi-layer approach, mapping can have different qualifications: explicit/implicit, simple/complex or static/dynamic. The difference between static and dynamic is whether synthesis parameters values depend only on the actual gesture parameters, or whether there is a relation with past values [21].

Other details about practical questions on mapping can be found in [33], dealing with the use of adaptive effects.

2.5 About Feedback

Feedback uses different modalities: sight, touch, hearing; to use feedback, the essential point is the coherence between the action and the perception. Obviously, the auditory feedback is the produced sound and is essential in music: generally, musicians are hearing the sound they produce. The tactile feedback can be passive (physical behavior of the device) or active, like force feedback [8], whether the device reacts to the gestures or can be controlled. The visual feedback has the advantage of spatial discrimination that helps the user to dispose of much information simultaneously. The sight can be used in an informative level to help the performer, as for displaying the values of some parameters, but can also be part of the interaction with the instrument, like with graphical user interfaces.

3 Creating Instruments

3.1 Making Modular Instruments

One of the most important topics in the creation of our digital instrument is to use modularity: for a given synthesis method, changing a gesture controller with another has to be possible and easy. One can also use the same gesture device with different synthesis techniques. The mapping choices will decide if the instrument is modular or not. Our three layers model of mapping, with perceptual spaces, was created to reinforce modularity in digital instrument design. The key point is the middle space, which is the space to create instrument. The simpler this space, the easier is the creation of an instrument.

As shown previously, musical gestural devices can be classified into three types: the controllers that are imitation of acoustical instruments, the hybrid controllers and the alternative controllers. Our study was deliberately focused on alternative controllers. The reason is we are going from sound to gesture and we want to give to the controllers an expressiveness in accordance with the actions we want to apply on the sound. Imitative or hybrid controllers are often imposing the expressivities of their models. Starting with basic data (position, pressure, speed, ...) enables to obtain the expressiveness we want to control our sound processes. The acoustical instruments have strong physical constraints on the gesture sensing, due to the intrinsic link between gesture and sound production; the alternative controllers are free from sound production.

The musical instruments we create use a computer with software program, Max/MSP [20], which is a modular environment to realize virtual instruments and play them in real time. Many today software programs enable real time synthesis and many of them provide a certain kind of modularity at different levels. Some of them, like Max-MSP, Jmax or PD, are complete graphical programming environments in which complex structures can be realized by combination of several primary elements. In those oriented object environments, one can manage data from external gestural controllers as well as produce and modify sound. Moreover, the user of such programs can create its own bricks, to enlarge the number of object in the environment. The modularity and the evolutivity of those softwares make them very effective tools to design digital musical instruments according to our methodology.

3.2 Three Examples of Instruments

3.2.1 The Voicer

The Voicer [17] is a digital musical instrument that imitates the vowels of a singing voice. the instrument is bimanual: the dominant hand drives the frequency and the other one navigates in a space of vowels. It uses a formantic vocal synthesis and it is driven by a graphic tablet [35] and a joystick. The choice of the vocal coloration is done by the position of the joystick. A source-filter synthesis model produces the sound. A 2D interpolator receives the x, y positions of the joystick and drives the filters in order to interpolate between 4 vowels. A specific mapping enables to drive the pitch on all the audio frequency range, to make vibratos and frequency slides as well as stable intonations.

The "Voicer" is used in a musical work called "D'ici et d'ailleurs" as a soloist instrument in a jazz-like band; this work is articulated around an oriental mode in which the "Voicer" finds its expression field in accordance with its portamento, vibrato and micro-modulations possibilities as well as its vocal-like articulation.

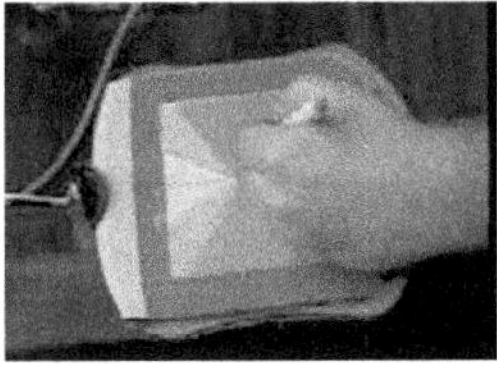

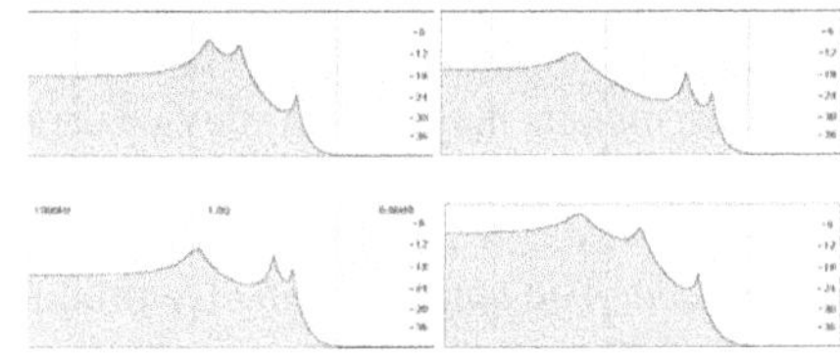

Fig. 3. A picture on the tablet helps the performer to control the frequencies; On the right, the frequency representation of the filter configurations corresponding to the 4 key vowels.

3.2.2 Scanned Synthesis Synthesizer

Scanned Synthesis [34] [7] is used in two different configurations in order to create two instruments. The principle of those instruments is the following: thanks to gesture by specific controllers, one interacts with a monodimensional shape (a string that can be circular) that moves at low frequencies, corresponding to the speed of our gestures. Gestures can put in motion the string or can modify its motion.

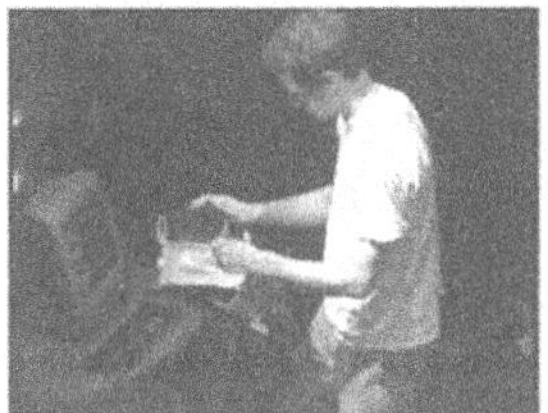

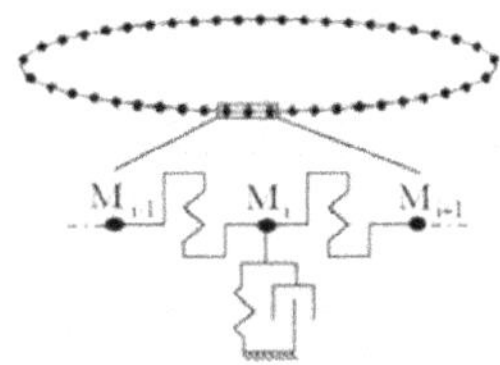

Fig. 4. The instrument uses a graphic tablet and a multi-touch tactile surface to control a string modeled by an assembly of masses, springs and dampers.

The shape of the string is used to produce sound in two configurations that are musically distinct: the Scanned Synthesis instrument, where the shape is scanned to an audio frequency and the "filtering string", where the shape is used to control the equivalent of a graphical equalizer.

In the Scanned Synthesis instrument [12], a tactile surface [31] is used to control dynamically the shape of the string (circular). Many presets have been created, providing different tones; those presets consist of the different values and the repartitions of these values on the string. The scanning frequency, that is the fundamental frequency of the sound, is controlled by the graphical tablet with the angular frequency control of the "Voicer".

In the second implementation [4], the "filtering string", we only use the shape of the string provided by our object, in order to modify the gains of a filter bank in a graphical equalizer. In this configuration, the graphical tablet controls the string parameters (stiffness, tension, damping) and the multi-touch surface controls the forces applied on the string, with a special mapping that enables the musician to give the string the shape he wants with his fingers.

In the work "Le rêve du funambule", the input sound is a white noise that enables to produces complex sounds. The string shape is displayed on a screen during live performances and gives to the public a visual feedback that is totally representative of the sound process.

3.2.3 Photosonic Synthesis Emulator

The photosonic emulator [3] emulates the sound and gesture obtained on the photosonic instrument, an optical device created by Jacques Dudon at the Atelier d'Exploration Harmonique. The optical instrument uses a light, a photosonic disk upon which is inscribed a series of rings. A filter is interposed between the disk and a solar photocell. The sound is directly produced by the interruption of the light by the disk and the filter.

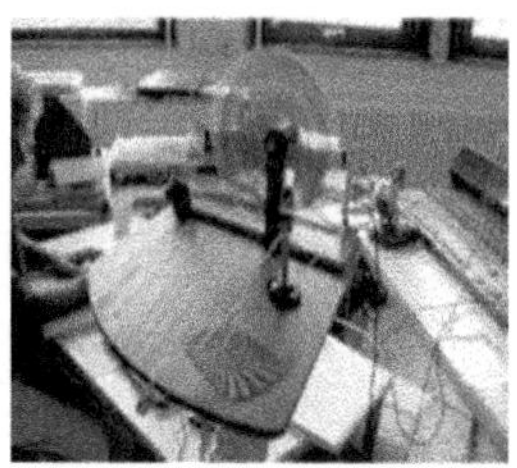

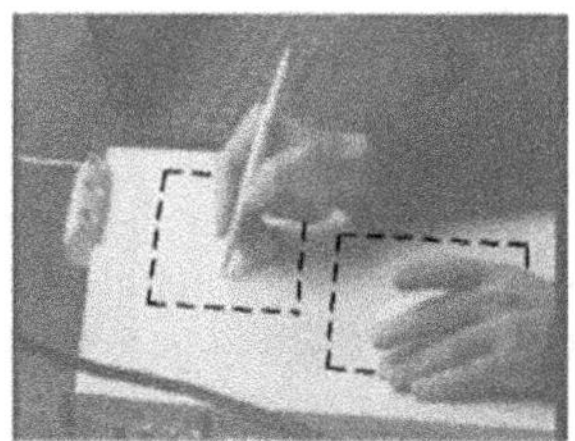

Fig. 5. On the left, the optical instrument; on the right, the tablet workspace is divided in two zones devoted to the control of the light and to the control of the filter.

The emulation of the instrument is realised in Max-Msp. The bimanual control is realised with two objects: a mouse and a stylet upon a graphic tablet; one makes the same gesture as moving a light and a celluloid filter in the photosonic (optical) instrument. This instrument is thus specific in the mimicking of the gestures of the "real instrument". More than 800 disks have been created for the optical instrument, and some have been used in the emulator.

The photosonic emulator has been used in duet with the optical instrument: "Patchwork 605" emphasises a similarity between the palettes of the two instruments, "821, de l'autre côté de l'arc en ciel" display unusual sonic games due to new filters and rapid movements and "duo sur ondes fractales 905" makes up a dialogue on the exploration of a palette of fractal sounds. The emulator has also been used in "les dauphins" with a an electronic cello giving an ecological flavour, and in "disque 729" a trio with electronic percussion and cello takes benefit of a long recursive delay to display a carpet of small photosonic sounds leaving place to some improvisation of the other instruments.

4 Conclusion

We have done here an overview of all the steps that we have ourselves followed in order to create our instruments and what we can do with them. We hope it will help others to understand the whole process of linking gesture to sound in order to perform on stage.

References

1. Arfib, D., "Digital synthesis of complex spectra by means of multiplication of non-linear distorted sine waves". Journal of the Audio Engineering Society 27-10, 1979.

2. Arfib D., Kessous L., "Gestural control of sound synthesis and processing algorithms", Gesture workshop 2001, ed. Ipke Wachsmuth & Timo Sowa, Springer-Verlag, Lecture Notes in Computer Science, LNAI 2298.
3. Arfib D., Dudon J. : "A digital emulator of the photosonic instrument", Proceedings of the 2002 Conference on New Instruments for Musical Expression (NIME-02), Dublin, Ireland, May 24-26, 2002, proceedings also on line at http://www.nime.org
4. Arfib D., Couturier J.-M., Kessous L. (2002) : "Gestural stategies for specific filtering processes", proceedings of DAFx02 conference, Hamburg, 26-28 sept 2002, pp. 1-6.
5. Arfib D., Couturier J.M., Kessous L., Verfaille V., "Mapping strategies between gesture control parameters and synthesis models parameters using perceptual spaces", Organised Sound 7(2), Cambridge University Press, pp. 135-152, 2002.
6. Boulanger R., The Csound Book, MIT Press, 2000.
7. Boulanger R., Smaragdis P., Ffitch J., "Scanned Synthesis : An introduction and demonstration of a new synthesis and signal processing technique", Proceedings of the 2000 International Computer Music Conference, pp. 372-375, Berlin Zannos editor, ICMA, 2000.
8. Cadoz C., Luciani A. and Florens J-L., "Synthèse musicale par simulation des mécanismes instrumentaux, transducteurs gestuels rétroactifs pour l'étude du jeu instrumental", *Revue d'Acoustique*, vol. 59, pp. 279-292, 1981.
9. Cadoz, C., Les réalités virtuelles, Dominos, Flammarion, 1994.
10. Cadoz C. « musique, geste, technologie » dans Les nouveaux gestes de la musique direction : Hugues Genevois et Raphaël de Vivo, Éditions Parenthèses, 1999, p 47-92.
11. Chowning J., "The synthesis of comples audio spectra by means of frequency modulation", "Journal of the Audio Engineering Society", vol 1 n°2, p :526-534, 1977.
12. Couturier J.M., "A scanned synthesis virtual instrument", Proceedings of the 2002 Conference on New Instruments for Musical Expression (NIME-02), Dublin, Ireland, May 24-26, 2002.
13. Couturier J.M., "La synthèse par balayage et son contrôle gestuel", Proceedings of the 9th Journées d'Informatique Musicale (JIM 02), Marseille, France, May 29-31, 2002.
14. Crowley J. L., "Vision for man machine interaction", Proceedings of Engineering Human Computer Interaction, EHCI'95, Grand Targhee, USA, August 1995, Chapman&Hall Publ.
15. Gather J. P., Amsterdam Catalog of Csound Computer Instruments, http://www.csounds.com/accci/index.html
16. Hunt, A. Wanderley, M. Kirk, R., Towards a Model for Instrumental Mapping in Expert Musical Interaction. Proceedings of the International Computer Music Conference (ICMC'2000, Berlin), ICMA, 209-12, 2000.
17. Kessous L., "A two-handed controller with angular fundamental frequency control and sound color navigation", Proceedings of the 2002 Conference on New Instruments for Musical Expression (NIME-02), Dublin, Ireland, May 24-26, 2002.
18. Lebrun M., "waveshaping synthesis", *Journal of the Audio Engineering Society*, vol 27, pp. 250-266, April 1979.
19. Mathews M. and Kohut J., "Electronic simulation of violin resonances," Journal of the Acoustical Society of America, vol. 53, no. 6, pp. 1620–1626, 1973.
20. Max/MSP, http://www.cycling74.com/products/maxmsp.html.
21. Menzies D., "New Performance Instruments for Electroacoustical Music", Dphil Thesis, 1999, http://www.zenprobe.com/dylan/pubs
22. Miranda E., "computer Sound Design", 2nd edition, focal press ed., 2002
23. Moore, F. R., "Elements of Computer Music", Englewood Cliffs, NJ: Prentice Hall, 1990.
24. Palombini, C., "Pierre Schaeffer's Typo-Morphology of Sonic Objects", Ph.D. University of Durham, 1993, http://www.sun.rhbnc.ac.uk/Music/Archive/Disserts/palombin.html
25. Paradiso J., Electronic Music Interfaces: New Ways to Play J. Paradiso, IEEE Spectrum Magazine, Vol. 34, No. 12, pp. 18-30 (Dec., 1997).

26. Penttinen H., Härmä A., and Karjalainen M., "Digital Guitar Body Mode Modulation With One Driving Parameter", Proceedings of the DAFx-00 Conference, Verona, Italy, December 7-9, pp. 31-36, 2000.
27. Risset, J.C. (1969). An introductory catalog of computer-synthesized sounds. Reprinted with C.D. Wergo 2033-2, The historical CD of digital sound synthesis (1995), 88-254.
28. Roads C., "Introduction to Granular Synthesis", Computer Music Journal, 12, 2, 11-13, 1988.
29. Roads C., "Sound Composition with Pulsars", *Journal of the Audio Engineering Society* 49(3): 134-147, March 2001.
30. Sapir S, "Gestural Control of Digital Audio Environments", Special Issue: "Musical Implications of Digital Audio Effects", Journal of New Music Research, Guest Editor D. Arfib, Number 2, June 2002.
31. Tactex, touch surfaces, http://www.tactex.com/.
32. Todoroff T., "Control of digital audio effects", DAFX digital audio effects, U. Zolzer Ed., J. Wiley & Sons, 2002, pp. 465-497.
33. Verfaille V., Arfib D. (2002) : "Implementation strategies for Adaptive Digital Audio Effects", proceedings of DAFx02 conference, Hamburg, 26-28 sept 2002, pp. 21-26.
34. Verplank B., Mathews M., Shaw R., "Scanned Synthesis", Proceedings of the 2000 International Computer Music Conference, pp. 368-371, Berlin, Zannos editor, ICMA, 2000.
35. Wacom tablets, http://www.wacom.com/
36. Wanderley M., Battier M., Ed, CD-ROM Trends in Gestural control of music, Ircam, 2000.
37. Wanderley, M. 2001. "Performer-Instrument Interaction: Applications to Gestural Control of Music", PhD Thesis, Paris, France, University Pierre et Marie Curie - Paris VI. http://www.ircam.fr/wanderle/Thesis/Thesis_comp.pdf.
38. Zolzer U., DAFX digital audio effects, J. Wiley & Sons, 2002,

Analysis of a Genuine Scratch Performance

Kjetil Falkenberg Hansen and Roberto Bresin

Dept. of Speech, Music and Hearing
KTH, Royal Institute of Technology
SE-100 44 Stockholm, Sweden
{hansen,roberto}@speech.kth.se

Abstract. The art form of manipulating vinyl records done by disc jockeys (DJs) is called scratching, and has become very popular since its start in the seventies. Since then turntables are commonly used as expressive musical instruments in several musical genres. This phenomenon has had a serious impact on the instrument-making industry, as the sales of turntables and related equipment have boosted. Despite of this, the acoustics of scratching has been barely studied until now. In this paper, we illustrate the complexity of scratching by measuring the gestures of one DJ during a performance. The analysis of these measurements is important to consider in the design of a scratch model.

1 Introduction

To scratch means to push and pull a vinyl record against the needle on an ordinary turntable along the grooves. This way of producing sounds has during the last two decades made the turntable become a popular instrument for both solo and ensemble playing in different musical styles. The turntable is mostly popular in the hip-hop style where disk jockeys (DJs) first started to scratch. However, all musical forms seem to keenly adopt the turntables into their instrumental scenery. Composers in traditions such as rock, metal, pop, disco, jazz, experimental music, film music, contemporary music and numerous others have been experimenting with DJs the past years. Experimental DJs and most hip-hop DJs now frequently call themselves "turntablists", and the music style of scratching and extensive cut-and-paste mixing is called "turntablism". These terms, derived from "turntable", are now generally accepted. It is also generally accepted that a turntablist is a musician and that the turntable is to be considered an instrument. The acoustics of scratching has been barely studied until now. On the other end, the business market of DJs equipment is quite large. It is therefore interesting to study the phenomenon of turntablism from a scientific point of view.

In this paper, one experiment is presented. Aim of this experiment is to understand how an expressive scratch performance is carried out by the artist. Previous investigations of turntable scratching shows that the DJs use a wide range of different techniques [1], and that these techniques can be used to model

A. Camurri and G. Volpe (Eds.): GW 2003, LNAI 2915, pp. 519–528, 2004.

scratching [2]. With better understanding of the performance practices, modelling scratching can be improved. This experiment investigates a real performance with aid of sensors on the equipment in order to determine what kinds of problems and parameter variation a model will need to deal with.

1.1 Method

Measurements. One of the things we needed to measure was the movement of the vinyl record itself without considering the turntable platter or motor. The slipmat placed between the platter and the record reduces friction depending on the fabric and material. For these measurements, the DJ used his preferred felt slipmat, which allowed the record to be moved quite effortlessly regardless of the platter and motor movement.

The second element we measured was the movement of the crossfader. To get a reliable signal we measured directly on the circuit board.

The third signal we recorded was the sound output from the manipulated record. In order to let the musician play in a realistic manner he was allowed to choose the sound to perform with.

Subject. Only one subject was used in the experiment. He is Alexander Danielsson, *DJ 1210 Jazz*, a professional DJ from Sweden. He volunteered for the experiment. 1210 Jazz (as he will be called throughout the paper) has no formal musical training, but has for almost 15 years been considered among the best turntablists in Sweden and Europe. He has made three records for DJ use, one of which was used during the recording sessions.

Equipment. The equipment used for the experiment is summarised in Table 1.

Table 1. Equipment used for the experiment

Equipment	Description		
Turntable	Technics SL-1210 Mk2 with felt slipmat		
Cartridge	Shure M44-7		
DJ-mixer	Vestax PMC-06 Pro with Vestax PMC-06 Pro faders		
Record	1210 Jazz - Book of Five Scratches. Book 2.[3]		
Potentiometer	Bourns 3856A-282-103A 10K		
DAT-recorder	Teak RD-200T	Channel 1 (20 kHz)	Potentiometer
	Multichannel	Channel 2 (10 kHz)	Crossfader
		Channel 3 (10 kHz)	Sound
Wave analysis	Soundswell Signal Workstation[4]		
software	Wavesurfer [5]		

A potentiometer was used for mapping the vinyl movement. The $3\frac{3}{4}$ rounds $(1220\,^\circ)$ potentiometer was mounted to the vinyl with the help of a stand and a cylinder attached to the record centre. Output was recorded to a multichannel

DAT. The potentiometer was chosen based on how easily it turned. No effect could be noticed in the performance and friction on the vinyl when the potentiometer was attached to it, and the DJ felt comfortable with the set-up. See Fig. 1.

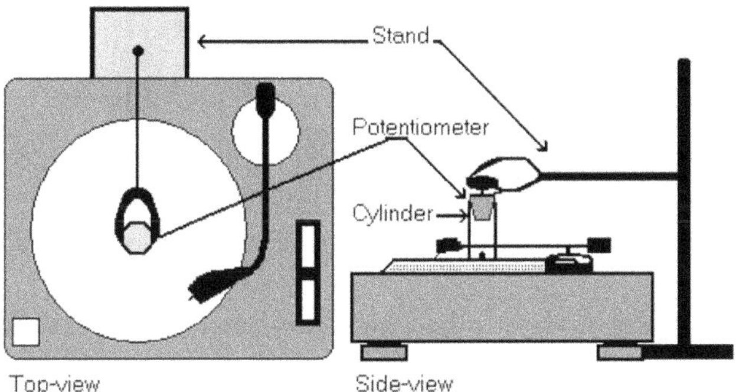

Fig. 1. Potentiometer set-up with above and lateral views of the turntable

Modern mixers give the DJ opportunity to change the fading curves of the crossfader. To get a reliable signal, we decided to find the slider position from reading the output voltage, not physical position. Two cables connected from the circuit board to the multichannel DAT recorder tracked the slider movement, but not automatically the sound level. To read the approximate sound output level from the position of the crossfader, every millimetre position was mapped to a dB level (using a tone generator). The crossfader run is 45 mm, but the interesting part, from silence to full volume, spans only two-three millimetres some millimetres' distance from the right end of the slider. Positioned to the right, the crossfader let no sound through, and moved a few millimetres to the left it let all sound through.

Only the right channel of the stereo sound output signal was recorded to the multichannel DAT, but that was sufficient, and purposeful, for evaluating the record movement output against the sound output. The original sound from the record had no significant stereo effects, and both right and left channel appeared similar.

Instrument Line-Up. 1210 Jazz placed mixer on the left and turntable on the right, as he uses his strongest hand (right) on the record. The turntable was connected to stereo-in on the mixer. The right channel was output to a DAT recorder, while the left channel was output to a headphone mixer so the DJ could hear himself. See Fig. 2.

Material. The recordings used in this experiment were done at KTH in Stockholm during October 2001. In the recording sessions, eight performances were

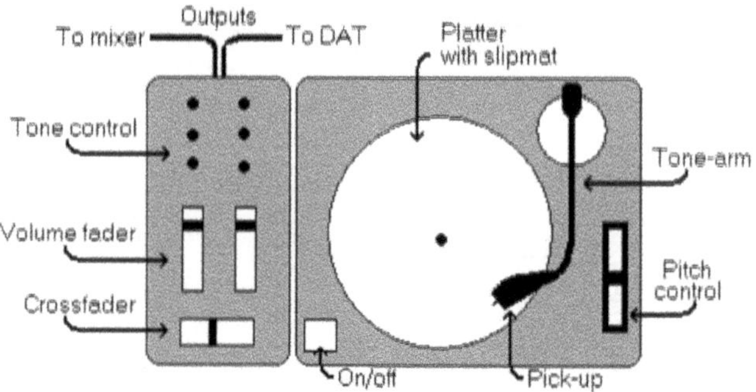

Fig. 2. Instrument set-up with mixer on the left and turntable on the right side

executed, all of which without a backing drum track. Since 1210 Jazz is an experienced performer, the lack of backing track was not considered a restraining or unnatural condition even though scratching often is performed to a looped beat.

The DJ was asked to play in a normal way, as he would do in an ordinary improvisation. He was not allowed to use other volume-controller than the crossfader, but as the crossfader is by far most used in a performance, and the other controllers are used in a manner to achieve the same sounding results, this did not affect the artistic result. The performances from that session are by all means representative examples of improvised solo scratching with a clearly identifiable rhythmic structure, and one of those will be used here. 30 seconds of music are analysed. All sounds produced are originated from the popular "ahhh" sound from "Change the beat" [6]. This sampled part is found on most battle-records, including the 1210 Jazz [3] record used in the experiment.

2 Analysis

In order to acquire knowledge about how scratching is performed and how it works and behaves musically, an analysis of several aspects of playing was necessary. Results from this analysis can be used as a starting point for implementing future scratch models. By only looking at the individual technique taken out of the musical context, it is easy to get an impression of scratching as being very well defined and straightforward. This is not always the case. Techniques are not often played subsequently in full, but rather shortened or abruptly changed, going into next technique. Also, many moves does not necessarily classify as a technique, as intention or imperfections in the performance let a record movement get unexpected crossfader movements.

The analysis was done with three signals: the crossfader, the record movement and a waveform of the recorded sound. The audio track was used as control. Comparison with previous recordings of the separate techniques provides valuable information, and emphasizes the importance of knowledge of these techniques.

To facilitate its analysis, the recorded performance was described in terms of *beats*, *bars* and time. This choice necessarily calls for interpretations, and especially at the end of the piece it is questionable if the performance is strictly rhythmical or not. In this analysis, however, that is a minor concern. With our interpretation the piece consists of 12 bars in four-fourth time. The tempo and rhythm is fairly consistent throughout with an overall tempo of about 96 beats per minute (bpm). Figure 3 shows an excerpt of the readings and illustrates how the structuring to beats and bars was done. The upper panel is the low pass-filtered signal from the crossfader in volts, the middle panel is the audio signal and the lower panel is the potentiometer signal (or rotation angle), in degrees. The excerpt in Fig. 3 is from bar 7.

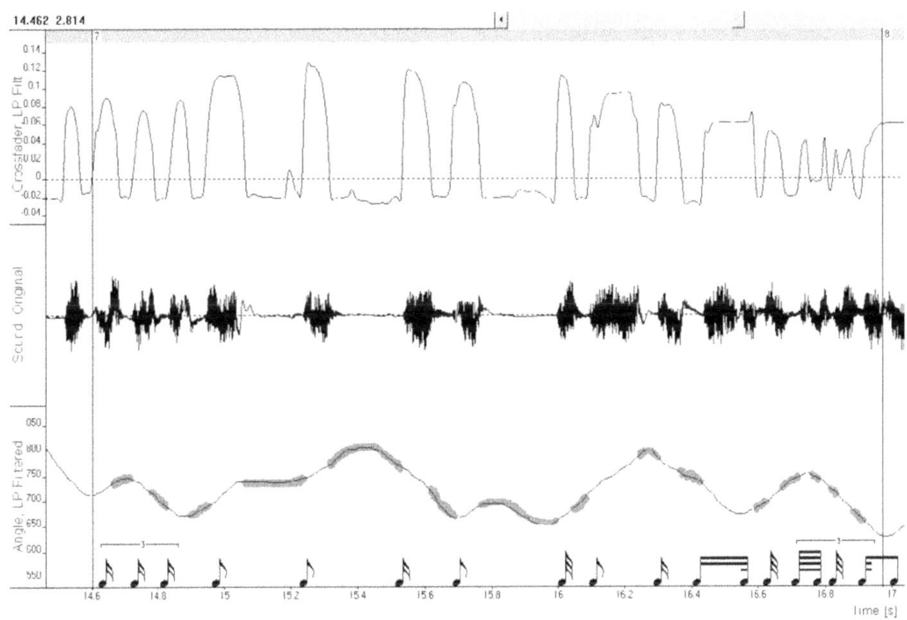

Fig. 3. Bar 7 transcribed into musical notation. Grey areas mark time intervals when the crossfader silence the signal. Upper panel shows the low pass-filtered signal from the crossfader in volts. In the middle panel is the audio signal, and in the lower panel the rotation angle in degrees is shown

In the analysis, some key elements will be considered, namely the workings on the vinyl in terms of directional changes, angles and areas, speed and timing, the crossfader and volume, occurrences of predefined techniques, and finally occurrences of different kinds of patterns. The three variables considered in the measurements were crossfader movements, record movements, and associated sound signal.

Sounding Directional Changes. One principle of scratching is that moving the record forward and backward is the main means of producing sound. This implies that the record will change direction continually during playing. Directional changes can be grouped in three categories: (1) the ones where the crossfader masks the change, (2) the silent ones where the change is done on a part of the record where there is no signal (i.e. outside a sound), and (3) the ones where the sound is heard, here called *turns* for short. In the following, the turns are further be categorised in *significant* and *insignificant turns* according to how well the directional change can be heard.

A significant turn inside the sound will produce the attack of the next tone. An insignificant turn appears when only a little part of the sound from the returning record is heard, either intentionally or by imprecision, also producing a kind of attack, although less audible.

In the analysed piece of music, the record direction is changed 135 times, in average 4.5 times per second. 21.5 % of the directional changes are heard; 18.5 % of them are significant turns and 6 % insignificant. A technique like *scribble* would influence this result considerably, as it implies fast and small forward and backward movements (about 20 turns per second) with sound constantly on. This excerpt has two instances of short *scribble*-scratches, representing 36 % of the significant turns. It seems that in a normal scratch improvisation (at least for this subject), about 70-90 % of the directional changes are silenced.

Further investigation is needed in order to explain why so many directional changes are silenced. More data from other DJs need to be collected and analysed. However, one possible reason could be that the highly characteristic and recognizable sound of a record changing direction is no longer a desirable sound among DJs wanting to express themselves without too much use of clichés, risking prejudice. These characteristic sounds of a record changing direction are associated with the early, simple techniques.

Angles and Area. DJs can only change the record speed by applying a force either in or against the direction of the record. Pushing the record hand will increase the speed, and pulling it will play the record backwards. In the following, a *push* means a forward hand/record movement, a *pull* means a backward hand/record movement, and a *stroke* means a movement in either direction.

The length of a sample naturally limits the working area on the record for the musician, and moving the record can be obstructed by the turntable's tone arm. About a quarter of the platter area is taken up by the tone arm in the worst case, i.e. when the S-shaped tone arm (used in most turntable brands) is close to the record centre. Big arm movements are difficult to perform fast with precision, resulting in a narrowing down, as the technical level evolves, to an average of about 90°. Although not measured, recordings of DJs from mid-eighties seem to show generally longer and slower movements. We consider long movements to be those that exceed 100°. In the performance analysed here, a little less than 50 % are long movements.

The occurrence of equally long movements in both directions is quite low. About 30 % of the pairing movements cover the same area. Only 25 % of the push-pull movements starts and ends on the same spot. Backward strokes tend to be longer than the forward ones, and almost every long forward results from letting the record go (releasing it). It is easier for a DJ to control pulling than pushing, so long backward strokes can be performed to do difficult crossfader patterns, but also to bring the record back to an exact spot, i.e. the start of a sound.

Issues Concerning Rhythm and Timing. An attempt to transcribe the piece to traditional notation will necessarily mean that some subjective decisions and interpretations have to be made. Still some information can be seen more easily from a musical analysis point of view. This transcription allows an analysis of timing in relation to the various scratching techniques by looking at the speed of movements of both record and crossfader and its relation to the corresponding waveform.

All bars starts with a pushing movement, with the exception of the tenth bar. In seven bars, the fourth beat is a long (released) forward movement followed by a fast pull to prepare the next bar. In a few cases, the push starts before the first beat, and the crossfader is used to cut in the sound on beat. Apart from the start and the fourth beat of the mentioned bars, DJ 1210 Jazz performs strokes freely within his rhythmical framework with movements producing eights, triplets and more intricate rhythmical figures.

Speed. About half of all movements are done slower than the original tempo in this recording, in both directions. The backward moves are more often performed faster than the forward moves, 33 % compared to 26 %. Different factors make it difficult to perform a movement with constant speed, i.e. the platter's inertia and muscle control for pushing and pulling. Also, holding on to a vinyl record forces movements that follows the rounded path of a rotating turntable. The majority of all movements tend to have unstable speed and does not give straight lines in the potentiometer output.

Sound Position. Even though a DJ has great control over where a sound is positioned on the record, aided by visual marks such as coloured stickers, a minor inaccuracy can spoil the result greatly. Here 1210 Jazz only has one sound (and position) to focus on, so he does not make any serious mistakes that cause unexpected attacks or silences. The sound used is also quite easy to deal with. Accuracy is more critical when the DJ is performing with continuous changes of sound samples, or controlling sharper sounds like drumbeats and words with two or more syllables.

Crossfader. This analysis will not distinguish extensively between crossfader movements done with the hand or by bouncing with the fingers, but some evident cases can be pointed out. It may seem that the crossfader should be left open for a number of techniques, but the longest constant openings in this performance have duration shorter than half a second, or about a dotted eight note in 96 bpm. The crossfader is turned or clicked on about 170 times in 30 seconds (more than five times per second). The total amount of sound and silence is approximately equal.

53.3 % of the strokes have one sound only, and 11.8 % of the strokes are silenced. Of the remaining strokes, 24.4 % have two sounds, 6.6 % have three sounds and 3.7 % of the strokes have four separate sounds. Multiple sounds per draw are distributed quite evenly on pushes and pulls, except for the five strokes carrying four tones; all are done when pulling the record.

Techniques. The aesthetics of today's musicians roots in a mutual understanding and practice of attentively explained techniques. However, the actual improvising does not necessarily turn out to be a series of perfectly performed basic techniques. Scratch research so far has naturally been most interested in the separate techniques and the record moving part. An overview of the techniques being used in this piece clearly shows the need for a new approach considering combinations of techniques and basic movements. All recognised techniques are here associated to the bar number they appear in.

Forwards (where the record is released to play a sound as it is) appear in the same place in almost every bar. There are 9 *forwards* in 12 bars; 7 occur on the fourth beat (in bars 1, 2, 3, 4, 6, 10 and 12) and 2 *forwards* on the first beat (in bars 6 and 9). All *forwards* on the fourth beat are followed by a pickup-beat to the next bar, except for the last *forward.* Most forward movements exceeding 145 ° are *forwards.*

Tear-like figures appear from time to time when the sound is clicked off during the pull, but will not sound much like *tears* because the breakdown in the backward draw is silenced. Three of these *tear*-likes are executed, in bars 6, 10 and 11. Normally several *tears* are performed in a series, and leaves the sound on for its entire duration.

Chops normally require a silenced return, and 10 of the silences are part of *chops.* They are found in bars 3, 4, 5, 7, 8 and 11. A *chop* can be followed by other techniques as in bars 5, 7 and 11, but the whole forward move is used by the chop. *Stabs* (forward) and *drags* (backward) are similar to *chops,* but performed faster by using more force. They both appear in bar 8.

The majority of playing techniques use crossfader so that one single, fast record hand movement can produce multiple tone attacks, normally from 2 to 5 and sometimes even more. Many strokes (35 %) have a swift crossfader use. There are two states of crossfader position during scratching; with the sound initially off, the sound will be temporarily let in, and oppositely with the sound initially on, the sound will be temporarily cut out. Main techniques of sound-off state are different *transform*-scratches, while *chirps*, *crabs* and especially *flares* are typical for sound-on state. Sound-on state should give more significant turns. Most of the significant (and insignificant) turns happen with variations on the *flare* scratch.

Some common techniques were not found in the recording of the analysed performance, including *baby*, *hydroplane*, *chirp* and *tweak.* The reasons for this could be many; *baby* scratching will often seem old-fashioned while *tweaking* can only be performed with the motor turned off, so it is not obvious or usual for the performer to incorporate it in a short phrase. The absence of *hydroplane* and *chirp* can be explained as artistic choice or coincidence, as they are widely used techniques.

Patterns. Some movements and series of movements are repeated frequently. Patterns are not considered to be unique techniques, and they are not necessarily so-called "combos" either. A combo is a combination of two or more techniques, performed subsequently or simultaneously.

Often a significant turn will be followed by a silenced change and a new significant (or insignificant) turn. This particular sequence is performed 6 times (in bars 1, 4, 6, 11, 12) in both directions.

In the performance analysed, only five long (more than 100 °) pushes are followed by another long push, and there are never more than two long pushes in a row. On the pulls, long strokes happen more frequently. 16 long pulls are followed by another long pull; on three occasions three long pulls come in a row, and once 6 long pulls come in a row.

No push is ever silenced, while 16 pulls are silenced with the crossfader. One silenced stroke is a long one of 220 °, the rest are all less than 75 °. As the *chop* technique uses small movements and involves a silenced return, this technique is often evident around these silences.

Two bars, bars 4 and 5, are performed almost identically; the major difference is that bar 4 has a *forward* on the fourth beat while bar 5 has a *chop* on the third offbeat.

Twin Peaks. One returning pattern is a long push with a slightly shorter pull followed by a new long push (shorter than the first) and a pull returning to the starting point. This distinctive sequence looks in the record angle view like two peaks standing next to each other, the left one being the highest, and as it returns eight times in 30 seconds it was for convenience called *twin peaks* (from the TV-series "Twin Peaks" by David Lynch, with a picture of a mountain in the opening scene).

The *twin peaks* pattern is repeated eight times with striking similarity. The first peak is the highest in all cases, ranging from 100 ° to 175 ° (132.5 ° in average) going up (forward), and from 85 ° to 150 ° (120 ° in average) going down (backward). The second peak ranges from 50 ° to 100 ° (77.5 ° in average) going up, and from 75 ° to 150 ° (128.75 ° in average) going down. All have about 10 crossfader attacks (from 7 to 11), and more on the second peak than the first. The second peak is always a variant of a *flare* scratch. *Twin peaks*-patterns take up almost one third of the performance in time.

3 Discussion

Modelling scratching in hardware and software can be done with several different approaches. One is to just make a virtual turntable that is controlled with existing or specially designed input devices. From a playing practice point of view, this approach is straight-forward as the performer will need to learn to play in the same way as on real equipment. A second approach is to have a sort of "scratch sampler" with synthesised techniques that can be performed in real time. This approach is static in the sense that techniques will follow each other in sequences and probably not in a very realistic way. A third approach is to design a computer program with scratch techniques and patterns in software without the possibility to perform it in real time.

The three approaches to scratch modelling have been implemented in commercial products, but they do not easily allow the performer to play convincingly. How important the scratch techniques are, is still an unanswered question. For a better understanding of musical content in scratching, more recordings should be analysed as only twelve bars and one subject do not suffice for formulating general conclusions.

References

1. K. F. Hansen. Turntablisme - his master's voice: The art of the record player. Master's thesis, NTNU, 1999.
2. K. F. Hansen. The Basics of Scratching. *Journal of New Music Research*, 2002, Vol. 31, No. 4: 357–367.
3. DJ 1210 Jazz. Book of five scratches. Book 2. Snickars Rec., SR1206, 2001.
4. Hitech Development. Soundswell signal workstation. `http://www.hitech.se/development/products/soundswell.htm`.
5. K. Sjolander and J. Beskow. Wavesurfer - an open source speech tool. `http://www.speech.kth.se/wavesurfer/`.
6. Fab Five Freddie. Change the beat. 12" Celluloid Records CEL 156, 1982.

Conducting Audio Files via Computer Vision

Declan Murphy, Tue Haste Andersen, and Kristoffer Jensen

Computer Science Department, University of Copenhagen
{declan,haste,krist}@diku.dk

Abstract. This paper presents a system to control the playback of audio files by means of the standard classical conducting technique. Computer vision techniques are developed to track a conductor's baton, and the gesture is subsequently analysed. Audio parameters are extracted from the sound-file and are further processed for audio beat tracking. The sound-file playback speed is adjusted in order to bring the audio beat points into alignment with the gesture beat points. The complete system forms all parts necessary to simulate an orchestra reacting to a conductor's baton.

1 Introduction

The technique of classical conducting is the most established protocol for mapping free gesture to orchestral music. Having developed since the baroque period out of the practical necessity for an ensemble to play together in time, it has evolved into the most sophisticated such mapping [1] of gesture to music despite the recent flourish of research activity in this area [2].

The presented system consists of a computer vision part to track the gestures of an ordinary baton, a second part that extracts a parameter from the audio in order to track the beat, and a third part that performs time scaling of the audio. A schematic overview of the complete system appears in Fig. 1.

Gesture tracking is performed using a combination of computer vision techniques and a 3D model of the baton. The system outputs the beat time points based on the position and velocity of the baton tip. Two modes are employed: a seek mode to locate the baton initially and a track mode to follow the baton position in time.

Audio beat estimation is based on the extraction of an audio parameter, combined with a high-level beat model. The peaks of the extracted parameter indicate note onsets that are related to the beats of the music. The beat estimation is improved by updating a beat probability vector with the note onsets.

The coupling of conductor's beats and audio beats is done using two different approaches. The first approach, viz. an event based coupling of the beats, is possible if the overall latency of the system is low and in the case of sparse event based music, while the second approach of delayed handling is suitable in all situations.

Max Mathews' Radio Baton [5] from 1991 is generally regarded as the first computerised baton conducting system. It monitors the positions of two batons

A. Camurri and G. Volpe (Eds.): GW 2003, LNAI 2915, pp. 529–540, 2004.

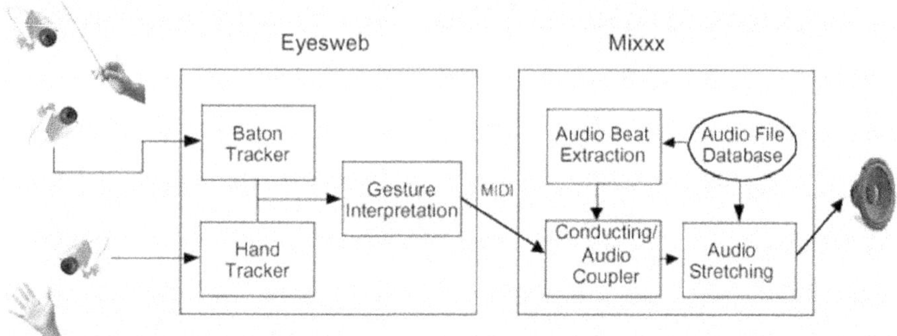

Fig. 1. The complete system. It consists of a computer vision module implemented in EyesWeb [3] and an audio processing system implemented in Mixxx [4].

which are fitted with radio transmitters by means of directional antennas. The Buchla Lightning-II [6] is a versatile MIDI device consisting of a pair of wands fitted with infra-red sources whose locations are monitored by a special remote unit. Borchers et al. [7] use the Lightning-II with pre-stretched audio tracks across a range of pitches, so that the audio can be scaled live more easily and with better quality. Magnetic sensors were used by Ilmonen and Takala [8] for tracking the conductor's movements and they used artificial neural networks for determining the conductor's tempo. The Digital Baton developed by Marrin and Paradiso [9] adopts a hybrid approach of accelerometers, pressure sensors and an infra-red LED mounted in the tip which is monitored by a position-sensitive photo-diode behind a camera lens. Marrin later developed the Conductor's Jacket [10] which is designed to be worn by a conductor during performance and is fitted with sensors to monitor electromyography (a measure of muscle tension), breathing, heart rate, skin conductivity and temperature. CCD cameras were used by Carosi and Bertini [11] to trigger computer generated parts while conducting an ensemble. Segen et al. use two cameras for segmentation and apply a linear filter to boundaries represented as a curvature plot [12] to track a baton in order to conduct a ballet dancing avatar [13]. Further systems are briefly reviewed in [14].

Disadvantages with the instrumented batons are that they are fatiguing for prolonged use, that they do not feel like "the real thing", and that they involve special hardware. Most of the vision based systems are relatively crude by comparison in terms of their precision: they use heuristics to extract the main beat of an up-down movement rather than tracking and recognising the various beat gestures. The system presented here may be used with an ordinary conductor's baton and inexpensive CMOS cameras. Furthermore, this system is independent of musical style in that it can be used with any sound file having a clear beat.

2 The Nature of Conducting Gestures

In the light of gesture research, conducting is a rather interesting example because of the complexity of multiple layers of meaning at the same time, and by virtue of the combination of both formal technique and subjective body language. Indeed, almost the entire gamut of a gesture taxonomy can be present at a given moment: from control gestures with a clearly defined meaning associated with a clearly defined movement, through to the equivalent of co-verbal gestures, through to emotive gesticulation. Indeed, following McNeill [15], there are direct equivalents of the full range of co-verbal gestures. The baton gestures qualify as both beats and cohesives: the physical form[1] and semantic content are canonically that of a beat as it punctuates and emphasises the underlying pulse of the music, while they are cohesive in their form by being repetitious and in their function by tying together temporally disjoint yet structurally related points. The non-baton hand generally executes iconics and metaphorics: an iconic could typically be a mimesis of bowing action by way of instruction to the strings while a metaphoric could typically be an upward movement of the upturned palm calling for a crescendo. Both hands and eyes execute deictics: the baton and eyes to give cues, and the non-baton hand by pointing directly to the intended recipient.

The overall body language of the conductor generally sets the desired mood for the musicians' phrasing, whilst the specific gestures – how the conducting patterns are executed – give more technical lower-level instruction to the musicians.

There is a great deal to be said about how to conduct *well* from a musicological point of view. This involves being aware of the most salient musical events at every stage of the piece, an understanding of phrasing, orchestration and the physical constraints of all instruments involved, good social communication and an understanding of rehearsal group dynamics, amongst other attributes. See, for example, [16]. Rudolf made a comprehensive survey of orchestral conducting technique in his classic text [1], in which he defines the formal grammar of beat structure and how it may be embellished by gestural variations, again illustrating how conducting functions simultaneously both linguistically and as co-verbal gestures.

This paper presents a prototype system for conducting audio files by extracting the tempo information from the user's baton gestures and by scaling the audio playback accordingly. A more complete conducting system is the subject of the first author's current research. This involves a representation of the score with beat pattern annotations (which is realistic since the players and conductor know what to expect from each other and from the music through their rehearsals), a subsystem for recognising the deviations from the expected tempo and volume as indicated by the sampled baton locations, and live generated output. This in turn forms part of the authors' research on how gesture may used for composition and performance of music.

[1] Indeed, the "beat" gesture has been termed the "baton" by several authors.

3 Baton Tracking

The tracker has two modes of operation: seek mode and track mode. In seek mode, the system tries to locate the baton without any knowledge from previous frames. In track mode, the system knows where to expect to find the baton and so is more tolerant of blurred or noisy images and less likely to switch to tracking something other than the targeted baton. The system starts in seek mode and switches automatically into track mode when it is sure that the baton has been localised. It switches back into seek mode if the track mode looses its confidence in its result or upon momentary request of the user.

A camera is placed directly in front of the user. In the case of a second camera being available, it takes a profile view of the conductor and thus always sees the baton in its full length and always has a clear view of the vertical component of the baton's trajectory. The first (and perhaps only) camera faces the conductor directly, and thus has a better view of the baton's trajectory in both horizontal and vertical components, but only sees the baton's length as ranging between zero and less than its actual length which makes the recognition more difficult. Once the baton has been located in both views, a three dimensional reconstruction of the baton is modeled, and the correspondence of the two views is a tracking criterion in subsequent frames.

It is assumed that there is only one baton in view, and that it is uniformly bright against a reasonably contrasting background. Once tracked, the baton reduces to a single point: its tip pointing away from the conductor. Periodic samples of the tip's trajectory are sent to the gesture interpretation algorithm. In the following sections, a brief introduction to the baton tracker is given; a more complete description appears in [17].

3.1 Seek Mode

In seek mode, the tracker begins with Canny edge detection [18] that identifies and follows pixels using a hysteresis function on blurred images. This outputs a number of pixel-wide line segments corresponding to the edges of the baton and other objects in the image. The stationary baton has a very characteristic edge trace of two parallel line segments of the same length, running side by side, with a fixed perpendicular distance apart. These are detected by a finite state machine. In a typical image, however, there will be many other edges satisfying this criterion (coming from the user's body and the background), and the real baton edges will be fragmented. Nevertheless, this substantially and efficiently reduces the search area.

To identify the baton, a trace along pixels of maximum intensity is made on a Gaussian blurred copy of the original image, starting at locations corresponding to in-between each pair of candidate line segment pairs in the edge detection image. See Fig. 2. A count is made of the number of edge pixels flanking these traces, and the one of greatest count (not exceeding the maximum length) is subjected to gauging techniques as in [19].

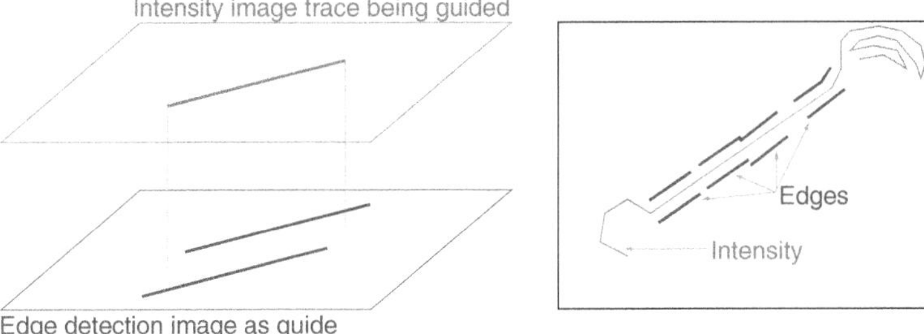

Fig. 2. Illustrating (left) how the seek mode uses the extracted edges (lower plane) to guide an intensity trace (upper plane) and (right) how ranking the flanking edges avoids the disadvantages of using both edges and intensity.

During development, it was found that the above-mentioned maximum intensity tracing, when applied to all image pixels without the previous edge detection stages, resulted in spurious quantisation along digitisation boundaries and an over-sensitivity to non-baton traces despite elaborate gauging. On the other hand, working with edge detection alone requires elaborate filtering to establish "straightness" (both geometric methods and the Hough transform were tried) and even more elaborate techniques in order to deal with the branching of detected edges (where edges overlap) and the gaps invariably left out. The presented combination method uses a very simple and efficient finite state machine to filter the detected edges, and by collating this with maximal tracing it simultaneously avoids spurious tracing and the complexity of curved, branching and broken edges.

3.2 Track Mode

A problem with baton tracking by camera is that, if the baton is relatively close to the camera then it gives blurred images when it moves quickly (see Fig. 3), whereas if it is relatively far away from the camera then it cannot be seen well enough due to its slight cross-section. The solution pursued is a hybrid approach combining a more tolerant version of the above seek mode with optical flow [20]. The "slack seek" tracking is suitable for when the baton has little or no motion as seen by the camera. Optical flow calculates a vector field corresponding to the apparent motion of brightness patterns between successive frames as seen by the camera. It diminishes to background noise for a stationary baton but it is immune from motion blur and thus very suitable for tracking higher speed movement. Both of these methods start with knowledge of the expected location and velocity as calculated from previous frames. If a profile camera is used, the expected location of the baton in the frontal image is known with greater likelihood and accuracy.

After optical flow is calculated, the sum of the scalar (or dot) products of each vector with its immediate neighbours is calculated and thresholded. This was found to be rather more noise resilient than simply taking the magnitudes

Fig. 3. Note how a moving baton appears as a wedge with an intensity gradient in the camera frame (right) giving the general form illustrated with an artificial border (left).

for revealing the baton's location. A further advantage to using optical flow is that it gives a measure of the baton's velocity. A local average is taken of a small region of non-border pixels close to the tip, and this value is passed on to the gesture analysis algorithm.

3.3 Gesture Recognition

At this stage, the baton has been reduced to a single tracked point in a plane and the objective is to follow where this point is in relation to a standard conductor's beat pattern. The user is instructed to face and gesture directly towards the frontal camera so that the tracked point's trajectory lies approximately in a plane parallel to the camera image plane. This avoids unnecessary camera 3D calibration and projective geometry. The user is also expected to conduct such that the field of beating occupies most of the image frame while being contained within it.

Figure 4 shows just two of the many standard conductor's beat patterns from Rudolf [1]. The standard patterns along with their standard variations are encoded as parametric template functions of an even tempo. The periodic updates of position and velocity from the tracker are used to monitor the user's execution of the beat pattern. Changes in tempo, dynamics and registration are simultaneously resolved and output via MIDI to the conducting/audio coupler.

4 Audio Beat Estimation

The estimation of the underlying beat of the conductor's movements is now to be coupled with the beat of the music, in order to perform the necessary time scaling of the audio.

Audio beat estimation is non-trivial, in particular taking into account problems such as weak/strong beats, tempo change, and off-beat rhythmic information. In this work beat is defined to represent what humans perceive as a binary regular pulse underlying the music.

The beat in music is often marked by transient sounds, e.g. note onsets of instruments. Some onset positions may correspond to the position of a beat, while other onsets fall off beat. By detecting the onsets in the acoustic signal, and using this as input to a beat induction model, the beat is estimated.

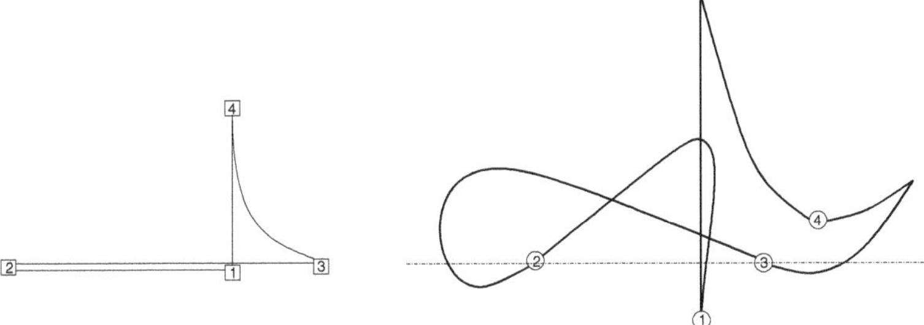

Fig. 4. The standard $\frac{4}{4}$ light-staccato (left) and expressive-legato (right) conducting beat patterns (conductor's view). For light-staccato, the baton pauses at each beat point with a quick flick in-between. For expressive-legato, the baton passes through the beat points without stopping with a more tense movement in-between.

The system presented here estimates the beat from a sampled waveform in real-time, and consists of a feature extraction module from which note onset information is extracted and a beat induction model based on a probability function which gives beat probability as a function of the note onset intervals. The probability function ensures a stable beat estimation, while local variations are detected directly from the estimated note onsets.

4.1 Parameter Extraction

The parameter is estimated from the given sound files, and used to detect note onsets. The note onset detection is based on the assumption that the attack has more high frequency energy than the sustain and release of a note. This is generally true for most musical instruments.

To capture the start of each new note, peaks are detected on the maximum of the time derivative of the parameter. In [21] a number of different parameters were compared. It was shown that the high frequency content (HFC) [22] is the most appropriate parameter for the detection of note onsets, and it is therefore used in the onset detection routine. The HFC is calculated as the sum of the magnitudes of a Short Time Fourier Transform, weighted by the frequencies squared. A short segment of the time derivative HFC is shown in Fig. 5 (top), from which the note onsets are clearly visible.

4.2 Beat Probability Vector

It is not unreasonable to assume that any given melody will have an underlying beat, which is perceived through recurring note onset intervals. This is modeled in the beat probability vector, in which note onset intervals have their weight increased by a Gaussian shape each time the interval occurs. This is a variation of the algorithm presented in [23]. To maintain a dynamic behavior, the memory weights are scaled down at each time step. In [23] and [24], weights at multiples of the interval are also increased. Since the intervals are found from the audio

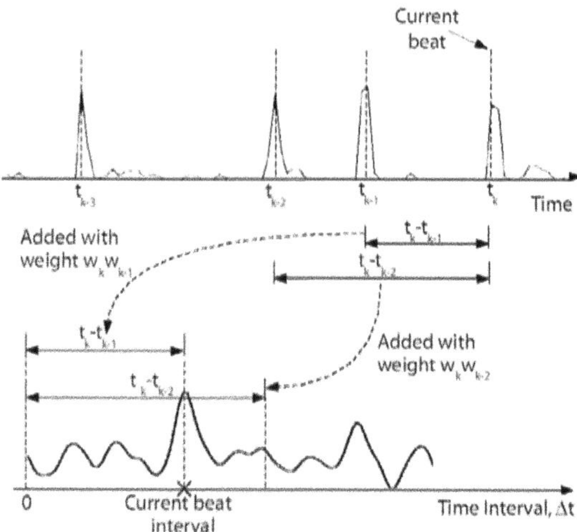

Fig. 5. Short example of HFC, including the detected peaks at time t_k (top), and selection of beats in the beat probability vector (bottom). For each new peak, a number of previous intervals are scaled and added to the beat probability vector. If an interval is found near the maximum of the beat probability vector, it is selected as the current interval.

file in this work, the erroneous intervals are generally not multiples of the beat. Another method must therefore be used to identify the important beat interval.

To avoid a situation where spurious peaks create a maximum in the probability vector with an interval that does not match the current beat, the vector is updated in a novel way. By weighting each new note and taking previous note onsets into account, the probability vector of time intervals $H(\Delta t)$ is updated at each note onset time t_k, with N previous weighted intervals that lie within the allowed beat interval,

$$H(\Delta t) = W^{t_k - t_{k-1}} H(\Delta t) + (1 - W^{t_k - t_{k-1}}) \sum_{i=1}^{N} w_k w_{k-i} G(t_k - t_{k-i}, \Delta t),$$

where G is a Gaussian shape which is non-zero at a limited range centered around $t_k - t_{k-i}$. W is the time scaling factor that ensures a dynamic behavior of the beat probability vector. w_k is the value of the HFC at time t_k. This model gives a strong indication of note boundaries at common intervals of the analysed music, which permits the identification of the current beat. An example of the beat probability vector is shown in Fig. 5 (bottom) together with an illustration of how it is created from the peaks of the HFC.

5 System Construction

The gesture tracking and analysis algorithms are implemented as EyesWeb blocks [25]. EyesWeb provides a suitable platform for framegrabber camera input and MIDI output while serving as highly adaptable environment for prototyping [3]. The MIDI output is directed to Mixxx [4], but it can be used in other systems, in particular it is intended to be used in PatternPlay [26].

Mixxx is an open source digital DJ system, developed to perform interaction studies in relation to the DJ performance scenario. Mixxx emulates two turntables and a mixer by integrating two sound file players with functionality similar to that of an analogue mixer. Mixxx has been designed to be easily extendible through a modular sound processing system, and by a flexible mapping of control values to incoming MIDI messages.

Mixxx includes an implementation of a phase vocoder for time scaling, described in Sect. 5.2, and audio beat extraction as described in Sect. 4. The coupling of the MIDI based timer events and the audio beats is described in Sect. 5.1.

5.1 Coupling

A certain latency of the system, when measured from the time when the conductor marks a beat to the beat from the music is heard, is unavoidable. The hardware and operating system latencies of audio playback is at best around 3 ms, but the camera and image streaming have larger latency.

Dependent on the total latency of the system and the music material, different approaches for synchronization can be taken. In the *event based approach* the beat is played as soon as possible, thereby cutting or extending audio, by performing interpolation over very short periods of time. This solution works well if the latency of the overall system is sufficiently low, and the music consists of relatively sparse percussive instruments. The event based approach is similar to how sequences of MIDI files are played back in other baton control systems.

If, however, the latency is large, this approach is not possible. In the *delayed approach* the audio tempo is adjusted one beat behind the baton beats. This results in delayed response, but it permits the playback of beats synchronously to the conductor's beats.

The audio is scaled according to the current tempo, and played back. If the conductor changes the tempo, the playback speed of the audio is scaled so the next beat falls at the estimated point in time of the new baton beat. Because of latency, the audio tempo must overcompensate during one beat so that the next beat falls in synchronization. An illustration of the relative playback speed when the tempo is changed is shown in Fig. 6. This approach is described in more detail in [7].

5.2 Time Scaling

The naïve approach of changing the speed of audio playback has the effect of also changing the pitch correspondingly, as with a record player (although this pitch alteration is highly undesirable for orchestral music, it is perfectly normal for turntablists). Different approaches exist to try to keep the pitch as it was. The approach used here, and implemented in Mixxx, is based on the phase vocoder [27]. It is a combination of time and frequency processing techniques. It

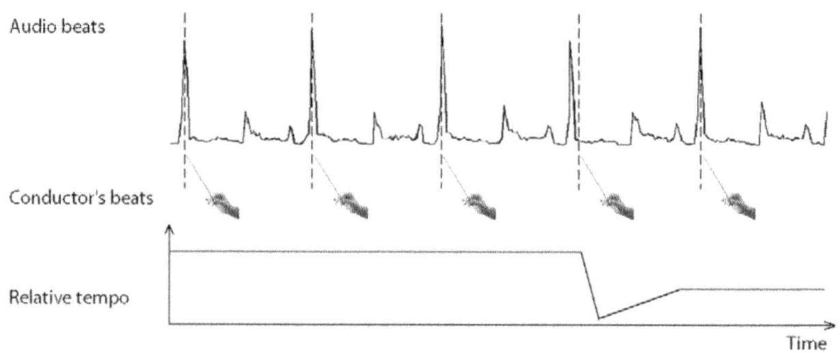

Fig. 6. Example of relative playback speed adjustments over time in delayed latency handling. Because the conductor's beat falls later than expected, the current audio beat is out of phase. To correct for this, the sound is played at an even lower speed so the next audio beat is in phase with the conductor's new tempo.

works by processing the sound in blocks, whose sizes are determined by a non-overlapping sliding window of length R_a. Each block is passed through an FFT followed by an inverse FFT of a different size R_s. To form a smooth audio track from the resulting blocks, each block is divided with the same type of window as used in the analysis. Interpolation between consecutive blocks is performed by adding them together using a triangular window, as described in [28]. The overlap factor corresponds to the block size used in the Mixxx playback system. By controlling the scale factor R_a/R_s, the audio is stretched or compressed to match the conductor's beat and tempo prediction messages received via MIDI.

6 Conclusion

In this paper a complete system for the simulation of an orchestra's reaction to a conductor's baton is presented. It consists of a vision based baton tracking system, an automatic real-time audio beat estimation module, and a system for coupling the conducting beats with the audio beats by scaling the audio playback accordingly.

The baton tracking system successfully tracks the velocity of the tip of the baton using one or two cameras. The baton may be mapped to a 3D model to improve the stability of the estimated position. The system operates in two modes: an initial seek mode to retrieve a start position of the baton, and a subsequent tracking mode. The tip of the baton is subsequently used to estimate velocity and beat time points.

The audio beat estimation module is based on a computationally simple parameter. The peaks of the estimated parameter are used for identifying the temporal location of the beats and the errors are removed by weighting the estimated intervals and merging them into a running beat probability vector.

Two approaches for mapping baton beats to audio beats are used. If the visual and audio systems operate at low latencies, an event based coupling of the beats is used. Otherwise a delayed approach is employed.

In this way, the vision based system corresponds to the musicians observing the conductor, the audio beat estimation module corresponds to the conductor listening to the orchestra, and the coupling and time-scaling modules correspond to the musicians performing the music.

The visual tracking is freely available as EyesWeb modules from [25]. Mixxx is available from [29].

Further work includes refinement of the conducting gesture recognition algorithm and its inclusion into a more complete conducting system. To provide an improved orchestral simulation, expressive parameters other than beat could be included in the modelling. By extracting such information from the audio, or by providing it with manual annotation, it could be used in the rendering of the audio playback, thereby giving the conductor control of these other expressive parameters.

References

1. Rudolf, M.: The Grammar of Conducting: A Comprehensive Guide to Baton Technique and Interpretation. Third edn. Macmillan (1993)
2. Wanderley, M., Battier, M., eds.: Trends in Gestural Control of Music. IRCAM (2000)
3. Camurri, A., Hashimoto, S., Ricchetti, M., Trocca, R.: Eyesweb – towards gesture and affect recognition in dance/music interactive systems. Computer Music Journal **24** (2000) 57–69 `www.musart.dist.unige.it/site_inglese/research/r_current/eyesweb.html`.
4. Andersen, T.H.: Mixxx: Towards novel DJ interfaces. In: New Interfaces for Musical Expression, Montreal, Canada (2003) 30–35
5. Boulanger, R., Mathews, M.: The 1997 Mathews radio-baton improvisation modes. In: Proceedings of the International Computer Music Conference, Thessaloniki, Greece, ICMA (1997) 395–398
6. Rich, R., Buchla, D.: Lightning II. Electronic Musician **12** (1996) 118–124
7. Borchers, J.O., Samminger, W., Mühlhäuser, M.: Engineering a realistic real-time conducting system for the audio/video rendering of a real orchestra. In: Fourth International Symposium on Multimedia Software Engineering, California, USA, IEEE MSE (2002)
8. Ilmonen, T., Takala, T.: Conductor following with artificial neural networks. In: Proceedings of the International Computer Music Conference, Beijing, China, ICMA (1999) 367–370
9. Marrin, T., Paradiso, J.: The digital baton: a versatile performance instrument. In: Proceedings of the International Computer Music Conference, Thessaloniki, Greece, ICMA (1997) 313–316
10. Marrin, T.: Inside the Conductor's Jacket: analysis interpretation and musical synthesis of expressive gesture. Ph.D thesis, MIT (2000)
11. Carosi, P., Bertini, G.: The light baton: A system for conducting computer music performance. In: Proceedings of the International Computer Music Conference, San Francisco, CA, USA (1992) 73–76
12. Segen, J., Kumar, S., Gluckman, J.: Visual interface for conducting virtual orchestra. In: Proceedings of the International Conference on Pattern Recognition (ICPR). Volume 1., Barcelona, Spain, IEEE (2000) 1276–1279

13. Segen, J., Majumder, A., Gluckman, J.: Virtual dance and music conducted by a human conductor. In Gross, M., Hopgood, F.R.A., eds.: Eurographics. Volume 19(3)., EACG (2000)
14. Gerver, R.: Conducting algorithms. WWW (2001) `http://www.stanford.edu/~rgerver/conducting.htm`.
15. McNeill, D.: Hand and Mind: What Gestures Reveal About Thought. University of Chicago Press (1992)
16. Humphries, L.: What to think about when you conduct: Perception, language, and musical communication. WWW (2000) `http://www.ThinkingApplied.com`.
17. Murphy, D.: Tracking a conductor's baton. In Olsen, S., ed.: Proceedings of the 12th Danish Conference on Pattern Recognition and Image Analysis. Volume 2003/05 of DIKU report., Copenhagen, Denmark, DSAGM, HCØ Tryk (2003) 59–66
18. Canny, J.: A computational approach to edge detection. IEEE Transactions on Pattern Analysis and Machine Intelligence **PAMI-8** (1986) 697–698
19. Murphy, D.: Extracting arm gestures for VR using EyesWeb. In Buyoli, C.L., Loureiro, R., eds.: Workshop on Current Research Directions in Computer Music, Barcelona, Spain, Audiovisual Institute, Pompeu Fabra University (2001) 55–60
20. Lucas, B., Kanade, T.: An iterative image registration technique with an application to stereo vision. In: Proceedings of 7th International Joint Conference on Artificial Intelligence (IJCAI). (1981) 674–679
21. Jensen, K., Andersen, T.H.: Real-time beat estimation using feature selection. Volume 2771 of Lecture Notes in Computer Science., Springer-Verlag (2003)
22. Masri, P., Bateman, A.: Improved modelling of attack transient in music analysis-resynthesis. In: Proceedings of the International Computer Music Conference, Hong-Kong (1996) 100–104
23. Desain, P.: A (de)composable theory of rhythm. Music Perception **9** (1992) 439–454
24. Jensen, K., Murphy, D.: Segmenting melodies into notes. In Olsen, S., ed.: Proceedings of the 10th Danish Conference on Pattern Recognition and Image Analysis. Volume 2001/04 of DIKU report., Copenhagen, Denmark, DSAGM, HCØ Tryk (2001) 115–119
25. Murphy, D.: Baton tracker. WWW (2002) Includes user guide. `http://www.diku.dk/~declan/projects/baton-tracker.html`.
26. Murphy, D.: Pattern play. In Smaill, A., ed.: Additional Proceedings of the 2nd International Conference on Music and Artificial Intelligence. On-line tech. report series of the Division of Informatics, University of Edinburgh, Scotland, UK, `http://dream.dai.ed.ac.uk/group/smaill/icmai/b06.pdf` (2002)
27. Dolson, M.: The phase vocoder: A tutorial. Computer Music Journal **4** (1986) 14–27
28. Rodet, X., Dapalle, P.: Spectral envelopes and inverse FFT synthesis. In: Proceedings of the 93rd AES Convention, San Francisco, USA (1992) Preprint 3393
29. Andersen, T.H., Andersen, K.H.: Mixxx. WWW (2003) `http://mixxx.sourceforge.net/`.

A Video System for Recognizing Gestures by Artificial Neural Networks for Expressive Musical Control

Paul Modler[1] and Tony Myatt[2]

[1] Hochschule für Gestaltung, 76135 Karlsruhe, Germany
pmodler@hfg-karlsruhe.de
[2] University of York, Music Department ,YO10 5DD York, UK
am12@york.ac.uk

Abstract. In this paper we describe a system to recognize gestures to control musical processes. For that we applied a Time Delay Neuronal Network to match gestures processed as variation of luminance information in video streams. This resulted in recognition rates of about 90% for 3 different types of hand gestures and it is presented here as a prototype for a gestural recognition system that is tolerant to ambient conditions and environments. The neural network can be trained to recognize gestures difficult to be described by postures or sign language. This can be used to adapt to unique gestures of a performer or video sequences of arbitrary moving objects. We will discuss the outcome of extending the system to learn successfully a set of 17 hand gestures. The application was implemented in jMax to achieve real-time conditions and easy integration into a musical environment. We will describe the design and learning procedure of the using the Stuttgart Neuronal Network Simulator. The system aims to integrate into an environment that enables expressive control of musical parameters (KANSEI).

1 Motivation

The discussions relating to gestural data processing for musical applications have emerged in recent years. This discussion developed from the background of interactive computer music systems and their use in performance, but also from the experience of novel interfaces to control the generation of sound and musical processes. Several data processing paradigms have been established inspired by the availability of a larger range of sensor systems and the increasing processing power These all use gestural data to control musical parameters (or light etc.) within artistic environments. Issues of mapping control data to musical parameters are related to these paradigms and the detection of higher level expressive information of music parameters are of great interest (RIMM, MEGA, Wanderley/Battier).

This paper describes a video-based system developed for the recognition of gestural data. It analyses body movements to extract high level (gestural) information about the movements which then can be used as artistic material for parameter control.

A. Camurri and G. Volpe (Eds.): GW 2003, LNAI 2915, pp. 541–548, 2004.

2 Video Based Data Acquisition

The use of a video-based system offers the advantage of common and widely available input device. The setup process for a system of this type is straightforward and the resulting data directly comparable to the visual interpretation of gestures by humans.

The drawbacks for video-based systems are the high data rate and processing complexity evolving from multi-dimensional data. Additionally, the complex and sophisticated ability of human visual data processing increases the aspiration of video systems.

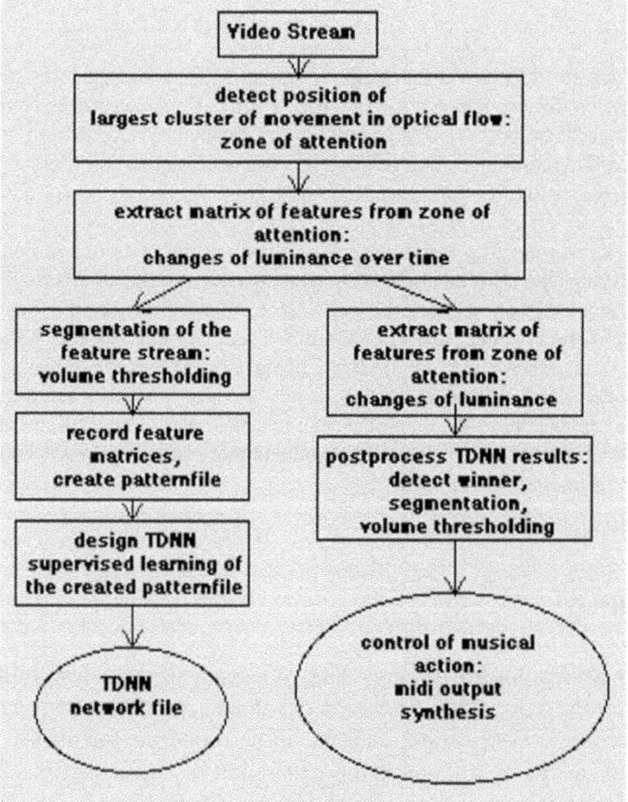

Fig. 1. Dataflow

Available video tracking systems are based on color detection or the change between successive video frames and are used in a wide range of musical and artistic applications (*EyesWeb*, *Fingerprint*, *Palindrom*, *SoftVNS*, *BigEye*).

Gestural processing is strongly related to the amount of movement or energy within the gesture (Cuttler, 1998). This assumption prompted an approach where the rate of change of luminance points in consecutive video frames became the main feature for the recognition process.

3 System Overview

The video stream from a standard dv-camera was analyzed and information relating to luminance magnitudes of consecutive video frames was extracted and presented to an artificial neural network. The output of the neural network was evaluated using a post processing function that resulted in a binary output signifying the recognition of a trained gesture. Video digitization and visualization, recording and editing of data as well as real-time gesture recognition was realised on a Pentium 4, Linux system running at 1.7 GHz with jMax 2.5.1. A standard consumer video camera as well as a low cost webcam, were successfully used.

4 Trained Gestures

As an initial experiment we used video data from three different hand gestures to teach the TDNN. The recorded data for one gesture type were 3 gesture samples with different gestural speed each recorded twice. This gave a set of 6 samples for each gesture. The gestures were taped to be able to reproduce the gestures exactly.

Trained gestures:

- open and close hand (openClose)
- move open hand parallel to lens (waving)
- move fingers without thumb (flatter)

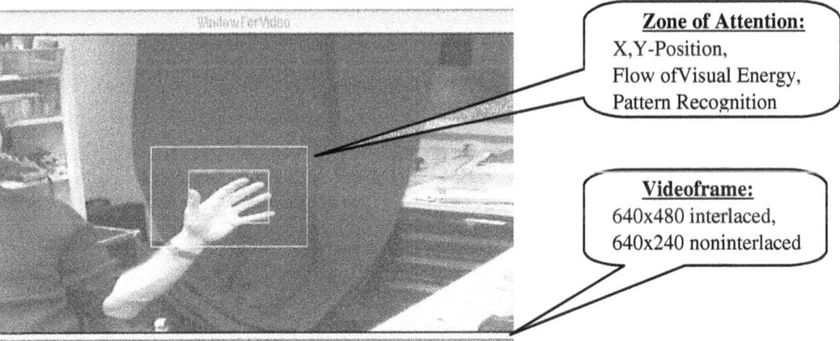

Fig. 2. Video Input and Zone of Attention

5 Preprocessing and Feature Extraction

The luminance values of consecutive frames were extracted from the RGB data of the video stream at relevant pixel positions and their rates of change were computed. To reduce the amount of data to be processed, but maintain relevant gestural information we used a combination of pixel resolutions.

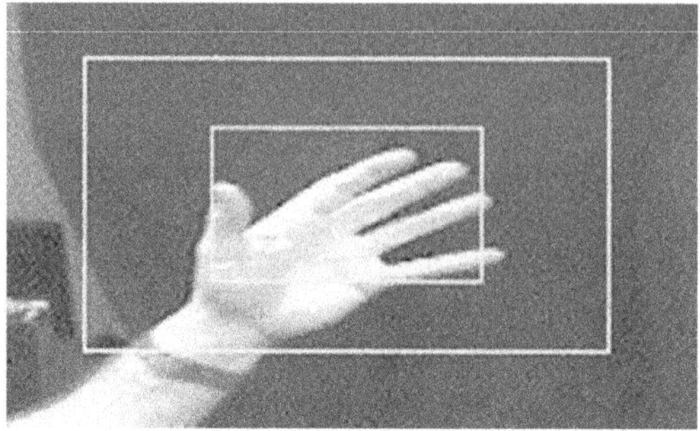

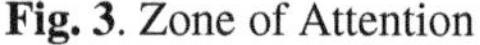

Fig. 3. Zone of Attention

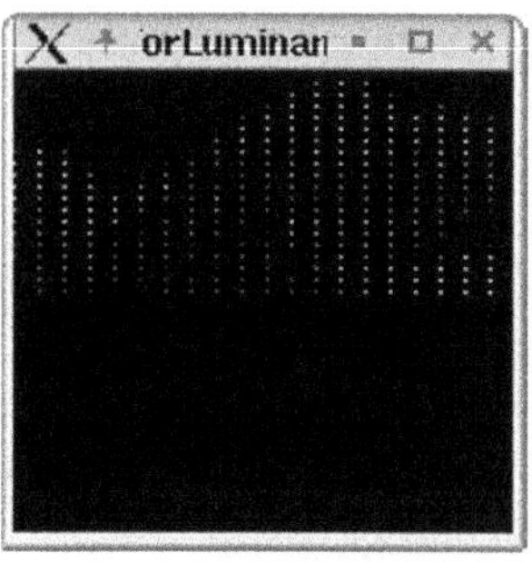

Fig. 4. Feature Extraction

A clustering process is used to detect the overall location of the gesture. The aim of this is to achieve a position independent subframe and also to increase the resolution of the relevant video data only for the relevant parts of the visual stream. In other words: the whole picture is inspected to indicate a small zone for higher resolution data capture (zone of attention).

6 Creation of Training Patterns, Automatic Segmentation of Gestural Data

To teach the Neuronal Network we preprocessed the recorded gesture samples as described in 5. The resulting feature stream, in our case a matrix of luminance rates from within the zone of attention was recorded for each gesture sample. All recorded patterns were completed with the appropriate values for the output neurons and then stored as a pattern-file in the format of the Stuttgart Neuronal Net Simulator (SNNS).

To achieve fast acquisition of training data the video stream was segmented through a threshold algorithm detecting start and end of a gesture. The threshold was triggered by the level of optical energy present in the zone of attention.

7 Extending the Trainings Data through Variations of Patterns

To increase the recognition rates of the network we added to the set of training patterns variations of the recorded patterns. For that we operated linear affine transformations on each recorded gesture to multiply the recorded training patterns automatically. The transformations were applied in the following order:

1. stretching in the x, y direction
2. rotation in the x, y plane around the center of gravity of the gesture
3. shifting in the x, y plane

8 Design of the Artificial Neural Network: TDNN

For the recognition of the gestures we used a Time Delay Neural Network architecture. The TDNN was developed for phoneme recognition (Waibel, Berthold) but has been successfully applied in gestural processing (Modler, Zannos 1997) as well as in musical audio applications (Marolt 1999). A certain form of Time Delay Networks was successfully applied for recognition of image sequences for gestural control (Vassilakis, Howell, 2001).

This neural network architecture provides recognition of timed patterns at low processing power requirements independent from the pattern speed reference.

The network is designed to have one input layer with 900x6 input units, one hidden layer with 50x4 units and one output layer with 3 units. For each frame of the video stream the network is presented a new set of pixels plus the previous 5 sets. This can be seen as a windowing function over the whole data stream. (Zell, 1994).

The TDNN was design and trained in SNNS with the patterns created as described above. The time needed to teach the TDNN varies depending on the size of the network, the size of each pattern and the number of instances for each gesture type, and on the number of cycles a pattern-set has to be taught before the pattern set is learnt sufficiently. On a Pentium 4, 2.8GHz one cycle of learning of a pattern set based on 18 patterns (2 x 3 instances x 3 gestures) and approximately 1300 variations for each gesture was accomplished in about 1 h.

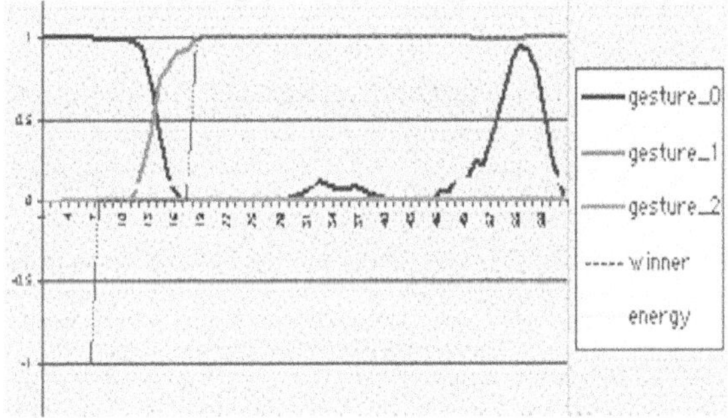

Fig. 5. Result of the Output Neurons for openClose (0), flatter (1), waving(2)

9 Post Processing

The output of the neural network was processed with threshold and filter functions. Together with the overall level of the luminance rate the onset and offset of a gesture as well as the type of the gesture was estimated. The output of the recognition process was displayed on the screen as well as sent to external devices via midi as note-ons and not-offs.

10 Recognition Rates

Various parameters of the experiment, like distance, location, rotation and size of the gestural object (here: the hand) in the video frame have influence on the recognition results. Overall light conditions, gesture speed etc, also have an impact on recognition rates.

Figure 6 shows the resulting values of the three output neurons and the overall energy of the optical flow over time. A value close to 1.0 indicates the network assumes the output unit as recognized. We estimated the recognition rates by presenting the neural network 10 samples of each trained gesture. The 10 test samples for one gesture type were similar in location and rotation, but different in gestural speed. The estimated recognition rates were about 90%.

11 Learning More Gestures

Extending the described Neural Network to a larger number of output neurons we increased the number of gestures the network was able to recognize. We successfully taught such a neural network 17 gestures of different types and different amounts of optical flow. Although we achieved similar recognition rates for the network trained with 17 gestures as for that trained with three gestures the position independence of the gestures in a video frame was unsatisfying. The recognition rate decreased when the hand position was altered relative to the camera. Moving the hand in the x,y plane was difficult for a performer to reproduce a gesture similar relative to a camera. This was due to the bio-mechanics of the hand but also to the concept of processing pure image sequences. Extending the system by using a Model Based approach (Bowden 1999) or by extracting and using additional features like the Quantity of Motion or Contraction Index (Camurri 2002) as used in the KANSEI approach could be integrated to overcome this drawback.

12 Integration into a Performance Environment

To integrate the process into a performance environment we realized all parts of the process in jMax as following external objects (Modler, 2002):

The results of the recognition process as well as values of the extracted features can be sent to external devices through the standard jMax midi-port.

In a test setup we mapped the output of the winner detection to trigger three different audio samples from within jMax. Additional parameters like the position of the zone of attention or the volume of the luminance inside the zone can be used as sub-gestural control information for the sound process. We also mapped the output of the neurons directly to the volume of sine-wave generators running at different frequencies.

Table 1. External jMax Objects

Object	*Purpose*
grabber	video input
window	video output and data visualization:
recorder	recording editing and saving of multidimensional data
Feature	feature extraction
Nn	TDNN and pattern-files, gesture recognition

13 Conclusions

Our aim was to investigate the use of a low-cost setup to achieve a gesture recognition tool that can be used in a wide range of interactive, artistic applications such as dance, installations, novel interfaces and more.

For that we developed a video-based system based on a Time Delay Neural Network architecture. The luminance rates technique promise an increased independence in different lighting conditions, especially varying light temperature and light intensity. It also significantly reduces the amount of video data to be processed.

The segmentation and clustering mechanisms resulted both in a certain level of position independence of the gesture in the video frame a further reduction in the data to be processed by the neural network.

Further work in this area will provide details about the number of different gestures, which sufficiently can be learned from a chosen network design and about the use of different gesture types, such as hand gestures or full body gestures.

Also more work has to be done combining analysis tools like Model Based Analysis (Bowden 1999) or KANSEI tools (Camurri 2002) into the system. This should increase the recognition rates as well as reduce the computational needs.

So far the system provides an environment for the detection of a wide range of gestures in different surroundings suitable for interactive compositions, performances, dance and installations.

References

1. Berthold, R. Michael.: A Time Delay Radial Basis Function Network for Phoneme Recognition. In Proceedings of IEEE International Conference on Neural Networks, volume 7, pages 4470-- 4473, Orlando, FL, 1994. IEEE Computer Society Press.
2. Bowden, R., Learning Nonlinear Models of Shape and Motion, PhD Thesis, Brunel University 1999
3. A.Camurri, R.Trocca, G.Volpe , Interactive Systems Design: A KANSEI-based Approach, Proc. NIME2002, Dublin, May 2002

4. de Cecco, M., Dechelle, F., jMax/FTS Documentation, http://www.ircam.fr, 1999
5. Cuttler, R., Turk, M., View-based Interpretation of Real-time Optical Flow for Gesture Recognition, Proceedings of the 3. IEEE International Conference of Face and Gesture Recognition, 1998
6. Marolt, Matia, A Comparison of feed forward neural network architectures for piano music transcription, Proceedings of the ICMC 1999, ICMA 1999
7. MEGA, Multisensory Expressive Gesture Applications, V Framework Programme IST Project No.1999-20410, 2002, http://www.megaproject.org/
8. Modler, Paul, Zannos, Ioannis, Emotional Aspects of Gesture Recognition by Neural Networks, using dedicated Input Devices, in Antonio Camurri (ed.) Proc. of KANSEI The Technology of Emotion, AIMI International Workshop, Universita Genova, Genova 1997
9. Modler, Paul, A General Purpose Open Source Artificial Neural Network Simulator for jMax, IRCAM-Forum, Nov. 2002, Paris
10. Myatt, A: Strategies for interaction in *construction 3*, Organised Sound, Volume 7 Number 3, CUP, Cambridge UK 2002, pp157-169
11. Palindrome, http://www.palindrome.de/
12. The RIMM Project, Real-time Interactive Multiple Media Content Generation Using High Performance Computing and Multi-Parametric Human-Computer Interfaces, European Commission 5th Framework programme Information, Societies, Technology 2002, http://www.york.ac.uk/res/rimm/
13. Rokeby, David, SoftVNS Motion Tracking system, http://www.interlog.com/~drokeby/softVNS.html
14. SNNS, Stuttgarter Neural Network Simulator, User Manual 4.1, Stuttgart, University of Stuttgart, 1995.
15. Vassilakis H.,Howell, J. A., Buxton, H. I, Comparison of Feedforward (TDRBF) and Generative (TDRGBN) Network for Gesture Based Control, Proceedings of the Int. Gesture Workshop 2001,
16. Waibel, A., T. Hanazawa, G. Hinton, K. Shikano, and K.J. Lang, Phoneme recognition using time-delay neural networks, IEEE Transactions On Acoustics, Speech, and Signal Processing, Vol 37, No. 3, pp. 328-339, March 1989.
17. Wanderley, Marcelo, Battier Marc, Trends in Gestural Control of Music, CD-Rom, 2000, IRCAM, Paris,
18. Zell, Andres, Simulation Neuronaler Netze, Bonn, Paris: Addison Wesley, 1994.

Ghost in the Cave – An Interactive Collaborative Game Using Non-verbal Communication

Marie-Louise Rinman[1], Anders Friberg[2], Bendik Bendiksen[3], Demian Cirotteau[5], Sofia Dahl[2], Ivar Kjellmo[3], Barbara Mazzarino[4], and Antonio Camurri[4]

[1] Centre of User Oriented IT-design, KTH, Stockholm
rinman@nada.kth.se
[2] Speech Music and Hearing, KTH, Stockholm
{andersf,sofiad}@speech.kth.se
[3] Octaga / Telenor, Oslo
{ivar.kjellmo,bendik.bendiksen}@octaga.com
[4] InfoMus Lab, DIST-University of Genoa, Genoa
music@dist.unige.it, bunny@infomus.dist.unige.it
[5] CSC – Center of Computational Sonology, DEI – Dept of Information Engineering
University of Padua
Cirotteau@csc.unipd.it

Abstract. The interactive game environment, *Ghost in the Cave*, presented in this short paper, is a work still in progress. The game involves participants in an activity using non-verbal emotional expressions. Two teams use expressive gestures in either voice or body movements to compete. Each team has an avatar controlled either by singing into a microphone or by moving in front of a video camera. Participants/players control their avatars by using acoustical or motion cues. The avatar is navigated in a 3D distributed virtual environment using the Octagon server and player system. The voice input is processed using a musical cue analysis module yielding performance variables such as tempo, sound level and articulation as well as an emotional prediction. Similarly, movements captured from a video camera are analyzed in terms of different movement cues. The target group is young teenagers and the main purpose to encourage creative expressions through new forms of collaboration.

1 Introduction

Collaboration and communication are frequently discussed issues not the least concerning senior level school classes. How could communication and collaboration be facilitated among young teenagers with different social and cultural background? Games of all kinds, sports, children's play and games, computer games and so forth, are part of our everyday lives. As such they are recognisable to most people despite cultural and social background and may therefore serve as a means for establishing a common ground. What elements and properties in games are common enough to serve as a platform for collaboration? Win-or-lose games focusing on either individual results (tennis, "shoot-them-up" computer games) or teamwork such as football (and various networked computer games) seem to be preferred to reflective collaborative ones. Furthermore games generally consist of a set of acknowledged rules and conventions. As a suggestion an interactive collaborative game environment favour-

A. Camurri and G. Volpe (Eds.): GW 2003, LNAI 2915, pp. 549–556, 2004.

ing participation, collaboration and communication should contain a well-balanced mix of constraints as well as allowing free scope for participants according to Rinman [12]. In such a game the following set of qualities and elements could be included: 1. Well-defined rules and tasks that should be executed within a limited time and space. 2. A well-defined structure. The classical drama, or traditional narrative, has a beginning, middle and end, which in turn includes an introduction (revealing context), a climax (search for a solution of a task), and the final discovery, or change from ignorance to knowledge. The similar structure occurs in "Ghost" when participants find out how to control their avatar. As for allowing participants a certain amount of freedom, "Ghost" uses emotional non-verbal communication in music and dance to communicate and interact with an avatar, which allows participants to "play around" with the environment as well as communicating freely with each other. Expressive Gesture, as applied in "Ghost", is using recent models of expressive communication in music and dance developed by Camurri and others [4,] [2], [5] and [9] within the frames of the EU project MEGA. These models are based upon a large body of research in expressive communication [10], [6].

The aim of the interactive game environment, "Ghost in the cave", as presented in this paper, is to test the applicability and intelligibility of expressive gesture in a new setting. First, could expressive gesture, e.g. music and dance, be used as a basis for collaboration and participation? And second, could it be used as an input control in an interactive game environment?

2 The Interactive Game Environment: "Ghost in the Cave"

The group of participants (a school class) are divided into two teams, each team consisting of one small group of 1-3 players and an assisting team helping the players in various ways. One player in each team controls an avatar either by singing into a microphone or by moving in front of a video camera. The other two players may discuss alternative solutions helping the navigator executing his or her task. The challenge for each team is to 1) figure out how to use the gestures in order to control the navigation of the avatar in the sea world and 2) make the avatar change mood to an emotion corresponding to that of a ghost inside each cave. Here the avatar changes colour and shape depending on the acoustical and motion cues conveyed by the players. The assisting teams generate speed as well as a music background by moving and dancing (overall quantity of motion captured by two cameras, one for each team). They may follow the game via two screens onto which each team's avatar is projected showing a third person view of the virtual game world. Figure 1 gives an overview of game environment.

3 Detailed Properties of "Ghost in the Cave"

Main features and aims: A multi-user real-time activity including multi-sensory interaction and modality.

Categories and properties: A traditional game of competition and struggle aiming at proving one's superiority based on a set of strict rules. Game narrative as a consuming

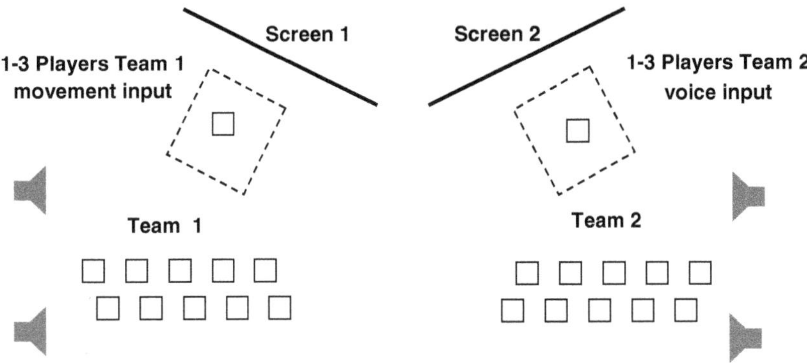

Fig. 1. Overview of game setup.

object. On the other hand the complete opposite also holds: a game solving riddles and puzzles based on teamwork. Cheating may be part of the game, making it less respectful and more humorous and playful.

Virtual game environment: A 3D animated sea world

Avatars: Team 1 (Purple) controls a Stingray; Team 2 (Blue) controls a Dolphin.

Task/mission: The first task is to navigate through a fish tank, locate and enter caves, three all together. When a player has found a cave their avatar is locked in position outside the cave waiting for the competing team's player to catch up. Each cave has a ghost representing a different emotion and colour: cave number one (1) blue/sad; number two (2) red/angry; and finally in cave number three (3) yellow/happy. The second task is to change the avatar into the same mood as the ghost in the cave using voice or movements, a task that is interchanged between the three players. Players (with assistance from other players and team members) have to find out what gestures correspond to the specific emotion by means of sound of voice or movements.

Concept: There is a (very) simple narrative, or story, in the game, i.e. a sequence of casually and thematically related events. Although there is no character development, no actual relation between characters and events, a more complex narrative occurs in the communicative and collaborative process between players and team members (narrative as social construction).

Means of controlling, navigating and changing the avatar: Players in Team 1 (T1) control their avatar through sound, and Team 2 (T2) through the use of movements. Navigational possibilities: forward, right and left.

Rules and points: When a player succeeds in finding a cave it gives one point, and changing the avatar's mood one point. Both avatar's points are displayed in the corner of each screen. Teams may also score points by presenting original solutions to the game.

Time limits: The tasks have to be executed within a certain limit of time. For instance, emotions have to be within three minutes.

Perspective in virtual world: Third person (back), inside cave (front of both avatars in order to be able to see the "face" of the avatars when changing facial expression).

Table 1. Game and drama structure in 3D environment. Each section, or scene, could be divided into smaller units in order to facilitate design of participation, functions, interface etc.

Drama structure Game Structure (Rules – Points)	Beginning: Introduction (revealing context) Start				Middle: Climax (search for solution)				End: Discovery Finish
Acts Emotions	Act 1 Sad				Act 2 Angry				Act 3 Happy
Scenes Points	Scene1	S 2	S 3 1 p	S 4 + 1 p	S1	S2	S3 + 1p	S4 + 1 p	S 1 + 1 = 5 p
Setting: 3 D sea world	Start	Sea world	Out-side C1	Inside C 1	Start in tank	Sea world	Out-side C2	In-side C2	Direct from C2 to C3
Action players: S 1-3: navigation S 4: mood:	out of cave	Search	En-trance:	Change To sad	→				
Action Teams:	Increase speed Create music		Action music	Emotional music	→				
Characters: Players Teams	Avatars are pre-programmed. Possibilities: move around, change shape and colour Players and team members, development: from individual to collaborative action								
Obstacles: Players	How to navigate Voice/movements	-		Change mood	→				
T 1 + T 2	Correct motions			Corre-sponding music					
Trains: Abilities Favours: Skills	Coordinated movements, singing, sounding, collaboration, communication Motor skills, cognitive skills								

4 Expressiveness in Music and Dance

Music performances can be described by their performance variables such as tone interonsets interval (IOI), tone sound level, articulation, and intonation. Overall measures of these performance variables over a section, henceforth as cues, have a strong coupling to the performed and perceived emotional expressive content in the performance [8]. For example, happiness is communicated by fast tempo, staccato articulation, high sound level, and fast tone attacks, while sadness is communicated by slow tempo, low sound level, legato articulation, and slow tone attacks. These rather general descriptions have been collected from a large number of investigations and are surprisingly consistent for different music examples, performers or listeners.

Dance performance may be analysed in a similar way using overall motion cues such as quantity of motion, velocity, amount of motion/rest, and fluency [3]. Here too, there is a coupling between these cues and the expressive character of the dance according to Camurri, Lagerlöf and Volpe [4].

Recently, real-time computer tools for analysing expressive gestures in music and dance have been developed within the MEGA project (www.megaproject.org). These tools have been developed within the software platforms EyesWeb and pd. The body gesture analysis package in EyesWeb has a large number of different gesture cues and is using imaging algorithms applied to video input. The musical gesture analysis is using signal processing algorithms applied on audio input and outputs both the basic musical cues such as tempo and sound level, but also the emotional intent [6] [7].

5 Technical Implementation

The implementation was mainly in forms of patches within the software environments Octagon, EyesWeb, and pd. The virtual 3D environment is run in the Octagon server and player system. This system is a distributed virtual reality system, that uses MPEG4 and VRML file formats. Multiple users may be represented in the virtual world by their own figure or avatar. Here they are present in the same shared virtual environment and can interact with each other. The distribution goes through a network using the MPEG4 protocol. (More on Octaga and the Octagon system at: www.octaga.com).

To control the avatars the players can use two types of expressive input: voice or movements. The player using the voice input steers by talking, singing or producing any kind of sound into two microphones, and different music performance variables are analysed using the musical cue analysis software [7]. Simply by using the left or right microphone the avatar turns left or right, using both microphones sets the direction forward. The number of detected note onsets determines the velocity of the avatar. However, this velocity can also be scaled by the overall movement of the supporting team members.

Similarly, the player using movement input controls his/her avatar by moving the left, right or both arms in front of a video camera connected to an EyesWeb patch. The overall movement gives the velocity of the avatar. As for the audio navigation control this can also be scaled by the overall movement of the supporting team members.

For the task of matching the avatars to the mood of each cave, different audio and movement "cues" are used. The audio input uses the sound level, articulation and tempo, so that a medium fast tempo, staccato articulation and medium high sound level corresponds to "happy". For the video input the player is supposed to move/dance and different overall motion cues are analysed using a cue analysis patch implemented in the EyesWeb software. The cues used are the overall quantity of motion, the contraction index (i.e. how "collected" the body is), and upward gesture tempo (i.e. the time between gestures in the vertical direction). In the current mapping a "happy" performance corresponds to high quantity of motion, low contraction index and a medium upward gesture tempo. EyesWeb is connected to each Octagon client so the clients can receive expressive parameters. In this case the avatars receive the parameters and change according to them.

The overall movement of the team members are not directly involved in controlling the avatar influences both the velocity of the avatar as well as controlling the music "scheme".

6 Design Problems in Interactive Environments

The complex mix of interaction between people as well as with the environment in a setting like "Ghost" brings to the forefront several similarities between theatre and human-computer interaction (HCI). "Player" and "user" differ from each other concerning intentions and goals (entertaining vs. fulfilling certain purposes). In a mixed reality performance users become participants; they are co-writers and co-directors influencing the outcome of a game [12] a fact that may be a challenge, or cause problems, for the designers. "Ghost" is a "staged" game where the user takes on different roles such as player, assisting team member, spectator and so forth. The player actually steps up on a stage and interacts with a virtual character projected on a screen.

The first design problem is "communication", which may be defined in terms of sharing and participation. In interactive environments communication is not principally instrumental or utilitarian, the attitude of the participants is more likely to be playful or personally committed [12], whereas applicability and usability may be major goals from an HCI perspective. Despite these differences, designers from the different areas deal with the same problem: communication, relationships and human experiences.

The second issue is to identify the degree and category of user/participant involvement and interaction. In drama relationships are central as well as in various types of games. Relationships may consist of different constellations between people, between people and ideas and between people and the environment.

The third issue is the notion of a multiple interface that goes along with the development of settings that involve people in multiple-relationships and real-time conversation. When a practice is considered a unit of activity, such as a complex performance setting, one could speak of *interfaces* rather than of an interface. The interface then becomes a resource for social action and interaction according to Bowers and Rodden [1]. They claim the interface includes political, social, organisational, and technical as well as emotional properties.

7 Organising "User" Participation Using Drama as Foundation

Performance theories and practices deal by tradition with the issue of orchestrating audience experience, engagement and reactions. This knowledge could contribute to design dealing with human – machine interaction in general.

In the early nineties Brenda Laurel proposed the idea of using theatre and drama to get a deeper understanding of human-computer activity. "Dramatic arts have a tradition of several thousand years in thought, study, and experimentation with human experience with a variety of modes of interaction" [11]. Theatre and games basically deal with orchestrating emotions, forms of interaction, collaboration and relationships. Engagement is created through a balance between restrictions and possibilities. To orchestrate and make social as well as human-machine interaction possible in interactive environments this balance is pivotal. Furthermore participants should to a certain extent be able to influence the outcome of the event. In "Ghost" the team members communicate and try to solve a task according to a (limited) set of rules. These rules serve as common ground and shared understanding that make collaboration possible [12].

In a play the actor takes on a role as participants do in a game session when accepting rules and conditions. A player who trespasses against or ignores the rules is a "spoilsport". The spoilsport is not the same as the false player, the cheat, for the latter pretends to be playing the game and in doing so still acknowledges a world of illusions. The spoilsport however shatters the play-world itself robbing play of its illusion. Rules may be broken and interpreted differently by participants in the game.

8 Evaluation

Basis for evaluation: The evaluation is partly based on video recordings of a game event within the frames of a whole evening's performance at the SMAC conference in Stockholm, August 6, and partly on a questionnaire given to the participants (answering rate: 33 out of approx. 200 people). Apart from the conference delegates a number of invited guests and their children participated in the game event.

User role: Depending on the role people, or users, had in the game the more positive the attitude towards the activity. The higher degree of control participants felt they had the more engaged and tolerant towards shortcomings they were. Players (controlling the avatar) tended to be more enthusiastic and understanding of the game's logic than the assisting team members. Their enthusiasm depended to some extent on proximity to the screens and players. Spectators were the most sceptical.

Problems and critique: Some problems with sound/movement interface. Immediate feedback to motion and sound input is important as well as time limits in terms of solving tasks. Moreover the game requires a thorough introduction to be comprehensible and accessible, which is demanding in terms of people and time.

Finally, could expressive gesture, e.g. music and dance, be used as a basis for collaboration and as a means for communication in interactive game environments? Conclusions drawn from this one occasion are positive although the "Ghost" needs to be refined. It could as well serve as a means to inspire teenagers to physical exercise as well as to collaborate using non-verbal communication.

Acknowledgements

This work is partially supported by the EU project MEGA IST-20410 and the competence centre CID, KTH, Stockholm.

References

1. Bowers J and Rodden T (1993) Exploding the Interface: Experiences of a CSCW Network. In Proceedings of INTERCHI'93 the conference on Human factors in computing systems, Amsterdam, The Netherlands.
2. Camurri A (2002) Interactive Systems Design: a KANSEI-based Approach, in NIME-02 Intl. Conference on New Interfaces for Musical Expression, Dublin, Ireland
3. Camurri A, Coletta P, Mazzarino B, Trocca R, Volpe G (2002). Improving the man-machine interface through the analysis of expressiveness in human movement. Proc. Intl. Conf. IEEE ROMAN-2002, Sept. 2002, Berlin. IEEE CS Press.
4. Camurri A, Lagerhof I, Volpe G (2003). Recognizing Emotion from Dance Movement: Comparison of Spectator Recognition and Automated Techniques, International Journal of Human-Computer Studies, Vol. 59, 213-255.
5. Canazza S (in press) An abstract control space for communication of sensory expressive intentions in music performance, Computer Music Journal.

6. Friberg A and Battel G, U. (2002). Structural Communication. In (R. Parncutt & G. E. McPherson, Eds.) The Science and Psychology of Music Performance: Creative Strategies for Teaching and Learning. New York: Oxford University Press, 199-218.
7. Friberg A, Schoonderwaldt E, Juslin, PN and Bresin, R (2002) Automatic Real-Time Extraction of Musical Expression. In Proceedings of the International Computer Music Conference 2002, San Francisco: International Computer Music Association, 365-367.
8. Juslin P N (2001) Communication of emotion in music performance: A review and a theoretical framework. In P. N. Juslin & J. A. Sloboda (Eds.), Music and emotion: Theory and research (pp. 309-337). New York: Oxford University Press.
9. Juslin, P N, Friberg A and Bresin, R (2002). Toward a computational model of expression in performance: The GERM model. Musicae Scientiae special issue 2001-2002: 63-122.
10. Juslin P N and Sloboda, J A, eds. (2002) Music and emotion: Theory and research. New York: Oxford University Press.
11. Laurel B (1991, 1993) Computers as Theatre. Addison-Wesley Publishing Company, Inc.
12. Rinman M-L (2002) Forms of Interaction in Mixed Reality Performance – A study of the artistic event Desert Rain. Licentiate thesis, Royal Institute of Technology (KTH), Stockholm

Author Index

Lecture Notes in Artificial Intelligence (LNAI)

Vol. 2953: K. Konrad, Model Generation for Natural Language Interpretation and Analysis. XIII, 166 pages. 2004.

Vol. 2934: G. Lindemann, D. Moldt, M. Paolucci (Eds.), Regulated Agent-Based Social Systems. X, 301 pages. 2004.

Vol. 2930: F. Winkler, Automated Deduction in Geometry. VII, 231 pages. 2004.

Vol. 2923: V. Lifschitz, I. Niemelä (Eds.), Logic Programming and Nonmonotonic Reasoning. IX, 365 pages. 2004.

Vol. 2915: A. Camurri, G. Volpe (Eds.), Gesture-Based Communication in Human-Computer Interaction. XIII, 558 pages. 2004.

Vol. 2913: T.M. Pinkston, V.K. Prasanna (Eds.), High Performance Computing - HiPC 2003. XX, 512 pages. 2003.

Vol. 2903: T.D. Gedeon, L.C.C. Fung (Eds.), AI 2003: Advances in Artificial Intelligence. XVI, 1075 pages. 2003.

Vol. 2902: F.M. Pires, S.P. Abreu (Eds.), Progress in Artificial Intelligence. XV, 504 pages. 2003.

Vol. 2892: F. Dau, The Logic System of Concept Graphs with Negation. XI, 213 pages. 2003.

Vol. 2891: J. Lee, M. Barley (Eds.), Intelligent Agents and Multi-Agent Systems. X, 215 pages. 2003.

Vol. 2882: D. Veit, Matchmaking in Electronic Markets. XV, 180 pages. 2003.

Vol. 2871: N. Zhong, Z.W. Raś, S. Tsumoto, E. Suzuki (Eds.), Foundations of Intelligent Systems. XV, 697 pages. 2003.

Vol. 2854: J. Hoffmann, Utilizing Problem Structure in Planing. XIII, 251 pages. 2003.

Vol. 2843: G. Grieser, Y. Tanaka, A. Yamamoto (Eds.), Discovery Science. XII, 504 pages. 2003.

Vol. 2842: R. Gavaldá, K.P. Jantke, E. Takimoto (Eds.), Algorithmic Learning Theory. XI, 313 pages. 2003.

Vol. 2838: N. Lavrač, D. Gamberger, L. Todorovski, H. Blockeel (Eds.), Knowledge Discovery in Databases: PKDD 2003. XVI, 508 pages. 2003.

Vol. 2837: N. Lavrač, D. Gamberger, L. Todorovski, H. Blockeel (Eds.), Machine Learning: ECML 2003. XVI, 504 pages. 2003.

Vol. 2835: T. Horváth, A. Yamamoto (Eds.), Inductive Logic Programming. X, 401 pages. 2003.

Vol. 2821: A. Günter, R. Kruse, B. Neumann (Eds.), KI 2003: Advances in Artificial Intelligence. XII, 662 pages. 2003.

Vol. 2807: V. Matoušek, P. Mautner (Eds.), Text, Speech and Dialogue. XIII, 426 pages. 2003.

Vol. 2801: W. Banzhaf, J. Ziegler, T. Christaller, P. Dittrich, J.T. Kim (Eds.), Advances in Artificial Life. XVI, 905 pages. 2003.

Vol. 2797: O.R. Zaïane, S.J. Simoff, C. Djeraba (Eds.), Mining Multimedia and Complex Data. XII, 281 pages. 2003.

Vol. 2792: T. Rist, R. Aylett, D. Ballin, J. Rickel (Eds.), Intelligent Virtual Agents. XV, 364 pages. 2003.

Vol. 2782: M. Klusch, A. Omicini, S. Ossowski, H. Laamanen (Eds.), Cooperative Information Agents VII. XI, 345 pages. 2003.

Vol. 2780: M. Dojat, E. Keravnou, P. Barahona (Eds.), Artificial Intelligence in Medicine. XIII, 388 pages. 2003.

Vol. 2777: B. Schölkopf, M.K. Warmuth (Eds.), Learning Theory and Kernel Machines. XIV, 746 pages. 2003.

Vol. 2752: G.A. Kaminka, P.U. Lima, R. Rojas (Eds.), RoboCup 2002: Robot Soccer World Cup VI. XVI, 498 pages. 2003.

Vol. 2741: F. Baader (Ed.), Automated Deduction – CADE-19. XII, 503 pages. 2003.

Vol. 2705: S. Renals, G. Grefenstette (Eds.), Text- and Speech-Triggered Information Access. VII, 197 pages. 2003.

Vol. 2703: O.R. Zaïane, J. Srivastava, M. Spiliopoulou, B. Masand (Eds.), WEBKDD 2002 - MiningWeb Data for Discovering Usage Patterns and Profiles. IX, 181 pages. 2003.

Vol. 2700: M.T. Pazienza (Ed.), Extraction in the Web Era. XIII, 163 pages. 2003.

Vol. 2699: M.G. Hinchey, J.L. Rash, W.F. Truszkowski, C.A. Rouff, D.F. Gordon-Spears (Eds.), Formal Approaches to Agent-Based Systems. IX, 297 pages. 2002.

Vol. 2691: V. Mařík, J.P. Müller, M. Pechoucek (Eds.), Multi-Agent Systems and Applications III. XIV, 660 pages. 2003.

Vol. 2684: M.V. Butz, O. Sigaud, P. Gérard (Eds.), Anticipatory Behavior in Adaptive Learning Systems. X, 303 pages. 2003.

Vol. 2671: Y. Xiang, B. Chaib-draa (Eds.), Advances in Artificial Intelligence. XIV, 642 pages. 2003.

Vol. 2663: E. Menasalvas, J. Segovia, P.S. Szczepaniak (Eds.), Advances in Web Intelligence. XII, 350 pages. 2003.

Vol. 2661: P.L. Lanzi, W. Stolzmann, S.W. Wilson (Eds.), Learning Classifier Systems. VII, 231 pages. 2003.

Vol. 2654: U. Schmid, Inductive Synthesis of Functional Programs. XXII, 398 pages. 2003.

Vol. 2650: M.-P. Huget (Ed.), Communications in Multiagent Systems. VIII, 323 pages. 2003.

Vol. 2645: M.A. Wimmer (Ed.), Knowledge Management in Electronic Government. XI, 320 pages. 2003.

Vol. 2639: G. Wang, Q. Liu, Y. Yao, A. Skowron (Eds.), Rough Sets, Fuzzy Sets, Data Mining, and Granular Computing. XVII, 741 pages. 2003.

Vol. 2637: K.-Y. Whang, J. Jeon, K. Shim, J. Srivastava, Advances in Knowledge Discovery and Data Mining. XVIII, 610 pages. 2003.

Vol. 2636: E. Alonso, D. Kudenko, D. Kazakov (Eds.), Adaptive Agents and Multi-Agent Systems. XIV, 323 pages. 2003.

Vol. 2627: B. O'Sullivan (Ed.), Recent Advances in Constraints. X, 201 pages. 2003.

Vol. 2600: S. Mendelson, A.J. Smola (Eds.), Advanced Lectures on Machine Learning. IX, 259 pages. 2003.

Vol. 2592: R. Kowalczyk, J.P. Müller, H. Tianfield, R. Unland (Eds.), Agent Technologies, Infrastructures, Tools, and Applications for E-Services. XVII, 371 pages. 2003.

Vol. 2586: M. Klusch, S. Bergamaschi, P. Edwards, P. Petta (Eds.), Intelligent Information Agents. VI, 275 pages. 2003.

Vol. 2583: S. Matwin, C. Sammut (Eds.), Inductive Logic Programming. X, 351 pages. 2003.

Vol. 2581: J.S. Sichman, F. Bousquet, P. Davidsson (Eds.), Multi-Agent-Based Simulation. X, 195 pages. 2003.

Vol. 2577: P. Petta, R. Tolksdorf, F. Zambonelli (Eds.), Engineering Societies in the Agents World III. X, 285 pages. 2003.

Vol. 2569: D. Karagiannis, U. Reimer (Eds.), Practical Aspects of Knowledge Management. XIII, 648 pages. 2002.

Vol. 2560: S. Goronzy, Robust Adaptation to Non-Native Accents in Automatic Speech Recognition. XI, 144 pages. 2002.

Vol. 2557: B. McKay, J. Slaney (Eds.), AI 2002: Advances in Artificial Intelligence. XV, 730 pages. 2002.

Vol. 2554: M. Beetz, Plan-Based Control of Robotic Agents. XI, 191 pages. 2002.

Vol. 2543: O. Bartenstein, U. Geske, M. Hannebauer, O. Yoshie (Eds.), Web Knowledge Management and Decision Support. X, 307 pages. 2003.

Vol. 2541: T. Barkowsky, Mental Representation and Processing of Geographic Knowledge. X, 174 pages. 2002.

Vol. 2533: N. Cesa-Bianchi, M. Numao, R. Reischuk (Eds.), Algorithmic Learning Theory. XI, 415 pages. 2002.

Vol. 2531: J. Padget, O. Shehory, D. Parkes, N.M. Sadeh, W.E. Walsh (Eds.), Agent-Mediated Electronic Commerce IV. Designing Mechanisms and Systems. XVII, 341 pages. 2002.

Vol. 2527: F.J. Garijo, J.-C. Riquelme, M. Toro (Eds.), Advances in Artificial Intelligence - IBERAMIA 2002. XVIII, 955 pages. 2002.

Vol. 2522: T. Andreasen, A. Motro, H. Christiansen, H.L. Larsen (Eds.), Flexible Query Answering Systems. X, 383 pages. 2002.

Vol. 2514: M. Baaz, A. Voronkov (Eds.), Logic for Programming, Artificial Intelligence, and Reasoning. XIII, 465 pages. 2002.

Vol. 2507: G. Bittencourt, G.L. Ramalho (Eds.), Advances in Artificial Intelligence. XIII, 417 pages. 2002.

Vol. 2504: M.T. Escrig, F. Toledo, E. Golobardes (Eds.), Topics in Artificial Intelligence. XI, 427 pages. 2002.

Vol. 2499: S.D. Richardson (Ed.), Machine Translation: From Research to Real Users. XXI, 254 pages. 2002.

Vol. 2484: P. Adriaans, H. Fernau, M. van Zaanen (Eds.), Grammatical Inference: Algorithms and Applications. IX, 315 pages. 2002.

Vol. 2479: M. Jarke, J. Koehler, G. Lakemeyer (Eds.), KI 2002: Advances in Artificial Intelligence. XIII, 327 pages. 2002.

Vol. 2475: J.J. Alpigini, J.F. Peters, A. Skowron, N. Zhong (Eds.), Rough Sets and Current Trends in Computing. XV, 640 pages. 2002.

Vol. 2473: A. Gómez-Pérez, V.R. Benjamins (Eds.), Knowledge Engineering and Knowledge Management. Ontologies and the Semantic Web. XI, 402 pages. 2002.

Vol. 2466: M. Beetz, J. Hertzberg, M. Ghallab, M.E. Pollack (Eds.), Advances in Plan-Based Control of Robotic Agents. VIII, 291 pages. 2002.

Vol. 2464: M. O'Neill, R.F.E. Sutcliffe, C. Ryan, M. Eaton, N.J.L. Griffith (Eds.), Artificial Intelligence and Cognitive Science. XI, 247 pages. 2002.

Vol. 2448: P. Sojka, I. Kopecek, K. Pala (Eds.), Text, Speech and Dialogue. XII, 481 pages. 2002.

Vol. 2447: D.J. Hand, N.M. Adams, R.J. Bolton (Eds.), Pattern Detection and Discovery. XII, 227 pages. 2002.

Vol. 2446: M. Klusch, S. Ossowski, O. Shehory (Eds.), Cooperative Information Agents VI. XI, 321 pages. 2002.

Vol. 2445: C. Anagnostopoulou, M. Ferrand, A. Smaill (Eds.), Music and Artificial Intelligence. VIII, 207 pages. 2002.

Vol. 2443: D. Scott (Ed.), Artificial Intelligence: Methodology, Systems, and Applications. X, 279 pages. 2002.

Vol. 2432: R. Bergmann, Experience Management. XXI, 393 pages. 2002.

Vol. 2431: T. Elomaa, H. Mannila, H. Toivonen (Eds.), Principles of Data Mining and Knowledge Discovery. XIV, 514 pages. 2002.

Vol. 2430: T. Elomaa, H. Mannila, H. Toivonen (Eds.), Machine Learning: ECML 2002. XIII, 532 pages. 2002.

Vol. 2427: M. Hannebauer, Autonomous Dynamic Reconfiguration in Multi-Agent Systems. XXI, 284 pages. 2002.

Vol. 2424: S. Flesca, S. Greco, N. Leone, G. Ianni (Eds.), Logics in Artificial Intelligence. XIII, 572 pages. 2002.

Vol. 2417: M. Ishizuka, A. Sattar (Eds.), PRICAI 2002: Trends in Artificial Intelligence. XX, 623 pages. 2002.

Vol. 2416: S. Craw, A. Preece (Eds.), Advances in Case-Based Reasoning. XII, 656 pages. 2002.

Vol. 2413: K. Kuwabara, J. Lee (Eds.), Intelligent Agents and Multi-Agent Systems. X, 221 pages. 2002.

Vol. 2408: A.C. Kakas, F. Sadri (Eds.), Computational Logic: Logic Programming and Beyond. XII, 628 pages. 2002.

Vol. 2407: A.C. Kakas, F. Sadri (Eds.), Computational Logic: Logic Programming and Beyond. XII, 678 pages. 2002.

Vol. 2403: M. d'Inverno, M. Luck, M. Fisher, C. Preist (Eds.), Foundations and Applications of Multi-Agent Systems. X, 261 pages. 2002.

GPSR Compliance
The European Union's (EU) General Product Safety Regulation (GPSR) is a set of rules that requires consumer products to be safe and our obligations to ensure this.

If you have any concerns about our products, you can contact us on

ProductSafety@springernature.com

In case Publisher is established outside the EU, the EU authorized representative is:

Springer Nature Customer Service Center GmbH
Europaplatz 3
69115 Heidelberg, Germany

www.ingramcontent.com/pod-product-compliance
Ingram Content Group UK Ltd.
Pitfield, Milton Keynes, MK11 3LW, UK
UKHW021901190726
13853UKWH00003B/1374

* 9 7 8 3 6 6 2 2 1 3 8 9 6 *